THE ESSENTIAL
DEWEY

VOLUME 1

Pragmatism, Education, Democracy

THE ESSENTIAL
DEWEY

VOLUME 1

Pragmatism, Education, Democracy

Edited by **Larry A. Hickman** *and* **Thomas M. Alexander**

Indiana University Press / Bloomington and Indianapolis

The paper used in this publication meets the minimum requirements of American National Standard for Information Sciences— Permanence of Paper for Printed Library Materials, ANSI Z39.48– 1984.

MANUFACTURED IN THE UNITED STATES OF AMERICA

Library of Congress Cataloging-in-Publication Data
Dewey, John, 1859–1952.
The essential Dewey / edited by Larry A. Hickman and Thomas M. Alexander.
    p.   cm.
Includes index.
Contents: v. 1. Pragmatism, education, democracy — v. 2. Ethics, logic, psychology.
ISBN 0-253-33390-3 (cl : v. 1 : alk. paper). — ISBN 0-253-21184-0 (pbk. : v. 1 : alk. paper). — ISBN 0-253-33391-1 (cl : v. 2 alk. paper). — ISBN 0-253-21185-9 (pbk. : v. 2 : alk. paper)
1. Philosophy.   I. Hickman, Larry.   II. Alexander, Thomas M., date.   III. Title.
B 945.D41H53   1998
191—dc21   97-43936
1 2 3 4 5 03 02 01 00 99 98

CONTENTS

ACKNOWLEDGMENTS

These volumes were prepared at the Center for Dewey Studies during 1996 and 1997. They were produced from the text of *The Collected Works of John Dewey, 1882–1953: The Electronic Edition*, edited by Larry A. Hickman (Charlottesville, Virginia: InteLex Corporation, 1996), which is in turn based on the critical edition of Dewey's works, *The Collected Works of John Dewey, 1882–1953*, edited by Jo Ann Boydston (Carbondale and Edwardsville: Southern Illinois University Press, 1969–1991). All selections are reprinted with the permission of Southern Illinois University Press.

Three members of the Center's staff devoted extensive time and effort toward their timely completion. Diane Meierkort and Barbara Levine exercised care with respect to matters of style and proofreading that has been characteristic of their work during more than twenty years at the Center, and Karen O'Brien spent many hours at her computer preparing and checking the copy.

Standard references to John Dewey's work are to the critical edition, *The Collected Works of John Dewey, 1882–1953,* edited by Jo Ann Boydston (Carbondale and Edwardsville: Southern Illinois University Press, 1969–1991), and published as *The Early Works: 1882–1898* (EW), *The Middle Works: 1899–1924* (MW), and *The Later Works: 1925–1953* (LW). These designations are followed by volume and page number. For example, page 101 of volume 12 of the *Later Works* would be cited as "LW 12:101." An electronic edition, based on the critical edition, is now available as *The Collected Works of John Dewey, 1882–1953: The Electronic Edition*, edited by Larry A. Hickman (Charlottesville, Virginia: InteLex Corporation, 1996). In order to maintain uniformity of citation, the line and page breaks of the critical edition have been maintained in the electronic edition. Page numbers in the footnotes refer to the volume of *The Collected Works* from which the selection is excerpted.

INTRODUCTION

Pragmatism, Education, Democracy

In addition to being one of the greatest technical philosophers of the twentieth century, John Dewey (1859-1952) was also an educational innovator, a Progressive Era reformer, and one of his country's last great public intellectuals. In Henry Commager's trenchant appraisal, he was "the guide, the mentor, and the conscience of the American people: it is scarcely an exaggeration to say that for a generation no major issue was clarified until Dewey had spoken." The *New York Times* once hailed Dewey as no less than "America's Philosopher."

Many of the issues that engaged Dewey's attention, and about which he wrote with unflagging energy and intelligence, are still with us. Dewey's insights into the problems of public education, immigration, the prospects for democratic government, and the relation of faith to science are as fresh today as when they were first published. His penetrating treatments of the nature and function of philosophy, the ethical and aesthetic dimensions of life, and the role of inquiry in human experience are of increasing relevance to thoughtful people everywhere.

Dewey's massive *Collected Works*—thirty-seven volumes in all—thus stands ready to help guide our journey into the twenty-first century. But how are we to assess so large a body of work? How are we to find our way about within its complex structure?

The two volumes of *The Essential Dewey* present for the first time a collection of Dewey's essays and book chapters that is both manageable and comprehensive. The materials selected for these volumes exhibit Dewey's intellectual development over time, but they also represent his mature thinking on every major issue to which he turned his attention. Some of the essays, familiar to several generations of readers, have been in print for almost a century. Others have only recently been published and so have not yet received the attention they deserve. Some were published in journals of opinion. Others were published in books addressed primarily to other technical philosophers. Taken as a whole, *The Essential Dewey* presents Dewey's unique understanding of the problems and prospects of human existence, and therefore of the philosophical enterprise.

PART I: DEWEY IN CONTEXT

John Dewey was an American, and he became the foremost spokesman of American pragmatism. The essays in this part place him within that context. "The Development of American Pragmatism" (1925) is Dewey's account of the versions of pragmatism advanced by his predecessors C. S. Peirce and William James, and of the relation of his work to theirs. In this essay he details the differences between his own instrumentalism and both the realism of Peirce and the nominalism of James.

A deeply private man despite his immense public persona, Dewey wrote very little in the way of autobiography. On the occasion of his 70th birthday, however, he published two essays that sketched his intellectual development and distilled his personal beliefs. The first, "From Absolutism to Experimentalism" (1930), traces an intellectual journey that stretches from his boyhood in Vermont to his retirement from the faculty of Columbia University. In this essay Dewey draws our attention to four waymarkers of his intellectual journey that are also central themes of his work as a whole. The second, "What I Believe" (1930), reflects Dewey's lifelong attempt to recast the language of traditional religious faith in terms of a new pragmatic faith in the methods of experimental intelligence. "A philosophic faith," he writes, "being a tendency to action, can be tried and tested only in action."

"Pragmatic America" (1922) is one of Dewey's many attempts to dispel the notion, propagated by Bertrand Russell and others, that pragmatism was little more than an apology for crass American commercialism. In "The Pragmatic Acquiescence" (1927) Dewey responds to what he takes to be Lewis Mumford's misunderstanding of his ideas, and strives to place his full-bodied version of pragmatism, which he termed "instrumentalism," within its wider American cultural context.

PART 2: RECONSTRUCTING PHILOSOPHY

This part presents Dewey's call for the demolition of much of traditional western philosophy and his blueprint for its renovation. In "The Influence of Darwinism on Philosophy" (1909) Dewey draws a parallel between one of Darwin's central ideas and one of his own. Darwin had argued that biologists must abandon the idea of fixed species and focus instead on change and transition. Dewey argues that the 2,500-year philosophical quest for permanence and perfection must be replaced by a philosophy that acknowledges growth and development, and that seeks to come to terms with the rough-and-tumble of lived experience.

By 1917, when "The Need for a Recovery of Philosophy" was published, Dewey had worked out the details of his version of pragmatism and was ready to offer an expanded account of his plan for the reform of philosophy. Whereas traditional philosophy, especially in its modern period, has understood experience as subjective and knowledge as a personal possession, pragmatism is concerned with the objective experiences of organisms as they interact with their surrounding conditions. And whereas traditional philosophy has attempted to reach a foundation of certainty grounded in sensory or logical particulars, pragmatism stresses the importance of continuities and relations.

Dewey's assault on the traditional identification of philosophy as a form of knowledge reaches high intensity in "Philosophy and Democracy" (1919). A philosophy worthy of its name, he writes, must be a form of desire, and a "working program of action, a prophesy of the future, but one disciplined by serious thought and knowledge." In "Philosophy and Civilization" (1927) Dewey builds upon his remarks in "Philosophy and Democracy." This essay provides an excellent transition to his extensive presentation in chapter ten of *Experience and Nature*, included as the next essay in this collection, where Dewey articulates philosophy as the criticism of culture.

Many of Dewey's readers regard "Existence, Value and Criticism" (1925), as one of the high-water marks of his career. It constitutes his most detailed statement of what philosophy is and how it should function. If experienced objects and events are to be managed in such a way that they become valuable, he argues, then judgments, or *valuations* must continually be made. It is the function of philosophy, as a generalized theory of valuation, to provide a continual supply of tools and instruments by the means of which such judgments can be appraised.

Originally delivered as a part of his Gifford Lectures at the University of Edinburgh in 1929, "Philosophy's Search for the Immutable"—chapter two of *The Quest for Certainty*—adds an historical dimension to the analysis that Dewey provides in "Existence, Value and Criticism." Since the time of the Greeks, he observes, the quest for certainty has dominated philosophical and religious endeavors. Now the time has come for philosophy to follow the example of scientific technology: it must begin to integrate theory and practice toward the end of enhancing effective control over the criticism of values.

PART 3: EVOLUTIONARY NATURALISM

This part is the first of several which present essays where Dewey turns his attention to some of the specific problems that he thought require philosophical reconstruction. "The Postulate of Immediate Empiricism" (1905) is an early, radical statement that demonstrates the implications of Dewey's novel concept of experience for metaphysics. It is in this essay that he first articulates his claim that knowing is only one mode of experiencing. He contends that the point of philosophy is to find out *how* things are experienced when they are known. His critique of traditional epistemology, and especially of representational realism, is further refined in "Pure Experience and Reality: A Disclaimer" (1907). "Does Reality Possess Practical Character?" (1908) is one of the most powerful presentations of Dewey's conception of a world in which interaction, change, and process are not only real, but manifested in practical action rather than pure theory. In the seventh chapter of *Experience and Nature*, "Nature, Life and Body-Mind" (1925), Dewey provides an even more detailed analysis of the ideas of growth, continuity and emergence in nature. The two concluding essays in this part, "Nature in Experience" (1940) and "Anti-Naturalism in Extremis" (1943), illustrate Dewey's mature naturalism, and they also contain responses to some of his critics.

PART 4: PRAGMATIC METAPHYSICS

The issues raised in Part 3 receive even closer scrutiny in this part, which focuses on Dewey's radical reconstruction of traditional metaphysical concepts. "The Subject-Matter of Metaphysical Inquiry" (1915) is an early essay that anticipates *Experience and Nature* in its discussion of metaphysics as a descriptive enterprise that deals with the evolutionary, generic features of nature. "Events and the Future" (1926) reconstructs the notion of time, especially the future, and the implications of such a recon-

struction for traditional concepts of Being. "Appearing and Appearance" (1927) is a mature piece that illustrates Dewey's radical recasting of this distinction, which has been honored within western metaphysics since the time of Plato. "Qualitative Thought" (1930) and *Context and Thought* (1931) are closely related masterpieces that bring together key themes from Dewey's logic, aesthetics, ethics, and theory of meaning in terms of his contextual metaphysics. The final essay in this section, "Time and Individuality" (1940), is a late essay that reveals the relationship of Dewey's thought with process philosophy in terms of the emphasis that the two outlooks place on creative individuality as a feature of nature.

PART 5: THE AIMS OF EDUCATION

This section contains some of the best of Dewey's writings about education. "My Pedagogic Creed" (1897) remains one of the most concise of Dewey's statements of his educational aims. In *The Child and the Curriculum* (1902), still a classic in its field, Dewey argues against two extremes of educational theory. The first view, held in Dewey's time by W. T. Harris, who was the U.S. Commissioner of Education from 1889 to 1906, is that subject matter should be emphasized at the expense of the child's individual peculiarities. The second, held by psychologist G. Stanley Hall, is that the personality and character of the child are more important than subject matter. Dewey rejects both of these attempts to bifurcate educational practice. He seeks to replace them with a pedagogy that integrates the best elements of each view. In "The Moral Training Given by the School Community," chapter two of *Moral Principles in Education* (1909), Dewey presents what takes place in the classroom as an integral part of the activities of the wider community.

Two chapters from *Democracy and Education* (1916) further develop these themes. Chapter eight, "Aims in Education," argues that educational aims cannot successfully be imposed upon material from the outside, but must flow from the intelligent practice of teaching and learning. Chapter nine, "Natural Development and Social Efficiency as Aims," argues that natural development and social efficiency as educational aims must be defined in terms of a larger cultural context, where "culture" is taken as "the capacity for constantly expanding the range and accuracy of one's perception of meanings."

In "Nationalizing Education" (1916) Dewey calls upon teachers to form a bulwark against the forces that would fragment the national culture by fostering fear and hatred of minorities, immigrants, and others who have traditionally been the targets of such demagoguery. A "national" education would recognize both the complexities of its cultural context and its place in a community of nations. "Education as Engineering" (1922) constitutes a call for Americans to devote the same intellectual and financial resources to education that they have to the great projects of scientific technology. Finally, in "Education in Relation to Form," a selection from chapter five of *How We Think* (1933), Dewey discusses the vital meaning for education of the term "logical." It signifies, he argues, "the *regulation* of natural and spontaneous processes of observation, suggestion, and testing; that is, thinking as an *art*."

PART 6: THE INDIVIDUAL, THE COMMUNITY, AND DEMOCRACY

One of the most complex and controversial areas of Dewey's thought concerns his attempts to justify his faith in democracy as a mode of community action. In this section those attempts are exhibited in full relief within essays on the public-private distinction, the nature and prospects of liberalism, and the reasons why democracy must be radical in its outlook and purposes.

In "Search for the Public" and "Search for the Great Community"—chapters one and five of *The Public and Its Problems* (1927)—Dewey applies his social behaviorism to the problem of distinguishing what is private from what is public, and he examines the role of scientific technology and the arts in the construction of the instrumentalities by means of which associated living can be transformed into the spirit of a "Great Community."

In "The Inclusive Philosophic Idea" (1928) Dewey argues against the Lockean notion of atomic individualism, suggesting in-

stead that political philosophy must take seriously the social as a category. The individual, he argues, can only be properly understood in terms of the social. In a companion piece, "A Critique of American Civilization" (1928), Dewey returns to a theme that permeates his social and political philosophy. A civilization is only as strong as its weakest members. It is therefore incumbent on any civilization that wishes to persevere that it establish and nourish institutions that will promote the liberation of the talents and potentialities of all of its citizens. Individualism, he suggests, is something to be worked toward, and not something given in advance.

Dewey returns to this theme in "Renascent Liberalism," chapter three of *Liberalism and Social Action* (1935). Written during the depths of the Great Depression, this essay calls for a radical liberalism, that is, one that would make it clear that intelligence is a social asset and that it is social cooperation, and not what Dewey elsewhere calls "ragged individualism," that will have to be honored if progress is to be achieved. In "Democracy Is Radical" (1937) Dewey restates some of these ideas in a more popular form. Written during a time when fascism was ascendant in Europe and perceived as attractive by many in the United States, Dewey reminds his readers that democracy is not only a goal, but a means as well. Temporary dictatorship as a means to greater democracy, he argues, is a contradiction in terms.

Finally, in a benchmark essay on the subject, Dewey argues in "Creative Democracy—The Task Before Us" (1939) that democracy is "a way of life controlled by a working faith in the possibilities of human nature." This would involve, in turn, faith in the capacities of each individual, and a faith in education as a means of liberating those capacities.

PART 7: PRAGMATISM AND CULTURE: SCIENCE AND TECHNOLOGY, ART, AND RELIGION

Dewey was above all a philosopher of culture. He had a profound understanding of the essential role that philosophy has in the interpretation of its culture. In the essays contained in this section he takes up some of the most persistent problems of American culture.

In "Fundamentals" (1924), published just one year before the famous Scopes "monkey trial" in Tennessee, Dewey attacks literalist interpretations of Hebrew and Christian scriptures. He suggests that those who hold such views have misnamed themselves, since a true fundamentalist would inquire after needed foundations rather than just announcing a preferred doctrine as the only acceptable viewpoint. Dewey sees liberal religion as a bulwark against extremism of this type, and calls upon its proponents to articulate a clearer vision of their own program. During 1924 Dewey also published "Science, Belief and the Public," in which he returned to a theme that had occupied him since his 1909 essay "The Influence of Darwin on Philosophy." He is distressed at the lack of science education in the schools, and faults the dead weight of religious and cultural prejudice for impeding progress in this area.

In another essay published in 1924, "Logical Method and Law," Dewey argues that legal rules are only working hypotheses, and that they must constantly be tested in the light of experience. In two related articles, "Science and Society" (1931) and "Social Science and Social Control" (1931), Dewey addresses the relations between the natural sciences and the social sciences. In the first he argues that the "greatest scientific revolution" is yet to come. That revolution will only occur, if it does at all, once knowledge is organized for the management of social relations in the same ways that scientific technology has been used to manage the affairs of nature. In the second he offers a plan for the development of more robust social sciences. "By Nature and by Art" (1944) is perhaps Dewey's clearest statement of his view of the relation of science to technology. Avoiding the pitfalls of scientism, it nevertheless constitutes a call for the wider application, within the humanities, of the methods that have proven valuable in scientific technology.

"Common Sense and Scientific Inquiry," chapter four of *Logic: The Theory of Inquiry* (1938), argues that there is a continuity between common sense and science in terms of their common methods of inquiry, and that the only real difference between them is a difference in the logical forms they employ. Science grows out of common sense as its tools of inquiry become more refined. This chapter also contains an excellent discussion of one of Dewey's most problematic technical terms, "the situation."

In "The Live Creature," the first chapter of *Art as Experience* (1934), Dewey establishes a connection between the "refined" arts and everyday experiences by denying the traditionally accepted split between organism and environment. It is as the organism attends to its own struggles and achievements, and then seeks to express those experiences in ways that consolidate and enrich them, that art enters into the world.

"Religion versus the Religious" is the first chapter of *A Common Faith* (1934). Here Dewey denies that there is any such thing as religion in the singular, and that there is any single element or "essence" that all religions have in common. He then proposes that the noun "religion" be replaced by the adjective "religious," which would signify that quality of any experience which leads to a "composing and harmonizing of the various elements of our being."

The essays brought together in the two volumes of *The Essential Dewey* present Dewey's thought in a way that is clear, concise, and relevant to the problems and prospects of contemporary philosophy. They demonstrate Dewey's concern to establish continuities within experiences that would otherwise be inchoate or fragmented, and his demand that philosophy be pertinent to the daily lives of men and women. Above all, they provide testimony to his continuing relevance as a preeminent philosopher of American culture.

C H R O N O L O G Y

THE ESSENTIAL
DEWEY

VOLUME 1

Pragmatism, Education, Democracy

PART I

Dewey in Context

The purpose of this article is to define the principal theories of the philosophical movements known under the names of Pragmatism, Instrumentalism, or Experimentalism. To do this we must trace their historical development; for this method seems to present the simplest way of comprehending these movements and at the same time avoiding certain current misunderstandings of their doctrines and their aims.

The origin of Pragmatism goes back to Charles Sanders Peirce, the son of one of the most celebrated mathematicians of the United States, and himself very proficient in the science of mathematics; he is one of the founders of the modern symbolic logic of relations. Unfortunately Peirce was not at all a systematic writer and never expounded his ideas in a single system. The pragmatic method which he developed applies only to a very narrow and limited universe of discourse. After William James had extended the scope of the method, Peirce wrote an exposition of the origin of pragmatism as he had first conceived it; it is from this exposition that we take the following passages.

The term "pragmatic," contrary to the opinion of those who regard pragmatism as an exclusively American conception, was suggested to him by the study of Kant. In the *Metaphysic of Morals* Kant established a distinction between *pragmatic* and *practical*. The latter term applies to moral laws which Kant regards as *a priori*, whereas the former term applies to the rules of art and technique which are based on experience and are applicable to experience. Peirce, who was an empiricist, with the habits of mind, as he put it, of the laboratory, consequently refused to call his system "practicalism," as some of his friends suggested. As a logician he was interested in the art and technique of real thinking, and especially interested, as far as pragmatic method is concerned, in the art of making concepts clear, or of construing adequate and effective definitions in accord with the spirit of scientific method.

Following his own words, for a person "who still thought in Kantian terms most readily, '*praktisch*' and '*pragmatisch*' were as far apart as the two poles; the former belonging in

The Development of American Pragmatism

(1925)

a region of thought where no mind of the experimental type can ever make sure of solid ground under his feet, the latter expressing relation to some definite human purpose. Now quite the most striking feature of the new theory was its recognition of an inseparable connection between rational cognition and rational purpose."[1]

In alluding to the experimental type of mind, we are brought to the exact meaning given by Peirce to the word "pragmatic." In speaking of an experimentalist as a man whose intelligence is formed in the laboratory, he said: "Whatever assertion you may make to him, he will either understand as meaning that if a given prescription for an experiment ever can be and ever is carried out in act, an experience of a given description will result, or else he will see no sense at all in what you say." And thus Peirce developed the theory that "the rational purport of a word or other expression, lies exclusively in its conceivable bearing upon the conduct of life; so that, since obviously nothing that might not result from experiment can have any direct bearing upon conduct, if one can define accurately all the conceivable experimental phenomena which the affirmation or denial of a concept could imply, one will have therein a complete definition of the concept."[2]

The essay in which Peirce developed his theory bears the title: "How to Make Our Ideas Clear."[3] There is a remarkable similarity here to Kant's doctrine. Peirce's effort was to interpret the universality of concepts in the domain of *experience* in the same way in which Kant established the law of practical reason in the domain of the *a priori*. "The rational meaning of every proposition lies in the future. . . . But of the myriads of forms into which a proposition may be translated, what is that one which is to be called its very meaning? It is, according to the pragmatist, that form in which the proposition becomes applicable to human conduct, not in these or those special circumstances, nor when one entertains this or that special design, but that form which is most directly applicable to self-control under every situation, and to every purpose."[4] So also, "the pragmatist does not make the *summum bonum* to consist in action, but makes it to consist in

that process of evolution whereby the existent comes more and more to embody generals . . . "[5]—in other words—the process whereby the existent becomes, with the aid of action, a body of rational tendencies or of habits generalized as much as possible. These statements of Peirce are quite conclusive with respect to two errors which are commonly committed in regard to the ideas of the founder of pragmatism. It is often said of pragmatism that it makes action the end of life. It is also said of pragmatism that it subordinates thought and rational activity to particular ends of interest and profit. It is true that the theory according to Peirce's conception implies essentially a certain relation to action, to human conduct. But the role of action is that of an intermediary. In order to be able to attribute a meaning to concepts, one must be able to apply them to existence. Now it is by means of action that this application is made possible. And the modification of existence which results from this application constitutes the true meaning of concepts. Pragmatism is, therefore, far from being that glorification of action for its own sake which is regarded as the peculiar characteristic of American life.

It is also to be noted that there is a scale of possible applications of concepts to existence, and hence a diversity of meanings. The greater the extension of the concepts, the more they are freed from the restrictions which limit them to particular cases, the more is it possible for us to attribute the greatest generality of meaning to a term. Thus the theory of Peirce is opposed to every restriction of the meaning of a concept to the achievement of a particular end, and still more to a personal aim. It is still more strongly opposed to the idea that reason or thought should be reduced to being a servant of any interest which is pecuniary or narrow. This theory was American in its origin in so far as it insisted on the necessity of human conduct and the fulfillment of some aim in order to clarify thought. But at the same time, it disapproves of those aspects of American life which make action an end in itself, and which conceive ends too narrowly and too "practically." In considering a system of philosophy in its relation to national factors it is necessary to keep in mind not only the aspects of life which are incorporated in the system, but also the aspects against which the system is a protest. There never was a philosopher who has merited the name for the simple reason that he glorified the tendencies and characteristics of his social environment; just as it is also true that there never has been a philosopher who has not seized upon certain aspects of the life of his time and idealized them.

The work commenced by Peirce was continued by William James. In one sense James narrowed the application of Peirce's pragmatic method, but at the same time he extended it. The articles which Peirce wrote in 1878 commanded almost no attention from philosophical circles, which were then under the dominating influence of the neo-Kantian idealism of Green, of Caird, and of the Oxford School, excepting those circles in which the Scottish philosophy of common sense maintained its supremacy. In 1898 James inaugurated the new pragmatic movement in an address entitled, "Philosophical Conceptions and Practical Results," later reprinted in the volume, *Collected Essays and Reviews.* Even in this early study one can easily notice the presence of those two tendencies to restrict and at the same time to extend early pragmatism. After having quoted the psychological remark of Peirce that "beliefs are really rules for action, and the whole function of thinking is but one step in the production of habits of action," and that every idea which we frame for ourselves of an object is really an idea of the possible effects of that object, he expressed the opinion that all these principles could be expressed more broadly than Peirce expressed them. "The ultimate test for us of what a truth means is indeed the conduct it dictates or inspires. But it inspires that conduct because it first foretells some particular turn to our experience which shall call for just that conduct from us. And I should prefer to express Peirce's principle by saying that the effective meaning of any philosophic proposition can always be brought down to some particular consequence, in our future practical experience, whether active or passive; the point lying rather in the fact that the experience must be particular, than in the fact that it must be active."[6] In an essay written in 1908 James repeats this statement and states

that whenever he employs the term "the practical," he means by it, "the distinctively concrete, the individual, the particular and effective as opposed to the abstract, general and inert—'Pragmata' are things in their plurality—particular consequences can perfectly well be of a theoretic nature."[7]

William James alluded to the development which he gave to Peirce's expression of the principle. In one sense one can say that he enlarged the bearing of the principle by the substitution of particular consequences for the general rule or method applicable to future experience. But in another sense this substitution limited the application of the principle since it destroyed the importance attached by Peirce to the greatest possible application of the rule, or the habit of conduct—its extension to universality. That is to say, William James was much more of a nominalist than Peirce.

One can notice an extension of pragmatism in the above passage. James there alludes to the use of a method of determining the meaning of truth. Since truth is a term and has consequently a meaning, this extension is a legitimate application of pragmatic method. But it should be remarked that here this method serves only to make clear the meaning of the term "truth," and has nothing to do with the truth of a particular judgment. The principal reason which led James to give a new color to pragmatic method was that he was preoccupied with applying the method to determine the meaning of philosophical problems and questions and that moreover, he chose to submit to examination philosophical notions of a theological or religious nature. He wished to establish a criterion which would enable one to determine whether a given philosophical question has an authentic and vital meaning or whether, on the contrary, it is trivial and purely verbal; and in the former case, what interests are at stake, when one accepts and affirms one or the other of two theses in dispute. Peirce was above all a logician; whereas James was an educator and humanist and wished to force the general public to realize that certain problems, certain philosophical debates have a real importance for mankind, because the beliefs which they bring into play lead to very different modes of conduct. If this important distinction is not grasped, it is impossible to understand the majority of the ambiguities and errors which belong to the later period of the pragmatic movement.

James took as an example the controversy between theism and materialism. It follows from this principle that if the course of the world is considered as completed, it is equally legitimate to assert that God or matter is its cause. Whether one way or the other, the facts are what they are, and it is they which determine whatever meaning is to be given to their cause. Consequently the name which we can give to this cause is entirely arbitrary. It is entirely different if we take the future into account. God then has the meaning of a power concerned with assuring the final triumph of ideal and spiritual values, and matter becomes a power indifferent to the triumph or defeat of these values. And our life takes a different direction according as we adopt one or the other of these alternatives. In the lectures on pragmatism published in 1907, he applies the same criticism to the philosophical problem of the One and the Many, that is to say of Monism and Pluralism, as well as to other questions. Thus he shows that Monism is equivalent to a rigid universe where everything is fixed and immutably united to others, where indetermination, free choice, novelty, and the unforeseen in experience have no place; a universe which demands the sacrifice of the concrete and complex diversity of things to the simplicity and nobility of an architectural structure. In what concerns our beliefs, Monism demands a rationalistic temperament leading to a fixed and dogmatic attitude. Pluralism, on the other hand, leaves room for contingence, liberty, novelty, and gives complete liberty of action to the empirical method, which can be indefinitely extended. It accepts unity where it finds it, but it does not attempt to force the vast diversity of events and things into a single rational mold.

From the point of view of an educator or of a student or, if you will, of those who are thoroughly interested in these problems, in philosophical discussions and controversies, there is no reason for contesting the value of this application of pragmatic method, but it is no less important to determine the nature of this application. It affords a means of discovering the implications for human life of philosophical conceptions which are often treated as of no importance and of a purely dialectical nature. It furnishes a criterion for determining the vital implications of beliefs which present themselves as alternatives in any theory. Thus as he himself said, "the whole function of philosophy ought to be to find the characteristic influences which you and I would undergo at a determinate moment of our lives, if one or the other formula of the universe were true." However, in saying that the whole function of philosophy has this aim, it seems that he is referring rather to the teaching than to the construction of philosophy. For such a statement implies that the world formulas have already all been made, and that the necessary work of producing them has already been finished, so that there remains only to define the consequences which are reflected in life by the acceptance of one or the other of these formulas as true.

From the point of view of Peirce, the object of philosophy would be rather to give a fixed meaning to the universe by formulas which correspond to our attitudes or our most general habits of response to the environment; and this generality depends on the extension of the applicability of these formulas to specific future events. The *meaning* of concepts of "matter" and of "God" must be fixed before we can even attempt to reach an understanding concerning the *value* of our belief in these concepts. Materialism would signify that the world demands on our part a single kind of constant and general habits; and God would signify the demand for another type of habits; the difference between materialism and theism would be tantamount to the difference in the habits required to face all the detailed facts of the universe. The world would be one in so far as it would be possible for us to form a single habit of action which would take account of all future existences and would be applicable to them. It would be many in so far as it is necessary for us to form several habits, differing from each other and irreducible to each other, in order to be able to meet the events in the world and control them. In short, Peirce wrote as a logician and James as a humanist.

William James accomplished a new advance in Pragmatism by his theory of the will to believe, or as he himself later called it, the right to believe. The discovery of the fundamental consequences of one or another belief has without fail a certain influence on that belief itself. If a man cherishes novelty, risk, opportunity and a variegated esthetic reality, he will certainly reject any belief in Monism, when he clearly perceives the import of this system. But if, from the very start, he is attracted by esthetic harmony, classic proportions, fixity even to the extent of absolute security and logical coherence, it is quite natural that he should put faith in Monism. Thus William James took into account those motives of instinctive sympathy which play a greater role in our choice of a philosophic system than do formal reasonings; and he thought that we should be rendering a service to the cause of philosophical sincerity if we would openly recognize the motives which inspire us. He also maintained the thesis that the greater part of philosophic problems and especially those which touch on religious fields are of such a nature that they are not susceptible of decisive evidence one way or the other. Consequently he claimed the right of a man to choose his beliefs not only in the presence of proofs or conclusive facts, but also in the absence of all such proof. Above all when he is forced to choose between one meaning or another, or when by refusing to choose he has a right to assume the risks of faith, his refusal is itself equivalent to a choice. The theory of the will to believe gives rise to misunderstandings and even to ridicule; and therefore it is necessary to understand clearly in what way James used it. We are always obliged to act in any case; our actions and with them their consequences actually change according to the beliefs which we have chosen. Moreover it may be that, in order to discover the proofs which will ultimately be the intellectual justification of certain beliefs—the belief in freedom, for example, or the belief in God—it is necessary to begin to act in accordance with this belief.

In his lectures on Pragmatism, and in his volume of essays bearing the title *The Meaning of Truth*, which appeared in 1909, James extended the use of the pragmatic method to the problem of the nature of truth. So far we have considered the pragmatic method as an instrument in determining the meaning of words and the vital importance of philosophic beliefs. Now and then we have made allusion to the future consequences which are implied. James showed, among other things, that in certain philosophic conceptions, the affirmation of certain beliefs could be justified by means of the nature of their consequences, or by the differences which these beliefs make in existence. But then why not push the argument to the point of maintaining that the meaning of truth in general is determined by its consequences? We must not forget here that James was an empiricist before he was a pragmatist, and repeatedly stated that pragmatism is merely empiricism pushed to its legitimate conclusions. From a general point of view, the pragmatic attitude consists in "looking away from first things, principles, 'categories,' supposed necessities; and of looking towards last things, fruits, consequences, facts." It is only one step further to apply the pragmatic method to the problem of truth. In the natural sciences there is a tendency to identify truth in any particular case with a verification. The verification of a theory, or of a concept, is carried on by the observation of particular facts. Even the most scientific and harmonious physical theory is merely an hypothesis until its implications, deduced by mathematical reasoning or by any other kind of inference, are verified by observed facts. What direction therefore, must an empirical philosopher take who wishes to arrive at a definition of truth by means of an empirical method? He must, if he wants to apply this method, and without bringing in for the present the pragmatic formula, first find particular cases from which he then generalizes. It is therefore in submitting conceptions to the control of experience, in the process of verifying them, that one finds examples of what is called truth. Therefore any philosopher who applies this empirical method, without the least prejudice in favor of pragmatic doctrine, can be led to conclude that truth "means" verification, or if one prefers, that verification either actual or possible, is the definition of truth.

In combining this conception of empirical

method with the theory of pragmatism, we come upon other important philosophical results. The classic theories of truth in terms of the coherence or compatibility of terms, and of the correspondence of an idea with a thing, hereby receive a new interpretation. A merely mental coherence without experimental verification does not enable us to get beyond the realm of hypothesis. If a notion or a theory makes pretense of corresponding to reality or to the facts, this pretense cannot be put to the test and confirmed or refuted except by causing it to pass over into the realm of action and by noting the results which it yields in the form of the concrete observable facts to which this notion or theory leads. If, in acting upon this notion, we are brought to the fact which it implies or which it demands, then this notion is true. A theory corresponds to the facts when it leads to the facts which are its consequences, by the intermediary of experience. And from this consideration the pragmatic generalization is drawn that all knowledge is prospective in its results, except in the case where notions and theories after having been first prospective in their application, have already been tried out and verified. Theoretically, however, even such verifications or truths could not be absolute. They would be based upon practical or moral certainty, but they are always subject to being corrected by unforeseen future consequences or by observed facts which had been disregarded. Every proposition concerning truths is really in the last analysis hypothetical and provisional, although a large number of these propositions have been so frequently verified without failure that we are justified in using them as if they were absolutely true. But logically absolute truth is an ideal which cannot be realized, at least not until all the facts have been registered, or as James says "bagged," and until it is no longer possible to make other observations and other experiences.

Pragmatism, thus, presents itself as an extension of historical empiricism, but with this fundamental difference, that it does not insist upon antecedent phenomena but upon consequent phenomena; not upon the precedents but upon the possibilities of action. And this change in point of view is almost revolutionary in its consequences. An empiricism which is content with repeating facts already past has no place for possibility and for liberty. It cannot find room for general conceptions or ideas, at least no more than to consider them as summaries or records. But when we take the point of view of pragmatism we see that general ideas have a very different role to play than that of reporting and registering past experiences. They are the bases for organizing future observations and experiences. Whereas, for empiricism, in a world already constructed and determined, reason or general thought has no other meaning than that of summing up particular cases, in a world where the future is not a mere word, where theories, general notions, rational ideas have consequences for action, reason necessarily has a constructive function. Nevertheless the conceptions of reasoning have only a secondary interest in comparison with the reality of facts, since they must be confronted with concrete observations.[8]

Pragmatism thus has a metaphysical implication. The doctrine of the value of consequences leads us to take the future into consideration. And this taking into consideration of the future takes us to the conception of a universe whose evolution is not finished, of a universe which is still, in James' term, "in the making," "in the process of becoming," of a universe up to a certain point still plastic.

Consequently reason, or thought, in its more general sense, has a real, though limited function, a creative, constructive function. If we form general ideas and if we put them in action, consequences are produced which could not be produced otherwise. Under these conditions the world will be different from what it would have been if thought had not intervened. This consideration confirms the human and moral importance of thought and of its reflective operation in experience. It is therefore not true to say that James treated reason, thought and knowledge with contempt, or that he regarded them as mere means of gaining personal or even social profits. For him reason has a creative function, limited because specific, which helps to make the world other than it would have been without it. It makes the world really more reasonable; it gives to it an intrinsic value. One will understand the philosophy of James better if one considers it in its totality as a revision of English empiricism, a revision which replaces the value of past experience, of what is already given, by the future, by that which is as yet mere possibility.

These considerations naturally bring us to the movement called instrumentalism. The survey which we have just made of James' philosophy shows that he regarded conceptions and theories purely as instruments which can serve to constitute future facts in a specific manner. But James devoted himself primarily to the moral aspects of this theory, to the support which it gave to "meliorism" and moral idealism, and to the consequences which followed from it concerning the sentimental value and the bearing of various philosophical systems, particularly to its destructive implications for monistic rationalism and for absolutism in all its forms. He never attempted to develop a complete theory of the forms or "structures" and of the logical operations which are founded on this conception. Instrumentalism is an attempt to establish a precise logical theory of concepts, of judgments and inferences in their various forms, by considering primarily how thought functions in the experimental determinations of future consequences. That is to say, it attempts to establish universally recognized distinctions and rules of logic by deriving them from the reconstructive or mediative function ascribed to reason. It aims to constitute a theory of the general forms of conception and reasoning, and not of this or that particular judgment or concept related to its own content, or to its particular implications.

As far as the historical antecedents of instrumentalism are concerned, two factors are particularly important, over and above this matter of experimental verification which we have already mentioned in connection with James. The first of these two factors is psychological, and the second is a critique of the theory of knowledge and of logic which has resulted from the theory proposed by neo-Kantian idealism and expounded in the logical writings of such philosophers as Lotze, Bosanquet, and F. H. Bradley. As we have already said, neo-Kantian influence was very marked in the United States during the last decade of the nineteenth century. I myself, and those who have collaborated with me in the exposition of instrumentalism, began by being neo-Kantians, in the same way that Peirce's point of departure was Kantianism and that of James was the empiricism of the British School.

The psychological tendencies which have exerted an influence on instrumentalism are of a biological rather than a physiological nature. They are, more or less, closely related to the important movement whose promoter in psychology has been Doctor John Watson and to which he has given the name of Behaviourism. Briefly, the point of departure of this theory is the conception of the brain as an organ for the coordination of sense stimuli (to which one should add modifications caused by habit, unconscious memory, or what are called today "conditioned reflexes") for the purpose of effecting appropriate motor responses. On the basis of the theory of organic evolution it is maintained that the analysis of intelligence and of its operations should be compatible with the order of known biological facts, concerning the intermediate position occupied by the central nervous system in making possible responses to the environment adequate to the needs of the living organism. It is particularly interesting to note that in the *Studies in Logical Theory* (1903), which were their first declaration, the instrumentalists recognized how much they owed to William James for having forged the instruments which they used, while at the same time, in the course of the studies, the authors constantly declared their belief in a close union of the "normative" principles of logic and the real processes of thought, in so far as these are determined by an objective or biological psychology and not by an introspective psychology of states of consciousness. But it is curious to note that the "instruments" to which allusion is made, are not the considerations which were of the greatest service to James. They precede his pragmatism and it is among some of the pages of his *Principles of Psychology* that one must look for them. This important work (1890) really developed two distinct theses.

The one is a re-interpretation of introspective psychology, in which James denies that sensations, images and ideas are discrete and in which he replaces them by a continuous stream which he calls "the stream of consciousness." This conception necessitates a consideration of relations as an immediate part of the field of consciousness, having the same status as qualities. And throughout his *Psychology* James gives a philosophical tinge to this conception by using it in criticising the atomism of Locke and of Hume as well as the *a-priorism* of the synthesis of rational principles by Kant and his successors, among whom should be mentioned in England, Thomas Hill Green, who was then at the height of his influence.

The other aspect of his *Principles of Psychology* is of a biological nature. It shows itself in its full force in the criterion which James established for discovering the existence of mind. "The pursuance of future ends and the choice of means for their attainment are thus the mark and criterion of the presence of mentality in a phenomenon."[9] The force of this criterion is plainly shown in the chapter on Attention, and its relation to Interest considered as the force which controls it, and its teleological function of selection and integration; in the chapter on Discrimination and Comparison (Analysis and Abstraction), where he discusses the way in which ends to be attained and the means for attaining them evoke and control intellectual analysis; and in the chapter on Conception, where he shows that a general idea is a mode of signifying particular things and not merely an abstraction from particular cases or a super-empirical function,—that it is a teleological instrument. James then develops this idea in the chapter on reasoning where he says that "the only meaning of essence is teleological, and that classification and conception are purely teleological weapons of mind."

One might complete this brief enumeration by mentioning also the chapter of James' book in which he discusses the Nature of Necessary Truths and the Effects of Experience, and affirms in opposition to Herbert Spencer, that many of our most important modes of perception and conception of the world of sensible objects are not the cumulative products of particular experience, but rather original biological sports, spontaneous variations

which are maintained because of their applicability to concrete experiences after once having been created. Number, space, time, resemblance and other important "categories" could have been brought into existence, he says, as a consequence of some particular cerebral instability, but they could by no means, have been registered on the mind by outside influence. Many significant and useless concepts also arise in the same manner. But the fundamental categories have been cumulatively extended and reinforced because of their value when applied to concrete instances and things of experience. It is therefore not the origin of a concept, it is its application which becomes the criterion of its value; and here we have the whole of pragmatism in embryo. A phrase of James' very well summarizes its import: "the popular notion that 'Science' is forced on the mind *ab extra*, and that our interests have nothing to do with its constructions, is utterly absurd."

Given the point of view which we have just specified, and the interest attaching to a logical theory of conception and judgment, and there results a theory of the following description. The adaptations made by inferior organisms, for example their effective and coordinated responses to stimuli, become teleological in man and therefore give occasion to thought. Reflection is an indirect response to the environment, and the element of indirection can itself become great and very complicated. But it has its origin in biological adaptive behaviour and the ultimate function of its cognitive aspect is a prospective control of the conditions of the environment. The function of intelligence is therefore not that of copying the objects of the environment, but rather of taking account of the way in which more effective and more profitable relations with these objects may be established in the future.

How this point of view has been applied to the theory of judgment is too long a story to be told here. We shall confine ourselves here to saying that, in general, the "subject" of a judgment represents that portion of the environment to which a reaction must be made; the predicate represents the possible response or habit or manner in which one should behave towards the environment; the copula represents the organic and concrete act by which the connection is made between the fact and its signification; and finally the conclusion, or the definitive object of judgment, is simply the original situation transformed, a situation which implies a change as well in the original subject (including its mind) as in the environment itself. The new and harmonious unity thus attained verifies the bearing of the data which were at first chosen to serve as subject and of the concepts introduced into the situation during the process as teleological instruments for its elaboration. Until this final unification is attained the perceptual data and the conceptual principles, theories, are merely hypotheses from a logical point of view. Moreover, affirmation and negation are intrinsically a-logical: they are acts.

Such a summary survey can hardly pretend to be either convincing or suggestive. However, in noting the points of resemblance and difference between this phase of pragmatism and the logic of neo-Hegelian idealism, we are bringing out a point of great importance. According to the latter logic, thought constitutes in the last analysis its object and even the universe. It is necessary to affirm the existence of a series of forms of judgment, because our first judgments, which are nearest to sense, succeed in constituting objects in only a partial and fragmentary fashion, even to the extent of involving in their nature an element of contradiction. There results a dialectic which permits each inferior and partial type of judgment to pass into a more complete form until we finally arrive at the total judgment where the thought which comprehends the entire object or the universe is an organic whole of interrelated mental distinctions. It is evident that this theory magnifies the role of thought beyond all proportion. It is an objective and rational idealism which is opposed to and distinct from the subjective and perceptual idealism of Berkeley's school. Instrumentalism, however, assigns a positive function to thought, that of *reconstituting* the present stage of things instead of merely knowing it. As a consequence, there cannot be intrinsic degrees, or a hierarchy of forms of judgments. Each type has its own end, and its validity is entirely determined by its efficacy in the pursuit of its end. A limited perceptual judgment, adapted to the situation which has given it birth, is as true in its place as is the most complete and significant philosophic or scientific judgment. Logic, therefore, leads to a realistic metaphysics in so far as it accepts things and events for what they are independently of thought, and to an idealistic metaphysics in so far as it contends that thought gives birth to distinctive acts which modify future facts and events in such a way as to render them more reasonable, that is to say, more adequate to the ends which we propose for ourselves. This ideal element is more and more accentuated by the inclusion progressively of social factors in human environment over and above natural factors; so that the needs which are fulfilled, the ends which are attained are no longer of a merely biological or particular character, but include also the ends and activities of other members of society.

It is natural that continental thinkers should be interested in American philosophy as it reflects, in a certain sense, American life. Thus it should be clear after this rapid survey of the history of pragmatism that American thought continues European thought. We have imported our language, our laws, our institutions, our morals, and our religion from Europe, and we have adapted them to the new conditions of our life. The same is true of our ideas. For long years our philosophical thought was merely an echo of European thought. The pragmatic movement which we have traced in the present essay as well as neo-realism, behaviourism, the absolute idealism of Royce, the naturalistic idealism of Santayana, are all attempts at re-adaptation; but they are not creations *de novo*. They have their roots in British and European thought. Since these systems are re-adaptations they take into consideration the distinctive traits of the environment of American life. But as has already been said, they are not limited to reproducing what is worn and imperfect in this environment. They do not aim to glorify the energy and the love of action which the new conditions of American life exaggerated. They do not reflect the excessive mercantilism of American life. Without doubt all these traits of the environment have not been without a certain influence on American philosophical thought; our philosophy would not be national or spontaneous if it were not subject to this influence. But the fundamental idea which the movements of which we have just spoken, have attempted to express, is the idea that action and opportunity justify themselves only to the degree in which they render life more reasonable and increase its value. Instrumentalism maintains in opposition to many contrary tendencies in the American environment, that action should be intelligent and reflective, and that thought should occupy a central position in life. That is the reason for our insistence on the teleological phase of thought and knowledge. If it must be teleological in particular and not merely true in the abstract, that is probably due to the practical element which is found in all the phases of American life. However that may be, what we insist upon above all else is that intelligence be regarded as the only source and sole guarantee of a desirable and happy future. It is beyond doubt that the progressive and unstable character of American life and civilization has facilitated the birth of a philosophy which regards the world as being in continuous formation, where there is still place for indeterminism, for the new and for a real future. But this idea is not exclusively American, although the conditions of American life have aided this idea in becoming self-conscious. It is also true that Americans tend to underestimate the value of tradition and of rationality considered as an achievement of the past. But the world has also given proof of irrationality in the past and this irrationality is incorporated in our beliefs and our institutions. There are bad traditions as there are good ones: it is always important to distinguish. Our neglect of the traditions of the past, with whatever this negligence implies in the way of spiritual impoverishment of our life, has its compensation in the idea that the world is re-commencing and being re-made under our eyes. The future as well as the past can be a source of interest and consolation and give meaning to the present. Pragmatism and instrumental experimentalism bring into prominence the importance of the individual. It is he who is the carrier of creative thought, the author of action, and of its application. Subjectivism is an old story in philosophy; a story which began in Europe and not in America. But American philosophy, in the systems which we have expounded, has given to the subject, to the individual mind, a practical rather than an epistemological function. The individual mind is important because only the individual mind is the organ of modifications in traditions and institutions, the vehicle of experimental creation. One-sided and egoistic individualism in American life has left its imprint on our practices. For better or for worse, depending on the point of view, it has transformed the esthetic and fixed individualism of the old European culture into an active individualism. But the idea of a society of individuals is not foreign to American thought; it penetrates even our current individualism which is unreflective and brutal. And the individual which American thought idealises is not an individual *per se*, an individual fixed in isolation and set up for himself, but an individual who evolves and develops in a natural and human environment, an individual who can be educated.

If I were asked to give an historical parallel to this movement in American thought I would remind my reader of the French philosophy of the enlightenment. Every one knows that the thinkers who made that movement illustrious were inspired by Bacon, Locke, and Newton; what interested them was the application of scientific method and the conclusions of an experimental theory of knowledge to human affairs, the critique and reconstruction of beliefs and institutions. As Höffding writes, they were animated by "a fervent faith in intelligence, progress, and humanity." And certainly they are not accused today, just because of their educational and social significance, of having sought to subordinate intelligence and science to ordinary utilitarian aims. They merely sought to free intelligence from its impurities and to render it sovereign. One can scarcely say that those who glorify intelligence and reason in the abstract, because of their value for those who find personal satisfaction in their possession, estimate intelligence more truly than those who wish to make it the indispensable guide of intellectual and social life. When an American critic says of instrumentalism that it regards ideas as mere servants which make for success in life, he only reacts, without reflection, to the ordinary verbal associations of the word "instrumental," as many others have reacted in the same manner to the use of the word "practical." Similarly a recent Italian writer after having said that pragmatism and instrumentalism are characteristic products of American thought, adds that these systems "regard intelligence as a mere mechanism of belief, and consequently attempt to re-establish the dignity of reason by making of it a machine for the production of beliefs useful to morals and society." This criticism does not hold. It is by no means the production of beliefs useful to morals and society which these systems pursue. It is the formation of a faith in intelligence, as the one and indispensable belief necessary to moral and social life. The more one appreciates the intrinsic esthetic, immediate value of thought and of science, the more one takes into account what intelligence itself adds to the joy and dignity of life, the more one should feel grieved at a situation in which the exercise and joy of reason are limited to a narrow, closed and technical social group and the more one should ask how it is possible to make all men participators in this inestimable wealth.

NOTES

[First published in *Studies in the History of Ideas*, ed. Department of Philosophy, Columbia University (New York: Columbia University Press, 1925), 2:353–77. LW 2:3–21.]

1. *Monist,* vol. 15, p. 163.
2. *Monist,* vol. 15, p. 162.
3. *Popular Science Monthly,* 1878.
4. *Monist,* vol. 15, pp. 173–74.
5. *Monist,* vol. 15, p. 178.
6. *Collected Essays and Reviews,* p. 412.
7. *The Meaning of Truth,* pp. 209–211. In a footnote James gave an example of the errors which are committed in connection with the term "Practical," quoting M. Bourdeau who had written that "Pragmatism is an Anglo-Saxon reaction against the intellectualism and rationalism of the Latin mind. . . . It is a philosophy without words, a philosophy of gestures and of acts, which abandons what is general and holds only to what is particular." In his lecture at California, James brought out the idea that his pragmatism was inspired to a considerable extent by the thought of the British philosophers, Locke, Berkeley, Hume, Mill, Bain, and Shadworth Hodgson. But he contrasted this method with German transcendentalism, and particularly with that of Kant. It is especially interesting to notice this difference between Peirce and James: the former attempted to give an experimental, not an *a priori* interpretation of Kant, whereas James tried to develop the point of view of the British thinkers.

8. William James said, in a happy metaphor, that they must be "cashed in," by producing specific consequences. This expression means that they must be able to lead to concrete facts. But for those who are not familiar with American idioms, James' formula was taken to mean that the consequences themselves of our rational conceptions must be narrowly limited by their pecuniary value. Thus Mr. Bertrand Russell wrote recently that pragmatism is merely a manifestation of American commercialism.

9. *Psychology,* vol. 1, p. 8.

From Absolutism to Experimentalism

(1930)

In the late 'seventies, when I was an undergraduate, "electives" were still unknown in the smaller New England colleges. But in the one I attended, the University of Vermont, the tradition of a "senior-year course" still subsisted. This course was regarded as a kind of intellectual coping to the structure erected in earlier years, or, at least, as an insertion of the keystone of the arch. It included courses in political economy, international law, history of civilization (Guizot), psychology, ethics, philosophy of religion (Butler's *Analogy*), logic, etc., not history of philosophy, save incidentally. The enumeration of these titles may not serve the purpose for which it is made; but the idea was that after three years of somewhat specialized study in languages and sciences, the last year was reserved for an introduction into serious intellectual topics of wide and deep significance—an introduction into the world of ideas. I doubt if in many cases it served its alleged end; however, it fell in with my own inclinations, and I have always been grateful for that year of my schooling. There was, however, one course in the previous year that had excited a taste that in retrospect may be called philosophical. That was a rather short course, without laboratory work, in Physiology, a book of Huxley's being the text. It is difficult to speak with exactitude about what happened to me intellectually so many years ago, but I have an impression that there was derived from that study a sense of interdependence and interrelated unity that gave form to intellectual stirrings that had been previously inchoate, and created a kind of type or model of a view of things to which material in any field ought to conform. Subconsciously, at least, I was led to desire a world and a life that would have the same properties as had the human organism in the picture of it derived from study of Huxley's treatment. At all events, I got great stimulation from the study, more than from anything I had had contact with before; and as no desire was awakened in me to continue that particular branch of learning, I date from this time the awakening of a distinctive philosophic interest.

The University of Vermont rather prided itself upon its tradition in philosophy. One of its earlier teachers, Dr. Marsh, was almost the first person in the United States to venture upon the speculative and dubiously orthodox seas of German thinking—that of Kant, Schelling, and Hegel. The venture, to be sure, was made largely by way of Coleridge; Marsh edited an American edition of Coleridge's *Aids to Reflection*. Even this degree of speculative generalization, in its somewhat obvious tendency to rationalize the body of Christian theological doctrines, created a flutter in ecclesiastical dovecots. In particular, a controversy was carried on between the Germanizing rationalizers and the orthodox representatives of the Scottish school of thought through the representatives of the latter at Princeton. I imagine— although it is a very long time since I have had any contact with this material—that the controversy still provides data for a section, if not a chapter, in the history of thought in this country.

Although the University retained pride in its pioneer work, and its atmosphere was for those days theologically "liberal"—of the Congregational type—the teaching of philosophy had become more restrained in tone, more influenced by the still dominant Scotch school. Its professor, Mr. H. A. P. Torrey, was a man of genuinely sensitive and cultivated mind, with marked esthetic interest and taste, which, in a more congenial atmosphere than that of northern New England in those days, would have achieved something significant. He was, however, constitutionally timid, and never really let his mind go. I recall that, in a conversation I had with him a few years after graduation, he said: "Undoubtedly pantheism is the most satisfactory form of metaphysics intellectually, but it goes counter to religious faith." I fancy that remark told of an inner conflict that prevented his native capacity from coming to full fruition. His interest in philosophy, however, was genuine, not perfunctory; he was an excellent teacher, and I owe to him a double debt, that of turning my thoughts definitely to the study of philosophy as a life-pursuit, and of a generous gift of time to me during a year devoted privately under his direction to a reading of classics in the history of philosophy and learning to read philosophic German. In our walks and talks during this year, after three years on my part of high-school teaching, he

let his mind go much more freely than in the class-room, and revealed potentialities that might have placed him among the leaders in the development of a freer American philosophy—but the time for the latter had not yet come.

Teachers of philosophy were at that time, almost to a man, clergymen; the supposed requirements of religion, or theology, dominated the teaching of philosophy in most colleges. Just how and why Scotch philosophy lent itself so well to the exigencies of religion I cannot say; probably the causes were more extrinsic than intrinsic; but at all events there was a firm alliance established between religion and the cause of "intuition." It is probably impossible to recover at this date the almost sacrosanct air that enveloped the idea of intuitions; but somehow the cause of all holy and valuable things was supposed to stand or fall with the validity of intuitionalism; the only vital issue was that between intuitionalism and a sensational empiricism that explained away the reality of all higher objects. The story of this almost forgotten debate, once so urgent, is probably a factor in developing in me a certain scepticism about the depth and range of purely contemporary issues; it is likely that many of those which seem highly important to-day will also in a generation have receded to the status of the local and provincial. It also aided in generating a sense of the value of the history of philosophy; some of the claims made for this as a sole avenue of approach to the study of philosophic problems seem to me misdirected and injurious. But its value in giving perspective and a sense of proportion in relation to immediate contemporary issues can hardly be over-estimated.

I do not mention this theological and intuitional phase because it had any lasting influence upon my own development, except negatively. I learned the terminology of an intuitional philosophy, but it did not go deep, and in no way did it satisfy what I was dimly reaching for. I was brought up in a conventionally evangelical atmosphere of the more "liberal" sort; and the struggles that later arose between acceptance of that faith and the discarding of traditional and institutional creeds came from personal experiences and not from the effects of philosophical teaching. It was not, in other words, in this respect that philosophy either appealed to me or influenced me—though I am not sure that Butler's *Analogy*, with its cold logic and acute analysis, was not, in a reversed way, a factor in developing "scepticism."

During the year of private study, of which mention has been made, I decided to make philosophy my life-study, and accordingly went to Johns Hopkins the next year (1884) to enter upon that new thing, "graduate work." It was something of a risk; the work offered there was almost the only indication that there were likely to be any self-supporting jobs in the field of philosophy for others than clergymen. Aside from the effect of my study with Professor Torrey, another influence moved me to undertake the risk. During the years after graduation I had kept up philosophical readings and I had even written a few articles which I sent to Dr. W. T. Harris, the well-known Hegelian, and the editor of the *Journal of Speculative Philosophy*, the only philosophic journal in the country at that time, as he and his group formed almost the only group of laymen devoted to philosophy for non-theological reasons. In sending an article I asked Dr. Harris for advice as to the possibility of my successfully prosecuting philosophic studies. His reply was so encouraging that it was a distinct factor in deciding me to try philosophy as a professional career.

The articles sent were, as I recall them, highly schematic and formal; they were couched in the language of intuitionalism; of Hegel I was then ignorant. My deeper interests had not as yet been met, and in the absence of subject-matter that would correspond to them, the only topics at my command were such as were capable of a merely formal treatment. I imagine that my development has been controlled largely by a struggle between a native inclination toward the schematic and formally logical, and those incidents of personal experience that compelled me to take account of actual material. Probably there is in the consciously articulated ideas of every thinker an over-weighting of just those things that are contrary to his natural tendencies, an emphasis upon those things that are contrary to his intrinsic bent, and which, therefore, he has to

struggle to bring to expression, while the native bent, on the other hand, can take care of itself. Anyway, a case might be made out for the proposition that the emphasis upon the concrete, empirical, and "practical" in my later writings is partly due to considerations of this nature. It was a reaction against what was more natural, and it served as a protest and protection against something in myself which, in the pressure of the weight of actual experiences, I knew to be a weakness. It is, I suppose, becoming a commonplace that when anyone is unduly concerned with controversy, the remarks that seem to be directed against others are really concerned with a struggle that is going on inside himself. The marks, the stigmata, of the struggle to weld together the characteristics of a formal, theoretic interest and the material of a maturing experience of contacts with realities also showed themselves, naturally, in style of writing and manner of presentation. During the time when the schematic interest predominated, writing was comparatively easy; there were even compliments upon the clearness of my style. Since then thinking and writing have been hard work. It is easy to give way to the dialectic development of a theme; the pressure of concrete experiences was, however, sufficiently heavy, so that a sense of intellectual honesty prevented a surrender to that course. But, on the other hand, the formal interest persisted, so that there was an inner demand for an intellectual technique that would be consistent and yet capable of flexible adaptation to the concrete diversity of experienced things. It is hardly necessary to say that I have not been among those to whom the union of abilities to satisfy these two opposed requirements, the formal and the material, came easily. For that very reason I have been acutely aware, too much so, doubtless, of a tendency of other thinkers and writers to achieve a specious lucidity and simplicity by the mere process of ignoring considerations which a greater respect for concrete materials of experience would have forced upon them.

It is a commonplace of educational history that the opening of Johns Hopkins University marked a new epoch in higher education in the United States. We are probably not in a condition as yet to estimate the extent to which its foundation and the development of graduate schools in other universities, following its example, mark a turn in our American culture. The 'eighties and 'nineties seem to mark the definitive close of our pioneer period, and the turn from the civil war era into the new industrialized and commercial age. In philosophy, at least, the influence of Johns Hopkins was not due to the size of the provision that was made. There was a half-year of lecturing and seminar work given by Professor George Sylvester Morris, of the University of Michigan; belief in the "demonstrated" (a favorite word of his) truth of the substance of German idealism, and of belief in its competency to give direction to a life of aspiring thought, emotion, and action. I have never known a more single-hearted and whole-souled man—a man of a single piece all the way through; while I long since deviated from his philosophic faith, I should be happy to believe that the influence of the spirit of his teaching has been an enduring influence.

While it was impossible that a young and impressionable student, unacquainted with any system of thought that satisfied his head and heart, should not have been deeply affected, to the point of at least a temporary conversion, by the enthusiastic and scholarly devotion of Mr. Morris, this effect was far from being the only source of my own "Hegelianism." The 'eighties and 'nineties were a time of new ferment in English thought; the reaction against atomic individualism and sensationalistic empiricism was in full swing. It was the time of Thomas Hill Green, of the two Cairds, of Wallace, of the appearance of the *Essays in Philosophical Criticism*, cooperatively produced by a younger group under the leadership of the late Lord Haldane. This movement was at the time the vital and constructive one in philosophy. Naturally its influence fell in with and reinforced that of Professor Morris. There was but one marked difference, and that, I think, was in favor of Mr. Morris. He came to Kant through Hegel instead of to Hegel by way of Kant, so that his attitude toward Kant was the critical one expressed by Hegel himself. Moreover, he retained something of his early Scotch philosophical training in a common-sense belief in the existence of the external

world. He used to make merry over those who thought the *existence* of this world and of matter were things to be proved by philosophy. To him the only philosophical question was as to the *meaning* of this existence; his idealism was wholly of the objective type. Like his contemporary, Professor John Watson, of Kingston, he combined a logical and idealistic metaphysics with a realistic epistemology. Through his teacher at Berlin, Trendelenburg, he had acquired a great reverence for Aristotle, and he had no difficulty in uniting Aristoteleanism with Hegelianism.

There were, however, also "subjective" reasons for the appeal that Hegel's thought made to me; it supplied a demand for unification that was doubtless an intense emotional craving, and yet was a hunger that only an intellectualized subject-matter could satisfy. It is more than difficult, it is impossible, to recover that early mood. But the sense of divisions and separations that were, I suppose, borne in upon me as a consequence of a heritage of New England culture, divisions by way of isolation of self from the world, of soul from body, of nature from God, brought a painful oppression—or, rather, they were an inward laceration. My earlier philosophic study had been an intellectual gymnastic. Hegel's synthesis of subject and object, matter and spirit, the divine and the human, was, however, no mere intellectual formula; it operated as an immense release, a liberation. Hegel's treatment of human culture, of institutions and the arts, involved the same dissolution of hard-and-fast dividing walls, and had a special attraction for me.

As I have already intimated, while the conflict of traditional religious beliefs with opinions that I could myself honestly entertain was the source of a trying personal crisis, it did not at any time constitute a leading philosophical problem. This might look as if the two things were kept apart; in reality it was due to a feeling that any genuinely sound religious experience could and should adapt itself to whatever beliefs one found oneself intellectually entitled to hold—a half unconscious sense at first, but one which ensuing years have deepened into a fundamental conviction. In consequence, while I have, I hope, a due degree of personal sympathy with individuals who are undergoing the throes of a personal change of attitude, I have not been able to attach much importance to religion as a philosophic problem; for the effect of that attachment seems to be in the end a subornation of candid philosophic thinking to the alleged but factitious needs of some special set of convictions. I have enough faith in the depth of the religious tendencies of men to believe that they will adapt themselves to any required intellectual change, and that it is futile (and likely to be dishonest) to forecast prematurely just what forms the religious interest will take as a final consequence of the great intellectual transformation that is going on. As I have been frequently criticized for undue reticence about the problems of religion, I insert this explanation: it seems to me that the great solicitude of many persons, professing belief in the universality of the need for religion, about the present and future of religion proves that in fact they are moved more by partisan interest in a particular religion than by interest in religious experience.

The chief reason, however, for inserting these remarks at this point is to bring out a contrast effect. Social interests and problems from an early period had to me the intellectual appeal and provided the intellectual sustenance that many seem to have found primarily in religious questions. In undergraduate days I had run across, in the college library, Harriet Martineau's exposition of Comte. I cannot remember that his law of "the three stages" affected me particularly; but his idea of the disorganized character of Western modern culture, due to a disintegrative "individualism," and his idea of a synthesis of science that should be a regulative method of an organized social life, impressed me deeply. I found, as I thought, the same criticisms combined with a deeper and more far-reaching integration in Hegel. I did not, in those days when I read Francis Bacon, detect the origin of the Comtean idea in him, and I had not made acquaintance with Condorcet, the connecting link.

I drifted away from Hegelianism in the next fifteen years; the word "drifting" expresses the slow and, for a long time, imperceptible character of the movement, though it does not convey the impression that there was an adequate cause for the change. Nevertheless I should never think of ignoring, much less denying, what an astute critic occasionally refers to as a novel discovery—that acquaintance with Hegel has left a permanent deposit in my thinking. The form, the schematism, of his system now seems to me artificial to the last degree. But in the content of his ideas there is often an extraordinary depth; in many of his analyses, taken out of their mechanical dialectical setting, an extraordinary acuteness. Were it possible for me to be a devotee of any system, I still should believe that there is greater richness and greater variety of insight in Hegel than in any other single systematic philosopher—though when I say this I exclude Plato, who still provides my favorite philosophic reading. For I am unable to find in him that all-comprehensive and overriding system which later interpretation has, as it seems to me, conferred upon him as a dubious boon. The ancient sceptics overworked another aspect of Plato's thought when they treated him as their spiritual father, but they were nearer the truth, I think, than those who force him into the frame of a rigidly systematized doctrine. Although I have not the aversion to system as such that is sometimes attributed to me, I am dubious of my own ability to reach inclusive systematic unity, and in consequence, perhaps, of that fact also dubious about my contemporaries. Nothing could be more helpful to present philosophizing than a "Back to Plato" movement; but it would have to be back to the dramatic, restless, cooperatively inquiring Plato of the *Dialogues*, trying one mode of attack after another to see what it might yield; back to the Plato whose highest flight of metaphysics always terminated with a social and practical turn, and not to the artificial Plato constructed by unimaginative commentators who treat him as the original university professor.

The rest of the story of my intellectual development I am unable to record without more faking than I care to indulge in. What I have so far related is so far removed in time that I can talk about myself as another person; and much has faded, so that a few points stand out without my having to force them into the foreground. The philosopher, if I may apply that word to myself, that I became as I moved away from German idealism, is too much the self that I still am and is still too much in process of change to lend itself to record. I envy, up to a certain point, those who can write their intellectual biography in a unified pattern, woven out of a few distinctly discernible strands of interest and influence. By contrast, I seem to be unstable, chameleon-like, yielding one after another to many diverse and even incompatible influences; struggling to assimilate something from each and yet striving to carry it forward in a way that is logically consistent with what has been learned from its predecessors. Upon the whole, the forces that have influenced me have come from persons and from situations more than from books—not that I have not, I hope, learned a great deal from philosophical writings, but that what I have learned from them has been technical in comparison with what I have been forced to think upon and about because of some experience in which I found myself entangled. It is for this reason that I cannot say with candor that I envy completely, or envy beyond a certain point, those to whom I have referred. I like to think, though it may be a defense reaction, that with all the inconveniences of the road I have been forced to travel, it has the compensatory advantage of not inducing an immunity of thought to experiences—which perhaps, after all, should not be treated even by a philosopher as the germ of a disease to which he needs to develop resistance.

While I cannot write an account of intellectual development without giving it the semblance of a continuity that it does not in fact own, there are four special points that seem to stand out. One is the importance that the practice and theory of education have had for me: especially the education of the young, for I have never been able to feel much optimism regarding the possibilities of "higher" education when it is built upon warped and weak foundations. This interest fused with and brought together what might otherwise have been separate interests—that in psychology and that in social institutions and social life. I can recall but one critic who has suggested that my thinking has been too much permeated by interest in education. Although a book called *Democracy and Education* was for many years that in which my philosophy, such as it is, was most fully expounded, I do not know that philosophic critics, as distinct from teachers, have ever had recourse to it. I have wondered whether such facts signified that philosophers in general, although they are themselves usually teachers, have not taken education with sufficient seriousness for it to occur to them that any rational person could actually think it possible that philosophizing should focus about education as the supreme human interest in which, moreover, other problems, cosmological, moral, logical, come to a head. At all events, this handle is offered to any subsequent critic who may wish to lay hold of it.

A second point is that as my study and thinking progressed, I became more and more troubled by the intellectual scandal that seemed to me involved in the current (and traditional) dualism in logical standpoint and method between something called "science" on the one hand and something called "morals" on the other. I have long felt that the construction of a logic, that is, a method of effective inquiry, which would apply without abrupt breach of continuity to the fields designated by both of these words, is at once our needed theoretical solvent and the supply of our greatest practical want. This belief has had much more to do with the development of what I termed, for lack of a better word, "instrumentalism," than have most of the reasons that have been assigned.

The third point forms the great exception to what was said about no very fundamental vital influence issuing from books; it concerns the influence of William James. As far as I can discover one specifiable philosophic factor which entered into my thinking so as to give it a new direction and quality, it is this one. To say that it proceeded from his *Psychology* rather than from the essays collected in the volume called *Will to Believe*, his *Pluralistic Universe*, or *Pragmatism*, is to say something that needs explanation. For there are, I think, two unreconciled strains in the *Psychology*. One is found in the adoption of the subjective tenor of prior psychological tradition; even when the special tenets of that tradition are radically criticized, an underlying subjectivism is retained, at least in vocabulary—and the difficulty in finding a vocabulary which will intelligibly convey a genuinely new idea is perhaps the obstacle that most retards the easy progress of philosophy. I may cite as an illustration the substitution of the "stream of consciousness" for discrete elementary states: the advance made was enormous. Nevertheless the point of view remained that of a realm of consciousness set off by itself. The other strain is objective, having its roots in a return to the earlier biological conception of the *psyche*, but a return possessed of a new force and value due to the immense progress made by biology since the time of Aristotle. I doubt if we have as yet begun to realize all that is due to William James for the introduction and use of this idea; as I have already intimated, I do not think that he fully and consistently realized it himself. Anyway, it worked its way more and more into all my ideas and acted as a ferment to transform old beliefs.

If this biological conception and mode of approach had been prematurely hardened by James, its effect might have been merely to substitute one schematism for another. But it is not tautology to say that James's sense of life was itself vital. He had a profound sense, in origin artistic and moral, perhaps, rather than "scientific," of the difference between the categories of the living and of the mechanical; some time, I think, someone may write an essay that will show how the most distinctive factors in his general philosophic view, pluralism, novelty, freedom, individuality, are all connected with his feeling for the qualities and traits of that which lives. Many philosophers have had much to say about the idea of organism; but they have taken it structurally and hence statically. It was reserved for James to think of life in terms of life in action. This point, and that about the objective biological factor in James's conception of thought (discrimination, abstraction, conception, generalization), is fundamental when the role of psychology in philosophy comes under consideration. It is true that the effect of its introduction into philosophy has often, usually, been to dilute and distort the latter. But that is because the psychology was bad psychology.

I do not mean that I think that in the end the connection of psychology with philosophy is, in the abstract, closer than is that of other branches of science. Logically it stands on the same plane with them. But historically and at the present juncture the revolution introduced by James had, and still has, a peculiar significance. On the negative side it is important, for it is indispensable as a purge of the heavy charge of bad psychology that is so embedded in the philosophical tradition that it is not generally recognized to be psychology at all. As an example, I would say that the problem of "sense data," which occupies such a great bulk in recent British thinking, has to my mind no significance other than as a survival of an old and outworn psychological doctrine—although those who deal with the problem are for the most part among those who stoutly assert the complete irrelevance of psychology to philosophy. On the positive side we have the obverse of this situation. The newer objective psychology supplies the easiest way, pedagogically if not in the abstract, by which to reach a fruitful conception of thought and its work, and thus to better our logical theories—provided thought and logic have anything to do with one another. And in the present state of men's minds the linking of philosophy to the significant issues of actual experience is facilitated by constant interaction with the methods and conclusions of psychology. The more abstract sciences, mathematics and physics, for example, have left their impress deep upon traditional philosophy. The former, in connection with an exaggerated anxiety about formal certainty, has more than once operated to divorce philosophic thinking from connection with questions that have a source in existence. The remoteness of psychology from such abstractions, its nearness to what is distinctively human, gives it an emphatic claim for a sympathetic hearing at the present time.

In connection with an increasing recognition of this human aspect, there developed the influence which forms the fourth heading of this recital. The objective biological approach of the Jamesian psychology led straight to the perception of the importance of distinctive social categories, especially communication and participation. It is my conviction that a great deal of our philosophizing needs to be done over again from this point of view, and that there will ultimately result an integrated synthesis in a philosophy congruous with modern science and related to actual needs in education, morals, and religion. One has to take a broad survey in detachment from immediate prepossessions to realize the extent to which the characteristic traits of the science of to-day are connected with the development of social subjects—anthropology, history, politics, economics, language and literature, social and abnormal psychology, and so on. The movement is both so new, in an intellectual sense, and we are so much of it and it so much of us, that it escapes definite notice. Technically the influence of mathematics upon philosophy is more obvious; the great change that has taken place in recent years in the ruling ideas and methods of the physical sciences attracts attention much more easily than does the growth of the social subjects, just because it is farther away from impact upon us. Intellectual prophecy is dangerous; but if I read the cultural signs of the times aright, the next synthetic movement in philosophy will emerge when the significance of the social sciences and arts has become an object of reflective attention in the same way that mathematical and physical sciences have been made the objects of thought in the past, and when their full import is grasped. If I read these signs wrongly, nevertheless the statement may stand as a token of a factor significant in my own intellectual development.

In any case, I think it shows a deplorable deadness of imagination to suppose that philosophy will indefinitely revolve within the scope of the problems and systems that two thousand years of European history have bequeathed to us. Seen in the long perspective of the future, the whole of western European history is a provincial episode. I do not expect to see in my day a genuine, as distinct from a forced and artificial, integration of thought. But a mind that is not too egotistically impatient can have faith that this unification will issue in its season. Meantime a chief task of those who call themselves philosophers is to help get rid of the useless lumber that blocks our highways of thought, and strive to make straight and open the paths that lead to the future. Forty years spent in wandering in a wilderness like that of the present is not a sad fate—unless one attempts to make himself believe that the wilderness is after all itself the promised land.

NOTES

[LW 5:147–60.]

What
I Believe

(1930)

I

Faith was once almost universally thought to be acceptance of a definite body of intellectual propositions, acceptance being based upon authority—preferably that of revelation from on high. It meant adherence to a creed consisting of set articles. Such creeds are recited daily in our churches. Of late there has developed another conception of faith. This is suggested by the words of an American thinker: "Faith is tendency toward action." According to such a view, faith is the matrix of formulated creeds and the inspiration of endeavor. Change from the one conception of faith to the other is indicative of a profound alteration. Adherence to any body of doctrines and dogmas based upon a specific authority signifies distrust in the power of experience to provide, in its own ongoing movement, the needed principles of belief and action. Faith in its newer sense signifies that experience itself is the sole ultimate authority.

Such a faith has in it all the elements of a philosophy. For it implies that the course and material of experience give support and stay to life, and that its possibilities provide all the ends and ideals that are to regulate conduct. When these implications are made explicit, there emerges a definite philosophy. I have no intention here of trying to unfold such a philosophy, but rather to indicate what a philosophy based on experience as the ultimate authority in knowledge and conduct means in the present state of civilization, what its reactions are upon what is thought and done. For such a faith is not at present either articulate or widely held. If it were, it would be not so much a philosophy as a part of common sense.

In fact, it goes contrary to the whole trend of the traditions by which mankind is educated. On the whole it has been denied that experience and life can regulate themselves and provide their own means of direction and inspiration. Except for an occasional protest, historic philosophies have been "transcendental." And this trait of philosophies is a reflex of the fact that dominant moral codes and religious beliefs have appealed for support to something above and beyond experience. Experience has been systematically disparaged in contrast with something taken to be more fundamental and superior in worth.

Life as it is actually lived has been treated as a preparation for something outside of it and after it. It has been thought lawless, without meaning and value, except as it was taken to testify to a reality beyond itself. The creeds that have prevailed have been founded upon the supposed necessity of escape from the confusion and uncertainties of experience. Life has been thought to be evil and hopeless unless it could be shown to bear within itself the assured promise of a higher reality. Philosophies of escape have also been philosophies of compensation for the ills and sufferings of the experienced world.

Mankind has hardly inquired what would happen if the possibilities of experience were seriously explored and exploited. There has been much systematic exploration in science and much frantic exploitation in politics, business, and amusement. But this attention has been, so to say, incidental and in contravention to the professedly ruling scheme of belief. It has not been the product of belief in the power of experience to furnish organizing principles and directive ends. Religions have been saturated with the supernatural—and the supernatural signifies precisely that which lies beyond experience. Moral codes have been allied to this religious supernaturalism and have sought their foundation and sanction in it. Contrast with such ideas, deeply embedded in all Western culture, gives the philosophy of faith in experience a definite and profound meaning.

II

Why have men in the past resorted to philosophies of that which is above and beyond experience? And why should it be now thought possible to desist from such recourse? The answer to the first question is, undoubtedly, that the experience which men had, as well as any which they could reasonably anticipate, gave no signs of ability to furnish the means of its own regulation. It offered promises it refused to fulfill; it awakened desires only to frustrate them; it created hopes and blasted

them; it evoked ideals and was indifferent and hostile to their realization. Men who were incompetent to cope with the troubles and evils that experience brought with it, naturally distrusted the capacity of experience to give authoritative guidance. Since experience did not contain the arts by which its own course could be directed, philosophies and religions of escape and consolatory compensation naturally ensued.

What are the grounds for supposing that this state of affairs has changed and that it is now possible to put trust in the possibilities of experience itself? The answer to this question supplies the content of a philosophy of experience. There are traits of present experience which were unknown and unpossessed when the ruling beliefs of the past were developed. Experience now owns as a part of itself scientific methods of discovery and test; it is marked by ability to create techniques and technologies—that is, arts which arrange and utilize all sorts of conditions and energies, physical and human. These new possessions give experience and its potentialities a radically new meaning. It is a commonplace that since the seventeenth century science has revolutionized our beliefs about outer nature, and it is also beginning to revolutionize those about man.

When our minds dwell on this extraordinary change, they are likely to think of the transformation that has taken place in the subject matter of astronomy, physics, chemistry, biology, psychology, anthropology, and so on. But great as is this change, it shrinks in comparison with the change that has occurred in method. The latter is the author of the revolution in the content of beliefs. The new methods have, moreover, brought with them a radical change in our intellectual attitude and its attendant morale. The method we term "scientific" forms for the modern man (and a man is not modern merely because he lives in 1930) the sole dependable means of disclosing the realities of existence. It is the sole authentic mode of revelation. This possession of a new method, to the use of which no limits can be put, signifies a new idea of the nature and possibilities of experience. It imports a new morale of confidence, control, and security.

The change in knowledge has its overt and practical counterpart in what we term the Industrial Revolution, with its creation of arts for directing and using the energies of nature. Technology includes, of course, the engineering arts that have produced the railway, steamship, automobile, and airplane, the telegraph, telephone, and radio, and the printing press. But it also includes new procedures in medicine and hygiene, the function of insurance in all its branches, and, in its potentiality if not actualization, radically new methods in education and other modes of human relationship. "Technology" signifies all the intelligent techniques by which the energies of nature and man are directed and used in satisfaction of human needs; it cannot be limited to a few outer and comparatively mechanical forms. In the face of its possibilities, the traditional conception of experience is obsolete.

Different theories have expressed with more or less success this and that phase of the newer movements. But there is no integration of them into the standing habits and the controlling outlook of men and women. There are two great signs and tests of this fact. In science and in industry the fact of constant change is generally accepted. Moral, religious, and articulate philosophic creeds are based upon the idea of fixity. In the history of the race, change has been feared. It has been looked upon as the source of decay and degeneration. It has been opposed as the cause of disorder, chaos, and anarchy. One chief reason for the appeal to something beyond experience was the fact that experience is always in such flux that men had to seek stability and peace outside of it. Until the seventeenth century, the natural sciences shared in the belief in the superiority of the immutable to the moving, and took for their ideal the discovery of the permanent and changeless. Ruling philosophies, whether materialistic or spiritual, accepted the same notion as their foundation.

In this attachment to the fixed and immutable, both science and philosophy reflected the universal and pervasive conviction of religion and morals. Impermanence meant insecurity; the permanent was the sole ground of assurance and support amid the vicissitudes of existence. Christianity proffered a fixed revelation of absolute, unchanging Being and truth; and the revelation was elaborated into a system of definite rules and ends for the direction of life. Hence "morals" were conceived as a code of laws, the same everywhere and at all times. The good life was one lived in fixed adherence to fixed principles.

III

In contrast with all such beliefs, the outstanding fact in all branches of natural science is that to exist is to be in process, in change. Nevertheless, although the idea of movement and change has made itself at home in the physical sciences, it has had comparatively little influence on the popular mind as the latter looks at religion, morals, economics, and politics. In these fields it is still supposed that our choice is between confusion, anarchy, and something fixed and immutable. It is assumed that Christianity is the final religion; Jesus the complete and unchanging embodiment of the divine and the human. It is assumed that our present economic régime, at least in principle, expresses something final, something to endure—with, it is incidentally hoped, some improvements in detail. It is assumed, in spite of evident flux in the actual situation, that the institutions of marriage and family that developed in medieval Europe are the last and unchanging word.

These examples hint at the extent to which ideals of fixity persist in a moving world. A philosophy of experience will accept at its full value the fact that social and moral existences are, like physical existences, in a state of continuous if obscure change. It will not try to cover up the fact of inevitable modification, and will make no attempt to set fixed limits to the extent of changes that are to occur. For the futile effort to achieve security and anchorage in something fixed, it will substitute the effort to determine the character of changes that are going on and to give them in the affairs that concern us most some measure of intelligent direction. It is not called upon to cherish Utopian notions about the imminence of such intelligent direction of social changes. But it is committed to faith in the possibility of its slow effectuation in the degree in which men realize the full import of the revolution that has already been effected in physical and technical regions.

Wherever the thought of fixity rules, that of all-inclusive unity rules also. The popular philosophy of life is filled with desire to attain such an all-embracing unity, and formal philosophies have been devoted to an intellectual fulfillment of the desire. Consider the place occupied in popular thought by search for *the* meaning of life and *the* purpose of the universe. Men who look for a single purport and a single end either frame an idea of them according to their private desires and tradition, or else, not finding any such single unity, give up in despair and conclude that there is no genuine meaning and value in any of life's episodes.

The alternatives are not exhaustive, however. There is no need of deciding between no meaning at all and one single, all-embracing meaning. There are many meanings and many purposes in the situations with which we are confronted—one, so to say, for each situation. Each offers its own challenge to thought and endeavor, and presents its own potential value.

It is impossible, I think, even to begin to imagine the changes that would come into life—personal and collective—if the idea of a plurality of interconnected meanings and purposes replaced that of *the* meaning and purpose. Search for a single, inclusive good is doomed to failure. Such happiness as life is capable of comes from the full participation of all our powers in the endeavor to wrest from each changing situation of experience its own full and unique meaning. Faith in the varied possibilities of diversified experience is attended with the joy of constant discovery and of constant growing. Such a joy is possible even in the midst of trouble and defeat, whenever life-experiences are treated as potential disclosures of meanings and values that are to be used as means to a fuller and more significant future experience. Belief in a single purpose distracts thought and wastes energy that would help make the world better if it were directed to attainable ends.

IV

I have stated a general principle, because philosophy, I take it, is more than an enumeration of items of belief with respect to this and that question. But the principle can acquire definiteness only in application to actual issues. How about religion? Does renunciation of the extra-empirical compel also an abandonment of all religion? It certainly exacts a surrender of that supernaturalism and fixed dogma and rigid institutionalism with which Christianity has been historically associated. But as I read human nature and history, the intellectual content of religions has always finally adapted itself to scientific and social conditions after they have become clear. In a sense, it has been parasitic upon the latter.

For this reason I do not think that those who are concerned about the future of a religious attitude should trouble themselves about the conflict of science with traditional doctrines—though I can understand the perplexity of fundamentalists and liberals alike who have identified religion with a special set of beliefs. Concern about the future of religion should take, I think, a different direction. It is difficult to see how religion, after it has accommodated itself to the disintegrating effect of knowledge upon the dogmas of the church, can accommodate itself to traditional social institutions and remain vital.

It seems to me that the chief danger to religion lies in the fact that it has become so respectable. It has become largely a sanction of what socially exists—a kind of gloss upon institutions and conventions. Primitive Christianity was devastating in its claims. It was a religion of renunciation and denunciation of the "world"; it demanded a change of heart that entailed a revolutionary change in human relationships. Since the Western world is now alleged to be Christianized, a world of outworn institutions is accepted and blessed. A religion that began as a demand for a revolutionary change and that has become a sanction to established economic, political, and international institutions should perhaps lead its sincere devotees to reflect upon the sayings of the one worshiped as its founder: "Woe unto you when all men shall speak well of you," and, "Blessed are ye when men shall revile you and persecute you."

I do not mean by this that the future of religion is bound up with a return to the apocalyptic vision of the speedy coming of a heavenly kingdom. I do not mean that I think early Christianity has within itself even the germs of a ready-made remedy for present ills and a ready-made solution for present problems. Rather I would suggest that the future of religion is connected with the possibility of developing a faith in the possibilities of human experience and human relationships that will create a vital sense of the solidarity of human interests and inspire action to make that sense a reality. If our nominally religious institutions learn how to use their symbols and rites to express and enhance such a faith, they may become useful allies of a conception of life that is in harmony with knowledge and social needs.

Since existing Western civilization is what it is so largely because of the forces of industry and commerce, a genuinely religious attitude will be concerned with all that deeply affects human work and the leisure that is dependent upon the conditions and results of work. That is, it will acknowledge the significance of economic factors in life instead of evading the issue. The greatest obstacle that exists to the apprehension and actualization of the possibilities of experience is found in our economic régime. One does not have to accept the doctrine of economic determination of history and institutions to be aware that the opportunities of men in general to engage in an experience that is artistically and intellectually rich and rewarding in the daily modes of human intercourse is dependent upon economic conditions. As long as the supreme effort of those who influence thought and set the conditions under which men act is directed toward maintenance of the existing money economy and private profit, faith in the possibilities of an abundant and significant experience, participated in by all, will remain merely philosophic. While this matter was led up to by a consideration of religion, its significance extends far beyond the matter of religion. It affects every range and aspect of life.

Many persons have become acutely conscious of economic evils as far as they bear upon the life of wage earners, who form the great mass of mankind. It requires somewhat more imagination to see how the experience of those who are, as we say, well-to-do or are "comfortably off" is restricted and distorted. They seem to enjoy the advantages of the present situation. But they suffer as deeply from its defects. The artist and scientific inquirer are pushed outside the main currents of life and become appendages to its fringe or caterers to its injustices. All aesthetic and intellectual interests suffer in consequence. Useless display and luxury, the futile attempt to secure happiness through the possession of things, social position, and economic power over others, are manifestations of the restriction of experience that exists among those who seemingly profit by the present order. Mutual fear, suspicion, and jealousy are also its products. All of these things deflect and impoverish human experience beyond any calculation.

There may have been a time when such things had to be endured because mankind had neither the knowledge nor the arts by which to attain an abundant life shared by all. As it becomes increasingly evident that science and technology have given us the resources for dealing effectively with the workings of economic forces, the philosophy of the possibilities of experience takes on concrete meaning.

V

Our international system (since, with all its disorder, it is a system) presents another example, writ large, of the restriction of experience created by exclusiveness and isolation. In the arts and technical sciences, there already exist contacts and exchanges undreamed of even a century ago. Barring our execrable tariff walls, the same is true of commerce in physical commodities. But at the same time, race and color prejudice have never had such opportunity as they have now to poison the mind, while nationalism is elevated into a religion called patriotism. Peoples and nations exist in a state of latent antagonism when not engaged in overt conflict. This state of affairs narrows and impoverishes the experience of every individual in countless ways. An outward symbol of this restriction is found in the oft cited fact that eighty per cent of our national expenditure goes to pay for the results of past wars and preparing for future wars. The conditions of a vitally valuable experience for the individual are so bound up with complex, collective, so-cial relationships that the individualism of the past has lost its meaning. Individuals will always be the centre and the consummation of experience, but what an individual actually *is* in his life-experience depends upon the nature and movement of associated life. This is the lesson enforced by both our economic and our international systems.

Morals is not a theme by itself because it is not an episode nor department by itself. It marks the issue of all the converging forces of life. Codes that set up fixed and unchanging ends and rules have necessarily relaxed in the face of changing science and society. A new and effective morale can emerge only from an exploration of the realities of human association. Psychology and the social disciplines are beginning to furnish the instrumentalities of this inquiry. In no field has disrespect for experience had more disastrous consequences, for in no other has there been such waste. The experience of the past is largely thrown away. There has been no deliberate, cumulative process, no systematic transmission of what is learned in the contacts and intercourse of individuals with one another. It has been thought enough to hand on fixed rules and fixed ends. Controlled moral progress can begin only where there is the sifting and communication of the results of all relevant experiences of human association, such as now exists as a matter of course in the experiences of science with the natural world.

In popular speech, morals usually signifies matters of sex relationship. Phenomena of a period of acute transition like those of the present are poor material upon which to base prediction and foresight. But it is clear that the codes which still nominally prevail are the result of one-sided and restricted conditions. Present ideas of love, marriage, and the family are almost exclusively masculine constructions. Like all idealizations of human interests that express a dominantly one-sided experience, they are romantic in theory and prosaic in operation. Sentimental idealization on one side has its obverse in a literally conceived legal system. The realities of the relationships of men, women, and children to one another have been submerged in this fusion of senti-mentalism and legalism. The growing freedom of women can hardly have any other outcome than the production of more realistic and more human morals. It will be marked by a new freedom, but also by a new severity. For it will be enforced by the realities of associated life as they are disclosed to careful and systematic inquiry, and not by a combination of convention and an exhausted legal system with senti-mentality.

VI

The chief intellectual characteristic of the present age is its despair of any constructive philosophy—not just in its technical meaning, but in the sense of any integrated outlook and attitude. The developments of the last century have gone so far that we are now aware of the shock and overturn in older beliefs. But the formation of a new, coherent view of nature and man based upon facts consonant with science and actual social conditions is still to be had. What we call the Victorian Age seemed to have such a philosophy. It was a philosophy of hope, of progress, of all that is called liberalism. The growing sense of unsolved social problems, accentuated by the war, has shaken that faith. It is impossible to recover its mood.

The result is disillusionment about all comprehensive and positive ideas. The possession of constructive ideals is taken to be an admission that one is living in a realm of fantasy. We have lost confidence in reason because we have learned that man is chiefly a creature of habit and emotion. The notion that habit and impulse can themselves be rendered intelligent on any large and social scale is felt to be only another illusion. Because the hopes and expectations of the past have been discredited, there is cynicism as to all far-reaching plans and policies. That the very knowledge which enables us to detect the illusory character of past hopes and aspirations—a knowledge denied those who held them—may enable us to form purposes and expectations that are better grounded, is overlooked.

In fact, the contrast with the optimism of the Victorian Age is significant of the need and possibility of a radically different type of philosophy. For that era did not question the essential validity of older ideas. It recognized that the new science demanded a certain purification of traditional beliefs—such, for example, as the elimination of the supernatural. But in the main, Victorian thought conceived of new conditions as if they merely put in our hands effective instruments for realizing old ideals. The shock and uncertainty so characteristic of the present marks the discovery that the older ideals themselves are undermined. Instead of science and technology giving us better means for bringing them to pass, they are shaking our confidence in all large and comprehensive beliefs and purposes.

Such a phenomenon is, however, transitory. The impact of the new forces is for the time being negative. Faith in the divine author and authority in which Western civilization confided, inherited ideas of the soul and its destiny, of fixed revelation, of completely stable institutions, of automatic progress, have been made impossible for the cultivated mind of the Western world. It is psychologically natural that the outcome should be a collapse of faith in all fundamental organizing and directive ideas. Skepticism becomes the mark and even the pose of the educated mind. It is the more influential because it is no longer directed against this and that article of the older creeds but is rather a bias against any kind of far-reaching ideas, and a denial of systematic participation on the part of such ideas in the intelligent direction of affairs.

It is in such a context that a thoroughgoing philosophy of experience, framed in the light of science and technique, has its significance. For it, the breakdown of traditional ideas is an opportunity. The possibility of producing the kind of experience in which science and the arts are brought unitedly to bear upon industry, politics, religion, domestic life, and human relations in general, is itself something novel. We are not accustomed to it even as an idea. But faith in it is neither a dream nor a demonstrated failure. It is a faith. Realization of the faith, so that we may work in larger measure by sight of things achieved, is in the future. But the conception of it as a possibility when it is worked out in a coherent body of ideas, critical and constructive, forms a philosophy, an organized attitude of outlook, interpretation, and construction. A philosophic faith, being a tendency to action, can be tried and tested only in action. I know of no viable alternative in the present day to such a philosophy as has been indicated.

NOTES

[First published in *Forum* 83 (March 1930): 176–82, as part of a series. LW 5:267–78.]

In a recent number of the *Freeman* Bertrand Russell writes: "The two qualities which I consider superlatively important are love of truth and love of our neighbour. I find love of truth in America obscured by commercialism of which pragmatism is the philosophical expression; and love of our neighbour kept in fetters by Puritan morality." The statement comes to us with double importance. For it is obviously dictated by Mr. Russell's own love of truth and love for us as his neighbor. Police records and newspaper columns do not seem to indicate that Puritanism is effective in fettering our love for our neighbor's wife however much it restricts our love for him. If pragmatism is the intellectual reflection of commercialism, pragmatists seem to be assured of a speedy victory of their philosophy in England and the continent of Europe; for there are rumors, apparently authentic, that commercialism exists in strength in these outlying parts of the world. But such matters may be passed over, especially as Mr. Russell tells us that he is aware that the evils he finds in us are not unknown in the rest of the world, and that he urges their potency among us because we are more complacent, more boastful of our "idealism," less possessed of a critical minority than is the old world.

Mr. Russell is probably not entirely alone in the world in regarding love of truth and of neighbor as the two supreme human excellences. In the United States there are those who agree, at least in profession. The fact that the belief had some currency before he voiced it makes it the more important to consider the state of these virtues, and the power of their enemies among us. One otherwise attractive line of discussion is closed to us. We cannot cite evidence that we compare favorably with the rest of humanity in love of truth, and possibly a little more than favorably in respect to love of neighbors. For such a method turns against us. It is just another sample of our obdurate complacency, of the rationalizing idealization with which we obscure our critical perception of the truth.

The suggestion that pragmatism is the intellectual equivalent of commercialism need not, however, be taken too seriously. It is of that order of interpretation which would say

Pragmatic America

(1922)

that English neo-realism is a reflection of the aristocratic snobbery of the English; the tendency of French thought to dualism an expression of an alleged Gallic disposition to keep a mistress in addition to a wife; and the idealism of Germany a manifestation of an ability to elevate beer and sausage into a higher synthesis with the spiritual values of Beethoven and Wagner. Nor does the figure of William James exist in exact correspondence with a glorification of commercialism. The man who wrote that "callousness to abstract justice is *the* sinister feature of U.S. civilization," that this callousness is a "symptom of the moral flabbiness born of the exclusive worship of the bitch-goddess SUCCESS," and that this worship "together with the squalid cash interpretation put upon the word success is our national disease" was not consciously nor unconsciously engaged in an intellectual formulation of the spirit he abhorred. Nor was Charles Peirce conspicuous for conformity to commercial standards. Emotional irritation coexists in our humanity with the consideration that love of truth is a superlative good, and it is capable upon occasion of blinding that love.

Nevertheless, there is something instructive about our spiritual estate in the fact that pragmatism was born upon American soil, and that pragmatism presents consequences as a test and a responsibility of the life of reason. Historically the fact is testimony to "Anglo-Saxon" kinship; it is testimony to spiritual kinship with Bacon, who wrote that "truth and utility are the very same thing, and works themselves are of greater value as pledges of truth than as contributing to the comforts of life"; who taught that the end and the test of science and philosophy are their fruits for the relief and betterment of the estate of humanity; while also holding that converting science and philosophy to immediate fruitage for lucre and reputation is their curse. American pragmatism is testimony that the tradition of Bacon carried on in divers ways by Hobbes, Locke and Hume has taken root here.

Yet there is special significance in the fact that this tradition was first revived and then made central by Peirce and James in the United States. Anyone who wishes to take a census of our spiritual estate (along with the censorship implied in a census) will assuredly find the pragmatic spirit important. It is a commonplace, however, that strength and weakness, excellence and defect, go together, because they are the two sides of the same thing. If, therefore, love of truth is to express itself in a discriminating way, it must be willing to attach itself to our sense that consequences are the test and the token of responsibility in the operation of intelligence until its significance is extracted. It is not in the first instance a question of the truth of this feeling. The disposition may be, if you please, as obnoxious to ultimate philosophic truth as it is repellent to certain temperaments. But first we have to find out what it means, what it means for both good and bad. Love of truth is manifest in desire to understand rather than in hurry to praise and blame.

A conviction that consequences in human welfare are a test of the worth of beliefs and thoughts has some obvious beneficial aspects. It makes for a fusion of the two superlatively important qualities, love of truth and love of neighbor. It discourages dogmatism and its child, intolerance. It arouses and heartens an experimental spirit which wants to know how systems and theories work before giving complete adhesion. It militates against too sweeping and easy generalizations, even against those which would indict a nation. Compelling attention to details, to particulars, it safeguards one from seclusion in universals; one is obliged, as William James was always saying, to get down from noble aloofness into the muddy stream of concrete things. It fosters a sense of the worth of communication of what is known. This takes effect not only in education, but in a belief that we do not fully know the meaning of anything till it has been imparted, shared, made common property. I well remember the remark of an unschooled American pioneer, who said of a certain matter that some day it would not only be found out, but it would be known. He was ignorant of books, but he declared the profound philosophy that nothing is really known till it operates in the common life.

Any such attitude is clearly a faith, not a demonstration. It too can be demonstrated only in *its* works, its fruits. Therefore it is not a facile thing. It commits us to a supremely difficult task. Perhaps the task is too hard for human nature. The faith may demonstrate its own falsity by failure. We may be arrested on the plane of commercial "success"; we may be diverted to search for consequences easier to achieve, and may noisily acclaim superficial and even disastrous "works" and fruits as proof of genuine success instead of evidence of failure. We not only may do so, but we actually are doing so. If the course of history be run, if our present estate be final, no honest soul can claim that success exceeds failure. Perhaps this will always remain the case. Humanity is not conspicuous for having made a successful job of life anywhere. But an honest soul will also admit that the failure is not due to inherent defects in the faith, but to the fact that its demands are too high for human power; that mankind is not up to making good the requirements of the faith, or at least that that part of a common humanity which inhabits these United States is not up to it, and that the experiment must be passed on to another place and time.

Yet the gloomiest view reminds us of another phase of the pragmatic faith. Undoubtedly in expressing his sense of a world still open, a world still in the making, William James reported, perhaps with some superfluous accretions of romanticism to his native idiom, a characteristic feature of the American scene. Be the evils what they may, the experiment is not yet played out. The United States are not yet made; they are not a finished fact to be categorically assessed. Mr. James' assertion that the world is still making does not import a facile faith. He knew well that the world has also its madeness, and that what is done and over with fearfully complicates the task of making the future that human better we should like it to be.

A discriminating spiritual census of the United States will, therefore, ask about the already made things which we inherit and which mix with our creative making to arrest, divert and pervert it. After all we inherit from a Europe which was, compared with our scene, a made affair. Every day our cities are eloquent of the past fruits of a feudal Europe. His power far exceeds mine who can tell just how much

of our present ill is due to the commercialism which is of our making and how much is due to deposit of an ancient feudalism. Commerce itself, let us dare to say it, is a noble thing. It is intercourse, exchange, communication, distribution, sharing of what is otherwise secluded and private. Commercialism like all isms is evil. That we have not as yet released commerce from bondage to private interests is proof of the solidity and tenacity of our European heritage. Commerce in knowledge, in intelligence, is still a side-issue, precarious, spasmodic, corrupt. Pragmatic faith walks in chains, not erect.

One other heritage of things already made still has to be reckoned with, reckoned with in social practice as well as in formulation. These United States were born when the pragmatic and experimental faith of the English tradition was in eclipse. Bacon did not exaggerate the control of nature to be obtained from study of nature. But he enormously underestimated that inertia of social forces which would resist free application of the new power to the relief and betterment of the human estate, and which would effect a private monopolization of the fruits of the new power of knowledge. Those who were called liberals lost their faith in experimental method. They were seduced into desiring a creed as absolute, as final, as eternal as that wielded by their opponents. The dogma of natural rights of the individual was the product. The pioneer, agrarian American scene was a congenial home for the new dogma. We tied ourselves down to political and legal practices and institutions radically hostile to our native disposition and endeavor. Legalism, along with feudalized commercialism, wedded to form modern commercialism, is the anti-pragmatic "made" which hinders and perverts our pragmatic makings. It is incarnate in constitutions and courts. The resulting situation is not one which calls for complacency. But the beginning of improvement is to place responsibility where it belongs.

Our noisy and nauseating "idealism" is an expression of the emotions which would cover and disguise a mixed situation. There is a genuine idealism of faith in the future, in experiment directed by intelligence, in the communication of knowledge, in the rights of the common man to a common share in the fruits of the spirit. This spirit when it works does not need to talk. But its workings are paralyzed here, arrested there, and more or less corrupted everywhere by a feudalized commercialism and a legalism which we cover up with eloquent speeches because we do not honestly confront them. Discrimination is the first fruit of love of truth and of love of neighbor. Till we discriminate we shall oscillate between wholesale revulsion and the sloppy idealism of popular emotion.

NOTES

[First published in *New Republic* 30 (1922): 185–87. Republished in *Characters and Events*, ed. Joseph Ratner (New York: Henry Holt and Co., 1929), 2:542–47. MW 13:306–10.]

The Pragmatic Acquiescence

(1927)

There are myths and myths. Some are inspiriting; some are benumbing. Nature myths, at least in their first form, inspire because they are spontaneous responses of imagination to the scene that confronts it. Myths of literary criticism and historic interpretation are deadening. They do not enliven; they force subject-matter into ready-made patterns and thus dull sensitivity of perception. Such myths grow up in interpretations of past philosophies and always tend to overlay and conceal the realities of past reflection. They flourish in those literary versions by which the ideas of philosophers reach the public—for philosophers themselves are usually too much preoccupied with the technique, the professional rules, of their calling to have a public—except one another. Even such new movements as pragmatism and instrumentalism already have their accretion of myths which stand in place of the ideas themselves. Probably the unfortunate names themselves invite the creation and encourage the spread of these myths. The names account alike for some of the vogue of the doctrines and for some of the condemnation they receive.

One reading of the myth is embodied in the words which form the caption of what I am writing. They are borrowed from Lewis Mumford's *The Golden Day*; they sum up his essential criticism. "William James," he says, "gave this attitude of compromise and acquiescence a name: he called it pragmatism." Not content with this epithet, he headlines the idea of acquiescence; "the pragmatism that followed it was a paralysis." And again, "pragmatism was a blessed anesthetic." What is denoted by "this attitude"? And in what did James acquiesce? The America of his own time, according to Mr. Mumford, the America of the Gilded Age that followed the Civil War. More concerned with making clear his pattern than he is with William James he goes as far as to say, "James was only warming over again in philosophy the hash of everyday experience in the Gilded Age." And this of William James, the arch-heretic of his day, the intellectual nonconformist, the constant protester against everything institutionalized in action and belief, the valiant fighter for causes which if not lost were unpopular and conventionally ignored! Such are the exigencies and dangers of a myth. If one were to apply Mr. Mumford's method to his own treatment, one might regard him as the acquiescent prophet of the Slogan Age of the 1920's.

For some reason, Mr. Mumford is fairer to me than he is to William James. But to bring me into line with his formula he has to attribute to me ideas of democracy and of "adjustment" which I not only have never held, but against which I have consistently, if vainly, taught and written. As evidence of a willing surrender on my part to industrial utilitarianism, he cites the following passage from my writings: "Fine art, consciously undertaken as such, is peculiarly instrumental in quality. It is a device in experimentation carried on for the sake of education. It exists for the sake of a specialized use, use being a training of new modes of perception," etc. The reader of the passage would inevitably infer what Mr. Mumford intends him to infer, that the passage represents my view of fine art, namely, that it is merely instrumental in character. But the entire chapter from which it is extracted is a statement that all art which is really fine exhibits experience when it attains completion or a "final," consummatory character, and, while it is urged that such art is also contributory, that to which it is held to be auxiliary is "renewal of spirit," not, it would seem, a base end, and certainly not a utilitarian one. The passage cited is directed against those views of fine art which treat it as an experience apart and for the few, an esoteric experience, instead of as a perfecting of the potentialities of any and all experience. This reference is implied in the quoted phrase "consciously undertaken as such"; it is explicitly stated in words which immediately precede what is cited, namely "seclusive estheticians," the point being that fine art conceived in *their* sense is "instrumental," so that while all value is not denied to it, its value consists in opening "new objects to be observed and enjoyed." The next sentence after those which Mr. Mumford quotes, reads as follows: "This is a genuine service, but only an age of combined confusion and conceit will arrogate to works that perform this special utility the exclusive name of fine art." My literary style must indeed be "fuzzy and formless," as Mr. Mumford calls it, to have led him to assign to me a definition of fine art which I assert indicates combined confusion and conceit.

William James, however, hardly needs defense, certainly not against shaping him to a pattern which inverts his whole spirit and thought, and I do not think that a few more misconceptions of my own ideas are of such importance as to justify writing the present article. What has been said is introductory to an issue which is of genuine significance. What is the relation of criticism to the social life criticized? What, more particularly, is the relation of philosophy to its social medium and generation? I doubt if any competent student of the history of thought would say that there has existed any philosophy which amounted to anything which was merely a formulated acquiescence in the immediately predominating traits of its day. Such things need no formulation, not even an apologetics; they dominate and that is enough for them. Yet there is probably also no historic philosophy which is not in some measure a reflection, an idealization, a justification of some of the tendencies of its own age. Yet what makes it a work of reflection and criticism is that the elements and values selected are set in opposition to other factors, and those perhaps the ones most in evidence, the most clamorous, the most insistent: which is to say that all serious thinking combines in some proportion and perspective the actual and the possible, where actuality supplies contact and solidity while possibility furnishes the ideal upon which criticism rests and from which creative effort springs. The question whether the possibility appealed to is a possibility of the actual, or is externally imported and applied, is crucial.

There is a sense, then, in which pragmatic philosophy is a report of actual social life; in the same sense it is true of any philosophy that is not a private and quickly forgotten intellectual excrescence. Not that philosophers set out to frame such reports. They are usually too much preoccupied with the special traditions within which their work is done to permit the assumption of any such task. They are concerned with doing the best they can with problems and issues which come to them from the conflict of their professional traditions, which, therefore, are specialized and technical, and through which they see the affairs of the contemporary scene only indirectly and, alas, darkly. Nevertheless being human they may retain enough humanity to be, sub-consciously at least, sensitive to the non-technical, non-professional, tendencies and issues of their own civilizations, and to find in the peculiar characteristics of this civilization subjects for inquiry and analysis. In any case, it is as necessary as it is legitimate that their methods and results should, in their leading features, be translated out of their proper technical context and set in a freer and more public landscape. The product of the dislocation may surprise no one more than the author of the technical doctrines. But without it the ulterior and significant meaning of the doctrines is neither liberated nor tested. The office of the literary and social critic in dealing with the broader human relationship of specialized philosophical thinking is, accordingly, to be cherished. But the office is a difficult one to perform, more difficult to do well than that of technical philosophizing itself, just as any truly liberal human work is harder to achieve than is a technical task. Preconceptions, fixed patterns, too urgent desire to point a moral, are almost fatal. A pattern is implied in such critical interpretation, but it must be tridimensional and flowing, not linear and tight.

What, then, is to be said of pragmatism and of instrumentalism when they are viewed as reflective reports of the American scene? More specifically, admitting a certain connection between the thought of James and the pioneer phase of American life and between instrumentalism and our industrialism, how is that connection to be understood? Mr. Mumford recognizes that the reflection by James of pioneer life is genuine and significant as far as it goes. But, he says, a "valuable philosophy must take into account a greater range of experience than the dominating ones of a single generation." Doubtless: nevertheless the dominating tendencies of two or three centuries may reveal to a genial mind something of vast significance for all generations. Their very exaggeration may disclose something hitherto concealed, while the lack of that something

may have introduced such distortion and thinness into the earlier intellectual picture that its disclosure operates as a transformation. Mr. Mumford says that James lacked a Welt-Anschauung. No sentence he could have uttered affords such a measure of his competency to state the relation which the thought of James bore to pioneerdom. The idea of a universe which is not all closed and settled, which is still in some respects indeterminate and in the making, which is adventurous and which implicates all who share in it, whether by acting or believing, in its own perils, may appear to Mr. Mumford a commonplace, and not to be reckoned as a Welt-Anschauung. But one who has not studied James patiently enough to learn how this idea is wrought into his treatment of all special topics, from the will to believe to his pluralism, from his radical empiricism to his moral and religious ideas, has not got far in knowledge of James. That the controlling Welt-Anschauung does not appear in formal and pompous logical parade in discussion of special topics may not make the task of the would-be critic easy. But the style shows how genuinely and spontaneously the leading idea pervades his thinking. No other mode of literary presentation could have been so faithful to the central thought.

Perhaps one has to be old enough to recall, with some fullness of impression, the intellectual atmosphere in which James's work was carried on to realize that James brought with him not only a Welt-Anschauung but a revolutionary one. His professional contemporaries did not even trouble to criticize his philosophy; it was enough to laugh. Was it not self-evidently a more or less delightful whimsy of a tyro in philosophy who happened at the same time to be temperamentally something of a genius in psychology? Not until he gathered together the ideas which long previously he had profusely scattered in his other writings under the rather unfortunate title of pragmatism did he receive serious attention. And long after "pragmatism" in any sense save as an application of his Welt-Anschauung shall have passed into a not unhappy oblivion, the fundamental idea of an open universe in which uncertainty, choice, hypotheses, novelties and possibilities are naturalized will remain associated with the name of James; the more he is studied in his historic setting the more original and daring will the idea appear. And if perchance the future historian associates the generation of the idea with a pioneer America—in which James had no personal share—that historian may be trusted to see that such an idea is removed as far as pole from pole from the temper of an age whose occupation is acquisition, whose concern is with security, and whose creed is that the established economic régime is peculiarly "natural" and hence immutable in principle.

But America is now industrial and technological, not pioneering. Perhaps the later form of pragmatism called instrumentalism is the anodyne to reconcile the imagination and desire of man to the brutalities and perversions of this aspect of our life? Well, natural science and the technology which has issued from it are dominant tendencies of present culture, more conspicuously prominent in the United States than elsewhere, but everywhere all but universal in scope. That preoccupation with them should, whether consciously or subconsciously, have played a part in generating "instrumentalism" is a not unreasonable hypothesis. What then? If one confronts this phenomenon and does not withdraw for consolation to the "pillaging" of other climes and epochs, what is to be done with it? It needs criticism, not acquiescence: granted. But there is no criticism without understanding. And no matter how much one may draw upon contrasting phases of life, Greek, Indian with Mr. Santayana, or the Golden Day of Emerson, Thoreau and Whitman with Mr. Mumford, for aid in this understanding, it is also true that without an understanding of natural science and technology in their own terms, understanding is external, arbitrary, and criticism is "transcendent" and ultimately of one's own private conceit.

Words, especially epithets, in philosophy are far from self-explaining. But the term "instrumentalism" might suggest to a mind not too precommitted, that natural science and technology are conceived as instruments, and that the logical intellect of mind which finds its congenial materials in these subjects is also instrumental—that is to say, not final, not complete, not the truth or reality of the world and life. Instruments imply, I should suppose, ends to which they are put, purposes that are not instruments which control them, values for which tools and agencies are to be used. The record of philosophy doubtless presents instances of almost utter self-contradiction and self-stultification. But it would require a mind unusually devoid both of sense of logic and a sense of humor—if there be any difference between them—to try to universalize instrumentalism, to set up a doctrine of tools which are not tools for anything except for more tools. The counterpart of "instrumentalism" is precisely that the values by which Mr. Mumford sets such store are the ends for the attainment of which natural science and all technologies and industries and industriousnesses are intrinsically, not externally and transcendentally, or by way of exhortation, contributory. The essential and immanent criticism of existing industrialism and of the dead weight of science is that instruments are made into ends, that they are deflected from their intrinsic quality and thereby corrupted. The implied idealization of science and technology is not by way of acquiescence. It is by way of appreciation that the ideal values which dignify and give meaning to human life have themselves in the past been precarious in possession, arbitrary, accidental and monopolized in distribution, because of lack of means of control; by lack, in other words, of those agencies and instrumentalities with which natural science through technologies equips mankind. Not all who say Ideals, Ideals, shall enter the kingdom of the ideal, but those who know and who respect the roads that conduct to the kingdom.

NOTES

[First published in *New Republic* 49 (1927): 186–89. LW 3:145–51.]

PART 2

Reconstructing Philosophy

I

That the publication of the *Origin of Species* marked an epoch in the development of the natural sciences is well known to the layman. That the combination of the very words origin and species embodied an intellectual revolt and introduced a new intellectual temper is easily overlooked by the expert. The conceptions that had reigned in the philosophy of nature and knowledge for two thousand years, the conceptions that had become the familiar furniture of the mind, rested on the assumption of the superiority of the fixed and final; they rested upon treating change and origin as signs of defect and unreality. In laying hands upon the sacred ark of absolute permanency, in treating the forms that had been regarded as types of fixity and perfection as originating and passing away, the *Origin of Species* introduced a mode of thinking that in the end was bound to transform the logic of knowledge, and hence the treatment of morals, politics and religion.

No wonder then that the publication of Darwin's book, a half-century ago, precipitated a crisis. The true nature of the controversy is easily concealed from us, however, by the theological clamor that attended it. The vivid and popular features of the anti-Darwinian row tended to leave the impression that the issue was between science on one side and theology on the other. Such was not the case—the issue lay primarily within science itself, as Darwin himself early recognized. The theological outcry he discounted from the start, hardly noticing it save as it bore upon the "feelings of his female relatives." But for two decades before final publication he contemplated the possibility of being put down by his scientific peers as a fool or as crazy; and he set, as the measure of his success, the degree in which he should affect three men of science: Lyell in geology, Hooker in botany and Huxley in zoology.

Religious considerations lent fervor to the controversy, but they did not provoke it. Intellectually, religious emotions are not creative but conservative. They attach themselves readily to the current view of the world and consecrate it. They steep and dye intellectual fabrics in the seething vat of emotions; they do

The Influence of Darwinism on Philosophy[1]

(1909)

not form their warp and woof. There is not, I think, an instance of any large idea about the world being independently generated by religion. Although the ideas that rose up like armed men against Darwinism owed their intensity to religious associations, their origin and meaning are to be sought in science and philosophy, not in religion.

II

Few words in our language foreshorten intellectual history as much as does the word species. The Greeks, in initiating the intellectual life of Europe, were impressed by characteristic traits of the life of plants and animals; so impressed indeed that they made these traits the key to defining nature and to explaining mind and society. And truly life is so wonderful that a seemingly successful reading of its mystery might well lead men to believe that the key to the secrets of heaven and earth was in their hands. The Greek rendering of this mystery, the Greek formulation of the aim and standard of knowledge, was in the course of time embodied in the word species, and it controlled philosophy for two thousand years. To understand the intellectual face-about expressed in the phrase "Origin of Species," we must, then, understand the long dominant idea against which it is a protest.

Consider how men were impressed by the facts of life. Their eyes fell upon certain things slight in bulk, and frail in structure. To every appearance, these perceived things were inert and passive. Suddenly, under certain circumstances, these things—henceforth known as seeds or eggs or germs—begin to change, to change rapidly in size, form and qualities. Rapid and extensive changes occur, however, in many things—as when wood is touched by fire. But the changes in the living thing are orderly; they are cumulative; they tend constantly in one direction; they do not, like other changes, destroy or consume, or pass fruitless into wandering flux; they realize and fulfil. Each successive stage, no matter how unlike its predecessor, preserves its net effect and also prepares the way for a fuller activity on the part of its successor. In living beings, changes do not happen as they seem to happen elsewhere,

any which way; the earlier changes are regulated in view of later results. This progressive organization does not cease till there is achieved a true final term, a τελὸς, a completed, perfected end. This final form exercises in turn a plenitude of functions, not the least noteworthy of which is production of germs like those from which it took its own origin, germs capable of the same cycle of self-fulfilling activity.

But the whole miraculous tale is not yet told. The same drama is enacted to the same destiny in countless myriads of individuals so sundered in time, so severed in space, that they have no opportunity for mutual consultation and no means of interaction. As an old writer quaintly said, "things of the same kind go through the same formalities"—celebrate, as it were, the same ceremonial rites.

This formal activity which operates throughout a series of changes and holds them to a single course; which subordinates their aimless flux to its own perfect manifestation; which, leaping the boundaries of space and time, keeps individuals distant in space and remote in time to a uniform type of structure and function: this principle seemed to give insight into the very nature of reality itself. To it Aristotle gave the name, εἶδος. This term the scholastics translated as *species*.

The force of this term was deepened by its application to everything in the universe that observes order in flux and manifests constancy through change. From the casual drift of daily weather, through the uneven recurrence of seasons and unequal return of seed time and harvest, up to the majestic sweep of the heavens— the image of eternity in time—and from this to the unchanging pure and contemplative intelligence beyond nature lies one unbroken fulfilment of ends. Nature, as a whole, is a progressive realization of purpose strictly comparable to the realization of purpose in any single plant or animal.

The conception of eidos, species, a fixed form and final cause, was the central principle of knowledge as well as of nature. Upon it rested the logic of science. Change as change is mere flux and lapse; it insults intelligence. Genuinely to know is to grasp a permanent end that realizes itself through changes, holding them thereby within the metes and bounds of fixed truth. Completely to know is to relate all special forms to their one single end and good: pure contemplative intelligence. Since, however, the scene of nature which directly confronts us is in change, nature as directly and practically experienced does not satisfy the conditions of knowledge. Human experience is in flux, and hence the instrumentalities of sense-perception and of inference based upon observation are condemned in advance. Science is compelled to aim at realities lying behind and beyond the processes of nature, and to carry on its search for these realities by means of rational forms transcending ordinary modes of perception and inference.

There are, indeed, but two alternative courses. We must either find the appropriate objects and organs of knowledge in the mutual interactions of changing things; or else, to escape the infection of change, we *must* seek them in some transcendent and supernal region. The human mind, deliberately as it were, exhausted the logic of the changeless, the final and the transcendent, before it essayed adventure on the pathless wastes of generation and transformation. We dispose all too easily of the efforts of the schoolmen to interpret nature and mind in terms of real essences, hidden forms and occult faculties, forgetful of the seriousness and dignity of the ideas that lay behind. We dispose of them by laughing at the famous gentleman who accounted for the fact that opium put people to sleep on the ground it had a dormitive faculty. But the doctrine, held in our own day, that knowledge of the plant that yields the poppy consists in referring the peculiarities of an individual to a type, to a universal form, a doctrine so firmly established that any other method of knowing was conceived to be unphilosophical and unscientific, is a survival of precisely the same logic. This identity of conception in the scholastic and anti-Darwinian theory may well suggest greater sympathy for what has become unfamiliar as well as greater humility regarding the further unfamiliarities that history has in store.

Darwin was not, of course, the first to question the classic philosophy of nature and of knowledge. The beginnings of the revolution are in the physical science of the sixteenth and seventeenth centuries. When Galileo said: "It is my opinion that the Earth is very noble and admirable by reason of so many and so different alterations and generations which are incessantly made therein," he expressed the changed temper that was coming over the world; the transfer of interest from the permanent to the changing. When Descartes said: "The nature of physical things is much more easily conceived when they are beheld coming gradually into existence, than when they are only considered as produced at once in a finished and perfect state," the modern world became self-conscious of the logic that was henceforth to control it, the logic of which Darwin's *Origin of Species* is the latest scientific achievement. Without the methods of Copernicus, Kepler, Galileo and their successors in astronomy, physics and chemistry, Darwin would have been helpless in the organic sciences. But prior to Darwin the impact of the new scientific method upon life, mind and politics, had been arrested, because between these ideal or moral interests and the inorganic world intervened the kingdom of plants and animals. The gates of the garden of life were barred to the new ideas; and only through this garden was there access to mind and politics. The influence of Darwin upon philosophy resides in his having conquered the phenomena of life for the principle of transition, and thereby freed the new logic for application to mind and morals and life. When he said of species what Galileo had said of the earth, *e pur si muove*, he emancipated, once for all, genetic and experimental ideas as an organon of asking questions and looking for explanations.

III

The exact bearings upon philosophy of the new logical outlook are, of course, as yet, uncertain and inchoate. We live in the twilight of intellectual transition. One must add the rashness of the prophet to the stubbornness of the partisan to venture a systematic exposition of the influence upon philosophy of the Darwinian method. At best, we can but inquire as to its general bearing—the effect upon mental temper and complexion, upon that body of half-conscious, half-instinctive intellectual aversions and preferences which determine, after all, our more deliberate intellectual enterprises. In this vague inquiry there happens to exist as a kind of touchstone a problem of long historic currency that has also been much discussed in Darwinian literature. I refer to the old problem of design *versus* chance, mind *versus* matter, as the causal explanation, first or final, of things.

As we have already seen, the classic notion of species carried with it the idea of purpose. In all living forms, a specific type is present directing the earlier stages of growth to the realization of its own perfection. Since this purposive regulative principle is not visible to the senses, it follows that it must be an ideal or rational force. Since, however, the perfect form is gradually approximated through the sensible changes, it also follows that in and through a sensible realm a rational ideal force is working out its own ultimate manifestation. These inferences were extended to nature: (*a*) She does nothing in vain; but all for an ulterior purpose. (*b*) Within natural sensible events there is therefore contained a spiritual causal force, which as spiritual escapes perception, but is apprehended by an enlightened reason. (*c*) The manifestation of this principle brings about a subordination of matter and sense to its own realization, and this ultimate fulfilment is the goal of nature and of man. The design argument thus operated in two directions. Purposefulness accounted for the intelligibility of nature and the possibility of science, while the absolute or cosmic character of this purposefulness gave sanction and worth to the moral and religious endeavors of man. Science was underpinned and morals authorized by one and the same principle, and their mutual agreement was eternally guaranteed.

This philosophy remained, in spite of sceptical and polemic outbursts, the official and the regnant philosophy of Europe for over two thousand years. The expulsion of fixed first and final causes from astronomy, physics and chemistry had indeed given the doctrine something of a shock. But, on the other hand, increased acquaintance with the details of plant and animal life operated as a counterbalance and perhaps even strengthened the argument from design. The marvelous adaptations of organisms to their environment, of organs to the organism, of unlike parts of a complex organ—like the eye—to the organ itself; the foreshadowing by lower forms of the higher; the preparation in earlier stages of growth for organs that only later had their functioning— these things were increasingly recognized with the progress of botany, zoology, paleontology and embryology. Together they added such prestige to the design argument that by the late eighteenth century it was, as approved by the sciences of organic life, the central point of theistic and idealistic philosophy.

The Darwinian principle of natural selection cut straight under this philosophy. If all organic adaptations are due simply to constant variation and the elimination of those variations which are harmful in the struggle for existence that is brought about by excessive reproduction, there is no call for a prior intelligent causal force to plan and preordain them. Hostile critics charged Darwin with materialism and with making chance the cause of the universe.

Some naturalists, like Asa Gray, favored the Darwinian principle and attempted to reconcile it with design. Gray held to what may be called design on the installment plan. If we conceive the "stream of variations" to be itself intended, we may suppose that each successive variation was designed from the first to be selected. In that case, variation, struggle and selection simply define the mechanism of "secondary causes" through which the "first cause" acts; and the doctrine of design is none the worse off because we know more of its *modus operandi*.

Darwin could not accept this mediating proposal. He admits or rather he asserts that it is "impossible to conceive this immense and wonderful universe including man with his capacity of looking far backwards and far into futurity as the result of blind chance or necessity."[2] But nevertheless he holds that since variations are in useless as well as useful directions, and since the latter are sifted out simply by the stress of the conditions of struggle for existence, the design argument as applied to living beings is unjustifiable; and its lack of support there deprives it of scientific value as applied to nature in general. If the variations of the pigeon, which under artificial selection give the pouter pigeon, are not preordained for the sake of the breeder, by what logic do we argue that variations resulting in natural species are pre-designed?[3]

IV

So much for some of the more obvious facts of the discussion of design *versus* chance as causal principles of nature and of life as a whole. We brought up this discussion, you recall, as a crucial instance. What does our touchstone indicate as to the bearing of Darwinian ideas upon philosophy? In the first place, the new logic outlaws, flanks, dismisses—what you will—one type of problems and substitutes for it another type. Philosophy forswears inquiry after absolute origins and absolute finalities in order to explore specific values and the specific conditions that generate them.

Darwin concluded that the impossibility of assigning the world to chance as a whole and to design in its parts indicated the insolubility of the question. Two radically different reasons, however, may be given as to why a problem is insoluble. One reason is that the problem is too high for intelligence; the other is that the question in its very asking makes assumptions that render the question meaningless. The latter alternative is unerringly pointed to in the celebrated case of design *versus* chance. Once admit that the sole verifiable or fruitful object of knowledge is the particular set of changes that generate the object of study, together with the consequences that then flow from it, and no intelligible question can be asked about what, by assumption, lies outside. To assert—as is often asserted—that specific values of particular truth, social bonds and forms of beauty, if they can be shown to be generated by concretely knowable conditions, are meaningless and in vain; to assert that they are justified only when they and their particular causes and effects have all at once been gathered up into some inclusive first cause and some exhaustive final goal, is intellectual atavism. Such argumentation is reversion to the logic that explained the extinction of fire by water through the formal essence of aqueousness and the quenching of thirst by water

through the final cause of aqueousness. Whether used in the case of the special event or that of life as a whole, such logic only abstracts some aspect of the existing course of events in order to reduplicate it as a petrified eternal principle by which to explain the very changes of which it is the formalization.

When Henry Sidgwick casually remarked in a letter that as he grew older his interest in what or who made the world was altered into interest in what kind of a world it is anyway, his voicing of a common experience of our own day illustrates also the nature of that intellectual transformation effected by the Darwinian logic. Interest shifts from the wholesale essence back of special changes to the question of how special changes serve and defeat concrete purposes; shifts from an intelligence that shaped things once for all to the particular intelligences which things are even now shaping; shifts from an ultimate goal of good to the direct increments of justice and happiness that intelligent administration of existent conditions may beget and that present carelessness or stupidity will destroy or forego.

In the second place, the classic type of logic inevitably set philosophy upon proving that life *must* have certain qualities and values—no matter how experience presents the matter—because of some remote cause and eventual goal. The duty of wholesale justification inevitably accompanies all thinking that makes the meaning of special occurrences depend upon something that once and for all lies behind them. The habit of derogating from present meanings and uses prevents our looking the facts of experience in the face; it prevents serious acknowledgment of the evils they present and serious concern with the goods they promise but do not as yet fulfil. It turns thought to the business of finding a wholesale transcendent remedy for the one and guarantee for the other. One is reminded of the way many moralists and theologians greeted Herbert Spencer's recognition of an unknowable energy from which welled up the phenomenal physical processes without and the conscious operations within. Merely because Spencer labeled his unknowable energy "God," this faded piece of metaphysical goods was greeted as an important and grateful concession to the reality of the spiritual realm. Were it not for the deep hold of the habit of seeking justification for ideal values in the remote and transcendent, surely this reference of them to an unknowable absolute would be despised in comparison with the demonstrations of experience that knowable energies are daily generating about us precious values.

The displacing of this wholesale type of philosophy will doubtless not arrive by sheer logical disproof, but rather by growing recognition of its futility. Were it a thousand times true that opium produces sleep because of its dormitive energy, yet the inducing of sleep in the tired, and the recovery to waking life of the poisoned, would not be thereby one least step forwarded. And were it a thousand times dialectically demonstrated that life as a whole is regulated by a transcendent principle to a final inclusive goal, none the less truth and error, health and disease, good and evil, hope and fear in the concrete, would remain just what and where they now are. To improve our education, to ameliorate our manners, to advance our politics, we must have recourse to specific conditions of generation.

Finally, the new logic introduces responsibility into the intellectual life. To idealize and rationalize the universe at large is after all a confession of inability to master the courses of things that specifically concern us. As long as mankind suffered from this impotency, it naturally shifted a burden of responsibility that it could not carry over to the more competent shoulders of the transcendent cause. But if insight into specific conditions of value and into specific consequences of ideas is possible, philosophy must in time become a method of locating and interpreting the more serious of the conflicts that occur in life, and a method of projecting ways for dealing with them: a method of moral and political diagnosis and prognosis.

The claim to formulate *a priori* the legislative constitution of the universe is by its nature a claim that may lead to elaborate dialectic developments. But it is also one that removes these very conclusions from subjection to experimental test, for, by definition, these results make no differences in the detailed course of events. But a philosophy that humbles its pre-

tensions to the work of projecting hypotheses for the education and conduct of mind, individual and social, is thereby subjected to test by the way in which the ideas it propounds work out in practice. In having modesty forced upon it, philosophy also acquires responsibility.

Doubtless I seem to have violated the implied promise of my earlier remarks and to have turned both prophet and partisan. But in anticipating the direction of the transformations in philosophy to be wrought by the Darwinian genetic and experimental logic, I do not profess to speak for any save those who yield themselves consciously or unconsciously to this logic. No one can fairly deny that at present there are two effects of the Darwinian mode of thinking. On the one hand, there are making many sincere and vital efforts to revise our traditional philosophic conceptions in accordance with its demands. On the other hand, there is as definitely a recrudescence of absolutistic philosophies; an assertion of a type of philosophic knowing distinct from that of the sciences, one which opens to us another kind of reality from that to which the sciences give access; an appeal through experience to something that essentially goes beyond experience. This reaction affects popular creeds and religious movements as well as technical philosophies. The very conquest of the biological sciences by the new ideas has led many to proclaim an explicit and rigid separation of philosophy from science.

Old ideas give way slowly; for they are more than abstract logical forms and categories. They are habits, predispositions, deeply engrained attitudes of aversion and preference. Moreover, the conviction persists—though history shows it to be a hallucination—that all the questions that the human mind has asked are questions that can be answered in terms of the alternatives that the questions themselves present. But in fact intellectual progress usually occurs through sheer abandonment of questions together with both of the alternatives they assume—an abandonment that results from their decreasing vitality and a change of urgent interest. We do not solve them: we get over them. Old questions are solved by disappearing, evaporating, while new questions corresponding to the changed attitude of endeavor and preference take their place. Doubtless the greatest dissolvent in contemporary thought of old questions, the greatest precipitant of new methods, new intentions, new problems, is the one effected by the scientific revolution that found its climax in the *Origin of Species*.

NOTES

[First published in *Popular Science Monthly* 75 (1909): 90–98, with the title "Darwin's Influence upon Philosophy." Revised and reprinted in *The Influence of Darwin on Philosophy* (New York: Henry Holt and Co., 1910), pp. 1–19, with the title "The Influence of Darwinism on Philosophy." MW 4:3–14.]

1. A lecture in a course of public lectures on "Charles Darwin and His Influence on Science," given at Columbia University in the winter and spring of 1909.

2. *Life and Letters*, Vol. I, p. 282; cf. 285.

3. *Life and Letters*, Vol. II, pp. 146, 170, 245; Vol. I, pp. 283–84. See also the closing portion of his *Variations of Animals and Plants under Domestication*.

The
Need
for a Recovery
of Philosophy

(1917)

Intellectual advance occurs in two ways. At times increase of knowledge is organized about old conceptions, while these are expanded, elaborated and refined, but not seriously revised, much less abandoned. At other times, the increase of knowledge demands qualitative rather than quantitative change; alteration, not addition. Men's minds grow cold to their former intellectual concerns; ideas that were burning fade; interests that were urgent seem remote. Men face in another direction; their older perplexities are unreal; considerations passed over as negligible loom up. Former problems may not have been solved, but they no longer press for solution.

Philosophy is no exception to the rule. But it is unusually conservative—not, necessarily, in proffering solutions, but in clinging to problems. It has been so allied with theology and theological morals as representatives of men's chief interests, that radical alteration has been shocking. Men's activities took a decidedly new turn, for example, in the seventeenth century, and it seemed as if philosophy, under the lead of thinkers like Bacon and Descartes, was to execute an about-face. But, in spite of the ferment, it turned out that many of the older problems were but translated from Latin into the vernacular or into the new terminology furnished by science.

The association of philosophy with academic teaching has reinforced this intrinsic conservatism. Scholastic philosophy persisted in universities after men's thoughts outside of the walls of colleges had moved in other directions. In the last hundred years intellectual advances of science and politics have in like fashion been crystallized into material of instruction and now resist further change. I would not say that the spirit of teaching is hostile to that of liberal inquiry, but a philosophy which exists largely as something to be taught rather than wholly as something to be reflected upon is conducive to discussion of views held by others rather than to immediate response. Philosophy when taught inevitably magnifies the history of past thought, and leads professional philosophers to approach their subject-matter through its formulation in received systems. It tends, also, to emphasize points upon which men have divided into schools, for these lend themselves to retrospective definition and elaboration. Consequently, philosophical discussion is likely to be a dressing out of antithetical traditions, where criticism of one view is thought to afford proof of the truth of its opposite (as if formulation of views guaranteed logical exclusives). Direct preoccupation with contemporary difficulties is left to literature and politics.

If changing conduct and expanding knowledge ever required a willingness to surrender not merely old solutions but old problems it is now. I do not mean that we can turn abruptly away from all traditional issues. This is impossible; it would be the undoing of the one who attempted it. Irrespective of the professionalizing of philosophy, the ideas philosophers discuss are still those in which Western civilization has been bred. They are in the backs of the heads of educated people. But what serious-minded men not engaged in the professional business of philosophy most want to know is what modifications and abandonments of intellectual inheritance are required by the newer industrial, political, and scientific movements. They want to know what these newer movements mean when translated into general ideas. Unless professional philosophy can mobilize itself sufficiently to assist in this clarification and redirection of men's thoughts, it is likely to get more and more sidetracked from the main currents of contemporary life.

This essay may, then, be looked upon as an attempt to forward the emancipation of philosophy from too intimate and exclusive attachment to traditional problems. It is not in intent a criticism of various solutions that have been offered, but raises a question *as to the genuineness, under the present conditions of science and social life, of the problems.*

The limited object of my discussion will, doubtless, give an exaggerated impression of my conviction as to the artificiality of much recent philosophizing. Not that I have willfully exaggerated in what I have said, but that the limitations of my purpose have led me not to say many things pertinent to a broader purpose. A discussion less restricted would strive to enforce the genuineness, in their own context, of questions now discussed mainly because they have been discussed rather than because contemporary conditions of life suggest them. It would also be a grateful task to dwell upon the precious contributions made by philosophic systems which as a whole are impossible. In the course of the development of unreal premises and the discussion of artificial problems, points of view have emerged which are indispensable possessions of culture. The horizon has been widened; ideas of great fecundity struck out; imagination quickened; a sense of the meaning of things created. It may even be asked whether these accompaniments of classic systems have not often been treated as a kind of guarantee of the systems themselves. But while it is a sign of an illiberal mind to throw away the fertile and ample ideas of a Spinoza, a Kant, or a Hegel, because their setting is not logically adequate, it is surely a sign of an undisciplined one to treat their contributions to culture as confirmations of premises with which they have no necessary connection.

I

A criticism of current philosophizing from the standpoint of the traditional quality of its problems must begin somewhere, and the choice of a beginning is arbitrary. It has appeared to me that the notion of experience implied in the questions most actively discussed gives a natural point of departure. For, if I mistake not, it is just the inherited view of experience common to the empirical school and its opponents which keeps alive many discussions even of matters that on their face are quite remote from it, while it is also this view which is most untenable in the light of existing science and social practice. Accordingly I set out with a brief statement of some of the chief contrasts between the orthodox description of experience and that congenial to present conditions.

(i) In the orthodox view, experience is regarded primarily as a knowledge-affair. But to eyes not looking through ancient spectacles, it assuredly appears as an affair of the intercourse of a living being with its physical and social environment. (ii) According to tradition experience is (at least primarily) a psychical thing, infected throughout by "subjectivity." What experience suggests about itself is a genuinely objective world which enters into the actions and sufferings of men and undergoes modifications through their responses. (iii) So far as anything beyond a bare present is recognized by the established doctrine, the past exclusively counts. Registration of what has taken place, reference to precedent, is believed to be the essence of experience. Empiricism is conceived of as tied up to what has been, or is, "given." But experience in its vital form is experimental, an effort to change the given; it is characterized by projection, by reaching forward into the unknown; connexion with a future is its salient trait. (iv) The empirical tradition is committed to particularism. Connexions and continuities are supposed to be foreign to experience, to be by-products of dubious validity. An experience that is an undergoing of an environment and a striving for its control in new directions is pregnant with connexions. (v) In the traditional notion experience and thought are antithetical terms. Inference, so far as it is other than a revival of what has been given in the past, goes beyond experience; hence it is either invalid, or else a measure of desperation by which, using experience as a springboard, we jump out to a world of stable things and other selves. But experience, taken free of the restrictions imposed by the older concept, is full of inference. There is, apparently, no conscious experience without inference; reflection is native and constant.

These contrasts, with a consideration of the effect of substituting the account of experience relevant to modern life for the inherited account, afford the subject-matter of the following discussion.

Suppose we take seriously the contribution made to our idea of experience by biology,—not that recent biological science discovered the facts, but that it has so emphasized them that there is no longer an excuse for ignoring them or treating them as negligible. Any account of experience must now fit into the consideration that experiencing means living; and that living goes on in and because of an environing medium, not in a vacuum. Where there is experience, there is a living being. Where there is life, there is a double connexion maintained with the environment.

In part, environmental energies constitute organic functions; they enter into them. Life is not possible without such direct support by the environment. But while all organic changes depend upon the natural energies of the environment for their origination and occurrence, the natural energies sometimes carry the organic functions prosperously forward, and sometimes act counter to their continuance. Growth and decay, health and disease, are alike continuous with activities of the natural surroundings. The difference lies in the bearing of what happens upon future life-activity. From the standpoint of this future reference environmental incidents fall into groups: those favorable to life-activities, and those hostile.

The successful activities of the organism, those within which environmental assistance is incorporated, react upon the environment to bring about modifications favorable to their own future. The human being has upon his hands the problem of responding to what is going on around him so that these changes will take one turn rather than another, namely, that required by its own further functioning. While backed in part by the environment, its life is anything but a peaceful exhalation of environment. It is obliged to struggle—that is to say, to employ the direct support given by the environment in order indirectly to effect changes that would not otherwise occur. In this sense, life goes on by means of controlling the environment. Its activities must change the changes going on around it; they must neutralize hostile occurrences; they must transform neutral events into cooperative factors or into an efflorescence of new features.

Dialectic developments of the notion of self-preservation, of the *conatus essendi*, often ignore all the important facts of the actual process. They argue as if self-control, self-development, went on directly as a sort of unrolling push from within. But life endures only in virtue of the support of the environment. And since the environment is only incompletely enlisted in our behalf, self-preservation—or self-realization or whatever—is always indirect—always an affair of the way in which our present activities affect the direction taken by independent changes in the surroundings. Hindrances must be turned into means.

We are also given to playing loose with the conception of adjustment, as if that meant something fixed—a kind of accommodation once for all (ideally at least) of the organism *to* an environment. But as life requires the fitness of the environment to the organic functions, adjustment to the environment means not passive acceptance of the latter, but acting so that the environing changes take a certain turn. The "higher" the type of life, the more adjustment takes the form of an adjusting of the factors of the environment to one another in the interest of life; the less the significance of living, the more it becomes an adjustment to a given environment till at the lower end of the scale the differences between living and the non-living disappear.

These statements are of an external kind. They are about the conditions of experience, rather than about experiencing itself. But assuredly experience as it concretely takes place bears out the statements. Experience is primarily a process of undergoing: a process of standing something; of suffering and passion, of affection, in the literal sense of these words. The organism has to endure, to undergo, the consequences of its own actions. Experience is no slipping along in a path fixed by inner consciousness. Private consciousness is an incidental outcome of experience of a vital objective sort; it is not its source. Undergoing, however, is never mere passivity. The most patient patient is more than a receptor. He is also an agent—a reactor, one trying experiments, one concerned with undergoing in a way which may influence what is still to happen. Sheer endurance, side-stepping evasions, are, after all, ways of treating the environment with a view to what such treatment will accomplish. Even if we shut ourselves up in the most clam-like fashion, we are doing something; our passivity is an active attitude, not an extinction of response. Just as there is no assertive action, no aggressive attack upon things as they are, which is all action, so there is no undergoing which is not on our part also a going on and a going through.

Experience, in other words, is a matter of *simultaneous* doings and sufferings. Our undergoings are experiments in varying the course of events; our active tryings are trials and tests of ourselves. This duplicity of experience shows itself in our happiness and misery, our successes and failures. Triumphs are dangerous when dwelt upon or lived off from; successes use themselves up. Any achieved equilibrium of adjustment with the environment is precarious because we cannot evenly keep pace with changes in the environment. These are so opposed in direction that we must choose. We must take the risk of casting in our lot with one movement or the other. Nothing can eliminate all risk, all adventure; the one thing doomed to failure is to try to keep even with the whole environment at once—that is to say, to maintain the happy moment when all things go our way.

The obstacles which confront us are stimuli to variation, to novel response, and hence are occasions of progress. If a favor done us by the environment conceals a threat, so its disfavor is a potential means of hitherto unexperienced modes of success. To treat misery as anything but misery, as for example a blessing in disguise or a necessary factor in good, is disingenuous apologetics. But to say that the progress of the race has been stimulated by ills undergone, and that men have been moved by what they suffer to search out new and better courses of action is to speak veraciously.

The preoccupation of experience with things which are coming (are now coming, not just to come) is obvious to any one whose interest in experience is empirical. Since we live forward; since we live in a world where changes are going on whose issue means our weal or woe; since every act of ours modifies these changes and hence is fraught with promise, or charged with hostile energies—what should experience be but a future implicated in a present! Adjustment is no timeless state; it is a continuing process. To say that a change takes time may be to say something about the event which is external and uninstructive. But adjustment of organism to environment takes time in the pregnant sense; every step in the process is conditioned by reference to further changes which it effects. What is going on in the environment is the concern of the organism; not what is already "there" in accomplished and finished form. In so far as the issue of what is going on may be affected by intervention of the organism, the moving event is a challenge which stretches the agent-patient to meet what is coming. Experiencing exhibits things in their unterminated aspect moving toward determinate conclusions. The finished and done with is of import as affecting the future, not on its own account: in short, because it is not, really, done with.

Anticipation is therefore more primary than recollection; projection than summoning of the past; the prospective than the retrospective. Given a world like that in which we live, a world in which environing changes are partly favorable and partly callously indifferent, and experience is bound to be prospective in import; for any control attainable by the living creature depends upon what is done to alter the state of things. Success and failure are the primary "categories" of life; achieving of good and averting of ill are its supreme interests; hope and anxiety (which are not self-enclosed states of feeling, but active attitudes of welcome and wariness) are dominant qualities of experience. Imaginative forecast of the future is this forerunning quality of behavior rendered available for guidance in the present. Day-dreaming and castle-building and esthetic realization of what is not practically achieved are offshoots of this practical trait, or else practical intelligence is a chastened fantasy. It makes little difference. Imaginative recovery of the bygone is indispensable to successful invasion of the future, but its status is that of an instrument. To ignore its import is the sign of an undisciplined agent; but to isolate the past, dwelling upon it for its own sake and giving it the eulogistic name of knowledge, is to substitute the reminiscence of old-age for effective intelligence. The movement of the agent-patient to meet the future is partial and passionate; yet detached and impartial study of the past is the only alternative to luck in assuring success to passion.

II

This description of experience would be but a rhapsodic celebration of the commonplace were it not in marked contrast to orthodox philosophical accounts. The contrast indicates that traditional accounts have not been em-

pirical, but have been deductions, from unnamed premises, of what experience *must* be. Historic empiricism has been empirical in a technical and controversial sense. It has said, Lord, Lord, Experience, Experience; but in practice it has served ideas *forced into* experience, not *gathered from* it.

The confusion and artificiality thereby introduced into philosophical thought is nowhere more evident than in the empirical treatment of relations or dynamic continuities. The experience of a living being struggling to hold its own and make its way in an environment, physical and social, partly facilitating and partly obstructing its actions, is of necessity a matter of ties and connexions, of bearings and uses. The very point of experience, so to say, is that it doesn't occur in a vacuum; its agent-patient instead of being insulated and disconnected is bound up with the movement of things by most intimate and pervasive bonds. Only because the organism is in and of the world, and its activities correlated with those of other things in multiple ways, is it susceptible to undergoing things and capable of trying to reduce objects to means of securing its good fortune. That these connexions are of diverse kinds is irresistibly proved by the fluctuations which occur in its career. Help and hindrance, stimulation and inhibition, success and failure mean specifically different modes of correlation. Although the actions of things in the world are taking place in one continuous stretch of existence, there are all kinds of specific affinities, repulsions, and relative indifferencies.

Dynamic connexions are qualitatively diverse, just as are the centres of action. *In this sense*, pluralism, not monism, is an established empirical fact. The attempt to establish monism from consideration of the very nature of a relation is a mere piece of dialectics. Equally dialectical is the effort to establish by a consideration of the nature of relations an ontological Pluralism of Ultimates: *simple and independent beings*. To attempt to get results from a consideration of the "external" nature of relations is of a piece with the attempt to deduce results from their "internal" character. Some things are relatively insulated from the influence of other things; some things are easily invaded by others; some things are fiercely attracted to conjoin their activities with those of others. Experience exhibits every kind of connexion[1] from the most intimate to mere external juxtaposition.

Empirically, then, active bonds or continuities of all kinds, together with static discontinuities, characterize existence. To deny this qualitative heterogeneity is to reduce the struggles and difficulties of life, its comedies and tragedies to illusion: to the non-being of the Greeks or to its modern counterpart, the "subjective." Experience is an affair of facilitations and checks, of being sustained and disrupted, being let alone, being helped and troubled, of good fortune and defeat in all the countless qualitative modes which these words pallidly suggest. The existence of genuine connexions of all manner of heterogeneity cannot be doubted. Such words as conjoining, disjoining, resisting, modifying, saltatory, and ambulatory (to use James's picturesque term) only hint at their actual heterogeneity.

Among the revisions and surrenders of historic problems demanded by this feature of empirical situations, those centering in the rationalistic-empirical controversy may be selected for attention. The implications of this controversy are twofold: First, that connexions are as homogeneous in fact as in name; and, secondly, if genuine, are all due to thought, or, if empirical, are arbitrary by-products of past particulars. The stubborn particularism of orthodox empiricism is its outstanding trait; consequently the opposed rationalism found no justification of bearings, continuities, and ties save to refer them in gross to the work of a hyper-empirical Reason.

Of course, not all empiricism prior to Hume and Kant was sensationalistic, pulverizing "experience" into isolated sensory qualities or simple ideas. It did not all follow Locke's lead in regarding the entire content of generalization as the "workmanship of the understanding." On the Continent, prior to Kant, philosophers were content to draw a line between empirical generalizations regarding matters of fact and necessary universals applying to truths of reason. But logical atomism was implicit even in this theory. Statements referring to empirical fact were mere quantitative summaries of particular instances. In the sensationalism which sprang from Hume (and which was left unquestioned by Kant as far as any strictly empirical element was concerned) the implicit particularism was made explicit. But the doctrine that sensations and ideas are so many separate existences was not derived from observation nor from experiment. It was a logical deduction from a prior unexamined concept of the nature of experience. From the same concept it followed that the appearance of stable objects and of general principles of connexion was but an appearance.[2]

Kantianism, then, naturally invoked universal bonds to restore objectivity. But, in so doing, it accepted the particularism of experience and proceeded to supplement it from non-empirical sources. A sensory manifold being all which is really empirical in experience, a reason which transcends experience must provide synthesis. The net outcome might have suggested a correct account of experience. For we have only to forget the apparatus by which the net outcome is arrived at, to have before us the experience of the plain man—a diversity of ceaseless changes connected in all kinds of ways, static and dynamic. This conclusion would deal a deathblow to both empiricism and rationalism. For, making clear the non-empirical character of the alleged manifold of unconnected particulars, it would render unnecessary the appeal to functions of the understanding in order to connect them. With the downfall of the traditional notion of experience, the appeal to reason to supplement its defects becomes superfluous.

The tradition was, however, too strongly entrenched; especially as it furnished the subject-matter of an alleged science of states of mind which were directly known in their very presence. The historic outcome was a new crop of artificial puzzles about relations; it fastened upon philosophy for a long time the quarrel about the *a priori* and the *a posteriori* as its chief issue. The controversy is to-day quiescent. Yet it is not at all uncommon to find thinkers modern in tone and intent who regard any philosophy of experience as necessarily committed to denial of the existence of genuinely general propositions, and who take empiricism to be inherently averse to the recognition of the importance of an organizing and constructive intelligence.

The quiescence alluded to is in part due, I think, to sheer weariness. But it is also due to a change of standpoint introduced by biological conceptions; and particularly the discovery of biological continuity from the lower organisms to man. For a short period, Spencerians might connect the doctrine of evolution with the old problem, and use the long temporal accumulation of "experiences" to generate something which, for human experience, is *a priori*. But the tendency of the biological way of thinking is neither to confirm or negate the Spencerian doctrine, but to shift the issue. In the orthodox position *a posteriori* and *a priori* were affairs of knowledge. But it soon becomes obvious that while there is assuredly something *a priori*—that is to say, native, unlearned, original—in human experience, that something is *not* knowledge, but is activities made possible by means of established connexions of neurones. This empirical fact does not solve the orthodox problem; it dissolves it. It shows that the problem was misconceived, and solution sought by both parties in the wrong direction.

Organic instincts and organic retention, or habit-forming, are undeniable factors in actual experience. They are factors which effect organization and secure continuity. They are among the specific facts which a description of experience cognizant of the correlation of organic action with the action of other natural objects will include. But while fortunately the contribution of biological science to a truly empirical description of experiencing has outlawed the discussion of the *a priori* and *a posteriori*, the transforming effect of the same contributions upon other issues has gone unnoticed, save as pragmatism has made an effort to bring them to recognition.

III

The point seriously at issue in the notion of experience common to both sides in the older controversy thus turns out to be the place of thought or intelligence in experience. Does reason have a distinctive office? Is there a characteristic order of relations contributed by it?

Experience, to return to our positive conception, is primarily what is undergone in connexion with activities whose import lies in their objective consequences—their bearing upon future experiences. Organic functions deal with things as things in course, in operation, in a state of affairs not yet given or completed. What is done with, what is just "there," is of concern only in the potentialities which it may indicate. As ended, as wholly given, it is of no account. But as a sign of what may come, it becomes an indispensable factor in behavior dealing with changes, the outcome of which is not yet determined.

The only power the organism possesses to control its own future depends upon the way its present responses modify changes which are taking place in its medium. A living being may be comparatively impotent, or comparatively free. It is all a matter of the way in which its present reactions to things influence the future reactions of things upon it. Without regard to its wish or intent every act it performs makes some difference in the environment. The change may be trivial as respects its own career and fortune. But it may also be of incalculable importance; it may import harm, destruction, or it may procure well-being.

Is it possible for a living being to increase its control of welfare and success? Can it manage, in any degree, to assure its future? Or does the amount of security depend wholly upon the accidents of the situation? Can it learn? Can it gain ability to assure its future in the present? These questions centre attention upon the significance of reflective intelligence in the process of experience. The extent of an agent's capacity for inference, its power to use a given fact as a sign of something not yet given, measures the extent of its ability systematically to enlarge its control of the future.

A being which can use given and finished facts as signs of things to come; which can take given things as evidences of absent things, can, in that degree, forecast the future; it can form reasonable expectations. It is capable of achieving ideas; it is possessed of intelligence. For use of the given or finished to anticipate the consequence of processes going on is precisely what is meant by "ideas," by "intelligence."

As we have already noted, the environment is rarely all of a kind in its bearing upon organic welfare; its most whole-hearted support of life-activities is precarious and temporary. Some environmental changes are auspicious; others are menacing. The secret of success—that is, of the greatest attainable success—is for the organic response to cast in its lot with present auspicious changes to strengthen them and thus to avert the consequences flowing from occurrences of ill-omen. Any reaction is a venture; it involves risk. We always build better or worse than we can foretell. But the organism's fateful intervention in the course of events is blind, its choice is random, except as it can employ what happens to it as a basis of inferring what is likely to happen later. In the degree in which it can read future results in present on-goings, its responsive choice, its partiality to this condition or that, become intelligent. Its bias grows reasonable. It can deliberately, intentionally, participate in the direction of the course of affairs. Its foresight of different futures which result according as this or that present factor predominates in the shaping of affairs permits it to partake intelligently instead of blindly and fatally in the consequences its reactions give rise to. Participate it must, and to its own weal or woe. Inference, the use of what happens, to anticipate what will—or at least may—happen, makes the difference between directed and undirected participation. And this capacity for inferring is precisely the same as that use of natural occurrences for the discovery and determination of consequences—the formation of new dynamic connexions—which constitutes knowledge.

The fact that thought is an intrinsic feature of experience is fatal to the traditional empiricism which makes it an artificial by-product. But for that same reason it is fatal to the historic rationalisms whose justification was the secondary and retrospective position assigned to thought by empirical philosophy. According to the particularism of the latter, thought was inevitably only a bunching together of hard-and-fast separate items; thinking was but the gathering together and tying of items already completely given, or else an equally artificial untying—a mechanical adding and subtracting of the given. It was but a cumulative registration, a consolidated merger; generality was a matter of bulk, not of quality. Thinking was therefore treated as lacking constructive power; even its organizing capacity was but simulated, being in truth but arbitrary pigeon-holing. Genuine projection of the novel, deliberate variation and invention, are idle fictions in such a version of experience. If there ever was creation, it all took place at a remote period. Since then the world has only recited lessons.

The value of inventive construction is too precious to be disposed of in this cavalier way. Its unceremonious denial afforded an opportunity to assert that in addition to experience the subject has a ready-made faculty of thought or reason which transcends experience. Rationalism thus accepted the account of experience given by traditional empiricism, and introduced reason as extra-empirical. There are still thinkers who regard any empiricism as necessarily committed to a belief in a cut-and-dried reliance upon disconnected precedents, and who hold that all systematic organization of past experiences for new and constructive purposes is alien to strict empiricism.

Rationalism never explained, however, how a reason extraneous to experience could enter into helpful relation with concrete experiences. By definition, reason and experience were antithetical, so that the concern of reason was not the fruitful expansion and guidance of the course of experience, but a realm of considerations too sublime to touch, or be touched by, experience. Discreet rationalists confined themselves to theology and allied branches of abstruse science, and to mathematics. Rationalism would have been a doctrine reserved for academic specialists and abstract formalists had it not assumed the task of providing an apologetics for traditional morals and theology, thereby getting into touch with actual human beliefs and concerns. It is notorious that historic empiricism was strong in criticism and in demolition of outworn beliefs, but weak for purposes of constructive social direction. But we frequently overlook the fact that whenever rationalism cut free from conservative apologetics, it was also simply an instrumentality for pointing out inconsistencies and absurdities in existing beliefs—a sphere in which it was immensely useful, as the Enlightenment shows. Leibniz and Voltaire were contemporary rationalists in more senses than one.[3]

The recognition that reflection is a genuine factor within experience and an indispensable factor in that control of the world which secures a prosperous and significant expansion of experience undermines historic rationalism as assuredly as it abolishes the foundations of historic empiricism. The bearing of a correct idea of the place and office of reflection upon modern idealisms is less obvious, but no less certain.

One of the curiosities of orthodox empiricism is that its outstanding speculative problem is the existence of an "external world." For in accordance with the notion that experience is attached to a private subject as its exclusive possession, a world like the one in which we appear to live must be "external" to experience instead of being its subject-matter. I call it a curiosity, for if anything seems adequately grounded empirically it is the existence of a world which resists the characteristic functions of the subject of experience; which goes its way, in some respects, independently of these functions, and which frustrates our hopes and intentions. Ignorance which is fatal; disappointment; the need of adjusting means and ends to the course of nature, would seem to be facts sufficiently characterizing empirical situations as to render the existence of an external world indubitable.

That the description of experience was arrived at by forcing actual empirical facts into conformity with dialectic developments from a concept of a knower outside of the real world of nature is testified to by the historic alliance of empiricism and idealism.[4] According to the most logically consistent editions of orthodox empiricism, all that can be experienced is the fleeting, the momentary, mental state. That alone is absolutely and indubitably present; therefore, it alone is cognitively certain. It alone is *knowledge*. The existence of the past (and of the future), of a decently stable world and of other selves—indeed, of one's own self—falls outside this datum of experience. These can be arrived at only by inference which is "ejective"—a name given to an alleged type of inference that jumps from experience, as from a springboard, to something beyond experience.

I should not anticipate difficulty in showing that this doctrine is, dialectically, a mass of inconsistencies. Avowedly it is a doctrine of desperation, and as such it is cited here to show the desperate straits to which ignoring empirical facts has reduced a doctrine of experience. More positively instructive are the objective idealisms which have been the offspring of the marriage between the "reason" of historic rationalism and the alleged immediate psychical stuff of historic empiricism. These idealisms have recognized the genuineness of connexions and the impotency of "feeling." They have then identified connexions with logical or rational connexions, and thus treated "the real World" as a synthesis of sentient consciousness by means of a rational self-consciousness introducing objectivity: stability and universality of reference.

Here again, for present purposes, criticism is unnecessary. It suffices to point out that the value of this theory is bound up with the genuineness of the problem of which it purports to be a solution. If the basic concept is a fiction, there is no call for the solution. The more important point is to perceive how far the "thought" which figures in objective idealism comes from meeting the empirical demands made upon actual thought. Idealism is much less formal than historic rationalism. It treats thought, or reason, as constitutive of experience by means of uniting and constructive functions, not as just concerned with a realm of eternal truths apart from experience. On such a view thought certainly loses its abstractness and remoteness. But, unfortunately, in thus gaining the whole world it loses its own self. A world already, in its intrinsic structure, dominated by thought is not a world in which, save by contradiction of premises, thinking has anything to do.

That the doctrine logically results in making change unreal and error unaccountable are consequences of importance in the technique of professional philosophy; in the denial of empirical fact which they imply they seem to many a *reductio ad absurdum* of the premises from which they proceed. But, after all, such consequences are of only professional import. What is serious, even sinister, is the implied sophistication regarding the place and office of reflection in the scheme of things. A doctrine which exalts thought in name while ignoring its efficacy in fact (that is, its use in bettering life) is a doctrine which cannot be entertained and taught without serious peril. Those who are not concerned with professional philosophy but who are solicitous for intelligence as a factor in the amelioration of actual conditions can but look askance at any doctrine which holds that the entire scheme of things is already, if we but acquire the knack of looking at it aright, fixedly and completely rational. It is a striking manifestation of the extent in which philosophies have been compensatory in quality.[5] But the matter cannot be passed over as if it were simply a question of not grudging a certain amount of consolation to one amid the irretrievable evils of life. For as to these evils no one knows how many are retrievable; and a philosophy which proclaims the ability of a dialectic theory of knowledge to reveal the world as already and eternally a self-luminous rational whole, contaminates the scope and use of thought at its very spring. To substitute the otiose insight gained by manipulation of a formula for the slow cooperative work of a humanity guided by reflective intelligence is more than a technical blunder of speculative philosophers.

A practical crisis may throw the relationship of ideas to life into an exaggerated Brocken-like spectral relief, where exaggeration renders perceptible features not ordinarily noted. The use of force to secure narrow because exclusive aims is no novelty in human affairs. The deploying of all the intelligence at command in order to increase the effectiveness of the force used is not so common, yet presents nothing intrinsically remarkable. The identification of force—military, economic, and administrative—with moral necessity and moral culture is, however, a phenomenon not likely to exhibit itself on a wide scale except where intelligence has already been suborned by an idealism which identifies "the actual with the rational," and thus finds the measure of reason in the brute event determined by superior force. If we are to have a philosophy which will intervene between attachment to rule of thumb muddling and devotion to a systematized subordination of intelligence to preexistent ends, it can be found only in a philosophy which finds the ultimate measure of intelligence in consideration of a desirable future and in search for the means of bringing it progressively into existence. When professed idealism turns out to be a narrow pragmatism—narrow because taking for granted the finality of ends determined by historic conditions—the time has arrived for a pragmatism which shall be empirically idealistic, proclaiming the essential connexion of intelligence with the unachieved future—with possibilities involving a transfiguration.

IV

Why has the description of experience been so remote from the facts of empirical situations? To answer this question throws light upon the submergence of recent philosophizing in epistemology—that is, in discussions of the nature, possibility, and limits of knowledge in general, and in the attempt to reach conclusions regarding the ultimate nature of reality from the answers given to such questions.

The reply to the query regarding the currency of a non-empirical doctrine of experience (even among professed empiricists) is that the traditional account is derived from a conception once universally entertained regarding the subject or bearer or centre of experience. The description of experience has been forced into conformity with this prior conception; it has been primarily a deduction from it, actual empirical facts being poured into the molds of the deductions. The characteristic feature of this prior notion is the assumption that experience centres in, or gathers about, or proceeds from a centre or subject which is outside the course of natural existence, and set over against it:—it being of no importance, for present purposes, whether this antithetical subject is termed soul, or spirit, or mind, or ego, or consciousness, or just knower or knowing subject.

There are plausible grounds for thinking that the currency of the idea in question lies in the form which men's religious preoccupations took for many centuries. These were deliberately and systematically other-worldly. They centered about a Fall which was not an event in nature, but an aboriginal catastrophe that corrupted Nature; about a redemption made possible by supernatural means; about a life in another world—essentially, not merely spatially, Other. The supreme drama of destiny took place in a soul or spirit which, under the circumstances, could not be conceived other than as non-natural—extra-natural, if not, strictly speaking, supernatural. When Descartes and others broke away from medieval interests, they retained as commonplaces its intellectual apparatus: Such as, knowledge is exercised by a power that is extra-natural and set over against the world to be known. Even if they had wished to make a complete break, they had nothing to put as knower in the place of the soul. It may be doubted whether there was any available empirical substitute until science worked out the fact that physical changes are functional correlations of energies, and that man is continuous with other forms of life, and until social life had developed an intellectually free and responsible individual as its agent.

But my main point is not dependent upon any particular theory as to the historic origin of the notion about the bearer of experience. The point is there on its own account. The essential thing is that the bearer was conceived as outside of the world; so that experience consisted in the bearer's being affected through a type of operations not found anywhere in the world, while knowledge consists in surveying the world, looking at it, getting the view of a spectator.

The theological problem of attaining knowledge of God as ultimate reality was transformed in effect into the philosophical problem of the possibility of attaining knowledge of reality. For how is one to get beyond the limits of the subject and subjective occurrences? Familiarity breeds credulity oftener than contempt. How can a problem be artificial when men have been busy discussing it for almost three hundred years? But if the assumption that experience is something set over against the world is contrary to fact, then the problem of how self or mind or subjective experience or consciousness can reach knowledge of an external world is assuredly a meaningless problem. Whatever questions there may be about knowledge, they will not be the kind of problems which have formed epistemology.

The problem of knowledge as conceived in the industry of epistemology is the problem of knowledge *in general*—of the possibility, extent, and validity of knowledge in general. What does this "in general" mean? In ordinary life there are problems a-plenty of knowledge in particular; every conclusion we try to reach, theoretical or practical, affords such a problem. But there is no problem of knowledge in general. I do not mean, of course, that general statements cannot be made about knowledge, or that the problem of attaining these general statements is not a genuine one. On the contrary, specific instances of success and failure in inquiry exist, and are of such a character that one can discover the conditions conducing to success and failure. Statement of these conditions constitutes logic, and is capable of being an important aid in proper guidance of further attempts at knowing. But this logical problem of knowledge is at the opposite pole from the epistemological. Specific problems are about right conclusions to be reached—which means, in effect, right ways of going about the business of inquiry. They imply a difference between knowledge and error consequent upon right and wrong methods of inquiry and testing; not a difference between experience and the world. The problem of knowledge *überhaupt* exists because it is assumed that there is a knower in general, who is outside of the world to be known, and who is defined in terms antithetical to the traits of the world. With analogous assumptions, we could invent and discuss a problem of digestion in general. All that would be required would be to conceive the stomach and food-material as inhabiting different worlds. Such an assumption would leave on our hands the question of the possibility, extent, nature, and genuineness of any transaction between stomach and food.

But because the stomach and food inhabit a continuous stretch of existence, because digestion is but a correlation of diverse activities in one world, the problems of digestion are specific and plural: What are the particular correlations which constitute it? How does it proceed in different situations? What is favorable and what unfavorable to its best performance?—and so on. Can one deny that if we were to take our clue from the present empirical situation, including the scientific notion of evolution (biological continuity) and the existing arts of control of nature, subject and object would be treated as occupying the same natural world as unhesitatingly as we assume the natural conjunction of an animal and its food? Would it not follow that knowledge is one way in which natural energies cooperate? Would there be any problem save discovery of the peculiar structure of this cooperation, the conditions under which it occurs to best effect, and the consequences which issue from its occurrence?

It is a commonplace that the chief divisions of modern philosophy, idealism in its different kinds, realisms of various brands, so-called common-sense dualism, agnosticism, relativism, phenomenalism, have grown up around the epistemological problem of the general relation of subject and object. Problems not openly epistemological, such as whether the relation of changes in consciousness to physical changes is one of interaction, parallelism, or automatism have the same origin. What becomes of philosophy, consisting largely as it does of different answers to these questions, in case the assumptions which generate the questions have no empirical standing? Is it not time that philosophers turned from the attempt to determine the comparative merits of various replies to the questions to a consideration of the claims of the questions?

When dominating religious ideas were built up about the idea that the self is a stranger and pilgrim in this world; when morals, falling in line, found true good only in inner states of a self inaccessible to anything but its own private introspection; when political theory assumed the finality of disconnected and mutually exclusive personalities, the notion that the bearer of experience is antithetical to the world instead of being in and of it was congenial. It at least had the warrant of other beliefs and aspirations. But the doctrine of biological continuity or organic evolution has destroyed the scientific basis of the conception. Morally, men are now concerned with the amelioration of the conditions of the common lot in this world. Social sciences recognize that associated life is not a matter of physical juxtaposition, but of genuine intercourse—of community of experience in a non-metaphorical sense of community. Why should we longer try to patch up and refine and stretch the old solutions till they seem to cover the change of thought and practice? Why not recognize that the trouble is with the problem?

A belief in organic evolution which does not extend unreservedly to the way in which the subject of experience is thought of, and which does not strive to bring the entire theory of experience and knowing into line with biological and social facts, is hardly more than Pickwickian. There are many, for example, who hold that dreams, hallucinations, and errors cannot be accounted for at all except on the theory that a self (or "consciousness") exercises a modifying influence upon the "real object." The logical assumption is that consciousness is outside of the real object; that it is something different in kind, and therefore has the power of changing "reality" into appearance, of introducing "relativities" into things as they are in themselves—in short, of infecting real things with subjectivity. Such writers seem unaware of the fact that this assumption makes consciousness supernatural in the literal sense of the word; and that, to say the least, the conception can be accepted by one who accepts the doctrine of biological continuity only after every other way of dealing with the facts has been exhausted.

Realists, of course (at least some of the Neo-realists), deny any such miraculous intervention of consciousness. But they[6] admit the reality of the problem; denying only this particular solution, they try to find some other way out, which will still preserve intact the notion of knowledge as a relationship of a general sort between subject and object.

Now dreams and hallucinations, errors, pleasures, and pains, possibly "secondary" qualities, do not occur save where there are organic centres of experience. They cluster about a subject. But to treat them as things which inhere exclusively in the subject; or as posing the problem of a distortion of *the* real object by a knower set over against the world, or as presenting facts to be explained primarily as cases of contemplative knowledge, is to testify that one has still to learn the lesson of evolution in its application to the affairs in hand.

If biological development be accepted, the subject of experience is at least an animal, continuous with other organic forms in a process of more complex organization. An animal in turn is at least continuous with chemico-physical processes which, in living things, are so organized as really to constitute the activities of life with all their defining traits. And experience is not identical with brain action; it is the entire organic agent-patient in all its interaction with the environment, natural and social. The brain is primarily an organ of a certain kind of behavior, not of knowing the world. And to repeat what has already been said, experiencing *is* just certain modes of interaction, of correlation, of natural objects among which the organism happens, so to say, to be one. It follows with equal force that experience means primarily not knowledge, but ways of doing and suffering. Knowing must be described by discovering what particular mode—qualitatively unique—of doing and suffering it is. As it is, we find experience assimilated to a non-empirical concept of knowledge, derived from an antecedent notion of a spectator outside of the world.[7]

In short, the epistemological fashion of conceiving dreams, errors, "relativities," etc., depends upon the isolation of mind from intimate participation with other changes in the same continuous nexus. Thus it is like contending that when a bottle bursts, the bottle is, in some self-contained miraculous way, exclusively responsible. Since it is the nature of a bottle to be whole so as to retain fluids, bursting is an abnormal event—comparable to an hallucination. Hence it cannot belong to the "real" bottle; the "subjectivity" of glass is the cause. It is obvious that since the breaking of glass is a case of specific correlation of natural energies, its accidental and abnormal character has to do with *consequences*, not with causation. Accident is interference with the con-

sequences for which the bottle is intended. The bursting considered apart from its bearing on these consequences is on a plane with any other occurrence in the wide world. But from the standpoint of a desired future, bursting is an anomaly, an interruption of the course of events.

The analogy with the occurrence of dreams, hallucinations, etc., seems to me exact. Dreams are not something outside of the regular course of events; they are in and of it. They are not cognitive distortions of real things; they are *more* real things. There is nothing abnormal in their existence, any more than there is in the bursting of a bottle.[8] But they may be abnormal, from the standpoint of their influence, of their operation as stimuli in calling out responses to modify the future. Dreams have often been taken as prognostics of what is to happen; they have modified conduct. A hallucination may lead a man to consult a doctor; such a consequence is right and proper. But the consultation indicates that the subject regarded it as an indication of consequences which he feared: as a symptom of a disturbed life. Or the hallucination may lead him to anticipate consequences which in fact flow only from the possession of great wealth. Then the hallucination is a disturbance of the normal course of events; the occurrence is wrongly *used* with reference to eventualities.

To regard reference to use and to desired and intended consequences as involving a "subjective" factor is to miss the point, for this has regard to the future. The uses to which a bottle is put are not mental; they do not consist of psychical states; they are further correlations of natural existences. Consequences in use are genuine natural events; but they do not occur without the intervention of behavior involving anticipation of a future. The case is not otherwise with an hallucination. The differences it makes are in any case differences in the course of the one continuous world. The important point is whether they are good or bad differences. To use the hallucination as a sign of organic lesions that menace health means the beneficial result of seeing a physician; to respond to it as a sign of consequences such as actually follow only from being persecuted is to fall into error—to be abnormal. The persecutors are "unreal"; that is, there are no things which act as persecutors act; but the hallucination exists. Given its conditions it is as natural as any other event, and poses only the same kind of problem as is put by the occurrence of, say, a thunderstorm. The "unreality" of persecution is not, however, a subjective matter; it means that conditions do not exist for producing the *future* consequences which are now anticipated and reacted to. Ability to anticipate future consequences and to respond to them as stimuli to present behavior may well *define* what is meant by a mind or by "consciousness."[9] But this is only a way of saying just what kind of a real or natural existence the subject is; it is not to fall back on a preconception about an unnatural subject in order to characterize the occurrence of error.

Although the discussion may be already labored, let us take another example—the occurrence of disease. By definition it is pathological, abnormal. At one time in human history this abnormality was taken to be something dwelling in the intrinsic nature of the event—in its existence irrespective of future consequences. Disease was literally extranatural and to be referred to demons or to magic. No one to-day questions its naturalness—its place in the order of natural events. Yet it is abnormal—for it operates to effect results different from those which follow from health. The difference is a genuine empirical difference, not a mere mental distinction. From the standpoint of bearing on a subsequent course of events disease is unnatural, in spite of the naturalness of its occurrence and origin.

The habit of ignoring reference to the future is responsible for the assumption that to admit human participation in any form is to admit the "subjective" in a sense which alters the objective into the phenomenal. There have been those who, like Spinoza, regarded health and disease, good and ill, as equally real and equally unreal. However, only a few consistent materialists have included truth along with error as merely phenomenal and subjective. But if one does not regard movement toward possible consequences as genuine, wholesale denial of existential validity to all these distinctions is the only logical course. To select truth as objective and error as "subjective" is,

on this basis, an unjustifiably partial procedure. Take everything as fixedly given, and both truth and error are arbitrary insertions into fact. Admit the genuineness of changes going on, and capacity for its direction through organic action based on foresight, and both truth and falsity are alike existential. It is human to regard the course of events which is in line with our own efforts as the *regular* course of events, and interruptions as abnormal, but this partiality of human desire is itself a part of what actually takes place.

It is now proposed to take a particular case of the alleged epistemological predicament for discussion, since the entire ground cannot be covered. I think, however, the instance chosen is typical, so that the conclusion reached may be generalized.

The instance is that of so-called relativity in perception. There are almost endless instances; the stick bent in water; the whistle changing pitch with change of distance from the ear; objects doubled when the eye is pushed; the destroyed star still visible, etc., etc. For our consideration we may take the case of a spherical object that presents itself to one observer as a flat circle, to another as a somewhat distorted elliptical surface. This situation gives empirical proof, so it is argued, of the difference between a real object and mere appearance. Since there is but one object, the existence of two *subjects* is the sole differentiating factor. Hence the two appearances of the one real object is proof of the intervening distorting action of the subject. And many of the Neo-realists who deny the difference in question, admit the case to be one of knowledge and accordingly to constitute an epistemological problem. They have in consequence developed wonderfully elaborate schemes of sundry kinds to maintain "epistemological monism" intact.

Let us try to keep close to empirical facts. In the first place the two unlike appearances of the one sphere are physically necessary because of the laws of reaction of light. If the one sphere did *not* assume these two appearances under given conditions, we should be confronted with a hopelessly irreconcilable discrepancy in the behavior of natural energy. That the result is natural is evidenced by the fact that two cameras—or other arrangements of apparatus for reflecting light—yield precisely the same results. Photographs are as genuinely physical existences as the original sphere; and they exhibit the two geometrical forms.

The statement of these facts makes no impression upon the confirmed epistemologist; he merely retorts that as long as it is admitted that the organism is the cause of a sphere being seen, from different points, as a circular and as an elliptical surface, the essence of his contention—the modification of the real object by the subject—is admitted. To the question why the same logic does not apply to photographic records he makes, as far as I know, no reply at all.

The source of the difficulty is not hard to see. The objection assumes that the alleged modifications of *the* real object are cases of *knowing* and hence attributable to the influence of a *knower*. Statements which set forth the doctrine will always be found to refer to the organic factor, to the eye, as an observer or a percipient. Even when reference is made to a lens or a mirror, language is sometimes used which suggests that the writer's naïveté is sufficiently gross to treat these physical factors as if they were engaged in perceiving the sphere. But as it is evident that the lens operates as a physical factor in correlation with other physical factors—notably light—so it ought to be evident that the intervention of the optical apparatus of the eye is a purely noncognitive matter. The relation in question is not one between a sphere and a would-be knower of it, unfortunately condemned by the nature of the knowing apparatus to alter the thing he would know; it is an affair of the dynamic interaction of two physical agents in producing a third thing, an effect;—an affair of precisely the same kind as in any physical conjoint action, say the operation of hydrogen and oxygen in producing water. To regard the eye as primarily a knower, an observer, of things, is as crass as to assign that function to a camera. But unless the eye (or optical apparatus, or brain, or organism) be so regarded, there is absolutely no problem of observation or of knowledge in the case of the occurrence of elliptical and circular surfaces. Knowledge

does not enter into the affair at all till *after* these forms of refracted light have been produced. About them there is nothing unreal. Light is really, physically, existentially, refracted into these forms. If the same spherical form upon refracting light to physical objects in two quite different positions produced the same geometric forms, there would, indeed, be something to marvel at—as there would be if wax produced the same results in contact simultaneously with a cold body and with a warm one. Why talk about *the real* object in relation to *a knower* when what is given is one real thing in dynamic connection with another real thing?

The way of dealing with the case will probably meet with a retort; at least, it has done so before. It has been said that the account given above and the account of traditional subjectivism differ only verbally. The essential thing in both, so it is said, is the admission that an activity of a self or subject or organism makes a difference in the real object. Whether the subject makes this difference in the very process of knowing or makes it prior to the act of knowing is a minor matter; what is important is that the known thing has, by the time it is known, been "subjectified."

The objection gives a convenient occasion for summarizing the main points of the argument. On the one hand, the retort of the objector depends upon talking about *the* real object. Employ the term "*a* real object," and the change produced by the activity characteristic of the optical apparatus is of just the same kind as that of the camera lens or that of any other physical agency. Every event in the world marks a difference made to one existence in active conjunction with some other existence. And, as for the alleged subjectivity, if subjective is used merely as an adjective to designate the specific activity of a particular existence, comparable, say, to the term feral, applied to tiger, or metallic, applied to iron, then of course reference to subjective is legitimate. But it is also tautological. It is like saying that flesh eaters are carnivorous. But the term "subjective" is so consecrated to other uses, usually implying invidious contrast with objectivity (while subjective in the sense just suggested means specific mode *of* objectivity), that it is difficult to maintain this innocent sense. Its use in any disparaging way in the situation before us—any sense implicating contrast with a real object—assumes that the organism *ought* not to make any difference when it operates in conjunction with other things. Thus we run to earth that assumption that the subject is heterogeneous from every other natural existence; it is to be the one otiose, inoperative thing in a moving world—our old assumption of the self as outside of things.[10]

What and where is knowledge in the case we have been considering? Not, as we have already seen, in the production of forms of light having a circular and elliptical surface. These forms are natural happenings. They may enter into knowledge or they may not, according to circumstances. Countless such refractive changes take place without being noted.[11] When they become subject-matter for knowledge, the inquiry they set on foot may take on an indefinite variety of forms. One may be interested in ascertaining more about the structural peculiarities of the forms themselves; one may be interested in the mechanism of their production; one may find problems in projective geometry, or in drawing and painting—all depending upon the specific matter-of-fact context. The forms may be *objectives* of knowledge—of reflective examination—or they may be means of knowing something else. It may happen—under some circumstances it does happen—that the objective of inquiry is the nature of the geometric form which, when refracting light, gives rise to these other forms. In this case the sphere is the thing known, and in this case, the forms of light are signs or evidence of the conclusion to be drawn. There is no more reason for supposing that they *are* (mis)knowledges of the sphere—that the sphere is necessarily and from the start what one is trying to know—than for supposing that the position of the mercury in the thermometer tube is a cognitive distortion of atmospheric pressure. In each case (that of the mercury and that of, say, a circular surface) the primary datum is a physical happening. In each case it may be used, upon occasion, as a sign or evidence of the nature of the causes which brought it about. Given the position in question, the circular form would be an intrin-

sically *unreliable* evidence of the nature and position of the spherical body only in case it, as the direct datum of perception, were *not* what it is—a circular form.

I confess that all this seems so obvious that the reader is entitled to inquire into the motive for reciting such plain facts. Were it not for the persistence of the epistemological problem it would be an affront to the reader's intelligence to dwell upon them. But as long as such facts as we have been discussing furnish the subject-matter with which philosophizing is peculiarly concerned, these commonplaces must be urged and reiterated. They bear out two contentions which are important at the juncture, although they will lose special significance as soon as these are habitually recognized: Negatively, a prior and non-empirical notion of the self is the source of the prevailing belief that experience as such is primarily cognitional—a knowledge affair; positively, *knowledge is always a matter of the use that is made of experienced natural events*, a use in which given things are treated as indications of what will be experienced under different conditions.

Let us make one effort more to clear up these points. Suppose it is a question of knowledge of water. The thing to be known does not present itself primarily as a matter of knowledge-and-ignorance at all. It occurs as a stimulus to action and as the source of certain undergoings. It is something to react to:—to drink, to wash with, to put out fire with, and also something that reacts unexpectedly to our reactions, that makes us undergo disease, suffocation, drowning. In this twofold way, water or anything else enters into experience. Such presence in experience has of itself nothing to do with knowledge or consciousness; nothing that is in the sense of depending upon them, though it has everything to do with knowledge and consciousness in the sense that the latter depends upon prior experience of this non-cognitive sort. Man's experience is what it is because his response to things (even successful response) and the reactions of things to his life, are so radically different from knowledge. The difficulties and tragedies of life, the stimuli to acquiring knowledge, lie in the radical disparity of presence-in-experience and presence-in-knowing. Yet the immense importance of knowledge experience, the fact that turning presence-in-experience over into presence-in-a-knowledge-experience is the sole mode of control of nature, has systematically hypnotized European philosophy since the time of Socrates into thinking that all experiencing is a mode of knowing, if not good knowledge, then a low-grade or confused or implicit knowledge.

When water is an adequate stimulus to action or when its reactions oppress and overwhelm us, it remains outside the scope of knowledge. When, however, the bare presence of the thing (say, as optical stimulus) ceases to operate directly as stimulus to response and begins to operate in connection with a forecast of the consequences it will effect when responded to, it begins to acquire meaning—to be known, to be an object. It is noted as something which is wet, fluid, satisfies thirst, allays uneasiness, etc. The conception that we begin with a known visual quality which is thereafter enlarged by adding on qualities apprehended by the other senses does not rest upon experience; it rests upon making experience conform to the notion that every experience *must* be a cognitive noting. As long as the visual stimulus operates as a stimulus on its own account, there is no apprehension, no noting, of color or light at all. To much the greater portion of sensory stimuli we react in precisely this wholly non-cognitive way. In the attitude of suspended response in which consequences are anticipated, the direct stimulus becomes a sign or index of something else—and thus matter of noting or apprehension or acquaintance, or whatever term may be employed. This difference (together, of course, with the consequences which go with it) is the difference which the natural event of knowing makes to the natural event of direct organic stimulation. It is no change of a reality into an unreality, of an object into something subjective; it is no secret, illicit, or epistemological transformation; it is a genuine acquisition of new and distinctive features through entering into relations with things with which it was not formerly connected—namely, possible and future things.

But, replies some one so obsessed with the epistemological point of view that he assumes that the prior account is a rival epistemology in disguise, all this involves no change in Reality, no difference made to Reality. Water was all the time all the things it is ever found out to be. Its real nature has not been altered by knowing it; any such alteration means a mis-knowing.

In reply let it be said,—once more and finally,—there is no assertion or implication about *the* real object or *the* real world or *the* reality. Such an assumption goes with that epistemological universe of discourse which has to be abandoned in an empirical universe of discourse. The change is of *a* real object. An incident of the world operating as a physiologically direct stimulus is assuredly a reality. Responded to, it produces specific consequences in virtue of the response. Water is not drunk unless somebody drinks it; it does not quench thirst unless a thirsty person drinks it—and so on. Consequences occur whether one is aware of them or not; they are integral facts in experience. But let one of these consequences be anticipated and let it, as anticipated, become an indispensable element in the stimulus, and then there is a known object. It is not that knowing *produces* a change, but that it *is* a change of the specific kind described. A serial process, the successive portions of which are as such incapable of simultaneous occurrence, is telescoped and condensed into an object, a unified inter-reference of contemporaneous properties, most of which express potentialities rather than completed data.

Because of this change, an *object* possesses truth or error (which the physical occurrence as such never has); it is classifiable as fact or fantasy; it is of a sort or kind, expresses an essence or nature, possesses implications, etc., etc. That is to say, it is marked by specifiable *logical* traits not found in physical occurrences as such. Because objective idealisms have seized upon these traits as constituting the very essence of Reality is no reason for proclaiming that they are ready-made features of physical happenings, and hence for maintaining that knowing is nothing but an appearance of things on a stage for which "consciousness" supplies the footlights. For only the epistemological predicament leads to "presentations" being regarded as cognitions of things which were previously unpresented. In any empirical situation of everyday life or of science, knowledge signifies something stated or inferred of another thing. Visible water is not a more or less erroneous presentation of H_2O, but H_2O is a knowledge about the thing we see, drink, wash with, sail on, and use for power.

A further point and the present phase of discussion terminates. Treating knowledge as a presentative relation between the knower and object makes it necessary to regard the mechanism of *presentation* as constituting the act of knowing. Since things may be presented in sense-perception, in recollection, in imagination and in conception, and since the mechanism in every one of these four styles of presentation is sensory-cerebral the problem of knowing becomes a mind-body problem.[12] The psychological, or physiological, mechanism of presentation involved in seeing a chair, remembering what I ate yesterday for luncheon, imagining the moon the size of a cart wheel, conceiving a mathematical continuum is identified with the operation of knowing. The evil consequences are twofold. The problem of the relation of mind and body has become a part of the problem of the possibility of knowledge in general, to the further complication of a matter already hopelessly constrained. Meantime the actual process of knowing, namely, operations of controlled observation, inference, reasoning, and testing, the only process with *intellectual* import, is dismissed as irrelevant to the theory of knowing. The methods of knowing practiced in daily life and science are excluded from consideration in the philosophical theory of knowing. Hence the constructions of the latter become more and more elaborately artificial because there is no definite check upon them. It would be easy to quote from epistemological writers statements to the effect that these processes (which supply the only empirically verifiable facts of knowing) are *merely* inductive in character, or even that they are of purely psychological significance. It would be difficult to find a more complete inversion of the facts than in the latter statement, since presentation constitutes in fact the psychological affair. A confusion of logic with physiological psychology has bred hybrid epistemology, with the amazing result that the

technique of effective inquiry is rendered irrelevant to the theory of knowing, and those physical events involved in the occurrence of data for knowing are treated as if they constituted the act of knowing.

V

What are the bearings of our discussion upon the conception of the present scope and office of philosophy? What do our conclusions indicate and demand with reference to philosophy itself? For the philosophy which reaches such conclusions regarding knowledge and mind must apply them, sincerely and whole-heartedly, to its idea of its own nature. For philosophy claims to be one form or mode of knowing. If, then, the conclusion is reached that knowing is a way of employing empirical occurrences with respect to increasing power to direct the consequences which flow from things, the application of the conclusion must be made to philosophy itself. It, too, becomes not a contemplative survey of existence nor an analysis of what is past and done with, but an outlook upon future possibilities with reference to attaining the better and averting the worse. Philosophy must take, with good grace, its own medicine.

It is easier to state the negative results of the changed idea of philosophy than the positive ones. The point that occurs to mind most readily is that philosophy will have to surrender all pretension to be peculiarly concerned with ultimate reality, or with reality as a complete (i.e., completed) whole: with *the* real object. The surrender is not easy of achievement. The philosophic tradition that comes to us from classic Greek thought and that was reinforced by Christian philosophy in the Middle Ages discriminates philosophical knowing from other modes of knowing by means of an alleged peculiarly intimate concern with supreme, ultimate, true reality. To deny this trait to philosophy seems to many to be the suicide of philosophy; to be a systematic adoption of skepticism or agnostic positivism.

The pervasiveness of the tradition is shown in the fact that so vitally a contemporary thinker as Bergson, who finds a philosophic revolution involved in abandonment of the traditional identification of the truly real with the fixed (an identification inherited from Greek thought), does not find it in his heart to abandon the counterpart identification of philosophy with search for the truly Real; and hence finds it necessary to substitute an ultimate and absolute flux for an ultimate and absolute permanence. Thus his great empirical services in calling attention to the fundamental importance of considerations of time for problems of life and mind get compromised with a mystic, non-empirical "Intuition"; and we find him preoccupied with solving, by means of his new idea of ultimate reality, the traditional problems of realities-in-themselves and phenomena, matter and mind, free-will and determinism, God and the world. Is not that another evidence of the influence of the classic idea about philosophy?

Even the new realists are not content to take their realism as a plea for approaching subject-matter directly instead of through the intervention of epistemological apparatus; they find it necessary first to determine the status of *the* real object. Thus they too become entangled in the problem of the possibility of error, dreams, hallucinations, etc., in short, the problem of evil. For I take it that an uncorrupted realism would accept such things as real events, and find in them no other problems than those attending the consideration of any real occurrence—namely, problems of structure, origin, and operation.

It is often said that pragmatism, unless it is content to be a contribution to mere methodology, must develop a theory of Reality. But the chief characteristic trait of the pragmatic notion of reality is precisely that no theory of Reality in general, *überhaupt*, is possible or needed. It occupies the position of an emancipated empiricism or a thoroughgoing naïve realism. It finds that "reality" is a *denotative* term, a word used to designate indifferently everything that happens. Lies, dreams, insanities, deceptions, myths, theories are all of them just the events which they specifically are. Pragmatism is content to take its stand with science; for science finds all such events to be subject-matter of description and inquiry— just like stars and fossils, mosquitoes and malaria, circulation and vision. It also takes its

stand with daily life, which finds that such things really have to be reckoned with as they occur interwoven in the texture of events.

The only way in which the term reality can ever become more than a blanket denotative term is through recourse to specific events in all their diversity and thatness. Speaking summarily, I find that the retention by philosophy of the notion of a Reality feudally superior to the events of everyday occurrence is the chief source of the increasing isolation of philosophy from common sense and science. For the latter do not operate in any such region. As with them of old, philosophy in dealing with real difficulties finds itself still hampered by reference to realities more real, more ultimate, than those which directly happen.

I have said that identifying the cause of philosophy with the notion of superior reality is the cause of an *increasing* isolation from science and practical life. The phrase reminds us that there was a time when the enterprise of science and the moral interests of men both moved in a universe invidiously distinguished from that of ordinary occurrence. While all that happens is equally real—since it really happens—happenings are not of equal worth. Their respective consequences, their import, varies tremendously. Counterfeit money, although real (or rather *because* real), is really different from valid circulatory medium, just as disease is really different from health; different in specific structure and so different in consequences. In occidental thought, the Greeks were the first to draw the distinction between the genuine and the spurious in a generalized fashion and to formulate and enforce its tremendous significance for the conduct of life. But since they had at command no technique of experimental analysis and no adequate technique of mathematical analysis, they were compelled to treat the difference of the true and the false, the dependable and the deceptive, as signifying two kinds of existence, the truly real and the apparently real.

Two points can hardly be asserted with too much emphasis. The Greeks were wholly right in the feeling that questions of good and ill, as far as they fall within human control, are bound up with discrimination of the genuine from the spurious, of "being" from what only pretends to be. But because they lacked adequate instrumentalities for coping with this difference in specific situations, they were forced to treat the difference as a wholesale and rigid one. Science was concerned with vision of ultimate and true reality; opinion was concerned with getting along with apparent realities. Each had its appropriate region permanently marked off. Matters of opinion could never become matters of science; their intrinsic nature forbade. When the practice of science went on under such conditions, science and philosophy were one and the same thing. Both had to do with ultimate reality in its rigid and insuperable difference from ordinary occurrences.

We have only to refer to the way in which medieval life wrought the philosophy of an ultimate and supreme reality into the context of practical life to realize that for centuries political and moral interests were bound up with the distinction between the absolutely real and the relatively real. The difference was no matter of a remote technical philosophy, but one which controlled life from the cradle to the grave, from the grave to the endless life after death. By means of a vast institution, which in effect was state as well as church, the claims of ultimate reality were enforced; means of access to it were provided. Acknowledgment of The Reality brought security in this world and salvation in the next. It is not necessary to report the story of the change which has since taken place. It is enough for our purposes to note that none of the modern philosophies of a superior reality, or *the* real object, idealistic or realistic, holds that its insight makes a difference like that between sin and holiness, eternal condemnation and eternal bliss. While in its own context the philosophy of ultimate reality entered into the vital concerns of men, it now tends to be an ingenious dialectic exercised in professorial corners by a few who have retained ancient premises while rejecting their application to the conduct of life.

The increased isolation from science of any philosophy identified with the problem of *the* real is equally marked. For the growth of science has consisted precisely in the invention of an equipment, a technique of appliances and procedures, which, accepting all occurrences as homogeneously real, proceeds to distinguish the authenticated from the spurious, the true from the false, by specific modes of treatment in specific situations. The procedures of the trained engineer, of the competent physician, of the laboratory expert, have turned out to be the only ways of discriminating the counterfeit from the valid. And they have revealed that the difference is not one of antecedent fixity of existence, but one of mode of treatment and of the consequences thereon attendant. After mankind has learned to put its trust in specific procedures in order to make its discriminations between the false and the true, philosophy arrogates to itself the enforcement of the distinction at its own cost.

More than once, this essay has intimated that the counterpart of the idea of invidiously real reality is the spectator notion of knowledge. If the knower, however defined, is set over against the world to be known, knowing consists in possessing a transcript, more or less accurate but otiose, of real things. Whether this transcript is presentative in character (as realists say) or whether it is by means of states of consciousness which represent things (as subjectivists say), is a matter of great importance in its own context. But, in another regard, this difference is negligible in comparison with the point in which both agree. Knowing is viewing from outside. But if it be true that the self or subject of experience is part and parcel of the course of events, it follows that the self *becomes* a knower. It becomes a mind in virtue of a distinctive way of partaking in the course of events. The significant distinction is no longer between the knower *and* the world; it is between different ways of being in and of the movement of things; between a brute physical way and a purposive, intelligent way.

There is no call to repeat in detail the statements which have been advanced. Their net purport is that the directive presence of future possibilities in dealing with existent conditions is what is meant by knowing; that the self becomes a knower or mind when anticipation of future consequences operates as its stimulus. What we are now concerned with is the effect of this conception upon the nature of philosophic knowing.

As far as I can judge, popular response to pragmatic philosophy was moved by two quite different considerations. By some it was thought to provide a new species of sanctions, a new mode of apologetics, for certain religious ideas whose standing had been threatened. By others, it was welcomed because it was taken as a sign that philosophy was about to surrender its otiose and speculative remoteness; that philosophers were beginning to recognize that philosophy is of account only if, like everyday knowing and like science, it affords guidance to action and thereby makes a difference in the event. It was welcomed as a sign that philosophers were willing to have the worth of their philosophizing measured by responsible tests.

I have not seen this point of view emphasized, or hardly recognized, by professional critics. The difference of attitude can probably be easily explained. The epistemological universe of discourse is so highly technical that only those who have been trained in the history of thought think in terms of it. It did not occur, accordingly, to non-technical readers to interpret the doctrine that the meaning and validity of thought are fixed by differences made in consequences and in satisfactoriness to mean consequences in personal feelings. Those who were professionally trained, however, took the statement to mean that consciousness or mind in the mere act of looking at things modifies them. It understood the doctrine of test of validity by consequences to mean that apprehensions and conceptions are true if the modifications effected by them were of an emotionally desirable tone.

Prior discussion should have made it reasonably clear that the source of this misunderstanding lies in the neglect of temporal considerations. The change made in things by the self in knowing is not immediate and, so to say, cross-sectional. It is longitudinal—in the redirection given to changes already going on. Its analogue is found in the changes which take place in the development of, say, iron ore into a watch-spring, not in those of the miracle of transubstantiation. For the static, cross-sectional, non-temporal relation of subject and object, the pragmatic hypothesis substitutes apprehension of a thing in terms of the results in other things which it is tending to effect. For the unique epistemological relation, it substitutes a practical relation of a familiar type:—responsive behavior which changes in time the subject-matter to which it applies. The unique thing about the responsive behavior which constitutes knowing is the specific difference which marks it off from other modes of response, namely, the part played in it by anticipation and prediction. Knowing is the act, stimulated by this foresight, of securing and averting consequences. The success of the achievement measures the standing of the foresight by which response is directed. The popular impression that pragmatic philosophy means that philosophy shall develop ideas relevant to the actual crises of life, ideas influential in dealing with them and tested by the assistance they afford, is correct.

Reference to practical response suggests, however, another misapprehension. Many critics have jumped at the obvious association of the word pragmatic with practical. They have assumed that the intent is to limit all knowledge, philosophic included, to promoting "action," understanding by action either just any bodily movement, or those bodily movements which conduce to the preservation and grosser well-being of the body. James's statement that general conceptions must "cash in" has been taken (especially by European critics) to mean that the end and measure of intelligence lies in the narrow and coarse utilities which it produces. Even an acute American thinker, after first criticizing pragmatism as a kind of idealistic epistemology, goes on to treat it as a doctrine which regards intelligence as a lubricating oil facilitating the workings of the body.

One source of the misunderstanding is suggested by the fact that "cashing in" to James meant that a general idea must always be capable of verification in specific existential cases. The notion of "cashing in" says nothing about the breadth or depth of the specific consequences. As an empirical doctrine, it could not say anything about them in general; the specific cases must speak for themselves. If one conception is verified in terms of eating beefsteak, and another in terms of a favorable credit balance in the bank, that is not because of anything in the theory, but because of the specific nature of the conceptions in question, and because there exist particular events like hunger and trade. If there are also existences in which the most liberal esthetic ideas and the most generous moral conceptions can be verified by specific embodiment, assuredly so much the better. The fact that a strictly empirical philosophy was taken by so many critics to imply an *a priori* dogma about the kind of consequences capable of existence is evidence, I think, of the inability of many philosophers to think in concretely empirical terms. Since the critics were themselves accustomed to get results by manipulating the concepts of "consequences" and of "practice," they assumed that even a would-be empiricist must be doing the same sort of thing. It will, I suppose, remain for a long time incredible to some that a philosopher should really intend to go to specific experiences to determine of what scope and depth practice admits, and what sort of consequences the world permits to come into being. Concepts are so clear; it takes so little time to develop their implications; experiences are so confused, and it requires so much time and energy to lay hold of them. And yet these same critics charge pragmatism with adopting subjective and emotional standards!

As a matter of fact, the pragmatic theory of intelligence means that the function of mind is to project new and more complex ends—to free experience from routine and from caprice. Not the use of thought to accomplish purposes already given either in the mechanism of the body or in that of the existent state of society, but the use of intelligence to liberate and liberalize action, is the pragmatic lesson. Action restricted to given and fixed ends may attain great technical efficiency; but efficiency is the only quality to which it can lay claim. Such action is mechanical (or becomes so), no matter what the scope of the pre-formed end, be it the Will of God or *Kultur*. But the doctrine that intelligence develops within the sphere of action for the sake of possibilities not yet given is the opposite of a doctrine of mechanical efficiency. Intelligence *as* intelligence is inherently forward-looking; only by ignoring its primary function does it become a mere means for an end already given. The latter *is* servile,

even when the end is labeled moral, religious, or esthetic. But action directed to ends to which the agent has not previously been attached inevitably carries with it a quickened and enlarged spirit. A pragmatic intelligence is a creative intelligence, not a routine mechanic.

All this may read like a defense of pragmatism by one concerned to make out for it the best case possible. Such is not, however, the intention. The purpose is to indicate the extent to which intelligence frees action from a mechanically instrumental character. Intelligence is, indeed, instrumental *through* action to the determination of the qualities of future experience. But the very fact that the concern of intelligence is with the future, with the as-yet-unrealized (and with the given and the established only as conditions of the realization of possibilities), makes the action in which it takes effect generous and liberal; free of spirit. Just that action which extends and approves intelligence has an intrinsic value of its own in being instrumental:—the intrinsic value of being informed with intelligence in behalf of the enrichment of life. By the same stroke, intelligence becomes truly liberal: knowing is a human undertaking, not an esthetic appreciation carried on by a refined class or a capitalistic possession of a few learned specialists, whether men of science or of philosophy.

More emphasis has been put upon what philosophy is not than upon what it may become. But it is not necessary, it is not even desirable, to set forth philosophy as a scheduled program. There are human difficulties of an urgent, deep-seated kind which may be clarified by trained reflection, and whose solution may be forwarded by the careful development of hypotheses. When it is understood that philosophic thinking is caught up in the actual course of events, having the office of guiding them towards a prosperous issue, problems will abundantly present themselves. Philosophy will not solve these problems; philosophy is vision, imagination, reflection—and these functions, apart from action, modify nothing and hence resolve nothing. But in a complicated and perverse world, action which is not informed with vision, imagination, and reflection, is more likely to increase confusion and conflict than to straighten things out. It is not easy for generous and sustained reflection to become a guiding and illuminating method in action. Until it frees itself from identification with problems which are supposed to depend upon Reality as such, or its distinction from a world of Appearance, or its relation to a Knower as such, the hands of philosophy are tied. Having no chance to link its fortunes with a responsible career by suggesting things to be tried, it cannot identify itself with questions which actually arise in the vicissitudes of life. Philosophy recovers itself when it ceases to be a device for dealing with the problems of philosophers and becomes a method, cultivated by philosophers, for dealing with the problems of men.

Emphasis must vary with the stress and special impact of the troubles which perplex men. Each age knows its own ills, and seeks its own remedies. One does not have to forecast a particular program to note that the central need of any program at the present day is an adequate conception of the nature of intelligence and its place in action. Philosophy cannot disavow responsibility for many misconceptions of the nature of intelligence which now hamper its efficacious operation. It has at least a negative task imposed upon it. It must take away the burdens which it has laid upon the intelligence of the common man in struggling with his difficulties. It must deny and eject that intelligence which is naught but a distant eye, registering in a remote and alien medium the spectacle of nature and life. To enforce the fact that the emergence of imagination and thought is relative to the connexion of the sufferings of men with their doings is of itself to illuminate those sufferings and to instruct those doings. To catch mind in its connexion with the entrance of the novel into the course of the world is to be on the road to see that intelligence is itself the most promising of all novelties, the revelation of the meaning of that transformation of past into future which is the reality of every present. To reveal intelligence as the organ for the guidance of this transformation, the sole director of its quality, is to make a declaration of present untold significance for action. To elaborate these convictions of the connexion of intelli-gence with what men undergo because of their doings and with the emergence and direction of the creative, the novel, in the world is of itself a program which will keep philosophers busy until something more worth while is forced upon them. For the elaboration has to be made through application to all the disciplines which have an intimate connexion with human conduct:—to logic, ethics, esthetics, economics, and the procedure of the sciences formal and natural.

I also believe that there is a genuine sense in which the enforcement of the pivotal position of intelligence in the world and thereby in control of human fortunes (so far as they are manageable) is the peculiar problem in the problems of life which come home most closely to ourselves—to ourselves living not merely in the early twentieth century but in the United States. It is easy to be foolish about the connexion of thought with national life. But I do not see how any one can question the distinctively national color of English, or French, or German philosophies. And if of late the history of thought has come under the domination of the German dogma of an inner evolution of ideas, it requires but a little inquiry to convince oneself that that dogma itself testifies to a particularly nationalistic need and origin. I believe that philosophy in America will be lost between chewing a historic cud long since reduced to woody fibre, or an apologetics for lost causes (lost to natural science), or a scholastic, schematic formalism, unless it can somehow bring to consciousness America's own needs and its own implicit principle of successful action.

This need and principle, I am convinced, is the necessity of a deliberate control of policies by the method of intelligence, an intelligence which is not the faculty of intellect honored in text-books and neglected elsewhere, but which is the sum-total of impulses, habits, emotions, records, and discoveries which forecast what is desirable and undesirable in future possibilities, and which contrive ingeniously in behalf of imagined good. Our life has no background of sanctified categories upon which we may fall back; we rely upon precedent as authority only to our own undoing—for with us there is such a continuously novel situation that final reliance upon precedent entails some class interest guiding us by the nose whither it will. British empiricism, with its appeal to what has been in the past, is, after all, only a kind of *a priorism*. For it lays down a fixed rule for future intelligence to follow; and only the immersion of philosophy in technical learning prevents our seeing that this is the essence of *a priorism*.

We pride ourselves upon being realistic, desiring a hardheaded cognizance of facts, and devoted to mastering the means of life. We pride ourselves upon a practical idealism, a lively and easily moved faith in possibilities as yet unrealized, in willingness to make sacrifice for their realization. Idealism easily becomes a sanction of waste and carelessness, and realism a sanction of legal formalism in behalf of things as they are—the rights of the possessor. We thus tend to combine a loose and ineffective optimism with assent to the doctrine of take who take can: a deification of power. All peoples at all times have been narrowly realistic in practice and have then employed idealization to cover up in sentiment and theory their brutalities. But never, perhaps, has the tendency been so dangerous and so tempting as with ourselves. Faith in the power of intelligence to imagine a future which is the projection of the desirable in the present, and to invent the instrumentalities of its realization, is our salvation. And it is a faith which must be nurtured and made articulate: surely a sufficiently large task for our philosophy.

NOTES

[First published in *Creative Intelligence: Essays in the Pragmatic Attitude* (New York: Henry Holt and Co., 1917), pp. 3–69. MW 10:3–48.]

1. The word relation suffers from ambiguity. I am speaking here of *connexion,* dynamic and functional interaction. "Relation" is a term used also to express logical reference. I suspect that much of the controversy about internal and external relations is due to this ambiguity. One passes at will from existential connexions of things to logical relationship of terms. Such an identification of existences with *terms* is congenial to idealism, but is paradoxical in a professed realism.

2. There is some gain in substituting a doctrine of flux and interpenetration of psychical states, *à la* Bergson, for that of rigid discontinuity. But the substitution leaves untouched the fundamental mis-statement of experience, the conception of experience as directly and primarily "inner" and psychical.

3. Mathematical science in its formal aspects, or as a branch of formal logic, has been the empirical stronghold of rationalism. But an empirical empiricism, in contrast with orthodox deductive empiricism, has no difficulty in establishing its jurisdiction as to deductive functions.

4. It is a shame to devote the word idealism, with its latent moral, practical connotations, to a doctrine whose tenets are the denial of the existence of a physical world, and the psychical character of all objects—at least as far as they are knowable. But I am following usage, not attempting to make it.

5. See Horace M. Kallen, "Value and Existence in Philosophy, Art and Religion," in *Creative Intelligence: Essays in the Pragmatic Attitude*, pp. 409–67.

6. The "they" means the "some" of the prior sentence—those whose realism is epistemological, instead of being a plea for taking the facts of experience as we find them without refraction through epistemological apparatus.

7. It is interesting to note that some of the realists who have assimilated the cognitive relation to other existential relations in the world (instead of treating it as an unique or epistemological relation) have been forced in support of their conception of knowledge as a "presentative" or spectatorial affair to extend the defining features of the latter to all relations among things, and hence to make all the "real" things in the world pure "simples," wholly independent of one another. So conceived the doctrine of external relations appears to be rather the doctrine of complete externality of *things*. Aside from this point, the doctrine is interesting for its dialectical ingenuity and for the elegant development of assumed premises, rather than convincing on account of empirical evidence supporting it.

8. In other words, there is a general "problem of error" only because there is a general problem of evil, concerning which see Dr. Kallen's "Value and Existence."

9. Compare Boyd H. Bode, "Consciousness and Psychology," in *Creative Intelligence: Essays in the Pragmatic Attitude*, pp. 228–81.

10. As the attempt to retain the epistemological problem and yet to reject idealistic and relativistic solutions has forced some Neo-realists into the doctrine of isolated and independent simples, so it has also led to a doctrine of Eleatic pluralism. In order to maintain the doctrine the subject makes no difference to anything else, it is held that *no* ultimate real makes any difference to anything else— all this rather than surrender once for all the genuineness of the problem and to follow the lead of

empirical subject-matter.

11. There is almost no end to the various dialectic developments of the epistemological situation. When it is held that all the relations of the type in question are cognitive, and yet it is recognized (as it must be) that many such "transformations" go unremarked, the theory is supplemented by introducing "unconscious" psychical modifications.

12. Conception-presentation has, of course, been made by many in the history of speculation an exception to this statement; "pure" memory is also made an exception by Bergson. To take cognizance of this matter would, of course, accentuate, not relieve, the difficulty remarked upon in the text.

Why such a title as Philosophy and Democracy? Why Philosophy and Democracy, any more than Chemistry and Oligarchy, Mathematics and Aristocracy, Astronomy and Monarchy? Is not the concern of philosophy with truth, and can truth vary with political and social institutions any more than with degrees of latitude and meridians of longitude? Is there one ultimate reality for men who live where suffrage is universal and another and different reality where limited suffrage prevails? If we should become a socialistic republic next week would that modify the nature of the ultimates and absolutes with which philosophy deals any more than it would affect the principles of arithmetic or the laws of physics?

Such questions, I fancy, lurk in your minds when they are confronted by a title like that which is chosen for this evening. It is well that these questions should not be allowed to lurk in subconscious recesses, but should be brought out into the open. For they have to do with what is the first and last problem for a student of philosophy: The problem of what after all is the business and province of philosophy itself. What is it about? What is it after? What would it have to be possessed of in order to be satisfied? To such questions as these must the remarks of the evening be chiefly addressed, leaving the nominal and explicit subject of the relation of democracy to philosophy to figure for the most part as a corollary or even as a postscript.

If then we return to the imaginary interrogations with which we set out we shall find that a certain assumption underlies them—or rather two assumptions. One is that philosophy ranks as a science, that its business is with a certain body of fixed and finished facts and principles. Philosophy is viewed not as its etymology would lead us to expect as a form of love or desire, but as a form of knowledge, of apprehension and acknowledgment of a system of truths comparable in its independence of human wish and effort with the truths of physics. Such, I take it, is the first assumption. The second is that since the realities or truths to be known must be marked off from those of physics and mathematics in order that philosophy may be itself a distinctive form of

Philosophy and Democracy

(1919)

knowledge, philosophy somehow knows reality more *ultimately* than do the other sciences. It approaches truth with an effort at a more comprehensive, a more completely total vision, and takes reality at a deeper and more fundamental level than do those subjects which orthodox philosophers have loved to call the *special* sciences. What they take piecemeal and therefore more or less erroneously (since a fragment arbitrarily torn from the organic whole is not truly a truth) philosophy takes *teres et rotundus*. What they take superficially, in, so to say, its appearance, philosophy takes at that deeper level where connections and relations within the whole are found.

Some such suppositions as these have, I think, been fostered by many philosophers. They are in the back of the minds of many students when they come to the study of philosophy. They are equally in the minds of many foes of philosophy who also compare philosophy with science, but only to contrast them—at the expense of philosophy. Philosophy, they say, is circular and disputatious; it settles nothing, for its schools are still divided much as they were in the times of the Greeks, engaged in arguing the same questions. Science is progressive; it settles some things and moves on to others. Philosophy moreover is sterile. Where are its works? Where are its concrete applications and living fruits? Hence they conclude that while philosophy is a form of knowledge or science, it is a pretentious and pseudo-form, an effort at a kind of knowledge which is impossible—impossible at all events to human minds.

Yet every generation, no matter how great the advance of positive knowledge, nor how great the triumphs of the special sciences, shows in its day discontent with all these proved and ascertained results and turns afresh and with infinite hope to philosophy, as to a deeper, more complete and more final revelation. Something is lacking in even the most demonstrated of scientific truths which breeds dissatisfaction, and a yearning for something more conclusive and more mind-filling.

In the face of such perplexities as these there is, I think, another alternative, another way out. Put baldly, it is to deny that philosophy is in any sense whatever a form of knowl-

edge. It is to say that we should return to the original and etymological sense of the word, and recognize that philosophy is a form of desire, of effort at action—a love, namely, of wisdom; but with the thorough proviso, not attached to the Platonic use of the word, that wisdom, whatever it is, is not a mode of science or knowledge. A philosophy which was conscious of its own business and province would then perceive that it is an intellectualized wish, an aspiration subjected to rational discriminations and tests, a social hope reduced to a working program of action, a prophecy of the future, but one disciplined by serious thought and knowledge.

These are statements at once sweeping and vague. Let us recur to the question of whether there is such a thing as a philosophy which is distinctively that of a social order, a distinctive type appropriate to a democracy or to a feudalism. Let us consider the matter not theoretically but historically. In point of fact, nobody would deny that there has been a German, a French, an English philosophy in a sense in which there have not been national chemistries or astronomies. Even in science there is not the complete impersonal detachment which some views of it would lead us to expect. There is difference in color and temper, in emphasis and preferred method characteristic of each people. But these differences are inconsiderable in comparison with those which we find in philosophy. There the differences have been differences in standpoint, outlook and ideal. They manifest not diversities of intellectual emphasis so much as incompatibilities of temperament and expectation. They are different ways of construing life. They indicate different practical ethics of life, not mere variations of intellectual assent. In reading Bacon, Locke, Descartes, Comte, Hegel, Schopenhauer, one says to oneself this could have proceeded only from England, or France, or Germany, as the case may be. The parallelisms with political history and social needs are obvious and explicit.

Take the larger divisions of thought. The conventional main division of philosophy is into ancient, medieval and modern. We may make a similar division in the history of science. But there the meaning is very different.

We either mean merely to refer to the stage of ignorance and of knowledge found in certain periods, or we mean not science at all but certain phases of philosophy. When we take science proper, astronomy or geometry, we do not find Euclid especially Greek in his demonstrations. No, ancient, medieval, modern, express in philosophy differences of interest and of purpose characteristic of great civilizations, great social epochs, differences of religious and social desire and belief. They are applicable to philosophy only because economic, political and religious differences manifest themselves in philosophy in fundamentally the same ways that they are shown in other institutions. The philosophies embodied not colorless intellectual readings of reality, but men's most passionate desires and hopes, their basic beliefs about the sort of life to be lived. They started not from science, not from ascertained knowledge, but from moral convictions, and then resorted to the best knowledge and the best intellectual methods available in their day to give the form of demonstration to what was essentially an attitude of will, or a moral resolution to prize one mode of life more highly than another, and the wish to persuade other men that this was the wise way of living.

And this explains what is meant by saying that love of wisdom is not after all the same thing as eagerness for scientific knowledge. By wisdom we mean not systematic and proved knowledge of fact and truth, but a conviction about moral values, a sense for the better kind of life to be led. Wisdom is a moral term, and like every moral term refers not to the constitution of things already in existence, not even if that constitution be magnified into eternity and absoluteness. As a moral term it refers to a choice about something to be done, a preference for living this sort of life rather than that. It refers not to accomplished reality but to a desired future which our desires, when translated into articulate conviction, may help bring into existence.

There are those who think that such statements give away the whole case for philosophy. Many critics and foes of philosophy coming from the camp of science would doubtless claim they were admissions of the claims that philosophy has always been a false light, a pretentious ambition; and that the lesson is that philosophers should sit down in humility and accept the ascertainments of the special sciences, and not go beyond the task of weaving these statements into a more coherent fabric of expression. Others would go further and find in such statements a virtual confession of the futility of all philosophizing.

But there is another way of taking the matter. One might rather say that the fact that the collective purpose and desire of a given generation and people dominates its philosophy is evidence of the sincerity and vitality of that philosophy; that failure to employ the known facts of the period in support of a certain estimate of the proper life to lead would show lack of any holding and directing force in the current social ideal. Even wresting facts to a purpose, obnoxious as it is, testifies to a certain ardency in the vigor with which a belief about the right life to be led is held. It argues moral debility if the slave Epictetus and the Emperor Aurelius entertain just the same philosophy of life, even though both belong to the same Stoic school. "A community devoted to industrial pursuits, active in business and commerce, is not likely to see the needs and possibilities of life in the same way as a country with high aesthetic culture and little enterprise in turning the energies of nature to mechanical account. A social group with a fairly continuous history will respond mentally to a crisis in a very different way from one which has felt the shock of distinct breaks." Different hues of philosophic thought are bound to result. Women have as yet made little contribution to philosophy. But when women who are not mere students of other persons' philosophy set out to write it, we cannot conceive that it will be the same in viewpoint or tenor as that composed from the standpoint of the different masculine experience of things. Institutions, customs of life, breed certain systematized predilections and aversions. The wise man reads historic philosophies to detect in them intellectual formulations of men's habitual purposes and cultivated wants, not to gain insight into the ultimate nature of things or information about the make-up of reality. As far as what is loosely called reality figures in philosophies, we may be sure that it signifies those selected aspects of the world which are chosen because they lend themselves to the support of men's judgment of the worth-while life, and hence are most highly prized. In philosophy, "reality" is a term of value or choice.

To deny however that philosophy is in any essential sense a form of science or of knowledge, is not to say that philosophy is a mere arbitrary expression of wish or feeling or a vague suspiration after something, nobody knows what. All philosophy bears an intellectual impress because it is an effort to convince some one, perhaps the writer himself, of the reasonableness of some course of life which has been adopted from custom or instinct. Since it is addressed to man's intelligence, it must employ knowledge and established beliefs, and it must proceed in an orderly way, logically. The art of literature catches men unaware and employs a charm to bring them to a spot whence they see vividly and intimately some picture which embodies life in a meaning. But magic and immediate vision are denied the philosopher. He proceeds prosaically along the highway, pointing out recognizable landmarks, mapping the course, and labeling with explicit logic the stations reached. This means of course that philosophy must depend upon the best science of its day. It can intellectually recommend its judgments of value only as it can select relevant material from that which is recognized to be established truth, and can persuasively use current knowledge to drive home the reasonableness of its conception of life. It is this dependence upon the method of logical presentation and upon scientific subject matter which confers upon philosophy the garb, though not the form, of knowledge.

Scientific form is a vehicle for conveying a non-scientific conviction, but the carriage is necessary, for philosophy is not mere passion but a passion that would exhibit itself as a reasonable persuasion. Philosophy is therefore always in a delicate position, and gives the heathen and Philistine an opportunity to rage. It is always balancing between sophistry, or pretended and illegitimate knowledge, and vague, incoherent mysticism—not of necessity mysticism in its technical definition, but in that sense of the mysterious and misty which

affects the popular meaning of the word. When the stress is too much on intellectual form, when the original moral purpose has lost its vitality, philosophy becomes learned and dialectical. When there is cloudy desire, unclarified and unsustained by the logical exhibition of attained science, philosophy becomes hortatory, edifying, sentimental, or fantastic and semi-magical. The perfect balance may hardly be attained by man, and there are few indeed who can even like Plato rhythmically alternate with artistic grace from one emphasis to the other. But what makes philosophy hard work and also makes its cultivation worth while, is precisely the fact that it assumes the responsibility for setting forth some ideal of a collective good life by the methods which the best science of the day employs in its quite different task, and with the use of the characteristic knowledge of its day. The philosopher fails when he avoids sophistry, or the conceit of knowledge, only to pose as a prophet of miraculous intuition or mystic revelation or a preacher of pious nobilities of sentiment.

Perhaps we can now see why it is that philosophers have so often been led astray into making claims for philosophy which when taken literally are practically insane in their inordinate scope, such as the claim that philosophy deals with some supreme and total reality beyond that with which the special sciences and arts have to do. Stated sincerely and moderately, the claim would take the form of pointing out that no knowledge as long as it remains just knowledge, just apprehension of fact and truth, is complete or satisfying. Human nature is such that it is impossible that merely finding out that things are thus and so can long content it. There is an instinctive uneasiness which forces men to go beyond any intellectual grasp or recognition, no matter how extensive. Even if a man had seen the whole existent world and gained insight into its hidden and complicated structure, he would after a few moments of ecstacy at the marvel thus revealed to him become dissatisfied to remain at that point. He would begin to ask himself what of it? What is it all about? What does it all mean? And by these questions he would not signify the absurd search for a knowledge greater than all knowledge, but would indicate the need for projecting even the completest knowledge upon a realm of another dimension—namely, the dimension of action. He would mean: What am I to do about it? What course of activity does this state of things require of me? What possibilities to be achieved by my own thought turned over into deed does it open up to me? What new responsibilities does this knowledge impose? To what new adventures does it invite? All knowledge in short makes a difference. It opens new perspectives and releases energy to new tasks. This happens anyway and continuously, philosophy or no philosophy. But philosophy tries to gather up the threads into a central stream of tendency, to inquire what more fundamental and general attitudes of response the trend of knowledge exacts of us, to what new fields of action it calls us. It is in this sense, a practical and moral sense, that philosophy can lay claim to the epithets of universal, basic and superior. Knowledge *is* partial and incomplete, any and all knowledge, till we have placed it in the context of a future which cannot be known, but only speculated about and resolved upon. It is, to use in another sense a favorite philosophical term, a matter of *appearance*, for it is not self-enclosed, but an indication of something to be done.

As was intimated at the outset, considerable has been said about philosophy, but nothing as yet about democracy. Yet, I hope, certain implications are fairly obvious. There has been, roughly speaking, a coincidence in the development of modern experimental science and of democracy. Philosophy has no more important question than a consideration of how far this may be mere coincidence, and how far it marks a genuine correspondence. Is democracy a comparatively superficial human expedient, a device of petty manipulation, or does nature itself, as that is uncovered and understood by our best contemporaneous knowledge, sustain and support our democratic hopes and aspirations? Or, if we choose to begin arbitrarily at the other end, if to construct democratic institutions is our aim, how then shall we construe and interpret the natural environment and natural history of humanity in order to get an intellectual warrant for our endeavors, a reasonable persuasion that

our undertaking is not contradicted by what science authorizes us to say about the structure of the world? How shall we read what we call reality (that is to say the world of existence accessible to verifiable inquiry) so that we may essay our deepest political and social problems with a conviction that they are to a reasonable extent sanctioned and sustained by the nature of things? Is the world as an object of knowledge at odds with our purposes and efforts? Is it merely neutral and indifferent? Does it lend itself equally to all our social ideals, which means that it gives itself to none, but stays aloof, ridiculing as it were the ardor and earnestness with which we take our trivial and transitory hopes and plans? Or is its nature such that it is at least willing to cooperate, that it not only does not say us nay, but gives us an encouraging nod?

Is not this, you may ask, taking democracy too seriously? Why not ask the question about say presbyterianism or free verse? Well, I would not wholly deny the pertinency of similar questions about such movements. All deliberate action of mind is in a way an experiment with the world to see what it will stand for, what it will promote and what frustrate. The world is tolerant and fairly hospitable. It permits and even encourages all sorts of experiments. But in the long run some are more welcomed and assimilated than others. Hence there can be no difference save one of depth and scope between the questions of the relation of the world to a scheme of conduct in the form of church government or a form of art and that of its relation to democracy. If there be a difference, it is only because democracy is a form of desire and endeavor which reaches further and condenses into itself more issues.

This statement implies a matter of definition. What is meant by democracy? It can certainly be defined in a way which limits the issue to matters which if they bear upon philosophy at all affect it only in limited and technical aspects. Anything that can be said in the way of definition in the remaining moments must be, and confessedly is, arbitrary. The arbitrariness may however, be mitigated by linking up the conception with the historic formula of the greatest liberal movement of history—the formula of liberty, equality and fraternity. In referring to this, we only exchange arbitrariness for vagueness. It would be hard indeed to arrive at any consensus of judgment about the meaning of any one of the three terms inscribed on the democratic banner. Men did not agree in the eighteenth century and subsequent events have done much to accentuate their differences. Do they apply purely politically, or do they have an economic meaning?—to refer to one great cleavage which in the nineteenth century broke the liberal movement into two factions, now opposed to one another as liberal and conservative were once opposed.

Let us then take frank advantage of the vagueness and employ the terms with a certain generosity and breadth. What does the demand for liberty imply for philosophy, when we take the idea of liberty as conveying something of decided moral significance? Roughly speaking, there are two typical ideas of liberty. One of them says that freedom is action in accord with the consciousness of fixed law; that men are free when they are rational, and they are rational when they recognize and consciously conform to the necessities which the universe exemplified. As Tolstoi says, even the ox would be free if it recognized the yoke about its neck and took the yoke for the law of its own action instead of engaging in a vain task of revolt which escapes no necessity but only turns it in the direction of misery and destruction. This is a noble idea of freedom embodied, both openly and disguisedly, in classic philosophies. It is the only view consistent with any form of absolutism whether materialistic or idealistic, whether it considers the necessary relations which form the universe to be physical in character or spiritual. It holds of any view which says that reality exists under the form of eternity, that it is, to use a technical term, a *simul totum*, an all at once and forever affair, no matter whether the all at once be of mathematical-physical laws and structures, or a comprehensive and exhaustive divine consciousness. Of such a conception one can only say that however noble, it is not one which is spontaneously congenial to the idea of liberty in a society which has set its heart on democracy.

A philosophy animated, be it uncon-sciously or consciously, by the strivings of men to achieve democracy will construe liberty as meaning a universe in which there is real uncertainty and contingency, a world which is not all in, and never will be, a world which in some respect is incomplete and in the making, and which in these respects may be made this way or that according as men judge, prize, love and labor. To such a philosophy any notion of a perfect or complete reality, finished, existing always the same without regard to the vicissitudes of time, will be abhorrent. It will think of time not as that part of reality which for some strange reason has not yet been traversed, but as a genuine field of novelty, of real and unpredictable increments to existence, a field for experimentation and invention. It will indeed recognize that there is in things a grain against which we cannot successfully go, but it will also insist that we cannot even discover what that grain is except as we make this new experiment and that fresh effort, and that consequently the mistake, the effort which is frustrated in direct execution, is as true a constituent of the world as is the act which most carefully observes law. For it is the grain which is rubbed the wrong way which more clearly stands out. It will recognize that in a world where discovery is genuine, error is an inevitable ingredient of reality, and that man's business is not to avoid it—or to cultivate the illusion that it is mere appearance—but to turn it to account, to make it fruitful. Nor will such a philosophy be mealy-mouthed in admitting that where contingency is real and experiment is required, good fortune and bad fortune are facts. It will not construe all accomplishment in terms of merit and virtue, and all loss and frustration in terms of demerit and just punishment. Because it recognizes that contingency cooperates with intelligence in the realization of every plan, even the one most carefully and wisely thought out, it will avoid conceit and intellectual arrogance. It will not fall into the delusion that consciousness is or can be everything as a determiner of events. Hence it will be humbly grateful that a world in which the most extensive and accurate thought and reason can only take advantage of events is also a world which gives room to move about in, and which offers the delights of consummations that are new revelations, as well as those defeats that are admonishments to conceit.

The evident contrast of equality is inequality. Perhaps it is not so evident that inequality means practically inferiority and superiority. And that this relation works out practically in support of a regime of authority or feudal hierarchy in which each lower or inferior element depends upon, holds from, one superior from which it gets direction and to which it is responsible. Let one bear this idea fully in mind and he will see how largely philosophy has been committed to a metaphysics of feudalism. By this I mean it has thought of things in the world as occupying certain grades of value, or as having fixed degrees of truth, ranks of reality. The traditional conception of philosophy to which I referred at the outset, which identifies it with insight into supreme reality or ultimate and comprehensive truth, shows how thoroughly philosophy has been committed to a notion that inherently some realities are superior to others, are better than others. Now any such philosophy inevitably works in behalf of a regime of authority, for it is only right that the superior should lord it over the inferior. The result is that much of philosophy has gone to justifying the particular scheme of authority in religion or social order which happened to exist at a given time. It has become unconsciously an apologetic for the established order, because it has tried to show the rationality of this or that existent hierarchical grading of values and schemes of life. Or when it has questioned the established order it has been a revolutionary search for some rival principle of authority. How largely indeed has historic philosophy been a search for an indefeasible seat of authority. Greek philosophy began when men doubted the authority of custom as a regulator of life; it sought in universal reason or in the immediate particular, in being or in flux, a rival source of authority, but one which as a rival was to be as certain and definite as ever custom had been. Medieval philosophy was frankly an attempt to reconcile authority with reason, and modern philosophy began when man doubting the authority of revelation began a search for some authority which should have all the weight, certainty and inerrancy previously ascribed to the will of God embodied in the divinely instituted church.

Thus for the most part the democratic practice of life has been at an immense intellectual disadvantage. Prevailing philosophies have unconsciously discountenanced it. They have failed to furnish it with articulation, with reasonableness, for they have at bottom been committed to the principle of a single, final and unalterable authority from which all lesser authorities are derived. The men who questioned the divine right of kings did so in the name of another absolute. The voice of the people was mythologized into the voice of God. Now a halo may be preserved about the monarch. Because of his distance, he can be rendered transcendentally without easy detection. But the people are too close at hand, too obviously empirical, to be lent to deification. Hence democracy has ranked for the most part as an intellectual anomaly, lacking philosophical basis and logical coherency, but upon the whole to be accepted because somehow or other it works better than other schemes and seems to develop a more kindly and humane set of social institutions. For when it has tried to achieve a philosophy it has clothed itself in an atomistic individualism, as full of defects and inconsistencies in theory as it was charged with obnoxious consequences when an attempt was made to act upon it.

Now whatever the idea of equality means for democracy, it means, I take it, that the world is not to be construed as a fixed order of species, grades or degrees. It means that every existence deserving the name of existence has something unique and irreplaceable about it, that it does not exist to illustrate a principle, to realize a universal or to embody a kind or class. As philosophy it denies the basic principle of atomistic individualism as truly as that of rigid feudalism. For the individualism traditionally associated with democracy makes equality quantitative, and hence individuality something external and mechanical rather than qualitative and unique. In social and moral matters, equality does not mean mathematical equivalence. It means rather the inapplicability of considerations of greater and less, superior and inferior. It means that no matter how great the quantitative differences of ability, strength, position, wealth, such differences are negligible in comparison with something else—the fact of individuality, the manifestation of something irreplaceable. It means, in short, a world in which an existence must be reckoned with on its own account, not as something capable of equation with and transformation into something else. It implies, so to speak, a metaphysical mathematics of the incommensurable in which each speaks for itself and demands consideration on its own behalf.

If democratic equality may be construed as individuality, there is nothing forced in understanding fraternity as continuity, that is to say, as association and interaction without limit. Equality, individuality, tends to isolation and independence. It is centrifugal. To say that what is specific and unique can be exhibited and become forceful or actual only in relationship with other like beings is merely, I take it, to give a metaphysical version to the fact that democracy is concerned not with freaks or geniuses or heroes or divine leaders but with associated individuals in which each by intercourse with others somehow makes the life of each more distinctive.

All this, of course, is but by way of intimation. In spite of its form it is not really a plea for a certain kind of philosophizing. For if democracy be a serious, important choice and predilection it must in time justify itself by generating its own child of wisdom, to be justified in turn by its children, better institutions of life. It is not so much a question as to whether there will be a philosophy of this kind as it is of just who will be the philosophers associated with it. And I cannot conclude without mentioning the name of one through whom this vision of a new mode of life has already spoken with beauty and power—William James.

NOTES

[First published in *University* [of California] *Chronicle* 21 (1919): 39–54, from an address to the Philosophical Union of the University of California, 29 November 1918. Republished in *Characters and Events*, ed. Joseph Ratner (New York: Henry Holt and Co., 1929), 2:841–55. MW 11:41–53.]

Volumes have been written about each term of our theme. What *is* civilization? philosophy? Yet time passes, and ambiguities and complexities cannot be eliminated by definition; we can only circumvent them by begging questions. But as to one of the terms at least, namely, philosophy, we shall frankly make what is begged explicit. A statement of the relations of philosophy to the history of civilization will, after all, only expound, in some indirect manner, the view of philosophy to which one is already committed. Unless this fact is faced, we shall not only beg the issue, but we shall deceive ourselves into thinking that we are setting forth the conclusions of an original inquiry, undertaken and executed independently of our own philosophical conceptions.

As for myself, then, the discussion is approached with the antecedent idea that philosophy, like politics, literature, and the plastic arts, is itself a phenomenon of human culture. Its connection with social history, with civilization, is intrinsic. There is current among those who philosophize the conviction that, while past thinkers have reflected in their systems the conditions and perplexities of their own day, present-day philosophy in general, and one's own philosophy in particular, is emancipated from the influence of that complex of institutions which forms culture. Bacon, Descartes, Kant, each thought with fervor that he was founding philosophy anew because he was placing it securely upon an exclusive intellectual basis, exclusive, that is, of everything but intellect. The movement of time has revealed the illusion; it exhibits as the work of philosophy the old and ever new undertaking of adjusting that body of traditions which constitute the actual mind of man to scientific tendencies and political aspirations which are novel and incompatible with received authorities. Philosophers are parts of history, caught in its movement; creators perhaps in some measure of its future, but also assuredly creatures of its past.

Those who assert in the abstract definition of philosophy that it deals with eternal truth or reality, untouched by local time and place, are forced to admit that philosophy as a concrete

Philosophy and Civilization

(1927)

existence is historical, having temporal passage and a diversity of local habitations. Open your histories of philosophy, and you find written throughout them the same periods of time and the same geographical distributions which provide the intellectual scheme of histories of politics, industry, or the fine arts. I cannot imagine a history of philosophy which did not partition its material between the Occident and the Orient; which did not find the former falling into ancient, mediaeval, and modern epochs; which in setting forth Greek thought did not specify Asiatic and Italian colonies and Athens. On the other hand, those who express contempt for the enterprise of philosophy as a sterile and monotonous preoccupation with unsolvable or unreal problems, cannot, without convicting themselves of Philistinism, deny that, however it may stand with philosophy as a revelation of eternal truths, it is tremendously significant as a revelation of the predicaments, protests, and aspirations of humanity.

The two views of the history of thought are usually proffered as unreconcilable opposites. According to one, it is the record of the most profound dealings of the reason with ultimate being; according to the other, it is a scene of pretentious claims and ridiculous failures. Nevertheless, there is a point of view from which there is something common to the two notions, and this common denominator is more significant than the oppositions. Meaning is wider in scope as well as more precious in value than is truth, and philosophy is occupied with meaning rather than with truth. Making such a statement is dangerous; it is easily misconceived to signify that truth is of no great importance under any circumstances; while the fact is that truth is so infinitely important when it is important at all, namely, in records of events and descriptions of existences, that we extend its claims to regions where it has no jurisdiction. But even as respects truths, meaning is the wider category; truths are but one class of meanings, namely, those in which a claim to verifiability by their consequences is an intrinsic part of their meaning. Beyond this island of meanings which in their own nature are true or false lies the ocean of meanings to which truth and falsity are irrelevant. We do not inquire whether Greek civilization was true or false, but we are immensely concerned to penetrate its meaning. We may indeed ask for the truth of Shakespeare's *Hamlet* or Shelley's "Skylark," but by truth we now signify something quite different from that of scientific statement and historical record.

In philosophy we are dealing with something comparable to the meaning of Athenian civilization or of a drama or a lyric. Significant history is lived in the imagination of man, and philosophy is a further excursion of the imagination into its own prior achievements. All that is distinctive of man, marking him off from the clay he walks upon or the potatoes he eats, occurs in his thought and emotions, in what we have agreed to call consciousness. Knowledge of the structure of sticks and stones, an enterprise in which, of course, truth is essential, apart from whatever added control it may yield, marks in the end but an enrichment of consciousness, of the area of meanings. Thus scientific thought itself is finally but a function of the imagination in enriching life with the significance of things; it is of its peculiar essence that it must also submit to certain tests of application and control. Were significance identical with existence, were values the same as events, idealism would be the only possible philosophy.

It is commonplace that physically and existentially man can but make a superficial and transient scratch upon the outermost rind of the world. It has become a cheap intellectual pastime to contrast the infinitesimal pettiness of man with the vastnesses of the stellar universes. Yet all such comparisons are illicit. We cannot compare existence and meaning; they are disparate. The characteristic life of man is itself the meaning of vast stretches of existences, and without it the latter have no value or significance. There is no common measure of physical existence and conscious experience because the latter is the only measure there is for the former. The significance of being, though not its existence, is the emotion it stirs, the thought it sustains.

It follows that there is no specifiable difference between philosophy and its role in the history of civilization. Discover and define the right characteristic and unique function in civilization, and you have defined philosophy itself. To try to define philosophy in any other way is to search for a will-o'-the-wisp; the conceptions which result are of purely private interpretation for they only exemplify the particular philosophies of their authorship and interpretation. Take the history of philosophy from whatever angle and in whatever cross-section you please, Indian, Chinese, Athenian, the Europe of the twelfth or the twentieth century, and you find a load of traditions proceeding from an immemorial past. You find certain preoccupying interests that appear hypnotic in their rigid hold upon imagination and you also find certain resistances, certain dawning rebellions, struggles to escape and to express some fresh value of life. The preoccupations may be political and artistic as in Athens; they may be economic and scientific as today. But in any case, there is a certain intellectual work to be done; the dominant interest working throughout the minds of masses of men has to be clarified, a result which can be accomplished only by selection, elimination, reduction, and formulation; the interest has to be intellectually forced, exaggerated, in order to be focused. Otherwise it is not intellectually in consciousness, since all clear consciousness by its very nature marks a wrenching of something from its subordinate place to confer upon it a centrality which is existentially absurd. Where there is sufficient depth and range of meanings for consciousness to arise at all, there is a function of adjustment, of reconciliation of the ruling interest of the period with preoccupations which had a different origin and an irrelevant meaning. Consider, for example, the uneasy, restless effort of Plato to adapt his new mathematical insights and his political aspirations to the traditional habits of Athens; the almost humorously complacent union of Christian supernaturalism in the Middle Ages with the naturalism of pagan Greece; the still fermenting effort of the recent age to unite the new science of nature with inherited classic and mediaeval institutions. The life of all thought is to effect a junction at some point of the new and the old, of deep-sunk customs and unconscious dispositions, that are brought to the light of attention by some conflict with newly emerging directions of activity. Philosophies which emerge at distinctive periods define the larger patterns of continuity which are woven in effecting the enduring junctions of a stubborn past and an insistent future.

Philosophy thus sustains the closest connection with the history of culture, with the succession of changes in civilization. It is fed by the streams of tradition, traced at critical moments to their sources in order that the current may receive a new direction; it is fertilized by the ferment of new inventions in industry, new explorations of the globe, new discoveries in science. But philosophy is not just a passive reflex of civilization that persists through changes, and that changes while persisting. It is itself a change; the patterns formed in this junction of the new and the old are prophecies rather than records; they are policies, attempts to forestall subsequent developments. The intellectual registrations which constitute a philosophy are generative just because they are selective and eliminative exaggerations. While purporting to say that such and such is and always *has* been the purport of the record of nature, in effect they proclaim that such and such *should* be the significant value to which mankind should loyally attach itself. Without evidence adduced in its behalf such a statement may seem groundless. But I invite you to examine for yourselves any philosophical idea which has had for any long period a significant career and find therein your own evidence. Take, for example, the Platonic patterns of cosmic design and harmony; the Aristotelian perpetually recurrent ends and grooved potentialities; the Kantian fixed forms of intellectual synthesis; the conception of nature itself as it figured in seventeenth and eighteenth century thought. Discuss them as revelations of eternal truth, and something almost childlike or something beyond possibility of decision enters in; discuss them as selections from existing culture by means of which to articulate forces which the author believed should and would dominate the future, and they become preciously significant aspects of human history.

Thus philosophy marks a change of culture. In forming patterns to be conformed to in future thought and action, it is additive and transforming in its role in the history of civilization. Man states anything at his peril; once stated, it occupies a place in a new perspective; it attains a permanence which does not belong to its existence; it enters provokingly into wont and use; it points in a troubling way to need of new endeavors. I do not mean that the creative element in the role of philosophy is necessarily the dominant one; obviously its formulations have been often chiefly conservative, justificatory of selected elements of traditions and received institutions. But even these preservative systems have had a transforming if not exactly a creative effect; they have lent the factors which were selected a power over later human imagination and sentiment which they would otherwise have lacked. And there are other periods, such as those of the seventeenth and eighteenth centuries in Europe, when philosophy is overtly revolutionary in attitude. To their authors, the turn was just from complete error to complete truth; to later generations looking back, the alteration in strictly factual content does not compare with that in desire and direction of effort.

Of the many objections which may be brought against the conception that philosophy not only *has* a role, but that it *is* a specifiable role in the development of human culture, there are two misconceptions which I wish to touch upon. What has been said, taken without qualifying additions, might suggest a picture of a dominant system of philosophy at each historic period. In fact there are diverse currents and aspirations in almost every historic epoch; the divergence of philosophic systems instead of being a reproach (as of course it is from the standpoint of philosophy as a revelation of truth) is evidence of sincerity and vitality. If the ruling and the oppressed elements in a population, if those who wished to maintain the *status quo* and those concerned to make changes, had, when they became articulate, the same philosophy, one might well be skeptical of its intellectual integrity. The other point is much more important. In making a distinction between meaning and truth and asserting that the latter is but one type of meaning, important under definite conditions, I have expressed the idea as if there might be in the processes of human life meanings which

are wholly cut off from the actual course of events. Such is not the intent; meanings are generated and in some degree sustained by existence. Hence they cannot be wholly irrelevant to the world of existence; they all have some revelatory office which should be apprehended as correctly as possible. This is true of politics, religion, and art as well as of philosophy. They all tell something of the realm of existence. But in all of them there is an exuberance and fertility of meanings and values in comparison with which correctness of telling is a secondary affair, while in the function termed science accuracy of telling is the chief matter.

In the historic role of philosophy, the scientific factor, the element of correctness, of verifiable applicability, has a place, but it is a negative one. The meanings delivered by confirmed observation, experimentation, and calculation, scientific facts and principles, serve as tests of the values which tradition transmits and of those which emotion suggests. Whatever is not compatible with them must be eliminated in any sincere philosophizing. This fact confers upon scientific knowledge an incalculably important office in philosophy. But the criterion is negative; the exclusion of the inconsistent is far from being identical with a positive test which demands that only what has been scientifically verifiable shall provide the entire content of philosophy. It is the difference between an imagination that acknowledges its responsibility to meet the logical demands of ascertained facts, and a complete abdication of all imagination in behalf of a prosy literalism.

Finally, it results from what has been said that the presence and absence of native born philosophies is a severe test of the depth of unconscious tradition and rooted institutions among any people, and of the productive force of their culture. For sake of brevity, I may be allowed to take our own case, the case of civilization in the United States. Philosophy, we have been saying, is a conversion of such culture as exists into consciousness, into an imagination which is logically coherent and is not incompatible with what is factually known. But this conversion is itself a further movement of civilization; it is not something performed upon the body of habits and tendencies from without, that is, miraculously. If American civilization does not eventuate in an imaginative formulation of itself, if it merely re-arranges the figures already named and placed, in playing an inherited European game, that fact is itself the measure of the culture which we have achieved. A deliberate striving for an American Philosophy as such would be only another evidence of the same emptiness and impotency. There is energy and activity among us, enough and to spare. Not an inconsiderable part of the vigor that once went into industrial accomplishment now finds its way into science; our scientific "plant" is coming in its way to rival our industrial plants. Especially in psychology and the social sciences an amount of effort is putting forth which is hardly equalled in any one other part of the world. He would be a shameless braggart who claimed that the result is as yet adequate to the activity. What is the matter? It lies, I think, with our lack of imagination in generating leading ideas. Because we are afraid of speculative ideas, we do, and do over and over again, an immense amount of dead, specialized work in the region of "facts." We forget that such facts are only data; that is, are only fragmentary, uncompleted meanings, and unless they are rounded out into complete ideas—a work which can only be done by hypotheses, by a free imagination of intellectual possibilities— they are as helpless as are all maimed things and as repellent as are needlessly thwarted ones.

Please do not imagine that this is a plea in disguise for any particular type of philosophizing. On the contrary, any philosophy which is a sincere outgrowth and expression of our own civilization is better than none, provided it speaks the authentic idiom of an enduring and dominating corporate experience. If we are really, for instance, a materialistic people, we are at least materialistic in a new fashion and on a new scale. I should welcome then a consistent materialistic philosophy, if only it were sufficiently bold. For in the degree in which, despite attendant aesthetic repulsiveness, it marked the coming to consciousness of a group of ideas, it would formulate a coming to self-consciousness of our civilization. Thereby it would furnish ideas, supply an intellectual polity, direct further observations and experiments, and organize their results on a grand scale. As long as we worship science and are afraid of philosophy we shall have no great science; we shall have a lagging and halting continuation of what is thought and said elsewhere. As far as any plea is implicit in what has been said, it is, then, a plea for the casting off of that intellectual timidity which hampers the wings of imagination, a plea for speculative audacity, for more faith in ideas, sloughing off a cowardly reliance upon those partial ideas to which we are wont to give the name of facts. I have given to philosophy a more humble function than that which is often assigned it. But modesty as to its final place is not incompatible with boldness in the maintenance of that function, humble as it may be. A combination of such modesty and courage affords the only way I know of in which the philosopher can look his fellow man in the face with frankness and with humanity.

NOTES

[First published in *Philosophical Review* 36 (1927): 1–9, from an address to the Sixth International Congress of Philosophy, Harvard University, 15 Sept. 1926. LW 3:3–10.]

Existence, Value and Criticism

From *Experience and Nature* (1925)

Recent philosophy has witnessed the rise of a theory of value. Value as it usually figures in this discussion marks a desperate attempt to combine the obvious empirical fact that objects are qualified with good and bad, with philosophic deliverances which, in isolating man from nature, qualitative individualities from the world, render this fact anomalous. The philosopher erects a "realm of values" in which to place all the precious things which are extruded from natural existence because of isolations artificially introduced. Poignancy, humor, zest, tragedy, beauty, prosperity and bafflement, although rejected from a nature which is identified with mechanical structure, remain just what they empirically are, and demand recognition. Hence they are gathered up into the realm of values, contradistinguished from the realm of existence. Then the philosopher has a new problem with which to wrestle: What is the relationship of these two "worlds"? Is the world of value that of ultimate and transcendent Being from which the world of existence is a derivation or a fall? Or is it but a manifestation of human subjectivity, a factor somehow miraculously supervening upon an order complete and closed in physical structure? Or are there scattered at random through objective being, detached subsistences as "real" as are physical events, but having no temporal dates and spatial locations, and yet at times and places miraculously united with existences?

Choice among such notions of value is arbitrary, because the problem is arbitrary. When we return to the conceptions of potentiality and actuality, contingency and regularity, qualitatively diverse individuality, with which Greek thought operated, we find no room for a theory of values separate from a theory of nature. Yet if we are to recur to the Greek conceptions, the return must be a return with a difference. It must surrender the identification of natural ends with good and perfection; recognizing that a natural end, apart from endeavor expressing choice, has no intrinsic eulogistic quality, but is the boundary which writes "Finis" to a chapter of history inscribed by a moving system of energies. Failure by exhaustion as well as by triumph may constitute an end; death, ignorance, as well as life, are finalities.

Again, the return must abandon the notion of a predetermined limited number of ends inherently arranged in an order of increasing comprehensiveness and finality. It will have to recognize that natural termini are as infinitely numerous and varied as are the individual systems of action they delimit; and that since there is only relative, not absolute, impermeability and fixity of structure, new individuals with novel ends emerge in irregular procession. It must recognize that limits, closures, ends are experimentally or dynamically determined, presenting, like the boundaries of political individuals or states, a moving adjustment of various energy-systems in their cooperative and competitive interactions, not something belonging to them of their own right. Consequently, it will surrender the separation in nature from each other of contingency and regularity, the hazardous and the assured; it will avoid that relegation of them to distinct orders of Being which is characteristic of the classic tradition. It will note that they intersect everywhere; that it is uncertainty and indeterminateness that create the need for and the sense of order and security; that whatever is most complete and liberal in being and possession is for that very reason most exposed to vicissitude, and most needful of watchful safeguarding art.

The connotation of "value" in recent thought contains some hint of the changes which experience has compelled in the classic notion of natural ends. For by implication at least values are recognized to be fugitive and precarious, to be negative and positive, and indefinitely diversified in quality. Even that metaphysical theory of super-idealism which finds them to be eternal, and the eternal foundation and source of shifting temporal events, bases its argument upon the undeniable insecurity, the interminable elusiveness, the appearance and disappearance, of values in actual experience. Because of this sense of the evanescence and uncertainty of what used to be called ends but are now called values, the important consideration and concern is not a theory of values but a theory of criticism; a method of discriminating among goods on the basis of the conditions of their appearance, and of their consequences.

Values are values, things immediately having certain intrinsic qualities. Of them as values there is accordingly nothing to be said; they are what they are. All that can be said of them concerns their generative conditions and the consequences to which they give rise. The notion that things as direct values lend themselves to thought and discourse rests upon a confusion of causal categories with immediate qualities. Objects, for example, may be distinguished as contributory or as fulfilling, but this is distinction of place with respect to causal relationship; it is not a distinction of values. We may be interested in a thing, be concerned with it or like it, for a reason. The reason for appreciation, for an enjoyed appropriation, is often that the object in question serves as a means to something; or the reason is that it stands as the culmination of an antecedent process. But to take into account the reason for liking and enjoyment concerns the cause of the existence of a value, and has nothing to do with the intrinsicalness or nature of the value-quality, which either does or does not exist. Things that are means and things that are fulfillments have different qualities; but so do symphonies, operas and oratorios among themselves. The difference is not one that has anything to do with the immediacy or intrinsicalness of value-quality; it is a difference between one affair and quality and another.

It is self-contradictory to suppose that when a fulfillment possesses immediate value, its means of attainment do not. The person to whom the cessation of a tooth-ache has value, by that very fact finds value in going to a dentist, or in whatever else is means of fulfillment. For fulfillment is as relative to means as means are to realization. Means-consequences constitute a single undivided situation. Consequently when thought and discussion enter, when theorizing sets in, when there is anything beyond bare immediate enjoyment and suffering, it is the means-consequence relationship that is considered. Thought goes beyond immediate existence to its relationships, the conditions which mediate it and the things to which it is in turn mediatory. And such a procedure is criticism. The all but universal confusion in theories of value of determined position in causative or sequential relationship with value proper is indirect testimony to the fact that every intelligent appreciation is also criticism, judgment, of the thing having immediate value. Any *theory* of values is perforce entrance into the field of criticism. Value as such, even things having value, cannot in their immediate existence be reflected upon; they either are or are not; are or are not enjoyed. To pass beyond direct occurrence, even though the passage be restricted to an attempt to define value, is to begin a process of discrimination which implies a reflective criterion. In themselves, values may be just pointed at; to attempt a definition by complete pointing is however bootless. Sooner or later, with respect to positive or negative value, designation will have to include everything.

These remarks are preparatory to presenting a conception of philosophy; namely, that philosophy is inherently criticism, having its distinctive position among various modes of criticism in its generality; a criticism of criticisms, as it were. Criticism is discriminating judgment, careful appraisal, and judgment is appropriately termed criticism wherever the subject-matter of discrimination concerns goods or values. Possession and enjoyment of goods passes insensibly and inevitably into appraisal. First and immature experience is content simply to enjoy. But a brief course in experience enforces reflection; it requires but brief time to teach that some things sweet in the having are bitter in after-taste and in what they lead to. Primitive innocence does not last. Enjoyment ceases to be a datum and becomes a problem. As a problem, it implies intelligent inquiry into the conditions and consequences of a value-object; that is, criticism. If values were as plentiful as huckleberries, and if the huckleberry-patch were always at hand, the passage of appreciation into criticism would be a senseless procedure. If one thing tired or bored us, we should have only to turn to another. But values are as unstable as the forms of clouds. The things that possess them are exposed to all the contingencies of existence, and they are indifferent to our likings and tastes.

Good things change and vanish not only with changes in the environing medium but with changes in ourselves. Continued perception, except when it has been cultivated through prior criticism, dulls itself; it is soon satiated, exhausted, blasé. The infinite flippancy of the natural man is a standing theme for discourse by shrewd observers of human nature. Cultivated taste alone is capable of prolonged appreciation of the same object; and it is capable of it because it has been trained to a discriminating procedure which constantly uncovers in the object new meanings to be perceived and enjoyed. Add to exhaustion of the organs of perception and enjoyment, all the other organic causes which render enjoyed objects unstable, and then add the external vicissitudes to which they are subjected, and there is no cause to wonder at the evanescence of immediate goods; nor at the so-called paradoxes of pleasure and virtue, according to which they are not secured by aiming at them but by attention to other things;—a fact however, which is not a paradox in a world where nothing is attained in any other way than by attention to its causal conditions.

When criticism and the critical attitude are legitimately distinguished from appreciation and taste, we are in the presence of one case of the constant rhythm of "perchings and flights" (to borrow James's terms), characteristic of alternate emphasis upon the immediate and mediate, the consummatory and instrumental, phases of all conscious experience. If we are misled into ignoring the omnipresence in all observations and ideas of this rhythm, it is largely because, under the influence of formal theories, we attach too elaborate and too remote a signification to "appreciation" and "criticism." Values of some sort or other are not traits of rare and festal occasions; they occur whenever any object is welcomed and lingered over; whenever it arouses aversion and protest; even though the lingering be but momentary and the aversion a passing glance toward something else.

Similarly, criticism is not a matter of formal treatises, published articles, or taking up important matters for consideration in a serious way. It occurs whenever a moment is devoted to looking to see what sort of value is present; whenever instead of accepting a value-object wholeheartedly, being rapt by it, we raise even a shadow of a question about its worth, or modify our sense of it by even a passing estimate of its probable future. It is well upon the whole that we use the terms "appreciation" and "criticism" honorifically, to designate conspicuous instances. But it is fatal to any understanding of them to fail to note that formally emphatic instances are of exactly the same nature as the rhythmic alternation between slight agreeable acceptances, annoyed rejections and passing questionings and estimates, which make up the entire course of our waking experience, whether in revery, in controlled inquiry or in deliberate management of affairs.

The rhythmic succession of the two modes of perception suggests that the difference is one of emphasis, or degree. Critical appreciation, and appreciative, warmly emotionalized criticism occur in every matured sane experience. After the first dumb, formless experience of a thing as a good, subsequent perception of the good contains at least a germ of critical reflection. For this reason, and only for this reason, elaborate and formulated criticism is subsequently possible. The latter, if just and pertinent, can but develop the reflective implications found within appreciation itself. Criticism would be the most wilful of undertakings if the possession and enjoyment of good objects had no element of memory and foresight in it; if it lacked all circumspection and judgment. Criticism is reasonable and to the point, in the degree in which it extends and deepens these factors of intelligence found in immediate taste and enjoyment.

Conscience in morals, taste in fine arts and conviction in beliefs pass insensibly into critical judgments; the latter pass also into a more and more generalized form of criticism called philosophy. How is the assertion of "canons" of taste and criticism compatible with the declaration that there is no discussing tastes? What is meant by a distinction between apparent good and real good? How can the distinction between seeming and being be capable of application to what is good? Is critical appraisal possible without a standard measure of values? Is the standard of values itself a value? Is it derived from the value-objects to which it is applied? If so, what authority does it possess

over and beyond that of particular cases? What right has it to pass judgment upon its own source and authors? Does a standard exist transcendentally in independence of concrete cases judged? If so, what is its source, and what is the ground and guarantee of its applicability to alien material? Is taste, immediate appreciation, sense and moral sense, ultimate, its own final judge in every case as it arises? What, in that event, saves us from chaotic anarchy? Is there among men a common measure of value? If so, is it grounded outside of man, in an independent objective form of Being?

Such questions as these, which may be multiplied as one pleases, indicate that no great difficulty would attend an effort to derive all the stock issues of philosophy from the problems of value and their relationship to critical judgment. Whether it be a question of the good and bad in conviction and opinion, or in matters of conduct, or in appreciated scenes of nature and art, there occurs in every instance a conflict between the immediate value-object and the ulterior value-object: the given good, and that reached and justified by reflection; the now apparent and the eventual. In knowledge, for example there are beliefs *de facto* and beliefs *de jure*. In morals, there are immediate goods, the desired, and reasonable goods, the desirable. In esthetics, there are the goods of an undeveloped or perverted taste and there are the goods of cultivated taste. With respect to any of these distinctions, the true, real, final, or objective good is no *more* good as an immediate existence than is the contrasting good, called false, specious, illusory, showy, meretricious, *le faux bon*. The difference in adjectives designates a difference instituted in critical judgment; the validity of the difference between good which is approved and that which is good (immediately) but is *judged bad*, depends therefore upon the value of reflection in general, and of a particular reflective operation in especial. Even if good of the reflective object is different from that of the good of the non-reflective object, it does not follow that it is a better good, much less that it is such a difference in goodness as makes the non-reflective good *bad*:—except upon one proviso, namely, that there is something unique in the value or goodness of reflection.

Either, then, the difference between genuine, valid, good and a counterfeit, specious good is unreal, or it is a difference consequent upon reflection, or criticism, and the significant point is that this difference is equivalent to that made by discovery of relationships, of conditions and consequences. With this conclusion are bound up two other propositions: Of immediate values as such, values which occur and which are possessed and enjoyed, there is no theory at all; they just occur, are enjoyed, possessed; and that is all. The moment we begin to discourse about these values, to define and generalize, to make distinctions in kinds, we are passing beyond value-objects themselves; we are entering, even if only blindly, upon an inquiry into causal antecedents and causative consequents, with a view to appraising the "real," that is the eventual, goodness of the thing in question. We are criticizing, not for its own sake, but for the sake of instituting and perpetuating more enduring and extensive values.

The other proposition is that philosophy is and can be nothing but this critical operation and function become aware of itself and its implications, pursued deliberately and systematically. It starts from actual situations of belief, conduct and appreciative perception which are characterized by immediate qualities of good and bad, and from the modes of critical judgment current at any given time in all the regions of value; these are its data, its subject-matter. These values, criticisms, and critical methods, it subjects to further criticism as comprehensive and consistent as possible. The function is to regulate the further appreciation of goods and bads; to give greater freedom and security in those acts of direct selection, appropriation, identification and of rejection, elimination, destruction which enstate and which exclude objects of belief, conduct and contemplation.

Such a conclusion wears an air of strangeness. It may appear to indicate an attempt by a dialectic trick to make the category of good-and-bad supreme in its jurisdiction over intellectual life and over all objects. This impression will, I think, be readily dissipated by consideration of the actual meaning of what is said. Objects of belief and of refusals to believe are value-objects; for each object is some thing acquiesced in, accepted, adopted, appropriated. This is the same as saying it is found good or satisfactory to believe or disbelieve; truistically, whatever is accepted is as such and in so far good. There is no occult significance in this statement; it is not preliminary to an argument which shall sweep away the properties which objects possess independent of their being objects of belief, or of their being values. It does not annihilate the difference among beliefs; it does not set up the *fact* that an object believed in is perforce found good as if it were a *reason* for belief. On the contrary: the statement is preliminary. The all-important matter is what lies back of and causes acceptance and rejection; whether or no there is method of discrimination and assessment which makes a difference in what is assented to and denied. Properties and relations that *entitle* an object to be found good in belief are extraneous to the qualities that are its immediate good; they are causal, and hence found only by search into the antecedent and the eventual. The conception that there are some objects or some properties of objects which carry their own adequate credentials upon their face is the snare and delusion of the whole historic tradition regarding knowledge, infecting alike sensational and rational schools, objective realisms and introspective idealisms.

Concerning beliefs and their objects taken in their immediacy "*non-disputandum*" holds, as truly as it does concerning tastes and their objects. If a man believes in ghosts, devils, miracles, fortune-tellers, the immutable certainty of the existing economic régime, and the supreme merits of his political party and its leaders, he does so believe; these are immediate goods to him, precisely as some color and tone combinations are lovely, or the mistress of his heart is charming. When the question is raised as to the "real" value of the object for belief, the appeal is to criticism, intelligence. And the court of appeal decides by the law of conditions and consequences. Inquiry duly pursued leads to the enstatement of an object which is directly accepted, good in belief, but an object whose character now depends upon the reflective operations whose conclusion it is. Like the object of dogmatic and uncritical belief, it marks an "end," a static arrest; but unlike it, the "end" is a *conclusion*; hence it carries credentials.

Were not objects of belief immediate goods, false beliefs would not be the dangerous things which they are. For it is because these objects are good to believe, to admit and assert, that they are cherished so intolerantly and unremittingly. Beliefs about God, Nature, society and man are precisely the things that men most cling to and most ardently fight for. It is easier to wean a miser from his hoard, than a man from his deeper opinions. And the tragedy is that in so many cases the *causes* which lead to the thing in question being a value are not *reasons* for its being a good, while the fact that it is an immediate good tends to preclude that search for causes, that dispassionate judgment, which is prerequisite to the conversion of goods *de facto* into goods *de jure*. Here, again and preeminently, since reflection is the instrumentality of securing freer and more enduring goods, reflection is a unique intrinsic good. Its instrumental efficacy determines it to be a candidate for a distinctive position as an immediate good, since beyond other goods it has power of replenishment and fructification. In it, apparent good and real good enormously coincide.

In traditional discussion the fact is overlooked that the subject-matter of belief is a good, since belief means assimilation and assertion. It is overlooked that its immediate goodness is both the obstacle to reflective examination and the source of its necessity. The "true" is indeed set up along with the good and the beautiful as a transcendent good, but the role of empirical good, of value, in the sweep of ordinary beliefs is passed by. The counterpart of this error, which isolates the subject-matter of intellect from the scope of values and valuations, is a corresponding isolation of the subject-matter of esthetic contemplation and immediate enjoyment from judgment. Between these two realms, one of intellectual objects without value and the other of value-objects without intellect, there is an equivocal mid-country in which moral objects are placed, with rival claimants striving to annex them either to the region of purely immediate goods (in this case termed pleasures) or to that of

purely rational objects. Hence the primary function of philosophy at present is to make it clear that there is no such difference as this division assumes between science, morals, and esthetic appreciation. All alike exhibit the difference between immediate goods casually occurring and immediate goods which have been reflectively determined by means of critical inquiry. If bare liking is an adequate determinant of values in one case, it is in the others. If intelligence, criticism, is required in one, it is in the others. If the end to be attained in any case is an enhanced and purified immediate appreciative, experienced object, so it is in the others. All cases manifest the same duality and present the same problem; that of embodying intelligence in action which shall convert casual natural goods, whose causes and effects are unknown, into goods valid for thought, right for conduct and cultivated for appreciation.

Philosophic discourse partakes both of scientific and literary discourse. Like literature, it is a comment on nature and life in the interest of a more intense and just appreciation of the meanings present in experience. Its business is reportorial and transcriptive only in the sense in which the drama and poetry have that office. Its primary concern is to clarify, liberate and extend the goods which inhere in the naturally generated functions of experience. It has no call to create a world of "reality" *de novo*, nor to delve into secrets of Being hidden from common sense and science. It has no stock of information or body of knowledge peculiarly its own; if it does not always become ridiculous when it sets up as a rival of science, it is only because a particular philosopher happens to be also, as a human being, a prophetic man of science. Its business is to accept and to utilize for a purpose the best available knowledge of its own time and place. And this purpose is criticism of beliefs, institutions, customs, policies with respect to their bearing upon good. This does not mean their bearing upon *the* good, as something itself attained and formulated in philosophy. For as philosophy has no private store of knowledge or of methods for attaining truth, so it has no private access to good. As it accepts knowledge of facts and principles from those competent in inquiry and discovery, so it accepts the goods that are diffused in human experience. It has no Mosaic nor Pauline authority of revelation entrusted to it. But it has the authority of intelligence, of criticism of these common and natural goods.

At this point, it departs from the arts of literary discourse. They have a freer office to perform—to perpetuate, enhance and vivify in imagination the natural goods; all things are forgiven to him who succeeds. But philosophic criticism has a stricter task, with a greater measure of responsibility to what lies outside its own products. It has to appraise values by taking cognizance of their causes and consequences; only by this straight and narrow path may it contribute to expansion and emancipation of values. For this reason the conclusions of science about matter-of-fact efficiencies of nature are its indispensable instruments. If its eventual concern is to render goods more coherent, more secure and more significant in appreciation, its road is the subject-matter of natural existence as science discovers and depicts it.

Only in verbal form is there anything novel in this conception of philosophy. It is a version of the old saying that philosophy is love of wisdom, of wisdom which is not knowledge and which nevertheless cannot be without knowledge. The need of an organon of criticism which uses knowledge of relations among events to appraise the casual, immediate goods that obtain among men is not a fact of philosophy, but of nature and life. We can conceive a happier nature and experience than flourishes among us wherein the office of critical reflection would be carried on so continuously and in such detail that no particular apparatus would be needed. But actual experience is such a jumble that a degree of distance and detachment are a prerequisite of vision in perspective. Thinkers often withdraw too far. But a withdrawal is necessary, unless they are to be deafened by the immediate clamor and blinded by the immediate glare of the scene. What especially makes necessary a generalized instrument of criticism, is the tendency of objects to seek rigid non-communicating compartments. It is natural that nature, variegatedly qualified, should exhibit various trends

when it achieves experience of itself, so that there is a distribution of emphases such as are designated by the adjectives scientific, industrial, political, religious, artistic, educational, moral and so on.

But however natural from the standpoint of causation may be the institutionalizing of these trends, their separation effects an isolation which is unnatural. Narrowness, superficiality, stagnation follow from lack of the nourishment which can be supplied only by generous and wide interactions. Goods isolated as professionalism and institutionalization isolate them, petrify; and in a moving world solidification is always dangerous. Resistant force is gained by precipitation, but no one thing gets strong enough to defy everything. Over-specialization and division of interests, occupations and goods create the need for a generalized medium of intercommunication, of mutual criticism through all-around translation from one separated region of experience into another. Thus philosophy as a critical organ becomes in effect a messenger, a liaison officer, making reciprocally intelligible voices speaking provincial tongues, and thereby enlarging as well as rectifying the meanings with which they are charged.

The difficulty is that philosophy, even when professing catholicity, has often been suborned. Instead of being a free messenger of communication it has been a diplomatic agent of some special and partial interest; insincere, because in the name of peace it has fostered divisions that lead to strife, and in the name of loyalty has promoted unholy alliances and secret understandings. One might say that the profuseness of attestations to supreme devotion to truth on the part of philosophy is matter to arouse suspicion. For it has usually been a preliminary to the claim of being a peculiar organ of access to highest and ultimate truth. Such it is not; and it will not lose its esoteric and insincere air until the profession is disclaimed. Truth is a collection of truths; and these constituent truths are in the keeping of the best available methods of inquiry and testing as to matters-of-fact; methods, which are, when collected under a single name, science. As to truth, then, philosophy has no preeminent status; it is a recipient, not a donor. But the realm of meanings is wider than that of true-and-false meanings; it is more urgent and more fertile. When the claim of meanings to truth enters in, then truth is indeed preeminent. But this fact is often confused with the idea that truth has a claim to enter everywhere; that it has monopolistic jurisdiction. Poetic meanings, moral meanings, a large part of the goods of life are matters of richness and freedom of meanings, rather than of truth; a large part of our life is carried on in a realm of meanings to which truth and falsity as such are irrelevant. And the claim of philosophy to rival or displace science as a purveyor of truth seems to be mostly a compensatory gesture for failure to perform its proper task of liberating and clarifying meanings, including those scientifically authenticated. For, assuredly, a student prizes historic systems rather for the meanings and shades of meanings they have brought to light than for the store of ultimate truths they have ascertained. If accomplishment of the former office were made the avowed business of philosophy, instead of an incidental by-product, its position would be clearer, more intelligent and more respected.

It is sometimes suggested, however, that such a view of philosophy derogates from its dignity, degrading it into an instrument of social reforms, and that it is a view congenial only to those who are insensitive to the positive achievements of culture and over-sensitive to its evils. Such a conception overlooks outstanding facts. "Social reform" is conceived in a Philistine spirit, if it is taken to mean anything less than precisely the liberation and expansion of the meanings of which experience is capable. No doubt many schemes of social reform are guilty of precisely this narrowing. But for that very reason they are futile; they do not succeed in even the special reforms at which they aim, except at the expense of intensifying other defects and creating new ones. Nothing but the best, the richest and fullest experience possible, is good enough for man. The attainment of such an experience is not to be conceived as the specific problem of "reformers" but as the common purpose of men. The contribution which philosophy can make to this common aim is criticism. Criticism certainly includes a heightened con-sciousness of deficiencies and corruptions in the scheme and distribution of values that obtains at any period.

No just or pertinent criticism in its negative phase can possibly be made, however, except upon the basis of a heightened appreciation of the positive goods which human experience has achieved and offers. Positive concrete goods of science, art and social companionship are the basic subject-matter of philosophy as criticism; and only because such positive goods already exist is their emancipation and secured extension the defining aim of intelligence. The more aware one is of the richness of meanings which experience possesses, the more will a generous and catholic thinker be conscious of the limits which prevent sharing in them; the more aware will he be of their accidental and arbitrary distribution. If instrumental efficacies need to be emphasized, it is not for the sake of instruments but for the sake of that full and more secure distribution of values which is impossible without instrumentalities.

If philosophy be criticism, what is to be said of the relation of philosophy to metaphysics? For metaphysics, as a statement of the generic traits manifested by existences of all kinds without regard to their differentiation into physical and mental, seems to have nothing to do with criticism and choice, with an effective love of wisdom. It begins and ends with analysis and definition. When it has revealed the traits and characters that are sure to turn up in every universe of discourse, its work is done. So at least an argument may run. But the very nature of the traits discovered in every theme of discourse, since they are ineluctable traits of natural existence, forbids such a conclusion. Qualitative individuality and constant relations, contingency and need, movement and arrest are common traits of all existence. This fact is source both of values and of their precariousness; both of immediate possession which is casual and of reflection which is a precondition of secure attainment and appropriation. Any theory that detects and defines these traits is therefore but a ground-map of the province of criticism, establishing base lines to be employed in more intricate triangulations.

If the general traits of nature existed in water-tight compartments, it might be enough to sort out the objects and interests of experience among them. But they are actually so intimately intermixed that all important issues are concerned with their degrees and the ratios they sustain to one another. Barely to note and register that contingency is a trait of natural events has nothing to do with wisdom. To note, however, contingency in connection with a concrete situation of life is that fear of the Lord which is at least the beginning of wisdom. The detection and definition of nature's end is in itself barren. But the undergoing that actually goes on in the light of this discovery brings one close to supreme issues: life and death.

The more sure one is that the world which encompasses human life is of such and such a character (no matter what his definition), the more one is committed to try to direct the conduct of life, that of others as well as of himself, upon the basis of the character assigned to the world. And if he finds that he cannot succeed, that the attempt lands him in confusion, inconsistency and darkness, plunging others into discord and shutting them out from participation, rudimentary precepts instruct him to surrender his assurance as a delusion; and to revise his notions of the nature of nature till he makes them more adequate to the concrete facts in which nature is embodied. Man needs the earth in order to walk, the sea to swim or sail, the air to fly. Of necessity he acts within the world, and in order to be, he must in some measure adapt himself as one part of nature to other parts.

In mind, thought, this situation, this predicament becomes aware of itself. Instead of the coerced adaptation of part to part with coerced failure or success as consequence, there is search for the meaning of things with respect to acts to be performed, plans and policies to be formed; there is search for the meaning of proposed acts with respect to objects they induce and preclude. The one cord that is never broken is that between the energies and acts which compose nature. Knowledge modifies the tie. But the idea that knowledge breaks the tie, that it inserts something opaque between the interactions of things, is

hardly less than infantile. Knowledge as science modifies the particular interactions that come within its reach, because it is itself a modification of interactions, due to taking into account their past and future. The generic insight into existence which alone can define metaphysics in any empirically intelligible sense is itself an added fact of interaction, and is therefore subject to the same requirement of intelligence as any other natural occurrence: namely, inquiry into the bearings, leadings and consequences of what it discovers. The universe is no infinite self-representative series, if only because the addition within it of a representation makes it a different universe.

By an indirect path we are brought to a consideration of the most far-reaching question of all criticism: the relationship between existence and value, or as the problem is often put, between the real and ideal.

Philosophies have usually insisted upon a wholesale relationship. Either the goods which we most prize and which are therefore termed ideal are identified completely and throughout with real Being; or the realms of existence and of the ideal are wholly severed from each other. In the European tradition in its orthodox form the former alternative has prevailed. *Ens* and *verum, bonum* are the same. Being, in the full sense, is perfection of power to be; the measure of degrees of perfection and of degrees of reality is extent of power. Evil and error are impotences; futile gestures against omnipotence—against Being. Spinoza restated to this effect medieval theology in terms of the new outlook of science. Modern professed idealisms have taught the same doctrine. After magnifying thought and the objects of thought, after magnifying the ideals of human aspiration, they have then sought to prove that after all these things are not ideal but are real—real not *as* meanings and ideals, but as existential being. Thus the assertion of faith in the ideal belies itself in the making; these "idealists" cannot trust their ideal till they have converted it into existence—that is, into the physical or the psychical, which, since it lacks the properties of the empirically physical and psychophysical becomes a peculiar kind of existence, called metaphysical.

There are also philosophies, rarer in occurrence, which allege that the ideal is too sacredly ideal to have any point of contact whatever with existence; they think that contact is contagion and contagion infection. At first sight such a view seems to display a certain nobility of faith and fineness of abnegation. But an ideal realm that has no roots in existence has no efficacy nor relevancy. It is a light which is darkness, for shining in the void it illumines nothing and cannot reveal even itself. It gives no instruction, for it cannot be translated into the meaning and import of what actually happens, and hence it is barren; it cannot mitigate the bleakness of existence nor modify its brutalities. It thus abnegates itself in abjuring footing in natural events, and ceases to be ideal, to become whimsical fantasy or linguistic sophistication.

These remarks are made not so much by way of hostile animadversion as by way of indicating the sterility of wholesale conceptions of the relation of existence and value. By negative implication, they reveal the only kind of doctrine that can be effectively critical, taking effect in discriminations which emancipate, extend, and clarify. Such a theory will realize that the meanings which are termed ideal as truly as those which are termed sensuous are generated by existences; that as far as they continue in being they are sustained by events; that they are indications of the possibilities of existences, and are, therefore, to be used as well as enjoyed; used to inspire action to procure and buttress their causal conditions. Such a doctrine criticizes particular occurrences by the particular meanings to which they give rise; it criticizes also particular meanings and goods as their conditions are found to be sparse, accidental, incapable of conservation, or frequent, pliant, congruous, enduring; and as their consequences are found to afford enlightenment and direction in conduct, or to darken counsel, narrow the horizon of vision, befog judgment and distort perspective. A good is a good anyhow, but to reflection those goods approve themselves, whether labelled beauty or truth or righteousness, which steady, vitalize and expand judgments in creation of new goods and conservation of old goods. To common sense this statement is a truism. If to philosophy it is a stumbling-block, it is be-cause tradition in philosophy has set itself in stiff-necked fashion against discriminations within the realm of existences, on account of the pluralistic implications of discrimination. It insists upon having all or none; it cannot choose in favor of some existences and against others because of prior commitment to a dogma of perfect unity. Such distinctions as it makes are therefore always hierarchical; degrees of greater and less, superior and inferior, in one homogeneous order.

I gladly borrow the glowing words of one of our greatest American philosophers; with their poetry they may succeed in conveying where dry prose fails. Justice Holmes has written: "The mode in which the inevitable comes to pass is through effort. Consciously or unconsciously we all strive to make the kind of world that we like. And although with Spinoza we may regard criticism of the past as futile, there is every reason for doing all that we can to make a future such as we desire." He then goes on to say, "there is every reason also for trying to make our desires intelligent. The trouble is that our ideals for the most part are inarticulate, and that even if we have made them definite we have very little experimental knowledge of the way to bring them about." And this effort to make our desires, our strivings and our ideals (which are as natural to man as his aches and his clothes) articulate, to define them (not in themselves which is impossible) in terms of inquiry into conditions and consequences is what I have called criticism; and when carried on in the grand manner, philosophy. In a further essay, Justice Holmes touches upon the relation of philosophy (thus conceived) to our scientific and metaphysical insight into the kind of a world in which we live.

"When we come to our attitude toward the universe I do not see any rational ground for demanding the superlative—for being dissatisfied unless we are assured that our truth is cosmic truth, if there is such a thing. . . . If a man sees no reason for believing that significance, consciousness and ideals are more than marks of the human, that does not justify what has been familiar in French sceptics; getting upon a pedestal and professing to look with haughty scorn upon a world in ruins. The real conclusion is that the part can not swallow the whole. . . . If we believe that we came out of the universe, not it out of us, we must admit that we do not know what we are talking about when we speak of brute matter. We do know that a certain complex of energies can wag its tail and another can make syllogisms. These are among the powers of the unknown, and if, as may be, it has still greater powers that we cannot understand . . . why should we not be content? Why should we employ the energy that is furnished to us by the cosmos to defy it and to shake our fist at the sky? It seems to me silly."

"That the universe has in it more than we understand, that the private soldiers have not been told the plan of campaign, or even that there is one . . . has no bearing on our conduct. We still shall fight—all of us because we want to live, some, at least, because we want to realize our spontaneity and prove our powers, for the joy of it, and we may leave to the unknown the supposed final valuation of that which in any event has value to us. It is enough for us that the universe has produced us and has within it, as less than it, all that we believe and love. If we think of our existence not as that of a little god outside, but as that of a ganglion within, we have the infinite behind us. It gives us our only but our adequate significance. If our imagination is strong enough to accept the vision of ourselves as parts inseparable from the rest, and to extend our final interest beyond the boundary of our skins, it justifies even the sacrifice of our lives for ends outside of ourselves. The motive to be sure is the common wants and ideals that we find in man. Philosophy does not furnish motives, but it shows men that they are not fools for doing what they already want to do. It opens to the forlorn hopes on which we throw ourselves away, the vista of the farthest stretch of human thought, the chords of a harmony that breathes from the unknown."

Men move between extremes. They conceive of themselves as gods, or feign a powerful and cunning god as an ally who bends the world to do their bidding and meet their wishes. Disillusionized, they disown the world that disappoints them; and hugging ideals to themselves as their own possession, stand in haughty aloofness apart from the hard course of events that pays so little heed to our hopes and aspirations. But a mind that has opened itself to experience and that has ripened through its discipline knows its own littleness and impotencies; it knows that its wishes and acknowledgments are not final measures of the universe whether in knowledge or in conduct, and hence are, in the end, transient. But it also knows that its juvenile assumption of power and achievement is not a dream to be wholly forgotten. It implies a unity with the universe that is to be preserved. The belief, and the effort of thought and struggle which it inspires are also the doing of the universe, and they in some way, however slight, carry the universe forward. A chastened sense of our importance, apprehension that it is not a yard-stick by which to measure the whole, is consistent with the belief that we and our endeavors are significant not only for themselves but in the whole.

Fidelity to the nature to which we belong, as parts however weak, demands that we cherish our desires and ideals till we have converted them into intelligence, revised them in terms of the ways and means which nature makes possible. When we have used our thought to its utmost and have thrown into the moving unbalanced balance of things our puny strength, we know that though the universe slay us still we may trust, for our lot is one with whatever is good in existence. We know that such thought and effort is one condition of the coming into existence of the better. As far as we are concerned it is the only condition, for it alone is in our power. To ask more than this is childish; but to ask less is a recreance no less egotistic, involving no less a cutting of ourselves from the universe than does the expectation that it meet and satisfy our every wish. To ask in good faith as much as this from ourselves is to stir into motion every capacity of imagination, and to exact from action every skill and bravery.

While, therefore, philosophy has its source not in any special impulse or staked-off section of experience, but in the entire human predicament, this human situation falls wholly within nature. It reflects the traits of nature; it gives indisputable evidence that in nature itself qualities and relations, individualities and uniformities, finalities and efficacies, contingencies and necessities are inextricably bound together. The harsh conflicts and the happy coincidences of this interpenetration make experience what it consciously is; their manifest apparition creates doubt, forces inquiry, exacts choice, and imposes liability for the choice which is made. Were there complete harmony in nature, life would be spontaneous efflorescence. If disharmony were not in both man and nature, if it were only between them, man would be the ruthless overlord of nature, or its querulous oppressed subject. It is precisely the peculiar intermixture of support and frustration of man by nature which constitutes experience. The standing antitheses of philosophic thought, purpose and mechanism, subject and object, necessity and freedom, mind and body, individual and general, are all of them attempts to formulate the fact that nature induces and partially sustains meanings and goods, and at critical junctures withdraws assistance and flouts its own creatures.

The striving of man for objects of imagination is a continuation of natural processes; it is something man has learned from the world in which he occurs, not something which he arbitrarily injects into that world. When he adds perception and ideas to these endeavors, it is not after all he who adds; the addition is again the doing of nature and a further complication of its own domain. To act, to enjoy and suffer in consequence of action, to reflect, to discriminate and make differences in what had been but gross and homogeneous good and evil, according to what inquiry reveals of causes and effects; to act upon what has been learned, thereby to plunge into new and unconsidered predicaments, to test and revise what has been learned, to engage in new goods and evils is human, the course which manifests the course of nature. They are the manifest destiny of contingency, fulfillment, qualitative individualization and generic uniformities in nature. To note, register and define the constituent structure of nature is not then an affair neutral to the office of criticism. It is a preliminary outline of the field of criticism, whose chief import is to afford understanding of the necessity and nature of the office of intelligence.

If I mistake not, the actual animus of subjectivity in modern philosophy is not where its antagonists have placed it. Its actual animus and its obnoxious burden are exemplified in the doctrine of its hostile critics. For they assign to knowledge alone valid reference to existence. Desires, beliefs, "practical" activity, values are attributed exclusively to the human subject; this division is what makes subjectivity a snare and peril. The case of belief is crucial. For it is admitted that belief involves a phase of acquiescence or assertion; it presents qualities which involve *personal* factors, and (whatever definition of value be employed) value. A sharp line of demarcation has therefore to be drawn between belief and knowledge, for the latter has been defined in terms of pure objectivity. The need to control belief is admitted; knowledge figures, even though according to these theories only *per accidens*, as the organon of such control. Practically then, in effect, knowledge, science, truth, is the method of criticizing beliefs. It is the method of determining right participation in beliefs on the part of personal factors. Why then keep up any other distinction between knowledge and beliefs, save that between methodical agencies, efficacious instrumentalities, and the accepted objects which being conclusions, are hence marked by characters due to the method of their production, in contrast with objects of belief blindly and accidentally generated? Why perturbation at the intimation that science is inherently an instrument of critically determining what is good and bad in the way of acceptance and rejection?

I can see but one answer. The realm of desire, belief, search, choice is thought of as "subjective" in a sense which isolates it from natural existence and which makes it an inexplicable irruption. This is the reason for sharp separation of belief and knowledge. Aversion to making science a means of determining the right operation of personal factors, just as the technical and material apparatus of a painter determines his product, is well grounded if the personal is outside of nature. Made a means to something personal conceived in this sense, science loses its objectivity, and becomes infected with the traits which characterize the merely private and arbitrary.

There is involved, however, in the conclusion an unexamined and uncriticized assumption. The reason for isolating doubt, striving, purpose, the variegated colored play of goods and bads, rejections and acceptances, is they do not belong in the block universe which forms the object of generalized knowledge, whether the block be conceived as mechanical or as rational in structure. The argument thus moves in a vicious circle; the question is begged at the outset. If individualized qualities, status arrests, limiting "ends," and contingent changes characterize nature, then they manifest themselves in the uses, enjoyments and sufferings, the searchings and strivings which form conscious experience. These are as realistic, as "objectively" natural, as are the constituents of the object of cognitional experience. There is then no ground for denying or evading the full import of the fact that the latter are the means and the only means of regulative appraisals of values, of their revision, rectification, of their regulated generation and fortification.

The habitual avoidance in theories of knowledge of any reference to the fact that knowledge is a case of belief, operates as a device for ignoring the monstrous consequences of regarding the latter as existentially subjective, personal and private. No such device is available in dealing with esthetic and moral goods. Here the obnoxious one-sided conception operates in full force. The usual current procedure is to link values with likings as merely personal affairs, ignoring the inconvenient fact that the theory logically thereby makes all *beliefs* also matters of arbitrary, undiscussable preference. It is no cause for wonder therefore that there is next to no consensus in esthetic and moral theories. Since their subject-matter is totally segregated from that of science, since they are assigned to independent non-participating realms of existence, the only possible method of achieving agreement has been exiled in advance.

Practically this consequence is intolerable;

accordingly it is rarely faced. "Standards" of value suddenly make their appearance to serve as criteria of taste and conscience. The distinction between likings and that which is worth liking, between the desired and the desirable, between the is and the ought, descends out of the blue. There are, it seems, immediate values, but there also are standard values, and the latter may be used to judge and measure immediate goods and bads. Thus the reflective distinction between the true and the false, the genuine and the spurious is brought upon the scene. In strict logic, however, it enters only to disappear. For if the standard is itself a value, then it is by definition only another name for the object of a particular liking, on the part of some particular subjective creature. If the liking for it conflicts with some other liking, the strongest wins. There is no question of false and true, of real and seeming, but only of stronger and weaker. The question of which one *should* be stronger is as meaningless as it would be in a cock-fight.

Such a conclusion puts an end to all attempt at consistency and organization and calls out in reaction an opposite theory. The "standard" is not, it is decided, for us at least, a good. It is rather a principle rationally apprehended. It is that which is "right" rather than that which is good; and since it is the right, it is the standard for judging all goods. If right is also good, the identification subsists in some transcendental realm; in some eternal, non-empirical realm of Being which is also a realm of values. The standard of good thus conceived as a principle of reason and as a form of supreme Being, is set over against the outside of actual desires, striving, satisfactions and frustrations. It ought to enter into their determination but for the most part it does not. The distinction between is and ought is one of kind, and a separation. It is not surprising that the wheel completes a full circle, and that the finale is a retort that the alleged standard is itself but another dignified disguise for some one's arbitrary liking—the *ipse dixit* of some one accidentally clothed with extraneous authority.

It is as irritating to have experience of beauty and moral goodness reduced to groundless whims as to have that of truth. Common sense has an inexpugnable conviction that there are immediate goods of enjoyment and conduct, and that there are principles by which they may be appraised and rectified. Common sense entertains this firm conviction because it is innocent of any rigid demarcation between knowledge on one side and belief, conduct and esthetic appreciation on the other. It is guiltless of the division between objective reality and subjective events. It takes striving, purposing, inquiring, wanting, the life of "practice," to be as much facts of nature as are the themes of scientific discourse; to it, indeed, the former has a more direct and urgent reality. Hence it has no difficulty with the idea of rational or objective criticism and rectification of immediate goods. If it were articulate, it would say that the same natural processes which generate goods and evils generate also the striving to secure the one and avoid the other, and generate judgments to regulate the strivings. Its weakness is that it fails to recognize that deliberate and systematized science is a precondition of adequate judgments and hence of adequate striving and adequate choice. Its organs of criticism are for the most part half-judgments, uncriticized products of custom, chance circumstance and vested interests. Hence common sense when it begins to reflect upon its own convictions easily falls a victim to traditional theories; and the vicious circle begins over again. It is sound as to the need and possibility of objective criticism of values, it is weak as to the method of accomplishing.

Yet all this time there is an example of the way out in the case of beliefs. There was a time when beliefs about external events were largely matters of what it was found immediately good to accept or reject; as far as there was a distinction made between the immediately good in belief and the real or true, it lay chiefly in the fact that the latter was the object sanctioned by authorities of church and state. Yet it is now all but commonplace that every belief-value must be subjected to criticism; in scientific undertakings, it is a commonplace that criticism does not depend upon reference to a transcendent standard truth. The distinction between an immediate belief-value, which is but a challenge to inquiry, and an eventual object of belief that concludes critical inquiry, and has the value of fulfilling the causal relationships discovered, is made in the course of intelligent experiment. The result is a distinction between the apparent and the real good. Gradually a reluctant world is persuaded that meanings so determined define what is good for acceptance and assertion. Meantime beliefs determined by passion, class-interest, routine and authority remain sufficiently prevalent to enforce the perception that it makes all the difference in the world in the value of a belief how its object is formed and arrived at. Thus the lesson is enforced that critical valuations of immediate goods proceed in terms of the generation and consequences of objects qualified with good.

In outward forms, experimental science is infinitely varied. In principle, it is simple. We know an object when we know how it is made, and we know how it is made in the degree in which we ourselves make it. Old tradition compels us to call thinking "mental." But "mental" thought is but partial experimentation, terminating in preliminary readjustments, confined within the organism. As long as thinking remained at this stage, it protected itself by regarding this introverted truncation as evidence of an immaterial reason superior to and independent of body. As long as thought was thus cooped up, overt action in the "outer" natural scene was inevitably shorn of its full meed of meaning; it was to that extent arbitrary and routine. When "outer" and "inner" activity came together in a single experimental operation, used as the only adequate method of discovery and proof, effective criticism, consistent and ordered valuation, emerged. Thought aligned itself with other arts that shape objects by informing things with meanings.

Psychology, which reflects the old dualistic separation of mind from nature, has made current the notion that the processes which terminate in knowledge fare forth from innocent sensory data, or from pure logical principles, or from both together, as original starting points and material. As a natural history of mind this notion is wholly mythological. All knowing and effort to know starts from some belief, some received and asserted meaning which is a deposit of prior experience, personal and communal. In every instance, from passing query to elaborate scientific undertaking, the art of knowing criticizes a belief which has passed current as genuine coin, with a view to its revision. It terminates when freer, richer and more secure objects of belief are instituted as goods of immediate acceptance. The operation is one of doing and making in the literal sense. Starting from one good, treated as apparent and questionable, and ending in another which is tested and substantiated, the final act of knowing is acceptance and intellectual appreciation of what is significantly conclusive.

Is there any reason for supposing that the situation is any different in the case of other values and valuations? Is there any intrinsic difference between the relation of scientific inquiry to belief-values, of esthetic criticism to esthetic values, and of moral judgments to moral goods? Is there any difference in logical method? If we adopt a current theory, and say that immediate values occur wherever there is liking, interest, bias, it is clear that this liking is an act, if not an overt one, at least a dispositional tendency and direction. But most likings, all likings in their first appearance, are blind and gross. They do not know what they are about nor why they attach themselves to this or that object. Moreover, every such act takes a risk and assumes a liability, and does so ignorantly. For there are always in existence rival claimants for liking. To prefer *this* is to exclude *that*. Any liking is choice, unwittingly performed. There is no selection without rejection; interest and bias are selective, preferential. To take this for a good is to declare in act, though not at first in thought, that it is better than something else. This decision is arbitrary, capricious, unreasoned because made without thought of the other object, and without comparison. To say that an object is a good may seem to be an absolute and intrinsic declaration particularly when the assertion is made in direct act rather than in thought. But when we recognize that in effect the assertion is that one thing is better than another thing, the issues shift to something comparative, relational, causal, intellectual and objective. *Immediately* nothing is better or worse than anything else; it is just what it is. Comparison is

comparison of things, things in their efficacies, their promotions and hindrances. The better is that which will do more in the way of security, liberation and fecundity for other likings and values.

To make a valuation, to judge appraisingly, is then to bring to conscious perception relations of productivity and resistance and thus to make value significant, intelligent and intelligible. In becoming discriminately aware of the causal conditions of the object liked and preferred, we become aware of its eventual operations. If in the case of esthetic and moral goods, the causal conditions which reflection reveals as determinants of the good object are found to lie within organic constitution in greater degree than is the case with objects of belief, this finding is of enormous importance for the technique of critical judgment. But it does not modify the logic which obtains in knowledge of the relationship of values and valuations to each other. It indicates the particular subject-matter which has to be controlled and used in the conscious art of remaking goods. As inquiries which aim at knowledge start from pre-existent beliefs, so esthetic and moral criticism start from antecedent natural goods of contemplative enjoyment and social intercourse. Its purpose is to make it possible to like and choose knowingly and with meaning, instead of blindly. All criticism worthy of the title is but another name for that revealing discovery of conditions and consequences which enables liking, bias, interest to express themselves in responsible and informed ways instead of ignorantly and fatalistically.

The meaning of the theory advanced concerning the relationship of goods and criticism may be illustrated by ethical theory. Few I suppose would deny that in spite of the attention devoted to this subject by many minds of a high order of intention and intellectual equipment, the outcome, judged from the standpoint of scientific consensus, is rather dismaying. The outcome is due in part to the importance of the subject, its intimate connection with man's deepest concerns, with his most cherished traditions and with the most acutely perplexing problems of his contemporary social life. Objective detachment and development of adequate intellectual instruments are necessarily difficult under such conditions. But I think that we find, amid all the diversity, one common intellectual preconception which inevitably defers the possibility of attainment of scientific method. This is the assumption, implicit or overt, that moral theory is concerned with ends, values rather than with criticism of ends and values; the latter being in fact not only independent of moral theory but not themselves having even moral quality. To discover and define once for all the *bonum* and the *summum bonum* in a way which rationally subserves all virtues and duties, is the traditional task of morals; to deny that moral theory has any such office will seem to many equivalent to denial of the possibility of moral philosophy. Yet in other things repeated failure of achievement is regarded as evidence that we are going at the affair in a wrong way. And to a mind willing to surrender the traditional preconception, failure to achieve consensus in method and even in generic conclusions in morals as a branch of philosophy may be similarly explained.

It is not meant of course that the tradition assumes that the good and the highest good are created by moral theory. The assumption is not so bad as that; it is to the effect that it is the province of moral theory to reveal moral goods; to bring them to consciousness and to enforce their character in perception. As empirical fact, however, the arts, those of converse and the literary arts which are the enhanced continuations of social converse, have been the means by which goods are brought home to human perception. The writings of moralists have been efficacious in this direction upon the whole not in their professed intent as theoretical doctrines, but in as far as they have genially participated in the arts of poetry, fiction, parable and drama. Conversion into doctrinal teachings of the imaginative relations of life with which great moral artists have dowered humanity has been the great cause of their ossification into harsh dogmas; illuminating insight into the relations and goods of life has been lost, and an arbitrary code of precepts and rules substituted. Direct appeal of experience concentrated, vivified and intensified by the insight of an artist and embodied in literary creations similar in kind to the revelation of meanings which is the work of any artist, has been treated as a discovery and definition of things true to scientific or philosophic reason.

Meantime the work which theoretical criticism might do has not been done; namely, discovery of the conditions and consequences, the existential relations, of goods which are accepted as goods not because of theory but because they are such in experience. The cause in large measure is doubtless because the prerequisite tools of physics, physiology and economics were not at hand. But now when these potential instrumentalities are more adequately prepared they will not be employed until it is recognized that the business of moral theory is not at all with consummations and goods as such, but with discovery of the conditions and consequences of their appearance, a work which is factual and analytic, not dialectic, hortatory, nor prescriptive. The argument does not forget that there have been would-be naturalistic and empirical ethics which have asserted that goods are such prior to moral conduct as well as to moral theory, and that they become moral only when employed in conduct as objects of reflective choice and endeavor. But the apparent exception proves the rule. For these forms of moral theory while releasing morals from the obligation of telling man what goods are, leaving that office to life itself, have failed to note that the office of moral philosophy is criticism; and that the performance of this office by discovery of existential conditions and consequences involves a qualitative transformation, a re-making in subsequent action which experimentally tests the conclusions of theory.

Therefore like the Aristotelian ethics, they have been dialectic, defining and classifying in hierarchical order antecedent goods and terminating in a notion of *the* good, the *summum bonum*; or, like hedonistic ethics, they have made a dialectic abstraction of a feature of concrete goods, their pleasantness; and instead of providing a method of analysis of concrete situations have laid down rules of calculation and prescribed policies to be pursued as fixed, not intellectually experimental, results of prior calculations. When they were, like Jeremy Bentham, persons of human sensitiveness to evils from which men suffer in virtue of institutions which may be altered; or, like John Stuart Mill, of genial insight into the constituents of a liberal and humane happiness, they have stirred their generation to beneficent action. But the connection between their theories and the practical outcome was adventitious; their ideas operated when all is said and done as literary rather than as scientific apparatus, as much so as in the case of reforms to which Charles Dickens not meanly contributed.

The implications of the position which has been taken import a "practical" element into philosophy as effective and verifiable criticism, obnoxious to the traditional view. Yet if man is within nature, not a little god outside, and is within as a mode of energy inseparably connected with other modes, interaction is the one unescapable trait of every human concern; thinking, even philosophic thinking, is not exempt. This interaction is subject to partiality because the human factor has bent and bias. But partiality is not obnoxious just because it is partial. A world characterized by qualitative histories with their own beginnings, directions and terminations is of necessity a world in which any interaction is intensive change—a world of partialities, particulars. What is obnoxious in partiality is due to the illusion that there are states and acts which are not also interactions. Immature and undisciplined mind believes in actions which have their seat and source in a particular and separate being, from which they issue. This is the very belief which the advance of intelligent criticism destroys. The latter transforms the notion of isolated one-sided acts into acknowledged interactions. The view which isolates knowledge, contemplation, liking, interest, value, or whatever from action is itself a survival of the notion that there are things which can exist and be known apart from active connection with other things.

When man finds he is not a little god in his active powers and accomplishments, he retains his former conceit by hugging to his bosom the notion that nevertheless in some realm, be it knowledge or esthetic contemplation, he is still outside of and detached from the ongoing sweep of inter-acting and changing events; and being there alone and irresponsible save to himself, is as a god. When he perceives clearly and adequately that he is within nature, a part of its interactions, he sees that the line to be drawn is not between action and thought, or action and appreciation, but between blind, slavish, meaningless action and action that is free, significant, directed and responsible. Knowledge, like the growth of a plant and the movement of the earth, is a mode of interaction; but it is a mode which renders other modes luminous, important, valuable, capable of direction, causes being translated into means and effects into consequences.

All reason which is itself reasoned, is thus method, not substance; operative, not "end in itself." To imagine it the latter is to transport it outside the natural world, to convert it into a god, whether a big and original one or a little and derived one, outside of the contingencies of existence and untouched by its vicissitudes. This is the meaning of the "reason" which is alleged to envisage reality *sub specie aeternitatis*. It is indeed true that all relations, all universals and laws as such are timeless. Even an order of time as an order is timeless, for it is relational. But to give irrelevancy to time the name of eternal in an eulogistic sense, is but to proclaim that irrelevancy to any existence forms a higher kind of existence. Orders, relations, universals are significant and invaluable as objects of knowledge. They are so because they apply to intensive and extensive, individualized, existences; to things of spacious and temporal qualities. Application is not for the sake of something extraneous, for the sake of something designated an utility. It is for the sake of the laws, principles, ideals. Had they not been detached for the purpose of application, they would not have meaning; intent and potentiality of application in the course of events lends them all their significance. Without *actuality* of application, without effort to realize their intent, they are meanings, but they possess neither truth nor falsity, since without application they have no bearing and test. Thus they cease to be objects of knowledge, or even reflection; and become detached objects of contemplation. They may then have the esthetic value possessed by the objects of a dream. But after all we have not left temporal experience, human desire, liking, and passion behind or below us. We have merely painted nature with the colors of an all too local and transitory flight from the hardships of life. These eternal objects abstracted from the course of events, although labeled Reality, in opposition to Appearance, are in truth but the idlest and most evanescent of appearances, born of personal craving and shaped by private fantasy.

Because intelligence is critical method applied to goods of belief, appreciation and conduct, so as to construct freer and more secure goods, turning assent and assertion into free communication of shareable meanings, turning feeling into ordered and liberal sense, turning reaction into response, it is the reasonable object of our deepest faith and loyalty, the stay and support of all reasonable hopes. To utter such a statement is not to indulge in romantic idealization. It is not to assert that intelligence will ever dominate the course of events; it is not even to imply that it will save from ruin and destruction. The issue is one of choice, and choice is always a question of alternatives. What the method of intelligence, thoughtful valuation will accomplish, if once it be tried, is for the result of trial to determine. Since it is relative to the intersection in existence of hazard and rule, of contingency and order, faith in a wholesale and final triumph is fantastic. But

some procedure has to be tried; for life is itself a sequence of trials. Carelessness and routine, Olympian aloofness, secluded contemplation are themselves choices. To claim that intelligence is a better method than its alternatives, authority, imitation, caprice and ignorance, prejudice and passion, is hardly an excessive claim. These procedures have been tried and have worked their will. The result is not such as to make it clear that the method of intelligence, the use of science in criticizing and re-creating the casual goods of nature into intentional and conclusive goods of art, the union of knowledge and values in production, is not worth trying. There may be those to whom it is treason to think of philosophy as the critical method of developing methods of criticism. But this conception of philosophy also waits to be tried, and the trial which shall approve or condemn lies in the eventual issue. The import of such knowledge as we have acquired and such experience as has been quickened by thought is to evoke and justify the trial.

NOTES

[LW 1:295–326.]

Philosophy's Search for the Immutable

From *The Quest for Certainty* (1929)

In the previous chapter, we noted incidentally the distinction made in the classic tradition between knowledge and belief, or, as Locke put it, between knowledge and judgment. According to this distinction the certain and knowledge are co-extensive. Disputes exist, but they are whether sensation or reason affords the basis of certainty; or whether existence or essence is its object. In contrast with this identification, the very word "belief" is eloquent on the topic of certainty. We *believe* in the absence of knowledge or complete assurance. Hence the quest for certainty has always been an effort to transcend belief. Now since, as we have already noted, all matters of practical action involve an element of uncertainty, we can ascend from belief to knowledge only by isolating the latter from practical doing and making.

In this chapter we are especially concerned with the effect of the ideal of certainty as something superior to belief upon the conception of the nature and function of philosophy. Greek thinkers saw clearly—and logically—that experience cannot furnish us, as respects cognition of existence, with anything more than contingent probability. Experience cannot deliver to us necessary truths; truths completely demonstrated by reason. Its conclusions are particular, not universal. Not being "exact" they come short of "science." Thus there arose the distinction between rational truths or, in modern terminology, truths relating to the relation of ideas, and "truths" about matters of existence, empirically ascertained. Thus not merely the arts of practice, industrial and social, were stamped matters of belief rather than of knowledge, but also all those sciences which are matters of inductive inference from observation.

One might indulge in the reflection that they are none the worse for all that, especially since the natural sciences have developed a technique for achieving a high degree of probability and for measuring, within assignable limits, the amount of probability which attaches in particular cases to conclusions. But historically the matter is not so simple as to permit of this retort. For empirical or observational sciences were placed in invidious contrast to rational sciences which dealt with eternal and universal objects and which therefore were possessed of necessary truth. Consequently all observational sciences as far as their material could not be subsumed under forms and principles supplied by rational science shared in the depreciatory view held about practical affairs. They are relatively low, secular and profane compared with the perfect realities of rational science.

And here is a justification for going back to something as remote in time as Greek philosophy. The whole classic tradition down to our day has continued to hold a slighting view of experience as such, and to hold up as the proper goal and ideal of true knowledge realities which even if they are located in empirical things cannot be known by experimental methods. The logical consequence for philosophy itself is evident. Upon the side of method, it has been compelled to claim for itself the possession of a method issuing from reason itself, and having the warrant of reason, independently of experience. As long as the view obtained that nature itself is truly known by the same rational method, the consequences—at least those which were evident—were not serious. There was no break between philosophy and genuine science—or what was conceived to be such. In fact, there was not even a distinction; there were simply various branches of philosophy, metaphysical, logical, natural, moral, etc., in a descending scale of demonstrative certainty. Since, according to the theory, the subject-matter of the lower sciences was inherently of a different character from that of true knowledge, there was no ground for rational dissatisfaction with the lower degree of knowledge called belief. Inferior knowledge or belief corresponded to the inferior state of subject-matter.

The scientific revolution of the seventeenth century effected a great modification. Science itself through the aid of mathematics carried the scheme of demonstrative knowledge over to natural objects. The "laws" of the natural world had that fixed character which in the older scheme had belonged only to rational and ideal forms. A mathematical science of nature couched in mechanistic terms claimed to be the only sound natural philosophy. Hence the older philosophies lost alliance with natural knowledge and the support that had been given to philosophy by them. Philosophy in maintaining its claim to be a superior form of knowledge was compelled to take an invidious and so to say malicious attitude toward the conclusions of natural science. The framework of the old tradition had in the meantime become embedded in Christian theology, and through religious teaching was made a part of the inherited culture of those innocent of any technical philosophy. Consequently, the rivalry between philosophy and the new science, with respect to the claim to know reality, was converted in effect into a rivalry between the spiritual values guaranteed by the older philosophic tradition and the conclusions of natural knowledge. The more science advanced the more it seemed to encroach upon the special province of the territory over which philosophy had claimed jurisdiction. Thus philosophy in its classic form became a species of apologetic justification for belief in an ultimate reality in which the values which should regulate life and control conduct are securely enstated.

There are undoubted disadvantages in the historic manner of approach to the problem which has been followed. It may readily be thought either that the Greek formulation which has been emphasized has no especial pertinency with respect to modern thought and especially to contemporary philosophy; or that no philosophical statement is of any great importance for the mass of non-philosophic persons. Those interested in philosophy may object that the criticisms passed are directed if not at a man of straw at least to positions that have long since lost their actuality. Those not friendly to any form of philosophy may inquire what import they have for any except professed philosophers.

The first type of objection will be dealt with somewhat *in extenso* in the succeeding chapter, in which I shall try to show how modern philosophies, in spite of their great diversity, have been concerned with problems of adjustment of the conclusions of modern science to the chief religious and moral tradition of the western world; together with the way in which these problems are connected with retention of the conception of the relation of knowledge to reality formulated in Greek thought. At the point in the discussion now reached, it suffices to point out that, in spite of great changes in detail, the notion of a separation between knowledge and action, theory and practice, has been perpetuated, and that the beliefs connected with action are taken to be uncertain and inferior in value compared with those inherently connected with objects of knowledge, so that the former are securely established only as they derived from the latter. Not the specific content of Greek thought is pertinent to present problems, but its insistence that security is measured by certainty of knowledge, while the latter is measured by adhesion to fixed and immutable objects, which therefore are independent of what men do in practical activity.

The other objection is of a different sort. It comes from those who feel that not merely Greek philosophy but philosophy in any form is remote from all significant human concern. It is willing to admit or rather assert that it is presumptuous for philosophy to lay claim to knowledge of a higher order than that given by natural science, but it also holds that this is no great matter in any case except for professional philosophers.

There would be force in this latter objection were it not that those who make it hold for the most part the same philosophy of certainty and its proper object that is held by philosophers, save in an inchoate form. They are not interested in the notion that philosophic thought is a special means of attaining this object and the certainty it affords, but they are far from holding, either explicitly or implicitly, that the arts of intelligently directed action are the means by which security of values are to be attained. With respect to certain ends and goods they accept this idea. But in thinking of these ends and values as material, as related to health, wealth, control of conditions for the sake of an inferior order of consequences, they retain the same division between a higher reality and a lower that is formulated in classic philosophy. They may be innocent of the vocabulary that speaks of reason, necessary truth, the universal, things in themselves and appearances. But they incline to believe that there is some other road than that of action, directed by knowledge, to

achieve ultimate security of higher ideals and purposes. They think of practical action as necessary for practical utilities, but they mark off practical utilities from spiritual and ideal values. Philosophy did not originate the underlying division. It only gave intellectual formulation and justification to ideas that were operative in men's minds generally. And the elements of these ideas are as active in present culture as they ever were in the past. Indeed, through the diffusion of religious doctrines, the idea that ultimate values are a matter of special revelation and are to be embodied in life by special means radically different from the arts of action that deal with lower and lesser ends has been accentuated in the popular mind.

Here is the point which is of general human import instead of concern merely to professional philosophers. What about the security of values, of the things which are admirable, honorable, to be approved of and striven for? It is probably in consequence of the derogatory view held of practice that the question of the secure place of values in human experience is so seldom raised in connection with the problem of the relation of knowledge and practice. But upon any view concerning the status of action, the scope of the latter cannot be restricted to self-seeking acts, nor to those of a prudential aspect, nor in general to things of expediency and what are often termed "utilitarian" affairs. The maintenance and diffusion of intellectual values, of moral excellencies, the esthetically admirable, as well as the maintenance of order and decorum in human relations are dependent upon what men do.

Whether because of the emphasis of traditional religion upon salvation of the personal soul or for some other reason, there is a tendency to restrict the ultimate scope of morals to the reflex effect of conduct on one's self. Even utilitarianism, with all its seeming independence of traditional theology and its emphasis upon the general good as the criterion for judging conduct, insisted in its hedonistic psychology upon private pleasure as the motive for action. The idea that the stable and expanding institution of all things that make life worth while throughout all human relationships is the real object of *all* intelligent conduct is depressed from view by the current conception of morals as a special kind of action chiefly concerned with either the virtues or the enjoyments of individuals in their personal capacities. In changed form, we still retain the notion of a division of activity into two kinds having very different worths. The result is the depreciated meaning that has come to be attached to the very meaning of the "practical" and the useful. Instead of being extended to cover all forms of action by means of which all the values of life are extended and rendered more secure, including the diffusion of the fine arts and the cultivation of taste, the processes of education and all activities which are concerned with rendering human relationships more significant and worthy, the meaning of "practical" is limited to matters of ease, comfort, riches, bodily security and police order, possibly health, etc., things which in their isolation from other goods can only lay claim to restricted and narrow value. In consequence, these subjects are handed over to technical sciences and arts; they are no concern of "higher" interests which feel that no matter what happens to inferior goods in the vicissitudes of natural existence, the highest values are immutable characters of the ultimately real.

Our depreciatory attitude toward "practice" would be modified if we habitually thought of it in its most liberal sense, and if we surrendered our customary dualism between two separate kinds of value, one intrinsically higher and one inherently lower. We should regard practice as the only means (other than accident) by which whatever is judged to be honorable, admirable, approvable can be kept in concrete experienceable existence. In this connection the entire import of "morals" would be transformed. How much of the tendency to ignore permanent objective consequences in differences made in natural and social relations; and how much of the emphasis upon personal and internal motives and dispositions irrespective of what they objectively produce and sustain are products of the habitual depreciation of the worth of action in comparison with forms of mental processes, of thought and sentiment, which make no objective difference in things themselves?

It would be possible to argue (and, I think, with much justice) that failure to make action central in the search for such security as is humanly possible is a survival of the impotency of men in those stages of civilization when he had few means of regulating and utilizing the conditions upon which the occurrence of consequences depend. As long as man was unable by means of the arts of practice to direct the course of events, it was natural for him to seek an emotional substitute; in the absence of actual certainty in the midst of a precarious and hazardous world, men cultivated all sorts of things that would give them the *feeling* of certainty. And it is possible that, when not carried to an illusory point, the cultivation of the feeling gave man courage and confidence and enabled him to carry the burdens of life more successfully. But one could hardly seriously contend that this fact, if it be such, is one upon which to found a reasoned philosophy.

It is to the conception of philosophy that we come back. No mode of action can, as we have insisted, give anything approaching absolute certitude; it provides insurance but no assurance. Doing is always subject to peril, to the danger of frustration. When men began to reflect philosophically it seemed to them altogether too risky to leave the place of values at the mercy of acts the results of which are never sure. This precariousness might hold as far as empirical existence, existence in the sensible and phenomenal world, is concerned; but this very uncertainty seemed to render it the more needful that ideal goods should be shown to have, by means of knowledge of the most assured type, an indefeasible and inexpugnable position in the realm of the ultimately real. So at least we may imagine men to have reasoned. And to-day many persons find a peculiar consolation in the face of the unstable and dubious presence of values in actual experience by projecting a perfect form of good into a realm of essence, if not into a heaven beyond the earthly skies, wherein their authority, if not their existence, is wholly unshakeable.

Instead of asking how far this process is of that compensatory kind with which recent psychology has made us familiar, we are inquiring into the effect upon philosophy. It will not be denied, I suppose, that the chief aim of those philosophies which I have called classical, has been to show that the realities which are the objects of the highest and most necessary knowledge are also endowed with the values which correspond to our best aspirations, admirations and approvals. That, one may say, is the very heart of all traditional philosophic idealisms. There is a pathos, having its own nobility, in philosophies which think it their proper office to give an intellectual or cognitive certification to the ontological reality of the highest values. It is difficult for men to see desire and choice set earnestly upon the good and yet being frustrated, without their imagining a realm in which the good has come completely to its own, and is identified with a Reality in which resides all ultimate power. The failure and frustration of actual life is then attributed to the fact that this world is finite and phenomenal, sensible rather than real, or to the weakness of our finite apprehension, which cannot see that the discrepancy between existence and value is merely seeming, and that a fuller vision would behold partial evil an element in complete good. Thus the office of philosophy is to project by dialectic, resting supposedly upon self-evident premises, a realm in which the object of completest cognitive certitude is also one with the object of the heart's best aspiration. The fusion of the good and the true with unity and plenitude of Being thus becomes the goal of classic philosophy.

The situation would strike us as a curious one were it not so familiar. Practical activity is dismissed to a world of low grade reality. Desire is found only where something is lacking and hence its existence is a sign of imperfection of Being. Hence one must go to passionless reason to find perfect reality and complete certitude. But nevertheless the chief philosophic interest is to prove that the essential properties of the reality that is the object of pure knowledge are precisely those characteristics which have meaning in connection with affection, desire and choice. After degrading practical affairs in order to exalt knowledge, the chief task of knowledge turns out to be to demonstrate the absolutely assured and permanent reality of the values with which practical activity is concerned! Can we fail to see the irony in a situation wherein desire and emo-

tion are relegated to a position inferior in every way to that of knowledge, while at the same time the chief problem of that which is termed the highest and most perfect knowledge is taken to be the existence of evil—that is, of desires errant and frustrated?

The contradiction involved, however, is much more than a purely intellectual one—which if purely theoretical would be innocuously lacking in practical consequences. The thing which concerns all of us as human beings is precisely the greatest attainable security of values in concrete existence. The thought that the values which are unstable and wavering in the world in which we live are eternally secure in a higher realm (which reason demonstrates but which we cannot experience), that all the goods which are defeated here are triumphant there, may give consolation to the depressed. But it does not change the existential situation in the least. The separation that has been instituted between theory and practice, with its consequent substitution of cognitive quest for absolute assurance for practical endeavor to make the existence of good more secure in experience, has had the effect of distracting attention and diverting energy from a task whose performance would yield definite results.

The chief consideration in achieving concrete security of values lies in the perfecting of *methods* of action. Mere activity, blind striving, gets nothing forward. Regulation of conditions upon which results depend is possible only by doing, yet only by doing which has intelligent direction, which takes cognizance of conditions, observes relations of sequence, and which plans and executes in the light of this knowledge. The notion that thought, apart from action, can warrant complete certitude as to the status of supreme good, makes no contribution to the central problem of development of intelligent methods of regulation. It rather depresses and deadens effort in that direction. That is the chief indictment to be brought against the classic philosophic tradition. Its import raises the question of the relation which action sustains to knowledge in fact, and whether the quest for certainty by other means than those of intelligent action does not mark a baneful diversion of thought from its proper office. It raises the question whether mankind has not now achieved a sufficient degree of control of methods of knowing and of the arts of practical action so that a radical change in our conceptions of knowledge and practice is rendered both possible and necessary.

That knowing, as judged from the actual procedures of scientific inquiry, has completely abandoned in fact the traditional separation of knowing and doing, that the experimental procedure is one that installs doing as the heart of knowing, is a theme that will occupy our attention in later chapters. What would happen to philosophy if it wholeheartedly made a similar surrender? What would be its office if it ceased to deal with the problem of reality and knowledge at large? In effect, its function would be to facilitate the fruitful interaction of our cognitive beliefs, our beliefs resting upon the most dependable methods of inquiry, with our practical beliefs about the values, the ends and purposes, that should control human action in the things of large and liberal human import.

Such a view renounces the traditional notion that action is inherently inferior to knowledge and preference for the fixed over the changing; it involves the conviction that security attained by active control is to be more prized than certainty in theory. But it does not imply that action is higher and better than knowledge, and practice inherently superior to thought. Constant and effective interaction of knowledge and practice is something quite different from an exaltation of activity for its own sake. Action, when directed by knowledge, is method and means, not an end. The aim and end is the securer, freer and more widely shared embodiment of values in experience by means of that active control of objects which knowledge alone makes possible.[1]

From this point of view, the problem of philosophy concerns the *interaction* of our judgments about ends to be sought with knowledge of the means for achieving them. Just as in science the question of the advance of knowledge is the question of *what to do*, what experiments to perform, what apparatus to invent and use, what calculations to engage in, what branches of mathematics to employ or to per-fect, so *the* problem of practice is what do we need to *know*, how shall we obtain that knowledge and how shall we apply it?

It is an easy and altogether too common a habit to confuse a personal division of labor with an isolation of function and meaning. Human beings as individuals tend to devote themselves either to the practice of knowing or to the practice of a professional, business, social or esthetic art. Each takes the other half of the circle for granted. Theorists and practitioners, however, often indulge in unseemly wrangles as to the importance of their respective tasks. Then the personal difference of callings is hypostatized and made into an intrinsic difference between knowledge and practice.

If one looks at the history of knowledge, it is plain that at the beginning men tried to know because they had to do so in order to live. In the absence of that organic guidance given by their structure to other animals, man had to find out what he was about, and he could find out only by studying the environment which constituted the means, obstacles and results of his behavior. The desire for intellectual or cognitive understanding had no meaning except as a means of obtaining greater security as to the issues of action. Moreover, even when after the coming of leisure some men were enabled to adopt knowing as their special calling or profession, *merely* theoretical uncertainty continues to have no meaning.

This statement will arouse protest. But the reaction against the statement will turn out when examined to be due to the fact that it is so difficult to find a case of purely intellectual uncertainty, that is one upon which nothing hangs. Perhaps as near to it as we can come is in the familiar story of the Oriental potentate who declined to attend a horse race on the ground that it was already well known to him that one horse could run faster than another. His uncertainty as to which of several horses could outspeed the others may be said to have been purely intellectual. But also in the story nothing depended from it; no curiosity was aroused; no effort was put forth to satisfy the uncertainty. In other words, he did not care; it made no difference. And it is a strict truism that no one would care about *any* exclusively theoretical uncertainty or certainty. For by definition in being *exclusively* theoretical it is one which makes no difference anywhere.

Revulsion against this proposition is a tribute to the fact that actually the intellectual and the practical are so closely bound together. Hence when we imagine we are thinking of an exclusively theoretical doubt, we smuggle in unconsciously some consequence which hangs upon it. We think of uncertainty arising in the course of an inquiry; in this case, uncertainty until it is resolved blocks the progress of the inquiry—a distinctly practical affair, since it involves conclusions and the means of producing them. If we had no desires and no purposes, then, as sheer truism, one state of things would be as good as any other. Those who have set such store by the demonstration that Absolute Being already contains in eternal safety within itself all values, have had as their interest the fact that while the demonstration would make no difference in the concrete existence of these values—unless perhaps to weaken effort to generate and sustain them—it would make a difference in their own personal attitudes—in a feeling of comfort or of release from responsibility, the consciousness of a "moral holiday" in which some philosophers have found the distinction between morals and religion.

Such considerations point to the conclusion that the ultimate ground of the quest for cognitive certainty is the need for security in the results of action. Men readily persuade themselves that they are devoted to intellectual certainty for its own sake. Actually they want it because of its bearing on safeguarding what they desire and esteem. The need for protection and prosperity in action created the need for warranting the validity of intellectual beliefs.

After a distinctively intellectual class had arisen, a class having leisure and in a large degree protected against the more serious perils which afflict the mass of humanity, its members proceeded to glorify their own office. Since no amount of pains and care in action can ensure complete certainty, certainty in knowledge was worshipped as a substitute. In minor matters, those that are relatively technical, professional, "utilitarian," men continued to resort to improving their methods of operation in order to be surer of results. But in affairs of momentous value the requisite knowledge is hard to come by and the bettering of methods is a slow process to be realized only by the cooperative endeavor of many persons. The arts to be formed and developed are social arts; an individual by himself can do little to regulate the conditions which will render important values more secure, though with shrewdness and special knowledge he can do much to further his own peculiar aims—given a fair share of luck. So because of impatience and because, as Aristotle was given to pointing out, an individual is self-sufficient in that kind of thinking which involves no action, the ideal of a cognitive certainty and truth having no connection with practice, and prized because of its lack of connection, developed. The doctrine worked out practically so as to strengthen dependence upon authority and dogma in the things of highest value, while increase of specialized knowledge was relied upon in everyday, especially economic, affairs. Just as belief that a magical ceremony will regulate the growth of seeds to full harvest stifles the tendency to investigate natural causes and their workings, so acceptance of dogmatic rules as bases of conduct in education, morals and social matters, lessens the impetus to find out about the conditions which are involved in forming intelligent plans.

It is more or less of a commonplace to speak of the crisis which has been caused by the progress of the natural sciences in the last few centuries. The crisis is due, it is asserted, to the incompatibility between the conclusions of natural science about the world in which we live and the realm of higher values, of ideal and spiritual qualities, which get no support from natural science. The new science, it is said, has stripped the world of the qualities which made it beautiful and congenial to men; has deprived nature of all aspiration towards ends, all preference for accomplishing the good, and presented nature to us as a scene of indifferent physical particles acting according to mathematical and mechanical laws.

This effect of modern science has, it is notorious, set the main problems for modern philosophy. How is science to be accepted and yet the realm of values to be conserved? This question forms the philosophic version of the popular conflict of science and religion. Instead of being troubled about the inconsistency of astronomy with the older religious beliefs about heaven and the ascension of Christ, or the differences between the geological record and the account of creation in Genesis, philosophers have been troubled by the gap in kind which exists between the fundamental principles of the natural world and the reality of the values according to which mankind is to regulate its life.

Philosophers, therefore, set to work to mediate, to find some harmony behind the apparent discord. Everybody knows that the trend of modern philosophy has been to arrive at theories regarding the nature of the universe by means of theories regarding the nature of knowledge—a procedure which reverses the apparently more judicious method of the ancients in basing their conclusions about knowledge on the nature of the universe in which knowledge occurs. The "crisis" of which we have just been speaking accounts for the reversal.

Since science has made the trouble, the cure ought to be found in an examination of the nature of knowledge, of the conditions which make science possible. If the conditions of the possibility of knowledge can be shown to be of an ideal and rational character, then, so it has been thought, the loss of an idealistic cosmology in physics can be readily borne. The physical world can be surrendered to matter and mechanism, since we are assured that matter and mechanism have their foundation in immaterial mind. Such has been the characteristic course of modern spiritualistic philosophies since the time of Kant; indeed, since that of Descartes, who first felt the poignancy of the problem involved in reconciling the conclusions of science with traditional religious and moral beliefs.

It would presumably be taken as a sign of extreme naïveté, if not of callous insensitiveness, if one were to ask why all this ardor to reconcile the findings of natural science with the validity of values? Why should any increase of knowledge seem like a threat to what we prize, admire and approve? Why should we not proceed to employ our gains in science to improve our judgments about values, and to regulate our actions so as to make values more secure and more widely shared in existence?

I am willing to run the risk of charge of naïveté for the sake of making manifest the difference upon which we have been dwelling. If men had associated their ideas about values with practical activity instead of with cognition of antecedent Being, they would *not* have been troubled by the findings of science. They would have welcomed the latter. For anything ascertained about the structure of actually existing conditions would be a definite aid in making judgments about things to be prized and striven for more adequate, and would instruct us as to the means to be employed in realizing them. But according to the religious and philosophic tradition of Europe, the valid status of all the highest values, the good, true and beautiful, was bound up with their being properties of ultimate and supreme Being, namely, God. All went well as long as what passed for natural science gave no offence to this conception. Trouble began when science ceased to disclose in the objects of knowledge the possession of any such properties. Then some roundabout method had to be devised for substantiating them.

The point of the seemingly crass question which was asked is thus to elicit the radical difference made when the problem of values is seen to be connected with the problem of intelligent action. If the validity of beliefs and judgments about values is dependent upon the consequences of action undertaken in their behalf, if the assumed association of values with knowledge capable of being demonstrated apart from activity, is abandoned, then the problem of the intrinsic relation of science to value is wholly artificial. It is replaced by a group of practical problems: How shall we employ what we know to direct the formation of our beliefs about value and how shall we direct our practical behavior so as to test these beliefs and make possible better ones? The question is seen to be just what it has always been empirically: What shall we *do* to make objects having value more secure in existence? And we approach the answer to the problem with all the advantages given us by increase of knowledge of the conditions and relations under which this doing must proceed.

But for over two thousand years the weight of the most influential and authoritatively orthodox tradition of thought has been thrown into the opposite scale. It has been devoted to the problem of a purely cognitive certification (perhaps by revelation, perhaps by intuition, perhaps by reason) of the antecedent immutable reality of truth, beauty and goodness. As against such a doctrine, the conclusions of natural science constitute the materials of a serious problem. The appeal has been made to the Court of Knowledge and the verdict has been adverse. There are two rival systems that must have their respective claims adjusted. The crisis in contemporary culture, the confusions and conflicts in it, arise from a division of authority. Scientific inquiry seems to tell one thing, and traditional beliefs about ends and ideals that have authority over conduct tell us something quite different. The problem of reconciliation arises and persists for one reason only. As long as the notions persist that knowledge is a disclosure of reality, of reality prior to and independent of knowing, and that knowing is independent of a purpose to control the quality of experienced objects, the failure of natural science to disclose significant values in its objects will come as a shock. Those seriously concerned with the validity and authority of value will have a problem on their hands. As long as the notion persists that values are authentic and valid only on condition that they are properties of Being independent of human action, as long as it is supposed that their right to regulate action is dependent upon their being independent of action, so long there will be needed schemes to prove that values are, in spite of the findings of science, genuine and known qualifications of reality in itself. For men will not easily surrender all regulative guidance in action. If they are forbidden to find standards in the course of experience they will seek them somewhere else, if not in revelation, then in the deliverance of a reason that is above experience.

This then is the fundamental issue for present philosophy. Is the doctrine justified that knowledge is valid in the degree in which it is a revelation of antecedent existences or Being? Is the doctrine justified that regulative ends and purposes have validity only when they can be shown to be properties belonging to things, whether as existences or as essences, apart from human action? It is proposed to make another start. Desires, affections, preferences, needs and interests at least exist in human experience; they are characteristics of it. Knowledge about nature also exists. What does this knowledge imply and entail with respect to the guidance of our emotional and volitional life? How shall the latter lay hold of what is known in order to make it of service?

These latter questions do not seem to many thinkers to have the dignity that is attached to the traditional problems of philosophy. They are proximate questions, not ultimate. They do not concern Being and Knowledge "in themselves" and at large, but the state of existence at specified times and places and the state of affection, plans and purposes under concrete circumstances. They are not concerned with framing a general theory of reality, knowledge and value once for all, but with finding how authentic beliefs about existence as they currently exist can operate fruitfully and efficaciously in connection with the practical problems that are urgent in actual life.

In restricted and technical fields, men now proceed unhesitatingly along these lines. In technology and the arts of engineering and medicine, men do not think of operating in any other way. Increased knowledge of nature and its conditions does not raise the problem of validity of the value of health or of communication in general, although it may well make dubious the validity of certain conceptions men in the past have entertained about the nature of health and communication and the best ways of attaining these goods in fact.

In such matters, science has placed in our hands the means by which we can better judge our wants, and has aided in forming the instruments and operations by which to satisfy them. That the same sort of thing has not happened in the moral and distinctly humane arts is evident. Here is a problem which might well trouble philosophers.

Why have not the arts which deal with the wider, more generous, more distinctly humane values enjoyed the release and expansion which have accrued to the technical arts? Can it be seriously urged that it is because natural science has disclosed to us the kind of world which it has disclosed? It is easy to see that these disclosures are hostile to some beliefs about values which have been widely accepted, which have prestige, which have become deeply impregnated with sentiment, and which authoritative institutions as well as the emotion and inertia of men are slow to surrender. But this admission, which practically enforces itself, is far from excluding the formation of new beliefs about things to be honored and prized by men in their supreme loyalties of action. The difficulty in the road is a practical one, a social one, connected with institutions and the methods and aims of education, not with science nor with value. Under such circumstances the first problem for philosophy would seem to be to clear itself of further responsibility for the doctrine that the supreme issue is whether values have antecedent Being, while its further office is to make clear the revisions and reconstructions that have to be made in traditional judgments about values. Having done this, it would be in a position to undertake the more positive task of projecting ideas about values which might be the basis of a new integration of human conduct.

We come back to the fact that the genuine issue is not whether certain values, associated with traditions and institutions, have Being already (whether that of existence or of essence), but what concrete judgments we are to form about ends and means in the regulation of practical behavior. The emphasis which has been put upon the former question, the creation of dogmas about the way in which values are already real independently of what we do, dogmas which have appealed not in vain to philosophy for support, have naturally bred, in the face of the changed character of science, confusion, irresolution and numbness of will. If men had been educated to think about broader humane values as they have now learned to think about matters which fall within the scope of technical arts, our whole present situation would be very different. The attention which has gone to achieving a purely theoretical certainty with respect to them would have been devoted to perfecting the arts by which they are to be judged and striven for.

Indulge for a moment in an imaginative flight. Suppose that men had been systematically educated in the belief that the existence of values can cease to be accidental, narrow and precarious only by human activity directed by the best available knowledge. Suppose also men had been systematically educated to believe that the important thing is not to get themselves personally "right" in relation to the antecedent author and guarantor of these values, but to form their judgments and carry on their activity on the basis of public, objective and shared consequences. Imagine these things and then imagine what the present situation might be.

The suppositions are speculative. But they serve to indicate the significance of the one point to which this chapter is devoted. The method and conclusions of science have without doubt invaded many cherished beliefs about the things held most dear. The resulting clash constitutes a genuine cultural crisis. But it is a crisis in culture, a social crisis, historical and temporal in character. It is not a problem in the adjustment of properties of reality to one another. And yet modern philosophy has chosen for the most part to treat it as a question of how the realities assumed to be the object of science can have the mathematical and mechanistic properties assigned to them in natural science, while nevertheless the realm of ultimate reality can be characterized by qualities termed ideal and spiritual. The cultural problem is one of definite criticisms to be made and of readjustments to be accomplished. Philosophy which is willing to abandon its supposed task of knowing ultimate reality and to devote itself to a proximate human office might be of great help in such a task. It may be doubted whether it can indefinitely pursue the task of trying to show that the results of science when they are *properly* interpreted do not mean what they seem to say, or of proving, by means of an examination of possibilities and limits of knowledge, that after all they rest upon a foundation congruous with traditional beliefs about values.

Since the root of the traditional conception of philosophy is the separation that has been made between knowledge and action, between theory and practice, it is to the problem of this separation that we are to give attention. Our main attempt will be to show how the actual procedures of knowledge, interpreted after the pattern formed by experimental inquiry, cancel the isolation of knowledge from overt action. Before engaging in this attempt, we shall in the next chapter show the extent to which modern philosophy has been dominated by effort to adjust to each other two systems of belief, one relating to the objects of knowledge and the other to objects of ideal value.

NOTES

[LW 4:21–39.]

1. In reaction against the age-long depreciation of practice in behalf of contemplative knowledge, there is a temptation simply to turn things upside down. But the essence of pragmatic instrumentalism is to conceive of *both* knowledge and practice as means of making goods—excellencies of all kinds—secure in experienced existence.

PART 3

Evolutionary Naturalism

The criticisms made upon that vital but still unformed movement variously termed radical empiricism, pragmatism, humanism, functionalism, according as one or another aspect of it is uppermost, have left me with a conviction that the *fundamental* difference is not so much in matters overtly discussed as in a presupposition that remains tacit: a presupposition as to what experience is and means. To do my little part in clearing up the confusion, I shall try to make my own presupposition explicit. The object of this paper is, then, to set forth what I understand to be the postulate and the criterion of *immediate empiricism*.[2]

Immediate empiricism postulates that things—anything, everything, in the ordinary or non-technical use of the term "thing"—are what they are experienced as. Hence, if one wishes to describe anything truly, his task is to tell what it is experienced as being. If it is a horse that is to be described, or the *equus* that is to be defined, then must the horse-trader, or the jockey, or the timid family man who wants a "safe driver," or the zoologist or the paleontologist tell us what the horse is which is experienced. If these accounts turn out different in some respects, as well as congruous in others, this is no reason for assuming the content of one to be exclusively "real," and that of others to be "phenomenal"; for each account of what is experienced will manifest that it is the account *of* the horse-dealer, or *of* the zoologist, and hence will give the conditions requisite for understanding the differences as well as the agreements of the various accounts. And the principle varies not a whit if we bring in the psychologist's horse, the logician's horse or the metaphysician's horse.

In each case, the nub of the question is, *what sort of experience* is denoted or indicated: a concrete and determinate experience, varying, when it varies, in specific real elements, and agreeing, when it agrees, in specific real elements, so that we have a contrast, not between *a* Reality, and various approximations to, or phenomenal representations of Reality, but between different reals of experience. And the reader is begged to bear in mind that from this standpoint, when "an experience" or "some sort of experience" is referred to, "some thing" or "some sort of thing" is always meant.

The Postulate of Immediate Empiricism[1]

(1905)

Now, this statement that things are what they are experienced to be is usually translated into the statement that things (or, ultimately, Reality, Being) *are* only and just what they are *known* to be or that things are, or Reality *is*, what it is for a conscious knower—whether the knower be conceived primarily as a perceiver or as a thinker being a further and secondary question. This is the root-paralogism of all idealisms, whether subjective or objective, psychological or epistemological. By our postulate, things are what they are experienced to be; and, unless knowing is the sole and only genuine mode of experiencing, it is fallacious to say that Reality is just and exclusively what it is or would be to an all-competent all-knower; or even that it *is*, relatively and piecemeal, what it is to a finite and partial knower. Or, put more positively, knowing is one mode of experiencing, and the primary philosophic demand (from the standpoint of immediatism) is to find out *what* sort of an experience knowing is—or, concretely how things are experienced when they are experienced *as* known things.[3] By concretely is meant, obviously enough (among other things), such an account of the experience of things as known that will bring out the characteristic traits and distinctions they possess as things of a knowing experience, as compared with things experienced aesthetically, or morally, or economically, or technologically. To assume that, because from the *standpoint of the knowledge experience* things *are* what they are known to be, therefore, metaphysically, absolutely, without qualification, everything in its reality (as distinct from its "appearance," or phenomenal occurrence) is what a knower would find it to be, is, from the immediatist's standpoint, if not the root of all philosophic evil, at least one of its main roots. For this leaves out of account what the knowledge standpoint is itself *experienced as*.

I start and am flustered by a noise heard. Empirically, that noise is fearsome; it *really* is, not merely phenomenally or subjectively so. That *is what* it is experienced as being. But, when I experience the noise as a *known* thing, I find it to be innocent of harm. It is the tapping of a shade against the window, owing to movements of the wind. The experience has

changed; that is, the thing experienced has changed—not that an unreality has given place to a reality, nor that some transcendental (unexperienced) Reality has changed,[4] not that truth has changed, but just and only the concrete reality experienced has changed. I now feel ashamed of my fright; and the noise as fearsome is changed to noise as a wind-curtain fact, and hence practically indifferent to my welfare. This is a change of experienced existence effected through the medium of cognition. The content of the latter experience cognitively regarded is doubtless *truer* than the content of the earlier; but it is in no sense more real. To call it truer, moreover, must, from the empirical standpoint, mean a concrete *difference* in actual things experienced.[5] Again, in many cases, only in retrospect is the prior experience cognitionally regarded at all. In such cases, it is only in regard to contrasted content *in* a subsequent experience that the determination "truer" has force.

Perhaps some reader may now object that as matter of fact the entire experience is cognitive, but that the earlier parts of it are only imperfectly so, resulting in a phenomenon that is not real; while the latter part, being a more complete cognition, results in what is relatively, at least, more real.[6] In short, a critic may say that, when I was frightened by the noise, I *knew* I was frightened; otherwise there would have been no experience at all. At this point, it is necessary to make a distinction so simple and yet so all-fundamental that I am afraid the reader will be inclined to pooh-pooh it away as a mere verbal distinction. But to see that to the empiricist this distinction is not verbal, but genuine, is the precondition of any understanding of him. The immediatist must, by his postulate, ask what is the fright experienced *as*. Is what is actually experienced, I-know-I-am-frightened, or I-*am*-frightened? I see absolutely no reason for claiming that the experience *must* be described by the former phrase. In all probability (and all the empiricist logically needs is just one case of this sort) the experience is simply and just of fright-at-the-noise. Later one may (or may not) have an experience describable *as* I-know-I-am- (or-was) and improperly or properly, frightened. But this is a different experience—that is, a different *thing*. And if the critic goes on to urge that the person "*really*" must have known that he was frightened, I can only point out that the critic is shifting the venue. He may be right, but, if so, it is only because the "really" is something not concretely experienced (whose nature accordingly is the critic's business); and this is to depart from the empiricist's point of view, to attribute to him a postulate he expressly repudiates.

The material point may come out more clearly if I say that we must make a distinction between a thing as *cognitive*, and one as *cognized*.[7] I should define a cognitive experience as one that has certain bearings or implications which induce and fulfill themselves in a subsequent experience in which the relevant thing is experienced *as* cognized, *as* a known object, and is thereby transformed, or reorganized. The fright-at-the-noise in the case cited is obviously *cognitive*, in this sense. By description, it induces an investigation or inquiry in which both noise and fright are objectively stated or presented—the noise as a shade-wind fact, the fright as an organic reaction to a sudden acoustic stimulus, a reaction that under the given circumstances was useless or even detrimental, a maladaptation. Now, pretty much all of experience is of this sort (the "is" meaning, of course, is experienced *as*), and the empiricist is false to his principle if he does not duly note this fact.[8] But he is equally false to his principle if he permits himself to be confused as to the concrete differences in the two things experienced.

There are two little words through explication of which the empiricist's position may be brought out—"*as*" and "*that*." We may express his presupposition by saying that things are what they are experienced *as* being; or that to give a just account of anything is to tell what *that* thing is experienced to be. By these words I want to indicate the absolute, final, irreducible and inexpugnable concrete *quale* which everything experienced not so much *has* as *is*. To grasp this aspect of empiricism is to see what the empiricist means by objectivity, by the element of control. Suppose we take, as a crucial case for the empiricist, an out and out illusion, say of Zöllner's lines. These are experienced as convergent; they are "truly" paral-

lel. If things are what they are experienced as being, how can the distinction be drawn between illusion and the true state of the case? There is no answer to this question except by sticking to the fact that the experience of the lines as divergent is a concrete qualitative thing or *that*. It is *that* experience which it is, and no other. And if the reader rebels at the iteration of such obvious tautology, I can only reiterate that the realization of the *meaning* of this tautology is the key to the whole question of the objectivity of experience, as that stands to the empiricist. The lines of *that* experience *are* divergent: not merely *seem* so. The question of truth is not as to whether Being or Non-Being, Reality or mere Appearance, is experienced, but as to the *worth* of a certain concretely experienced thing. The only way of passing upon this question is by sticking in the most uncompromising fashion to *that* experience as real. *That* experience is that two lines with certain cross-hatchings are apprehended as convergent; only by taking that experience as real and as fully real, is there any basis for or way of going to an experienced knowledge that the lines are parallel. It is in the concrete thing *as experienced* that all the grounds and clues to its own intellectual or logical rectification are contained. It is because this thing, afterwards adjudged false, is a concrete *that*, that it develops into a corrected experience (that is, experience of a corrected thing—we reform things just as we reform ourselves or a bad boy) whose full content is not a whit more real, but which is true or truer.[9]

If *any* experience, then a *determinate* experience; and this determinateness is the only, and is the adequate, principle of control, or "objectivity." The experience may be of the vaguest sort. I may not see any thing which I can identify as a familiar object—a table, a chair, etc. It may be dark; I may have only the vaguest impression that there is something which looks like a table. Or I may be completely befogged and confused, as when one rises quickly from sleep in a pitch-dark room. But this vagueness, this doubtfulness, this confusion is the thing experienced, and, *qua* real, is as "good" a reality as the self-luminous vision of an Absolute. It is not just vagueness, doubtfulness, confusion, at large or in general.

It is *this* vagueness, and no other; absolutely unique, absolutely what *it* is.[10] Whatever gain in clearness, in fullness, in trueness of content is experienced must grow out of some element in the experience of *this* experienced *as* what it is. To return to the illusion: If the experience of the lines as convergent is illusory, it is because of some elements in the thing as experienced, not because of something defined in terms of externality to this particular experience. If the illusoriness can be detected, it is because the thing experienced is real, having within its experienced reality elements whose *own mutual* tension effects its reconstruction. Taken concretely, the experience of convergent lines contains within itself the elements of the transformation of its own content. It is *this* thing, and not some separate truth, that clamors for its own reform. There is, then, from the empiricist's point of view, no need to search for some aboriginal *that* to which all successive experiences are attached, and which is somehow thereby undergoing continuous change. Experience is always of *thats*; and the most comprehensive and inclusive experience of the universe that the philosopher himself can obtain is the experience of a characteristic *that*. From the empiricist's point of view, this is as true of the exhaustive and complete insight of a hypothetical all-knower as of the vague, blind experience of the awakened sleeper. As reals, they stand on the same level. As trues, the latter has by definition the better of it; but if this insight is in any way the truth of the blind awakening, it is because the latter has, in its *own* determinate *quale*, elements of real continuity with the former; it is, *ex hypothesi*, transformable through a series of experienced reals without break of continuity, into the absolute thought-experience. There is no need of logical manipulation to effect the transformation, nor *could* any logical consideration effect it. If effected at all it is just by immediate experiences, each of which is just as real (no more, no less) as either of the two terms between which they lie. Such, at least, is the meaning of the empiricist's contention. So, when he talks of experience, he does not mean some grandiose, remote affair that is cast like a net around a succession of fleeting experiences; he does not mean an indefinite total, comprehensive experience which somehow engirdles an endless flux; he means that *things* are what they are experienced to be, and that every experience is *some* thing.

From the postulate of empiricism, then (or, what is the same thing, from a *general* consideration of the concept of experience), nothing can be deduced, not a single philosophical proposition.[11] The reader may hence conclude that all this just comes to the truism that experience is experience, or is what it is. If one attempts to draw conclusions from the bare concept of experience, the reader is quite right. But the real significance of the principle is that of a method of philosophical analysis— a method identical in kind (but differing in problem and hence in operation) with that of the scientist. If you wish to find out what subjective, objective, physical, mental, cosmic, psychic, cause, substance, purpose, activity, evil, being, quality—any philosophic term, in short—means, go to experience and see what the thing is experienced *as*.

Such a method is not spectacular; it permits of no offhand demonstrations of God, freedom, immortality, nor of the exclusive reality of matter, or ideas, or consciousness, etc. But it supplies a way of telling what all these terms mean. It may seem insignificant, or chillingly disappointing, but only upon condition that it be not worked. Philosophic conceptions have, I believe, outlived their usefulness considered as stimulants to emotion, or as a species of sanctions; and a larger, more fruitful and more valuable career awaits them considered as specifically experienced meanings.

[NOTE: The reception of this essay proved that I was unreasonably sanguine in thinking that the foot-note of warning, appended to the title, would forfend radical misapprehension. I see now that it was unreasonable to expect that the word "immediate" in a philosophic writing could be generally understood to apply to anything except *knowledge*, even though the body of the essay is a protest against such limitation. But I venture to repeat that the essay is not a denial of the necessity of "mediation," or reflection, in knowledge, but is an assertion that the inferential factor must *exist*, or must occur, and that all existence is direct and vital, so that philosophy can pass upon its nature—as upon the nature of all of the rest of its subject-matter—only by first ascertaining what it exists or occurs as.

I venture to repeat also another statement of the text: I do not mean by "immediate experience" any aboriginal stuff out of which things are evolved, but I use the term to indicate the necessity of employing in philosophy the direct descriptive method that has now made its way in all the natural sciences, with such modifications, of course, as the subject itself entails.

There is nothing in the text to imply that things exist in experience atomically or in isolation. When it is said that a thing as cognized is *different* from an earlier non-cognitionally experienced thing, the saying no more implies lack of continuity between the things, than the obvious remark that a seed is different from a flower or a leaf denies their continuity. The amount and kind of continuity or discreteness that exists is to be discovered by recurring to what actually occurs in experience.

Finally, there is nothing in the text that denies the existence of things temporally prior to human experiencing of them. Indeed, I should think it fairly obvious that we experience most things *as* temporally prior to our experiencing of them. The import of the article is to the effect that we are not entitled to draw philosophic (as distinct from scientific) conclusions as to the meaning of prior temporal existence till we have ascertained what it is to experience a thing as past. These four disclaimers cover, I think, all the misapprehensions disclosed in the four or five controversial articles (noted below) that the original essay evoked. One of these articles (that of Professor Woodbridge), raised a point of fact, holding that cognitional experience tells us, without alteration, just what the things of other types of experience are, and in that sense transcends other experiences. This is too fundamental an issue to discuss in a note, and I content myself with remarking that with respect to it, the bearing of the article is that the issue must be settled by a careful descriptive survey of things as experienced, to see whether modifications do not occur in existences when they are experienced *as* known; *i.e.*, as true or false in char-

acter. The reader interested in following up this discussion is referred to the following articles: Vol. II of the *Journal of Philosophy, Psychology and Scientific Methods*, two articles by Bakewell, p. 520 and p. 687; one by Bode, p. 658; one by Woodbridge, p. 573; Vol. III of the same Journal, by Leighton, p. 174.]

NOTES

[First published in *Journal of Philosophy, Psychology and Scientific Methods* 2 (1905): 393–99. Reprinted in *The Influence of Darwin on Philosophy* (New York: Henry Holt and Co., 1910), pp. 226–41. MW 3:158–67.]

1. Reprinted, with very slight change, from the *Journal of Philosophy, Psychology and Scientific Methods*, Vol. II, No. 15, July, 1905.

2. All labels are, of course, obnoxious and misleading. I hope, however, the term will be taken by the reader in the sense in which it is forthwith explained, and not in some more usual and familiar sense. Empiricism, as herein used, is as antipodal to sensationalistic empiricism, as it is to transcendentalism, and for the same reason. Both of these systems fall back on something which is defined in non-directly-experienced terms in order to justify that which is directly experienced. Hence I have criticized such empiricism (*Philosophical Review*, Vol. XI, No. 4, p. 364 [*Middle Works* 2:31]) as essentially absolutistic in character; and also (*Studies in Logical Theory*, pp. 30, 58 [*Middle Works* 2:322, 344]) as an attempt to build up experience in terms of certain methodological checks and cues of attaining *certainty*.

3. I hope the reader will not therefore assume that from the empiricist's standpoint knowledge is of small worth or import. On the contrary, from the empiricist's standpoint it has *all* the worth which it is concretely experienced as possessing—which is simply tremendous. But the exact *nature* of this worth is a thing to be found out in describing what we mean by experiencing objects as known—the actual differences made or found in experience.

4. Since the non-empiricist believes in things-in-themselves (which he may term "atoms," "sensations," transcendental unities, *a priori* concepts, *an* absolute experience, or whatever), and since he finds that the empiricist makes much of change (as he must, since change is continuously experienced) he assumes that the empiricist means *his own* non-empirical Realities are in continual flux, and he naturally shudders at having his divinities so violently treated. But, once recognize that the empiricist doesn't have any such Realities at all, and the entire problem of the relation of change to reality takes a very different aspect.

5. It would lead us aside from the point to try to tell just what is the nature of the experienced difference we call truth. Professor James's recent articles may well be consulted. The point to bear in mind here is just what sort of a thing the empiricist must mean by true, or truer (the noun Truth is, of course, a generic name for all cases of "Trues"). The adequacy of any particular account is not a matter to be settled by general reasoning, but by finding out what sort of an experience the truth-experience actually is.

6. I say "relatively," because the transcendentalist still holds that finally the cognition is imperfect, giving us only some symbol or phenomenon of Reality (which *is* only in the Absolute or in some Thing-in-Itself)—otherwise the curtain-wind fact would have as much ontological reality as the existence of the Absolute itself: a conclusion at which the non-empiricist perhorresces, for no reason obvious to me—save that it would put an end to his transcendentalism.

7. In general, I think the distinction between *-ive* and *-ed* one of the most fundamental of philosophic distinctions, and one of the most neglected. The same holds of *-tion* and *-ing*.

8. What is criticized, now as "geneticism" (if I may coin the word) and now as "pragmatism" is, in its truth, just the fact that the empiricist does take account of the experienced "drift, occasion and contexture" of things experienced—to use Hobbes's phrase.

9. Perhaps the point would be clearer if expressed in this way: Except as subsequent estimates of *worth* are introduced, "real" means only existent. The eulogistic connotation that makes the term Reality equivalent to *true* or *genuine* being has great pragmatic significance, but its confusion with reality as existence is the point aimed at in the above paragraph.

10. One does not so easily escape medieval Realism as one thinks. Either every experienced thing has its own determinateness, its own unsubstitutable, unredeemable reality, or else "generals" *are* separate existences after all.

11. Excepting, of course, some negative ones. One could say that certain views are certainly *not* true, because, by hypothesis, they refer to nonentities, *i.e.*, non-empiricals. But even here the empiricist must go slowly. From his own standpoint, even the most professedly transcendental statements are, after all, real as experiences, and hence negotiate some transaction with facts. For this reason, he cannot, in theory, reject them *in toto*, but has to show concretely how they arose and how they are to be corrected. In a word, his logical relationship to statements that profess to relate to things-in-themselves, unknowables, inexperienced substances, etc., is precisely that of the psychologist to the Zöllner lines.

It is hard to judge how far it is advisable to enter into controversial discussion in reply to criticism. Observation of its usual course tends to the conclusion that the time devoted to it might ordinarily better be spent upon independent analysis or construction. And if one's original writings, put forth without controversial entanglements, are so awkwardly phrased as to provoke serious misunderstanding, why give the philosophic brethren additional cause for offense? But "Silence gives assent," and may propagate misunderstanding in minds hitherto innocent. Moreover, Professor McGilvary's misconception of my position, as he sets it forth in the May number of the *Philosophical Review*, under the caption of "Pure Experience and Reality" (Vol. XVI, pp. 266–84), is so extreme that, to some extent, it may be categorically dealt with.

1. He refers to me as among those who hold that the "reality of anything is the reality it has as experienced and *only when experienced*" (p. 266, italics mine); and again "No *contemporaneous* experience, *no* reality" (p. 274). I do not hold, never have held, and, to the best of my knowledge and belief, have never intimated nor implied any such views. That experience means experienced things; that all philosophic conclusions are to be drawn from the things as experienced (not from the concept of experience, which I have held to be purely empty excepting as indicating a *method* of procedure and recourse); that things are what they are experienced *as*, or experienced *to be*, I have asserted. The "only when" in the quotation has no standing in anything I have written. And books, chairs, geological ages, etc., are experienced, so far as I am aware, *as* existent at other times than the moments *when* they are experienced. Does not Professor McGilvary *experience* them *as* that sort of thing, *to be* that sort of thing?

2. The question raised in the paper upon which Professor McGilvary bases his criticism is (granting the existence of things prior to experiencing organisms), "What is the better index, for philosophy, of reality: its earlier or its later form?" (These words are in the original text and are quoted by Professor McGilvary himself.) That is to say, shall philosophy build its interpretation of reality upon reality as exis-

Pure Experience and Reality: A Disclaimer

(1907)

tent prior to its experience, or upon the reality of *that as now experienced*? The answer given is in the latter sense that the earlier (say Eozoic geological age) is experienced as the condition of a present experience which expresses reality more adequately (for philosophy, not for science) than the conception of it as merely pre-existent. This may be a false conception, but it is a totally different idea from that to which Professor McGilvary devotes much poetry, eloquence, and humor. How could it be a *condition* of the present experience unless it existed prior in time? But Professor McGilvary is so well aware that the prior existence of one thing to another thing in time leaves entirely untouched the question of the nature of the reality of time, and hence of the reality, for philosophy, of the temporal sequence, that I do not understand the satisfaction he gets from writing as if I were totally ignorant of this rudimentary distinction. Moreover, if the doctrine be false, it is still one that Professor McGilvary himself holds. He writes: "No experience somewhere and somewhen, no meaningful reality anywhere and anytime. *This is the truth which is contained in Professor Dewey's contention*" (p. 274, italics mine). I should say it was; the only truth for which I contended. My enjoyment, accordingly, of the ludicrous position in which Professor McGilvary places the "pure empiricist," with me as *corpus vile*, is heightened by the fact, that in view of his expressed agreement, I can stand the joke—if he can.

3. Professor McGilvary quotes from me: "The present experience of the veriest unenlightened ditch-digger does philosophic justice to the earlier reality [whose existence he charges me with denying!] in a way which the scientific statement does not and cannot; *cannot*, that is, *as formulated knowledge*" (p. 273, italics mine). Unfortunately for his logic (though doubtless fortunately for his humor and poetic metaphor), he fails to quote, or take into account, the next sentence, which runs as follows: "As itself vital or direct experience . . . the latter is more valuable and is truer in the sense of worth more for other interpretations." The point at issue is not in the least whether the experience *creates* the things known, but whether the scientific formula as such or the

direct, vital experience as such is, for the philosopher, a better index of the nature of reality, it being expressly declared that a direct experience which *includes* the scientific formulation is better than one which does not. When Professor McGilvary himself comes out strongly for the *representative* character of knowledge, he seems to be again in favor of my contention that a direct experience is a better index for philosophy than the knowledge phase as such of an experience. But perhaps only the erring empiricist holds that direct is better than merely representative experience. If so, I am still content to err; and shall abide by my conviction that an experience in which a symbol is experienced in its fulfillment or embodiment, is better than one in which the symbol alone is experienced, just as it is also better than one which remains as yet unrepresentative. And there are certain echoes from one Hegel, who held that the mediation finds its fruition in a new immediacy which I hope still also reaches the ears of Professor McGilvary.

4. Professor McGilvary refers to *Studies in Logical Theory* as follows: "In that work he [*i.e.*, the present writer] insisted that the *object of thought*, when it has emerged from the experience of stress and strain and appears in a subsequent tranquil experience as the result of pragmatic adjustment, must not be read back anachronistically into the time preceding the adjustment. The reader was therefore left to infer that no *truth* made out by intellectual labor is *to be held valid* of anything real that may have existed before that labor was ended" (p. 267, italics mine).

The reader was not only left to "infer" this, but the reader who did infer it was "left." The point of the contention to which Professor McGilvary refers is the anachronism of referring back the "object of *thought*" (as characteristically a *thought* object) to reality prior to the thinking. The old-fashioned empiricist held that thinking has no forms or modes of its own at all, being merely a complex of sensations or a disintegration of a prior complex; the epistemological idealist held that such forms or categories not only exist but are characteristic of reality as such, which therefore is to be conceived, philosophically, as a system of thought-relations; that thought as such is constitutive of reality as such. Now one object of the *Studies* was to insist, as against the sensationalist, that thinking does determine a characteristic objective situation, and, *against the idealist*, that it determines an object in process, through doubt and inquiry, of *redetermination*. Its purport, in short, is that all thinking is reflective, and that it is constitutive not of reality *per se* or at large, but only of such reality as has been reorganized through specific thinking, the reorganization finally taking place through *an action* in which the thinking terminates and by which it is tested. Thought is thus conceived of as a control-phenomenon biological in origin, humane, practical, or moral in import, involving in its issue real transformation of real reality. Hence the text abounds in assertions of reality existing prior to thinking, prior to coming to know, which, through the organic issue of thinking in experimental action, is reconstructed.

That it should be possible for a thinker of Professor McGilvary's equipment—to say nothing of his command of wit and of the poetry of picturesque and catastrophic metaphor—completely to invert the sense of my writing, even after its obscure and awkward character is taken into account, would be finally discouraging, were it not that I am buoyed up by three considerations. In the first place, he holds that knowledge is by subjective images which acquire a "transsubjective reference" to the realities to which they subjectively mean to refer,—the connection of the intention with the image, unfortunately, not being elucidated. Hence it would not be surprising if an image of my logical beliefs should spring up in Professor McGilvary's subjective resort for such creatures which should be totally unlike its object. If such an "image" were

of great aesthetic brilliancy and of an unusually vivacious quality, it might easily impose upon him. Or the image might get switched off during its "transsubjective" travels and finally light upon my devoted head, though originally intended, say, for some sensationalistic idealist. It would be obviously unjust to hold Professor McGilvary responsible for such a *faux pas* on the part of his image after it left him.

Again, thinkers who have got habituated to a mode of psychological analysis, which, in the interests of psychology, resolves experience into certain transient acts and states of a person, into sensations and images of a psychophysical organism, may forget that others employ the term experience in a more vital, concrete, and pregnant sense. Hence, when others talk about experience, it is assumed that this means the psychological abstract which it means to the critic. Finally, modern philosophy has been built up on the foundations of epistemology; that is, it has held that reality is to be reached by the philosopher on the basis of an analysis of the procedure of knowledge. Hence, when a writer endeavors to take naïvely a frankly naturalistic, biological, and moral attitude, and to account for knowledge on the basis of the place it occupies in such a reality, he is treated as if his philosophy were only, after all, just another kind of epistemology.

NOTES

[First published in *Philosophical Review* 16 (1907): 419–22. For Evander Bradley McGilvary's article to which this is a reply, see MW 4:295–313, "Pure Experience and Reality," *Philosophical Review* 16 (1907): 266–84. MW 4:120–24.]

Does Reality Possess Practical Character?

(1908)

I

Recently I have had an experience which, insignificant in itself, seems to mean something as an index-figure of the present philosophic situation. In a criticism of the neo-Kantian conception that *a priori* functions of thought are necessary to constitute knowledge, it became relevant to deny its underlying postulate: viz., the existence of anything properly called mental states or subjective impressions precedent to all objective recognitions, and requiring accordingly some transcendental function to order them into a world of stable and consistent reference. It was argued that such so-called original mental data are in truth turning points of the readjustment, or making over, through a state of incompatibility and shock, of objective affairs. This doctrine was met by the cry of "subjectivism"! It had seemed to its author to be a criticism, on grounds at once naturalistic and ethical, of the ground proposition of subjectivism. Why this diversity of interpretations? So far as the writer can judge, it is due to the fact that certain things characteristic of practical life, such things as lack and need, conflict and clash, desire and effort, loss and satisfaction, had been frankly referred to reality; and to the further fact that the function and structure of knowing were systematically connected with these practical features. These conceptions are doubtless radical enough; the latter was perhaps more or less revolutionary. The probability, the antecedent probability, was that hostile critics would have easy work in pointing out specific errors of fact and interpretation. But no: the simpler, the more effective method, was to dismiss the whole thing as anarchic subjectivism.

This was and remains food for thought. I have been able to find but one explanation: In current philosophy, everything of a practical nature is regarded as "merely" personal, and the "merely" has the force of denying legitimate standing in the court of cosmic jurisdiction. This conception seems to me the great and the ignored assumption in contemporary philosophy: many who might shrink from the doctrine if expressly formulated hang desperately to its implications. Yet surely as an underlying assumption, it is sheer prejudice, a culture-survival. If we suppose the traditions of philosophic discussion wiped out and philosophy starting afresh from the most active tendencies of to-day,—those striving in social life, in science, in literature, and art,—one can hardly imagine any philosophic view springing up and gaining credence, which did not give large place, in its scheme of things, to the practical and personal, and to them without employing disparaging terms, such as phenomenal, merely subjective, and so on. Why, putting it mildly, should what gives tragedy, comedy, and poignancy to life, be excluded from things? Doubtless, what we call life, what we take to be genuinely vital, is not all of things, but it is a part of things; and is that part which counts most with the philosopher—unless he has quite parted with his ancient dignity of lover of wisdom. What becomes of philosophy so far as humane and liberal interests are concerned, if, in an age when the person and the personal loom large in politics, industry, religion, art, and science, it contents itself with this parrot cry of phenomenalism, whenever the personal comes into view? When science is carried by the idea of evolution into introducing into the world the principles of initiative, variation, struggle, and selection; and when social forces have driven into bankruptcy absolutistic and static dogmas as authorities for the conduct of life, it is trifling for philosophy to decline to look the situation in the face. The relegation, as matter of course, of need, of stress and strain, strife and satisfaction, to the merely personal and the merely personal to the limbo of something which is neither flesh, fowl, nor good red herring, seems the thoughtless rehearsal of ancestral prejudice.

When we get beyond the echoing of tradition, the sticking point seems to be the relation of knowledge to the practical function of things. Let reality be in itself as "practical" as you please, but let not this practical character lay profane hands on the ark of truth. Every new mode of interpreting life—every new gospel—is met with the charge of antinomianism. An imagination bound by custom apprehends the restrictions that are relaxed and the checks that are removed, but not the inevitable responsibilities and tests that the new idea brings in. And so the conception that knowledge makes a difference in and to things looks licentious to those who fail to see that the necessity of doing well this business, of making the right difference puts intelligence under bonds it never yet has known: most of all in philosophy, the most gayly irresponsible of the procedures, and the most irresponsively sullen, of the historic fruits of intelligence.

Why should the idea that knowledge makes a difference to and in things be antecedently objectionable? If one is already committed to a belief that Reality is neatly and finally tied up in a packet without loose ends, unfinished issues or new departures, one would object to knowledge making a difference just as one would object to any other impertinent obtruder. But if one believes that the world itself is in transformation, why should the notion that knowledge is the most important mode of its modification and the only organ of its guidance be *a priori* obnoxious?

There is, I think, no answer save that the theory of knowledge has been systematically built up on the notion of a static universe, so that even those who are perfectly free in accepting the lessons of physics and biology concerning moving energy and evolution, and of history concerning the constant transformation of man's affairs (science included), retain an unquestioning belief in a theory of knowledge which is out of any possible harmony with their own theory of the matters to be known. Modern epistemology, having created the idea that the way to frame right conceptions is to analyze knowledge, has strengthened this view. For it at once leads to the view that realities must themselves have a theoretic and intellectual complexion—not a practical one. This view is naturally congenial to idealists; but that realists should so readily play into the hands of idealists by asserting what, on the basis of a formal theory of knowledge, realities must be, instead of accepting the guidance of things in divining what knowledge *is*, is an anomaly so striking as to support the view that the notion of static reality has taken its last stand in ideas about knowledge. Take, for example, the most striking, because the extreme case—knowledge of a past event. It is absurd to suppose that knowledge makes a difference to the final or appropriate content of knowledge:

to the subject-matter which fulfils the requirements of knowing. In this case, it would get in its own way and trip itself up in endless regress. But it seems the very superstition of intellectualism to suppose that this fact about knowledge can decide what is the nature of that reference to the past which when rightly made is final. No doctrine about knowledge can hinder the belief—if there be sufficient specific evidence for it—that what we know as past may be something which has *irretrievably* undergone just the difference which knowledge makes.

Now arguments against pragmatism—by which I mean the doctrine that reality possesses practical character and that this character is most efficaciously expressed in the function of intelligence[1]—seem to fall blandly into this fallacy. They assume that to hold that knowledge makes a difference in existences is equivalent to holding that it makes a difference in the object *to be* known, thus defeating its own purpose; witless that the reality which is the appropriate object of knowledge in a given case may be precisely a reality in which knowing has succeeded in making the needed difference. This question is not one to be settled by manipulation of the concept of knowledge, nor by dialectic discussion of its essence or nature. It is a question of facts, a question of what knowing exists as in the scheme of existence. If things undergo change without thereby ceasing to be real, there can be no *formal* bar to knowing being one specific kind of change in things, nor to its test being found in the successful carrying into effect of the kind of change intended. If knowing be a change in a reality, then the more knowing reveals this change, the more transparent, the more adequate, it is. And if all existences are in transition, then the knowledge which treats them as if they were something of which knowledge is a kodak fixation is just the kind of knowledge which refracts and perverts them. And by the same token a knowing which actively participates in a change in the way to effect it in the needed fashion would be the type of knowing which is valid. If reality be itself in transition—and this doctrine originated not with the objectionable pragmatist but with the physicist and naturalist and moral historian—then the doctrine that

knowledge *is* reality making a particular and specified sort of change in itself seems to have the best chance at maintaining a theory of knowing which itself is in wholesome touch with the genuine and valid.

II

If the ground be cleared of *a priori* objections, and if it be evident that pragmatism cannot be disposed of by any formal or dialectic manipulations of "knowledge" or "truth," but only by showing that some specific things are not of the sort claimed, we may consider some common-sense affiliations of pragmatism. Common sense regards intelligence as having a purpose and knowledge as amounting to something. I once heard a physicist, quite innocent of the pragmatic controversy, remark that the knowledge of a mechanic or farmer was what the Yankee calls gumption—acknowledgment of things in their belongings and uses, and that to his mind natural science was only gumption on a larger scale: the convenient cataloguing and arranging of a whole lot of things with reference to their most efficacious services. Popularly, good judgment is judgment as to the relative values of things: good sense is horse sense, ability to take hold of things right end up, to fit an instrument to an obstacle, to select resources apt for a task. To be reasonable is to recognize things in their offices as obstacles and as resources. Intelligence, in its ordinary use, is a practical term; ability to size up matters with respect to the needs and possibilities of the various situations in which one is called to do something; capacity to envisage things in terms of the adjustments and adaptations they make possible or hinder. Our objective test of the presence or absence of intelligence is influence upon behavior. No capacity to make adjustments means no intelligence; conduct evincing management of complex and novel conditions means a high degree of reason. Such conditions at least suggest that a reality-to-be-known, a reality which is the appropriate subject-matter of knowledge is reality-of-use-and-in-use, direct or indirect, and that a reality which is not in any sort of use, or bearing upon use, may go hang, *so far as knowledge is concerned*.

No one, I suppose, would deny that all knowledge issues in some action which changes things to some extent—be the action only a more deliberate maintenance of a course of conduct already instinctively entered upon. When I see a sign on the street corner I can turn or go on, knowing what I am about. The perceptions of the scientist need have no such overt or "utilitarian" uses, but surely after them he behaves differently, as an inquirer if in no other way; and the cumulative effect of such changes finally modifies the overt action of the ordinary man. That knowing, *after the event*, makes a difference of this sort, few I suppose would deny: if that were all pragmatism means, it would perhaps be accepted as a harmless truism. But there is a further question of fact: just how is the "consequent" action related to the "precedent" knowledge? When *is* "after the event"? What degree of continuity exists? Is the difference between knowing and acting intelligently one of kind or simply one of dominant quality? How does a thing, if it is not already in change in the knowing, manage to issue at its term in action? Moreover, do not the changes actively effected constitute the whole *import* of the knowledge, and hence its final measure and test of validity? If it merely *happens* that knowing when it is done with passes into some action, by what miracle is the subsequent action so pat to the situation? Is it not rather true that the "knowledge" is instituted and framed in anticipation of the consequent issue, and, in the degree in which it is wise and prudent, is held open to revision during it? Certainly the moralist (one might quote, for example, Goethe, Carlyle, and Mazzini) and the common man often agree that full knowledge, adequate assurance, of reality is found only in the issue which fulfils ideas; that we have to do a doctrine to *know* its truth; otherwise it is only dogma or doctrinaire program. Experimental science is a recognition that no idea is entitled to be termed knowledge till it has passed into such overt manipulation of physical conditions as constructs the object to which the idea refers. If one could get rid of his traditional logical theories and set to work afresh to frame a theory of knowledge on the basis of the procedure of the common man, the moralist and the experimentalist, would it be the forced or the natural procedure to say that the realities which we *know*, which we are sure of, are precisely those realities that have taken shape in and through the procedures of knowing?

I turn to another type of consideration. Certainly one of the most genuine problems of modern life is the reconciliation of the scientific view of the universe with the claims of the moral life. Are judgments in terms of the redistribution of matter in motion (or some other closed formula) alone valid? Or are accounts of the universe in terms of possibility and desirability, of initiative and responsibility, also valid? There is no occasion to expatiate on the importance of the moral life, nor upon the supreme importance of intelligence within the moral life. But there does seem to be occasion for asking how moral judgments—judgments of the would and should—relate themselves to the world of scientific knowledge. To frame a theory of knowledge which makes it necessary to deny the validity of moral ideas, or else to refer them to some other and separate kind of universe from that of common sense and science, is both provincial and arbitrary. The pragmatist has at least tried to face, and not to dodge, the question of how it is that moral and scientific "knowledge" can both hold of one and the same world. And whatever the difficulties in his proffered solution, the conception that scientific judgments are to be assimilated to moral is closer to common sense than is the theory that validity is to be denied of moral judgments because they do not square with a preconceived theory of the nature of the world to which scientific judgments must refer. And all moral judgments are about changes to be made.

III

I turn to one affiliation of the pragmatic theory with the results of recent science. The necessity for the occurrence of an event in the way of knowledge, of an organism which reacts or behaves in a specific way, would seem to be as well established as any scientific proposition. It is a peculiar fact, a fact fit to stir curiosity, that the rational function seems to be intercalated in a scheme of practical adjustments. The parts and members of the organism are certainly not there primarily for pure intellection or for theoretic contemplation. The brain, the last physical organ of thought, is a part of the same practical machinery for bringing about adaptation of the environment to the life requirements of the organism, to which belong legs and hand and eye. That the brain frees organic behavior from complete servitude to immediate physical conditions, that it makes possible the liberation of energy for remote and ever expanding ends is, indeed, a precious fact, but not one which removes the brain from the category of organic devices of behavior.[2] That the organ of thinking, of knowledge, was at least originally an organ of conduct, few, I imagine, will deny. And even if we try to believe that the cognitive function has supervened as a different operation, it is difficult to believe that the transfiguration has been so radical that knowing has lost all traces of its connection with vital impulse. But unless we so assume, have we any alternatives except to hold that this continual presence of vital impulse is a disturbing and refracting factor which forever prevents knowledge from reaching its own aim; or else that a certain promoting, a certain carrying forward of the vital impulse, importing certain differences in things, is the aim of knowledge?

The problem cannot be evaded—save ostrich-wise—by saying that such considerations are "merely genetic," or "psychological," having to do only with the origin and natural history of knowing. For the point is that the organic reaction, the behavior of the organism, affects the content of awareness. The subject-matter of all awareness is thing-related-to-organism—related as stimulus direct or indirect or as material of response, present or remote, ulterior or achieved. No one—so far as I know—denies this with respect to the perceptual field of awareness. Pains, pleasures, hunger, and thirst, all "secondary" qualities, involve inextricably the "interaction" of organism and environment. The perceptual field is distributed and arranged as the possible field of selective reactions of the organism at its centre. Up and down, far and near, before and behind, right and left, hard and soft (as well as white and black, bass and alto), involve reference to a centre of behavior.

This material has so long been the stock in trade of both idealistic arguments and proclamations of the agnostic "relativity" of knowledge that philosophers have grown aweary of listening. But even this lethargy might be quickened by a moderate hospitality to the pragmatic interpretation. That red, or far and near, or hard and soft, or big and little, involve a relation between organism and environment, is no more an argument for idealism than is the fact that water involves a relation between hydrogen and oxygen.[3] It is, however, an argument for the ultimately practical value of these distinctions—that they are *differences* made in what things would have been without organic behavior—differences made not by "consciousness" or "mind," but by the organism as the active centre of a system of activities. Moreover, the whole agnostic sting of the doctrine of "relativity" lies in the assumption that the ideal or aim of knowledge is to repeat or copy a prior existence—in which case, of course, the making of contemporaneous differences by the organism in the very fact of awareness would get in the way and forever hinder the knowledge function from the fulfilment of its proper end. Knowledge, awareness, in this case suffers from an impediment which no surgery can better. But if the aim of knowing be precisely to make *certain* differences in an environment, to carry on to *favorable issue*, by the readjustment of the organism, certain changes going on indifferently in the environment, then the fact that the changes of the organism enter pervasively into the subject-matter of awareness is no restriction or perversion of knowledge, but part of the fulfilment of its end.

The only question would then be whether the *proper* reactions take place. The whole agnostic, positivistic controversy is flanked by a single move. The issue is no longer an ideally necessary but actually impossible copying, *versus* an improper but unavoidable modification of reality through organic inhibitions and stimulations: but it is the right, the economical, the effective, and, if one may venture, the useful and satisfactory reaction *versus* the wasteful, the enslaving, the misleading, and the confusing reaction. The presence of organic responses, influencing and modifying every content, every subject-matter of awareness, is the undoubted fact. But the significant thing is the *way* organic behavior enters in— the *way* it influences and modifies. We assign very different values to different types of "knowledge,"—or subject-matters involving organic attitudes and operations. Some are only guesses, opinions, suspicious characters; others are "knowledge" in the honorific and eulogistic sense—science; some turn out mistakes, blunders, errors. Whence and how this discrimination of character in what is taken at its own time to be good knowledge? Why and how is the matter of some "knowledge" genuine-knowing and of other mis-knowing? Awareness is itself a blanket term, covering, in the same bed, delusion, doubt, confusion, ambiguity, and definition, organization, logical conclusiveness assured by evidence and reason. Any naturalistic or realistic theory is committed to the idea that all of these terms bear impartially the same relation to things considered as sheer existences. What we must have in any case is the same existences—the same in kind—only differently arranged or linked up. But why then the tremendous difference in value? And if the unnaturalist, the non-realist, says the difference is one of existential kind, made by the working here malign, there benign, of "consciousness," "psychical" operations and states, upon the existences which are the direct subject-matter of knowledge, there is still the problem of discriminating the conditions and nature of the respective beneficent and malicious interventions of the peculiar "existence" labelled consciousness.[4] The realness of error, ambiguity, doubt and guess poses a problem. It is a problem which has perplexed philosophy so long and has led to so many speculative adventures, that it would seem worth while, were it only for the sake of variety, to listen to the pragmatic solution. It is the business of that organic adaptation involved in all knowing to make a *certain* difference in reality, but *not* to make any old difference, any casual difference. The right, the true and good, difference is that which carries out satisfactorily the specific purpose for the sake of which

knowing occurs. All manufactures are the product of an activity, but it does not follow that all manufactures are equally good. And so all "knowledges" are differences made in things by knowing, but some differences are not calculated or wanted in the knowing, and hence are disturbers and interlopers when they come—while others fulfil the intent of the knowing, being in such harmony with the consistent behavior of the organism as to reinforce and enlarge its functioning. A mistake is literally a mishandling; a doubt is a temporary suspense and vacillation of reactions; an ambiguity is the tension of alternative but incompatible mode of responsive treatment; an inquiry is a tentative and retrievable (because intra-organic) mode of activity entered upon prior to launching upon a knowledge which is public, ineluctable—without anchors to windward—*because* it has taken physical effect through overt action.

It is practically all one to say that the norm of honorable knowing is to make no difference in *its* object, and that its aim is to attain and buttress a specific kind of difference in reality. Knowing fails in its business if it makes a change in its *own* object—that is a mistake; but its own object is none the less a prior existence changed in a certain way. Nor is this a play upon the two senses—end and subject-matter—of "object." The organism has its appropriate functions. To maintain, to expand adequate functioning is its business. This functioning does not occur *in vacuo*. It involves cooperative and readjusted changes in the cosmic medium. Hence the appropriate subject-matter of awareness is not reality at large, a metaphysical heaven to be mimeographed at many removes upon a badly constructed mental carbon paper which yields at best only fragmentary, blurred, and erroneous copies. Its proper and legitimate object is that relationship of organism and environment in which functioning is most amply and effectively attained; or by which, in case of obstruction and consequent needed experimentation, its later eventual free course is most facilitated. As for the other reality, metaphysical reality at large, it may, so far as awareness is concerned, go to its own place.

For ordinary purposes, that is for practical purposes, the truth and the realness of things are synonymous. We are all children who say "really and truly." A reality which is so taken in organic response as to lead to subsequent reactions that are off the track and aside from the mark, while it is, existentially speaking, perfectly real, is not *good* reality. It lacks the hallmark of value. Since it is a certain *kind* of object which we want, that which will be as favorable as possible to a consistent and liberal or growing functioning, it is this kind, the *true* kind, which for us monopolizes the title of reality. Pragmatically, teleologically, this identification of truth and "reality" is sound and reasonable: rationalistically, it leads to the notion of the duplicate versions of reality, one absolute and static because exhausted; the other phenomenal and kept continually on the jump because otherwise its own inherent nothingness would lead to its total annihilation. Since it is only genuine or sincere things, things which are good for what they pretend to in the way of consequences, that we want or are after, *morally* they alone are "real."

IV

So far we have been dealing with awareness as a fact—a fact there like any fact—and have been concerned to show that the subject-matter of awareness is, in any case, things in process of change; and in such change that the knowing function takes a hand in trying to guide it or steer it, so that *some* (and *not* other) differences accrue. But what about the awareness itself? What happens when it is made the subject-matter of awareness? What sort of a thing is it? It is, I submit, mere sophistication (futile at that), to argue either that we cannot become aware of awareness without involving ourselves in an endless regress, or that whenever we are aware of anything we are thereby necessarily aware of awareness once for all, so that it has no character save this purely formal and empty one. Taken concretely, awareness is an event with certain specifiable conditions. We may indeed be aware of it formally, as a bare fact, just as we may be cognizant of an explosion without knowing anything of its nature. But we may also be aware of it in a curious and analytic spirit, undertaking to study it in detail. This inquiry, like any other inquiry, proceeds by determining conditions and consequences. Here awareness is a characteristic fact, presenting to inquiry its own characteristic ear-marks; and a valid knowledge of awareness is the same sort of thing as valid knowledge of the spectrum or of a trotting horse; it proceeds generically in the same way and must satisfy the same generic tests.

What, then, is awareness found to be? The following answer, dogmatically summary in form, involves positive difficulties, and glides over many points where our ignorance is still too great. But it represents a general trend of scientific inquiry, carried on, I hardly need say, on its own merits without respect to the pragmatic controversy. Awareness means *attention*, and attention means a crisis of some sort in an existent situation; a forking of the roads of some material, a tendency to go this way and that. It represents something the matter, something out of gear, or in some way menaced, insecure, problematical and strained. This state of tension, of ambiguous indications, projects and tendencies, is not merely in the "mind," it is nothing merely emotional. It is in the facts of the situation as transitive facts; the emotional or "subjective" disturbance is just a part of the larger disturbance. And if, employing the *language* of psychology, we say that attention is a phenomenon of conflicting habits, being the process of resolving this conflict by finding an act which functions all the factors concerned, this language does not make the facts "merely psychological"—whatever that means.[5] The habits are as biologic as they are "personal," and as cosmic as they are biologic. They are the total order of things expressed in one way; just as a physical or chemical phenomenon is the same order expressed in another way. The statement in terms of conflict and readjustment of habits is at most one way of locating the disturbance in *things*; it furnishes no substitute for, or rival of, reality, and no "psychical" duplication.

If this be true, then awareness, even in its most perplexed and confused state, a state of maximum doubt and precariousness of subject-matter, means things entering, *via* the particular thing known as organism, into a peculiar condition of differential—or additive—change. How can we refuse to raise and consider the question of how things in this condition are related to the prior state which emerges into it, and to the subsequent state of things into which it issues?[6]

Suppose the case to be awareness of a chair. Suppose that this awareness comes only when there is some problematic affair with which the chair is in some way—in whatever degree of remoteness—concerned. It may be a wonder whether that is a chair at all; or whether it is strong enough to stand on; or where I shall put it; or whether it is worth what I paid for it; or, as not infrequently happens, the situation involved in uncertainty may be some philosophic matter in which the perception of the chair is cited as evidence or illustration. (Humorously enough, the awareness of it may even be cited in the course of a philosophic argument intended to show that awareness has nothing to do with situations of incompleteness and ambiguity.) Now what of the change the chair undergoes in entering this way into a situation of perplexed inquiry? Is this any part of the genuineness of that chair with which we are concerned? If not, where is the change found? In something totally different called "consciousness"? In that case how can the operations of inquiry, of observation and memory and reflection, ever have any assurance of getting referred back to the *right* object? Positively the presumption is that the *chair-of-which-we-are-speaking*, is the chair *of-which-we-are-speaking*; it is the *same* thing that is out there which is involved also in the doubtful situation. Moreover, the reference to "consciousness" as the exclusive locus of the doubt only repeats the problem, for "consciousness," by the theory under consideration, means, after all, only the chair *as* concerned in the problematical situation. The *physical* chair remains unchanged, you say. Surely, if as is altogether likely, what is *meant* by physical is precisely *that part* of the chair as object of total awareness which remains unaffected, for certain possible purposes, by entering for certain other actual purposes into the situation of awareness. But how can we segregate, *antecedently* to experimental inquiry, the "physical" chair from the chair which is now the object to

be known; into what contradictions do we fall when we attempt to define the object of one awareness not in its own terms, but in terms of a selected type of object which is the appropriate subject-matter of some other cognizance!

But awareness means inquiry as well as doubt—these are the negative and positive, the retrospective and the prospective relationships of the thing. This means a genuinely *additive* quale—one of readjustment in prior things.[7] I know the dialectic argument that nothing can assume a new relation, because in order to do so it must already be completely related—when it comes from an absolutist I can understand why he holds it, even if I cannot understand the idea itself. But apart from this conceptual reasoning we must follow the lead of our subject-matter; and when we find a thing assuming new relations in the process of inquiry, must accept the fact and frame our theory of things and of knowing to include it, not assert that it is impossible because we already have a theory of knowledge which precludes it. In inquiry, the existence which has become doubtful always undergoes experimental reconstruction. This may be largely imaginative or "speculative." We may view certain things *as if* placed under varying conditions, and consider what then happens to them. But such differences are really transformative so far as they go,—and besides, such inquiries never reach conclusions finally justifiable. In important and persistent inquiry, we insist upon something in the way of actual physical making—be it only a diagram. In other words, *science*, or knowing in its honorific sense, is experimental, involving physical construction. We insist upon something being *done about* it, that we may see how the idea when carried into effect comports with the other things through which our activities are hedged in and released. To avoid this conclusion by saying that knowing makes no difference in the "truth," but merely is the preliminary exercise which discovers it, is that old friend whose acquaintance we have repeatedly made in this discussion: the fallacy of confusing an existence anteceding knowing with the object which terminates and fulfils it. For knowing to make a difference in its own final term is gross self-stultification; it is none the less so when the aim of knowing is precisely to guide things straight up to this term. When "truth" means the accomplished introduction of certain new differences into conditions, why be foolish enough to make other and more differences, which are not wanted since they are irrelevant and misleading?

Were it not for the teachings of sad experience, it would not be necessary to add that the change in environment made by knowing is not a total or miraculous change. Transformation, readjustment, reconstruction all imply prior existences: existences which have characters and behaviors of their own which must be accepted, consulted, humored, manipulated or made light of, in all kinds of differing ways in the different contexts of different problems. Making a difference in reality does not mean making any more difference than we find by experimentation can be made under the given conditions—even though we may still hope for different fortune another time under other circumstances. Still less does it mean making a thing into an unreality, though the pragmatist is sometimes criticised as if any change in reality must be a change into non-reality. There are difficulties indeed, both dialectic, and real or practical, in the fact of change—in the fact that only a permanent can change and that change is alteration of a permanent. But till we enjoin botanists and chemists from referring to changes and transformations in their subject-matter on the ground that for anything to change means for it to part with its reality, we may as well permit the logician to make similar references.

V

Sub specie aeternitatis? or *sub specie generationis*? I am susceptible to the aesthetic charm of the former ideal—who is not? There are moments of relaxation: there are moments when the demand for peace, to be let alone and relieved from the continual claim of the world in which we live that we be up and doing something about it, seems irresistible; when the responsibilities imposed by living in a moving universe seem intolerable. We contemplate with equal mind the thought of the eternal sleep. But, after all, this is a matter in which reality and not the philosopher is the court of final jurisdiction. Outside of philosophy, the question seems fairly settled; in science, in poetry, in social organization, in religion—wherever religion is not hopelessly at the mercy of a Frankenstein philosophy which it originally called into being as its own slave. Under such circumstances there is danger that the philosophy which tries to escape the form of generation by taking refuge under the form of eternity will only come under the form of a by-gone generation. To try to escape from the snares and pitfalls of time by recourse to traditional problems and interests—rather than that let the dead bury their own dead. Better it is for philosophy to err in active participation in the living struggles and issues of its own age and times than to maintain an immune monastic impeccability, without relevancy and bearing in the generating ideas of its contemporary present. In the one case, it will be respected, as we respect all virtue that attests its sincerity by sharing in the perplexities and failures, as well as in the joys and triumphs, of endeavor. In the other case, it bids fair to share the fate of whatever preserves its gentility, but not its activity, in descent from better days; namely, to be snugly ensconced in the consciousness of its own respectability.

NOTES

[First published in *Essays, Philosophical and Psychological*, in Honor of William James, Professor in Harvard University, by his Colleagues at Columbia University (New York: Longmans, Green, and Co., 1908), pp. 53–80. Reprinted in *Philosophy and Civilization* (New York: Minton, Balch and Co., 1931), pp. 36–55, with the title "The Practical Character of Reality." For McGilvary's reply, see MW 4:314–16. MW 4:125–42.]

1. This definition, in the present state of discussion, is an arbitrary or personal one. The text does not mean that "pragmatism" is currently used exclusively in this sense; obviously there are other senses. It does not mean it is the sense in which it *ought* to be used. I have no wish to legislate either for language or for philosophy. But it marks the sense in which it *is* used in this paper; and the pragmatic movement is still so loose and variable that I judge one has a right to fix his own meaning, provided he serves notice and adheres to it.

2. It is interesting to note how the metaphysical puzzles regarding "parallelism," "interaction," "automatism," the relation of "consciousness" to "body," evaporate when one ceases isolating the brain into a peculiar physical substrate of mind at large, and treats it simply as one portion of the body as the instrumentality of adaptive behavior.

3. I owe this illustration to my colleague, Dr. Montague.

4. Of course on the theory I am interested in expounding, the so-called action of "consciousness" means simply the organic releases in the way of behavior which are the conditions of awareness, and which also modify its content.

5. What does it mean? Does the objectivity of fact disappear when the biologist gives it a biological statement? Why not object to his conclusions on the ground that they are "merely" biological?

6. It is this question *of the relation to one another of different successive states of things* which the pragmatic method substitutes for the epistemological inquiry of how one sort of existence, purely mental, temporal but not spatial, immaterial, made up of sublimated gaseous consciousness, can get beyond itself and have valid reference to a totally different kind of existence—spatial and extended; and how it can receive impressions from the latter, etc.,—all the questions which constitute that species of confirmed intellectual lock-jaw called epistemology.

7. We have arrived here, upon a more analytic platform, at the point made earlier concerning the fact that knowing *issues* in action which changes things.

Nature, Life and Body-Mind

From *Experience and Nature* (1925)

A series of cultural experiences exhibits a series of diverging conceptions of the relation of mind to nature in general and to the organic body in particular. Greek experience included affairs that rewarded without want and struggle the contemplation of free men; they enjoyed a civic life full and rich with an equable adaptation to natural surroundings. Such a life seemed to be upon the whole for those in its full possession a gracious culmination of nature; the organic body was the medium through which the culmination took place. Since any created thing is subject to natural contingency, death was not a problem; a being who is generated shares while he may in mind and eternal forms, and then piously merges with the forces which generated him. But life does not always exist in this happy equilibrium: it is onerous and devastating, civil life corrupt and harsh. Under such circumstances, a spirit which believes that it was created in the image of a divine eternal spirit, in whose everlastingness it properly shares, finds itself an alien and pilgrim in a strange and fallen world. Its presence in that world and its residence in a material body which is a part of that world are an enigma. Again the scene shifts. Nature is conceived to be wholly mechanical. The existence within nature and as part of it of a body possessed of life, manifesting thought and enjoying consciousness is a mystery.

This series of experiences with their corresponding philosophies display characteristic factors in the problem of life and mind in relation to body. To the Greeks, all life was psyche, for it was self-movement and only soul moves itself. That there should be self-movement in a world in which movement was also up-and-down, to-and-fro, circular, was indeed interesting but not strange or untoward. Evidence of the fact of self-movement is directly had in perception; even plants exhibit it in a degree and hence have soul, which although only vegetative is a natural condition of animal soul and rational mind. Organic body occupies a distinctive position in the hierarchy of being; it is the highest actuality of nature's physical potentialities, and it is in turn the potentiality of mind. Greek thought, as well as Greek religion, Greek sculpture and recreation, is piously attentive to the human body.

In Pauline Christianity and its successors, the body is earthly, fleshly, lustful and passionate; spirit is Godlike, everlasting; flesh is corruptible; spirit incorruptible. The body was conceived in terms of a moral disparagement colored by supernatural religion. Since the body is material, the dyslogy extends to all that is material; the metaphysical discount put upon matter by Plato and Aristotle becomes in ascetic thought a moral and essential discount. Sin roots in the will; but occasions for sin come from the lusts of the body; appetites and desires spring from the body, distract attention from spiritual things; concupiscence, anger, pride, love of money and luxury, worldly ambition, result. Technically, the framework of Aristotelian thought is retained by the scholastics; St. Thomas Aquinas repeats his formulae concerning life and the body almost word for word. But actually and substantially this formal relationship has been distorted and corrupted through the seduction of spirit by flesh manifest in the fall of man and nature by Adam's sin. Add to moral fear of the flesh, interest in resurrection into the next world for eternal bliss or woe, and there is present a fullfledged antithesis of spirit and matter. In spite of this antithesis, however, they are conjoined in the body of man. Spirit is simple, one, permanent and indissoluble; matter is multiple, subject to change and dissolution. The possibility of the conjunction of two such opposite things formed a problem. But it would have been a remote, technical problem of no interest save to a few speculative thinkers, were it not given concreteness by the notion of an immortality to be spent in bliss or in woe unutterable, and the dependence of this ultimate destiny upon a life in which lust of the flesh along with the world of ambition and the devil of pride, was a standing temptation to sin and thereby an occasion of eternal damnation.

As long as the Aristotelian metaphysical doctrine persisted that nature is an ordered series from lower to higher of potentialities and actualizations, it was possible to conceive of the organic body as normally the highest term in a physical series and the lowest term in

a psychical series. It occupied just that intermediate position where, in being the actualization of the potentialities of physical qualities, body was also potentiality for manifestation of their ideal actualities. Aside from moral and religious questions, there was in medieval thought no special problem attaching to the relation of mind and body. It was just one case of the universal principle of potentiality as the substrate of ideal actuality. But when the time came when the moral and religious associations of spirit, soul, and body persisted in full vigor, while the classic metaphysics of the potential and actual fell into disrepute, the full burden of the question of the relation of body, nature and man, of mind, spirit, and matter, was concentrated in the particular problem of the relation of the body and soul. When men ceased to interpret and explain facts in terms of potentiality and actuality, and resorted to that of causality, mind and matter stood over against one another in stark unlikeness; there were no intermediates to shade gradually the black of body into the white of spirit.

Moreover, both classic and medieval thought supplied influential empirical impetus to the new conception in spite of their theoretically divergent foundation. The old distinction between vegetative, animal and rational souls was, when applied to men, a formulation and justification of class divisions in Greek society. Slaves and mechanical artisans living on the nutritional, appetitive level were for practical purposes symbolized by the body—as obstructions to ideal ends and as solicitations to acts contrary to reason. The good citizen in peace and war was symbolized by the soul proper, amenable to reason, employing thought, but confining its operations after all to mundane matters, infected with matter. Scientific inquirers and philosophers alone exemplified pure reason, operating with ideal forms for the sake of the latter. The claim of this class for inherent superiority was symbolized by *nous*, pure immaterial mind. In Hellenistic thought, the three-fold distinction became that of body, mind or soul and spirit; spirit being elevated above all world affairs and acts, even moral concerns, having purely "spiritual" (immaterial) and religious objects.

This doctrine fell in with the sharp separation made in Christianity for practical moral purposes, between flesh and spirit, sin and salvation, rebellion and obedience. Thus the abstract and technical Cartesian dualism found prepared for it a rich empirical field with which to blend, and one which afforded its otherwise empty formalism concrete meaning and substance.

The formalism and unreality of the problem remains, however, in the theories which have been offered as its "solutions." They range from the materialism of Hobbes, the apparatus of soul, pineal glands, animal spirits of Descartes, to interactionism, pre-established harmony, occasionalism, parallelism, pan-psychic idealism, epiphenomenalism, and the *élan vital*—a portentous array. The diversity of solutions together with the dialectical character of each doctrine which renders it impregnable to empirical attack, suggest that the trouble lies not so much in the solutions, as in the factors which determine statement of the problem. If this be so, the way out of the snarl is a reconsideration of the conceptions in virtue of which the problem exists. And these conceptions have primarily nothing to do with mind-body; they have to do with underlying metaphysical issues:—the denial of quality in general to natural events; the ignoring in particular of temporal quality and the dogma of the superior reality of "causes."

Empirically speaking, the most obvious difference between living and non-living things is that the activities of the former are characterized by needs, by efforts which are active demands to satisfy needs, and by satisfactions. In making this statement, the terms need, effort and satisfaction are primarily employed in a biological sense. By need is meant a condition of tensional distribution of energies such that the body is in a condition of uneasy or unstable equilibrium. By demand or effort is meant the fact that this state is manifested in movements which modify environing bodies in ways which react upon the body, so that its characteristic pattern of active equilibrium is restored. By satisfaction is meant this recovery of equilibrium pattern, consequent upon the changes of environment due to interactions with the active demands of the organism.

A plant needs water, carbon dioxide; upon occasion it needs to bear seeds. The need is neither an immaterial psychic force superimposed upon matter, nor is it merely a notional or conceptual distinction, introduced by thought after comparison of two different states of the organism, one of emptiness and one of repletion. It denotes a concrete state of events: a condition of tension in the distribution of energies such as involves pressure from points of high potential to those of low potential, which in turn effects distinctive changes such that the connection with the environment is altered, so that it acts differently upon the environment and is exposed to different influences from it. In this fact, taken by itself, there is nothing which marks off the plant from the physico-chemical activity of inanimate bodies. The latter also are subject to conditions of disturbed inner equilibrium, which lead to activity in relation to surrounding things, and which terminate after a cycle of changes—a terminus termed saturation, corresponding to satisfaction in organic bodies.

The difference between the animate plant and the inanimate iron molecule is not that the former has something in addition to physico-chemical energy; it lies in the *way* in which physico-chemical energies are interconnected and operate, whence different *consequences* mark inanimate and animate activity respectively. For with animate bodies, recovery or restoration of the equilibrium pattern applies to the complex integrated course or history. In inanimate bodies as such, "saturation" occurs indifferently, not in such a way as to tend to maintain a temporal pattern of activity. The interactions of the various constituent parts of a plant take place in such ways as to tend to continue a characteristically organized activity; they tend to utilize conserved consequences of past activities so as to adapt subsequent changes to the needs of the integral system to which they belong. Organization is a fact, though it is not an original organizing force. Iron as such exhibits characteristics of bias or selective reactions, but it shows no bias in favor of remaining simple iron; it had just as soon, so to speak, become iron-oxide. It shows no tendency in its interaction with water to modify the interaction so that consequences will perpetuate the characteristics of pure iron. If it did, it would have the marks of a living body, and would be called an organism. Iron as a genuine constituent of an *organized* body acts so as to tend to maintain the type of activity of the organism to which it belongs.

If we identify, as common speech does, the physical as such with the inanimate we need another word to denote the activity of organisms as such. Psycho-physical is an appropriate term. Thus employed, "psycho-physical" denotes the conjunctive presence in activity of need-demand-satisfaction, in the sense in which these terms have been defined. In the compound word, the prefix "psycho" denotes that physical activity has acquired additional properties, those of ability to procure a peculiar kind of interactive support of needs from surrounding media. Psycho-physical does not denote an abrogation of the physico-chemical; nor a peculiar mixture of something physical and something psychical (as a centaur is half man and half horse); it denotes the possession of certain qualities and efficacies not displayed by the inanimate.

Thus conceived there is no problem of the relation of physical *and* psychic. There are specifiable empirical events marked by distinctive qualities and efficacies. There is first of all, *organization* with all which is implied thereby. The problem involved is one of definite factual inquiry. Under exactly what conditions does organization occur, and just what are its various modes and their consequences? We may not be able to answer these questions satisfactorily; but the difficulties are not those of a philosophical mystery, but such as attend any inquiry into highly complex affairs. Organization is an empirical trait of some events, no matter how speculative and dubious theories about it may be; especially no matter how false are certain doctrines about it which have had great vogue—namely, those doctrines which have construed it as evidence of a special force or entity called life or soul. Organization is so characteristic of the nature of some events in their sequential linkages that no theory about it can be as speculative or absurd as those which ignore or deny its genuine existence. Denial is never based on empirical evidence, but is a dialectical conclusion from a preconception that whatever appears later in time must be metaphysically unreal as compared with what is found earlier, or from a preconception that since the complex is controlled by means of the simpler, the latter is more "real."

Whenever the activities of the constituent parts of an organized pattern of activity are of such a nature as to conduce to the perpetuation of the patterned activity, there exists the basis of sensitivity. Each "part" of an organism is itself organized, and so of the "parts" of the part. Hence its selective bias in interactions with environing things is exercised so as to maintain *itself*, while also maintaining the whole of which it is a member. The root-tips of a plant interact with chemical properties of the soil in such ways as to serve organized life activity; and in such ways as to exact from the rest of the organism their own share of requisite nutrition. This pervasive operative presence of the whole in the part and of the part in the whole constitutes susceptibility—the capacity of feeling—whether or no this potentiality be actualized in plant-life. Responses are not merely selective, but are discriminatory, in behalf of some results rather than others. This discrimination is the essence of sensitivity. Thus with organization, bias becomes interest, and satisfaction a good or value and not a mere satiation of wants or repletion of deficiencies.

However it may be with plants and lower animals, in animals in which locomotion and distance-receptors exist, sensitivity and interest are realized as feeling, even though only as vague and massive uneasiness, comfort, vigor and exhaustion. A sessile organism requires no premonitions of what is to occur, nor cumulative embodiments of what has occurred. An organism with locomotion is vitally connected with the remote as well as with the nearby; when locomotor organs are accompanied by distance-receptors, response to the distant in space becomes increasingly prepotent and equivalent in effect to response to the future in time. A response toward what is distant is in effect an expectation or prediction of a later contact. Activities are differentiated into the preparatory, or anticipatory, and the fulfilling or consummatory. The resultant is a peculiar tension in which each immediate preparatory response is suffused with the consummatory tone of sex or food or security to which it contributes. Sensitivity, the capacity, is then actualized as feeling; susceptibility to the useful and harmful in surroundings becomes premonitory, an occasion of eventual consequences within life.

On the other hand, a consummation or satisfaction carries with it the continuation, in allied and reinforcing form, of preparatory or anticipatory activities. It is not only a culmination out of them, but is an integrated cumulation, a funded conservation *of* them. Comfort or discomfort, fatigue or exhilaration, implicitly sum up a history, and thereby unwittingly provide a means whereby, (when other conditions become present) the past can be unravelled and made explicit. For it is characteristic of feeling that while it may exist in a formless condition, or without configured distinctions, it is capable of receiving and bearing distinctions without end. With the multiplication of sensitive discriminatory reactions to different energies of the environment (the differentiation of sense-organs, extero-ceptors and proprio-ceptors) and with the increase in scope and delicacy of movements (the development of motor-organs, to which internal glandular organs for effecting a requisite redistribution of energy correspond), feelings vary more and more in quality and intensity.

Complex and active animals *have*, therefore, feelings which vary abundantly in quality, corresponding to distinctive directions and phases—initiating, mediating, fulfilling or frustrating—of activities, bound up in distinctive connections with environmental affairs. They *have* them, but they do not know they have them. Activity is psycho-physical, but not "mental," that is, not aware of meanings. As life is a character of events in a peculiar condition of organization, and "feeling" is a quality of life-forms marked by complexly mobile and discriminating responses, so "mind" is an added property assumed by a feeling creature, when it reaches that organized interaction with other living creatures which is language, communication. Then the qualities of feeling become significant of objective differences in external things and of episodes past and to come. This state of things

in which qualitatively different feelings are not just had but are significant of objective differences, is mind. Feelings are no longer just felt. They have and they make *sense*; record and prophesy.

That is to say, differences in qualities (feelings) of acts when employed as indications of acts performed and to be performed and as signs of their consequences, *mean* something. And they mean it directly; the meaning is had as their own character. Feelings make sense; as immediate meanings of events and objects, they are sensations, or, more properly, sensa. Without language, the qualities of organic action that are feelings are pains, pleasures, odors, colors, noises, tones, only potentially and proleptically. With language they are discriminated and identified. They are then "objectified"; they are immediate traits of things. This "objectification" is not a miraculous ejection from the organism or soul into external things, nor an illusory attribution of psychical entities to physical things. The qualities never were "in" the organism; they always were qualities of interactions in which both extra-organic things and organisms partake. When named, they enable identification and discrimination of things to take place as means in a further course of inclusive interaction. Hence they are as much qualities of the things engaged as of the organism. For purposes of control they may be referred specifically to either the thing or to the organism or to a specified structure of the organism. Thus color which turns out not to be a reliable sign of external events becomes a sign of, say, a defect in visual apparatus. The notion that sensory affections discriminate and identify themselves, apart from discourse, as being colors and sounds, etc., and thus *ipso facto* constitute certain elementary modes of knowledge, even though it be only knowledge of their own existence, is inherently so absurd that it would never have occurred to any one to entertain it, were it not for certain preconceptions about mind and knowledge. Sentiency in itself is anoetic; it exists as any immediate quality exists, but nevertheless it is an indispensable means of any noetic function.

For when, through language, sentience is taken up into a system of signs, when for example a certain quality of the active relationship of organism and environment is named hunger, it is seen as an organic demand for an extra-organic object. To term a quality "hunger," to name it, is to refer to an object, to food, to that which will satisfy it, towards which the active situation moves. Similarly, to name another quality "red," is to direct an interaction between an organism and a thing to some object which fulfills the demand or need of the situation. It requires but slight observation of mental growth of a child to note that organically conditioned qualities, including those special sense-organs, are discriminated only as they are employed to designate objects; red, for instance, as the property of a dress or toy. The difficulty in the way of identifying the qualities of acts conditioned by proprio-ceptor organs is notoriously enormous. They just merge in the general situation. If they entered into communication as shared means to social consequences they would acquire the same objective distinctiveness as do qualities conditioned by the extero-ceptor organs. On the other hand, the qualities of the latter are just shades of the general tone of situations until they are used, in language, as common or shared means to common ends. Then they are identified as traits of objects. The child has to learn through social intercourse that certain qualities of action mean greediness or anger or fear or rudeness; the case is not otherwise with those qualities which are identified as red, musical tone, a foul odor. The latter may have instigated nausea, and "red" may have excited uneasiness (as blood makes some persons faint); but discrimination of the nauseating object *as* foul odor, and of the excitation *as* red occurs only when they are designated as signs.

The qualities of situations in which organisms and surrounding conditions interact, when discriminated, make sense. Sense is distinct from feeling, for it has a recognized reference; it is the qualitative characteristic of something, not just a submerged unidentified quality or tone. Sense is also different from signification. The latter involves use of a quality as a sign or index of something else, as when the red of a light signifies danger, and the need of bringing a moving locomotive to a stop. The sense of a thing, on the other hand, is an immediate and immanent meaning; it is mean-

ing which is itself felt or directly had. When we are baffled by perplexing conditions, and finally hit upon a clew, and everything falls into place, the whole thing suddenly, as we say, "makes sense." In such a situation, the clew has signification in virtue of being an indication, a guide to interpretation. But the meaning of the *whole* situation as apprehended is sense. This idiomatic usage of the word sense is much nearer the empirical facts than is the ordinary restriction of the word in psychological literature to a single simple recognized quality, like sweet or red: the latter simply designates a case of *minimum* sense, deliberately limited for purposes of intellectual safety-first. Whenever a situation has this double function of meaning, namely signification and sense, mind, intellect is definitely present.

The distinction between physical, psychophysical, and mental is thus one of levels of increasing complexity and intimacy of interaction among natural events. The idea that matter, life and mind represent separate kinds of Being is a doctrine that springs, as so many philosophic errors have sprung, from a substantiation of eventual functions. The fallacy converts consequences of interaction of events into causes of the occurrence of these consequences—a reduplication which is significant as to the *importance* of the functions, but which hopelessly confuses understanding of them. "Matter," or the physical, is a character of events when they occur at a certain level of interaction. It is not itself an event or existence; the notion that while "mind" denotes essence, "matter" denotes existence is superstition. It is more than a bare essence; for it is a property of a particular field of interacting events. But as it figures in *science* it is as much an essence as is acceleration, or the square root of minus one; which meanings also express derivative characters of events in interaction. Consequently, while the theory that life, feeling and thought are never independent of physical events may be deemed materialism, it may also be considered just the opposite. For it is reasonable to believe that the most adequate definition of the basic traits of natural existence can be had only when its properties are most fully displayed— a condition which is met in the degree of the scope and intimacy of interactions realized.

In any case, genuine objection to metaphysical materialism is neither moral nor esthetic. Historically speaking, materialism and mechanistic metaphysics—as distinct from mechanistic science—designate the doctrine that matter is the efficient cause of life and mind, and that "cause" occupies a position superior in reality to that of "effect." Both parts of this statement are contrary to fact. As far as the conception of causation is to be introduced at all, not matter but the natural events having matter as a character, "cause" life and mind. "Effects," since they mark the release of potentialities, are more adequate indications of the nature of nature than are just "causes." Control of the occurrence of the complex depends upon its analysis into the more elementary; the dependence of life, sentiency and mind upon "matter" is thus practical or instrumental. Lesser, more external fields of interaction are more manageable than are wider and more intimate ones, and only through managing the former can we direct the occurrence of the latter. Thus it is in virtue of the character of events which is termed matter that psychophysical and intellectual affairs can be differentially determined. Every discovery of concrete dependence of life and mind upon physical events is therefore an addition to our resources. If life and mind had no mechanism, education, deliberate modification, rectification, prevention and constructive control would be impossible. To damn "matter" because of honorific interest in spirit is but another edition of the old habit of eulogizing ends and disparaging the means on which they depend.

This, then, is the significance of our introductory statement that the "solution" of the problem of mind-body is to be found in a revision of the preliminary assumptions about existence which generate the problem. As we have already noted, fruitful science of nature began when inquirers neglected immediate qualities, the "sense" of events, wet and dry, hot and cold, light and heavy, up and down, in behalf of "primary," namely, signifying, qualities, and when they treated the latter, although called qualities, not as such but as relations. This device made possible a totally different dialectical treatment. Classic science operated in terms of properties already attached to qualitative phenomena of sense and custom. Hence it could only repeat these phenomena in a changed vocabulary;—the vocabulary of sensory forms and forces which were, after all nothing but the already given meanings of things reduplicated. But the new dialectic was that of mathematical equations and functions. It started from meanings which ignored obvious characters or meanings of phenomena; hence it could lead to radically new relationships and generalizations—new in kind, and not merely in detail. No longer was the connection or classification of one color simply with other colors, but with all events involving rhythmic rates of change. Thus events hitherto disjoined were brought together under principles of inclusive formulation and prediction. Temporal qualities were stated as spatial velocities; thereby mathematical functions directly applicable to spatial positions, directions and distances, made it possible to reduce sequence of events into calculable terms. Neglect of temporal qualities as such centered thought upon *order* of succession, an order convertible into one of coexistence.

All this in effect is equivalent to seizing upon relations of events as the proper objects of knowledge. The surrender of immediate qualities, sensory and significant, as objects of science, and as proper forms of classification and understanding, left in reality these immediate qualities just as they were; since they are *had* there is no need to *know* them. But, as we have had frequent occasion to notice, the traditional view that the object of knowledge is reality *par excellence* led to the conclusion that the proper object of science was preeminently metaphysically real. Hence immediate qualities, being extruded from the object of science, were left thereby hanging loose from the "real" object. Since their *existence* could not be denied, they were gathered together into a psychic realm of being, set over against the object of physics. Given this premise, all the problems regarding the relation of mind and matter, the psychic and the bodily, necessarily follow. Change the metaphysical premise; restore, that is to say, immediate qualities to their rightful position as qualities of inclusive situations, and the problems in question cease to be epistemological problems. They become specifiable scientific problems: questions, that is to say, of how such and such an event having such and such qualities actually occurs.

Greek science imputed efficacy to qualities like wet and dry, hot and cold, heavy and light and to such qualitative differences in movement as up and down, to and fro, around and around. The world was formulated and explained on the basis of the causal efficacy of these qualities. The scientific revolution of the seventeenth century took its departure from a denial of causal status (and hence of significance for science) of these and all other direct qualities. On account, however, of the conversion of this fact about scientific procedure into a denial of the existence of qualities outside of mind and consciousness, psycho-physical and mental functions became inexplicable anomalies, supernatural in the literal sense of the word. The error of Greek science lay not in assigning qualities to natural existence, but in misconceiving the locus of their efficacy. It attributed to qualities apart from organic action efficiencies which qualities possess only through the medium of an organized activity of life and mind. When life and mind are recognized to be characters of the highly complex and extensive interaction of events, it is possible to give natural existential status to qualities, without falling into the mistake of Greek science. Psycho-physical phenomena and higher mental phenomena may be admitted in their full empirical reality, without recourse to dualistic breach in historic, existential continuity.

When knowing inanimate things, qualities as such may be safely disregarded. They present themselves as intensities and vector directions of movement capable of statement in mathematical terms. Thus their immediate individuality is got around; it is impertinent for science, concerned as the latter is with relationships. The most that can be said about qualities in the inanimate field is that they mark the limit of the contact of historical affairs, being abrupt ends or termini, boundaries of beginning and closing where a particular interaction ceases. They are like a line of foam marking the impact of waves of different directions of movement. They have to be noted and accepted in order to delimit a field of inquiry, but they do not enter into the inquiry as factors or terms.

In life and mind they play an active role. The delimitation or individualization they constitute on this level is not external to events. It is all one with the organization which permeates them, and which in permeating them, converts prior limitations of intensity and direction of energy into actual and intrinsic qualities, or sentient differences. For in feeling a quality exists as quality, and not merely as an abrupt, discrete, unique delimitation of interaction. Red differs from green for purposes of physical science as that which gives specific meaning to two sets of numbers applied to vibrations, or to two different placements of lines in a spectrum. The difference is proleptically qualitative; it refers to a unique difference of potentiality in the affairs under consideration. But as far as calculation and prediction are concerned these differences remain designable by non-qualitative indices of number and form. But in an organic creature sensitive to light, these differences of potentiality may be realized as differences in immediate sentiency. To say that they are *felt*, is to say that they come to independent and intrinsic existence on their own account. The proposition does not mean that feeling has been extraneously superadded to something else, or that a mode of extrinsic cognitive access to a purely physical thing has entered intrusively into a world of psychical things. "Feeling" is in general a name for the newly actualized quality acquired by events previously occurring upon a physical level, when these events come into more extensive and delicate relationships of interaction. More specifically, it is a name for the coming to existence of those ultimate differences in affairs which mark them off from one another and give them discreteness; differences which upon the physical plane can be spoken of only in anticipation of subsequent realization, or in terms of different numerical formulae, and different space-time positions and contiguities.

Thus qualities characteristic of sentiency are qualities *of* cosmic events. Only because they are such, is it possible to establish the one to one correspondence which natural science does establish between series of numbers and spatial positions on one hand and the series and spectra of sensory qualities on the other. The notion that the universe is split into two separate and disconnected realms of existence, one psychical and the other physical, and then that these two realms of being, in spite of their total disjunction, specifically and minutely correspond to each other—as a serial order of numbered vibrations corresponds to the immediately felt qualities of vision of the prismatic spectrum—presents the acme of incredibility. The one-to-one agreement is intelligible only as a correspondence of properties and relations in one and the same world which is first taken upon a narrower and more external level of interaction, and then upon a more inclusive and intimate level. When we recall that by taking natural events on these two levels and instituting point to point correspondence (or "parallelism") between them, the richer and more complex display of characters is rendered amenable to prediction and deliberate guidance, the intelligibility of the procedure becomes concretely sensible.

Thus while modern science is correct in denying direct efficacy and position in the described sequence of events to say, red, or dry; yet Greek science was correct in its underlying naïve assumption that qualities count for something highly important. Apart from sentiency and life, the career of an event can indeed be fully described without any reference to its having red as a quality,—though even in this case, since description is an event which happens only through mental events, dependence upon an overt or actualized quality of red is required in order to delimit the phenomenon of which a mathematical-mechanical statement is made. Qualities actually become specifically effective however, in psycho-physical situations. Where animal susceptibility exists, a red or an odor or sound may instigate a determinate mode of action; it has selective power in maintenance of a certain pattern of energy-organization. So striking is this fact that we might even define the difference between an inanimate body and a vital and psycho-physical one, by saying that the latter responds to qualities while the former does not. In this response, qualities become

productive of results, and hence potentially significant. That is, in achieving effects, they become connected with consequences, and hence capable of meaning, knowable if not known. This explains the fact that while we are forced to ascribe qualities to events on the physical level, we cannot *know* them on this level; they have when assigned strictly to that level no consequences. But through the medium of living things, they generate effects, which, when qualities are used as means to produce them, are consequences. Thus qualities become intelligible, knowable.

In the higher organisms, those with distance-receptors of ear and eye and, in lesser degree, of smelling, qualities further achieve a difference which is the material basis or substratum of a distinction into activities having preparatory and having consummatory status. "Ends" are not necessarily fulfillments or consummations. They may be mere closures, abrupt cessations, as a railway line may by force of external conditions come to an end, although the end does not fulfill antecedent activities. So there are starts, beginnings which are in no sense preparatory, being rather disturbances and interferences. Events of the physical type have such ends and beginnings which mark them off qualitatively and individually. But as such they are not in any true sense possessed of instrumental nor fulfilling character. They neither initiate nor complete. But when these qualities are realized through organic action, giving rise to acts of utilization, of adaptation (response to quality), they are converted into a series, in which some acts are preparatory and others consummatory. An original contact-activity (including intra-organic disturbances or needs) renders distance receptors open to stimulation; the responses which take place in consequence tend to occur in such a way as to terminate in a further contact-activity in which original need is satisfied.

This series forms the immediate material of thought when social communication and discourse supervene. The beginning not only *is* the initial term in a *series* (as distinct from a *succession*), but it gains the *meaning* of subsequent activity moving toward a consequence of which it is the first member. The concluding term conserves within itself the meaning of the entire preparatory process. Thereby the original status of contact and distance activities is reversed. When activity is directed by distant things, contact activities must be inhibited or held in. They become instrumental; they function only as far as is needed to direct the distance-conditioned activities. The result is nothing less than revolutionary. Organic activity is liberated from subjection to what is closest at hand in space and time. Man is led or drawn rather than pushed. The immediate is significant in respect to what has occurred and will occur; the organic basis of memory and expectation is supplied. The subordination of contact-activity to distance-activity is equivalent to possibility of release from submergence in the merely given, namely, to abstraction, generalization, inference. It institutes both a difference and a connection between matters that prepare the way for other events and the affairs finally appropriated; it furnishes the material for the relation of thing signifying and thing signified—a relation that is actualized when discourse occurs. When this juncture of events is reached, there comes about the distinction mentioned between sense and signification. The latter denotes the possibility of a later fulfilling sense of things in immediate appropriations and enjoyments. But meanwhile there is a sentience that has to be transformed by subordination to the distance-conditioned activity; which till it is thus transformed is vacant, confused, demanding but lacking meaning. Meanwhile also the distance-conditioned activities acquire as an integral part of their own quality the consequences of their prior fulfillments. They have *significance* with respect to their consequences; but they have perspicuous and coherent *sense* of their own. Thus they become final, and the qualities of contact-activity instrumental. In short, hearing and vision are notoriously the intellectual *and* esthetic senses—an undeniable fact which throws much light on the doctrine of those theorists about value who attempt to divide thought and enjoyable liking from each other in their definitions of value, and who also—quite logically on this premise—sharply separate values into contributory and intrinsic.

The foregoing discussion is both too technical and not elaborately technical enough for adequate comprehension. It may be conceived as an attempt to contribute to what has come to be called an "emergent" theory of mind. But every word that we can use, organism, feeling, psycho-physical, sensation and sense, "emergence" itself, is infected by the associations of old theories, whose import is opposite to that here stated. We may, however attempt a recapitulation by premising that while there is no isolated occurrence in nature, yet interaction and connection are not wholesale and homogenous. Interacting events have tighter and looser ties, which qualify them with certain beginnings and endings, and which mark them off from other fields of interaction. Such relatively closed fields come into conjunction at times so as to interact with each other, and a critical alteration is effected. A new larger field is formed, in which new energies are released, and to which new qualities appertain. Regulation, conscious direction and science imply ability to smooth over the rough junctures, and to form by translation and substitution a homogenous medium. Yet these functions do not abrogate or deny qualitative differences and unlike fields or ranges of operation, from atoms to solar systems. They do just what they are meant to do: give facility and security in utilizing the simpler manageable field to predict and modify the course of the more complete and highly organized.

In general, three plateaus of such fields may be discriminated. The first, the scene of narrower and more external interactions, while qualitatively diversified in itself, is physical; its distinctive properties are those of the mathematical-mechanical system discovered by physics and which define matter as a general character. The second level is that of life. Qualitative differences, like those of plant and animal, lower and higher animal forms, are here even more conspicuous; but in spite of their variety they have qualities in common which define the psycho-physical. The third plateau is that of association, communication, participation. This is still further internally diversified, consisting of individualities. It is marked throughout its diversities, however, by common properties, which define mind as intellect; possession of and response to meanings.

Each one of these levels having its own characteristic empirical traits has its own categories. They are however categories of description, conceptions required to state the fact in question. They are not "explanatory" categories, as explanation is sometimes understood; they do not designate, that is, the operation of forces as "causes." They stick to empirical facts noting and denoting characteristic qualities and consequences peculiar to various levels of interaction. Viewed from this standpoint, the traditional "mechanical" and "teleological" theories both suffer from a common fallacy, which may be suggested by saying that they both purport to be explanatory in the old, non-historical sense of causality. One theory makes matter account for the existence of mind; the other regards happenings that precede the appearance of mind as preparations made for the sake of mind in a sense of preparation that is alleged to explain the occurrence of these antecedents.

Mechanistic metaphysics calls attention to the fact that the latter occurrence could not have taken place without the earlier; that given the earlier, the latter was bound to follow. Spiritualistic metaphysics calls attention to the fact that the earlier, material affairs, prepare the way for vital and ideal affairs, lead up to them; promote them. Both statements are equally true descriptively; neither statement is true in the explanatory and metaphysical meaning imputed to it.

The notion of causal explanation involved in both conceptions implies a breach in the continuity of historic process; the gulf created has then to be bridged by an emission or transfer of force. If one starts with the assumption that mind and matter are two separate things, while the evidence forces one to see that they are connected, one has no option save to attribute the power to make the connection, to carry from one to the other, to one or the other of the two things involved. The one selected is then "cause"; it accounts for the existence of the other. One person is struck by such affairs as that when a match is struck and paper is near-by the paper catches fire, whether any one wished or intended it to do so or not. He is struck by a compulsory power exercised by the earlier over the later; given the lighted match and contiguous paper and the latter *must* burst into flame. Another person is struck by the fact that matches and paper exist only because somebody has use for them; that the intent and purpose of use preceded the coming into being of match and paper. So he concludes that thought, purpose, starts an emission and transfer of force which brought things into existence in order to accomplish the object of thought. Or, if a little less devoted to human analogies, one notes the cunning continuity of nature, how neatly one thing leads up to another, and how elegantly the later registers and takes advantage of what has gone before, and, beholding that the later is the more complex and the more significant, decides that what goes before occurs for the sake of the later, in its behalf, on its account. The eventual has somehow been there from the start, "implicitly," "potentially," but efficaciously enough to attend to its own realization by using material conditions at every stage.

The gratuitous nature of both assumptions is seen if we set out with any acknowledged historic process,—say—the growth from infancy to maturity, or the development of a melodic theme. There are those who regard childhood as merely getting ready for the supreme dignity of adulthood, and there are those who seem quite sure that adult life is merely an unrolling by way of mechanical effects of the "causal" forces found in childhood. One of the theories makes youth a preliminary and intrinsically insignificant journey toward a goal; the other makes adulthood a projection, on a supernumerary screen, of a plate and pattern previously inserted in the projecting apparatus of childhood or of prenatal condition, or of heredity, or wherever the fixed and separated antecedent be located. Nevertheless the notion of growth makes it easy, I think, to detect the fallacy residing in both views: namely, the breaking up of a continuity of historical change into two separate parts, together with the necessity which follows from the breaking-in-two for some device by which to bring them together again.

The reality is the growth-process itself; childhood and adulthood are phases of a continuity, in which just because it is a history, the later cannot exist until the earlier exists ("mechanistic materialism" in germ); and in which the later makes use of the registered and cumulative outcome of the earlier—or, more strictly, is its utilization ("spiritualistic teleology" in germ). The real existence is the history in its entirety, the history as just what it is. The operations of splitting it up into two parts and then having to unite them again by appeal to causative power are equally arbitrary and gratuitous. Childhood is the childhood of and in a certain serial process of changes which is just what it is, and so is maturity. To give the traits of either phase a kind of independent existence, and then to use the form selected to account for or explain the rest of the process is a silly reduplication; reduplication, because we have after all only parts of one and the same original history; silly because we fancy that we have accounted for the history on the basis of an arbitrary selection of part of itself.

Substitute for such growth a more extensive history of nature and call it the evolution of mind from matter, and the conclusion is not different. In the old dispute as to whether a stag runs because he has long and slender legs, or has the legs in order that he may run, both parties overlook the natural descriptive statement; namely, that it is of the nature of what goes on in the world that the stag has long legs and that having them he runs. When mind is said to be implicit, involved, latent, or potential in matter, and subsequent change is asserted to be an affair of making it explicit, evolved, manifest, actual, what happens is that a natural history is first cut arbitrarily and unconsciously in two, and then the severance is consciously and arbitrarily cancelled. It is simpler not to start by engaging in such manoeuvers.

The discussion gives an understanding of the adaptation of nature and life and mind to one another. A mystery has not seldom been made of the fact that objective nature lends itself to man's sense of fitness, order and beauty; or, in another region of discourse, that objective nature submits to mental operations sufficiently to be known. Or, the mystery is conceived from the other end: it seems wonderful that man should be possessed of a sense of order, beauty and rightness; that he should have a capacity of thinking and knowing, so

that man is elevated far above nature and seated with angels. But the wonder and mystery do not seem to be other than the wonder and mystery that there should be such a thing as nature, as existential events, at all, and that in being they should be what they are. The wonder should be transferred to the whole course of things. Only because an arbitrary breach has previously been introduced by which the world is first conceived as something quite different from what it demonstrably is, does it then appear passing strange that after all it should be just what it is. The world is subject-matter for knowledge, because mind has developed in that world; a body-mind, whose structures have developed according to the structures of the world in which it exists, will naturally find some of its structures to be concordant and congenial with nature, and some phases of nature with itself. The latter are beautiful and fit, and others ugly and unfit. Since mind cannot evolve except where there is an organized process in which the fulfillments of the past are conserved and employed, it is not surprising that mind when it evolves should be mindful of the past and future, and that it should use the structures which are biological adaptations of organism and environment as its own and its only organs. In ultimate analysis the mystery that mind should use a body, or that a body should have a mind, is like the mystery that a man cultivating plants should use the soil; or that the soil which grows plants at all should grow those adapted to its own physico-chemical properties and relations.

The account which has been given will be repeated from a more analytic point of view, starting with evident empirical consideration. Every "mind" that we are empirically acquainted with is found in connection with some organized body. Every such body exists in a natural medium to which it sustains some adaptive connection: plants to air, water, sun, and animals to these things and also to plants. Without such connections, animals die; the "purest" mind would not continue without them. An animal can live only as long as it draws nutriment from its medium, finds their means of defence, and ejects into it waste and superfluous products of its own making. Since no particular organism lasts forever, life in general goes on only as an organism reproduces itself; and the only place where it can reproduce itself is in the environment. In all higher forms reproduction is sexual; that is, it involves the meeting of two forms. The medium is thus one which contains similar and conjunctive forms. At every point and stage, accordingly, a living organism and its life processes involve a world or nature temporally and spatially "external" to itself but "internal" to its functions.

The only excuse for reciting such commonplaces is that traditional theories have separated life from nature, mind from organic life, and thereby created mysteries. Restore the connection, and the problem of how a mind can know an external world or even know that there is such a thing, is like the problem of how an animal eats things external to itself; it is the kind of problem that arises only if one assumes that a hibernating bear living off its own stored substance defines the normal procedure, ignoring moreover the question where the bear got its stored material. The problem of how one person knows the existence of other persons, is, when the relation of mind and life is genuinely perceived, like the problem of how one animal can associate with other animals, since other is other. A creature generated in a conjunctive union, dependent upon others (as are at least all higher forms) for perpetuation of its being, and carrying in its own structure the organs and marks of its intimate connection with others will know other creatures if it knows itself. Since both the inanimate and the human environment are involved in the functions of life, it is inevitable, if these functions evolve to the point of thinking and if thinking is naturally serial with biological functions, that it will have as the material of thought, even of its erratic imaginings, the events and connections of this environment. And if the animal succeeds in putting to use any of its thinkings as means of sustaining its functions, those thoughts will have the characters that define knowledge.

In contrast with lower organisms, the more complex forms have distance receptors and a structure in which activators and effectors are allied to distance even more extensively than to contact receptors. What is done in response to things near-by is so tied to what is done in response to what is far away, that a higher organism acts with reference to a spread-out environment as a single situation. We find also in all these higher organisms that what is done is conditioned by consequences of prior activities; we find the fact of learning or habit-formation. In consequence, an organism acts with reference to a time-spread, a serial order of events, as a unit, just as it does in reference to a unified spatial variety. Thus an environment both extensive and enduring is immediately implicated in present behavior. Operatively speaking, the remote and the past are "in" behavior making it what it is. The action called "organic" is not just that of internal structures; it is an integration of organic-environmental connections. It may be a mystery that there should be thinking but it is no mystery that if there is thinking it should contain in a "present" phase, affairs remote in space and in time, even to geologic ages, future eclipses and far away stellar systems. It is only a question of how far what is "in" its actual experience is extricated and becomes focal.

It is also an obvious empirical fact that animals are connected with each other in inclusive schemes of behavior by means of signaling acts, in consequence of which certain acts and consequences are deferred until a joint action made possible by the signaling occurs. In the human being, this function becomes language, communication, discourse, in virtue of which the consequences of the experience of one form of life are integrated in the behavior of others. With the development of recorded speech, the possibilities of this integration are indefinitely widened—in principle the cycle of objective integration within the behavior of a particular organism is completed. Not merely its own distant world of space-time is involved in its conduct but the world of its fellows. When consequences which are unexperienced and future to one agent are experienced and past to another creature with which it is in communication, organic prudence becomes conscious expectation, and future affairs living present realities. Human learning and habit-forming present thereby an integration of organic-environmental connections so vastly superior to those of animals without language that its experience appears to be super-organic.

Another empirical fact follows. Strict repetition and recurrence decrease relatively to the novel. Apart from communication, habit-forming wears grooves; behavior is confined to channels established by prior behavior. In so far the tendency is toward monotonous regularity. The very operation of learning sets a limit to itself, and makes subsequent learning more difficult. But this holds only of *a* habit, a habit in isolation, a non-communicating habit. Communication not only increases the number and variety of habits, but tends to link them subtly together, and eventually to subject habit-forming in a particular case to the habit of recognizing that new modes of association will exact a new use of it. Thus habit is formed in view of possible future changes and does not harden so readily. As soon as a child secretes from others the manifestation of a habit there is proof that he is practically aware that he forms *a* habit subject to the requirements of others as to his further habit formations.

Now an animal given to forming habits, is one with an increasing number of needs, and of new relationships with the world about it. Each habit demands appropriate conditions for its exercise and when habits are numerous and complex, as with the human organism, to find these conditions involves search and experimentation; the organism is compelled to make variations, and exposed to error and disappointment. By a seeming paradox, increased power of forming habits means increased susceptibility, sensitiveness, responsiveness. Thus even if we think of habits as so many grooves, the power to acquire many and varied grooves denotes high sensitivity, explosiveness. Thereby an old habit, a fixed groove if one wishes to exaggerate, gets in the way of the process of forming a new habit while the tendency to form a new one cuts across some old habit. Hence instability, novelty, emergence of unexpected and unpredictable combinations. The more an organism learns—the more that is, the former terms of a historic process are retained and integrated in this present phase—the more it has to learn, in order to

keep itself going; otherwise death and catastrophe. If mind is a further process in life, a further process of registration, conservation and use of what is conserved, then it must have the traits it does empirically have: being a moving stream, a constant change which nevertheless has axis and direction, linkages, associations as well as initiations, hesitations and conclusions.

The thing essential to bear in mind is that living as an empirical affair is not something which goes on below the skin-surface of an organism: it is always an inclusive affair involving connection, interaction of what is within the organic body and what lies outside in space and time, and with higher organisms far outside. For this reason, organic acts are a kind of fore-action of mind; they look as if they were deliberate and consciously intelligent, because, of necessity, intelligent action in utilizing the mechanisms they supply, reproduces their patterns. The evidence usually adduced in support of the proposition that lower animals, animals without language, think, turns out, when examined, to be evidence that when men, organisms with power of social discourse, think, they do so with the organs of adaptation used by lower animals, and thus largely repeat in imagination schemes of overt animal action. But to argue from this fact to the conclusion that animals think is like concluding that because every tool, say a plow, originated from some pre-existing natural production, say a crooked root or forked branch, the latter was inherently and antecedently engaged in plowing. The connection is there, but it is the other way around.

Excuse for dwelling upon the fact that life goes on between and among things of which the organism is but one is because this fact is so much ignored and virtually denied by traditional theories. Consider for example, the definitions of life and mind given by Herbert Spencer: correspondence of an inner order with an outer order. It implies there is an inner order and an outer order, and that the correspondence consists in the fact that the terms in one order are related to one another as the terms or members of the other order are connected within themselves. The correspondence is like that of various phonographic records to one another; but the genuine correspondence of life and mind with nature is like the correspondence of two persons who "correspond" in order to learn each one of the acts, ideas and intents of the other one, in such ways as to modify one's own intents, ideas and acts, and to substitute partaking in a common and inclusive situation for separate and independent performances. If the organism merely repeats in the series of its own self-enclosed acts the order already given without, death speedily closes its career. Fire for instance consumes tissue; that is the sequence in the external order. Being burned to death is the order of "inner" events which corresponds with this "outer" order. What the organism actually does is to act so as to change its relationship to the environment; and as organisms get more complex and human this change of relationship involves more extensive and more enduring changes in the environmental order. The aim is not to protract a line of organic events parallel to external events, but to form a new scheme of affairs to which both organic and environmental relations contribute, and in which they both partake. Yet all schemes of psycho-physical parallelism, traditional theories of truth as correspondence, etc., are really elaborations of the same sort of assumptions as those made by Spencer: assumptions which first make a division where none exists, and then resort to an artifice to restore the connection which has been willfully destroyed.

If organic life denotes a phase of history in which natural affairs have reached a point in which characteristic new properties appear, and new ways of acting are released because of integration of fields hitherto unlinked, there does not seem to be anything extraordinary in the fact that what is known about the earlier "physical" series is applied to interpret and direct vital phenomena; nor in the fact that this application does not exhaust their character nor suffice wholly for their description. We cannot direct a course of interactions without counting and measuring, but the interactions are more than numbers, spaces and velocities. To explain is to employ one thing to elucidate, clear, shed light upon, put in better order, because in a wider context, another thing. It is thus subordinate to more adequate discourse,

which, applied to space-time affairs, assumes the style of narration and description. Speaking in terms of captions familiar in rhetoric, exposition and argument are always subordinate to a descriptive narration, and exist for the sake of making the latter clearer, more coherent and more significant.

Body-mind designates an affair with its own properties. A large part of the difficulty in its discussion—perhaps the whole of the difficulty in general apart from detailed questions—is due to vocabulary. Our language is so permeated with consequences of theories which have divided the body and mind from each other, making separate existential realms out of them, that we lack words to designate the actual existential fact. The circumlocutions we are compelled to resort to—exemplified in the previous discussion—thus induce us to think that analogous separations exist in nature, which can also only be got around by elaborate circuitous arrangements. But body-mind simply designates what actually takes place when a living body is implicated in situations of discourse, communication and participation. In the hyphenated phrase body-mind, "body" designates the continued and conserved, the registered and cumulative operation of factors continuous with the rest of nature, inanimate as well as animate; while "mind" designates the characters and consequences which are differential, indicative of features which emerge when "body" is engaged in a wider, more complex and interdependent situation.

Just as when men start to talk they must use sounds and gestures antecedent to speech, and as when they begin to hunt animals, catch fish or make baskets, they must employ materials and processes that exist antecedently to these operations, so when men begin to observe and think they must use the nervous system and other organic structures which existed independently and antecedently. That the use reshapes the prior materials so as to adapt them more efficiently and freely to the uses to which they are put, is not a problem to be solved: it is an expression of the common fact that anything changes according to the interacting field it enters. Sounds do not cease to be sounds when they become articulate speech;

but they do take on new distinctions and arrangements, just as do materials used in tools and machines, without ceasing to be the materials they formerly were. Thus the external or environmental affairs, primarily implicated in living processes and later implicated in discourse, undergo modifications in acquiring meanings and becoming objects of mind, and yet are as "physical" as ever they were.

Unless vital organizations were organizations *of* antecedent natural events, the living creature would have no natural connections; it would not be pertinent to its environment nor its environment relevant to it; the latter would not be usable, material of nutrition and defence. In similar fashion, unless "mind" was, in its existential occurrence, an organization *of* physiological or vital affairs and unless its functions developed out of the patterns of organic behavior, it would have no pertinency to nature, and nature would not be the appropriate scene of its inventions and plans, nor the subject-matter of its knowledge. If we suppose, per impossible or by a miracle, that a separate mind is inserted abruptly in nature, its operation would be wholly dialectical, and in a sense of dialectic which is non-existential not only for the time being, but forever; that is dialectic would be without any *possible* reference to existence. We are so used by tradition both to separating mind from the world and noting that its acts and consequences are relevant to the world-error—aberration and insanity can exist only with respect to relevancy—that we find it easier to make a problem out of the conjunction of two inconsistent premises than to rethink our premises.

Of pure dialectic it is a truism that it is neither materially true nor false, but only self-consistent or else self-contradictory. Were it not for the distorting influence of material bias, of preference that *existence* be thus and so rather than otherwise, and of desire that other creatures should believe as we do or should accept our conclusions, dialectic and calculation would however not be subject even to inconsistency. Some purely logical operations are better than others, even as purely logical, for they have greater scope and fertility, but none are truer or more correct than others. Purely formal errors are impossible, so-called

formal fallacies to the contrary notwithstanding. No one ever actually reasoned that since horses are quadrupeds and cows are quadrupeds, horses are cows. If in some cases, it is made to appear that formal reasoning falls into such fallacies, the reason is that material causes are brought in and their operation is overlooked. Dialectical relations are dialectical, not existential and therefore have no causative power; there is nothing in them to generate misconception. The principle of dialectic is identity; its opposite is not inconsistency to say nothing of falsity; it is nonsense. To say that dialectic as such is infallible is only to say it is truistic.

Nevertheless logic or the *use* of meanings in a dialectic manner is actually exposed to all sorts of mistakes. For every instance of dialectic is itself existential. Meanings are taken; they are employed for a purpose, just as other materials are; they are combined and disjoined. It is the act of *taking* which enables dialectic to exist or occur, and taking is fallible, it is often mis-taking. Using meanings is a particular act; into this act enter causative factors, physiological, social, moral. The most perfect structure may be employed for purposes to which it is not apt; wrongly employed for the right purpose, it will buckle or default. Thus in dialectic, reasoning may flag because of fatigue; it may take one meaning for another because of perverse sensory appreciations, due to organic maladjustments; haste, due to absence of inhibition, may lead one to take a meaning to be clear when it is cloudy or ambiguous with respect to the purpose for which it is used, although in itself it is neither clear nor obscure; a desire to show off or to confute an opponent may lead to inconsistency and extraneous irrelevancies. Thousands of things may cause fallacies, when meanings truistically infallible because just what they are, are *used* to reach an end or make a conclusion. Self-contradiction assuredly occurs but it is material and active, not formal and non-existential. We contradict ourselves precisely as we contradict another person and for much the same reasons.

The ownership of meanings or mind thus vests in nature; meanings are meanings *of*. The existence of error is proof, not disproof, of the fact that all meanings intrinsically have reference to natural events. The idealist who employs the existence of error and of detection and possible correction of error as evidence of the existence of a pre-existent truth in which errors are contained in their total relationship, and hence are not errors but constituents of truth, is right in the insistence that error involves objective reference. But in the same way digestion involves food-stuffs; and yet does not prove that there pre-exists a model digestion in which food is perfectly assimilated. Error involves a possibility of detection and corrections because it refers to things, but the possibility has an eventual, not a backward reference. It denotes the possibility of acts yet to be undertaken. Like the criterion of perfect efficiency in respect to machines, the notion of a complete judgment in which errors exist only as a rectified constituent of a perfect truth, is part of the art of examination and invention. Action and reaction are equal, to a hundred per cent of equality; but this formal "law" does not guarantee that in any particular system of action-reaction there is contained perfect efficiency. Similarly the objective reference of meanings is complete; it is a hundred per cent affair; but it takes errors as well as truth to make up the hundred per cent, as it takes waste as well as efficiency to make up the perfect equality of action and reaction.

We mark off certain uses of meanings as reveries in order to control better the cognitive reference of other meanings. So we mark off certain meanings as purely rational or ideal, as dialectical or non-existential, in order to control better an eventual existential reference. Meaning may *become* purely esthetic; it may be appropriated and enjoyed for what it is in the having. This also involves control; it is *such* a way of taking and using them as to suspend cognitive reference.[1] This suspension is an acquired art. It required long discipline to recognize poetry instead of taking it as history, instruction and prediction. The idea that meanings are originally floating and esthetic and become intellectual, or practical and cognitive, by a conjunction of happy accidents, puts the cart before the horse. Its element of truth is that there is genuine distinction between having a meaning and using it; the ele-

ment of falsity is in supposing that meanings, ideas, are first had and afterwards used. It required long experience to enforce recognition of the distinction; for originally any meaning had, is had in and for use. To hold an idea contemplatively and esthetically is a late achievement in civilization.

Organic and psycho-physical activities with their qualities are conditions which have to come into existence before mind, the presence and operation of meanings, ideas, is possible. They supply mind with its footing and connection in nature; they provide meanings with their existential stuff. But meanings, ideas, are also, when they occur, characters of a new interaction of events; they are characters which in their incorporation with sentiency transform organic action, furnishing it with new properties. Every thought and meaning has its substratum in some organic act of absorption or elimination of seeking, or turning away from, of destroying or caring for, of signaling or responding. It roots in some definite act of biological behavior; our physical names for mental acts like seeing, grasping, searching, affirming, acquiescing, spurning, comprehending, affection, emotion are not just "metaphors." But while a burnt child may shrink from flame just as the dog cowers at the sight of a stick, a child may in addition, when the conditions involved have become a matter of discourse and are ideas, respond to the burn-giving flame in playful, inventive, curious and investigative ways. He pokes a stick or piece of paper into it; he uses flame and the fact of its painful and burning consequence not just to keep away from it, but to do things with it in ways which will satisfy his want to have to do with fire but without getting burned. Biological acts persist, but have sense, meaning, as well as feeling, tone. Abrupt withdrawal having only negative, protective consequences is turned into significant and fruitful exploration and manipulation. Man combines meanings, like fire, nearness, remoteness, warmth, comfort, nice, pain, expansion, softening, so that fire enters into new interactions and effects new consequences. By an intra-organic re-enactment of partial animal reactions to natural events, and of accompanying reactions to and from others acquired in intercourse and communication, means-consequences are tried out in advance without the organism getting irretrievably involved in physical consequences. Thought, deliberation, objectively directed imagination, in other words, is an added efficacious function of natural events and hence brings into being new consequences. For images are not made of psychical stuff; they are qualities of *partial* organic behaviors, which are their "stuff." They are partial because not fully geared to extero-ceptor and muscular activities, and hence not complete and overt.

Domination by spatial considerations leads some thinkers to ask *where* mind is. Reserving the discussion of *conscious* behavior for the next chapter, and accepting for the moment the standpoint of the questioner (which ignores the locus of discourse, institutions and social arts), limiting the question to the organic individual, we may say that the "seat" or locus of mind—its static phase—is the qualities of organic action, as far as these qualities have been conditioned by language and its consequences. It is usual for those who are posed by the question of "where" and who are reluctant to answer that mind is "where" there is a spaceless separate realm of existence, to fall back in general on the nervous system, and specifically upon the brain or its cortex as the "seat" of mind. But the organism is not just a structure; it is a characteristic way of interactivity which is not simultaneous, all at once, but serial. It is a way impossible without structures for its mechanism, but it differs from structure as walking differs from legs or breathing from lungs. Prior to communication, the qualities of this action are what we have termed psycho-physical; they are not "mental." The consequences of partaking in communication modify organic ways of acting; the latter attain new qualities.

When I think such meanings as "friend" and "enemy," I refer to external and eventual consequences. But this naming does not involve miraculous "action at a distance." There is something present in organic action which acts as a surrogate for the remote things signified. The words make immediate sense as well as have signification. This something now present is not just the activity of the laryngeal and vocal apparatus. When shortcircuiting

through language is carried as far as limitation to this apparatus, words are mere counters automatically used, and language disappears. The ideas are qualities of events in all the parts of organic structure which have ever been implicated in actual situations of concern with extra-organic friends and enemies:—presumably in proprioreceptors and organ-receptors with *all* their connected glandular and muscular mechanisms. These qualities give body and stuff to the activity of the linguistic apparatus. The integration of the qualities of vocal apparatus allied through the nervous mechanism with the qualities of these other events, constitutes the immediate sense of friendliness and animosity. The more intimate the alliance of vocal activity with the total organic disposition toward friends and enemies, the greater is the immediate sense of the words. The nervous system is in no sense the "seat" of the idea. It is the mechanism of the connection or integration of acts.

"Socrates is mortal" is hardly more than a counter of logical text-books; S is M will do just as well—or better. But not so to the disciples of Socrates who had just heard of his condemnation to death. The connection of the auditory act with the totality of organic responses was then complete. In some linguistic situations, such emphatic immediate presence of sense occurs; language is then poetical. For other purposes, action is served by elimination of immediate sense as far as possible. The attitude is prosaic; it is best subserved by mathematical symbolism; mathematical not signifying something ready-made, but being simply the devices by which mind is rigidly occupied with instrumental objects, by means of artificial inhibition of immediate and consummatory qualities, the latter being distracting for the activity in hand. The consummatory phase cannot be suppressed or eliminated however; nature pitched through the door returns through the window. And the common form of its return today is falling down in worship or in fear before the resulting mathematico-mechanical object.

In conclusion, it may be asserted that "soul" when freed from all traces of traditional materialistic animism denotes the qualities of psycho-physical activities as far as these are organized into unity. Some bodies have souls preeminently as some conspicuously have fragrance, color, and solidity. To make this statement is to call attention to properties that characterize these bodies, not to import a mysterious non-natural entity or force. Were there not in actual existence properties of sensitivity and of marvelously comprehensive and delicate participative response characterizing living bodies, mythical notions about the nature of the soul would never have risen. The myths have lost whatever poetic quality they once had; when offered as science they are superstitious encumbrances. But the idiomatic non-doctrinal use of the word soul retains a sense of the realities concerned. To say emphatically of a particular person that he has soul or a great soul is not to utter a platitude, applicable equally to all human beings. It expresses the conviction that the man or woman in question has in marked degree qualities of sensitive, rich and coordinated participation in all the situations of life. Thus works of art, music, poetry, painting, architecture, have soul, while others are dead, mechanical.

When the organization called soul is free, moving and operative, initial as well as terminal, it is spirit. Qualities are both static, substantial, and transitive. Spirit quickens; it is not only alive, but spirit gives life. Animals are spirited, but man is a living spirit. He lives in his works and his works do follow him. Soul is form, spirit informs. It is the moving function of that of which soul is the substance. Perhaps the words soul and spirit are so heavily laden with traditional mythology and sophisticated doctrine that they must be surrendered; it may be impossible to recover for them in science and philosophy the realities designated in idiomatic speech. But the realities are there, by whatever names they be called.

Old ideas do not die when the beliefs which have been explicitly associated with them disappear; they usually only change their clothes. Present notions about the organism are largely a survival, with changed vocabulary, of old ideas about soul and body. The soul was conceived as inhabiting the body in an external way. Now the nervous system is conceived as a substitute, mysteriously within the body. But as the soul was "simple" and there-fore not diffused through the body, so the nervous system as the seat of mental events is narrowed down to the brain, and then to the cortex of the brain; while many physiological inquirers would doubtless feel enormously relieved if a specific portion of the cortex could be ascertained to be *the* seat of consciousness. Those who talk most of the organism, physiologists and psychologists, are often just those who display least sense of the intimate, delicate and subtle interdependence of all organic structures and processes with one another. The world seems mad in preoccupation with what is specific, particular, disconnected in medicine, politics, science, industry, education. In terms of a conscious control of inclusive wholes, search for those links which occupy key positions and which effect critical connections is indispensable. But recovery of sanity depends upon seeing and using these specifiable things *as* links functionally significant in a process. To see the organism *in* nature, the nervous system in the organism, the brain in the nervous system, the cortex in the brain is the answer to the problems which haunt philosophy. And when thus seen they will be seen to be *in*, not as marbles are in a box but as events are in history, in a moving, growing never finished process. Until we have a procedure in actual practice which demonstrates this continuity, we shall continue to engage in appealing to some other specific thing, some other broken off affair, to restore connectedness and unity—calling the specific religion or reform or whatever specific is the fashionable cure of the period. Thus we increase the disease in the means used to cure it.[2]

In matters predominantly physical we know that all control depends upon conscious perception of relations obtaining between things, otherwise one cannot be used to affect the other. We have been marvellously successful in inventing and constructing external machines, because with respect to such things we take for granted that success occurs only upon the conscious plane—that of conscious perception of the relations which things sustain to one another. We know that locomotives and aeroplanes and telephones and power-plants do not arise from instinct or the subconscious but from deliberately ascertained perception of connections and orders of connections. Now after a period in which advance in these respects was complacently treated as proof and measure of progress, we have been forced to adopt pessimistic attitudes, and to wonder if this "progress" is to end in the deterioration of man and the possible destruction of civilization.

Clearly we have not carried the plane of conscious control, the direction of action by perception of connections, far enough. We cannot separate organic life and mind from physical nature without also separating nature from life and mind. The separation has reached a point where intelligent persons are asking whether the end is to be catastrophe, the subjection of man to the industrial and military machines he has created. This situation confers peculiar poignancy upon the fact that just where connections and interdependences are most numerous, intimate and pervasive, in living, psycho-physical activity, we most ignore unity and connection, and trust most unreservedly in our deliberate beliefs to the isolated and specific—which signifies that in action we commit ourselves to the unconscious and subconscious, to blind instinct and impulse and routine, disguised and rationalized by all sorts of honorific titles. Thus we are brought to the topic of consciousness.

NOTES

[LW 1:191–225.]

1. This statement does not rest upon a confusion between objects as causal conditions of meanings and objects as cognitively meant. The distinction is a genuine one, not to be slighted. The former connection is antecedent, the latter is subsequential. But meanings or mind have both kinds of connection. Greek myths for example were adequately conditioned in existence; but they also have a diagnostic status. When not taken as meanings of the behavior of gods, they are taken as meanings of Greek life, just as a hallucinatory ghost when not taken as a spiritual apparition is taken as meaning another event, say, a nervous shock. *Having* a meaning is not a reference, but every meaning had is taken or used as well as had. "Dialectic" means to take it a certain way.

2. See F. Matthias Alexander's *Man's Supreme Inheritance*, and *Constructive Conscious Control of the Individual*.

Nature in Experience

(1940)

The topic announced for this session is capable of two interpretations. When it was communicated to me I took it to mean that the subject for discussion was the relation between the theory of experience and the theory of nature. When the two papers we have just heard were sent to me I found that impression borne out in part. But it also became clear that the topic could be interpreted broadly so that anything I have written concerning either nature or experience is open for consideration. I had then to decide how should I plan my reply. I have adopted the first of the two versions. It has the advantage of enabling me to centralize what I have to say, since I should otherwise have to disperse what I have to say over a large variety of topics. It has the disadvantage that it may seem to show lack of respect for some quite important criticisms that are passed over, and perhaps that of accepting as sound the interpretations upon which the criticisms rest.

In this dilemma the finally decisive consideration was that the course which enables me to introduce more unity and organization serves also to focus attention upon a problem which is so central in philosophy that it must be met and dealt with by all schools. The theme of the Carus Lectures, to which we are having the pleasure of listening, brings to our attention the importance of the category of perspectives, and this matter of perspectives is basic in the issue of the connection between nature and experience. I find that with respect to the hanging together of various problems and various hypotheses in a perspective determined by a definite point of view, I have a system. In so far I have to retract disparaging remarks I have made in the past about the need for system in philosophy.

The peculiar importance in philosophy of a point of view and of the perspective it institutes is enhanced by the fact that a fairly large number of alternative points of view have been worked out in the history of philosophy in terms of the ways in which the world looks from them; that is to say, in terms of the leading categories by which the things of the world are to be understood. The significations attached to words and ideas which recur in practically every system tend to become fixed till it seems as if no choice were left, save to give the names (and the problems to which they relate) the import sanctioned by some one or other past philosophic point of view. In the degree in which a philosophy involves a shift from older points of view and from what is seen in their perspectives, both its author and those to whom he addresses himself find themselves in difficulties. The former has to use words that have meanings fixed under conditions of more or less alien points of view and the latter have to engage in some kind of imaginative translation.

The bearing of this general remark upon the present theme has to do first of all with the word "experience" and the allied word "empiricism." There is a long tradition of empiricism in the story of philosophy; upon the whole the tradition is particularistic and nominalistic, if not overtly sensationalistic, in its logic and ontology. When empiricism has escaped from the limits thereby set it has, upon the whole, been through making human experience the broken but still usable ladder of ascent to an absolute experience, and there has been a flight to some form of cosmic idealism. Presentation of a view of experience which puts experience in connection with nature, with the cosmos, but which would nevertheless frame its view of experience on the ground of conclusions reached in the natural sciences, has trouble in finding ways of expressing itself which do not seem to lead into one or the other of these historically sanctioned alternative perspectives.

There is a circularity in the position taken regarding the connection of experience and nature. Upon one side, analysis and interpretation of nature is made dependent upon the conclusions of the natural sciences, especially upon biology, but upon a biology that is itself dependent upon physics and chemistry. But when I say "dependent" I mean that the intellectual instrumentalities, the organs, for understanding the new and distinctive material of experienced objects are provided by the natural sciences. I do *not* mean that the material of experienced things *qua* experienced must be translated into the terms of the material of the physical sciences; that view leads to a naturalism which denies distinctive significance to experience, thereby ending in the identification of naturalism with mechanistic materialism.

The other aspect of the circle is found in the fact that it is held that experience itself, even ordinary gross macroscopic experience, contains the materials and the processes and operations which, when they are rightly laid hold of and used, lead to the methods and conclusions of the natural sciences; namely, to the very conclusions that provide the means for forming a theory of experience. That this circle exists is not so much admitted as claimed. It is also claimed that the circle is not vicious; for instead of being logical it is existential and historic. That is to say, if we look at human history and especially at the historic development of the natural sciences, we find progress made from a crude experience in which beliefs about nature and natural events were very different from those now scientifically authorized. At the same time we find the latter now enable us to frame a theory of experience by which we can tell *how* this development out of gross experience into the highly refined conclusions of science has taken place.

I come now to certain topics and criticism to be dealt with on the basis of the idea of this circular relation. The most inclusive criticism of my friend Morris Cohen is suggested, I think, by the word "anthropocentric" in the title of his paper; it is expressed in the saying that my absorption in human experience prevents me from formulating any adequate theory of non-human or physical nature. In short, it is held that the fact—which is not denied to be a fact—that experience involves a human element limits a philosophy that makes experience primary to human affairs as its sole material; hence it does not admit of propositions about such things as, say, the origin of life on earth or the events of geological ages preceding the advent of man and hence, of necessity, human experience.

Now there is a problem here which every empirical philosophy must meet; it can evade the challenge only to its own damage. Yet the problem is not confined to empiricism; the existence of experience is a fact, and it is fact that the organs of experience, the body, the nervous system, hands and eyes, muscles and senses, are means by which we have access to the non-human world. It would seem then as if the philosophy which denies that it is possible for experienced things and processes to form a road into the natural world must be controlled by an underlying postulate that there is a breach of continuity between nature and man and hence between nature and human experience. At all events, a fundamental question is raised. Is experience itself natural, a doing or manifestation of nature? Or is it in some genuine sense extra-natural, sub-natural or super-natural, something superimposed and alien? At all events, this is the setting in which I shall place and interpret some of the more basic criticisms passed upon my views.

(1) There are traits, qualities, and relations found in things experienced, in the things that are typically and emphatically matters of human experience, which do not appear in the objects of physical science; namely, such things as immediate qualities, values, ends. Are such things inherently relevant and important for a philosophical theory of nature? I have held that philosophical empiricism must take the position that they are intrinsically pertinent. I have written (and Cohen has quoted): "It is as much a part of the real being of atoms that they give rise in time, under increasing complications of relationships, to qualities of blue and sweet, pain and beauty, as that they have, at a certain cross-section of time, extension, mass or weight." Now whether this statement is correct or false, it is simply an illustration of what any theory must hold which sees things in the perspective determined by the continuity of experience with nature.[1]

I also write that domination of man by desire and reverie is as pertinent to a philosophical theory of nature as is mathematical physics. The point of this statement is also truistic, given the point of view of the continuity of experience with nature. It certainly is not countered by the statement that "For the understanding of the general processes of nature throughout time and space, the existence of human reverie and desire is surely not as illuminating as are considerations of mathematical physics." For the whole point of the passage is that qualities of experienced things that are not the least bit illuminating for the understanding of nature in physical science are as

important for a philosophy of nature as the thing most illuminating, namely mathematical physics—a view, as I have said, which any theory making experience continuous with nature is bound to hold.

This point gains more general philosophical significance because of the fact that qualities and values, which are not traits of the objects of natural science as these are now ascertained to be, were once completely fused with the material of what was taken to be science. The whole classic cosmology or theory of nature is framed in this sense. It is the progress of natural science itself that has destroyed this cosmology. As the history of modern philosophy proves, this destruction brought about that crisis which is represented by the bifurcation expressed in the dualistic opposition of subjective and objective, mind and matter, experience and nature. The problem involved is one which all philosophies alike must face. Any one view, such as the one I have set forth, can be intelligently criticized only from the standpoint of some alternative theory, while theories of bifurcation have their own difficulties and troubles, as the history of modern thought abundantly proves.[2] Affirmation of the continuity of experience with nature has its difficulties. But they are not grasped nor the theory refuted by translating what it says into terms of a theory which assumes that the presence of the human factor in experience precludes getting from experience to the non-human or physical.

(2) The passage which has been cited about the "real being" of the atom contains an explicit contrast between nature as judged in a short-time span or "cross-section" and in a long temporal span—one long enough to cover the emergence of human beings and their experiences. In order to be understood, what I have said about genesis and function, about antecedents and consequences, has to be placed in the perspective suggested by this emphasis upon the need of formulating a theory of nature and of the connections of man *in* (not *to*) nature on the basis of a temporal continuum.

What is basically involved is that some changes, those for example which terminate in the things of human experience, form a *history*, or a set of changes marked by development or growth. The dichotomy of the old discussion as to whether antecedents or ends are of primary importance in forming a theory of nature is done away with when growth, development, history is taken to be primary. Genesis and ends are of equal importance, but their import is that of terms or boundaries which delimit a history, thereby rendering it capable of description. The sentence before the one about the atom, reads, for example, as follows: "For knowledge, 'cause' and 'effect' have a partial and truncated being"; the paragraph as a whole is devoted to criticizing the notion that causal conditions have a "reality" superior to that of outcomes or effects. It is argued that the prevalent view which attributes superior rank to them results from hypostatizing a *function*: the function of causal conditions as means of control (ultimately, the *sole* means of control) is converted into a direct ontological property. Moreover, the chapter of which the paragraph is a part is devoted to showing that while Existence as process and as history involves "ends," the change from ancient to modern science compels us to interpret ends relatively and pluralistically, because as limits of specifiable histories.

Of the many special points which follow from this basic element in my theory of the connection of experience with nature—as itself an historical outcome or "end," I shall here deal with only one. In what I have said about meanings my critic finds an undue importance attached to consequences; in what I say (in a discussion devoted to a special problem) about the background of Greek philosophy he finds an equally one-sided importance attached to genesis. That in discussion of one particular history the emphasis with respect to a particular problem falls upon results, and in another history discussed in respect to another particular problem, emphasis falls upon antecedents, involves no inconsistency. With respect to consequences in their connection with meaning and verification I have repeatedly and explicitly insisted upon the fact that there is no way of telling what the consequences are save by discovery of antecedents, so that the latter are necessary and yet are subordinate in function.[3]

(3) Another aspect of the perspective determined by the point of view expressed in the continuity of nature and experience concerns the relation of theory and practical ends, particularly of physical science and morals. It is about this point, unless I am mistaken, that the fundamental criticisms of Cohen cluster, since the passages upon which the criticisms are based are interpreted in another perspective than that in which they are stated. The fact that I have, quite consistently and persistently, as far as I am aware, insisted that inquiry should follow the lead of its subject-matter[4] and not be subordinated to any end or motive having an external source, is less important than the fact that any other view would be contradictory to my main theses regarding (i) the place of the natural sciences in the formation of the ends and values of practical life, and (ii) the importance of the experimental method of the natural sciences as the model for the sciences involving human practice, or the social and moral disciplines.

The view I have put forward about the nature of that to which the adjective "physical" applies is that, while it is arrived at by following out clews given in directly experimental matter, it constitutes the *conditions* upon which all the qualities and terminal values, the consummations, of experience, depend. Hence those things which are physical are the sole means that exist for control of values and qualities. To read anything extraneous into them, to tamper in any way with the integrity of the inquiry of which they are the product, would thus be to nullify the very function in terms of which the *physical* as such is defined. I have even gone so far as to ascribe the backwardness of the human, the practical, sciences in part to the long period of backwardness of the physical sciences themselves and in part to the refusal of moralists and social scientists to utilize the physical, especially the biological, material that is at their disposal.

(4) These considerations bring me to my view regarding the nature and function of philosophy, a point which I think will be found crucial for the interpretation, and hence the criticism, of the passages upon which Cohen bases his view that I have pretty systematically subordinated inquiry, reflection, and science to extraneous practical ends. For speaking of *philosophy* (not of science) I have constantly

insisted that since it contains value-considerations within itself, indispensable to its existence as philosophy—in distinction from science—it has a "practical," that is a *moral* function, and I have held that since this element is inherent, the failure of philosophies to recognize and make explicit its presence introduces undesirable properties into them, leading them on one side to make claims of being purely cognitive, which bring them into rivalry with science, and on the other side to neglect of the field in which they may be genuinely significant, that of possible guidance of human activity in the field of values.

The following passage is fairly typical of what I have said: "What would be its [philosophy's] office if it ceased to deal with the problem of reality and knowledge at large? In effect, its function would be to facilitate the fruitful interaction of our cognitive beliefs, our beliefs resting upon the most dependable methods of inquiry, with our practical beliefs about the values, the ends and purposes, that should control human action in the things of large and liberal human import."[5] Now whether this view of the nature of philosophic as distinct from distinctively scientific inquiry is correct or incorrect, the following points are so involved that the view cannot be understood without taking them into account: (i) It is one aspect of the general position of the experiential continuum constituted by the interaction of different modes of experienced things, in this case of the scientific and the moral; (ii) it gives philosophy a subject-matter distinct from the subject-matter of science and yet inherently connected with the latter, namely, the bearing of the conclusions reached in science ("the most dependable methods of inquiry") upon the value-factors involved in human action; (iii) there is no subordination of the results of knowledge to any preconceived scheme of values or predetermined practical ends (such as fixes the usual meaning of "reform"), but rather emphasis upon the reconstruction of existing ends and values in behalf of more generous and liberal human activities.

Now whether this view of philosophy is right or wrong (and my critic says nothing about what he takes to be the subject-matter and function of philosophy in connection with,

or distinction from, that of science), if what is said about philosophy is taken to be said about science or about reflection in general, the meanings which result will be justly exposed to all the criticisms passed upon them.[6] It is perhaps significant that Cohen himself virtually recognizes the presence of the human and moral factor in philosophy as distinct from science. For the "resignation" which he finds to be the lesson taught by a just theory of nature is surely a human and moral factor; it remains such even if I have over-emphasized the traits of courage and active responsibility, as I may have done in view of the fact that resignation and the purely consolatory office of philosophy have received more than enough emphasis in the historical tradition. But I have also pointed out that the classic or catholic version of that tradition recognizes that this lesson of passive resignation is not final; that it has to be supplemented by a divine institution which undertakes the positive function of guidance, and that in so far the practical logic of the situation is with the Church rather than with traditional philosophy which is minus institutional support and aid. As far as I am concerned the issue is between a theory of experience in nature which renders experienced things and operations impotent, and a theory which would search for and utilize the *things in experience* that are capable of progressively providing the needed support and guidance.[7] Finally, while I am grateful and deeply appreciative of Cohen's approval of my personal liberalism, I must add not only that this liberalism is definitely rooted in the very philosophy to which he takes exception, but that any theory of activity in social and moral matters, liberal or otherwise, which is not grounded in a comprehensive philosophy seems to me to be only a projection of arbitrary personal preference.

I come now, rather belatedly, to the criticisms of my other friendly critic, Ernest Hocking. If I grasp aright the point of view from which his criticisms are made, it does not involve the postulate of separation of experience from nature that is found in Cohen's criticisms, but rather a point of departure similar to mine. In that respect, Cohen's paper involves a criticism of Hocking as well as of me, and reciprocally. The trouble with my views lies, then, according to Hocking, in the account I have given of experience, primarily in my failure to give its due place and weight to thought in relation to knowledge and to the world of reality. I am grateful to Hocking for his explicit recognition of the place given in my theory of knowledge to thought and theory, to his recognition that in my theory "the scientific process is intellectualized to the last limit." His conclusion that, since I have done this, I am logically bound to go farther and take the position that "the more thought, the more reality," thus has a relevancy to my position not possessed by criticisms based upon the notion that I have adopted the depreciatory view of thought, theory, and abstraction characteristic of traditional nominalistic empiricism.

(1) However, in criticizing sensational and particularistic empiricism and in insisting upon the indispensable role of thought and theory in the determination of scientific objects, I have not gone so far as to deny the really indispensable role of observed material and the processes of observation. On the contrary, I have criticized traditional rationalism, not indeed for pointing out the necessary operational presence of thought, but for its failure to recognize the essential role of observation to bring into existence that material by which objects of thought are tested and validated—or the contrary—so as to be given something more than a hypothetical status. I quote from Hocking the following passage, speaking of such things as atoms and electrons: "Dewey will not say that I observe them, but only that I think them. I agree. But is the atom then less real than the chair?" My view more completely stated is that *at present* atom and electron are objects of thought *rather* than of observation. But, instead of denying the necessity of observed material, or even the possibility of observation of objects that are atomic in the scientific sense, I have held that the theoretical value of the atom consists in its ability, as a hypothesis or *thought*, to direct observations experimentally and to coordinate their results. The mere observation of something which if it were observed by a physicist would be an atom is not, however, observation

of an atom as a *scientific object* unless and only in so far as it meets the requirements of definition which has been attained by a set of systematic inferences, that is, of the function to which the name thought is given. The place of differential equations in the formulation of the atom as a scientific theoretical and hypothetical object is undeniable. But the equations as far as atoms as *existences* are concerned (in distinction from their function in facilitating and directing further inferences) state conditions to be satisfied by any observed material if it is to be warrantably asserted to *be* atomic.

(2) The formulation of the conditions to be satisfied takes a form which prescribes operations that are to be performed in instituting and interpreting observations. This fact leads to consideration of what Hocking says about operations. *If* thought and its object *as* object of thought were as complete and final apart from any connection with observed things as Hocking assumes them to be, then the operational view of scientific objects would indeed hang idly and unsupported in the void. To place, as Hocking does, interest in the entities of differential equations in opposition to interest in operations is to overlook, it seems to me, the fundamental thesis of operationalism; namely that these entities, as far as physics, including mathematical physics, is concerned, *are* formulations of operations to be performed in obtaining specified observed materials and determining whether or not that material answers to or satisfies certain conditions imposed upon it if it is to merit the name of a certain scientific object, atom, electron, or whatever. As I have frequently said, a given scientific person may occupy himself exclusively with the mathematical aspect of the matter, and do so fruitfully as far as the historic development of a science is concerned. But this fact taken by itself is not decisive about the actual place and function of the mathematical material.

(3) I come now to another criticism of Hocking's, connected with the "reality" part of his saying "the more thought, the more reality." My criticism of Hocking's criticism has up to this point concerned only the first part of his sentence. It amounts to saying that while he has not disrupted the continuity of experi-

ence with nature, he has, to my mind, broken off one aspect of experience, namely thought, from another aspect, that of perception. Further consequences of this artificial breach seem to me to be found in what he says about "reality." It is quite true, as he says, that one meaning of reality is the "independent being upon which other things depend"; and he finds this independent being in "the content of true judgment," a saying which seems to me to express in an almost flagrantly emphatic way the isolation of one mode of experience and its material from other modes and *their* things. For he goes on to say that Nature, as the content of true judgment or the object of perfect thought in its capacity of measure of knowledge, is the independent reality of which experience is the dependent derivative.

Now reality is, I fear, more than a double-barrelled word. Its ambiguity and slipperiness extend beyond the two significations which Hocking mentions in such a way as to affect the interpretation of "independence" and "dependence" in the view taken by him. For there is a definitely pragmatic meaning of "dependence" and "derivation," which affects the meaning of that most dangerous of all philosophical words, "reality." The objects of knowledge, when once attained, exercise, as I have already said, the function of *control* over other materials. Hence the latter in so far depend for their status and value upon the object of knowledge. The idea of the ether was dropped when it ceased to exercise any office of control over investigations. The idea of quanta has increased its role because of its efficacy and fertility in control of inquiries. But this interpretation of dependence is strictly functional. Instead of first isolating the object of knowledge or judgment and then setting it up in its isolation as a measure of the "reality" of other things, it connects the scientific object, genetically and functionally, with other things without casting the invidious shadow of a lesser degree of reality upon the latter.

(4) This consideration brings me to the fourth point in Hocking's paper upon which I shall comment. It is of course true that I have emphasized the temporal continuity of inquiry, and in consequence the dependence of conclusions reached at a given time upon the methods and results of previous investigations, and their subjection to modification in subsequent inquiries. But, as far as I can see, the idea that this view indefinitely defers possession and enjoyment of stable objects to the end of an infinite progression applies rather to Hocking's position than to mine. That is, if I held that thought is the only valid approach to "reality" and that the latter is the content of a perfect judgment, I should be troubled by the question of the worth, from the standpoint of reality, of all my present conclusions.

But I do not see that the question arises within the perspective of my own point of view. For in the latter, instead of there being isolation of the material of knowledge, there is its continual interaction with the things of other forms of experience, and the worth (or "reality") of the former is to be judged on the basis of the control exercised by it over the things of non-cognitive experiences and the increment of enriched meaning supplied to them. Even from the standpoint of knowledge by itself, inquiry produces such cumulative verification and stability that the prospect of future modification is an *added* value, just as in all other affairs of life those accomplishments that open up new prospects and new possibilities are enhanced, not depressed, by their power in this respect. But what is even more important is that, from the standpoint of the continuous interaction of the things of different modes of experience, the final test of the value of "contents of judgment" now attained is found not in their relation to the content of some final judgment, to be reached at the close of an infinite progression, but in what is done in the living present, what is done in giving enriched meaning to other things and in increasing our control over them.

In recurring to what I said at the outset about my choice of a theme, I wish to repeat that the limitation of my reply to criticisms passed upon my views only so far as they bear upon the problem of the connection of experience with nature is not intended to be evasive, nor does it evince lack of respect for criticisms I have not touched upon. I have not in the past been as unobservant or inattentive of criticisms as my good friend Ernest Hocking has humorously suggested. On the contrary, if my views have progressed either in clarity or in range, as I hope they have done, it is mainly because of what my critics have said and the thought I have given their criticisms. Given a point of view that determines a perspective and the nature and arrangement of things seen in that perspective, the point of view is, I suppose, the last thing to be seen. In fact it is never capable of being seen unless there is some change from the old point of view.

Criticisms are the means by which one is enabled to take, at least in imagination, a new point of view, and thus to re-see, literally to review and revise, what fell within one's earlier perspective. If I have succeeded today in making my views clearer to others than I have managed to do in my previous writings, it is because my critics have made their import clearer to myself. For that I am grateful to them, as I am deeply appreciative of the honor the Association and my friends Morris Cohen and Ernest Hocking have done me in giving time and thought to my writings.

NOTES

[First published in *Philosophical Review* 49 (March 1940): 244–58, from an address at the American Philosophical Association symposium on Dewey's Concepts of Experience and Nature, at Columbia University on 28 December 1939, in honor of his eightieth birthday. For addresses to which this is a reply, see Morris R. Cohen, "Some Difficulties in Dewey's Anthropocentric Naturalism," ibid., pp. 196–228, and William Ernest Hocking, "Dewey's Concepts of Experience and Nature," ibid., pp. 228–44 (print edition, Appendixes 1 and 2). LW 14:141–54.]

1. "Giving rise to" implies no particular theory as to causal determination, and the word "atom" is used illustratively. The point made would be the same if at some time in the future natural science abandoned the atomic theory and put something else in the place of atoms.

2. While Cohen, it seems to me, has somewhat overstated my opposition to Greek and medieval philosophy, it is just the fact of the enormous change that has taken place in the method and conclusions of natural science which is the ground of my insistence upon need for a radical change in the theory of nature and of knowledge. Upon this point, it seems to me that it is rather Cohen than myself who fails to attach sufficient importance to physical science in its relation to philosophy. Piety to classic thought is an admirable trait; but a revolution in the physical constituents of nature demands considerable change in cosmological theory, as change in the method of inquiry demands reconstruction *in* (though not *of*) logic.

3. My use of the compound word "genetic-functional" to describe what I regard as the proper method of philosophy is, then, directly linked to the position taken regarding the temporal continuum.

4. I would call attention to one passage, found on pp. 67–68 of *The Quest for Certainty* (cf. p. 228) [*Later Works* 4:55, 182]. The text states the nature of the ambiguity in the word "theoretical" which is the source of misunderstanding, the confusion of the attitude of the *inquirer* with the nature of the *subject-matter* inquired into. It is explicitly said that the former must be theoretical and cognitive, purged of personal desire and preference, marked by willingness to subordinate them to the lead of subject-matter. But it is also said that only inquiry itself can determine whether or not *subject-matter* contains practical conditions and qualities. To argue from the strictly theoretical character of the motives of the inquirer, from the necessity for "disinterested curiosity," to the nature of that investigated is a kind of "anthropocentrism" of which I should not wish to be guilty.

5. *The Quest for Certainty*, 36–37 [*Later Works* 4:29].

6. It often happens in addition that what is said about a particular type of philosophic system, in a context which qualifies what is said, is taken by Cohen absolutely, without qualification. For example, if the reader will consult the passage (*The Influence of Darwin*, 298–299 [*Early Works* 5:21]) containing the words "luxury," "nuisance," etc., it will be seen that instead of referring to philosophy in general or even to a particular historical school or schools—much less to impartial inquiry—it is qualified by a succession of "ifs." And the passage which says (*Creative Intelligence*, 60 [*Middle Works* 10:42]) that philosophy is of account only if it affords guidance to action, occurs in a paragraph dealing with the grounds for the difference between the popular and the professional reception of "pragmatism," not in a statement of my own view, although the idea that philosophy is love of wisdom as distinct from love of knowledge and that "philosophy is the guide of life" is not peculiarly new nor peculiarly a product of pragmatism.

7. Since readers cannot be expected to look up all quotations made from my writings, I will say that the sentence about the capacity of man to shape his own destiny is part of a passage about the atmosphere of the eighteenth-century thought which put forth the doctrine of the indefinite perfectibility of man. My own view is much more qualified.

Anti-Naturalism in Extremis

(1943)

Philosophical naturalism has a more distinguished ancestry than is usually recognized; there are, for example, the names of Aristotle and Spinoza. However, the Aristotle who has exercised the greatest influence upon modern philosophy was one whose naturalism did not prevent him from regarding the physical as the lowest stratum in the hierarchical order of Being and from holding that pure intellect, "pure" because free from contamination by any trace of matter, is at the apex. It is to be doubted, however, whether the work of Aristotle would have inured, as it has done, to the credit of anti-naturalism if he had not been adopted as the official philosopher of the Church, and if his writings had not found their way into modern culture through the transformation undergone in the medieval period.

For in this period, the out-and-out supernaturalism of the Roman Catholic Church was injected whenever possible into interpretation of Aristotle. The naturalistic elements in his teaching were overlaid, covered up, with supernatural beliefs; or, if that was not possible, were slurred over as the views of a pagan not enlightened by the Hebraic-Christian revelation from on high. The supernaturalism thus read into Aristotle united with elements in him which are genuinely non-naturalistic from the standpoint of present science. It resulted in his being held up by many modern writers as the founder, in conjunction with Plato, of spiritualistic anti-naturalistic philosophy.

However, when it is a question of moral theory, the naturalism of Aristotle lies so clearly on the face of what he said that medieval Christian theological philosophy was compelled to give it a radically different turn. How different was this turn may be inferred from words of Cardinal Newman which express the orthodox view: "The pattern-man, the just, the upright, the generous, the honourable, the conscientious, if he is all this not from a supernatural power, but from *mere natural virtue*" "has the prospect of heaven closed and refused him."[1] When such measure is meted out to such virtues as honor, uprightness, justice, and generosity, one readily gathers how conduct proceeding from appetite and desire will be judged. For the latter are even more deeply dyed with the Pauline and Augustinian view of the total corruption of the body and the carnal lusts of flesh. The historic source of the doctrine of the corruption of nature and the fallen estate of man may be relegated to the background. But the Western world was reared under the influence of the doctrines and sacraments of the Church. Contrast between the old Adam which is "natural" and a higher self which is "spiritual" remained the assumption of philosophers who avowedly repudiated supernaturalism—as in the striking case of Kant. The Church never forgot to remind its adherents of the lost condition that was due to their fallen estate. For otherwise there would have been no need for the work of redemption supernaturally entrusted to it. Similarly, the professedly non-supernatural philosopher who was anti-naturalist never ceased to dwell upon the merely sensuous and self-seeking character of the natural man and upon the morally seductive character of natural impulse and desire. For otherwise there would be no place for the doctrine that the truly moral factors in human relations are superimposed by a spiritual non-natural source and authority.

It is needful to use such terms as non-naturalist and anti-naturalist. For in addition to frank supernaturalism, there are philosophers who claim to rest their extra- if not super-naturalism upon a higher faculty of Reason or Intuition, or whatever, not upon special divine revelation. While I am personally convinced that their philosophy can be understood only as an historical heritage from frank supernaturalism, I shall not urge that view. I wish rather to call attention to a point of agreement and practical cooperation between the members of the two anti-naturalistic schools. Both of them identify naturalism with "materialism." They then employ the identification to charge naturalists with reduction of all distinctive human values, moral, esthetic, logical, to blind mechanical conjunctions of material entities—a reduction which is in effect their complete destruction. This identification thus permits anti-naturalists to substitute name-calling for a discussion of specific issues in their proper terms in connection with concrete evidence.

Regarding the identification in question, it suffices here to note that the naturalist is one who of necessity has respect for the conclusions of natural science. Hence he is quite aware that "matter" has in modern science none of the low, base, inert properties assigned to it in classic Greek and medieval philosophy:—properties that were the ground for setting it in stark opposition to all that is higher, and to which eulogistic adjectives may be applied. In consequence he is aware that since "matter" and "materialism" acquired their significance in contrast with something called "spirit" and "spiritualism," the fact that naturalism has no place for the latter deprives the former base epithets of philosophic significance. It would be difficult to find a greater distance between any two terms than that which separates "matter" in the Greek-medieval tradition and the technical signification, suitably expressed only in mathematical symbols, the word bears in science today.

Reference to science reminds us that nobody save perhaps the most dogmatic supernaturalist will deny that modern methods of experimental observation have wrought a profound transformation in the subject matters of astronomy, physics, chemistry and biology, or that the change wrought in them has exercised the deepest influence upon human relations. The naturalist adds to recognition of this fact, a further fact of fateful significance. He sees how anti-naturalism has operated to prevent the application of scientific methods in the whole field of human and social subject matter. It has thereby prevented science from completing its career and fulfilling its constructive potentialities, since it has held the human is extra-natural and hence reserved for organs and methods which are radically different from those that have given man the command he now possesses in all affairs, issues, and questions acknowledged to be natural. It is beyond human imagination to estimate the extent to which undesirable features of the present human situation are connected with the split, the division, confusion and conflict that is embodied in this half-way, mixed, unintegrated situation in respect to knowledge and attainment of truth. Democracy cannot obtain either adequate recognition of its own meaning or coherent practical realization as long as anti-naturalism operates to delay and frustrate the use of methods by which alone understanding of, and consequent ability to guide, social relationships can be attained.

In this connection, it is appropriate to say something which is more or less apart from the main topic of this paper. Philosophic naturalism still has a work to do in a field that so far it has hardly done more than touch. Because of the influence of supernatural religion, first Catholic and then Protestant, it is not just "matter" which continues to reflect the beliefs of a pre-scientific and pre-democratic period. Such words as mind, subject, self, person, *the* individual, to say nothing of "value," are more than tinged in their current usage—which affects willy-nilly philosophical formulations—with significations they absorbed from beliefs of an extra-natural character. There is almost no word employed in psychological and societal analysis and description that does not reflect this influence.

Hence comes the conclusion that the most pressing problem and the most urgent task of naturalism at the present time is to work out, on the basis of available evidence, a naturalistic interpretation of the things and events designated by the words that now exert almost complete control of psychological and societal inquiry and report. For example, no issue is more basic for naturalistic theory than the nature of observation. A survey of contemporary literature will, nevertheless, disclose that it is rarely discussed in its own terms:—that is of procedures employed by inquirers in astronomical observatories; in chemical, physical and biological laboratories; in the examinations conducted by physicians, and in what is done in field excursions of botanists and zoologists. Instead, it appears to be obligatory to substitute for observation of observation its reduction to terms of sensations, sensa, sense-data (the exact word is of little import), which are affected by an inheritance of non-naturalism.

The current discussion of language—also a topic of basic importance—affords another example. Students of this subject, from a logical and a social point of view, who regard themselves as anti-metaphysical scientific positivists, write as if words consisted of an "inner," private, mentalistic core or substance and an "outer" physical shell by means of which a subjective intrinsically incommunicable somewhat gets conveyed "trans-subjectively"! And they appear quite unaware of the extra-natural origin and status of their postulate. Until naturalists have applied their principles and methods to formulation of such topics as mind, consciousness, self, etc., they will be at a serious disadvantage. For writers of the "rational" philosophical variety of anti-naturalism almost always draw their premises from alleged facts of and about mind, consciousness, etc. They suppose the "facts" are accepted by naturalists. When they do not find the conclusions *they* draw, they accuse naturalists of holding an inconsistent and truncated position.

II

Since this topic is too large for discussion here, the rest of this paper is occupied with the contrast existing between charges brought against naturalism (because of its alleged identity with "materialism") and the facts of the case. At the present time there is a veritable eruption of such accusations. Many of them seem to regard the present tragic situation of the world as a heaven-sent occasion for accusing naturalism of responsibility for the manifold evils from which we are suffering. I begin with citing some specimen cases.

"Determinists, materialists, agnostics, behaviorists and their ilk can be sincere defenders of democracy only by being inconsistent; for their theories, whether they wish it or not, lead inevitably to justifying government by brute force and to denying all those rights and freedoms which we term inalienable." Naturalists are not included by name in the foregoing list. But a miscellaneous roll of writers that follows shows they fall within the "ilk" in question: "Kant and Carlyle, William James and Herbert Spencer, William McDougall and Henri Bergson, Gobineau and Chamberlain—all of them would be horrified at the complete product of Nazism—made such a philosophy [as that of government by brute force] not only possible but almost inevitable by their denial of one or more of the fundamentals on which any free and humanitarian and Christian concept of society must be built."[2]

The grouping together of men whose philosophies have nothing, or next to nothing, in common beyond denial or neglect of the dogmas of that Roman Catholic theological philosophy, which is held up by the adherents of this faith as the sole basis of a "free" and ordered society, is a commentary on the intellectual criteria employed by the writer. It is kind of gross carelessness that a naturalist would not dare to engage in. Only the confidence of one who thinks he is speaking for a divinely founded and divinely directed institution could lump together men of such contrary beliefs. Even more to the point is the fact that among those who are regarded as causes of the present social disorder is Kant—one who is a philosophical anti-naturalist, and who among other things formulated the doctrine that every human person is an end in himself, possessed of freedom because of membership in a realm above the natural world:—the Kant who regarded it as the function of history and the gradual improvement of social institutions to usher in republican government as the only one that conformed to the philosophical principles he laid down.

In view of the fact that Bergson is included in the list, it is interesting that the next quotation is from a writer, held up to Protestants as a specimen of the liberalism of the Catholic Church, who has publicly expressed peculiar indebtedness to this very Bergson: "What the world and civilization have needed in modern times in the intellectual order, what the temporal good of man has needed for four centuries, is Christian Philosophy. In their place arose a separate philosophy and an inhuman Humanism, a Humanism destructive of man because it wanted to be centered upon man and not upon God. We have drained the cup; we now see before our eyes that bloody anti-Humanism, that ferocious irrationalism and trend to slavery in which rationalist Humanism finally winds up."[3]

A "mere" naturalist would hesitate, even if he counted upon the ignorance or short memory of his audience, to assume that the world was in a state of blissful order and peace, free from blood and ferocity, before the rise of rationalism, naturalism and humanism. Even the ordinary reader might recall that some of the bloodiest and most cruel wars in human history were waged in the name of and with the explicit sanction of supernaturalism and of the ecclesiastic institution which dominated European culture until the last "four centuries," so significantly mentioned.

If, however, the reader is familiar with the articles of supernatural medieval philosophy, he will also recall that bloody and ferocious persecutions and oppressions are very different when carried on in the interests of the Church. For in this latter case they are intended to save from eternal damnation the souls of believers in heresies; or if that is not possible at least to protect others from being contaminated by literally "damnable" heresies. The interpretation put by St. Thomas Aquinas (now the official philosopher of *the* Church) upon the Biblical injunction "Love thy neighbor as thyself" is proof for the orthodox that since the love in question is love of an immortal soul which can be saved only by acceptance of the creed of the Church and by sharing in its sacraments, that injunction of Jesus is far from having the meaning that would naturally be assigned to it. For it is an express authorization of any and all means that will tend to save that soul from the tortures of hell. For what are peace, earthly and natural contentment, and a reasonable degree of happiness for a mere three score years and ten in comparison with supernatural eternity? Hence, the proper course to be taken by genuine "love"!

I come now to a statement which, if I mistake not, has both supernatural and philosophical anti-naturalists among its sponsors. "Men who hold to this naturalistic view in democratic countries are unaware of the dangers in their position. Influenced by the last remnants of philosophical Idealism, romantic Transcendentalism, or religious Theism in our day, they act as if they believed in the spiritual conception which they have intellectually repudiated. They try to maintain their feeling for the dignity of man, while paying homage to an essentially materialistic philosophy according to which man is simply (sic!) a highly developed animal. They are living off the spiritual capital which has come down to them from their classical and religious heritage. . . . Since this contradiction will prove to be intellectually intolerable, scholars and teachers *must* (!) recover and reaffirm the spiritual conception of man and his good which we have derived from Greek and Hebraic-Christian sources. If they fail to do this, not only religious reverence and moral responsibility, but also the scholarly activities with which they are directly concerned, will be greatly endangered. Already under totalitarian regimes and to a lesser extent in the democracies, these activities are being undermined."[4]

It is probable that the signers of this statement belong to both the supernatural and the rationalistic varieties of anti-naturalism. Reference to our classic *and* religious heritage, to Greek *and* Hebraic-Christian sources, indicates that such is the case. They agree for purposes of attack. But cross-examination would disclose a fundamental incompatibility. For example, philosophical anti-naturalists are obliged to confine themselves to dire prediction of terrible things to happen because of naturalism. Their companions of the supernatural variety are aware, however, of active and forcible means that were once employed to stay the spread of heresies like naturalism so as to prevent the frightful consequences from happening. If they are literate in their faith, they know that such methods are still required, but are prevented from now being put into execution by the spread of naturalistic liberalism in civilized countries. When members of this group think of the pains that were taken when the Church had the power to protect the faithful from "science falsely socalled," and from dangerous thoughts in scholarship, they might well smile at the innocence of their colleagues who imply that inquiry, scholarship, and teaching are completely unhampered where naturalism has not obtained a foothold. And they might certainly say of their merely philosophical confreres, that *they* are living off a capital derived from a supernatural heritage. A mere naturalist will content himself with wondering whether ignorance of history, or complacency or provincialism with respect to the non-Christian part of the world, or sheer rhetorical dogmatism is the outstanding trait of the pronunciamento. A historian of ideas would be able to contribute some interesting information as to the beliefs of the persons who have done the

most to make democracy and freedom of mind a reality in the modern world, and as to the beliefs of the persons who withstood their efforts at every turn until the march of events forced them to desist from that particular line of obscurantic obstructionism.

I conclude these citations with a passage written somewhat before the crisis had reached its present intensity. In a book G. K. Chesterton wrote after a visit to this country, he spoke as follows of the prospects of democracy in this country. "As far as that democracy becomes or remains Catholic and Christian, that democracy will remain democratic. . . . Men will more and more realise that there is no meaning in democracy if there is no meaning in anything; and that there is no meaning in anything if the universe has not a centre of significance and an authority that is the basis of our rights."

I should not have supposed that advance was to have been expected in greater realization of the truism that if there is no meaning in anything, there is no meaning in democracy. The nub of the passage clearly resides in assertion that the rights and freedom which constitute democracy have no validity or significance save as they are referable to some centre and authority entirely outside nature and outside men's connections with one another in society. This intrinsically sceptical, even cynical and pessimistic, view of human nature is at the bottom of all the asseverations that naturalism is destructive of the values associated with democracy, including belief in the dignity of man and the worth of human life. This disparaging view (to put it mildly) is the basis upon which rests the whole enterprise of condemning naturalism, no matter in what fine philosophical language the condemnation is set forth. The fact of the case is that naturalism finds the values in question, the worth and dignity of men and women, founded in human nature itself, in the connections, actual and potential, of human beings with one another in their natural social relationships. Not only that, but it is ready at any time to maintain the thesis that a foundation within man and nature is a much sounder one than is one alleged to exist outside the constitution of man and nature.

I do not suppose it is a matter of just expediency or policy in winning adherents that keeps in the dim background the historic origin of the view that human nature is inherently too depraved to be trusted. But it is well to recall that its source is the Pauline (and Augustinian) interpretation of an ancient Hebrew legend about Adam and Eve in the Paradise of Eden. Adherents of the Christian faith who have been influenced by geology, history, anthropology, and literary criticism prefer, quite understandably, to relegate the story to the field of symbolism. But the view that all nature was somehow thoroughly corrupted and that mankind is collectively and individually in a fallen estate, is the only ground upon which there can be urged the necessity of redemption by extra-natural means. And the diluted philosophic version of historic supernaturalism which goes by the name of rationalistic metaphysical spiritualism or idealism has no basis upon which to erect its "higher" non-natural organs and faculties, and the supernatural truths they are said to reveal, without a corresponding thoroughly pessimistic view of human nature.

III

I now come to the question of the moral and social consequences that flow from the base and degrading view of nature in general and of human nature in particular that inheres in every variety of anti-naturalistic philosophy. I begin with the fact that the whole tendency of this view has been to put a heavy discount upon resources that are potentially available for betterment of human life. In the case of any candid clear-eyed person, it is enough to ask one simple question: What is the inevitable effect of holding that anything remotely approaching a basic and serious amelioration of the human estate must be based upon means and methods that lie outside the natural and social world, while human capacities are so low that reliance upon them only makes things worse? Science cannot help; industry and commerce cannot help; political and jural arrangements cannot help; ordinary human affections, sympathies and friendships cannot help. Place these natural resources under the terrible

handicap put upon them by every mode of anti-naturalism, and what is the outcome? Not that these things have not accomplished anything in fact, but that their operation has always been weakened and hampered in just the degree in which supernaturalism has prevailed.

Take the case of science as a case of "natural" knowledge obtained by "natural" means and methods; together with the fact that after all, from the extra-naturalistic point of view, science is *mere* natural knowledge which must be put in stark opposition to a higher realm of truths accessible to extra-natural organs. Does any one believe that where this climate of opinion prevails, scientific method and the conclusions reached by its use can do what they are capable of? Denial of reasonable freedom and attendant responsibility to any group produces conditions which can then be cited as reasons why such group cannot be entrusted with freedom or given responsibility. Similarly, the low estimate put upon science, the idea that because it is occupied with the natural world, it is incapacitated from exercising influence upon values to which the adjectives "ideal" and "higher," (or any adjectives of eulogistic connotation) can be applied, restricts its influence. *The fruit of anti-naturalism is then made the ground of attack upon naturalism.*

If I stated that this low opinion of science in its natural state tended to lower the intellectual standards of anti-naturalists, to dull their sense of the importance of evidence, to blunt their sensitivity to the need of accuracy of statement, to encourage emotional rhetoric at the expense of analysis and discrimination, I might seem to be following too closely the model set by the aspersions (such as have been quoted) of anti-naturalists. It may be said, however, that while some writers of the anti-naturalistic school say a good deal, following Aristotle, about the "intellectual virtues," I fail to find any evidence that they have a perception of the way in which the rise of scientific methods has enlarged the range and sharpened the edge of these virtues. How could they, when it is a necessary part of their scheme to depreciate scientific method, in behalf of higher methods and organs of attaining extra-natural truths said to be of infinitely greater import?

Aside from displaying systematic disrespect for scientific method, supernaturalists deny the findings of science when the latter conflict with a dogma of their creed. The story of the conflict of theology and science is the result. It is played down at the present time. But, as already indicated, it throws a flood of light on the charge, brought in the manifesto previously quoted, that it is the naturalists who are endangering free scholarship. Philosophic anti-naturalists are ambiguous in their treatment of certain scientific issues. For example, competent scientific workers in the biological field are agreed in acceptance of some form of genetic development of all species of plants and animals, mankind included. This conclusion puts man definitely and squarely within the natural world. What, it may be asked, is the attitude of non-theological anti-naturalists toward this conclusion? Do those, for example, who sign a statement saying that naturalists regard man as "simply a highly developed animal" mean to deny the scientific biological conclusion? Do they wish to hold that philosophical naturalism and not scientific inquiry originated and upholds the doctrine of development? Or, do they wish to take advantage of the word "animal" to present naturalistic philosophers in a bad light?

Since the latter accept without discount and qualification facts that are authenticated by careful and thorough inquiry, they recognize in their full force observed facts that disclose the differences existing between man and other animals, as well as the strands of continuity that are discovered in scientific investigation. The idea that there is anything in naturalism that prevents acknowledgment of differential traits in their full significance, or that compels their "reduction" to traits characteristic of worms, clams, cats, or monkeys has no foundation. Lack of foundation is probably the reason why anti-naturalist critics find it advisable to represent naturalism as simply a variety of materialism. For the view attributed to naturalism is simply another instance of a too common procedure in philosophical controversy: Namely, representation of the position of an opponent in the terms it would have *if* the critic held it; that is, the meaning it has not in its own terms but after translation into the terms of an opposed theory. Upon the whole, the non-supernatural anti-naturalists are in such a dilemma that we should extend sympathetic pity to them. If they presented the naturalistic position in its own terms, they would have to take serious account of scientific method and its conclusions.

But if they should do that, they would inevitably be imbued with some of the ideas of the very philosophy they are attacking. Under these circumstances, the ambivalence of their own attitude is readily understood.

Lack of respect for scientific method, which after all is but systematic, extensive and carefully controlled use of alert and unprejudiced observation and experimentation in collecting, arranging and testing facts to serve as evidence, is attended by a tendency toward finalism and dogmatism. Non-theological anti-naturalists would probably deny that their views are marked by that quality of fanaticism which has marked the supernatural brand. And they have not displayed it in anything like the same intensity. But from the standpoint of logic, it must be said that their failure to do so is more creditable to their hearts than to their heads. For it is an essential part of their doctrine that above the inquiring, patient, ever-learning and tentative method of science there exists some organ or faculty which reveals ultimate and immutable truths, and that apart from the truths thus obtained there is no sure foundation for morals and for a humane order of society. As one critic of naturalism remarked (somewhat naively indeed), without these absolute and final truths, there would be in morals only the kind of certainty that exists in physics and chemistry.

Non-theological anti-naturalists write and speak as if there were complete agreement on the part of all absolutists as to standards, rules, and ideals with respect to the specific content of ultimate truths. Supernaturalists know better. They are aware of the conflict that exists; they are aware that conflict between truths claiming ultimate and complete authority is the most fundamental kind of discord that can exist. Hence, their claim to supernatural guidance; and hence fanaticism in carrying on a campaign to wipe out heresies which are dangerous in the degree they claim to rest on possession of ultimate truths. The non-supernatural variety in the more humane attitude it usually takes is living upon a capital which is inherited from the modern liberal developments professedly repudiated. Were its adherents to yield to the demands of logic, they would see how much more secure is the position of those who hold that given a body of ultimate and immutable truths, without which there is only moral and social confusion and conflict, a special institution is demanded which will make known and enforce these truths.

During periods in which social customs were static, and isolation of groups from one another was the rule, it was comparatively easy for men to live in complacent assurance as to the finality of their own practices and beliefs. That time has gone. The problem of attaining mutual understanding and a reasonable degree of amicable cooperation among different peoples, races, classes, is bound up with the problem of reaching by peaceful and democratic means some workable adjustment of the values, standards, and ends which are now in a state of conflict. Dependence upon the absolutist and totalitarian element involved in every form of anti-naturalism adds to the difficulty of this already extremely difficult undertaking.

To represent naturalistic morals as if they involved denial of the existence and the legitimacy of any sort of regulative end and standard is but another case of translation of a position into the terms of the position of its opponents. The idea that unless standards and rules are eternal and immutable they are not rules and criteria at all is childish. If there is anything confirmed by observation it is that human beings naturally cherish certain things and relationships, they naturally institute values. Having desires and having to guide themselves by aims and purposes, no other course is possible. It is also an abundantly confirmed fact of observation that standards and ends grew up and obtained their effectiveness over human behavior in all sorts of relatively accidental ways. Many of them reflect conditions of geographical isolation, social segregation, and absence of scientific methods. These conditions no longer obtaining, it requires a good

deal of pessimism to assume that vastly improved knowledge of nature, human nature included, cannot be employed or will not be employed to render human relationships more humane, just and liberal. The notion that such knowledge and such application, the things for which naturalism stands, will increase misunderstanding and conflict is an extraordinary "reversed charge" of results produced by dogmatic absolutism in appeal to extra-natural authority.

Reference to the pessimism which is involved reminds one of the chorus of voices now proclaiming that naturalism is committed to a dangerously romantic, optimistic, utopian view of human nature. This claim might be looked at as a welcome variation of the charge that naturalism looks upon everything human as "merely" animal. But it happens also to be aside from the mark. It is probably "natural" for those who engage in sweeping rationalistic generalizations to match their own pessimism by attributing an equally unrestrained optimism to their opponents. But since naturalists are committed to basing conclusions upon evidence, they give equal weight to observed facts that point in the direction of both non-social behavior and that of amity and cooperation. In neither case, however, are facts now existing taken to be final and fixed. They are treated as indications of things to be done.

Naturalism is certainly hopeful enough to reject the view expressed by Cardinal Newman when he said "She (the Church) regards this world and all that is in it, as dust and ashes, compared with the value of a single soul. . . . She considers the action of this world and the action of the soul simply incommensurate." Naturalism rejects this view because the "soul and its action" as supernatural are put in opposition to a natural world and its action, the latter being regarded as thoroughly corrupt. But naturalism does not fly to the opposite extreme. It holds to the possibility of discovering by natural means the conditions in human nature and in the environment which work in detail toward the production of concrete forms of both social health and social disease—as the possibility of knowledge and corresponding control in action by adequate knowledge is in process of actual demonstration in the case of medicine. The chief difficulty in the road is that in social and moral matters we are twenty-five hundred years behind the discovery of Hippocrates as to the natural quality of the cause of disease and health. We are also behind his dictum that all events are equally sacred and equally natural.

I mention one further instance of the contrast between the relative bearings of anti-naturalism and naturalism in connection with social problems. Because of the influence of a low view of human nature and of matter a sharp line has been drawn and become generally current between what is called *economic* and what is called *moral*:—and this in spite of facts which demonstrate that at present industry and commerce have more influence upon the actual relation of human groups to one another than any other single factor. The "economic" was marked off as a separate compartment because on the one hand it was supposed to spring from and to satisfy appetites and desires that are bodily and carnal, and on the other hand economic activities have to do with mere "matter."

Whether or not Karl Marx originated the idea that economic factors are the only ultimate causative factors in production of social changes, he did not originate the notion that such factors are "materialistic." He accepted that notion from the current and classic Greek-medieval-Christian tradition. I know of no way to judge how much of the remediable harshness and brutal inhumanity of existing social relationships is connected with denial of intrinsic moral significance to the activities by means of which men live. I do not mean that anti-naturalism is the original source of the evils that exist. But I do mean that the belief that whatever is natural is sub-normal and in tendency is anti-moral, has a great deal to do with perpetuating this state of affairs after we have natural means at command for rendering the situation more humane. Moreover, on the political side we fail to note that so-called laissez-faire individualism, with its extreme separatism and isolation of human beings from one another, is in fact a secularized version of the doctrine of a supernatural soul which has intrinsic connection only with God.

Fear and hate for that which is feared accompany situations of great stress and strain. The philosophic attempt to hold the rise of naturalism accountable for the evils of the present situation, as the ideological incarnation of the enemy democratic peoples are fighting, is greatly accentuated by the emotional perturbations that attend the present crisis. Intense emotion is an all-or-none event. It sees things in terms of only blackest black and purest shining white. Hence, persons of scholastic cultivation can write as if brutality, cruelty, and savage intolerance were unknown until the rise of naturalism. A *diabolus ex machina* is the natural emotionalized dramatic counterpart of the *deus ex machina* of supernaturalism. A naturalistic writer being human may yield to the influence of fear and hate. But in so far he abandons his humanistic naturalism. For it calls for observation of concrete natural causal conditions, and for projection of aims and methods that are consonant with the social conditions disclosed in inquiry. His philosophy commits him to continued use of all the methods of intelligent operation that are available. It commits him to aversion to the escapism and humanistic defeatism inherent in anti-naturalism.

As the war is a global war, so the peace must be a peace that has respect for all the peoples and "races" of the world. I mentioned earlier the provincialism which regards the non-Christians of the world, especially of Asia (and later Africa will come into the scene) as outside the fold, and which philosophical non-supernaturalism admits within the truly human compass only upon conditions its own metaphysics dictates. A philosophic naturalist cannot approve nor go along with those whose beliefs and whose actions, if the latter cohere with their theories, weaken dependence upon the natural agencies, cultural, scientific, economic, political, by which a more humane and friendly world must be built. On the contrary, to him the present tragic scene is a challenge to employ courageously, patiently, persistently and with wholehearted devotion all the *natural* resources that are now potentially at our command.

NOTES

[First published in *Partisan Review* 10 (January-February 1943): 24–39. LW 15:46–62.]

1. The word *mere* plays a large role in anti-naturalistic writings.

2. Thomas P. Neill, in the *Catholic World*, May 1942, p. 151.

3. From J. Maritain's "Contemporary Renewals in Religious Thought," p. 14, contained in *Religion and the Modern World*.

4. From a statement signed by a group of Princeton professors, published in Vol. II of the *Proceedings of the Conference on Science, Philosophy and Religion*. Although "science" appears in the title, the meetings and discussions of this Conference have been chiefly devoted to asserting some aspect of anti-naturalism; literary writers, being innocent of the philosophical issues involved, serving as cement of the amalgam.

PART 4

Pragmatic Metaphysics

A number of biologists holding to the adequacy of the mechanistic conception in biology have of late expressed views not unlike those clearly and succinctly set forth in the following quotation:

If we consider the organism simply as a system forming a part of external nature, we find no evidence that it possesses properties that may not eventually be satisfactorily analyzed by the methods of physico-chemical science; but we admit also that those peculiarities of ultimate constitution which have in the course of evolution led to the appearance of living beings in nature are such that we can not well deny the possibility or even legitimacy of applying a vitalistic or even biocentric conception to the cosmic process as a whole.[1]

The problems connected with the organism as a part of external nature are referred to in the context of the quotation as scientific problems; those connected with the peculiarities of ultimate constitution as metaphysical. The context also shows that ultimate constitution is conceived in a temporal sense. Metaphysical questions are said to be those having to do with "ultimate origins." Such questions lie quite beyond the application of scientific method. "Why it [nature] exhibits certain apparently innate potentialities and modes of action which have caused it to evolve in a certain way is a question which really lies beyond the sphere of natural science." These "apparently innate potentialities and modes of action" which have caused nature as a whole to evolve in the direction of living beings are identified with "ultimate peculiarities"; and it is with reference to them that the biocentric idea has a possible legitimate application. The argument implies that when we insist upon the adequacy of the physico-chemical explanation of living organisms, we are led, in view of the continuity of evolution of organisms from non-living things, to recognize that the world out of which life developed "held latent or potential within itself the possibility of life." In considering such a world and the nature of the potentiality which caused it to evolve living beings, we are forced, however, beyond the limits of scientific inquiry. We pass the boundary which separates it from metaphysics.

Thus is raised the question as to the na-

The Subject-Matter of Metaphysical Inquiry

(1915)

ture of metaphysical inquiry. I wish to suggest that while one may accept as a preliminary demarcation of metaphysics from science the more "ultimate traits" with which the former deals, it is not necessary to identify these ultimate traits with temporally original traits— that, in fact, there are good reasons why we should not do so. We may also mark off the metaphysical subject-matter by reference to certain irreducible traits found in any and every subject of scientific inquiry. With reference to the theme of evolution of living beings, the distinctive trait of metaphysical reflection would not then be its attempt to discover some temporally original feature which caused the development, but the irreducible traits of a world in which at least some changes take on an evolutionary form. A world where some changes proceed in the direction of the appearance of living and thinking creatures is a striking sort of a world. While science would trace the conditions of their occurrence in detail, connecting them in their variety with their antecedents, metaphysics would raise the question of the sort of world which *has* such an evolution, not the question of the sort of world which causes it. For the latter type of question appears either to bring us to an *impasse* or else to break up into just the questions which constitute scientific inquiry.

Any intelligible question as to causation seems to be a wholly scientific question. Starting from any given existence, be it a big thing like a solar system or a small thing like a rise of temperature, we may ask how it came about. We account for the change by linking up the thing in question with other specific existences acting in determinate ways—ways which collectively are termed physico-chemical. When we have traced back a present existence to the earlier existences with which it is connected, we may ask a like question about the occurrence of the earlier things, viewed as changes from something still earlier. And so on indefinitely; although, of course, we meet practical limits in our ability to push such questions beyond a certain indefinite point. Hence it may be said that a question about ultimate origin or ultimate causation is either a meaningless question, or else the words are used in a relative sense to designate the point in the

past at which a particular inquiry breaks off. Thus we might inquire as to the "ultimate" origin of the French language. This would take us back to certain definite antecedent existences, such as persons speaking the Latin tongue, others speaking barbarian tongues; the contact of these peoples in war, commerce, political administration, education, etc. But the term "ultimate" has meaning only in relation to the particular existence in question: French speech. We are landed in another historic set of existences, having their own specific antecedents. The case is not otherwise if we ask for the ultimate origin of human speech in general. The inquiry takes us back to animal cries, gestures, etc., certain conditions of intercourse, etc. The question is, how one set of specific existences gradually passed into another. No one would think of referring to latent qualities of the Latin speech as the cause of the evolution of French; one tries to discover actual and overt features which, *interacting* with other equally specific existences, brought about this particular change. If we are likely to fall into a different mode of speech with reference to human language in general, it is because we are more ignorant of the specific circumstances under which the transition from animal cries to articulate speech with a meaning took place. Upon analysis, reference to some immanent law or cause which forced the evolution will be found to be a lazy cloak for our ignorance of the specific facts needed in order to deal successfully with the question.

Suppose we generalize the situation still more. We may ask for the ultimate origin of the entire present state of things. Taken *en masse*, such a question is meaningless. Taken in detail, it means that we may apply the same procedure distributively to each and any of the things which now exist. In each case we may trace its history to an earlier state of things. But in each case, *its* history is what we trace, and the history always lands us at some state of things in the past, regarding which the same question might be asked. That scientific inquiry does not itself deal with any question of ultimate origins, except in the purely relative sense already indicated, is, of course, recognized. But it also seems to follow from what has been said that scientific inquiry does not generate, or leave over, such a question for some other discipline, such as metaphysics, to deal with. The contrary conception with respect to the doctrine of evolution is to be explained, I think, by the fact that theology used to have the idea of ultimate origin in connection with creation, and that at a certain juncture it was natural to regard the theory of evolution as a substitute or rival of the theological idea of creation.

If all questions of causation and origin are specific scientific questions, is there any place left for metaphysical inquiry at all? If its theme can not be ultimate origin and causation, is metaphysics anything but a kind of pseudo-science whose illusory character is now to be recognized? This question takes us to the matter of whether there are ultimate, that is, irreducible, traits of the very existences with which scientific reflection is concerned. In all such investigations as those referred to above we find at least such traits as the following: Specifically diverse existences, interaction, change. Such traits are found in any material which is the subject-matter of inquiry in the natural science. They are found equally and indifferently whether a subject-matter in question be dated 1915 or ten million years B.C. Accordingly, they would seem to deserve the name of ultimate, or irreducible, traits. As such they may be made the object of a kind of inquiry differing from that which deals with the genesis of a particular group of existences, a kind of inquiry to which the name metaphysical may be given.[2]

It may well seem as if the fact that the subject-matter of science is always a plurality of diverse interacting and changing existences were too obvious and commonplace to invite or reward investigation. Into this point I shall not go, beyond pointing out, in connection with the present theme, that certain negative advantages in the economizing of intellectual effort would at least accrue from the study. Bare recognition of the fact just stated would wean men from the futility of concern with ultimate origins and laws of causation with which the "universe" is supposed to have been endowed at the outset. For it would reveal that, whatever the date of the subject-matter which may be successfully reflected upon, we have the same situation that we have at present:

diversity, specificality, change. These traits have to be begged or taken in any case. If we face this fact without squeamishness we shall be saved from the recurrent attempts to reduce heterogeneity to homogeneity, diversity to sheer uniformity, quality to quantity, and so on. That considerations of quantity and mathematical order are indispensable to the successful prosecution of researches into particular occurrences is a precious fact. It exhibits certain irreducible traits *of* the irreducible traits we have mentioned, but it does not replace them. When it tries to do so it cuts the ground out from under its own feet.

Let me emphasize this point by comment on a further quotation.

If we assume constancy of the elementary natural processes, and constancy in the modes of connection between them—as exact observation forces us to do—there seems no avoiding the conclusion that—given an undifferentiated universe at the start—only one course of evolution can ever have been possible. Laplace long ago perceived this consequence of the mechanistic view of nature, and the inevitability of his conclusion has never been seriously disputed by scientific men. Nevertheless, this is a very strange result, and to many has seemed a *reductio ad absurdum* of the scientific view as applied to the whole of nature.

Note that the inevitable conclusion as to the predetermined course of evolution and the apparent incredibility of the conclusion both depend upon the premise "given an undifferentiated universe at the start." Now this is precisely a premise which a scientific view can not admit, for science deals with any particular existence only by tracing its occurrence to a plurality of prior changing interacting things. Any Laplacean formula would, in any case, be a formula for the structure of *some* existence *in* the world, not for the world as a "whole." The scientific grounds which make it impossible to take the world *en masse* at the present time and to give a comprehensive formula for it in its entirety apply even more strongly, if possible, to some earlier state of affairs. For such a formula can be reached only by tracing back a specific present phenomenon to its specific antecedents.

A curious illusion exists as to formulae for

the ancient states of nature. It is frequently assumed that they denote not merely some absolute original (which is impossible), but also one from which later events unroll in a mathematically predetermined fashion. We seem to be passing in a one-sided way from the earlier to the later. The illusion vanishes when we ask where the formula came from. How was it obtained? Evidently, by beginning with some present existence and tracing its earlier course, till at some time (relevant to the object of the inquiry) we stop and condense the main features of the course into a formula for the structure of the state of things at the date where we stop. Instead of really deducing or deriving the course of subsequent events from an original state, we are simply taking out of a formula the traits which we have put into it on the basis of knowledge of subsequent events. Let the present state be anything you please, as different as may be from what is actually found, and it will still be true that we could (theoretically) construct a comprehensive formula for its earlier estate. In short, as a matter of fact, a Laplacean formula merely summarizes what the actual course of events has been with respect to some selected features. How then can it be said to describe an original state of nature in virtue of which just such and such things have necessarily happened? A statement that the world is thus and so can not be tortured into a statement of how and why it must be as it is. The account of how a thing came to be as it is always starts and comes back to the fact that it is thus and so. How then can this fact be derived according to some law of predestination from the consideration of its own prior history? For, I repeat, this history is *its* history.[3]

This discussion, however, oversimplifies matters. It overlooks the extent to which inference as to a prior state of affairs is dependent upon the diversity and complexity of what is now observed. We should be in a hard case in trying to fix upon the structure of the Latin language if our sole datum were, say, the French language. As matter of fact, in considering the growth of the French tongue we have other Romance languages to fall back upon. Above all, we have independent evidence as to the characteristics of Latin speech. If we had not, we should be reasoning in a circle. Science

is rightly suspicious of accounts of things in terms of a hypothesis for whose existence nothing can be alleged save that if it existed it would or might account for something which is actually found. Independent evidence of the existence of such an object is required. This consideration has an interesting application to the question in hand. It brings out clearly the absurdity involved in supposing that any formula, of the Laplacean type, about some earlier state of existence, however comprehensive, is comprehensive enough to cover the whole scope of existence of that earlier time.

Let us suppose the formula to be descriptive of a primitive state of the solar system. Not only must it start from and be framed in terms of what *now* exists, but the present datum must be larger than the existing solar system if we are to escape reasoning in a circle. In such cosmological constructions, astronomers and geologists rely upon observation of what is going on outside of the solar system. Without such data, the inquiry would be hopelessly crippled. The stellar field now presents, presumably, systems in all stages of formation. Is there any reason for supposing that a like state of affairs did not present itself at any and every prior time? Whatever formula is arrived at for the beginning of our present solar system describes, therefore, only one structure existing amid a vaster complex. A state of things adequately and inclusively described by the formula would be, by conception, a state of things in which nothing could happen. To get change we have to assume other structures which interact with it, existences not covered by the formula.

As a matter of fact, the conception of a solar system seems to have exercised an hypnotic influence upon Newton's successors. The gathering together of sun, planets and their satellites, etc., into a system which might be treated as an individual having its own history was a wonderful achievement, and it impressed men's imaginations. It served for the time as a kind of symbol of the "universe." But as compared with the entire stellar field, the solar system is, after all, only a "right little, tight little island." Yet unless its complex context be ignored the idea of "an undifferentiated universe" which, by some immanent potential force, determined everything which has happened since, could hardly arise.[4] That the French language did not evolve out of Latin because of some immanent causality in the latter we have already noted. It is equally true that the contact and interaction of those speaking Latin with those speaking barbaric tongues were not due to the fact that they spoke Latin, but to independent variables. Internal diversity is as much a necessity as something externally heterogeneous.[5]

The consideration throws light, I think, upon the meaning of potentiality with reference to any state of things. We never apply the term except where there is change or a process of becoming. But we have an unfortunate tendency to conceive a fixed state of affairs and then appeal to a latent or potential something or other to effect change. But in reality the term refers to a characteristic of change. Anything changing might be said to exhibit potentiality with respect to two facts: first, that the change exhibits (in connection with interaction with new elements in its surroundings) qualities it did not show till it was exposed to them and, secondly, that the changes in which these qualities are shown run a certain course. To say that an apple has the potentiality of decay does not mean that it has latent or implicit within it a causal principle which will some time inevitably display itself in producing decay, but that its existing changes (in interaction with its surroundings) will take the form of decay, *if* they are exposed or subjected to certain conditions not now operating upon them. Potentiality thus signifies a certain limitation of present powers, due to the limited number of conditions with which they are in interaction plus the fact of the manifestation of new powers under different conditions. To generalize the idea, we have to add the fact that the very changes now going on have a tendency to expose the thing in question to these different conditions which will call out new modes of behavior, in other words, further changes of a different kind. Potentiality thus implies not merely diversity, but a progressively increasing diversification of a specific thing in a particular direction. So far is it from denoting a causal force immanent within a homogeneous something and leading it to change.

We may say then that an earlier condition of our earth was potential with life and mind. But this means that it was changing in a certain way and direction. Starting where we must start, with the present, the fact or organization shows that the world is of a certain kind. In spots, it *has* organization. Reference to the evolution of this organization out of an earlier world in which *such* organization was not found means something about that earlier condition—it means that it was characterized by a change having direction—that is, in the direction of vital and intelligent organization. I do not see that this justifies the conclusion that that earlier world was biocentric or vitalistic or psychic. Yet two conclusions seem to follow. One is negative. The fact that it is possible and desirable to state the processes of an organized being in chemico-physical terms does not eliminate, but rather takes for granted whatever peculiar features living beings have. It does not imply that the distinguishing features of living and thinking beings are to be explained away by resolution into the features found in non-living things. It is the *occurrence* of these peculiar features which is stated in physico-chemical terms. And, as we have already seen, the attempt to give an account of any occurrence involves the genuine and irreducible existence of the thing dealt with. A statement of the mechanism of vital and thinking creatures is a statement of *their* mechanism; an account of their production is an account of *their* production. To give such an account does not prove whether the existence in question is a good thing or a bad thing, but it proves nothing at all if it puts in doubt the specific existence of the subject-matter investigated.

The positive point is that the evolution of living and thinking beings out of a state of things in which life and thought were not found is a fact which must be recognized in any metaphysical inquiry into the irreducible traits of the world. For evolution appears to be just one of the irreducible traits. In other words, it is a fact to be reckoned with in considering the traits of diversity, interaction, and change which have been enumerated as among the traits taken for granted in all scientific subject-matter. If everything which is, is a changing thing, the evolution of life and mind indicates the nature of the changes of physico-chemical things and therefore something about those things. It indicates that as purely physical, they are still limited in their interactions; and that as they are brought into more and complex interactions they exhibit capacities not to be found in an exclusively mechanical world. To say, accordingly, that the existence of vital, intellectual, and social organization makes impossible a purely mechanistic metaphysics is to say something which the situation calls for. But it does not signify that the world "as a whole" is vital or sentient or intelligent. It is a remark of the same order as the statement that one is not adequately acquainted with water or iron until he has found it operating under a variety of different conditions, and hence a scientific doctrine which regards iron as essentially hard or water as essentially liquid is inadequate. Without a doctrine of evolution we might be able to say, not that matter *caused* life, but that matter under certain conditions of highly complicated and intensified interaction is living. With the doctrine of evolution, we can add to this statement that the interactions and changes of matter are themselves of a kind to bring about that complex and intensified interaction which is life. The doctrine of evolution implies that this holds good of any matter, irrespective of its date, for it is not the matter of 1915, as caused by matter that has now ceased to be, which lives. The matter which was active ten million years ago now lives: this is a feature of the matter of ten million years ago.

I am, however, getting beyond my main point. I am not concerned to develop a metaphysics; but simply to indicate one way of conceiving the problem of metaphysical inquiry as distinct from that of the special sciences, a way which settles upon the more ultimate traits of the world as defining its subject-matter, but which frees these traits from confusion with ultimate origins and ultimate ends—that is, from questions of creation and eschatology. The chief significance of evolution with reference to such an inquiry seems to be to indicate that while metaphysics takes the world irrespective of any particular time, yet time itself, or genuine change in a specific direction, is itself one of the ultimate traits of the world irrespective of date.

NOTES

[First published in *Journal of Philosophy, Psychology and Scientific Methods* 12 (1915): 337–45. For Ralph Stayner Lillie's article to which this is a reply, see MW 8:449–59, "The Philosophy of Biology: Vitalism *vs.* Mechanism," *Science*, n.s. 40 (1914): 840–46. MW 8:3–13.]

1. Professor Ralph S. Lillie, *Science*, Vol. XL, page 846. See also the references given in the article, which is entitled "The Philosophy of Biology: Vitalism *vs.* Mechanism."

2. The name at least has the sanction of the historical designation given to Aristotle's consideration of existence as existence. But it should be noted that we also find in Aristotle the seeds (which, moreover, have at places developed into flourishing growths in his own philosophy) of the conception of metaphysics rejected above. For he expressly gives the more general traits of existence the eulogistic title "divine" and identifies his first philosophy with theology, and so makes this kind of inquiry "superior" to all others, because it deals with the "highest of existing things." While he did not himself seek for this higher or supreme real in time, but rather located it, in its fullness of reality, just beyond space, this identification of existence as such with the divine led to such an identification the moment theology became supremely interested in "creation." But unless one approaches the study of the most general traits of the matter of scientific inquiry with theological presuppositions, there is, of course, no ground for the application to them of eulogistic predicates. There is no ground for thinking that they are any better or any worse, any higher or any lower, than other traits, or that any peculiar dignity attaches to a study of them.

3. Compare Woodbridge, "Evolution," *Philosophical Review*, Vol. XXI, page 137.

4. One who turns to Spencer's chapter on the "Instability of the Homogeneous" will perceive that his proof of its instability consists in showing that it was really already heterogeneous.

5. Some contemporary metaphysical theories attempt to start from pure "simple" entities and then refer change exclusively to "complexes." This overlooks the fact that without internal diversification in the alleged simple entity, a complex entity would no more exhibit change than a simple one. The history of the doctrine of atoms is instinctive. Such a metaphysics transgresses the conditions of intelligent inquiry in exactly the same way as the metaphysics of ultimate origins.

It is quite possible to use the word "event" as a fundamental term in science and yet carry over into the meaning of the term implications which belong to an order of scientific conceptions which "event" is employed to replace, and which are incompatible with satisfying the conditions which "event" is selected to meet. An illustration of this fact, and of the philosophical consequences of it, is found in Broad's *Scientific Thought*. Following Whitehead, Broad points out that "there are many types of objects whose characteristic qualities need a certain minimum of duration to inhere in." For example, if nothing is a mind which does not have memory, a long enough duration to permit memory is clearly necessary to the existence of a mind. Again, "Suppose that a certain sort of atom consisted of a nucleus and an electron rotating about it at a certain characteristic speed. Such an atom would need at least the duration of one complete rotation to display its characteristic properties. . . . If the duration of one complete rotation be sliced up into adjacent successive parts, *the contents of the parts will differ in quality from the contents of the whole*."[1]

I quote the passage because it gives an indispensable character of anything which may be termed an event: namely, a qualitative variation of parts with respect to the whole which requires duration in which to display itself. If we assume only qualitative homogeneity in a mind, we shall not have memory, and hence by definition not a mind. For the later portion of the total duration, even if *otherwise* exactly like the earlier, must, if there be memory, differ from it by recalling the previous state, and hence can not be a mere unchanged persistence of the earlier.

Unfortunately, however, Mr. Broad at once goes on to show that he does *not* regard qualitative variation to be involved in the definition of an event. He says "there may well be objects which are temporally homogeneous. This would mean that, however you divide up their *history*, the contents of the slices are the same as each other and as the whole in quality. . . . Now science regards the *ultimate* scientific objects as being spatio-temporally homogeneous. And it assumes that these ultimate scientific objects never begin or end. Thus the ultimate

Events
and
the Future

(1926)

scientific objects are regarded as *eternal* in the sense of existing throughout all time. The only ultimate scientific changes are the groupings and regroupings of such objects according to a single set of fundamental laws."[2]

Now I am not concerned here to try to show that there are no such *objects*. Mr. Broad says that he does not know whether the assumption that there are such objects is true or not, and I shall not profess to know that it is false. But one can assert on purely formal grounds that such objects are not events, nor parts of events. Eternal objects have no "history," much less a history which can be "divided." And if it is stated that such objects are the "temporally homogeneous" slabs out of which events or histories are composed, it is not evident how the union or co-adjacence of the timeless can give rise to time, nor how the qualitatively homogeneous can pass into the qualitatively heterogeneous; nor, to generalize, how "eternal objects" subject to a "single set of fundamental laws" can permit of *regroupings*, nor what conceivable meaning can attach to the phrase "ultimate scientific *changes*." The argument is not helped out by saying that the ultimate objects are eternal in the sense of "existing throughout all time." For unless there are changes and changes such that eternal objects can be put in correspondence with them, on the basis of which correspondence eternal objects may be said to have duration, there is no time for them to exist "throughout." There is also no sense in terming them *temporally* homogeneous. Their homogeneity with respect to temporality is utter irrelevancy to it. In short, the only logical significance which can be attached to the passage cited is one which makes "objects" logically prior to events, while it also sets serious barriers, to put it mildly, in the way of deriving events from objects as defined. While nominally much is made of events, the emphasis turns out Pickwickian.[3]

The bearing of the implication that (i) there are adjacent slabs of time which (ii) are qualitatively homogeneous with one another, appears in Broad's explicit discussion of time and the future, in an earlier part of the book, namely, Chapter Two. There he says that by event he is going to signify "anything which

endures at all, no matter how long it lasts or whether it be *qualitatively alike or qualitatively different* in adjacent stages in its history."[4] Here we have an express statement that there may be stages of history which are qualitatively like each other. It is my purpose to show that this assumption determines the results at which he arrives with respect to time, especially as regards futurity. Assuming that the definition means just what it says, and that by qualitative likeness he intends identity, and not merely close similarity—which, of course, admits heterogeneity—there appears to be no basis whatever for the idea of "adjacent stages." Bare persistence is not history and it has no stages; the moment they are referred to as stages qualitative change is introduced. Stages mean differences. A persistent "duration" without change may be alleged to be part of a history when enclosed in a larger whole in which there is qualitative variation, but it can not be itself a history. And without a history what is meant by imputing endurance to the thing called "event"? But where there are adjacent stages, every such stage is an event or history, and hence it has stages, which are events. Or, every event comprises events and is itself comprised in an event.[5]

The only other way in which we can intelligibly speak of adjacent stages in what persists as qualitatively the same is in relation to some *other* event. If we have taken genuine stages of difference in *M* and have assigned a certain date of beginning and end to each of these, then we may compare *M* as to these stages with *N*, and assign an identical duration (or some part of it) to *N*, and, by setting up a one-to-one correspondence between it and the stages of *M*, apportion it, in spite of its homogeneity. That we do thus divide into stages things which do not themselves exhibit *perceptible* differences is a well known fact. But to say that *a*, in spite of qualitative identity, is a temporal stage of *N*, is to assert that it can be put in one-to-one correspondence with α, which is a qualitative variation of *M*, standing in turn in specified relation to $\beta, \gamma, \delta, \ldots$ other qualitative variations of *M*.

Given the conception of an event as something internally unchanged, it is clear that the beginning of an event, and the occurrence of a qualitative variation in an event (if there be any distinction between these two things), is something other than an event. So Mr. Broad quite logically says that qualitative changes "involve the coming into existence of an event," and that such a change, which he calls a *becoming*, is of such a peculiar character that it is misleading to term it a change. "When we say that a thing changes in quality, or that an event changes in pastness, we are talking of events that exist both before and after the moment at which the change takes place. But when an event becomes, it *comes into existence*; and it was not anything at all until it had become" (p. 68, italics in original text). From this it follows logically that past and present events exist, since they *have* become; future events do not exist at all, since they have not become. Thus it follows from his conception of the intrinsically homogeneous character of an event that the future occupies a status existentially which is radically different from that of past and present events. The "future is simply nothing at all" (p. 70). "A present event is defined as one which is succeeded by nothing"; "there is no such thing as ceasing to exist; what has become exists henceforth for ever" (p. 68 and p. 69). Thus the sum total of existence is always increasing; something becomes; when this event is past, a fresh slice of existence has been added to the total history of the world.

The distinction between "event" and "becoming" follows logically from his definition of event. Events become but they are not becomings. What is given us by Broad is thus a lot of unchanging things, termed, nevertheless, events, with abrupt insertions of changes; time in the usual sense would appear to proceed by jerks or interruptions. How this view is adjusted to any notion of causal continuity does not here concern us. The point is that it is indispensable to Broad's argument to speak of events as *that which* come into existence. But if an event *is* a becoming, it is not intelligible to speak of the eventing of an event; or the becoming of a becoming. And an event is a becoming if as an event it involves qualitative variation or heterogeneity throughout itself. A distinction between event and becoming can be drawn only if an event is conceived as a solid homogeneous slab throughout, that is, is conceived of as *not* an event or a history. Broad carries over into his nominal use of the term "event" considerations pertinent to modes of thought which attach to what we may call the "pre-event" era of scientific history.

The bearing upon "time" and the future should be fairly evident. If existences are histories or events in the sense of becomings, then past-present-future are on the same level, because all are phases of any event or becoming. Any becoming is from, to, through. Its fromness, or out-of-ness, is *its* pastness; its towardness or intrinsic direction, is *its* futurity; that through which the becoming passes is *its* presentness. No becoming can be perceived or thought of except as out of something into something, and this involves a series of transitions which, taken distributively, belong both to the "out-of" and the "into," or form a "through." The present has thus nothing privileged about it; it is as legitimate to speak of the present century or the present geological age as of the present "moment." The present is defined in relation to an "out-of" and by a future or "into," as truly as the past by the present.

Since without change into, there is no becoming or event, futurity is comprised directly in any and every event which can be said to be present, or, better, be said to *have* a phase of presentness.

On this basis it is mere fiction that we know pastness and futurity only by means of inference from presentness. Any experience of anything in being an experience of a becoming or event contains within itself qualities which are named pastness, presentness, and futurity. To recall a specific past event or to foresee or predict a future specific event requires inference, but in the same sense it demands inference to make a determinately specific judgment about anything said to be present. Psychologically, expectancy stands on the same level as memory; in the same sense in which the latter can be said to refer directly to the past, the former can be said to refer directly to the future. In fact, it is questionable whether psychologically the attitude of expectancy is not more usually co-present with observations of what is going on than that of recall. It is even possible that we so commonly ignore it just because it is so omnipresent that there is no need to make it an object of explicit attention.

Mr. Broad gives what seems to me a correct account of *judgments* about the future, but to make a false use of his analysis. It is true that we can not refer intellectually to *a* future event, if the future is dissevered from the present, for then it does not exist for us to refer to. But when he says that it is not true that a judgment involving the future can "mean anything that begins with the statement: 'There is an event'" (p. 76), he says something gratuitously unnecessary. The judgment involving the future is: "There is a going-on or a becoming such that it has a specified directional movement." To make the judgment about the future explicit is not to refer to a non-existent; it is to infer the further becoming of what is going-on. "It will probably rain tomorrow" asserts a quality of toward-whichness characteristic of what is happening to-day defined in terms of yesterdays. In its completeness it is a judgment regarding some out-of-which-through-which-into-which.

When Mr. Broad says that any judgment that professes to be about the future seems to "involve two peculiar and not further analysable kinds of assertion," one of which "asserts that further events *will* become" (italics mine), and the other that so-and-so "*will* characterize some of the events which *will* become" (italics mine), he simply restores under the name of "will" what he officially denies under the name of futurity.[6] "Will be" and the future tense are equivalents and both go back to an "it-is-going-to," where the going-to characterizes what *is*. "Will become" is equivalent to futurity, precisely because it does not refer to some *other* event wholly disconnected from the present, but to an event or becoming which is going-on. Hence the "was," the "is," when temporally limited to a phase of the going-on, and the "will be" all stand on the same level with

respect to judgment. All of them as judgments are equally susceptible of error, but that is because all involve inference. For to say that every event, or going-on, has a phase of pastness, presentness, and futurity is not to say that *what* has been, is, and will be, is immediately self-revealing, or that it can be determined without an intellectual or mediating factor.

To save space I have written somewhat dogmatically. But the argument is hypothetical. It contrasts what follows *if* an event is a becoming or involves qualitative changes throughout, with what follows if something nominally termed an event is defined so as to exclude internal heterogeneity. In my opinion, Mr. Broad first nominally introduces duration into his "events" and then takes pains to eliminate all temporality from them. Having done that, he is obliged to re-introduce time by a succession of arbitrarily assumed interruptions or jerks, called becomings.

NOTES

[First published in *Journal of Philosophy* 23 (13 May 1926): 253–58. LW 2:62–68.]

1. Broad, *Scientific Thought*, p. 403, italics not in original.

2. *Ibid.*, p. 403, italics mine.

3. Contrast with Whitehead's: "Objects are entities recognised as appertaining to events," *Principles of Natural Knowledge*, p. 81. There was, of course, no obligation upon Broad to follow Whitehead, but the thought of the latter so hangs together that it is not possible to borrow his conception of events, and then place "*recognita*" or objects behind and under events, without getting into precisely such difficulties as the above.

4. *Op. cit.*, p. 54; italics not in original text.

5. Whitehead, *The Principles of Natural Knowledge*, p. 61, 77.

6. *Op. cit.*, pp. 76–77.

The idea of appearance has played a large and varied role in philosophic thought. In ancient philosophy, it was ontological in character, being used to denote a realm of being which was infected with defect or non-being and hence expressed itself in instability and change. In modern thinking, it has been chiefly an epistemic idea. Ontologically, there is but one kind of being; but this, as it affects the senses, or is itself affected by the faculties and conditions of knowing, becomes subjectivistically altered from its real estate. In both cases the distinction of appearance from reality is, of course, invidious. To an empiricist the distinction, however invalid he may consider it to be metaphysically or epistemologically, must have an empirical basis and origin which are misinterpreted in the traditional doctrines. It is accordingly incumbent upon him to give an analytic account of the origin and role of the meaning of appearance such as will acknowledge the empirical facts while eliminating historic misconstructions.

In its simplest and basic form, "appearance" denotes the fact that some things are at a particular time evident, patent, overt, open, outstanding, conspicuous, in contrast with others which are hidden, concealed, latent, covered up, remote. One of the things which itself soon "appears" or becomes obvious is that there is a connection between what is apparent and what is covert such that what appears has a representative function. It is a revelation, manifestation, exhibition. It can be understood only as a culminating eventuation of something beside itself which may be otherwise hidden—as prophets reveal the will of God—or may be overt in another connection—as trophies exhibit a victory won in war. A further specification of this function is so significant and so common as to deserve a class to itself. We take in the third place something which appears—in the first sense—as the clew to something hidden or unapparent, and as the basis of search for it: as sign, indication, evidence.

Appearing and Appearance

(1927)

I

The primary, innocent neutral meaning of appearance may best be expressed participially, by the word "appearing." The world is so constituted that things appear and disappear; the opposite to appearance is not reality but disappearance. Owing to rotation, the light of a beacon on the seas appears and disappears every so often. Similarly, owing to the rotation of the earth, the sun appears in the morning and disappears at night. In the spring-time leaves appear on the trees; they disappear in winter. Land disappears after a ship has got a distance at sea; another land appears after an interval of days. What is indicated by the term "appearance" is coming into view, sensibly or intellectually—as when the meaning of an obscure passage "dawns" on the mind, or the clew to a desired invention presents itself to an Edison. Appearance signifies conspicuousness, outstandingness, obviousness, being patent, evident in plain view. Its contrast is being obscured, hidden, concealed, absent, remote. A book appears on publication, a king appears once in a while to his subjects, an actor appears daily on the stage. An eclipse of the moon appears at calculable intervals.

If there is a metaphysical problem in the "world of appearances" there must also be one in a "world of disappearances." This correlativity of appearing and disappearing is in reality highly significant; it indicates the existence of a temporal process having phases. The fundamental importance of this temporal characteristic can be better dealt with at a later stage of our own account. At this point, I only want to emphasize that any existential question which arises can only concern stages in some temporal process that includes a cycle of phases. When a thing appears, its hereness and nowness are emphatically realized. If the Aristotelian categories of potentiality and actuality were in vogue, we could well say that appearing marks an actualization of a potential herenow. From any point of view, we must say that it marks a stage in the history of some object having different phases, owing to varied relations to other things. Thus the different appearances of the moon, as it waxes and wanes, are not matters of some unfolding from within any more than they are marks of degrees of reality; they are functions of its movement in relation to the movement of the earth.

It may, however, be objected that the epistemological aspect of the matter can not be so easily disposed of. It will be contended that since an appearance is always to somebody it involves dependence upon the mind or consciousness in or to which a thing appears; for this reason, I suppose, appearances are often called presentations, and presentations are then either identified with states of mind or at least with things modified by mind. But appearance does not denote a total or pervasive character, an intrinsic quality, but a relation which is additive. A lad appears in school; he answers present when the roll is called. No one thinks of supposing that this presence abrogates his being or reduces his reality. It marks a phase of his biography determined by his relations to school, class, and teachers, just as his absence marks a phase determined by other relations, vacation, illness, playing hookey, etc. So a presentation marks the existence of a thing in relation to an organism; the table before me is in view. If I close my eyes, it disappears from view:—a particular relationship ceases, namely, that with a certain part of my organism.

This relation is physical, existential, not epistemic. Its establishment is, indeed, a necessary condition of knowing, but it does not constitute knowledge, in either of its two senses: either as something actually known or as something *to be* known, a theme for inquiry, a subject of an investigation which shall terminate in knowledge. The sun is efficaciously present to the soil it warms, the plants whose growth it effects. Or, taking the case of the organism, its appearance may, just like the sounding of an alarm clock, operate as a signal to begin the round of daily duties. It may, indeed, be known, identified, for just what it is, or it may be present as an occasion of inquiry in order to discover what it is. But knowing in both these senses denotes that something in addition to the original appearance is taking place; that the thing appearing is entering into more complex relationships. In short, while the appearance is a precondition of knowing, it is not a case of knowing. Furthermore, we must note that the relation which determines a thing to appear is definite, specifiable, not wholesale. A table disappears—not absolutely but with respect to sight; when the eyes close, it may still be present to the hand. Failure to bear in mind the definite character of the organic relation that conditions an appearance is largely responsible for treating it as if it involved a unique problem.

II

The second sense of "appearance" is display, exhibition, manifestation, revelation. In some instances this meaning is but an intensification of that just dealt with. A vivid, spectacular, appearance of something is a "show" in an emphatic sense, just as an unusual ball-player or child musician is popularly called a "phenomenon." But in many cases the idea of showing, manifesting, implies something other than the merely striking character of the appearance in question. It calls attention explicitly to the connection between the whole temporal cycle and the phase of it prominent at a particular time in a particular context. This connection is implied in the first sense of appearing. But the idea of manifestation does something more than make the implicit explicit. It designates the appearance as a member of an inclusive *whole*. A display of fireworks may be only a striking appearance. But it may also be a commemoration of a notable event. A procession may be only a vivid pageant; but it may also be a celebration. The presentation is now a representation; it calls to mind a total situation such that *reference* to it gives the appearing object its meaning. It is the appearance *of* something in the sense of expression. Thus a particular act of ill-temper reveals a standing disposition; it is a transient ebullition of something enduring; similarly with a manifestation of greed, a display of courage. An actor appears, but not just in the sense that a man who has been absent is present. Appearance *as* an actor signifies the assumption of a role or part, and this implies the whole, the drama, in which the role is a contributing member. The subject-matter of the role would be, relatively, non-sense by itself and the drama would be defective without the part. A similar context is exemplified when a lawyer appears in behalf of a client. His presence is wholly representative, but it is a necessary phase in the realization of that which is represented. He takes a part in legal proceedings which exhibit a controversy in process of

solution. There is thus explicit in appearance as manifestation an added relation. The sun appears and its appearance is a phase of the sun's career. But it does not realize its special status by means of appearing on behalf of anything else, such that its representative office makes a definitive contribution to the whole. If, however, we take the rising of the sun in relation to the constitution of the entire system, the particular event may *then* be said to be a manifestation. On the one hand, it is seen to be a necessary part of the whole, and on the other hand, it can be understood only when it is placed in its relations within the organized system as a whole.

This second meaning leads to a third, the distinctively intellectual one, determining the logical import of "appearance." A representative exhibition may be more or less adequate or perfect—as in the case of lawyer, diplomat, and actor. We say they are or are not true, faithful, to their function. They may *mis*represent. Moreover, in the case of a delegate, a diplomat, credentials are demanded and offered. The question of *claim* and *right* enters in. When an appearance is taken as a manifestation, an organized whole is presupposed. The whole is known and the special place and role of the part is taken for granted. Suppose, however, a doubt arises as to whether the thing appearing is *entitled* to act in behalf of another; a claim is involved which must be investigated before "manifestation" may be predicated. Representative capacity instead of being assumed presents a problem, an inquiry to be undertaken. Yet we must not confuse the nature of the problem. We may assert that it is *false* that a man is an agent or representative of those whom he pretends to appear in behalf of. This does not mean that the "appearance" is false or unreal, but that the objective relations required to confer upon it the role which is claimed are lacking. Are the delegate's credentials in order? What is the nature of the body by whom he was chosen? There is an epistemic relation in the sense of knowledge of the relations which obtain to other objective things, but not an epistemological problem in the usual meaning of epistemology, namely, a direct and unique relation of a thing known to a knower.

A typical case of "appearance" wherein the

exact objective reference which constitutes a representative office (as a contribution in an inclusive whole) is at issue, is found when there is a question of legal liability in certain transactions. Did or did not a certain person "hold himself out" as agent for a certain principal? Or was a man who claimed to be an agent of another in making a certain agreement authorized to do so? Or, putting the two questions together, did he claim a representative character, and if so was he so authorized to act in that manner so that certain obligations are incumbent on a principal? In any such case, there is a question of whether a certain *allegation* was made or implied, and if so whether the relations to other things constituting the whole in question bear out the assertion. There is a problem, and there is inquiry. The solution of the problem one way or another depends upon what relations are discovered to exist to other things. If these objective relations are ignored, then "appearance" is taken to denote a relation to something behind or underneath which is wholly different in *kind* from what appears. The relation is taken in a lump, statically and in a co-existential cross-section. Hence the "reality" of what appears lies in a different realm of being. But in truth what is behind and covert is other things of the same kind but which have to be searched for in order to determine the genuineness of the representative office claimed. What is "back" is homogenous with what appears.

When there is doubt as to an alleged representative relation and it has to be settled by inquiry into connections with other things, we are obviously in a realm where "appearance" has an intellectual significance. What does the appearing thing *signify*? Is the claimed signifying capacity valid? Truth and falsity are involved. In this meaning there are further relations involved than in the second case where manifestation or exhibition is taken as an *undoubted* part of the situation. As the second sense of appearance makes explicit a connection with an inclusive whole, whose various manifestations are determined by the nature of the whole to be a serial order, so the third sense makes explicit the necessity of determining a *right* to inclusion within this whole; or, stated more generally, makes necessary the

determination of the interrelated whole of which it is actually a constituent. This determination involves a complex set of relations. In the proposition "The sun appears" there is implied the relation of the event termed "rising" to the sun as an enduring object which passes through a cycle of changes. When we say "The rising of the sun is a manifestation of the structure of the solar system" the relation is to the whole system of which the appearance of the sun at a determinate place and time is a function. The same is true in the proposition "Booth appears in the part of Hamlet," where the drama of Hamlet—or perhaps the entire Shakesperian system—is implied as the inclusive whole; so also in the proposition "Coolidge is the legal president of the United States." But in the last proposition "legal" introduces a relationship which is not explicit in the second sense, as is evident if we imagine the proposition denied. The question of validity, or right, enters in. The system is no longer taken for granted as including the part which "manifests" it in a particular phase but must be sought for. It is also necessary to determine the exact nature of the appearing object which is alleged to be a representative part of the whole.

III

There is involved in the latter determination a triadic set of relations. First, there is the relation which the man in his primary qualities sustains to himself as "holding himself out" as agent or as purporting to be an official. This is a reflexive relation. Secondly, as necessary for the *conclusive* determination of this relation there is the relation of the person claiming the office, role, or part to the principal or those represented. In the third place, depending upon this determination, there is a relation to those with whom he has dealings in virtue of the office. This third relationship constitutes the differential feature of the significance of appearance which is now before us. It is the consequences which follow when the claim to a certain office is legitimate and which do not follow when it is not justified which make it necessary in case of doubt to ascertain the rightfulness of the claim. In virtue of being an officer of the law a man has distinctive dealings with other persons; he has effective connections with them, which he does not have as a human being apart from the representative capacity. There is an obvious difference between Booth playing a certain role and a man *claiming* to be Booth taking the same part. In the first instance, those concerned, those affected by the playing of the part, either like it or do not like it. But if the claim is proved invalid, they have redress; they can exercise claims in return.

We have selected as typical illustrations instances of persons who put forth a representative claim. The purpose of the illustrative instances is to prepare the way for an examination of cases where an appearing object is *taken* to have a particular representative capacity and office, that of being a sign or evidence of other things: cases where the assertion is not made by a person on his own account, but is made by the one who takes the thing as evidence or sign of something else. The same triad of relations is found in both cases. Hence analysis of the cases in which the claim is self-asserted instead of depending upon some one's taking or using the appearing object as representative is relevant. When something is *taken* to be smoke and smoke is taken to be a sign of fire, there is also found the added and differential trait of relation to consequences, which consequences differ according as the representative role is or is not justified. When one takes the appearing object as a sign of fire, there are reactions and consequences appropriate to fire. Otherwise one merely reacts just to the appearing object in its own appearing or presented qualities and not as a sign. There is the same difference of treatment and consequences found in responding just to a sound and to a sound which is also a word, that is, to which a meaning is assigned, standing for something beyond itself. It is one and the same whether we say we deal with the whole which includes the manifestation or with the manifesting object as a member of the whole; the difference is purely verbal. But in the case of an appearance as sign or evidence of something else there is the need of determining how justified or valid is the claimed sign relationship, since responsive dealing and consequences depend upon the answer obtained to this question.

IV

The nub of the whole matter turns upon the nature of the reflexive relationship, the relation which an appearing object in its intrinsic qualities bears to the properties that capacitate it to be a sign of something else. That the appearing object is *in* evidence is a truism; the statement is tautologous. But *of* what is it evidence? The latter question introduces a distinction *within* the thing used as sign, a reflexive relation. That the relation to something else involved in being a sign of it is reflected into the appearing object itself is obvious from the fact that we take things as signs when we do not know *of* what they are signs. This happens in every inquiry, since inquiry implies first that some appearing object is a sign, and secondly that we do not as yet know of what it is a sign or evidence. This mode of taking would be impossible unless there were a distinction and relation set up within the appearing object between itself in its primary qualities and itself in its signifying office: just as a sheriff can neither identify his office as sheriff with all his personal peculiarities, needs, and capacities, nor yet wholly sink the latter in his official capacity. He must distinguish within himself characteristics which belong to him *qua* human being from characteristics belonging to him as officer, and at the same time relate them to each other. Unless he does the latter, his office becomes a purely disembodied function; it can become operative only through traits which belong to him as a human being, his hands, legs, tongue, and wits.

We may take as illustrative evidence the case of a sound used as a sign of something else—as a word in language. A child reacts first to a sound as a sound—as the adult reacts to sounds in a language he does not understand as gibberish or as quasi-musical. Taking it as a sign depends upon not treating it merely as a sound and also upon *not identifying* it with the thing meant. This is the same as saying that one must distinguish it as sound from its properties as signifying. The result is both a degradation and an enhancement. The former affects the sound in its primary existential qualities; the latter the sound as a sign. Mere sound is reduced to a vehicle or carrier; the latter gives the sound dignity and status. A good example is found in mathematical symbols where the direct quality of the appearing object is reduced as near a minimum as is consistent with having any appearance at all in order that there may be gain in effective representative import. Relationships react into the thing used as symbol to redetermine its *prior* estate.

This effect of the reflexive relation is of great importance. It is the clew to understanding the traditional misconstruction of the nature of appearances. The essence of this misinterpretation is that it notes and retains in mind the degradation of immediate existential quality, while it fails to note that this reduction is due to and for the sake of the performance of an office as sign of something else—as in our monetary system a bullion value is reduced existentially to a piece of paper while the paper at the same time gains value as a token of indebtedness. The degradation is taken to be something intrinsic, belonging to an existence as such. The appearing object certainly exists, but lacks self-justifying existence. It is therefore said to be only fragmentary, inherently defective, a puzzling anomaly in the order of being. There inevitably ensues the derogatory valuation of "appearance."

This analysis applies also to the "epistemological" misconstruction of the nature of appearance, though now with especial reference to the second of the triad of relations, that of the relation of the appearing thing as sign of some doubtful object to that of which it is a sign. The *legitimacy* of a case of "holding out" as agent does not depend upon a direct and unique relation of a man to those to whom he holds himself out but upon his antecedent relations to others. So the validity of using a thing as sign of this or that inferred object depends not on its direct relation to the knower, but upon its specific relations to other things. As long as these remain in question, we say that "apparently" it signifies this or that. "It *seems* to do so." "Apparently" and "seeming" have nothing to do with its direct and co-existential relation to the knower, nor with its intrinsic quality as affected by this relation. They designate the doubtful state of an inferred object. Whenever final judgment in in-

ference is suspended an appearing object gains a distinctive intellectual status, such as is conveyed in propositions like: "The bill seems to be counterfeit"; "the patient appears to have typhoid," etc.

Instead of denoting an intrinsic distortion of reality due to relation to a knower, "appearance" here marks a safeguard and precaution characteristic of all careful inferential inquiry. By use of "appears," "seems," attention is called to the as yet uncertain status of the inferred object, while at the same time a record is made of the fact that the thing which appears (in the first sense) has a certain amount of evidential force attached to it. Permit this distinctive phase of partial, inconclusive, representative capacity to be ignored, and "seeming" is inevitably taken to be a quality of what appears, due to relation of the thing in itself to a knower.

V

It is submitted that in the foregoing considerations is found the explanation of the category of "phenomena" as opposed to true realities that is found in Greek thought. Men are now in possession of methods of inquiry which have proved their efficacy to unravel the knots which come along with frustrated inference. There are still, of course, many cases in which we can not complete an attempted inference; when, that is, we can not tell just *what* some thing means although it is undoubted in its existential manifestation. But our technique of inquiry has succeeded in so many cases (and in so many cases we have managed to improve a defective technique until it has proved adequate) that in practise we recognize such cases as instances of blocked inference, and lay the subject-matter aside for further investigation. We employ the subject-matter to define a *problem* for research. But when the distinction between phenomena and noumena as two orders of Being was formulated, there was no technique of experimental analysis. The mechanical and the mathematical instruments of intellectual resolution were both lacking. Consequently, the world was full of anomalies— things which undoubtedly existed, but which could not be understood or duly connected with other things. It was an easy and not unnatural generalization to say that they constituted a realm on their own account. All that could be done, in the absence of methods which would link them into members of a course of events, thereby explaining them, was to *classify* them with one another as "phenomena."

This account is confirmed by the fact that the higher and contrasting realm of being was antithetically conceived to be noumena. Things which appear are present in sense-perception; the eye, ear, hand are the media of their determinate presence. Inferred objects that define their meaning and also constitute their full reality are, on the other hand, *qua* inferred, objects of *thought*. This statement is a truism, inference and thought being synonymous. Now at present our scientific technique is such that we can, speaking generally, experimentally control conditions so that an inferred object may itself be rendered perceptible, if not in its entirety, at least in respect to some of its defining features. The existential subject-matter arrived at by calculation is at least a candidate for observation. When the technique of observational analysis is not adequate to bring the calculated objects into view or render them apparent, they are treated as hypothetical. But Greek methods of inquiry made no provision for the "category" of the hypothetically existent any more than it did for the temporarily problematic. Hence the intelligible object which furnished meaning and stability to the perceptible object was treated as final, not as intermediate. It was intrinsically and wholly the object of thought, the noumenon, while in inference conducted by physical and mathematical methods there is no break in kind between the object which appears and the inferred object. For such inference proceeds by insertion of intermediaries which are sufficiently numerous and compact to be members of a temporal continuum. For lack of such methods, Greek speculation made a single jump from the apparent object to the object of thought; the absence of intermediary connecting links necessarily shoved the latter into a non-temporal realm.

The hard and fast distinction between the perceptible object as mere appearance and the intelligible object as ultimate reality is thus a projection, from a period when methods of inferential inquiry were deficient, into a period when methods actually practised leave no place for the distinction. The important thing to bear in mind is that when an ulterior object of inquiry is constituted, the perceptible or apparent object no longer stands over against what is inferred, but is included along with it in a comprehensive series or an inclusive whole. Any case of physical investigation illustrates what is here asserted. When, for example, the appearances or phenomena termed malaria are satisfactorily understood, they present themselves as part of the life-history of anopheles in connection with the life-history of the creature who is their host. When the inference is completed in the categorical assertion of an object, both the appearing (perceived) thing which has been employed as sign and the inferred (intelligible) object lose the isolation they possess during the process of inquiry and delayed inference. They both become members of an interrelated inclusive whole, so that the category of "manifestation" becomes applicable. A one-to-one relation in isolation between the appearing thing and what it means is characteristic only of the period of doubt and inquiry. The reason why our focal awareness fastens so exclusively upon the perceived or appearing object and the definite inferred or intelligible object is obvious. They are terms in a literal sense, defining terminals of the inclusive whole; nothing is gained by giving attention to the latter. The case is similar to the presence of a locked door and search for its key. The reality is the whole operation of opening the locked door. But the sought-for key is literally the key to this operation, just as the lock defines the problem. As soon as the key which fits is found, the operation takes place as a matter of course. It is passed over in explicit consciousness just because it is taken for granted as that which gives meaning to the key and to the search for it.

VI

We have, however, temporarily turned aside from the explanation of the epistemological misconstruction. Deferred inference, or relation to a missing but signified object, is expressed in such propositions as "This seems to be pure milk (but perhaps it is skimmed milk)." But such propositions as "It looks blue or chalky" have a distinctly different intellectual force. "The man down on the street looks very small from here"—the top of a high building. "That distant mountain appears blue." "The rails seem to converge; the stick appears bent; the coin seems elliptical." Such propositions (which have been made of late the object of much puzzled speculation) have a ready interpretation when taken in their logical status, that is, as involved in the use of appearing things as signs of something else. In the cases previously analyzed it was the inferred object which is merely "apparent," that is apparently but not surely signified. The propositions just stated refer to the way in which the object used as evidence presents itself. They state the appearing object as it appears—in our first neutral sense. But they state it with a purpose—that of defining the exact nature of the evidence at hand. "The stick seems bent in water" does not mean that the appearing object *seems* bent. It means that what appears *is* something bent, though not necessarily the stick; perhaps it is light.

The first step is to put ourselves on guard against depending upon the vague term "seems," "appears." We must specify the respect in which it appears, to eye, ear, touch, smell. If I say that a straight stick rising out of water *looks* bent (implying relation to the eye) I but state an objective fact, verified by a camera, and explained by well-known physical principles. In exactly the same way when I say that a moving whistle *sounds* higher or lower in pitch as it approaches or recedes, I state a fact of relationship to the ear. Incredible as it may appear, a serious problem has been made out of the fact that a fire feels colder as we move away from it. The process of creating the "problem" is as follows. The fire has really but one temperature. How is that fact to be reconciled with the fact that at different distances it *seems* to be of many different temperatures? Of course, it can not; but the statement is so mixed as to be absurd; the problem, not the solution, is at fault. The temperature of the air affected by the fire changes with distance; this is a physical fact, and what is *felt* is the tem-

perature of the air. Thus to say that the fire *feels* colder as we recede is to state an incontrovertible fact; there would be a problem only if it were not so.

It may seem like a trick to do away with this "problem" by substituting specific terms, "looks," "sounds," "feels," for the general term "appears," "seems." But the force of the substitution is to call attention to a specific relation, to that particular part of the nervous organism which is involved as a condition, a physical or causal condition, of the appearance of the thing which is to serve as sign. The propositions under discussion make explicit the exact nature of the thing to be used as evidence, before it is used.

This becomes evident if, instead of stating a definitive or concluded judgment such as "The straight stick looks bent in the water," we say merely "There is present a form which to the eye looks bent," a statement of fact, but of fact about the appearing object irrespective of any inferential use made of it. If we say "The round coin looks elliptical seen from this angle" we again state a correct judgment. If we say "There is present to the eye an elliptical form" we describe the nature of the appearance (in our first sense) preliminary to making inferential use of it. It may be said, however, that we have unduly simplified the situation in getting rid of the alleged problem. It may be objected that the real problem lies in the fact that there are many appearances, and that the question to be answered is which of these, if any, is or corresponds to the real object, a stick or penny. Why, for example, should the circular form, the thing appearing in perpendicular vision, be assigned any superiority over other appearances to the eye? The reply is that it is *not*; the superiority assigned to it is that of being a *better sign*. And that it is such is something learned by experience in making use of various appearing objects as bases of inferring other things.

A man sights with his eye along the edge of a board he has been planing and says "it *looks* straight." This is simply a statement of fact, of the same kind as when he says "it is a board." If he said "it *is* straight," he would have made an inference from what appears to his eye, perhaps a wrong one. When he confined himself to saying "it looks straight" he limits himself to a statement of the nature of what appears and suspends inferential judgment; it is just as if a geologist were to confine his report to saying that there are certain marks on the rock which *suggest* a trilobite, while he refrains from asserting that they *are* a fossil trilobite. In any such case, the one who makes the judgment recognizes in effect that the conditions of the appearing object are complex; they include both the edge of the board and his sensori-cerebral apparatus. Both conditions are involved in the temporal series of which the last term is the appearing object. No epistemic import is assigned to vision, but the visual apparatus is taken for what it is, one of the physically causal conditions of what appears or is present. Distrusting the adequacy of this appearance as sign or evidence, one then resorts to production of another appearance, the process being identical with any physical experiment where conditions are intentionally varied. One runs a finger over the edge and says "It feels uneven here and there." The implication is not that a tactile appearance is more real than a visual, but that for certain purposes it affords a better sign of a sought-for object. If one is still in doubt one may fall back upon mechanical appliances—upon relations to other things instead of relations to the organism—in order to determine that appearance which shall serve as a sign. As actual existence all "appearances" stand on the same level; as signs some are better than others, just as what one witness says is better evidence than what another says, although the utterances of each are equally actual occurrences.

VII

We conclude with a summary. The original and neutral sense of appearance is just that something previously remote, covert or obscure *appears*—comes into view, into actualized presence. When the thing appearing is referred without question to a whole of which it is a related member, it is termed an exhibition, manifestation, display, expression. But often this reference can not be made directly; what it belongs to has to be searched for. The evident object is now treated as evidence; it

gains the role of sign or index of something or other. In its reflexive relation it sets a problem to be inquired into. The appearance is now an appearance *of* something whose nature is to be determined by inference from the appearing objects and from others which may be aligned with it. Appearing now takes temporarily the form of seeming rather than of showing. But "seeming" does not signify that something seems to exist, but that a certain *object* seems to be *pointed* to: "seeming" denotes an essayed, but temporarily blocked, inference. Finally, it is often necessary in the interest of control of inference to state the causal conditions of that appearing thing which is used as sign. In this operation, organic conditions of touch, sight, hearing, smell, or taste are specified and "appears" is specified into feels, looks, sounds, smells, tastes thus and so. The process is no different from when a scientist specifies the physical apparatus which he has employed in producing the phenomena which are used as evidence in drawing an inference.

This point is worth dwelling upon. It has been implied throughout that the relation to organic apparatus involved in such terms as "looks," "sounds," "feels," "tastes" is a reference to a causal condition of the production of the particular object which appears, not a reference to a knower, an epistemological reference, and that this relation is specified as a safeguard of the use to be made of it in inference from it. The statement is thus precisely analogous to the pains which a scientific experimenter takes to specify exactly the apparatus through which he obtains the subject-matter from which he infers certain conclusions. If a man uses a microscope in obtaining his evidential subject-matter he tells of its nature and manner of employment so that another can decide *how* the objects were made to appear. The statement that a thing "looks thus and so" is of precisely the same sort; the difference being, on the one hand, the greater degree of refinement of causal condition in the case of the microscope, and on the other hand, the presence of an *organic* mechanism as a condition of the appearance of anything whatever. A similar principle applies to the use of a sense-organ under different conditions and to recourse to various sense organs: not because the appearance conditioned by one is more real existentially than that of any other, or less real than that of the thing inferred, but because in this way subject-matter better for purposes of inference is secured. So, in the laboratory, conditions are intentionally varied and precisely for the same reason: to obtain a fuller amount of evidential material and to use its various phases as means of checking the use of other portions.

The general notion of "appearance" we have broken up into a number of meanings each distinctive in a particular contextual situation. The elimination of traditional misconstruction is procured when we keep these meanings definite, each in its proper place, and do not transfer and mix traits of one with those of another. Four distinctive situations are stated in such propositions as the following: (I) The sun appears (rises, or emerges from a cloud)— the primitive and neutral meaning. (II) The sun's appearing at this place and time is a manifestation of certain characteristics of the structure of the system to which sun and earth belong; a type of proposition which states the conclusion of any completed inquiry accepted as valid knowledge. (III) The sun seems to move (apparently moves) from east to west across a stationary earth; the statement of an inferred object with an intimation of suspense and doubt concerning its correctness, or as preliminary to its rejection and the statement of another inferred total object such as "In reality, the earth rotates and its rotation, while the sun remains stationary with reference to the earth, accounts for the appearing objects which were used (wrongly) as the basis of the other inference." And finally (IV) The sun looks to the eye about the size of a twenty-five cent piece—a statement of a fact which is to serve as part of the matter of an inference as to its actual size, or an inference about its distance, etc.

In denying the metaphysical interpretation of appearance as an inferior order of being, it is not meant, of course, to deny all metaphysical implications in a certain sense of "metaphysical." On the contrary, the argument rests throughout on the fact that existential subject-matter in each of the four types of propositions is a series or temporal order of interrelated elements forming an inclusive whole of which the appearances are members. If this existential fact be denied, some form of bad metaphysics is bound to result. Nor is it implied that no general theory of knowledge is involved. On the contrary, the analysis points to the fact that knowledge requires as its precondition an appearing object which results from an integrated interaction of all factors, the organism included, and that the completed object of knowledge is precisely such an interrelated and self-manifesting whole as includes an appearance.

NOTES

[First published in *Journal of Philosophy* 24 (1927): 449–63. LW 3:55–72.]

The world in which we immediately live, that in which we strive, succeed, and are defeated is preeminently a qualitative world. What we act for, suffer, and enjoy are things in their qualitative determinations. This world forms the field of characteristic modes of thinking, characteristic in that thought is definitely regulated by qualitative considerations. Were it not for the double and hence ambiguous sense of the term "common-sense," it might be said that common-sense thinking, that concerned with action and its consequences, whether undergone in enjoyment or suffering, is qualitative. But since "common-sense" is also used to designate accepted traditions and is appealed to in support of them, it is safe at the outset to refer simply to that thought which has to do with objects involved in the concerns and issues of living.

The problem of qualitative objects has influenced metaphysics and epistemology but has not received corresponding attention in logical theory. The propositions significant in physical science are oblivious of qualitative considerations as such; they deal with "primary qualities" in distinction from secondary and tertiary; in actual treatment, moreover, these primary qualities are not qualities but relations. Consider the difference between movement as qualitative alteration, and motion as $F=ma$; between stress as involving effort and tension, and as force per unit surface; between the red of the blood issuing from a wound, and red as signifying 400 trillion vibrations per time unit. Metaphysics has been concerned with the existential status of qualitative objects as contrasted with those of physical science, while epistemology, having frequently decided that qualities are subjective and psychical, has been concerned with their relation in knowing to the properties of "external" objects defined in non-qualitative terms.

But a logical problem remains. What is the relation or lack of relations between the two types of propositions, one which refers to objects of physical science and the other to qualitative objects? What, if any, are the distinguishing logical marks of each kind? If it were true that things as things, apart from interaction with an organism, are qualityless, the logical problem would remain. For the truth would

Qualitative Thought

(1930)

concern the mode of production and existence of qualitative things. It is irrelevant to their logical status. Logic can hardly admit that it is concerned only with objects having one special mode of production and existence, and yet claim universality. And it would be fatal to the claims of logic to say that because qualities are psychical—supposing for the moment that they are—therefore logical theory has nothing to do with forms of thought characteristic of qualitative objects. It is even possible that some of the difficulties of metaphysical and epistemological theory about scientific and ordinary objects spring from neglect of a basic logical treatment.

A preliminary introduction to the topic may be found in the fact that Aristotelian logic, which still passes current nominally, is a logic based upon the idea that qualitative objects are existential in the fullest sense. To retain logical principles based on this conception along with the acceptance of theories of existence and knowledge based on an opposite conception is not, to say the least, conducive to clearness—a consideration that has a good deal to do with the existing dualism between traditional and the newer relational logics. A more obviously pertinent consideration is the fact that the interpretation of classic logic treats qualitative determinations as fixed properties of objects, and thus is committed to either an attributive or a classificatory doctrine of the import of propositions. Take the proposition: "The red Indian is stoical." This is interpreted either as signifying that the Indian in question is characterized by the property of stoicism in addition to that of redness, or that he belongs to the class of stoical objects. The ordinary direct sense of the proposition escapes recognition in either case. For this sense expresses the fact that the indigenous American was permeated throughout by a certain quality, instead of being an object possessing a certain quality along with others. He lived, acted, endured stoically.

If one thinks that the difference between the two meanings has no logical import, let him reflect that the whole current subject-predication theory of propositions is affected by the "property" notion, whether the theory speaks in the language of attribution or classification. A subject is "given"—ultimately apart from thinking—and then thought adds to what is given a further determination or else assigns it to a ready-made class of things. Neither theory can have any place for the integral development and reconstruction of subject-matter effected by the thought expressed in propositions. In effect it excludes thought from any share in the determination of the subject-matter of knowledge, confining it to setting forth the results (whether conceived as attributive or classificatory) of knowledge already attained in isolation from the method by which it is attained.

Perhaps, however, the consideration that will appeal to most people is the fact that the neglect of qualitative objects and considerations leaves thought in certain subjects without any logical status and control. In esthetic matters, in morals and politics, the effect of this neglect is either to deny (implicitly at least) that they have logical foundation or else, in order to bring them under received logical categories, to evacuate them of their distinctive meaning—a procedure which produces the myth of the "economic man" and the reduction of esthetics and morals, as far as they can receive any intellectual treatment at all, to quasi-mathematical subjects.

Consider for example a picture that is a work of art and not just a chromo or other mode of mechanical product. Its quality is not a property which it possesses in addition to its other properties. It is something which externally demarcates it from other paintings, and which internally pervades, colors, tones, and weights every detail and every relation of the work of art. The same thing is true of the "quality" of a person or of historic events. We follow, with apparently complete understanding, a tale in which a certain quality or character is ascribed to a certain man. But something said causes us to interject, "Oh, you are speaking of Thomas Jones, I supposed you meant John Jones." Every detail related, every distinction set forth remains just what it was before. Yet the significance, the color and weight, of every detail is altered. For the quality that runs through them all, that gives meaning to each and binds them together, is transformed.

Now my point is that unless such underlying and pervasive qualitative determinations are acknowledged in a distinct logical formulation, one or other of two results is bound to follow. Either thought is denied to the subject-matter in question, and the phenomena are attributed to "intuition" or "genius" or "impulse" or "personality" as ultimate and unanalyzable entities; or, worse yet, intellectual analysis is reduced to a mechanical enumeration of isolated items or "properties." As a matter of fact, such intellectual definiteness and coherence as the objects and criticisms of esthetic and moral subjects possess is due to their being controlled by the quality of subject-matter as a whole. Consideration of the meaning of regulation by an underlying and pervasive quality is the theme of this article.

What is intended may be indicated by drawing a distinction between something called a "situation" and something termed an "object." By the term situation in this connection is signified the fact that the subject-matter ultimately referred to in existential propositions is a complex existence that is held together in spite of its internal complexity by the fact that it is dominated and characterized throughout by a single quality. By "object" is meant some element in the complex whole that is defined in abstraction from the whole of which it is a distinction. The special point made is that the selective determination and relation of objects in thought is controlled by reference to a situation—to that which is constituted by a pervasive and internally integrating quality, so that failure to acknowledge the situation leaves, in the end, the logical force of objects and their relations inexplicable.

Now in current logical formulations, the beginning is always made with "objects." If we take the proposition "the stone is shaly," the logical import of the proposition is treated as if something called "stone" had complete intellectual import in and of itself and then some property, having equally a fixed content in isolation, "shaly" is attributed to it. No such self-sufficient and self-enclosed entity can possibly lead anywhere nor be led to; connection among such entities is mechanical and arbitrary, not intellectual. Any proposition about "stone" or "shaly" would have to be analytic in the Kantian sense, merely stating part of the content already known to be contained in the meaning of the terms. That a tautological proposition is a proposition only in name is well recognized. In fact, "stone," "shaly" (or whatever are subject and predicate) are determinations or distinctions instituted within the total subject-matter to which thought refers. When such propositions figure in logical textbooks, the actual subject-matter referred to is some branch of logical theory which is exemplified in the proposition.

This larger and inclusive subject-matter is what is meant by the term "situation." Two further points follow. The situation as such is not and cannot be stated or made explicit. It is taken for granted, "understood," or implicit in all propositional symbolization. It forms the universe of discourse of whatever is expressly stated or of what appears as a term in a proposition. The situation cannot present itself as an element in a proposition any more than a universe of discourse can appear as a member of discourse within that universe. To call it "implicit" does not signify that it is implied. It is present throughout as that of which whatever is explicitly stated or propounded is a distinction. A quart bowl cannot be held within itself or in any of its contents. It may, however, be contained in another bowl, and similarly what is the "situation" in one proposition may appear as a term in *another* proposition—that is, in connection with some *other* situation to which thought now refers.

Secondly, the situation controls the terms of thought, for they are *its* distinctions, and applicability to it is the ultimate test of their validity. It is this phase of the matter which is suggested by the earlier use of the idea of a pervasive and underlying quality. If the quart container affected the import of everything held within it, there would be a physical analogy, a consideration that may be awkwardly hinted at by the case of a person protesting to a salesman that he has not received a full quart; the deficiency affects everything that he has purchased. A work of art provides an apter illustration. In it, as we have already noted, the quality of the whole permeates, affects, and controls every detail. There are paintings, buildings, novels, arguments, in which an observer notes an inability of the author to sustain a unified attention throughout. The details fall to pieces; they are not distinctions of one subject-matter, because there is no qualitative unity underlying them. Confusion and incoherence are always marks of lack of control by a single pervasive quality. The latter alone enables a person to keep track of what he is doing, saying, hearing, reading, in whatever explicitly appears. The underlying unity of qualitativeness regulates pertinence or relevancy and force of every distinction and relation; it guides selection and rejection and the manner of utilization of all explicit terms. This quality enables us to keep thinking about one problem without our having constantly to stop to ask ourselves what it is after all that we are thinking about. We are aware of it not by itself but as the background, the thread, and the directive clue in what we do expressly think of. For the latter things are *its* distinctions and relations.[1]

If we designate this permeating qualitative unity in psychological language, we say it is felt rather than thought. Then, if we hypostatize it, we call it *a* feeling. But to term it a feeling is to reverse the actual state of affairs. The existence of unifying qualitativeness in the subject-matter defines the meaning of "feeling." The notion that "a feeling" designates a ready-made independent psychical entity is a product of a reflection which presupposes the direct presence of quality as such. "Feeling" and "felt" are names for a *relation* of quality. When, for example, anger exists, it is the pervading tone, color, and quality of persons, things, and circumstances, or of a situation. When angry we are not aware of anger but of these objects in their immediate and unique qualities. In another situation, anger may appear as a distinct term, and analysis may then call it a feeling or emotion. But we have now shifted the universe of discourse, and the validity of the terms of the later one depends upon the existence of the direct quality of the whole in a former one. That is, in saying that something was *felt* not thought of, we are analyzing in a new situation, having its own immediate quality, the subject-matter of a prior situation; we are making anger an object of analytic examination, not being angry.

When it is said that I have a feeling, or impression, or "hunch," that things are thus and so, what is actually designated is primarily the presence of a dominating quality in a situation as a whole, not just the existence of a feeling as a psychical or psychological fact. To say I have a feeling or impression that so and so is the case is to note that the quality in question is not yet resolved into determinate terms and relations; it marks a conclusion without statement of the reasons for it, the grounds upon which it rests. It is the first stage in the development of explicit distinctions. All thought in every subject begins with just such an unanalyzed whole. When the subject-matter is reasonably familiar, relevant distinctions speedily offer themselves, and sheer qualitativeness may not remain long enough to be readily recalled. But it often persists and forms a haunting and engrossing problem. It is a commonplace that a problem *stated* is well on its way to solution, for statement of the nature of a problem signifies that the underlying quality is being transformed into determinate distinctions of terms and relations or has become an object of articulate thought. But something presents itself as problematic before there is recognition of *what* the problem is. The problem is had or experienced before it can be stated or set forth; but it is had as an immediate quality of the whole situation. The sense of something problematic, of something perplexing and to be resolved, marks the presence of something pervading all elements and considerations. Thought is the operation by which it is converted into pertinent and coherent terms.

The word "intuition" has many meanings. But in its popular, as distinct from refined philosophic, usage it is closely connected with the single qualitativeness underlying all the details of explicit reasoning. It may be relatively dumb and inarticulate and yet penetrating; unexpressed in definite ideas which form reasons and justifications and yet profoundly right. To my mind, Bergson's contention that intuition precedes conception and goes deeper is correct. Reflection and rational elaboration spring from and make explicit a prior intuition. But there is nothing mystical about this fact, and it does not signify that there are two modes of knowledge, one of which is appropriate to one kind of subject-matter, and the other mode to the other kind. Thinking and theorizing about physical matters set out from an intuition, and reflection about affairs of life and mind consists in an ideational and conceptual transformation of what begins as an intuition. Intuition, in short, signifies the realization of a pervasive quality such that it regulates the determination of relevant distinctions or of whatever, whether in the way of terms or relations, becomes the accepted object of thought.

While some ejaculations and interjections are merely organic responses, there are those which have an intellectual import, though only context and the total situation can decide to which class a particular ejaculation belongs. "Alas," "Yes," "No," "Oh" may each of them be the symbol of an integrated attitude toward the quality of a situation as a whole; that it is thoroughly pitiful, acceptable, to be rejected, or is a matter of complete surprise. In this case, they characterize the existent situation and as such have a cognitive import. The exclamation "Good!" may mark a deep apprehension of the quality of a piece of acting on the stage, of a deed performed, or of a picture in its wealth of content. The actual judgment may find better expression in these symbols than in a long-winded disquisition. To many persons there is something artificial and repellent in discoursing about any consummatory event or object. It speaks so completely for itself that words are poor substitutes—not that thought fails, but that thought so completely grasps the dominant quality that translation into explicit terms gives a partial and inadequate result.

Such ejaculatory judgments supply perhaps the simplest example of qualitative thought in its purity. While they are primitive, it does not follow that they are always superficial and immature. Sometimes, indeed, they express an infantile mode of intellectual response. But they may also sum up and integrate prolonged previous experience and training, and bring to a unified head the results of severe and consecutive reflection. Only the situation symbolized and not the formal and propositional symbol can decide which is the case. The full content of meaning is best apprehended in case of the judgment of the esthetic expert in the presence of a work of art. But they come at the beginning and at the close of every scientific investigation. These open with the "Oh" of wonder and terminate with the "Good" of a rounded-out and organized situation. Neither the "Oh" nor the "Good" expresses a mere state of personal feeling. Each characterizes a subject-matter. "How beautiful" symbolizes neither a state of feeling nor the supervening of an external essence upon a state of existence but marks the realized appreciation of a pervading quality that is now translated into a system of definite and coherent terms. Language fails not because thought fails, but because no verbal symbols can do justice to the fullness and richness of thought. If we are to continue talking about "data" in any other sense than as reflective distinctions, the original datum is always such a qualitative whole.

The logic of artistic construction is worth more than a passing notice, whether its product be a painting, a symphony, a statue, a building, a drama, or a novel. So far as it is not evidence of conceit on the part of a specialized class, refusal to admit thought and logic on the part of those who make these constructions is evidence of the breakdown of traditional logic. There are (as we previously noted) alleged works of art in which parts do not hang together and in which the quality of one part does not reinforce and expand the quality of every other part. But this fact is itself a manifestation of the defective character of the thought involved in their production. It illustrates by contrast the nature of such works as are genuine intellectual and logical wholes. In the latter, the underlying quality that defines the work, that circumscribes it externally and integrates it internally, controls the thinking of the artist; his logic is the logic of what I have called qualitative thinking.

Upon subsequent analysis, we term the properties of a work of art by such names as symmetry, harmony, rhythm, measure, and proportion. These may, in some cases at least, be formulated mathematically. But the apprehension of these formal relationships is not primary for either the artist or the appreciative spectator. The subject-matter formulated by these terms is primarily qualitative, and is apprehended qualitatively. Without an independent qualitative apprehension, the characteristics of a work of art can be translated into explicit harmonies, symmetries, etc., only in a way which substitutes mechanical formulae for esthetic quality. The value of any such translation in esthetic criticism is measured, moreover, by the extent to which the propositional statements return to effect a heightening and deepening of a qualitative apprehension. Otherwise, esthetic appreciation is replaced by judgment of isolated technique.

The logic of artistic construction and esthetic appreciation is peculiarly significant because they exemplify in accentuated and purified form the control of selection of detail and of mode of relation, or integration, by a qualitative whole. The underlying quality demands certain distinctions, and the degree in which the demand is met confers upon the work of art that necessary or inevitable character which is its mark. Formal necessities, such as can be made explicit, depend upon the material necessity imposed by the pervasive and underlying quality. Artistic thought is not however unique in this respect but only shows an intensification of a characteristic of all thought. In a looser way, it is a characteristic of all non-technical, non-"scientific" thought. Scientific thought is, in its turn, a specialized form of art, with its own qualitative control. The more formal and mathematical science becomes, the more it is controlled by sensitiveness to a special kind of qualitative considerations. Failure to realize the qualitative and artistic nature of formal scientific construction is due to two causes. One is conventional, the habit of associating art and esthetic appreciation with a few popularly recognized forms. The other cause is the fact that a student is so concerned with the mastery of symbolic or propositional forms that he fails to recognize and to repeat the creative operations involved in their construction. Or, when they are mastered, he is more concerned with their further application than with realization of their intrinsic intellectual meaning.

The foregoing remarks are intended to suggest the significance to be attached to the term "qualitative thought." But as statements they are propositions and hence symbolic. Their meaning can be apprehended only by going beyond them, by using them as clues to call up qualitative situations. When an experience of the latter is had and they are re-lived, the realities corresponding to the propositions laid down may be had. Assuming that such a realization has been experienced, we proceed to consider some further questions upon which qualitative thought throws light.

First as to the nature of the predication. The difficulties connected with the problem of predication are of long standing. They were recognized in Greek thought, and the scepticism they induced was a factor in developing the Platonic theory of the same-and-the-other and the Aristotelian conception of potentiality-and-actuality. The sceptical difficulty may be summed up in the statement that predication is either tautological and so meaningless, or else falsifying or at least arbitrary. Take the proposition "that thing is sweet." If "sweet" already qualifies the meaning of "that thing," the predication is analytic in the Kantian sense, or forms a trivial proposition in the sense of Locke. But if "sweet" does not already qualify "that thing" what ground is there for tacking it on? The most that can be said is that some one who did not know before that it was sweet has now learned it. But such a statement refers only to an episode in the some one's intellectual biography. It has no logical force; it does not touch the question of predication that has objective reference and possible validity.

When, however, it is recognized that predication—any proposition having subject-predicate form—marks an attempt to make a qualitative whole which is directly and non-reflectively experienced into an object of thought for the sake of its own development, the case stands otherwise. What is "given" is not an object by itself nor a term having a meaning of its own. The "given," that is to say the existent, is precisely an undetermined and dominant complex quality. "Subject" and "predicate" are correlative determinations of this quality. The "copula" stands for the fact that one term is predicated of the other, and is thus a sign of the development of the qualitative whole by means of their distinction. It is, so to speak, the assertion of the fact that the distinctions designated in subject and predicate are correlative and work together in a common function of determination.

A certain quality is experienced. When it is inquired into or thought (judged), it differentiates into "that thing" on the one hand, and "sweet" on the other. Both "that thing" and "sweet" are analytic of the quality, but are additive, synthetic, ampliative, with respect to each other. The copula "is" marks just the effect of this distinction upon the correlative terms. They mark something like a division of labor, and the copula marks the function or work done by the structures that exhibit the division of labor. To say that "that thing is sweet" means "that thing" will *sweeten* some other object, say coffee, or a batter of milk and eggs. The intent of sweetening something formed the ground for converting a dumb quality into an articulate object of thought.

The logical force of the copula is always that of an active verb. It is merely a linguistic peculiarity, not a logical fact, that we say "that is red" instead of "that reddens," either in the sense of growing, becoming red, or in the sense of making something else red. Even linguistically our "is" is a weakened form of an active verb signifying "stays" or "stands." But the nature of any act (designated by the true verbal form) is best apprehended in its effect and issue; we say "is sweet" rather than "sweetens," "is red" rather than "reddens" because we define the active change by its anticipated or attained outcome. To say "the dog is ugly" is a way of setting forth what he is likely to *do*, namely to snarl and bite. "Man is mortal" indicates what man does or what actively is done to him, calling attention to a consequence. If we convert its verbal form into "men die," we realize the transitive and additive force of predication and escape the self-made difficulties of the attributive theory.

The underlying pervasive quality in the last instance, when it is put in words, involves care or concern for human destiny. But we must remember that this exists as a dumb quality until it is symbolized in an intellectual and propositional form. Out of this quality there emerges the idea of man and of mortality and of their existential connection with each other. No one of them has any meaning apart from the others, neither the distinctions, the terms, nor their relation, the predication. All the difficulties that attend the problem of

predication spring from supposing that we can take the terms and their connection as having meaning by themselves. The sole alternative to this supposition is the recognition that the object of thought, designated propositionally, is a quality that is first directly and unreflectively experienced or had.

One source of the difficulty and the error in the classic theory lies in a radical misconception of the treacherous idea of the "given." The only thing that is unqualifiedly given is the total pervasive quality; and the objection to calling it "given" is that the word suggests something *to* which it is given, mind or thought or consciousness or whatever, as well possibly as something that gives. In truth "given" in this connection signifies only that the quality immediately exists, or is brutely there. In this capacity, it forms that to which all objects of thought refer, although, as we have noticed, it is never part of the manifest subject-matter of thought. In itself, it is the big, buzzing, blooming confusion of which James wrote. This expresses not only the state of a baby's experience but the first stage and background of all thinking on any subject. There is, however, no inarticulate quality which is merely buzzing and blooming. It buzzes to some effect; it blooms toward some fruitage. That is, the quality, although dumb, has as a part of its complex quality a movement or transition in some direction. It can, therefore, be intellectually symbolized and converted into an object of thought. This is done by statement of limits and of direction of transition between them. "That" and "sweet" define the limits of the moving quality, the copula "tastes" (the real force of "is") defines the direction of movement between these limits. Putting the nature of the two limits briefly and without any attempt to justify the statement here, the subject represents the pervasive quality as means or condition and the predicate represents it as outcome or end.

These considerations define not only the subject-predicate structure of categorical propositions but they explain why the selective character of all such propositions with respect to the fullness of existence is not falsifying in character. Idealistic logicians, in calling attention to the partial or selective character of particular judgments, have used the fact to cast logical aspersion upon them, and to infer their need of correction first by transformation into conditional propositions and then finally into a judgment coextensive with the whole universe, arguing that only the latter can be truly true. But enough is always enough, and the underlying quality is itself the test of the "enough" for any particular case. All that is needed is to determine this quality by indicating the limits between which it moves and the direction or tendency of its movement. Sometimes the situation is simple and the most meagre indications serve, like the "safe" or "out" of a baseball umpire. At other times, a quality is complex and prolonged, and a multitude of distinctions and subordinate relations are required for its determinate statement. It would have been logically vicious on one occasion to propound more than "my kingdom for a horse," while under other circumstances it may need a volume to set forth the quality of the situation so as to make it comprehensible. Any proposition that serves the purpose for which it is made is logically adequate; the idea that it is inadequate until the whole universe has been included is a consequence of giving judgment a wrong office—an error that has its source in failure to see the domination of every instance of thought by a qualitative whole needing statement in order that it may function.

At this point a reference to what is termed association of ideas is in place. For while the subject is usually treated as psychological in nature, thinking as an existential process takes place through association; existentially, thinking *is* association as far as the latter is controlled. And the mechanics of thinking can hardly be totally irrelevant to its *logical* structure and function. I shall assume without much argument that "ideas" here signify objects, not psychical entities; objects, that is to say, as meanings to which reference may be made. When one, seeing smoke, thinks of fire he is associating objects, not just states in his own mind. And so when thinking of a hand, one thinks of grasping or of an organism. Thus, when association takes the form of thought, or is controlled and not loose day-dreaming, association is a name for a connection of objects or their elements in the total situation having a

qualitative unity. This statement signifies something different than does a statement that associated objects are physical parts of a physical whole. It happens to hold in the case of "hand-organism" and with some qualifications in the case of "smoke-fire." But a philosophical student might be led by the thought of hand to the thought of Aristotle on the ground of a remark made by Aristotle.

In any case an original contiguity (or similarity) is not the *cause* of an association. We do not associate *by* contiguity, for recognition of a whole in which elements are juxtaposed in space or in temporal sequence is the *result* of suggestion. The absurdity of the preposition "by" when applied to similarity is still more obvious. It is the reason why some writers reduce similarity to identity in differences, a position that will be examined later. That by which association is effected, by which suggestion and evocation of a distinct object of thought is brought about, is some acquired modification of the organism, usually designated habit. The conditioning mechanism may not be known at present in detail, but it cannot be an original contiguity because that contiguity is apprehended only in consequence of association. It may well be an organic attitude formed in consequence of a responsive act to things once coexistent or sequential. But this act was unitary; reference to it only accentuates the fact that the quality attending it was spread over and inclusive of the two things in question. That is, it was a response to a *situation* within which objects were related in space or time.

Given the conditions, the real problem is to say why objects once conjoined in a whole are now distinguished as two objects, one that which suggests, and the other that which is suggested. If I think of a chiffonier, the thought does not call up that of drawers as a distinct idea. For the drawers are a part of the object thought of. So when I originally saw, say a bird-in-a-nest, I saw a single total object. Why then does the sight or thought of a bird now call up that of a nest as a distinct idea? In general, the reason is that I have so often seen birds without seeing a nest and nests without birds. Moreover, it must be remembered that a person often sees a bird or nest, and instead of thinking of any other object, he reacts to it directly, as a man does when shooting at a bird or a boy climbing a tree to get the nest. While there is no association without habit, the natural tendency of habit is to produce an immediate reaction, not to evoke another distinct object of thought or idea. As the *dis*association of birds and nests in experience shows, this additional factor is some resistance to the attitude formed by the sight of nest-with-a-bird-in-it. Otherwise we should have the case over again of chiffonier and its drawers, or any object and its constitutive parts. Without the resistant or negative factor, there would be no tension to effect the change from a direct response, an immediate act, to an indirect one, a distinct object of thought.

Not only then is there no association *by* contiguity, but association is not *of* two objects separated yet contiguous in a prior experience. Its characteristic nature is that it presents as distinct but connected objects what originally were either two parts of one situational object, or (in the case that a man had previously always seen birds and nests separately from each other) that it presents in coexistence or sequence with one another objects previously separated in space and time. This consideration is fatal to the notion that the associated objects account by themselves or in their own isolated nature for association. It indicates that coexistence or sequence as a physical existential fact is not the ground of association. What alternative remains save that the quality of a situation as a whole operates to produce a functional connection? Acceptance of this alternative implies that association is an *intellectual* connection, thus aligning association with thought, as we shall now see.

There is nothing intellectual or logical in contiguity, in mere juxtaposition in space and time. If association were, then, either *of* or *by* contiguity, association would not have any logical force, any connection with thought.[2] But in fact association of bare contiguities is a myth. There is an indefinite number of particulars contiguous to one another in space and time. When I think of a nest why does a bird come into my mind? As a matter of contiguity, there are multitudinous leaves and twigs which are more frequently and more obviously

juxtaposed than is a bird. When I think of a hammer, why is the idea of nail so likely to follow? Such questions suggest, I hope, that even in seemingly casual cases of association, there is an underlying quality which operates to control the connection of objects thought of. It takes something else than contiguity to effect association; there must be relevancy of both ideas to a situation defined by unity of quality. There is coherence of some sort because of mutual pertinency of both ideas (or of all ideas in train) to a basis beyond any of them and beyond mere juxtaposition of objects in space and time.

The usual notion that association is merely *de facto* receives a still more obvious shock in the case of similarity. When I associate bird with nest, there may have been at least some previous conjunction in experience of the two objects, even though that conjunction is not by itself a sufficient condition of the later association. But when troublesome thought suggests the sting of an insect, or when change of fortune suggests the ebb and flow of the sea, there is *no* physical conjunction in the past to which appeal can be made. To try to explain the matter by saying that two objects are associated *because* they are similar is either to offer the problem as a solution or to attribute causal efficacy to "similarity"—which is to utter meaningless words. So-called association "by" similarity is a striking example of the influence of an underlying pervasive quality in determining the connection essential in thought.

There is, as far as I am aware, but one serious attempt to explain such association on some other basis. This is found in the view that there is in what is called similarity an actual existential identity among differences and that this identity works and then reinstates differences by contiguity. I fail to see how the explanation applies in many cases—such as that of the troublesome thought and the sting of an insect, or Socrates and a gadfly. "Identity" seems to be the result rather than the antecedent of the association. But I shall confine the discussion to instances in which it is claimed to work. Bradley has stated the theory in question most clearly and I shall use his illustration.[3]

Walking on the shore of England, one sees

a promontory and remarks how like it is to one in Wales. Bradley's explanation is that there is an actual identity of form in both and that this identical form suggests by contiguity in space certain elements which cannot be referred to the promontory now seen (size, color, etc., being incompatible) and thus constitutes in connection with identical form the content of the idea of the promontory in Wales. The seeming plausibility of this explanation is shattered by the fact that form is not one isolated element among others, but is an arrangement or pattern of elements. Identity of pattern, arrangement of form is something that can be apprehended only *after* the other promontory has been suggested, by comparison of the two objects.

The only way that form or pattern can operate as an immediate link is by the mode of a directly experienced *quality*, something present and prior to and independent of all reflective analysis, something of the same nature which controls artistic construction. In psychological language, it is felt, and the feeling is made explicit or a term of thought in the idea of another promontory. What operates is not an external existential identity between two things, but a present immediate quality—an explanation which is the only one applicable to some cases already cited, and to being reminded of blotting paper by a certain voice. The priority of regulative quality of the situation as a whole is especially obvious in the case of esthetic judgments. A man sees a picture and says at first sight that it is by Goya or by some one influenced by him. He passes the judgment long before he has made any analysis or any explicit identification of elements. It is the quality of the picture as a whole that operates. With a trained observer such a judgment based on pervasive quality may lead later to definite analysis of elements and details; the result of the analysis may confirm or may lead to rejection of the original ascription. But the basic appreciation of quality as a whole is a more dependable basis of such point by point analysis and its conclusion than is an external analysis performed by a critic who knows history and mechanical points of brushwork but who is lacking in sensitiveness to pervasive quality.

Another instance of Bradley's refers to Mill's denial that the suggestion of another triangle by a given triangle can be reduced to contiguity. For, Mill says, "the form of a triangle is not one single feature among others." Bradley thinks such a view absurd; he cannot, he says, even tell what is meant. The use of the term "feature" may be unfortunate. For when we speak of a nose as a feature of a face, we have in mind one element or part among others. Now triangularity is not such an isolable element. It is a characteristic of the disposition, arrangement, or pattern of all elements, and it must be capable of immediate realization. Even a nose as a feature of a man's face is not completely isolable. For it is characterized by the whole face as well as characterizing that face. A better instance is found, however, when we speak of a man's *expression*. That assuredly is a total effect of all elements in their relation to one another, not a "single feature among others." And so is triangularity. Family resemblances are often detected, and yet one is totally unable to specify the points of resemblance. Unanalyzed quality of the whole accounts for the identification as a *result*, and it is a radically different thing from identification of a man by finger prints.

The outcome of this brief discussion, in revealing the significance of dominant qualitativeness in suggestion and connection of ideas, shows why thinking as an existential process is all one with controlled association.[4] For the latter is not explained by any merely external conjunction or any external identity in things. If it were, association would itself be merely another case of existential sequence, coexistence, or identity and would be lacking in intellectual and logical import. But selection and coherence determined by an immediate quality that constitutes and delimits a situation are characteristics of "association." These traits are different in kind from existential conjunction and physical sameness, and identical with those of thought. The case of similarity or resemblance is almost uniquely significant. The problem of its nature is a crux of philosophies. The difficulty of dealing with it leads one on the one hand to thinking of it as purely psychical in nature, and, on the other hand, to the idealistic identification of the ontological and the logical *via* the principle of identity in difference. The recognition of pervasive quality enables us to avoid both extremes. By its means a voice is assimilated to blotting paper, and in more serious intellectual matters analogy becomes a guiding principle of scientific thought. On the basis of *assimilation* a further explicit recognition of similarity takes place. For assimilation is not itself the perception or judgment of similarity; the latter requires a further act made possible by symbols. It involves a proposition. The saying that there is a "tide in the affairs of men, etc." does not of itself involve any direct comparison of human affairs with the ocean and an explicit judgment of likeness. A pervasive quality has resulted in an assimilation. If symbols are at hand, this assimilation may lead to a further act—the judgment of similarity. But *de facto* assimilation comes first and need not eventuate in the express conception of resemblance.[5]

"Assimilation" denotes the efficacious operation of pervasive quality; "similarity" denotes a *relation. Sheer* assimilation results in the presence of a single object of apprehension. To identify a seen thing *as* a promontory is a case of assimilation. By some physiological process, not exactly understood at present but to which the name "habit" is given, the net outcome of prior experiences gives a dominant quality, designated "promontory" to a perceived existence. Passage from this object to some other implies resistance to mere assimilation and results in making distinctions. The pervasive quality is differentiated while at the same time these differentiations are connected. The result is an explicit statement or proposition.

I have touched, as I am well aware, only upon the fringes of a complex subject. But in view of the general neglect of the subject, I shall be satisfied if I have turned the attention of those interested in thought and its workings to an overlooked field. Omitting reference to ramifications, the gist of the matter is that the immediate existence of quality, and of dominant and pervasive quality, is the background, the point of departure, and the regulative principle of all thinking. Thought which denies the existential reality of qualitative things is therefore bound to end in self-contradiction

and in denying itself. "Scientific" thinking, that expressed in physical science, never gets away from qualitative existence. Directly, it always has its own qualitative background; indirectly, it has that of the world in which the ordinary experience of the common man is lived. Failure to recognize this fact is the source of a large part of the artificial problems and fallacies that infect our theory of knowledge and our metaphysics, or theories of existence. With this general conclusion goes another that has been emphasized in the preceding discussion. Construction that is artistic is as much a case of genuine thought as that expressed in scientific and philosophical matters, and so is all genuine esthetic appreciation of art, since the latter must in some way, to be vital, retrace the course of the creative process. But the development of this point in its bearing upon esthetic judgment and theory is another story.

NOTES

[First published in *Symposium* 1 (January 1930): 5–32. LW 5:243–62.]

1. The "fringe" of James seems to me to be a somewhat unfortunate way of expressing the role of the underlying qualitative character that constitutes a situation—unfortunate because the metaphor tends to treat it as an additional element instead of an all-pervasive influence in determining other contents.

2. The assumption that in the case of contiguity association is of a merely *de facto* or existential nature is the root of Lotze's (and others') theory that *a priori* logical forms are necessary in order to change juxtaposition of things into coherence of meaning.

3. *Logic*, Vol. I, Book II, Part 2, Ch. I, Sec. 30.

4. Were I to venture into speculative territory, I might apply this conception to the problem of "thinking" in animals, and what the *Gestalt* psychologists call "insight." That total quality operates with animals and sometimes secures, as with monkeys, results like those which we obtain by reflective analysis cannot, it seems to me, be doubted. But that this operation of quality in effecting results then goes out into symbolization and analysis is quite another matter.

5. Thus, to recur to Bradley's example, one may pass directly from the promontory in England to one in Wales and become absorbed in the latter without any judgment of the likeness of the two.

Context
and Thought

(1931)

In a supplementary essay in Ogden and Richards' *Meaning of Meaning*, Mr. Malinowski gives a striking example of the need for understanding context in connection with the use of language. The literal translation into English of an utterance of New Guinea natives runs as follows: "We run frontwards ourselves; we paddle in place; we turn, we see companion ours; he runs rearward behind their sea-arm Pilolu." As he says, the speech sounds like a meaningless jumble. If one is to understand it one must be informed about the situation in which the words were spoken and have them placed in their own context of culture. As a matter of fact, the utterance refers to a victory in an overseas trading expedition of the natives, in which several canoes have taken part in a competitive spirit. "This feature of rivalry (he adds) also explains the emotional nature of the utterance; it is not a mere statement of fact, but a boast, a piece of self-glorification, extremely characteristic of the Trobrianders' culture in general and of their ceremonial barter in particular."

After going into some detail of explanation, he remarks that in trying to give an adequate analysis of meaning "we are faced by a long and not altogether simple process of describing wide fields of custom, of social psychology, of tribal organisation, which correspond to one term or another. Linguistic analysis inevitably leads us into the study of all the subjects covered by Ethnographic fieldwork." Furthermore, as he points out, knowledge of ethnography will not remove all difficulties; even those of exclusively linguistic problems can, some of them, be solved only on the basis of psychological analysis. He sums up by saying that "in the reality of a spoken living language, the utterance has no meaning except in the context of a situation."

We should all, I suppose, admit this contention in the case of the speech of an alien and remote savage tribe. But it would be a great mistake to imagine that the principle is limited in application to such peoples. There is indeed a great contrast with our own modes of utterance. But the contrast is significant because it throws into relief familiar traits which very familiarity tends to conceal from us. We grasp the meaning of what is said in our own language not because appreciation of context is unnecessary but because context is so unescapably present. It is taken for granted; it is a matter of course, and accordingly is not explicitly specified. Habits of speech, including syntax and vocabulary, and modes of interpretation have been formed in the face of inclusive and defining situations of context. The latter are accordingly implicit in most of what is said and heard. We are not explicitly aware of the role of context just because our every utterance is so saturated with it that it forms the significance of what we say and hear.

The illustrative episode with which I began refers to language. But in it there is contained in germ all that I have to say for the indispensability of context for thinking, and therefore for a theory of logic and ultimately of philosophy itself. What is true of the meaning of words and sentences is true of all meaning. Such a statement need not, however, involve us in controversy about the relation of thought to language. If language is identified with speech, there is undoubtedly thought without speech. But if "language" is used to signify all kinds of signs and symbols, then assuredly there is no thought without language; while signs and symbols depend for their meaning upon the contextual situation in which they appear and are used.

For the meaning of symbols is not inherent but derived. This appears from the fact that they *are* symbols. It is true that when we talk and write the meaning of a particular verbal symbol is given us by the context of other symbols in which it occurs. It is also true that there are systems of symbols, notably in mathematics, where the system determines the meaning of any particular symbol. We cannot however infer from these facts that symbols are capable of supplying the ultimate context which provides meaning and understanding. Continued and systematic discourse enables us to determine the meaning of special symbols within the discourse only because it enables us to build up a non-verbal and non-symbolic context to which the whole refers. The mathematician does not stop to think of the ulterior context of existences, which gives his system of symbols import; long familiarity and a long tradition behind it have made the

connection highly indirect and tenuous. He would not only have difficulty in making the connection, but he would perhaps be irritated, as at a useless interruption and distraction, at any suggestion that he attempt to make the connection. But expertness in treating symbols as if they were things does not alter their symbolic character. Multiplication of symbols and increase in their intricacy facilitates manipulation. But reference of one symbol to another cannot destroy their character as symbols.

Now thought lives, moves, and has its being in and through symbols, and, therefore, depends for meaning upon context as do the symbols. We think *about* things, but not *by* things. Or rather when we do think by and with things, we are not experiencing the things in their own full nature and content. Sounds, for example, and marks in printed books are themselves existential things. But they operate in thought only as they stand for something else; if we become absorbed in them as things, they lose their value for thinking. If a man thinks, as he may do, by means of blocks and stones, he is not, as far as he is thinking, engaged in complete and intimate realization of them in their own intrinsic qualities. If he does become concerned with them in this fashion, he indulges in something that is either more or less than thought; more, if it is an esthetic absorption, less if it relapse into dumb stupor. The concern of thinking is with things as they carry the mind beyond themselves; they are vehicles not terminal stations.

These remarks have themselves an implicit context. Negatively, this context is the habit of philosophers of neglecting the indispensability of context, both in particular and in general. I should venture to assert that the most pervasive fallacy of philosophic thinking goes back to neglect of context. In the face to face communications of everyday life, context may be safely ignored. For, as we have already noted, it is irrevocably there. It is taken for granted, not denied, when it is passed over without notice. It gives point to everything said. A man engaged in a business transaction does not, for example, need to remind himself specifically of that fact—unless he is falling asleep. Context is incorporated in what is said and forms the arbiter of the value of every utterance. The same ideas and words apart from context would be the extravagances of a madman. But in philosophizing there is rarely an immediately urgent context which controls the course of thought. Neglect of specific acknowledgment of it is, then, too readily converted into a virtual denial.

Let us consider an instance or two of virtual denial of context in philosophy and its effect. Some philosophers have attacked the validity of analysis. They have held that while it is important in "science," that fact is itself evidence of the partial nature of science, of its abstraction from the "whole" with which philosophy is concerned. Other thinkers reach much the same conclusion when they assert that all valid analysis is attended by a synthetic act of thought which deliberately restores what is left out of account in the act of analysis. Now I do not see how a superadded act of synthesis can be other than arbitrary. But I can see how analysis falsifies when its results are interpreted as complete in themselves apart from any context. And it seems to me that the fault found with analysis would be more correctly as well as more simply directed against the ignoring of context. When a physician sets out to diagnose a disease he analyzes what is before him by the best technique at command. He does not at the end require another and further act of synthesis. The situation from the first has been one of disease and that situation provides the connection between the particular details analytically detected. One always identifies by discovering differences that are characteristic. This is true whether the identification be that of a criminal, of a plant or an animal, a metal, a disease, or a law. So far there is no defect in analysis and no demand for an added act of synthesis. But if the physician were to so forget the presence of a human being as a patient, if he were virtually to deny that context, he certainly would have a meaningless heap of atomic particulars on hand, and might be led to appeal to some transcendental synthesis to bring them to significant unity.

And so in philosophy. The trouble is not with analysis, but with the philosopher who ignores the context in which and for the sake of which the analysis occurs. In this sense, a characteristic defect of philosophy is connected with analysis. There are a multitude of ways of committing the analytic fallacy. It is found whenever the distinctions or elements that are discriminated are treated as if they were final and self-sufficient. The result is invariably some desiccation and atomizing of the world in which we live or of ourselves. The outcome has often been made the object of critical attack, as in the case of Locke and the Mills, and, indeed, in much of British thought. It has been rightly pointed out that the logical conclusion is denial of all connection and continuity, terminating in a doctrine of atomistic particularism. But unfortunately these same critics have not been content with the simple act of indicating neglect of context, but have assumed that the conclusion points to the necessity of some over-arching act of organic synthesis on the part of thought or "reason"— a method which, as I shall hope to show later, is the same disease of ignoring context in another form.

It is possible to find fresher straw to thresh than that of the systems of the thinkers just mentioned. Let me take an illustration from a field sufficiently remote from technical philosophical questions as not to arouse at once controversial associations. I have in mind the case of laboratory experimentation in psychology, say with respect to the discrimination of the least distinguishable color or sound, the finest possible discrimination of some sensory quality. Such qualities, when discriminated under conditions of refined control, have been assumed not only to be elements (which they are by definition, an element being only the last product of analysis), but to be original constituents out of which all mental life is built. They have been treated, in other words, as self-sufficient, independent in their isolation, so that all mental life is the result of their compounding.

Any such interpretation illustrates that ignoring of context which is virtually a denial of context. In fact there is present much besides the terminal elements. There is the background of the experimenter. This includes the antecedent state of theory which has given rise to his problem. It takes in his purpose in arranging the apparatus, including the technical knowledge which makes a controlled experiment possible. On the other side, there are the habits and present disposition of the subject, his capacity to give attention and to make verbal responses, etc., etc. Without the phase of context found on the side of the experimenter, there would be no scientific result at all, but an accident without theoretical import. The phase of context supplied from the side of the subject furnishes the causal factor determining the appearance of the quality discriminated. The latter, instead of being an isolated original unit out of which mental life is constructed by external composition, is the last term, for the time being, of an inclusive mental life. The immanent presence of the contextual setting of a moving experience provides connection. It renders unnecessary appeal to synthetic acts of thought, transcendental or otherwise, in order to supply connection. What takes place because of its connections does not require an act of thought to give it connection.

This remark brings me to what I called shortly ago the same disease in another form. The counterpart fallacy to that of analysis (as wrongly interpreted because of denial of context) is that of unlimited extension or universalization. When context is taken into account, it is seen that every generalization occurs under limiting conditions set by the contextual situation. When this fact is passed over or thrown out of court, a principle valid under specifiable conditions is perforce extended without limit. Any genuine case of thinking starts, for example, with considerations which as they stand are fragmentary and discrepant. Thinking then has the task of effecting unification in a single coherent whole. In this sense the goal of all thinking is the attaining of unity. But this unity is unification of just those data and considerations which in that situation are confused and incoherent. The fallacy of unlimited universalization is found when it is asserted, without any such limiting conditions, that the goal of thinking, particularly of philosophic thought, is to bring all things whatsoever into a single coherent and all inclusive whole. Then the idea of unity which has value and import under specifiable conditions is employed with such an unlimited extension that it loses its meaning.

All statements about the universe as a whole, reality as an unconditioned unity, involve the same fallacy. There is genuine meaning in the act of inquiring into the reality of a given situation. It is equivalent to an attempt to discover "the facts of the case," what is actually there or is actually happening—the addition of the adjective "real" to the substantive, "facts," being only for rhetorical emphasis. Within the limits of context found in any valid inquiry, "reality" thus means the confirmed outcome, actual or potential, of the inquiry that is undertaken. There is some specifiable confusion and dispersion which sets the inquiry going, and the latter terminates when the confusion is cleared away and definiteness accrues under conditions of suitable test. When "reality" is sought for at large, it is without intellectual import; at most the term carries the connotation of an agreeable emotional state. A like conclusion holds with reference to the "absolute," the "total," the "unconditioned," and many other terms held sacred on the lips of philosophers.

These statements do not however bring out *why* this fallacy of unlimited extension is the same ailment as that of unbridled analysis, in another form. We may have recourse to the instance already cited, that of mental life. Isolation from context of the distinctions found in a laboratory experiment induces the generalization that all varieties of mental life are compounds of independent units: whether the latter are called sensations, sensa, states of feeling or consciousness, or reflex arcs, or reactions to stimuli, or whatever is the prevailing fashion. This generalization into a sweeping theory is nothing but the logical statement of the conclusion which emerges when the context is suppressed. Given this suppression, elements become absolute, for they have no limiting conditions. Results of inquiry valid within specifiable limits of context are *ipso facto* converted into a sweeping metaphysical doctrine.

Further illustrations, if time permitted, would elucidate the nature of these two fallacies that tend to haunt philosophizing. I think, for example, that it could be shown that the predilections of many contemporaries for sensa and essences are products of neglect of context. I pass by, however, these possibilities to consider the use made in some aspects of contemporary philosophy of the concept of "events." That all existences are *also* events I do not doubt. For they are qualified by temporal transition. But that existences as such are *only* events strikes me as a proposition that can be maintained in no way except by a wholesale ignoring of context. For, in the first place, every occurrence is a *con*currence. An event is not a self-enclosed, self-executing affair—or it is not save by arbitrary definition. One may easily slip down a hill, but the slipping is not a self-contained entity, even though the *concept* of slipping may be self-contained—a transposition which makes it an essence, not an existence. The actual slide depends upon an interaction of several things, very many in an adequate account. Yet, unless I am mistaken in my interpretation, there is evidence that some contemporary writers tend to treat every existence as if to *be* an existence were to be a slide or a slip. To escape the difficulty by implying that the context of an event is simply other events is suspiciously like assuming that by putting enough slides together you can make a hill.

There are some cases of interaction which, relatively speaking, are merely displacements: like that which happens when one billiard ball impinges on another. What happens is then—or at least may be so treated for most purposes—merely a rearrangement. There are other transactions in which something happens to which the name interception can be given. In the interaction the product retains as it were something of the qualities of the concurring things. In this case, the event, viewed even as an event, is not merely an event. Such interception and coalescence of qualities hitherto distinct characterize anything that may be called an emergent. Put in a slightly different way, an event is both eventful and an eventuation.

Since every event is also an interaction of different things, it is inherently characterized by something from which and to which. The slide that starts with the slipping of the foot is not the same as that of a propelled sled; and it makes considerable difference to the slide as an event whether it terminates on rocks, water, or a pile of grass. The "from which" and "to which" qualify the event and make it, concretely, the distinctive event which it is. We may, indeed, by legitimate abstraction (legitimate for certain purposes) neglect the characteristic difference and reach the notion of slide in general. But the generalized abstraction would be impossible were there not events having their own qualitative traits. In other words, a *merely* general concept of "event" is undistinguishable from that of ascent, or perpendicular fall, or indeed from the meaning of any other term whatever which is equally treated as indifferent to all qualitative determination.

In the next place, when an event, because of neglect of context, is treated merely as an event, or as self-enclosed instead of as a change which takes place when qualitatively tempered things interact, it at once becomes necessary to invoke essences of eternal objects or some form of static eternal object to give any particular event an assignable character. The statement that interaction is constant and that consequently any existence at every point of its career is also an event, or that an existence may be looked at as *also* a serial set of events, seems to be authorized by the evidence. But to treat this proposition as equivalent to the proposition that every existence (apart from the entrance of an essence) is *merely* a collection of events is an instance of that unlimited extension that is entailed by neglect of context. The appeal to eternal objects has the same root, logically, as the appeal to an act of synthesis when the results of analysis, combined with ignoring of contextual connections, are taken to be the ground for invoking a further act of synthesis. As an added point we may note that a world of self-enclosed events, even when characterized by the entrance of eternal objects, requires something else to hold them together into anything like the semblance of one world. The supplementation takes the form of a framework of space-time—for an event as self-contained can have no change within it. It *is* a beginning and an end but it *has* no beginning nor end, and so an outside space-time must be superimposed.

Up to this point the discussion is negative in tone. It is meant to illustrate, though it cannot pretend to prove, that neglect of context is the greatest single disaster which philosophic thinking can incur. If we turn to consideration of the content and scope of the context that philosophizing should take into the reckoning, we approach the positive side of the discussion. Context includes at least those matters which for brevity I shall call background and selective interest. By "background" I mean the whole environment of which philosophy must take account in all its enterprises. A background is implicit in some form and to some degree in all thinking, although as background it does not come into explicit purview; that is, it does not form a portion of the subject matter which is consciously attended to, thought of, examined, inspected, turned over. Background is both temporal and spatial.

When we think, there are some things which we are immediately thinking *of*, considerations that are before us, and that are reflected upon, pondered over, etc. They are that with which we are wrestling, trying to overcome its difficulties and to reduce to order. Surrounding, bathing, saturating, the things of which we are explicitly aware is some inclusive situation which does not enter into the direct material of reflection. It does not come into question; it is taken for granted with respect to the particular question that is occupying the field of thinking. Since it does not come into question, it is stable, settled. To think of it in the sense of making it an object of thought's examination and scrutiny is an irrelevant and confusing distraction. It, or rather some part of it, comes into question, or into the explicit material of reflection, only when we suspect that it exercises such a *differential* effect upon what is consciously thought of as to be responsible for some of the confusion and perplexity we are trying to clear up. Then, of course, it enters into the immediate matter of thinking. But this transfer never disturbs the whole contextual background; it does not all come into question at once. There is always that which continues to be taken for granted, which is tacit, being "understood." If everything were literally unsettled at once, there would be nothing to which to tie those factors that, being unsettled, are in process of discovery and determination.

It was said that this background in thought is both spatial and temporal. The direct material of every reflection proceeds out of some precedent state of affairs in reference to which the existing state is disturbed or problematic or to which it is an "answer" or solution. In the episode related by Malinowski, the particular utterance served to sum up and record a previous struggle which issued in victory for one side. In the instance of the psychological experiment, the temporal background is the prior state of experimenter and subject. Take away the temporal background of the first incident and there is no triumph, nor any other significant happening; take away that of the second, and there is no experiment but merely an incident signifying nothing.

The temporal background of thinking in any case is intellectual as well as existential. That is, in the first cited instance there is a background of culture; in the second, of theory. There is no thinking which does not present itself on a background of tradition, and tradition has an intellectual quality that differentiates it from blind custom. Traditions are ways of interpretation and of observation, of valuation, of everything explicitly thought of. They are the circumambient atmosphere which thought must breathe; no one ever had an idea except as he inhaled some of this atmosphere. Aristotelian physics and Ptolemaic astronomy were for centuries the taken-for-granted background of all special inquiries in those fields. Then came the Newtonian background, for two centuries more imperious than any Tsar. So the fixity of species was the background of biological sciences until the time of Darwinism came; it then reigned so completely (I am speaking of the scientific inquirer) that Mendel's work did not cause even a ripple.

Meyerson has remarked that we can explain why medieval thinkers thought as they did and believed as they did, because we are outside their age. We cannot explain why we believe the things which we most firmly hold to because those things are a part of ourselves. We can no more completely escape them when we try to examine into them than we can get outside our physical skins so as to view them from without. Call these regulative traditions apperceptive organs or mental habits or whatever you will, there is no thinking without them. I do not mean, that a philosopher can take account of this context in the sense of making it a complete object of reflection. But he might realize the existence of such a context, and in doing so he would learn humility and would be debarred from a too unlimited and dogmatic universalization of his conclusions. He would not freeze the quotidian truths relevant to the problems that emerge in his own background of culture into eternal truths inherent in the very nature of things.

Spatial background covers all the contemporary setting within which a course of thinking emerges. That which is looked into, consciously scrutinized, has, like a picture, a foreground, middle distance, and a background—and as in some paintings the latter shades off into unlimited space. Demarcations so sharp that they amount to isolations do not occur in nature; their presence in thought is a sure sign that we, for some purpose, have taken a certain attitude toward the objective scene. Specify the contextual purpose and no harm arises. Forget it, and the fallacy of misinterpreted analysis ensues. This contextual setting is vague, but it is no mere fringe. It has a solidity and stability not found in the focal material of thinking. The latter denotes the part of the road upon which the spot light is thrown. The spatial context is the ground through which the road runs and for the sake of which the road exists. It is this setting which gives import to the road and to its consecutive illuminations. The path must be lighted if one is not to lose his way; the remoter territory may be safely left in the dark.

Another aspect of context is that which I have called "selective interest." Every particular case of thinking is what it is because of some attitude, some bias if you will; and no general theory can be framed which is not based upon what happens in particular cases. This attitude is no immediate part of what is consciously reflected upon, but it determines the selection of this rather than that subject-matter. The word "interest" may be questioned; it undoubtedly has connotations alien to the point I wish to make. But as to the fact which the word is used to denote that can hardly be in doubt. There is selectivity (and rejection) found in every operation of thought. There is care, concern, implicated in every act of thought. There is some one who has affection for some things over others; when he becomes a thinker he does not leave his characteristic affection behind. As a thinker, he is still differentially sensitive to some qualities, problems, themes. He may at times turn upon himself and inquire into and attempt to discount his individual attitudes. This operation will render some element in his attitude an object of thought. But it cannot eliminate all elements of selective concern; some deeper-lying ones will still operate. No regress will eliminate the attitude of interest that is as much involved in thinking about attitudes as it is in thinking about other things.

The aspect of context which I have called "interest" is known in philosophical terminology as the "subjective." The organism, self, ego, subject, give it whatever name you choose, is implicated in all thinking as in all eating, business, or play. Since it cannot in its entirety be made an explicit object of reflection and yet since it affects all matters thought of, it is legitimately called a phase of context. Subjectivism has a bad name, and as an 'ism it deserves its ill repute. But the subjective as determining attitude is not to be equated to this 'ism. It is not concern which is objectionable even when it takes the form of bias. It is certain kinds of bias that are obnoxious. Bias for impartiality is as much a bias as is partisan prejudice, though it is a radically different quality of bias. To be "objective" in thinking is to have a certain sort of selective interest operative. One can only see from a certain standpoint, but this fact does not make all standpoints of equal value. A standpoint which is nowhere in particular and from which things are not seen at a special angle is an absurdity. But one may have affection for a standpoint which gives a rich and ordered landscape rather than for one from which things are seen confusedly and meagerly.

Interest, as the subjective, is after all equivalent to individuality or uniqueness. There is no reason to limit its presence and operation to the organic and mental, although it is especially exemplified there. Everything which exists may be supposed to have its own unduplicated manner of acting and reacting, even atoms and electrons, although these individual traits are submerged in statistical statement. But in any event that which I have designated selective interest is a unique manner of entering into interaction with other things. It is not a part or constituent of subject-matter; but as a manner of action it selects subject-matter and leaves a qualitative impress upon it. One may call it genius or originality or give the more neutral and modest name of individuality. One realizes its nature best in thinking of genuine works of art. In the field of fine art, one never objects to that peculiar way of seeing, selecting, and arranging which defines the actual nature of the "subjective." One recognizes that its opposite is not the objective but the academic and mechanical, the merely repetitive. This quality is found in the subject-matter of all genuine thinking, for thinking is not the attribute of parrots. Newton may have supposed that he was thinking God's thoughts after him, but so far as he thought, he thought Newton's thoughts.

Such statements are easily misinterpreted both by those who make them and by those who deny them. They are sometimes taken to signify that the entire subject-matter of thought consists of states of consciousness or the material of a thinker's mind. The logical conclusion is then some form of solipsism. But individuality is not, as we have already said, subject-matter, but is a mode of selection that determines subject-matter. The subject-matter of science, physical and mathematical, may at first sight, seem to offer an insuperable objection to the statement that subjectivity, in the sense defined, is contextual in all the material of thinking. For in science there is elimination of connection with the mind of any one in particular. Science is science only as far as any especial tie to the mind of its authors can be left out of account. In the objection, however, there resides a confusion of the product of thought with its acceptance and further use. Newtonian conclusions reigned as science just because they were no longer taken as thought, but as given material to be employed in further investigations and interpretations.

One may find an exact enough analogy in the case of coins having an artistic design. The design in its origin bore the impress of individuality. But its further use, its status as legal tender, is not dependent upon that fact. The attitude controlling the selection and arrangement that forms the esthetic pattern is aside from the purposes of trade. Use in exchange is now the significant affair. In devotion to common social use, the design becomes a mere mechanical identifying sign, a mark of fitness to serve in exchange. If we apply the analogy to science we shall distinguish between science as a conclusion of reflective inquiry, and science as a ready-made body of organized subject-matter. In the first case, it and its status, its worth, reside in its connection with the quality of the inquiry of which it is the outcome and this quality bears the impress of an individual attitude. In the second case, its status and worth are dependent upon serviceability in the prosecution of further discovery and interpretation. From this standpoint, the impress of individuality is negligible because irrelevant; facility for repeated use is the important matter.

Even so, however, indispensability of reference to context still holds. It is easy and too usual to convert abstraction from *specific* context into abstraction from all context whatsoever: another instance of the fallacy of unlimited extension. The fallacy is indulged in whenever the formally logical traits of organized subject-matter are treated as if they were isolated from all material considerations. One of the necessary characters of subject-matter arranged for effective use is internal coherence and economy. When context is ignored this character is taken to be independent of existential material. But these formal characteristics have to do with conditions which must be fulfilled if the given scientific subject-matter is to secure the maximum of applicability in further inquiries and organizations. Only by a formulation in terms of equivalences can old subject-matter be rendered most effectively available in new intellectual undertakings. For only subject-matter stated in terms of reciprocal equivalences renders substitution and free translation possible in an efficient way. This context of use is ignored when formal traits are regarded as self-sufficient in their isolation.

It can hardly have escaped notice that my

underlying intention in this discussion concerns a desire to make a contribution to the theme of philosophic method. Thinking takes place in a scale of degrees of distance from the urgencies of an immediate situation in which something has to be done. The greater the degree of remoteness, the greater is the danger that a temporary and legitimate failure of express reference to context will be converted into a virtual denial of its place and import. Thinking is always thinking, but philosophic thinking is, upon the whole, at the extreme end of the scale of distance from the active urgency of concrete situations. It is because of this fact that neglect of context is the besetting fallacy of philosophical thought.

I should like to take my first example of the harmful working of this fallacy of philosophic method from the history of thought. The context of historic philosophies is too often treated as if it were simply other philosophies, instead of its being the perplexities, the troubles, and the issues of the period in which a philosophy arises. And strangely enough the limited context which is used in interpreting historic philosophy is frequently one which developed after the philosophy in question. I have just read an essay in literary criticism in which the writer remarks that a cursory examination of chronology will show that Aristotle's theory of poetry and tragedy was written subsequent to the production of the great dramatists of Athens, and that it is not likely that they wrote in order to prepare the way for Aristotelian theory. I wonder if the remark does not convey a lesson to interpreters of the history of thought. It may, for example, be reasonably asserted that Locke, Berkeley, and Hume wrote with reference to the intellectual conditions of their own times and not in order to initiate a movement which should find its consummation in Kant.

The significant positive content of this suggestion is the need of study of philosophical writings in their own vital context. I know that there are many persons to whom it seems derogatory to link a body of philosophic ideas to the social life and culture of their epoch. They seem to accept a dogma of immaculate conception of philosophical systems. I cannot argue the point here, but I can at least point to this attitude as an example of what I mean by neglect of context. The only alternative to the doctrine of the virginal birth of philosophies is recourse to the marriage of thinking with a tradition and a culture that are not themselves philosophical in character.

There exists at any period a body of beliefs and of institutions and practices allied to them. In these beliefs there are implicit broad interpretations of life and the world. These interpretations have consequences, often profoundly important. In their actual currency, however, the implications of origin, nature, and consequences are not examined and formulated. The beliefs and their associated practices express attitudes and responses which have operated under conditions of direct and often accidental stress. They constitute, as it seems to me, the *immediate* primary material of philosophical reflection. The aim of the latter is to criticize this material, to clarify it, to organize it, to test its internal coherence, and to make explicit its consequences. At the time of origin of every significant philosophy, this cultural context of beliefs and allied institutions is irretrievably there; reference to it is taken for granted and not made explicit. (I remark in passing, however, that part of the perennial significance of Plato's writings is due to the fact that in his dialogues the implied reference shines through much more than in most philosophic writings.) There are indeed historic philosophies in which reference to such cultural context is hard to detect. But examination will show that they are engaged in filling in chinks in other and more significant systems, or are engaged in a formal reconstruction of the latter.

If one is willing to adopt, even as a hypothesis for the time being, the idea that the immediate subject-matter for philosophy is supplied by the body of beliefs, religious, political, scientific, that determines the culture of a people and age, there follow certain conclusions regarding the problem and method of philosophy. The beliefs have their own context of origin, function, and determining interests or attitudes. But they are likely to be potent in the very degree in which these contexts are passed over in silence. Those who are most devoted to them take them as final revelations of truth, as spiritual Melchizedeks, without empirical generation. Moreover they "work"; they have consequences. But *how* they work, the connection of subsequent events and values, with them *as* consequences, is not subjected to examination. It is hardly even noted. Positive values, whatever their source, are treated as proper effects, while failures, evils, are attributed to some external source, even though examination would reveal that they flow directly from accepted beliefs in their institutional operation.

Here is the opportunity for that type of reflection which I should call philosophical. Philosophy is criticism; criticism of the influential beliefs that underlie culture; a criticism which traces the beliefs to their generating conditions as far as may be, which tracks them to their results, which considers the mutual compatibility of the elements of the total structure of beliefs. Such an examination terminates, whether so intended or not, in a projection of them into a new perspective which leads to new surveys of possibilities. This phase of reconstruction through criticism is as marked in justifying and systematizing philosophies as in avowedly skeptical ones, in the work of St. Thomas as of Hume. The clearer and more organized vision of the content of beliefs may have as an immediate outcome an enhanced sense of their worth and greater loyalty to them. But nevertheless the set of beliefs undergoes more than a sea-change in the process. It is dangerous to reflect seriously upon the nature, origin, and consequences of beliefs. The latter are safest when they are taken for granted without reasoned examination. To give reasons, even justifying ones, is to start a train of thoughts—that is, of questionings.

I have referred to religious, political, and scientific beliefs as instances of things that permeate and almost constitute a culture in their institutional accompaniments and their effects. One final example of the indispensability of reference to context will be alluded to, one taken from the relation of philosophy to science. It is sometimes assumed that this relation is exhausted in either an analytic examination of the logical foundations of the sciences, or in a synthesis of their conclusions, or both together. I would not derogate from the importance of such enterprises. But they are at best preparatory. For science itself operates within a context which is, relative to science, raw, crude, and primitive, and yet is pervasive and determining. To work exclusively within the context provided by the sciences themselves is to ignore their vital context. The place of science in life, the place of its peculiar subject-matter in the wide scheme of materials we experience, is a more ultimate function of philosophy than is any self-contained reflection upon science as such.

I am, of course, in this brief space of time only setting forth a possible hypothesis for your consideration. But I am confident that those who are willing to let their imaginations tarry with the hypothesis and follow its implications will at least get light upon the importance which some of us attach to "experience." If the finally significant business of philosophy is the disclosure of the context of beliefs, then we cannot escape the conclusion that experience is the name for the last inclusive context. A philosophy does not, of course, veritably acknowledge the significance of context merely by terming itself empirical. Sensational and nominalistic empiricism is perhaps as striking an example as can be found of the fallacy of neglecting context. But its error lay not in insisting upon experience as the basis and the terminus of philosophy but in its inadequate conception of experience. To refute the principle of empiricism by exposing the errors and defects of particular forms that self-avowed empiricisms have assumed is like supposing that when attention has been called to the eccentricities of a planetary orbit, the existence of an orbit has been disproved.

The significance of "experience" for philosophic method is, after all, but the acknowledgment of the indispensability of context in thinking when that recognition is carried to its full term. Let me recur for a moment to the illustration borrowed at the outset from Malinowski. Examination discloses three deepening levels or three expanding spheres of context. The narrowest and most superficial is that of the immediate scene, the competitive race. The next deeper and wider one is that of the culture of the people in question. The widest and deepest is found in recourse to the need of general understanding of the workings of human nature. We may without undue forcing find here an apt symbol of the necessary course of philosophical thinking.

The first, if most limited consideration, is the range and vitality of the experience of the thinker himself, that is, his most direct personal experience—which, however, only systematic misunderstanding construes to be merely an experience *of* his own person. However widely it reaches out into the world of things and persons, it is as personal, curtailed, one-sided, distorted. The remedy, however, is not divorce of thought from the intimacies of the direct contacts and intercourses of life, but a supplementation of limitations and a correction of biases through acquaintance with the experience of others, contemporary and as recorded in the history of the race. Dogmatism, adherence to a school, partisanship, class-exclusiveness, desire to show off and to impress, are all of them manifestations of disrespect for experience: for that experience which one makes one's own through sympathetic intercommunication. They are, as it were, deliberate perpetuations of the restrictions and perversions of personal experience.

Hence, the next wide circle or deepened stratum of context resides in what I have referred to as culture—in the sense in which anthropologists use the word. Philosophy proclaims its devotion to the universal. But as the profession of cosmopolitan philanthropy which is not rooted in neighborly friendliness is suspect, so I distrust the universals that are not reached by way of profound respect for the significant features and outcomes of human experience as found in human institutions, traditions, impelling interests, and occupations. A universal which has its home exclusively or predominantly in philosophy is a sure sign of isolation and artificiality.

Finally, there is the context of the make-up of experience itself. It is dangerous to begin at this point. Philosophies that have designated themselves empirical are full of warning to this effect. But the boundless multiplicity of the concrete experiences of humanity when they are dealt with gently and humanely, will naturally terminate in some sense of the structure of any and all experience. Biology, psychology, including social psychology and psychiatry, anthropology, all afford indications as to the nature of this structure, and these indications were never so numerous and so waiting for use as now. Those who try to interpret these indications may run the risk of being regarded by some other philosophers as not philosophers at all. They may, however, console themselves with the reflection that they are concerning themselves with that inclusive and pervasive context of experience in which philosophical thinking must, for good or ill, take place, and without reference to which such thinking is in the end but a beating of wings in the void.

NOTES:

[First published in University of California Publications in Philosophy, vol. 12, no. 3 (Berkeley: University of California Press, 1931), 203–24, from the George Holmes Howison Lecture for 1930, delivered at Berkeley on 14 January 1931. LW 6:3–21.]

The Greeks had a saying "Count no man happy till after his death." The adage was a way of calling attention to the uncertainties of life. No one knows what a year or even a day may bring forth. The healthy become ill; the rich poor; the mighty are cast down; fame changes to obloquy. Men live at the mercy of forces they cannot control. Belief in fortune and luck, good or evil, is one of the most widespread and persistent of human beliefs. Chance has been deified by many peoples. Fate has been set up as an overlord to whom even the Gods must bow. Belief in a Goddess of Luck is in ill repute among pious folk but their belief in providence is a tribute to the fact no individual controls his own destiny.

The uncertainty of life and one's final lot has always been associated with mutability, while unforeseen and uncontrollable change has been linked with time. Time is the tooth that gnaws; it is the destroyer; we are born only to die and every day brings us one day nearer death. This attitude is not confined to the ignorant and vulgar. It is the root of what is sometimes called the instinctive belief in immortality. Everything perishes in time but men are unable to believe that perishing is the last word. For centuries poets made the uncertainty which time brings with it the theme of their discourse—read Shakespeare's sonnets. Nothing stays; life is fleeting and all earthly things are transitory.

It was not then for metaphysical reasons that classic philosophy maintained that change, and consequently time, are marks of inferior reality, holding that true and ultimate reality is immutable and eternal. Human reasons, all too human, have given birth to the idea that over and beyond the lower realm of things that shift like the sands on the seashore there is the kingdom of the unchanging, of the complete, the perfect. The grounds for the belief are couched in the technical language of philosophy, but the cause for the grounds is the heart's desire for surcease from change, struggle, and uncertainty. The eternal and immutable is the consummation of mortal man's quest for certainty.

It is not strange then that philosophies which have been at odds on every other point have been one in the conviction that the ulti-

Time and Individuality

(1940)

217

mately real is fixed and unchanging, even though they have been as far apart as the poles in their ideas of its constitution. The idealist has found it in a realm of rational ideas; the materialist in the laws of matter. The mechanist pins his faith to eternal atoms and to unmoved and unmoving space. The teleologist finds that all change is subservient to fixed ends and final goals, which are the one steadfast thing in the universe, conferring upon changing things whatever meaning and value they possess. The typical realist attributes to unchanging essences a greater degree of reality than belongs to existences; the modern mathematical realist finds the stability his heart desires in the immunity of the realm of possibilities from vicissitude. Although classic rationalism looked askance at experience and empirical things because of their continual subjection to alteration, yet strangely enough traditional sensational empiricism relegated time to a secondary role. Sensations appeared and disappeared but in their own nature they were as fixed as were Newtonian atoms—of which indeed they were mental copies. Ideas were but weakened copies of sensory impressions and had no inherent forward power and application. The passage of time dimmed their vividness and caused their decay. Because of their subjection to the tooth of time, they were denied productive force.

In the late eighteenth and the greater part of the nineteenth centuries appeared the first marked cultural shift in the attitude taken toward change. Under the names of indefinite perfectability, progress, and evolution, the movement of things in the universe itself and of the universe as a whole began to take on a beneficent instead of a hateful aspect. Not every change was regarded as a sign of advance but the general trend of change, cosmic and social, was thought to be toward the better. Aside from the Christian idea of a millennium of good and bliss to be finally wrought by supernatural means, the Golden Age for the first time in history was placed in the future instead of at the beginning, and change and time were assigned a benevolent role.

Even if the new optimism was not adequately grounded, there were sufficient causes for its occurrence as there are for all great changes in intellectual climate. The rise of new science in the seventeenth century laid hold upon general culture in the next century. Its popular effect was not great, but its influence upon the intellectual elite, even upon those who were not themselves engaged in scientific inquiry, was prodigious. The enlightenment, the *éclaircissement*, the *Aufklärung*—names which in the three most advanced countries of Europe testified to the widespread belief that at last light had dawned, that dissipation of the darkness of ignorance, superstition, and bigotry was at hand, and the triumph of reason was assured—for reason was the counterpart in man of the laws of nature which science was disclosing. The reign of law in the natural world was to be followed by the reign of law in human affairs. A vista of the indefinite perfectability of man was opened. It played a large part in that optimistic theory of automatic evolution which later found its classic formulation in the philosophy of Herbert Spencer. The faith may have been pathetic but it has its own nobility.

At last, time was thought to be working on the side of the good instead of as a destructive agent. Things were moving to an event which was divine, even if far off.

This new philosophy, however, was far from giving the temporal an inherent position and function in the constitution of things. Change was working on the side of man but only because of *fixed* laws which governed the changes that take place. There was hope in change just because the laws that govern it do not change. The locus of the immutable was shifted to scientific natural law, but the faith and hope of philosophers and intellectuals were still tied to the unchanging. The belief that "evolution" is identical with progress was based upon trust in laws which, being fixed, worked automatically toward the final end of freedom, justice, and brotherhood, the natural consequences of the reign of reason.

Not till the late nineteenth century was the doctrine of the subordination of time and change seriously challenged. Bergson and William James, animated by different motives and proceeding by different methods, then installed change at the very heart of things. Bergson took his stand on the primacy of life and consciousness, which are notoriously in a state of flux. He assimilated that which is completely real in the natural world to them, conceiving the static as that which life leaves behind as a deposit as it moves on. From this point of view he criticized mechanistic and teleological theories on the ground that both are guilty of the same error, although from opposite points. Fixed laws which govern change and fixed ends toward which changes tend are both the products of a backward look, one that ignores the forward movement of life. They apply only to that which life has produced and has then left behind in its ongoing vital creative course, a course whose behavior and outcome are unpredictable both mechanically and from the standpoint of ends. The intellect is at home in that which is fixed only because it is done and over with, for intellect is itself just as much a deposit of *past* life as is the matter to which it is congenial. Intuition alone articulates in the forward thrust of life and alone lays hold of reality.

The animating purpose of James was, on the other hand, primarily moral and artistic. It is expressed, in his phrase, "block universe," employed as a term of adverse criticism. Mechanism and idealism were abhorrent to him because they both hold to a closed universe in which there is no room for novelty and adventure. Both sacrifice individuality and all the values, moral and aesthetic, which hang upon individuality, for according to absolute idealism, as to mechanistic materialism, the individual is simply a part determined by the whole of which he is a part. Only a philosophy of pluralism, of genuine indetermination, and of change which is real and intrinsic gives significance to individuality. It alone justifies struggle in creative activity and gives opportunity for the emergency of the genuinely new.

It was reserved, however, for the present century to give birth to the out and-out assertion in systematic form that reality *is* process, and that laws as well as things develop in the processes of unceasing change. The modern Heraclitean is Alfred North Whitehead, but he is Heraclitus with a change. The doctrine of the latter, while it held that all things flow like a river and that change is so continuous that a man cannot step into the same river even once (since it changes as he steps), nevertheless also held that there is a fixed order which controls the ebb and flow of the universal tide.

My theme, however, is not historical, nor is it to argue in behalf of any one of the various doctrines regarding time that have been advanced. The purpose of the history just roughly sketched is to indicate that the nature of time and change has now become in its own right a philosophical problem of the first importance. It is of time as a *problem* that I wish to speak. The aspect of the problem that will be considered is the connection of time with individuality, as the latter is exemplified in the living organism and especially in human beings.

Take the account of the life of any person, whether the account is a biography or an autobiography. The story begins with birth, a temporal incident; it extends to include the temporal existence of parents and ancestry. It does not end with death, for it takes in the influence upon subsequent events of the words and deeds of the one whose life is told. Everything recorded is an historical event; it is something temporal. The individual whose life history is told, be it Socrates or Nero, St. Francis or Abraham Lincoln, is an extensive event; or, if you prefer, it is a course of events each of which takes up into itself something of what went before and leads on to that which comes after. The skill, the art, of the biographer is displayed in his ability to discover and portray the subtle ways, hidden often from the individual himself, in which one event grows out of those which preceded and enters into those which follow. The human individual is himself a history, a career, and for this reason his biography can be related only as a temporal event. That which comes later explains the earlier quite as truly as the earlier explains the later. Take the individual Abraham Lincoln at one year, at five years, at ten years, at thirty years of age, and imagine everything later wiped out, no matter how minutely his life is recorded up to the date set. It is plain beyond the need of words that we then have not his biography but only a fragment of it, while the significance of that fragment is undisclosed. For he did not just exist in a time which externally surrounded him, but time was the heart of his existence.

Temporal seriality is the very essence, then, of the human individual. It is impossible for a biographer in writing, say the story of the first thirty years of the life of Lincoln, not to bear in mind his later career. Lincoln as an individual *is* a history; any particular event cut off from that history ceases to be a part of his life as an individual. As Lincoln is a particular development in time, so is every other human individual. Individuality is the uniqueness of the history, of the career, not something given once for all at the beginning which then proceeds to unroll as a ball of yarn may be unwound. Lincoln made history. But it is just as true that he made himself as an individual in the history he made.

I have been speaking about human individuality. Now an important part of the problem of time is that what is true of the human individual does not seem to be true of physical individuals. The common saying "as like as two peas" is a virtual denial to one kind of vegetable life of the kind of individuality that marks human beings. It is hard to conceive of the individuality of a given pea in terms of a unique history or career; such individuality as it appears to possess seems to be due in part to spatial separateness and in part to peculiarities that are externally caused. The same thing holds true of lower forms of animal life. Most persons would resent denial of some sort of unique individuality to their own dogs, but would be slow to attribute it to worms, clams, and bees. Indeed, it seems to be an exclusive prerogative of the romantic novelist to find anything in the way of a unique career in animal lives in general.

When we come to inanimate elements, the prevailing view has been that time and sequential change are entirely foreign to their nature. According to this view they do not have careers; they simply change their relations in space. We have only to think of the classic conception of atoms. The Newtonian atom, for example, moved and was moved, thus changing its position in space, but it was unchangeable in its own being. What it was at the beginning or without any beginning it is always and forever. Owing to the impact of other things it changes its direction and velocity of motion so that it comes closer and fur-

ther away from other things. But all this was believed to be external to its own substantial being. It had no development, no history, because it had no potentialities. In itself it was like a God, the same yesterday, today, and forever. Time did not enter into its being either to corrode or to develop it. Nevertheless, as an ultimate element it was supposed to have some sort of individuality, to be itself and not something else. Time, in physical science, has been simply a measure of motion in space.

Now, this apparently complete unlikeness in kind between the human and the physical individual is a part of the problem of time. Some philosophers have been content to note the difference and to make it the ground for affirming a sheer dualism between man and other things, a ground for assigning to man a spiritual being in contrast with material things. Others, fewer in numbers, have sought to explain away the seeming disparity, holding that the apparent uniqueness of human individuality is specious, being in fact the effect of the vast number of physical molecules, themselves complex, which make up his being, so that what looks like genuine temporal change or development is really but a function of the number and complexity of changes of constituent fixed elements. Of late, there have been a few daring souls who have held that temporal quality and historical career are a mark of everything, including atomic elements, to which individuality may be attributed.

I shall mention some of the reasons from the side of physical science that have led to this third idea. The first reason is the growing recognition that scientific objects are purely relational and have nothing to do with the intrinsic qualities of individual things and nothing to say about them. The meaning of this statement appears most clearly in the case of scientific laws. It is now a commonplace that a physical law states a correlation of changes or of ways and manners of change. The law of gravitation, for example, states a relation which holds between bodies with respect to distance and mass. It needs no argument to show that distance is a relation. Mass was long regarded as an inherent property of ultimate and individual elements. But even the

Newtonian conception was obliged to recognize that mass could be defined only in terms of inertia and that inertia could be defined only in terms, on the one hand, of the resistance it offered to the impact of other bodies, and, on the other hand, of its capacity to exercise impact upon them, impact being measured in terms of motion with respect to acceleration. The idea that mass is an inherent property which caused inertia and momentum was simply a holdover from an old metaphysical idea of force. As far as the findings of science are concerned, independent of the intrusion of metaphysical ideas, mass is inertia-momentum and these are strictly measures and relations. The discovery that mass changes with velocity, a discovery made when minute bodies came under consideration, finally forced surrender of the notion that mass is a fixed and inalienable possession of ultimate elements or individuals, so that time is now considered to be their fourth dimension.

It may be remarked incidentally that the recognition of the relational character of scientific objects completely eliminates an old metaphysical issue. One of the outstanding problems created by the rise of modern science was due to the fact that scientific definitions and descriptions are framed in terms in which qualities play no part. Qualities were wholly superfluous. As long as the idea persisted (an inheritance from Greek metaphysical science) that the business of knowledge is to penetrate into the inner being of objects, the existence of qualities like colors, sounds, etc., was embarrassing. The usual way of dealing with them is to declare that they are merely subjective, existing only in the consciousness of individual knowers. Given the old idea that the purpose of knowledge (represented at its best in science) is to penetrate into the heart of reality and reveal its "true" nature, the conclusion was a logical one. The discovery that the objects of scientific knowledge are purely relational shows that the problem is an artificial one. It was "solved" by the discovery that it needed no solution, since fulfillment of the function and business of science compels disregard of qualities. Using the older language, it was seen that so-called primary qualities are no more inherent properties of ultimate objects than are so-called secondary qualities of odors, sounds, and colors, since the former are also strictly relational; or, as Locke stated in his moments of clear insight, are "retainers" of objects in their connections with other things. The discovery of the nonscientific because of the empirically unverifiable and unnecessary character of absolute space, absolute motion, and absolute time gave the final *coup de grâce* to the traditional idea that solidity, mass, size, etc., are inherent possessions of ultimate individuals.

The revolution in scientific ideas just mentioned is primarily logical. It is due to recognition that the very method of physical science, with its primary standard units of mass, space, and time, is concerned with measurement of relations of change, not with individuals as such. This acknowledgment brought with it a further idea which, in spite of the resistance made to it by adherents of older metaphysical views, is making constant headway. This idea is that laws which purport to be statements of what actually occurs are statistical in character as distinct from so-called dynamic laws that are abstract and mathematical, and disguised definitions. Recognition of the statistical nature of physical laws was first effected in the case of gases when it became evident that generalizations regarding the behavior of swarms of molecules were not descriptions or predictions of the behavior of any individual particle. A single molecule is not and cannot be a gas. It is consequently absurd to suppose that the scientific law is about the elementary constituents of a gas. It is a statement of what happens when a very large number of such constituents interact with one another under certain conditions.

Statistical statements are of the nature of probability formulations. No insurance company makes any prediction as to what will happen to any given person in respect to death, or to any building with respect to destruction by fire. Insurance is conducted upon the basis of observation that out of a large number of persons of a given age such and such a proportionate number will probably live one year more, another proportionate number two years, and so on, while premiums are adjusted on the basis of these probability estimates. The validity of the estimates depends, as in the case of a swarm of molecules, upon the existence of a sufficiently large number of individuals, a knowledge which is a matter of the relative frequency of events of a certain kind to the total number of events which occur. No statement is made about what will take place in the case of an *individual*. The application to scientific formulations of the principle of probability statistically determined is thus a logical corollary of the principle already stated, that the subject matter of scientific findings is relational, not individual. It is for this reason that it is safe to predict the ultimate triumph of the statistical doctrine.

The third scientific consideration is found in Heisenberg's principle of uncertainty or indeterminacy, which may be regarded as a generalization of the ideas already stated. In form, this principle seems to be limited in its application. Classical science was based upon the belief that it is possible to formulate both the position and the velocity at one time of any given particle. It followed that knowledge of the position and velocity of a given number of particles would enable the future behavior of the whole collection to be accurately predicted. The principle of Heisenberg is that given the determination of position, its velocity can be stated only as of a certain order of probability, while if its velocity is determined the correlative factor of position can be stated only as of a certain order of probability. Both cannot be determined at once, from which it follows necessarily that the future of the whole collection cannot possibly be foretold except in terms of some order of probability.

Because of the fundamental place of the conceptions of position and velocity in physical science the principle is not limited in scope but is of the broadest possible significance.

Given the classic conception, Laplace stated its logical outcome when he said "we may conceive the present state of the universe as the effect of its past and the cause of its future. An intellect who at any given instant knew all the forces of animate nature and the mutual positions of the beings who compose it . . . could condense into a single formula the movement both of the greatest body in the universe and of its lightest atom. Nothing

would be uncertain to such an intellect, for the future, even as the past would be ever present before his eyes." No more sweeping statement of the complete irrelevancy of time to the physical world and of the complete unreality for individuals of time could well be uttered. But the principle of indeterminacy annihilates the premises from which the conclusion follows. The principle is thus a way of acknowledging the pertinency of real time to physical beings. The utmost possible regarding an individual is a statement as to some order of probability about the future. Heisenberg's principle has been seized upon as a basis for wild statements to the effect that the doctrine of arbitrary free will and totally uncaused activity are now scientifically substantiated. Its actual force and significance is generalization of the idea that the individual is a temporal career whose future cannot be *logically* deduced from its past.

As long as scientific knowledge was supposed to be concerned with individuals in their own intrinsic nature, there was no way to bridge the gap between the career of human individuals and that of physical individuals, save by holding that the seeming fundamental place of development and hence of time in the life histories of the former is only seeming or specious. The unescapable conclusion is that as human individuality can be understood only in terms of time as fundamental reality, so for physical individuals time is not simply a measure of predetermined changes in mutual positions, but is something that enters into their being. Laws do not "govern" the activity of individuals. They are a formulation of the frequency-distributions of the behavior of large numbers of individuals engaged in interactions with one another.

This statement does not mean that physical and human individuality are identical, nor that the things which appear to us to be non-living have the distinguishing characteristic of organisms. The difference between the inanimate and the animate is not so easily wiped out. But it does show that there is no fixed gap between them. The conclusion which most naturally follows, without indulging in premature speculations, is that the principle of a developing career applies to all things in nature, as well as to human beings—that they are born, undergo qualitative changes, and finally die, giving place to other individuals. The idea of development applied to nature involves differences of forms and qualities as surely as it rules out absolute breaches of continuity. The differences between the amoeba and the human organism are genuinely there even if we accept the idea of organic evolution of species. Indeed, to deny the reality of the differences and their immense significance would be to deny the very idea of development. To wipe out differences because of denial of complete breaks and the need for intervention of some outside power is just as surely a way to deny development as is assertion of gaps which can be bridged only by the intervention of some supernatural force. It is then in terms of development, or if one prefers the more grandiose term, evolution, that I shall further discuss the problem of time.

The issue involved is perhaps the most fundamental one in philosophy at the present time. Are the changes which go on in the world simply external redistributions, rearrangements in space of what previously existed, or are they genuine qualitative changes such as apparently take place in the physiological development of an organism, from the union of ovum and sperm to maturity, and as apparently take place in the personal life career of individuals? When the question is raised, certain misapprehensions must be first guarded against. Development and evolution have historically been eulogistically interpreted. They have been thought of as necessarily proceeding from the lower to the higher, from the relatively worse to the relatively better. But this property was read in from outside moral and theological preoccupations. The real issue is that stated above: Is what happens simply a spatial rearrangement of what existed previously or does it involve something qualitatively new? From this point of view, cancer is as genuinely a physiological development as is growth in vigor; criminals as well as heroes are a social development; the emergence of totalitarian states is a social evolution out of constitutional states independently of whether we like or approve them.

If we accept the intrinsic connection of time with individuality, they are not mere redistributions of what existed before.

Since it is a *problem* I am presenting, I shall assume that genuine transformations occur, and consider its implications. First and negatively, the idea (which is often identified with the essential meaning of evolution) is excluded that development is a process of unfolding what was previously implicit or latent. Positively it is implied that potentiality is a category of existence, for development cannot occur unless an individual has powers or capacities that are not actualized at a given time. But it also means that these powers are not unfolded from within, but are called out through interaction with other things. While it is necessary to revive the category of potentiality as a characteristic of individuality, it has to be revived in a different form from that of its classic Aristotelian formulation. According to that view, potentialities are connected with a *fixed* end which the individual endeavors by its own nature or essence to actualize, although its success in actualization depended upon the cooperation of external things and hence might be thwarted by the "accidents" of its surroundings—as not every acorn becomes a tree and few if any acorns become the typical oak.

When the idea that development is due to some indwelling end which tends to control the series of changes passed through is abandoned, potentialities must be thought of in terms of consequences of interactions with other things. Hence potentialities cannot be *known* till *after* the interactions have occurred. There are at a given time unactualized potentialities in an individual because and in as far as there are in existence other things with which it has not as yet interacted. Potentialities of milk are known today, for example, that were not known a generation ago, because milk has been brought into interaction with things other than organisms, and hence now has other than furnishing nutriment consequence. It is now predicted that in the future human beings will be wearing clothes made of glass and that the clothes will be cleaned by throwing them into a hot furnace. Whether this particular prediction is fulfilled or not makes no difference to its value as an illustration. Every new scientific discovery leads to some mode of technology that did not previously exist. As things are brought by new procedures into new contacts and new interactions, new consequences are produced and the power to produce these new consequences is a recognized potentiality of the thing in question. The idea that potentialities are inherent and fixed by relation to a predetermined end was a product of a highly restricted state of technology. Because of this restriction, the only potentialities recognized were those consequences which were customary in the given state of culture and were accordingly taken to be "natural." When the only possible use of milk was as an article of food, it was "natural" to suppose that it had an inherent tendency to serve that particular end. With the use of milk as a plastic, and with no one able to tell what future consequences may be produced by new techniques which bring it into new interactions, the only reasonable conclusion is that potentialities are not fixed and intrinsic, but are a matter of an indefinite range of interactions in which an individual may engage.

Return for a moment to the human individual. It is impossible to think of the historical career, which is the special individuality constituting Abraham Lincoln, apart from the particular conditions in which he lived. He did not create, for example, the conditions that formed the issues of States' rights and of slavery, the issues that influenced his development. What his being as an individual would have been without these interacting conditions it is idle to speculate upon. The conditions did not form him from without as wax is supposed to be shaped by external pressure. There is no such thing as interaction that is merely a one-way movement. There were many other persons living under much the same conditions whose careers were very different, because conditions acted upon them and were acted upon by them in different ways. Hence there is no account possible of Lincoln's life that does not portray him interacting day by day with special conditions, with his parents, his wife and children, his neighbors, his economic conditions, his school facilities, the incidents of his profession as a lawyer, and so on. The career which is his unique individuality is the series of interactions in which he was cre-

ated to be what he was by the ways in which he responded to the occasions with which he was presented. One cannot leave out either conditions *as opportunities* nor yet unique ways of responding to them. An occasion is an opportunity only when it is an evocation of a specific event, while a response is not a necessary effect of a cause but is a way of using an occasion to render it a constituent of an ongoing unique history.

Individuality conceived as a temporal development involves uncertainty, indeterminacy, or contingency. Individuality is the source of whatever is unpredictable in the world. The indeterminate is not change in the sense of violation of law, for laws state probable correlations of change and these probabilities exist no matter what the source of change may be. When a change occurs, *after* it has occurred it belongs to the observable world and is connected with other changes. The nomination of Lincoln for the presidency, his election, his Emancipation Proclamation, his assassination, after they took place can be shown to be related to other events; they can also be shown to have a certain connection with Lincoln's own past. But there was nothing in Lincoln's own life to cause by itself the conjunction of circumstances which brought about any one of these events. As far as he as an individual was concerned, the events were contingent, and as far as the conjunction of circumstances was concerned, his behavior at any given time in response to them was also contingent, or if you please fortuitous.

At critical junctures, his response could not be predicted either from his own past or from the nature of the circumstances, except as a probability. To say this is not arbitrarily to introduce mere chance into the world. It is to say that genuine individuality exists; that individuality is pregnant with new developments; that time is real. If we knew enough about Shakespeare's life we could doubtless show *after Hamlet* was produced how it is connected with other things. We could link it with sources; we could connect its mood with specific experiences of its author, and so on. But no one with the fullest knowledge of Shakespeare's past could have predicted the drama as it stands. If they could have done so, they would have been able to write it. Not even Shakespeare himself could have told in advance just what he was going to say—not if he was an individual, not a nodal point in the spatial redistribution of what already existed.

The mystery of time is thus the mystery of the existence of real individuals. It is a mystery because it is a mystery that anything which exists is just what it is. We are given to forgetting, with our insistence upon causation and upon the necessity of things happening as they do happen, that things exist as just what they qualitatively are. We can account for a change by relating it to other changes, but existences we have to accept for just what they are. Given a butterfly or an earthquake as an event, as a change, we can at least in theory find out and state its connection with other changes. But the individual butterfly or earthquake remains just the unique existence which it is. We forget in explaining its occurrence that it is only the *occurrence* that is explained, not the thing itself. We forget that in explaining the occurrence we are compelled to fall back on other individual things that have just the unique qualities they do have. Go as far back as we please in accounting for present conditions and we still come upon the mystery of things being just what they are.

Their occurrence, their manifestation, may be accounted for in terms of other occurrences, but their own quality of existence is final and opaque. The mystery is that the world is as it is—a mystery that is the source of all joy and all sorrow, of all hope and fear, and the source of development both creative and degenerative. The contingency of all into which time enters is the source of pathos, comedy, and tragedy. Genuine time, if it exists as anything else except the measure of motions in space, is all one with the existence of individuals as individuals, with the creative, with the occurrence of unpredictable novelties. Everything that can be said contrary to this conclusion is but a reminder that an individual may lose his individuality, for individuals become imprisoned in routine and fall to the level of mechanisms. Genuine time then ceases to be an integral element in their being. Our behavior becomes predictable because it is but an external rearrangement of what went before.

In conclusion, I would like to point out two considerations that seem to me to follow, two morals, if you wish to give them that name. I said earlier that the traditional idea of progress and evolution was based upon belief that the fixed structure of the universe is such as automatically brings it about. This optimistic and fatalistic idea is now at a discount. It is easy in the present state of the world to deny all validity whatever to the idea of progress, since so much of the human world seems bent on demonstrating the truth of the old theological doctrine of the fall of man. But the real conclusion is that, while progress is not inevitable, it is up to men as individuals to bring it about. Change is going to occur anyway, and the problem is the control of change in a given direction. The direction, the quality of change, is a matter of individuality. Surrender of individuality by the many to some one who is taken to be a superindividual explains the retrograde movement of society. Dictatorships and totalitarian states, and belief in the inevitability of this or that result coming to pass are, strange as it may sound, ways of denying the reality of time and the creativeness of the individual. Freedom of thought and of expression are not mere rights to be claimed. They have their roots deep in the existence of individuals as developing careers in time. Their denial and abrogation is an abdication of individuality and a virtual rejection of time as opportunity.

The ground of democratic ideas and practices is faith in the potentialities of individuals, faith in the capacity for positive developments if proper conditions are provided. The weakness of the philosophy originally advanced to justify the democratic movement was that it took individuality to be something given ready-made; that is, in abstraction from time, instead of as a power to develop.

The other conclusion is that art is the complement of science. Science as I have said is concerned wholly with relations, not with individuals. Art, on the other hand, is not only the disclosure of the individuality of the artist but is also a manifestation of individuality as creative of the future, in an unprecedented response to conditions as they were in the past. Some artists in their vision of might be but is not have been conscious rebels. But conscious protest and revolt is not the form which the labor of the artist in creation of the future must necessarily take. Discontent with things as they are is normally the expression of vision of what may be and is not, art in being the manifestation of individuality is this prophetic vision. To regiment artists, to make them servants of some particular cause does violence to the very springs of artistic creation. But it does more than that. It betrays the very cause of a better future it would serve, for in its subjection of the individuality of the artist it annihilates the source of that which is genuinely new. Were the regimentation successful, it would cause the future to be but a rearrangement of the past.

The artist in realizing his own individuality reveals potentialities hitherto unrealized. This revelation is the inspiration of other individuals to make the potentialities real, for it is not sheer revolt against things as they are which stirs human endeavor to its depths, but vision of what might be and is not. Subordination of the artists to any special cause no matter how worthy does violence not only to the artist but to the living source of a new and better future. Art is not the possession of the few who are recognized writers, painters, musicians; it is the authentic expression of any and all individuality. Those who have the gift of creative expression in unusually large measure disclose the meaning of the individuality of others to those others. In participating in the work of art, they become artists in their activity. They learn to know and honor individuality in whatever form it appears. The fountains of creative activity are discovered and released. The free individuality which is the source of art is also the final source of creative development in time.

NOTES

[First published in *Time and Its Mysteries*, series 2 (New York: New York University Press, 1940), pp. 85–109, from a lecture given on the James Arthur Foundation at New York University on 21 April 1938. LW 14:98–114.]

PART 5

The Aims of Education

ARTICLE ONE.
WHAT EDUCATION IS

I believe that all education proceeds by the participation of the individual in the social consciousness of the race. This process begins unconsciously almost at birth, and is continually shaping the individual's powers, saturating his consciousness, forming his habits, training his ideas, and arousing his feelings and emotions. Through this unconscious education the individual gradually comes to share in the intellectual and moral resources which humanity has succeeded in getting together. He becomes an inheritor of the funded capital of civilization. The most formal and technical education in the world cannot safely depart from this general process. It can only organize it; or differentiate it in some particular direction.

I believe that the only true education comes through the stimulation of the child's powers by the demands of the social situations in which he finds himself. Through these demands he is stimulated to act as a member of a unity, to emerge from his original narrowness of action and feeling and to conceive of himself from the standpoint of the welfare of the group to which he belongs. Through the responses which others make to his own activities he comes to know what these mean in social terms. The value which they have is reflected back into them. For instance, through the response which is made to the child's instinctive babblings the child comes to know what those babblings mean; they are transformed into articulate language and thus the child is introduced into the consolidated wealth of ideas and emotions which are now summed up in language.

I believe that this educational process has two sides—one psychological and one sociological; and that neither can be subordinated to the other or neglected without evil results following. Of these two sides, the psychological is the basis. The child's own instincts and powers furnish the material and give the starting point for all education. Save as the efforts of the educator connect with some activity which the child is carrying on of his own initiative independent of the educator, education becomes

My Pedagogic Creed

(1897)

reduced to a pressure from without. It may, indeed, give certain external results but cannot truly be called educative. Without insight into the psychological structure and activities of the individual, the educative process will, therefore, be haphazard and arbitrary. If it chances to coincide with the child's activity it will get a leverage; if it does not, it will result in friction, or disintegration, or arrest of the child nature.

I believe that knowledge of social conditions, of the present state of civilization, is necessary in order properly to interpret the child's powers. The child has his own instincts and tendencies, but we do not know what these mean until we can translate them into their social equivalents. We must be able to carry them back into a social past and see them as the inheritance of previous race activities. We must also be able to project them into the future to see what their outcome and end will be. In the illustration just used, it is the ability to see in the child's babblings the promise and potency of a future social intercourse and conversation which enables one to deal in the proper way with that instinct.

I believe that the psychological and social sides are organically related and that education cannot be regarded as a compromise between the two, or a superimposition of one upon the other. We are told that the psychological definition of education is barren and formal—that it gives us only the idea of a development of all the mental powers without giving us any idea of the use to which these powers are put. On the other hand, it is urged that the social definition of education, as getting adjusted to civilization, makes of it a forced and external process, and results in subordinating the freedom of the individual to a preconceived social and political status.

I believe each of these objections is true when urged against one side isolated from the other. In order to know what a power really is we must know what its end, use, or function is; and this we cannot know save as we conceive of the individual as active in social relationships. But, on the other hand, the only possible adjustment which we can give to the child under existing conditions, is that which arises through putting him in complete possession of all his powers. With the advent of democracy and modern industrial conditions, it is impossible to foretell definitely just what civilization will be twenty years from now. Hence it is impossible to prepare the child for any precise set of conditions. To prepare him for the future life means to give him command of himself; it means so to train him that he will have the full and ready use of all his capacities; that his eye and ear and hand may be tools ready to command, that his judgment may be capable of grasping the conditions under which it has to work, and the executive forces be trained to act economically and efficiently. It is impossible to reach this sort of adjustment save as constant regard is had to the individual's own powers, tastes, and interests—say, that is, as education is continually converted into psychological terms.

In sum, I believe that the individual who is to be educated is a social individual and that society is an organic union of individuals. If we eliminate the social factor from the child we are left only with an abstraction; if we eliminate the individual factor from society, we are left only with an inert and lifeless mass. Education, therefore, must begin with a psychological insight into the child's capacities, interests, and habits. It must be controlled at every point by reference to these same considerations. These powers, interests, and habits must be continually interpreted—we must know what they mean. They must be translated into terms of their social equivalents—into terms of what they are capable of in the way of social service.

ARTICLE TWO. WHAT THE SCHOOL IS

I believe that the school is primarily a social institution. Education being a social process, the school is simply that form of community life in which all those agencies are concentrated that will be most effective in bringing the child to share in the inherited resources of the race, and to use his own powers for social ends.

I believe that education, therefore, is a process of living and not a preparation for future living.

I believe that the school must represent present life—life as real and vital to the child as that which he carries on in the home, in the neighborhood, or on the playground.

I believe that education which does not occur through forms of life, forms that are worth living for their own sake, is always a poor substitute for the genuine reality and tends to cramp and to deaden.

I believe that the school, as an institution, should simplify existing social life; should reduce it, as it were, to an embryonic form. Existing life is so complex that the child cannot be brought into contact with it without either confusion or distraction; he is either overwhelmed by multiplicity of activities which are going on, so that he loses his own power of orderly reaction, or he is so stimulated by these various activities that his powers are prematurely called into play and he becomes either unduly specialized or else disintegrated.

I believe that, as such simplified social life, the school life should grow gradually out of the home life; that it should take up and continue the activities with which the child is already familiar in the home.

I believe that it should exhibit these activities to the child, and reproduce them in such ways that the child will gradually learn the meaning of them, and be capable of playing his own part in relation to them.

I believe that this is a psychological necessity, because it is the only way of securing continuity in the child's growth, the only way of giving a background of past experience to the new ideas given in school.

I believe it is also a social necessity because the home is the form of social life in which the child has been nurtured and in connection with which he has had his moral training. It is the business of the school to deepen and extend his sense of the values bound up in his home life.

I believe that much of present education fails because it neglects this fundamental principle of the school as a form of community life. It conceives the school as a place where certain information is to be given, where certain lessons are to be learned, or where certain habits are to be formed. The value of these is conceived as lying largely in the remote future; the child must do these things for the sake of something else he is to do; they are mere preparation. As a result they do not become a part of the life experience of the child and so are not truly educative.

I believe that moral education centres about this conception of the school as a mode of social life, that the best and deepest moral training is precisely that which one gets through having to enter into proper relations with others in a unity of work and thought. The present educational systems, so far as they destroy or neglect this unity, render it difficult or impossible to get any genuine, regular moral training.

I believe that the child should be stimulated and controlled in his work through the life of the community.

I believe that under existing conditions far too much of the stimulus and control proceeds from the teacher, because of neglect of the idea of the school as a form of social life.

I believe that the teacher's place and work in the school is to be interpreted from this same basis. The teacher is not in the school to impose certain ideas or to form certain habits in the child, but is there as a member of the community to select the influences which shall affect the child and to assist him in properly responding to these influences.

I believe that the discipline of the school should proceed from the life of the school as a whole and not directly from the teacher.

I believe that the teacher's business is simply to determine on the basis of larger experience and riper wisdom, how the discipline of life shall come to the child.

I believe that all questions of the grading of the child and his promotion should be determined by reference to the same standard. Examinations are of use only so far as they test the child's fitness for social life and reveal the place in which he can be of the most service and where he can receive the most help.

ARTICLE THREE. THE SUBJECT-MATTER OF EDUCATION

I believe that the social life of the child is the basis of concentration, or correlation, in all his training or growth. The social life gives the unconscious unity and the background of all his efforts and of all his attainments.

I believe that the subject-matter of the school curriculum should mark a gradual differentiation out of the primitive unconscious unity of social life.

I believe that we violate the child's nature and render difficult the best ethical results, by introducing the child too abruptly to a number of special studies, of reading, writing, geography, etc., out of relation to this social life.

I believe, therefore, that the true centre of correlation of the school subjects is not science, nor literature, nor history, nor geography, but the child's own social activities.

I believe that education cannot be unified in the study of science, or so-called nature study, because apart from human activity, nature itself is not a unity; nature in itself is a number of diverse objects in space and time, and to attempt to make it the centre of work by itself, is to introduce a principle of radiation rather than one of concentration.

I believe that literature is the reflex expression and interpretation of social experience; that hence it must follow upon and not precede such experience. It, therefore, cannot be made the basis, although it may be made the summary of unification.

I believe once more that history is of educative value in so far as it presents phases of social life and growth. It must be controlled by reference to social life. When taken simply as history it is thrown into the distant past and becomes dead and inert. Taken as the record of man's social life and progress it becomes full of meaning. I believe, however, that it cannot be so taken excepting as the child is also introduced directly into social life.

I believe accordingly that the primary basis of education is in the child's powers at work along the same general constructive lines as those which have brought civilization into being.

I believe that the only way to make the child conscious of his social heritage is to enable him to perform those fundamental types of activity which make civilization what it is.

I believe, therefore, in the so-called expressive or constructive activities as the centre of correlation.

I believe that this gives the standard for the place of cooking, sewing, manual training, etc., in the school.

I believe that they are not special studies which are to be introduced over and above a lot of others in the way of relaxation or relief, or as additional accomplishments. I believe rather that they represent, as types, fundamental forms of social activity; and that it is possible and desirable that the child's introduction into the more formal subjects of the curriculum be through the medium of these activities.

I believe that the study of science is educational in so far as it brings out the materials and processes which make social life what it is.

I believe that one of the greatest difficulties in the present teaching of science is that the material is presented in purely objective form, or is treated as a new peculiar kind of experience which the child can add to that which he has already had. In reality, science is of value because it gives the ability to interpret and control the experience already had. It should be introduced, not as so much new subject-matter, but as showing the factors already involved in previous experience and as furnishing tools by which that experience can be more easily and effectively regulated.

I believe that at present we lose much of the value of literature and language studies because of our elimination of the social element. Language is almost always treated in the books of pedagogy simply as the expression of thought. It is true that language is a logical instrument, but it is fundamentally and primarily a social instrument. Language is the device for communication; it is the tool through which one individual comes to share the ideas and feelings of others. When treated simply as a way of getting individual information, or as a means of showing off what one has learned, it loses its social motive and end.

I believe that there is, therefore, no succession of studies in the ideal school curriculum. If education is life, all life has, from the outset, a scientific aspect; an aspect of art and culture and an aspect of communication. It cannot, therefore, be true that the proper studies for one grade are mere reading and writing, and that at a later grade, reading, or literature, or science, may be introduced. The progress is not in the succession of studies but in the development of new attitudes towards, and new interests in, experience.

I believe finally, that education must be conceived as a continuing reconstruction of experience; that the process and the goal of education are one and the same thing.

I believe that to set up any end outside of education, as furnishing its goal and standard, is to deprive the educational process of much of its meaning and tends to make us rely upon false and external stimuli in dealing with the child.

ARTICLE FOUR. THE NATURE OF METHOD

I believe that the question of method is ultimately reducible to the question of the order of development of the child's powers and interests. The law for presenting and treating material is the law implicit within the child's own nature. Because this is so I believe the following statements are of supreme importance as determining the spirit in which education is carried on:

1. I believe that the active side precedes the passive in the development of the child nature; that expression comes before conscious impression; that the muscular development precedes the sensory; that movements come before conscious sensations; I believe that consciousness is essentially motor or impulsive; that conscious states tend to project themselves in action.

I believe that the neglect of this principle is the cause of a large part of the waste of time and strength in school work. The child is thrown into a passive, receptive or absorbing attitude. The conditions are such that he is not permitted to follow the law of his nature; the result is friction and waste.

I believe that ideas (intellectual and rational processes) also result from action and devolve for the sake of the better control of action. What we term reason is primarily the law of orderly or effective action. To attempt to develop the reasoning powers, the powers of judgment, without reference to the selection and arrangement of means in action, is the fundamental fallacy in our present methods of dealing with this matter. As a result we present the child with arbitrary symbols. Symbols are a necessity in mental development, but they have their place as tools for economizing effort; presented by themselves they are a mass of meaningless and arbitrary ideas imposed from without.

2. I believe that the image is the great instrument of instruction. What a child gets out of any subject presented to him is simply the images which he himself forms with regard to it.

I believe that if nine-tenths of the energy at present directed towards making the child learn certain things, were spent in seeing to it that the child was forming proper images, the work of instruction would be indefinitely facilitated.

I believe that much of the time and attention now given to the preparation and presentation of lessons might be more wisely and profitably expended in training the child's power of imagery and in seeing to it that he was continually forming definite, vivid, and growing images of the various subjects with which he comes in contact in his experience.

3. I believe that interests are the signs and symptoms of growing power. I believe that they represent dawning capacities. Accordingly the constant and careful observation of interests is of the utmost importance for the educator.

I believe that these interests are to be observed as showing the state of development which the child has reached.

I believe that they prophesy the stage upon which he is about to enter.

I believe that only through the continual and sympathetic observation of childhood's interests can the adult enter into the child's life and see what it is ready for, and upon what material it could work most readily and fruitfully.

I believe that these interests are neither to be humored nor repressed. To repress interest is to substitute the adult for the child, and so to weaken intellectual curiosity and alertness, to suppress initiative, and to deaden interest. To humor the interests is to substitute the transient for the permanent. The interest is always the sign of some power below; the important thing is to discover this power. To humor the interest is to fail to penetrate below the surface and its sure result is to substitute caprice and whim for genuine interest.

4. I believe that the emotions are the reflex of actions.

I believe that to endeavor to stimulate or arouse the emotions apart from their corresponding activities, is to introduce an unhealthy and morbid state of mind.

I believe that if we can only secure right habits of action and thought, with reference to the good, the true, and the beautiful, the emotions will for the most part take care of themselves.

I believe that next to deadness and dullness, formalism and routine, our education is threatened with no greater evil than sentimentalism.

I believe that this sentimentalism is the necessary result of the attempt to divorce feeling from action.

ARTICLE FIVE. THE SCHOOL AND SOCIAL PROGRESS

I believe that education is the fundamental method of social progress and reform.

I believe that all reforms which rest simply upon the enactment of law, or the threatening of certain penalties, or upon changes in mechanical or outward arrangements, are transitory and futile.

I believe that education is a regulation of the process of coming to share in the social consciousness; and that the adjustment of individual activity on the basis of this social consciousness is the only sure method of social reconstruction.

I believe that this conception has due regard for both the individualistic and socialistic ideals. It is duly individual because it recognizes the formation of a certain character as the only genuine basis of right living. It is socialistic because it recognizes that this right character is not to be formed by merely individual precept, example, or exhortation, but rather by the influence of a certain form of institutional or community life upon the individual, and that the social organism through the school, as its organ, may determine ethical results.

I believe that in the ideal school we have the reconciliation of the individualistic and the institutional ideals.

I believe that the community's duty to education is, therefore, its paramount moral duty. By law and punishment, by social agitation and discussion, society can regulate and form itself in a more or less haphazard and chance way. But through education society can formulate its own purposes, can organize its own means and resources, and thus shape itself with definiteness and economy in the direction in which it wishes to move.

I believe that when society once recognizes the possibilities in this direction, and the obligations which these possibilities impose, it is impossible to conceive of the resources of time, attention, and money which will be put at the disposal of the educator.

I believe it is the business of every one interested in education to insist upon the school as the primary and most effective instrument of social progress and reform in order that society may be awakened to realize what the school stands for, and aroused to the necessity of endowing the educator with sufficient equipment properly to perform his task.

I believe that education thus conceived marks the most perfect and intimate union of science and art conceivable in human experience.

I believe that the art of thus giving shape to human powers and adapting them to social service, is the supreme art; one calling into its service the best of artists; that no insight, sympathy, tact, executive power is too great for such service.

I believe that with the growth of psychological science, giving added insight into individual structure and laws of growth; and with growth of social science, adding to our knowledge of the right organization of individuals, all scientific resources can be utilized for the purposes of education.

I believe that when science and art thus join hands the most commanding motive for human action will be reached; the most genuine springs of human conduct aroused and the best service that human nature is capable of guaranteed.

I believe, finally, that the teacher is engaged, not simply in the training of individuals, but in the formation of the proper social life.

I believe that every teacher should realize the dignity of his calling; that he is a social servant set apart for the maintenance of proper social order and the securing of the right social growth.

I believe that in this way the teacher always is the prophet of the true God and the usherer in of the true kingdom of God.

NOTES

[First published in *School Journal*, LIV (Jan. 1897), 77–80. See A Note on the Texts for publishing history. EW 5:84–95.]

The Child and the Curriculum

(1902)

Profound differences in theory are never gratuitous or invented. They grow out of conflicting elements in a genuine problem—a problem which is genuine just because the elements, taken as they stand, are conflicting. Any significant problem involves conditions that for the moment contradict each other. Solution comes only by getting away from the meaning of terms that is already fixed upon and coming to see the conditions from another point of view, and hence in a fresh light. But this reconstruction means travail of thought. Easier than thinking with surrender of already formed ideas and detachment from facts already learned, is just to stick by what is already said, looking about for something with which to buttress it against attack.

Thus sects arise; schools of opinion. Each selects that set of conditions that appeal to it; and then erects them into a complete and independent truth, instead of treating them as a factor in a problem, needing adjustment.

The fundamental factors in the educative process are an immature, undeveloped being; and certain social aims, meanings, values incarnate in the matured experience of the adult. The educative process is the due interaction of these forces. Such a conception of each in relation to the other as facilitates completest and freest interaction is the essence of educational theory.

But here comes the effort of thought. It is easier to see the conditions in their separateness, to insist upon one at the expense of the other, to make antagonists of them, than to discover a reality to which each belongs. The easy thing is to seize upon something in the nature of the child, or upon something in the developed consciousness of the adult, and insist upon *that* as the key to the whole problem. When this happens a really serious practical problem—that of interaction—is transformed into an unreal, and hence insoluble, theoretic problem. Instead of seeing the educative steadily and as a whole, we see conflicting terms. We get the case of the child vs. the curriculum; of the individual nature vs. social culture. Below all other divisions in pedagogic opinion lies this opposition.

The child lives in a somewhat narrow world of personal contacts. Things hardly come within his experience unless they touch, intimately and obviously, his own well-being, or that of his family and friends. His world is a world of persons with their personal interests, rather than a realm of facts and laws. Not truth, in the sense of conformity to external fact, but affection and sympathy, is its keynote. As against this, the course of study met in the school presents material stretching back indefinitely in time, and extending outward indefinitely into space. The child is taken out of his familiar physical environment, hardly more than a square mile or so in area, into the wide world—yes, and even to the bounds of the solar system. His little span of personal memory and tradition is overlaid with the long centuries of the history of all peoples.

Again, the child's life is an integral, a total one. He passes quickly and readily from one topic to another, as from one spot to another, but is not conscious of transition or break. There is no conscious isolation, hardly conscious distinction. The things that occupy him are held together by the unity of the personal and social interests which his life carries along. Whatever is uppermost in his mind constitutes to him, for the time being, the whole universe. That universe is fluid and fluent; its contents dissolve and re-form with amazing rapidity. But, after all, it is the child's own world. It has the unity and completeness of his own life. He goes to school, and various studies divide and fractionize the world for him. Geography selects, it abstracts and analyzes one set of facts, and from one particular point of view. Arithmetic is another division, grammar another department, and so on indefinitely.

Again, in school each of these subjects is classified. Facts are torn away from their original place in experience and rearranged with reference to some general principle. Classification is not a matter of child experience; things do not come to the individual pigeonholed. The vital ties of affection, the connecting bonds of activity, hold together the variety of his personal experiences. The adult mind is so familiar with the notion of logically ordered facts that it does not recognize—it cannot realize—the amount of separating and reformulating which the facts of direct experience have to

undergo before they can appear as a "study," or branch of learning. A principle, for the intellect, has had to be distinguished and defined; facts have had to be interpreted in relation to this principle, not as they are in themselves. They have had to be regathered about a new centre which is wholly abstract and ideal. All this means a development of a special intellectual interest. It means ability to view facts impartially and objectively; that is, without reference to their place and meaning in one's own experience. It means capacity to analyze and to synthesize. It means highly matured intellectual habits and the command of a definite technique and apparatus of scientific inquiry. The studies as classified are the product, in a word, of the science of the ages, not of the experience of the child.

These apparent deviations and differences between child and curriculum might be almost indefinitely widened. But we have here sufficiently fundamental divergences: first, the narrow but personal world of the child against the impersonal but infinitely extended world of space and time; second, the unity, the single whole-heartedness of the child's life, and the specializations and divisions of the curriculum; third, an abstract principle of logical classification and arrangement, and the practical and emotional bonds of child life.

From these elements of conflict grow up different educational sects. One school fixes its attention upon the importance of the subject-matter of the curriculum as compared with the contents of the child's own experience. It is as if they said: Is life petty, narrow, and crude? Then studies reveal the great, wide universe with all its fullness and complexity of meaning. Is the life of the child egoistic, self-centered, impulsive? Then in these studies is found an objective universe of truth, law, and order. Is his experience confused, vague, uncertain, at the mercy of the moment's caprice and circumstance? Then studies introduce a world arranged on the basis of eternal and general truth; a world where all is measured and defined. Hence the moral: ignore and minimize the child's individual peculiarities, whims, and experiences. They are what we need to get away from. They are to be obscured or eliminated. As educators our work is precisely to substitute for these superficial and casual affairs stable and well-ordered realities; and these are found in studies and lessons.

Subdivide each topic into studies; each study into lessons; each lesson into specific facts and formulae. Let the child proceed step by step to master each one of these separate parts, and at last he will have covered the entire ground. The road which looks so long when viewed in its entirety, is easily traveled, considered as a series of particular steps. Thus emphasis is put upon the logical subdivisions and consecutions of the subject-matter. Problems of instruction are problems of procuring texts giving logical parts and sequences, and of presenting these portions in class in a similar definite and graded way. Subject-matter furnishes the end, and it determines method. The child is simply the immature being who is to be matured; he is the superficial being who is to be deepened; his is narrow experience which is to be widened. It is his to receive, to accept. His part is fulfilled when he is ductile and docile.

Not so, says the other sect. The child is the starting-point, the centre, and the end. His development, his growth, is the ideal. It alone furnishes the standard. To the growth of the child all studies are subservient; they are instruments valued as they serve the needs of growth. Personality, character, is more than subject-matter. Not knowledge or information, but self-realization, is the goal. To possess all the world of knowledge and lose one's own self is as awful a fate in education as in religion. Moreover, subject-matter never can be got into the child from without. Learning is active. It involves reaching out of the mind. It involves organic assimilation starting from within. Literally, we must take our stand with the child and our departure from him. It is he and not the subject-matter which determines both quality and quantity of learning.

The only significant method is the method of the mind as it reaches out and assimilates. Subject-matter is but spiritual food, possible nutritive material. It cannot digest itself; it cannot of its own accord turn into bone and muscle and blood. The source of whatever is dead, mechanical, and formal in schools is found precisely in the subordination of the life and experience of the child to the curriculum. It is because of this that "study" has become a synonym for what is irksome, and a lesson identical with a task.

This fundamental opposition of child and curriculum set up by these two modes of doctrine can be duplicated in a series of other terms. "Discipline" is the watchword of those who magnify the course of study; "interest" that of those who blazon "The Child" upon their banner. The standpoint of the former is logical; that of the latter psychological. The first emphasizes the necessity of adequate training and scholarship on the part of the teacher; the latter that of need of sympathy with the child, and knowledge of his natural instincts. "Guidance and control" are the catchwords of one school; "freedom and initiative" of the other. Law is asserted here; spontaneity proclaimed there. The old, the conservation of what has been achieved in the pain and toil of the ages, is dear to the one; the new, change, progress, wins the affection of the other. Inertness and routine, chaos and anarchism, are accusations bandied back and forth. Neglect of the sacred authority of duty is charged by one side, only to be met by counter-charges of suppression of individuality through tyrannical despotism.

Such oppositions are rarely carried to their logical conclusion. Common sense recoils at the extreme character of these results. They are left to theorists, while common sense vibrates back and forward in a maze of inconsistent compromise. The need of getting theory and practical common sense into closer connection suggests a return to our original thesis: that we have here conditions which are necessarily related to each other in the educative process, since this is precisely one of interaction and adjustment.

What, then, is the problem? It is just to get rid of the prejudicial notion that there is some gap in kind (as distinct from degree) between the child's experience and the various forms of subject-matter that make up the course of study. From the side of the child, it is a question of seeing how his experience already contains within itself elements—facts and truths—of just the same sort as those entering into the formulated study; and, what is of more importance, of how it contains within itself the attitudes, the motives, and the interests which have operated in developing and organizing the subject-matter to the plane which it now occupies. From the side of the studies, it is a question of interpreting them as outgrowths of forces operating in the child's life, and of discovering the steps that intervene between the child's present experience and their richer maturity.

Abandon the notion of subject-matter as something fixed and ready-made in itself, outside the child's experience; cease thinking of the child's experience as also something hard and fast; see it as something fluent, embryonic, vital; and we realize that the child and the curriculum are simply two limits which define a single process. Just as two points define a straight line, so the present standpoint of the child and the facts and truths of studies define instruction. It is continuous reconstruction, moving from the child's present experience out into that represented by the organized bodies of truth that we call studies.

On the face of it, the various studies, arithmetic, geography, language, botany, etc., are themselves experience—they are that of the race. They embody the cumulative outcome of the efforts, the strivings, and successes of the human race generation after generation. They present this, not as a mere accumulation, not as a miscellaneous heap of separate bits of experience, but in some organized and systematized way—that is, as reflectively formulated.

Hence, the facts and truths that enter into the child's present experience, and those contained in the subject-matter of studies, are the initial and final terms of one reality. To oppose one to the other is to oppose the infancy and maturity of the same growing life; it is to set the moving tendency and the final result of the same process over against each other; it is to hold that the nature and the destiny of the child war with each other.

If such be the case, the problem of the relation of the child and the curriculum presents itself in this guise: Of what use, educationally speaking, is it to be able to see the end in the beginning? How does it assist us in dealing with the early stages of growth to be able to anticipate its later phases? The studies, as we have agreed, represent the possibilities of development inherent in the child's immediate crude experience. But, after all, they are not parts of that present and immediate life. Why, then, or how, make account of them?

Asking such a question suggests its own answer. To see the outcome is to know in what direction the present experience is moving, provided it move normally and soundly. The far-away point, which is of no significance to us simply as far away, becomes of huge importance the moment we take it as defining a present direction of movement. Taken in this way it is no remote and distant result to be achieved, but a guiding method in dealing with the present. The systematized and defined experience of the adult mind, in other words, is of value to us in interpreting the child's life as it immediately shows itself, and in passing on to guidance or direction.

Let us look for a moment at these two ideas: interpretation and guidance. The child's present experience is in no way self-explanatory. It is not final, but transitional. It is nothing complete in itself, but just a sign or index of certain growth-tendencies. As long as we confine our gaze to what the child here and now puts forth, we are confused and misled. We cannot read its meaning. Extreme depreciations of the child morally and intellectually, and sentimental idealizations of him, have their root in a common fallacy. Both spring from taking stages of a growth or movement as something cut off and fixed. The first fails to see the promise contained in feelings and deeds which, taken by themselves, are unpromising and repellant; the second fails to see that even the most pleasing and beautiful exhibitions are but signs, and that they begin to spoil and rot the moment they are treated as achievements.

What we need is something which will enable us to interpret, to appraise, the elements in the child's present puttings forth and fallings away, his exhibitions of power and weakness, in the light of some larger growth-process in which they have their place. Only in this way can we discriminate. If we isolate the child's present inclinations, purposes, and experiences from the place they occupy and the part they have to perform in a developing experience, all stand upon the same level; all alike are equally good and equally bad. But in the movement of life different elements stand upon different planes of value. Some of the child's deeds are symptoms of a waning tendency; they are survivals in functioning of an organ which has done its part and is passing out of vital use. To give positive attention to such qualities is to arrest development upon a lower level. It is systematically to maintain a rudimentary phase of growth. Other activities are signs of a culminating power and interest; to them applies the maxim of striking while the iron is hot. As regards them, it is perhaps a matter of now or never. Selected, utilized, emphasized, they may mark a turning-point for good in the child's whole career; neglected, an opportunity goes, never to be recalled. Other acts and feelings are prophetic; they represent the dawning of flickering light that will shine steadily only in the far future. As regards them there is little at present to do but give them fair and full chance, waiting for the future for definite direction.

Just as, upon the whole, it was the weakness of the "old education" that it made invidious comparisons between the immaturity of the child and the maturity of the adult, regarding the former as something to be got away from as soon as possible and as much as possible; so it is the danger of the "new education" that it regard the child's present powers and interests as something finally significant in themselves. In truth, his learnings and achievements are fluid and moving. They change from day to day and from hour to hour.

It will do harm if child-study leave in the popular mind the impression that a child of a given age has a positive equipment of purposes and interests to be cultivated just as they stand. Interests in reality are but attitudes toward possible experiences; they are not achievements; their worth is in the leverage they afford, not in the accomplishment they represent. To take the phenomena presented at a given age as in any way self-explanatory or self-contained is inevitably to result in indulgence and spoiling. Any power, whether of child or adult, is indulged when it is taken on its given and present level in consciousness. Its genuine meaning is in the propulsion it affords toward a higher level. It is just some-

thing to do with. Appealing to the interest upon the present plane means excitation; it means playing with a power so as continually to stir it up without directing it toward definite achievement. Continuous initiation, continuous starting of activities that do not arrive, is, for all practical purposes, as bad as the continual repression of initiative in conformity with supposed interests of some more perfect thought or will. It is as if the child were forever tasting and never eating; always having his palate tickled upon the emotional side, but never getting the organic satisfaction that comes only with digestion of food and transformation of it into working power.

As against such a view, the subject-matter of science and history and art serves to reveal the real child to us. We do not know the meaning either of his tendencies or of his performances excepting as we take them as germinating seed, or opening bud, of some fruit to be borne. The whole world of visual nature is all too small an answer to the problem of the meaning of the child's instinct for light and form. The entire science of physics is none too much to interpret adequately to us what is involved in some simple demand of the child for explanation of some casual change that has attracted his attention. The art of Rafael or of Corot is none too much to enable us to value the impulses stirring in the child when he draws and daubs.

So much for the use of the subject-matter in interpretation. Its further employment in direction or guidance is but an expansion of the same thought. To interpret the fact is to see it in its vital movement, to see it in its relation to growth. But to view it as a part of a normal growth is to secure the basis for guiding it. Guidance is not external imposition. *It is freeing the life-process for its own most adequate fulfillment.* What was said about disregard of the child's present experience because of its remoteness from mature experience; and of the sentimental idealization of the child's naïve caprices and performances, may be repeated here with slightly altered phrase. There are those who see no alternative between forcing the child from without, or leaving him entirely alone. Seeing no alternative, some choose one mode, some another. Both fall into the same fundamental error. Both fail to see that development is a definite process, having its own law which can be fulfilled only when adequate and normal conditions are provided. Really to interpret the child's present crude impulses in counting, measuring, and arranging things in rhythmic series, involves mathematical scholarship—a knowledge of the mathematical formulae and relations which have, in the history of the race, grown out of just such crude beginnings. To see the whole history of development which intervenes between these two terms is simply to see what step the child needs to take just here and now; to what use he needs to put his blind impulse in order that it may get clarity and gain force.

If, once more, the "old education" tended to ignore the dynamic quality, the developing force inherent in the child's present experience, and therefore to assume that direction and control were just matters of arbitrarily putting the child in a given path and compelling him to walk there, the "new education" is in danger of taking the idea of development in altogether too formal and empty a way. The child is expected to "develop" this or that fact or truth out of his own mind. He is told to think things out, or work things out for himself, without being supplied any of the environing conditions which are requisite to start and guide thought. Nothing can be developed from nothing; nothing but the crude can be developed out of the crude—and this is what surely happens when we throw the child back upon his achieved self as a finality, and invite him to spin new truths of nature or of conduct out of that. It is certainly as futile to expect a child to evolve a universe out of his own mere mind as it is for a philosopher to attempt that task. Development does not mean just getting something out of the mind. It is a development of experience and into experience that is really wanted. And this is impossible save as just that educative medium is provided which will enable the powers and interests that have been selected as valuable to function. They must operate, and how they operate will depend almost entirely upon the stimuli which surround them, and the material upon which they exercise themselves. The problem of direction is thus the problem of selecting appropriate stimuli for instincts and impulses which it is desired to employ in the gaining of new experience. What new experiences are desirable, and thus what stimuli are needed, it is impossible to tell except as there is some comprehension of the development which is aimed at; except, in a word, as the adult knowledge is drawn upon as revealing the possible career open to the child.

It may be of use to distinguish and to relate to each other the logical and the psychological aspects of experience—the former standing for subject-matter in itself, the latter for it in relation to the child. A psychological statement of experience follows its actual growth; it is historic; it notes steps actually taken, the uncertain and tortuous, as well as the efficient and successful. The logical point of view, on the other hand, assumes that the development has reached a certain positive stage of fulfillment. It neglects the process and considers the outcome. It summarizes and arranges, and thus separates the achieved results from the actual steps by which they were forthcoming in the first instance. We may compare the difference between the logical and the psychological to the difference between the notes which an explorer makes in a new country, blazing a trail and finding his way along as best he may, and the finished map that is constructed after the country has been thoroughly explored. The two are mutually dependent. Without the more or less accidental and devious paths traced by the explorer there would be no facts which could be utilized in the making of the complete and related chart. But no one would get the benefit of the explorer's trip if it was not compared and checked up with similar wanderings undertaken by others; unless the new geographical facts learned, the streams crossed, the mountains climbed, etc., were viewed, not as mere incidents in the journey of the particular traveler, but (quite apart from the individual explorer's life) in relation to other similar facts already known. The map orders individual experiences, connecting them with one another irrespective of the local and temporal circumstances and accidents of their original discovery.

Of what use is this formulated statement of experience? Of what use is the map?

Well, we may first tell what the map is not. The map is not a substitute for a personal experience. The map does not take the place of an actual journey. The logically formulated material of a science or branch of learning, of a study, is no substitute for the having of individual experiences. The mathematical formula for a falling body does not take the place of personal contact and immediate individual experience with the falling thing. But the map, a summary, an arranged and orderly view of previous experiences, serves as a guide to future experience; it gives direction; it facilitates control; it economizes effort, preventing useless wandering, and pointing out the paths which lead most quickly and most certainly to a desired result. Through the map every new traveler may get for his own journey the benefits of the results of others' explorations without the waste of energy and loss of time involved in their wanderings—wanderings which he himself would be obliged to repeat were it not for just the assistance of the objective and generalized record of their performances. That which we call a science or study puts the net product of past experience in the form which makes it most available for the future. It represents a capitalization which may at once be turned to interest. It economizes the workings of the mind in every way. Memory is less taxed because the facts are grouped together about some common principle, instead of being connected solely with the varying incidents of their original discovery. Observation is assisted; we know what to look for and where to look. It is the difference between looking for a needle in a haystack, and searching for a given paper in a well-arranged cabinet. Reasoning is directed, because there is a certain general path or line laid out along which ideas naturally march, instead of moving from one chance association to another.

There is, then, nothing final about a logical rendering of experience. Its value is not contained in itself; its significance is that of standpoint, outlook, method. It intervenes between the more casual, tentative, and roundabout experiences of the past, and more controlled and orderly experiences of the future. It gives past experience in that net form which renders it most available and most significant, most fecund for future experience. The abstractions, generalizations, and classifications which it introduces all have prospective meaning.

The formulated result is then not to be opposed to the process of growth. The logical is not set over against the psychological. The surveyed and arranged result occupies a critical position in the process of growth. It marks a turning-point. It shows how we may get the benefit of past effort in controlling future endeavor. In the largest sense the logical standpoint is itself psychological; it has its meaning as a point in the development of experience, and its justification is in its functioning in the future growth which it insures.

Hence the need of reinstating into experience the subject-matter of the studies, or branches of learning. It must be restored to the experience from which it has been abstracted. It needs to be *psychologized*; turned over, translated into the immediate and individual experiencing within which it has its origin and significance.

Every study or subject thus has two aspects: one for the scientist as a scientist; the other for the teacher as a teacher. These two aspects are in no sense opposed or conflicting. But neither are they immediately identical. For the scientist, the subject-matter represents simply a given body of truth to be employed in locating new problems, instituting new researches, and carrying them through to a verified outcome. To him the subject-matter of the science is self-contained. He refers various portions of it to each other; he connects new facts with it. He is not, as a scientist, called upon to travel outside its particular bounds; if he does, it is only to get more facts of the same general sort. The problem of the teacher is a different one. As a teacher he is not concerned with adding new facts to the science he teaches; in propounding new hypotheses or in verifying them. He is concerned with the subject-matter of the science as *representing a given stage and phase of the development of experience*. His problem is that of inducing a vital and personal experiencing. Hence, what concerns him, as teacher, is the ways in which that subject may become a part of experience; what there is in the child's present that is usable with reference to it; how such elements are to be used; how his own knowledge of the subject-matter may assist in interpreting the child's needs and doings, and determine the medium in which the child should be placed in order that his growth may be properly directed. He is concerned, not with the subject-matter as such, but with the subject-matter as a related factor in a total and growing experience. Thus to see it is to psychologize it.

It is the failure to keep in mind the double aspect of subject-matter which causes the curriculum and child to be set over against each other as described in our early pages. The subject-matter, just as it is for the scientist, has no direct relationship to the child's present experience. It stands outside of it. The danger here is not a merely theortical one. We are practically threatened on all sides. Text-book and teacher vie with each other in presenting to the child the subject-matter as it stands to the specialist. Such modification and revision as it undergoes are a mere elimination of certain scientific difficulties, and the general reduction to a lower intellectual level. The material is not translated into life-terms, but is directly offered as a substitute for, or an external annex to, the child's present life.

Three typical evils result: In the first place, the lack of any organic connection with what the child has already seen and felt and loved makes the material purely formal and symbolic. There is a sense in which it is impossible to value too highly the formal and the symbolic. The genuine form, the real symbol, serve as methods in the holding and discovery of truth. They are tools by which the individual pushes out most surely and widely into unexplored areas. They are means by which he brings to bear whatever of reality he has succeeded in gaining in past searchings. But this happens only when the symbol really symbolizes—when it stands for and sums up in shorthand actual experiences which the individual has already gone through. A symbol which is induced from without, which has not been led up to in preliminary activities, is, as we say, a *bare* or *mere* symbol; it is dead and barren. Now, any fact, whether of arithmetic, or geography, or grammar, which is not led up to and into out of something which has previously

occupied a significant position in the child's life for its own sake, is forced into this position. It is not a reality, but just the sign of a reality which *might* be experienced if certain conditions were fulfilled. But the abrupt presentation of the fact as something known by others, and requiring only to be studied and learned by the child, rules out such conditions of fulfillment. It condemns the fact to be a hieroglyph: it would mean something if one only had the key. The clue being lacking, it remains an idle curiosity, to fret and obstruct the mind, a dead weight to burden it.

The second evil in this external presentation is lack of motivation. There are not only no facts or truths which have been previously felt as such with which to appropriate and assimilate the new, but there is no craving, no need, no demand. When the subject-matter has been psychologized, that is, viewed as an outgrowth of present tendencies and activities, it is easy to locate in the present some obstacle, intellectual, practical, or ethical, which can be handled more adequately if the truth in question be mastered. This need supplies motive for the learning. An end which is the child's own carries him on to possess the means of its accomplishment. But when material is directly supplied in the form of a lesson to be learned as a lesson, the connecting links of need and aim are conspicuous for their absence. What we mean by the mechanical and dead in instruction is a result of this lack of motivation. The organic and vital mean interaction—they mean play of mental demand and material supply.

The third evil is that even the most scientific matter, arranged in most logical fashion, loses this quality, when presented in external, ready-made fashion, by the time it gets to the child. It has to undergo some modification in order to shut out some phases too hard to grasp, and to reduce some of the attendant difficulties. What happens? Those things which are most significant to the scientific man, and most valuable in the logic of actual inquiry and classification, drop out. The really thought-provoking character is obscured, and the organizing function disappears. Or, as we commonly say, the child's reasoning powers, the faculty of abstraction and generalization, are not adequately developed. So the subject-matter is evacuated of its logical value, and, though it is what it is only from the logical standpoint, is presented as stuff only for "memory." This is the contradiction: the child gets the advantage neither of the adult logical formulation, nor of his own native competencies of apprehension and response. Hence the logic of the child is hampered and mortified, and we are almost fortunate if he does not get actual non-science, flat and commonplace residua of what was gaining scientific vitality a generation or two ago—degenerate reminiscence of what someone else once formulated on the basis of the experience that some further person had, once upon a time, experienced.

The train of evils does not cease. It is all too common for opposed erroneous theories to play straight into each other's hands. Psychological considerations may be slurred or shoved one side; they cannot be crowded out. Put out of the door, they come back through the window. Somehow and somewhere motive must be appealed to, connection must be established between the mind and its material. There is no question of getting along without this bond of connection; the only question is whether it be such as grows out of the material itself in relation to the mind, or be imported and hitched on from some outside source. If the subject-matter of the lessons be such as to have an appropriate place within the expanding consciousness of the child, if it grows out of his own past doings, thinkings, and sufferings, and grows into application in further achievements and receptivities, then no device or trick of method has to be resorted to in order to enlist "interest." The psychologized *is* of interest—that is, it is placed in the whole of conscious life so that it shares the worth of that life. But the externally presented material, that, conceived and generated in standpoints and attitudes remote from the child, and developed in motives alien to him, has no such place of its own. Hence the recourse to adventitious leverage to push it in, to factitious drill to drive it in, to artificial bribe to lure it in.

Three aspects of this recourse to outside ways for giving the subject-matter some psychological meaning may be worth mentioning. Familiarity breeds contempt, but it also breeds

something like affection. We get used to the chains we wear, and we miss them when removed. 'Tis an old story that through custom we finally embrace what at first wore a hideous mien. Unpleasant, because meaningless, activities may get agreeable if long enough persisted in. *It is possible for the mind to develop interest in a routine or mechanical procedure, if conditions are continually supplied which demand that mode of operation and preclude any other sort.* I frequently hear dulling devices and empty exercises defended and extolled because "the children take such an 'interest' in them." Yes, that is the worst of it; the mind, shut out from worthy employ and missing the taste of adequate performance, comes down to the level of that which is left to it to know and do, and perforce takes an interest in a cabined and cramped experience. To find satisfaction in its own exercise is the normal law of mind, and if large and meaningful business for the mind be denied, it tries to content itself with the formal movements that remain to it—and too often succeeds, save in those cases of more intense activity which cannot accommodate themselves, and that make up the unruly and *déclassé* of our school product. An interest in the formal apprehension of symbols and in their memorized reproduction becomes in many pupils a substitute for the original and vital interest in reality; and all because, the subject-matter of the course of study being out of relation to the concrete mind of the individual, some substitute bond to hold it in some kind of working relation to the mind must be discovered and elaborated.

The second substitute for living motivation in the subject-matter is that of contrast-effects; the material of the lesson is rendered interesting, if not in itself, at least in contrast with some alternative experience. To learn the lesson is more interesting than to take a scolding, be held up to general ridicule, stay after school, receive degradingly low marks, or fail to be promoted. And very much of what goes by the name of "discipline," and prides itself upon opposing the doctrines of a soft pedagogy and upon upholding the banner of effort and duty, is nothing more or less than just this appeal to "interest" in its obverse aspect—to fear, to dislike of various kinds of physical, social, and personal pain. The subject-matter does not appeal; it cannot appeal; it lacks origin and bearing in a growing experience. So the appeal is to the thousand and one outside and irrelevant agencies which may serve to throw, by sheer rebuff and rebound, the mind back upon the material from which it is constantly wandering.

Human nature being what it is, however, it tends to seek its motivation in the agreeable rather than in the disagreeable, in direct pleasure rather than in alternative pain. And so has come up the modern theory and practice of the "interesting," in the false sense of that term. The material is still left; so far as its own characteristics are concerned, just material externally selected and formulated. It is still just so much geography and arithmetic and grammar study; not so much potentiality of child-experience with regard to language, earth, and numbered and measured reality. Hence the difficulty of bringing the mind to bear upon it; hence its repulsiveness; the tendency for attention to wander; for other acts and images to crowd in and expel the lesson. The legitimate way out is to transform the material; to psychologize it—that is, once more, to take it and to develop it within the range and scope of the child's life. But it is easier and simpler to leave it as it is, and then by trick of method to *arouse* interest, to *make* it *interesting*; to cover it with sugar-coating; to conceal its barrenness by intermediate and unrelated material; and finally, as it were, to get the child to swallow and digest the unpalatable morsel while he is enjoying tasting something quite different. But alas for the analogy! Mental assimilation is a matter of consciousness; and if the attention has not been playing upon the actual material, that has not been apprehended, nor worked into faculty.

How, then, stands the case of Child *vs.* Curriculum? What shall the verdict be? The radical fallacy in the original pleadings with which we set out is the supposition that we have no choice save either to leave the child to his own unguided spontaneity or to inspire direction upon him from without. Action is response; it is adaptation, adjustment. There is no such thing as sheer self-activity possible— because all activity takes place in a medium, in a situation, and with reference to its conditions. But, again, no such thing as imposition of truth from without, as insertion of truth from without, is possible. All depends upon the activity which the mind itself undergoes in responding to what is presented from without. Now, the value of the formulated wealth of knowledge that makes up the course of study is that it may enable the educator *to determine the environment of the child*, and thus by indirection to direct. Its primary value, its primary indication, is for the teacher, not for the child. It says to the teacher: Such and such are the capacities, the fulfillments, in truth and beauty and behavior, open to these children. Now see to it that day by day the conditions are such that *their own activities* move inevitably in this direction, toward such culmination of themselves. Let the child's nature fulfill its own destiny, revealed to you in whatever of science and art and industry the world now holds as its own.

The case is of Child. It is his present powers which are to assert themselves; his present capacities which are to be exercised; his present attitudes which are to be realized. But save as the teacher knows, knows wisely and thoroughly, the race-experience which is embodied in that thing we call the Curriculum, the teacher knows neither what the present power, capacity, or attitude is, nor yet how it is to be asserted, exercised, and realized.

NOTES

[First published by University of Chicago Press, 1902. MW 2:273–91.]

The Moral Training Given by the School Community

From *Moral Principles in Education* (1909)

There cannot be two sets of ethical principles, one for life in the school, and the other for life outside of the school. As conduct is one, so also the principles of conduct are one. The tendency to discuss the morals of the school as if the school were an institution by itself is highly unfortunate. The moral responsibility of the school, and of those who conduct it, is to society. The school is fundamentally an institution erected by society to do a certain specific work,—to exercise a certain specific function in maintaining the life and advancing the welfare of society. The educational system which does not recognize that this fact entails upon it an ethical responsibility is derelict and a defaulter. It is not doing what it was called into existence to do, and what it pretends to do. Hence the entire structure of the school in general and its concrete workings in particular need to be considered from time to time with reference to the social position and function of the school.

The idea that the moral work and worth of the public-school system as a whole are to be measured by its social value is, indeed, a familiar notion. However, it is frequently taken in too limited and rigid a way. The social work of the school is often limited to training for citizenship, and citizenship is then interpreted in a narrow sense as meaning capacity to vote intelligently, disposition to obey laws, etc. But it is futile to contract and cramp the ethical responsibility of the school in this way. The child is one, and he must either live his social life as an integral unified being, or suffer loss and create friction. To pick out one of the many social relations which the child bears, and to define the work of the school by that alone, is like instituting a vast and complicated system of physical exercise which would have for its object simply the development of the lungs and the power of breathing, independent of other organs and functions. The child is an organic whole, intellectually, socially, and morally, as well as physically. We must take the child as a member of society in the broadest sense, and demand for and from the schools whatever is necessary to enable the child intelligently to recognize all his social relations and take his part in sustaining them.

To isolate the formal relationship of citizenship from the whole system of relations with which it is actually interwoven; to suppose that there is some one particular study or mode of treatment which can make the child a good citizen; to suppose, in other words, that a good citizen is anything more than a thoroughly efficient and serviceable member of society, one with all his powers of body and mind under control, is a hampering superstition which it is hoped may soon disappear from educational discussion.

The child is to be not only a voter and a subject of law; he is also to be a member of a family, himself in turn responsible, in all probability, for rearing and training of future children, thereby maintaining the continuity of society. He is to be a worker, engaged in some occupation which will be of use to society, and which will maintain his own independence and self-respect. He is to be a member of some particular neighborhood and community, and must contribute to the values of life, add to the decencies and graces of civilization wherever he is. These are bare and formal statements, but if we let our imagination translate them into their concrete details, we have a wide and varied scene. For the child properly to take his place in reference to these various functions means training in science, in art, in history; means command of the fundamental methods of inquiry and the fundamental tools of intercourse and communication; means a trained and sound body, skillful eye and hand; means habits of industry, perseverance; in short, habits of serviceableness.

Moreover, the society of which the child is to be a member is, in the United States, a democratic and progressive society. The child must be educated for leadership as well as for obedience. He must have power of self-direction and power of directing others, power of administration, ability to assume positions of responsibility. This necessity of educating for leadership is as great on the industrial as on the political side.

New inventions, new machines, new methods of transportation and intercourse are making over the whole scene of action year by year. It is an absolute impossibility to educate the child for any fixed station in life. So far as education is conducted unconsciously or con-

sciously on this basis, it results in fitting the future citizen for no station in life, but makes him a drone, a hanger-on, or an actual retarding influence in the onward movement. Instead of caring for himself and for others, he becomes one who has himself to be cared for. Here, too, the ethical responsibility of the school on the social side must be interpreted in the broadest and freest spirit; it is equivalent to that training of the child which will give him such possession of himself that he may take charge of himself; may not only adapt himself to the changes that are going on, but have power to shape and direct them.

Apart from participation in social life, the school has no moral end nor aim. As long as we confine ourselves to the school as an isolated institution, we have no directing principles, because we have no object. For example, the end of education is said to be the harmonious development of all the powers of the individual. Here no reference to social life or membership is apparent, and yet many think we have in it an adequate and thoroughgoing definition of the goal of education. But if this definition be taken independently of social relationship we have no way of telling what is meant by any one of the terms employed. We do not know what a power is; we do not know what development is; we do not know what harmony is. A power is a power only with reference to the use to which it is put, the function it has to serve. If we leave out the uses supplied by social life we have nothing but the old "faculty psychology" to tell what is meant by power and what the specific powers are. The principle reduces itself to enumerating a lot of faculties like perception, memory, reasoning, etc., and then stating that each one of these powers needs to be developed.

Education then becomes a gymnastic exercise. Acute powers of observation and memory might be developed by studying Chinese characters; acuteness in reasoning might be got by discussing the scholastic subtleties of the Middle Ages. The simple fact is that there is no isolated faculty of observation, or memory, or reasoning any more than there is an original faculty of black-smithing, carpentering, or steam engineering. Faculties mean simply that particular impulses and habits have been coordinated or framed with reference to accomplishing certain definite kinds of work. We need to know the social situations in which the individual will have to use ability to observe, recollect, imagine, and reason, in order to have any way of telling what a training of mental powers actually means.

What holds in the illustration of this particular definition of education holds good from whatever point of view we approach the matter. Only as we interpret school activities with reference to the larger circle of social activities to which they relate do we find any standard for judging their moral significance.

The school itself must be a vital social institution to a much greater extent than obtains at present. I am told that there is a swimming school in a certain city where youth are taught to swim without going into the water, being repeatedly drilled in the various movements which are necessary for swimming. When one of the young men so trained was asked what he did when he got into the water, he laconically replied, "Sunk." The story happens to be true; were it not, it would seem to be a fable made expressly for the purpose of typifying the ethical relationship of school to society. The school cannot be a preparation for social life excepting as it reproduces, within itself, typical conditions of social life. At present it is largely engaged in the futile task of Sisyphus. It is endeavoring to form habits in children for use in a social life which, it would almost seem, is carefully and purposely kept away from vital contact with the child undergoing training. The only way to prepare for social life is to engage in social life. To form habits of social usefulness and serviceableness apart from any direct social need and motive, apart from any existing social situation, is, to the letter, teaching the child to swim by going through motions outside of the water. The most indispensable condition is left out of account, and the results are correspondingly partial.

The much lamented separation in the schools of intellectual and moral training, of acquiring information and growing in character, is simply one expression of the failure to conceive and construct the school as a social institution, having social life and value within

itself. Except so far as the school is an embryonic typical community life, moral training must be partly pathological and partly formal. Training is pathological when stress is laid upon correcting wrong-doing instead of upon forming habits of positive service. Too often the teacher's concern with the moral life of pupils takes the form of alertness for failures to conform to school rules and routine. These regulations, judged from the standpoint of the development of the child at the time, are more or less conventional and arbitrary. They are rules which have to be made in order that the existing modes of school work may go on; but the lack of inherent necessity in these school modes reflects itself in a feeling, on the part of the child, that the moral discipline of the school is arbitrary. Any conditions that compel the teacher to take note of failures rather than of healthy growth give false standards and result in distortion and perversion. Attending to wrong-doing ought to be an incident rather than a principle. The child ought to have a positive consciousness of what he is about, so as to judge his acts from the standpoint of reference to the work which he has to do. Only in this way does he have a vital standard, one that enables him to turn failures to account for the future.

By saying that the moral training of the school is formal, I mean that the moral habits currently emphasized by the school are habits which are created, as it were, *ad hoc*. Even the habits of promptness, regularity, industry, non-interference with the work of others, faithfulness to tasks imposed, which are specially inculcated in the school, are habits that are necessary simply because the school system is what it is, and must be preserved intact. If we grant the inviolability of the school system as it is, these habits represent permanent and necessary moral ideas; but just in so far as the school system is itself isolated and mechanical, insistence upon these moral habits is more or less unreal, because the ideal to which they relate is not itself necessary. The duties, in other words, are distinctly school duties, not life duties. If we compare this condition with that of the well-ordered home, we find that the duties and responsibilities that the child has there to recognize do not belong to the family as a specialized and isolated institution, but flow from the very nature of the social life in which the family participates and to which it contributes. The child ought to have the same motives for right doing and to be judged by the same standards in the school, as the adult in the wider social life to which he belongs. Interest in community welfare, an interest that is intellectual and practical, as well as emotional—an interest, that is to say, in perceiving whatever makes for social order and progress, and in carrying these principles into execution—is the moral habit to which all the special school habits must be related if they are to be animated by the breath of life.

NOTES

[MW 4:269–74.]

Aims
in Education

From *Democracy
and Education* (1916)

I. THE NATURE OF AN AIM

The account of education given in our earlier chapters virtually anticipated the results reached in a discussion of the purport of education in a democratic community. For it assumed that the aim of education is to enable individuals to continue their education—or that the object and reward of learning is continued capacity for growth. Now this idea cannot be applied to *all* the members of a society except where intercourse of man with man is mutual, and except where there is adequate provision for the reconstruction of social habits and institutions by means of wide stimulation arising from equitably distributed interests. And this means a democratic society. In our search for aims in education, we are not concerned, therefore, with finding an end outside of the educative process to which education is subordinate. Our whole conception forbids. We are rather concerned with the contrast which exists when aims belong within the process in which they operate and when they are set up from without. And the latter state of affairs must obtain when social relationships are not equitably balanced. For in that case, some portions of the whole social group will find their aims determined by an external dictation; their aims will not arise from the free growth of their own experience, and their nominal aims will be means to more ulterior ends of others rather than truly their own.

Our first question is to define the nature of an aim so far as it falls within an activity, instead of being furnished from without. We approach the definition by a contrast of mere *results* with *ends*. Any exhibition of energy has results. The wind blows about the sands of the desert; the position of the grains is changed. Here is a result, an effect, but not an *end*. For there is nothing in the outcome which completes or fulfills what went before it. There is mere spatial redistribution. One state of affairs is just as good as any other. Consequently there is no basis upon which to select an earlier state of affairs as a beginning, a later as an end, and to consider what intervenes as a process of transformation and realization.

Consider for example the activities of bees in contrast with the changes in the sands when the wind blows them about. The results of the bees' actions may be called ends not because they are designed or consciously intended, but because they are true terminations or completions of what has preceded. When the bees gather pollen and make wax and build cells, each step prepares the way for the next. When cells are built, the queen lays eggs in them; when eggs are laid, they are sealed and bees brood them and keep them at a temperature required to hatch them. When they are hatched, bees feed the young till they can take care of themselves. Now we are so familiar with such facts, that we are apt to dismiss them on the ground that life and instinct are a kind of miraculous thing anyway. Thus we fail to note what the essential characteristic of the event is; namely, the significance of the temporal place and order of each element; the way each prior event leads into its successor while the successor takes up what is furnished and utilizes it for some other stage, until we arrive at the end, which, as it were, summarizes and finishes off the process.

Since aims relate always to results, the first thing to look to when it is a question of aims, is whether the work assigned possesses intrinsic continuity. Or is it a mere serial aggregate of acts, first doing one thing and then another? To talk about an educational aim when approximately each act of a pupil is dictated by the teacher, when the only order in the sequence of his acts is that which comes from the assignment of lessons and the giving of directions by another, is to talk nonsense. It is equally fatal to an aim to permit capricious or discontinuous action in the name of spontaneous self-expression. An aim implies an orderly and ordered activity, one in which the order consists in the progressive completing of a process. Given an activity having a time span and cumulative growth within the time succession, and aim means foresight in advance of the end or possible termination. If bees anticipated the consequences of their activity, if they perceived their end in imaginative foresight, they would have the primary element in an aim. Hence it is nonsense to talk about the aim of education—or any other undertaking— where conditions do not permit of foresight of results, and do not stimulate a person to look ahead to see what the outcome of a given activity is to be.

In the next place the aim as a foreseen end gives direction to the activity; it is not an idle view of a mere spectator, but influences the steps taken to reach the end. The foresight functions in three ways. In the first place, it involves careful observation of the given conditions to see what are the means available for reaching the end, and to discover the hindrances in the way. In the second place, it suggests the proper order or sequence in the use of means. It facilitates an economical selection and arrangement. In the third place, it makes choice of alternatives possible. If we can predict the outcome of acting this way or that, we can then compare the value of the two courses of action; we can pass judgment upon their relative desirability. If we know that stagnant water breeds mosquitoes and that they are likely to carry disease, we can, disliking that anticipated result, take steps to avert it. Since we do not anticipate results as mere intellectual onlookers, but as persons concerned in the outcome, we are partakers in the process which produces the result. We intervene to bring about this result or that.

Of course these three points are closely connected with one another. We can definitely foresee results only as we make careful scrutiny of present conditions, and the importance of the outcome supplies the motive for observations. The more adequate our observations, the more varied is the scene of conditions and obstructions that presents itself, and the more numerous are the alternatives between which choice may be made. In turn, the more numerous the recognized possibilities of the situation, or alternatives of action, the more meaning does the chosen activity possess, and the more flexibly controllable is it. Where only a single outcome has been thought of, the mind has nothing else to think of; the meaning attaching to the act is limited. One only steams ahead toward the mark. Sometimes such a narrow course may be effective. But if unexpected difficulties offer themselves, one has not as many resources at command as if he had chosen the same line of action after a broader survey of the possibilities of the field. He cannot make needed readjustments readily.

The net conclusion is that acting with an aim is all one with acting intelligently. To foresee a terminus of an act is to have a basis upon which to observe, to select, and to order objects and our own capacities. To do these things means to have a mind—for mind is precisely intentional purposeful activity controlled by perception of facts and their relationships to one another. To have a mind to do a thing is to foresee a future possibility; it is to have a plan for its accomplishment; it is to note the means which make the plan capable of execution and the obstructions in the way,—or, if it is really a *mind* to do the thing and not a vague aspiration—it is to have a plan which takes account of resources and difficulties. Mind is capacity to refer present conditions to future results, and future consequences to present conditions. And these traits are just what is meant by having an aim or a purpose. A man is stupid or blind or unintelligent—lacking in mind—just in the degree in which in any activity he does not know what he is about, namely, the probable consequences of his acts. A man is imperfectly intelligent when he contents himself with looser guesses about the outcome than is needful, just taking a chance with his luck, or when he forms plans apart from study of the actual conditions, including his own capacities. Such relative absence of mind means to make our feelings the measure of what is to happen. To be intelligent we must "stop, look, listen" in making the plan of an activity.

To identify acting with an aim and intelligent activity is enough to show its value—its function in experience. We are only too given to making an entity out of the abstract noun "consciousness." We forget that it comes from the adjective "conscious." To be conscious is to be aware of what we are about; conscious signifies the deliberate, observant, planning traits of activity. Consciousness is nothing which we have which gazes idly on the scene around one or which has impressions made upon it by physical things; it is a name for the purposeful quality of an activity, for the fact that it is directed by an aim. Put the other way about, to have an aim is to act with meaning, not like an automatic machine; it is to *mean* to do something and to perceive the meaning of things in the light of that intent.

II. THE CRITERIA OF GOOD AIMS

We may apply the results of our discussion to a consideration of the criteria involved in a correct establishing of aims. (1) The aim set up must be an outgrowth of existing conditions. It must be based upon a consideration of what is already going on; upon the resources and difficulties of the situation. Theories about the proper end of our activities—educational and moral theories—often violate this principle. They assume ends lying *outside* our activities; ends foreign to the concrete make-up of the situation; ends which issue from some outside source. Then the problem is to bring our activities to bear upon the realization of these externally supplied ends. They are something for which we *ought* to act. In any case such "aims" limit intelligence; they are not the expression of mind in foresight, observation, and choice of the better among alternative possibilities. They limit intelligence because, given ready-made, they must be imposed by some authority external to intelligence, leaving to the latter nothing but a mechanical choice of means.

(2) We have spoken as if aims could be completely formed prior to the attempt to realize them. This impression must now be qualified. The aim as it first emerges is a mere tentative sketch. The act of striving to realize it tests its worth. If it suffices to direct activity successfully, nothing more is required, since its whole function is to set a mark in advance; and at times a mere hint may suffice. But usually—at least in complicated situations—acting upon it brings to light conditions which had been overlooked. This calls for revision of the original aim; it has to be added to and subtracted from. An aim must, then, be *flexible*; it must be capable of alteration to meet circumstances. An end established externally to the process of action is always rigid. Being inserted or imposed from without, it is not supposed to have a working relationship to the concrete conditions of the situation. What happens in the course of action neither confirms, refutes, nor alters it. Such an end can only be insisted upon. The failure that results from its lack of adaptation is attributed simply to the perverseness of conditions, not to the fact that

the end is not reasonable under the circumstances. The value of a legitimate aim, on the contrary, lies in the fact that we can use it to change conditions. It is a method for dealing with conditions so as to effect desirable alterations in them. A farmer who should passively accept things just as he finds them would make as great a mistake as he who framed his plans in complete disregard of what soil, climate, etc., permit. One of the evils of an abstract or remote external aim in education is that its very inapplicability in practice is likely to react into a haphazard snatching at immediate conditions. A good aim surveys the present state of experience of pupils, and forming a tentative plan of treatment, keeps the plan constantly in view and yet modifies it as conditions develop. The aim, in short, is experimental, and hence constantly growing as it is tested in action.

(3) The aim must always represent a freeing of activities. The term *end in view* is suggestive, for it puts before the mind the termination or conclusion of some process. The only way in which we can define an activity is by putting before ourselves the objects in which it terminates—as one's aim in shooting is the target. But we must remember that the *object* is only a mark or sign by which the mind specifies the *activity* one desires to carry out. Strictly speaking, not the target but *hitting* the target is the end in view; one *takes* aim by means of the target, but also by the sight on the gun. The different objects which are thought of are means of *directing* the activity. Thus one aims at, say, a rabbit; what he wants is to shoot straight: a certain kind of activity. Or, if it is the rabbit he wants, it is not rabbit apart from his activity, but as a factor in activity; he wants to eat the rabbit, or to show it as evidence of his marksmanship—he wants to do something with it. The doing with the thing, not the thing in isolation, is his end. The object is but a phase of the active end,—continuing the activity successfully. This is what is meant by the phrase, used above, "freeing activity."

In contrast with fulfilling some process in order that activity may go on, stands the static character of an end which is imposed from without the activity. It is always conceived of as fixed; it is *something* to be attained and possessed. When one has such a notion, activity is a mere unavoidable means to something else; it is not significant or important on its own account. As compared with the end it is but a necessary evil; something which must be gone through before one can reach the object which is alone worth while. In other words, the external idea of the aim leads to a separation of means from end, while an end which grows up within an activity as plan for its direction is always both ends and means, the distinction being only one of convenience. Every means is a temporary end until we have attained it. Every end becomes a means of carrying activity further as soon as it is achieved. We call it end when it marks off the future direction of the activity in which we are engaged; means when it marks off the present direction. Every divorce of end from means diminishes by that much the significance of the activity and tends to reduce it to a drudgery from which one would escape if he could. A farmer has to use plants and animals to carry on his farming activities. It certainly makes a great difference to his life whether he is fond of them, or whether he regards them merely as means which he has to employ to get something else in which alone he is interested. In the former case, his entire course of activity is significant; each phase of it has its own value. He has the experience of realizing his end at every stage; the postponed aim, or end in view, being merely a sight ahead by which to keep his activity going fully and freely. For if he does not look ahead, he is more likely to find himself blocked. The aim is as definitely a *means* of action as is any other portion of an activity.

III. APPLICATIONS IN EDUCATION

There is nothing peculiar about educational aims. They are just like aims in any directed occupation. The educator, like the farmer, has certain things to do, certain resources with which to do, and certain obstacles with which to contend. The conditions with which the farmer deals, whether as obstacles or resources, have their own structure and operation independently of any purpose of his. Seeds sprout, rain falls, the sun shines, insects devour, blight comes, the seasons change. His aim is simply to utilize these various conditions; to make his activities and their energies work together, instead of against one another. It would be absurd if the farmer set up a purpose of farming, without any reference to these conditions of soil, climate, characteristics of plant growth, etc. His purpose is simply a foresight of the consequences of his energies connected with those of the things about him, a foresight used to direct his movements from day to day. Foresight of possible consequences leads to more careful and extensive observation of the nature and performances of the things he had to do with, and to laying out a plan—that is, of a certain order in the acts to be performed.

It is the same with the educator, whether parent or teacher. It is as absurd for the latter to set up their "own" aims as the proper objects of the growth of the children as it would be for the farmer to set up an ideal of farming irrespective of conditions. Aims mean acceptance of responsibility for the observations, anticipations, and arrangements required in carrying on a function—whether farming or educating. Any aim is of value so far as it assists observation, choice, and planning in carrying on activity from moment to moment and hour to hour; if it gets in the way of the individual's own common sense (as it will surely do if imposed from without or accepted on authority) it does harm.

And it is well to remind ourselves that education as such has no aims. Only persons, parents, and teachers, etc., have aims, not an abstract idea like education. And consequently their purposes are indefinitely varied, differing with different children, changing as children grow and with the growth of experience on the part of the one who teaches. Even the most valid aims which can be put in words will, as words, do more harm than good unless one recognizes that they are not aims, but rather suggestions to educators as to how to observe, how to look ahead, and how to choose in liberating and directing the energies of the concrete situations in which they find themselves. As a recent writer has said: "To lead this boy to read Scott's novels instead of old Sleuth's stories; to teach this girl to sew; to root out the habit of bullying from John's make up; to pre-

pare this class to study medicine,—these are samples of the millions of aims we have actually before us in the concrete work of education."

Bearing these qualifications in mind, we shall proceed to state some of the characteristics found in all good educational aims. (1) An educational aim must be founded upon the intrinsic activities and needs (including original instincts and acquired habits) of the given individual to be educated. The tendency of such an aim as preparation is, as we have seen, to omit existing powers, and find the aim in some remote accomplishment or responsibility. In general, there is a disposition to take considerations which are dear to the hearts of adults and set them up as ends irrespective of the capacities of those educated. There is also an inclination to propound aims which are so uniform as to neglect the specific powers and requirements of an individual, forgetting that all learning is something which happens to an individual at a given time and place. The larger range of perception of the adult is of great value in observing the abilities and weaknesses of the young, in deciding what they may amount to. Thus the artistic capacities of the adult exhibit what certain tendencies of the child are capable of; if we did not have the adult achievements we should be without assurance as to the significance of the drawing, reproducing, modeling, coloring activities of childhood. So if it were not for adult language, we should not be able to see the import of the babbling impulses of infancy. But it is one thing to use adult accomplishments as a context in which to place and survey the doings of childhood and youth; it is quite another to set them up as a fixed aim without regard to the concrete activities of those educated.

(2) An aim must be capable of translation into a method of cooperating with the activities of those undergoing instruction. It must suggest the kind of environment needed to liberate and to organize *their* capacities. Unless it lends itself to the construction of specific procedures, and unless these procedures test, correct, and amplify the aims, the latter is worthless. Instead of helping the specific task of teaching, it prevents the use of ordinary judgment in observing and sizing up the situa-

tion. It operates to exclude recognition of everything except what squares up with the fixed end in view. Every rigid aim just because it is rigidly given seems to render it unnecessary to give careful attention to concrete conditions. Since it *must* apply anyhow, what is the use of noting details which do not count?

The vice of externally imposed ends has deep roots. Teachers receive them from superior authorities; these authorities accept them from what is current in the community. The teachers impose them upon children. As a first consequence, the intelligence of the teacher is not free; it is confined to receiving the aims laid down from above. Too rarely is the individual teacher so free from the dictation of authoritative supervisor, textbook on methods, prescribed course of study, etc., that he can let his mind come to close quarters with the pupil's mind and the subject matter. This distrust of the teacher's experience is then reflected in lack of confidence in the responses of pupils. The latter receive their aims through a double or treble external imposition, and are constantly confused by the conflict between the aims which are natural to their own experience at the time and those in which they are taught to acquiesce. Until the democratic criterion of the intrinsic significance of every growing experience is recognized, we shall be intellectually confused by the demand for adaptation to external aims.

(3) Educators have to be on their guard against ends that are alleged to be general and ultimate. Every activity, however specific, is, of course, general in its ramified connections, for it leads out indefinitely into other things. So far as a general idea makes us more alive to these connections, it cannot be too general. But "general" also means "abstract," or detached from all specific context. And such abstractness means remoteness, and throws us back, once more, upon teaching and learning as mere means of getting ready for an end disconnected from the means. That education is literally and all the time its own reward means that no alleged study or discipline is educative unless it is worth while in its own immediate having. A truly general aim broadens the outlook; it stimulates one to take more consequences (connections) into account. This means a wider

and more flexible observation of means. The more interacting forces, for example, the farmer takes into account, the more varied will be his immediate resources. He will see a greater number of possible starting places, and a greater number of ways of getting at what he wants to do. The fuller one's conception of possible future achievements, the less his present activity is tied down to a small number of alternatives. If one knew enough, one could start almost anywhere and sustain his activities continuously and fruitfully.

Understanding then the term general or comprehensive aim simply in the sense of a broad survey of the field of present activities, we shall take up some of the larger ends which have currency in the educational theories of the day, and consider what light they throw upon the immediate concrete and diversified aims which are always the educator's real concern. We premise (as indeed immediately follows from what has been said) that there is no need of making a choice among them or regarding them as competitors. When we come to act in a tangible way we have to select or choose a particular act at a particular time, but any number of comprehensive ends may exist without competition, since they mean simply different ways of looking at the same scene. One cannot climb a number of different mountains simultaneously, but the views had when different mountains are ascended supplement one another: they do not set up incompatible, competing worlds. Or, putting the matter in a slightly different way, one statement of an end may suggest certain questions and observations, and another statement another set of questions, calling for other observations. Then the more general ends we have, the better. One statement will emphasize what another slurs over. What a plurality of hypotheses does for the scientific investigator, a plurality of stated aims may do for the instructor.

SUMMARY

An aim denotes the result of any natural process brought to consciousness and made a factor in determining present observation and choice of ways of acting. It signifies that an activity has become intelligent. Specifically it means foresight of the alternative consequences attendant upon acting in a given situation in different ways, and the use of what is anticipated to direct observation and experiment. A true aim is thus opposed at every point to an aim which is imposed upon a process of action from without. The latter is fixed and rigid; it is not a stimulus to intelligence in the given situation, but is an externally dictated order to do such and such things. Instead of connecting directly with present activities, it is remote, divorced from the means by which it is to be reached. Instead of suggesting a freer and better balanced activity, it is a limit set to activity. In education, the currency of these externally imposed aims is responsible for the emphasis put upon the notion of preparation for a remote future and for rendering the work of both teacher and pupil mechanical and slavish.

NOTES

[MW 9:107–17.]

I. NATURE AS SUPPLYING THE AIM

We have just pointed out the futility of trying to establish *the* aim of education—some one final aim which subordinates all others to itself. We have indicated that since general aims are but prospective points of view from which to survey the existing conditions and estimate their possibilities, we might have any number of them, all consistent with one another. As matter of fact, a large number have been stated at different times, all having great local value. For the *statement* of aim is a matter of emphasis at a given time. And we do not emphasize things which do not require emphasis—that is, such things as are taking care of themselves fairly well. We tend rather to frame our statement on the basis of the defects and needs of the contemporary situation; we take for granted, without explicit statement which would be of no use, whatever is right or approximately so. We frame our explicit aims in terms of some alteration to be brought about. It is, then, no paradox requiring explanation that a given epoch or generation tends to emphasize in its conscious projections just the things which it has least of in actual fact. A time of domination by authority will call out as response the desirability of great individual freedom; one of disorganized individual activities the need of social control as an educational aim.

The actual and implicit practice and the conscious or stated aim thus balance each other. At different times such aims as complete living, better methods of language study, substitution of things for words, social efficiency, personal culture, social service, complete development of personality, encyclopedic knowledge, discipline, aesthetic contemplation, utility, etc., have served. The following discussion takes up three statements of recent influence; certain others have been incidentally discussed in the previous chapters, and others will be considered later in a discussion of knowledge and of the values of studies. We begin with a consideration that education is a process of development in accordance with nature, taking Rousseau's statement, which opposed natural to social; and then pass over to the antitheti-

Natural Development and Social Efficiency as Aims

From *Democracy and Education* (1916)

cal conception of social efficiency, which often opposes social to natural.

(1) Educational reformers disgusted with the conventionality and artificiality of the scholastic methods they find about them are prone to resort to nature as a standard. Nature is supposed to furnish the law and the end of development; ours it is to follow and conform to her ways. The positive value of this conception lies in the forcible way in which it calls attention to the wrongness of aims which do not have regard to the natural endowment of those educated. Its weakness is the ease with which natural in the sense of *normal* is confused with the physical. The constructive use of intelligence in foresight, and contriving, is then discounted; we are just to get out of the way and allow nature to do the work. Since no one has stated in the doctrine both its truth and falsity better than Rousseau, we shall turn to him.

"Education," he says, "we receive from three sources—Nature, men, and things. The spontaneous development of our organs and capacities constitutes the education of Nature. The use to which we are taught to put this development constitutes that education given us by Men. The acquirement of personal experience from surrounding objects constitutes that of things. Only when these three kinds of education are consonant and make for the same end, does a man tend towards his true goal. . . . If we are asked what is this end, the answer is that of Nature. For since the concurrence of the three kinds of education is necessary to their completeness, the kind which is entirely independent of our control must necessarily regulate us in determining the other two." Then he defines Nature to mean the capacities and dispositions which are inborn, "as they exist prior to the modification due to constraining habits and the influence of the opinion of others."

The wording of Rousseau will repay careful study. It contains as fundamental truths as have been uttered about education in conjunction with a curious twist. It would be impossible to say better what is said in the first sentences. The three factors of educative development are (*a*) the native structure of our bodily organs and their functional activities; (*b*) the uses to which the activities of these organs are put under the influence of other persons; (*c*) their direct interaction with the environment. This statement certainly covers the ground. His other two propositions are equally sound; namely, (*a*) that only when the three factors of education are consonant and cooperative does adequate development of the individual occur, and (*b*) that the native activities of the organs, being original, are basic in conceiving consonance.

But it requires but little reading between the lines, supplemented by other statements of Rousseau, to perceive that instead of regarding these three things as factors which *must* work together to some extent in order that any one of them may proceed educatively, he regards them as separate and independent operations. Especially does he believe that there is an independent and, as he says, "spontaneous" development of the native organs and faculties. He thinks that this development can go on irrespective of the use to which they are put. And it is to this separate development that education coming from social contact is to be subordinated. Now there is an immense difference between a use of native activities in accord with those activities themselves—as distinct from forcing them and perverting them—and supposing that they have a normal development apart from any use, which development furnishes the standard and norm of all learning by use. To recur to our previous illustration, the process of acquiring language is a practically perfect model of proper educative growth. The start is from native activities of the vocal apparatus, organs of hearing, etc. But it is absurd to suppose that these have an independent growth of their own, which left to itself would evolve a perfect speech. Taken literally, Rousseau's principle would mean that adults should accept and repeat the babblings and noises of children not merely as the beginnings of the development of articulate speech—which they are—but as furnishing language itself—the *standard* for all teaching of language.

The point may be summarized by saying that Rousseau was right, introducing a much-needed reform into education, in holding that the structure and activities of the organs furnish the *conditions* of all teaching of the use of the organs; but profoundly wrong in intimating that they supply not only the conditions but also the *ends* of their development. As matter of fact, the native activities *develop*, in contrast with random and capricious exercise, through the uses to which they are put. And the office of the social medium is, as we have seen, to direct growth through putting powers to the best possible use. The instinctive activities may be called, metaphorically, spontaneous, in the sense that the organs give a strong bias for a certain sort of operation,—a bias so strong that we cannot go contrary to it, though by trying to go contrary we may pervert, stunt, and corrupt them. But the notion of a spontaneous normal development of these activities is pure mythology. The natural, or native, powers furnish the initiating and limiting forces in all education; they do not furnish its ends or aims. There is no learning except from a beginning in unlearned powers, but learning is not a matter of the spontaneous overflow of the unlearned powers. Rousseau's contrary opinion is doubtless due to the fact that he identified God with Nature; to him the original powers are wholly good, coming directly from a wise and good creator. To paraphrase the old saying about the country and the town, God made the original human organs and faculties, man makes the uses to which they are put. Consequently the development of the former furnishes the standard to which the latter must be subordinated. When men attempt to determine the uses to which the original activities shall be put, they interfere with a divine plan. This interference by social arrangements with Nature, God's work, is the primary source of corruption in individuals. Rousseau's passionate assertion of the intrinsic goodness of all natural tendencies was a reaction against the prevalent notion of the total depravity of innate human nature, and has had a powerful influence in modifying the attitude towards children's interests. But it is hardly necessary to say that primitive impulses are of themselves neither good nor evil, but become one or the other according to the objects for which they are employed. That neglect, suppression, and premature forcing of some instincts at the expense of others, are responsible for many avoidable ills, there can be no doubt. But the moral is not to leave them alone to follow their own "spontaneous development," but to provide an environment which shall organize them.

Returning to the elements of truth contained in Rousseau's statements, we find that natural development, as an aim, enables him to point the means of correcting many evils in current practices, and to indicate a number of desirable specific aims. (1) Natural development as an aim fixes attention upon the bodily organs and the need of health and vigor. The aim of natural development says to parents and teachers: Make health an aim; normal development cannot be had without regard to the vigor of the body—an obvious enough fact and yet one whose due recognition in practice would almost automatically revolutionize many of our educational practices. "Nature" is indeed a vague and metaphorical term, but one thing that "Nature" may be said to utter is that there are conditions of educational efficiency, and that till we have learned what these conditions are and have learned to make our practices accord with them, the noblest and most ideal of our aims are doomed to suffer—are verbal and sentimental rather than efficacious.

(2) The aim of natural development translates into the aim of respect for physical mobility. In Rousseau's words: "Children are always in motion; a sedentary life is injurious." When he says that "Nature's intention is to strengthen the body before exercising the mind" he hardly states the fact fairly. But if he had said that nature's "intention" (to adopt his poetical form of speech) is to develop the mind especially *by* exercise of the muscles of the body he would have stated a positive fact. In other words, the aim of following nature means, in the concrete, regard for the actual part played by use of the bodily organs in explorations, in handling of materials, in plays and games.

(3) The general aim translates into the aim of regard for individual differences among children. Nobody can take the principle of consideration of native powers into account without being struck by the fact that these powers differ in different individuals. The difference applies not merely to their intensity, but even more to their quality and arrangement. As Rousseau said: "Each individual is born with a

distinctive temperament. . . . We indiscriminately employ children of different bents on the same exercises; their education destroys the special bent and leaves a dull uniformity. Therefore after we have wasted our efforts in stunting the true gifts of nature we see the short-lived and illusory brilliance we have substituted die away, while the natural abilities we have crushed do not revive."

Lastly, the aim of following nature means to note the origin, the waxing, and waning, of preferences and interests. Capacities bud and bloom irregularly; there is no even four-abreast development. We must strike while the iron is hot. Especially precious are the first dawnings of power. More than we imagine, the ways in which the tendencies of early childhood are treated fix fundamental dispositions and condition the turn taken by powers that show themselves later. Educational concern with the early years of life—as distinct from inculcation of useful arts—dates almost entirely from the time of the emphasis by Pestalozzi and Froebel, following Rousseau, of natural principles of growth. The irregularity of growth and its significance is indicated in the following passage of a student of the growth of the nervous system. "While growth continues, things bodily and mental are lop-sided, for growth is never general, but is accentuated now at one spot, now at another. . . . The methods which shall recognise in the presence of these enormous differences of endowment the dynamic values of natural inequalities of growth, and utilise them, preferring irregularity to the rounding out gained by pruning will most closely follow that which takes place in the body and thus prove most effective."[1]

Observation of natural tendencies is difficult under conditions of restraint. They show themselves most readily in a child's spontaneous sayings and doings,—that is, in those he engages in when not put at set tasks and when not aware of being under observation. It does not follow that these tendencies are all desirable because they are natural; but it does follow that since they are there, they are operative and must be taken account of. We must see to it that the desirable ones have an environment which keeps them active, and that their activity shall control the direction the

others take and thereby induce the disuse of the latter because they lead to nothing. Many tendencies that trouble parents when they appear are likely to be transitory, and sometimes too much direct attention to them only fixes a child's attention upon them. At all events, adults too easily assume their own habits and wishes as standards, and regard all deviations of children's impulses as evils to be eliminated. That artificiality against which the conception of following nature is so largely a protest, is the outcome of attempts to force children directly into the mold of grown-up standards.

In conclusion, we note that the early history of the idea of following nature combined two factors which had no inherent connection with one another. Before the time of Rousseau educational reformers had been inclined to urge the importance of education by ascribing practically unlimited power to it. All the differences between peoples and between classes and persons among the same people were said to be due to differences of training, of exercise, and practice. Originally, mind, reason, understanding is, for all practical purposes, the same in all. This essential identity of mind means the essential equality of all and the possibility of bringing them all to the same level. As a protest against this view, the doctrine of accord with nature meant a much less formal and abstract view of mind and its powers. It substituted specific instincts and impulses and physiological capacities, differing from individual to individual (just as they differ, as Rousseau pointed out, even in dogs of the same litter), for abstract faculties of discernment, memory, and generalization. Upon this side, the doctrine of educative accord with nature has been reenforced by the development of modern biology, physiology, and psychology. It means, in effect, that great as is the significance of nurture, of modification, and transformation through direct educational effort, nature, or unlearned capacities, affords the foundation and ultimate resources for such nurture.

On the other hand, the doctrine of following nature was a political dogma. It meant a rebellion against existing social institutions, customs, and ideals. Rousseau's statement that everything is good as it comes from the hands of the Creator has its signification only in its contrast with the concluding part of the same sentence: "Everything degenerates in the hands of man." And again he says: "*Natural* man has an absolute value; he is a numerical unit, a complete integer and has no relation save to himself and to his fellow-man. Civilized man is only a relative unit, the numerator of a fraction whose value depends upon its denominator, its relation to the integral body of society. Good political institutions are those which make a man unnatural." It is upon this conception of the artificial and harmful character of organized social life as it now exists[2] that he rested the notion that nature not merely furnishes prime forces which initiate growth but also its plan and goal. That evil institutions and customs work almost automatically to give a wrong education which the most careful schooling cannot offset is true enough; but the conclusion is not to educate apart from the environment, but to provide an environment in which native powers will be put to better uses.

II. SOCIAL EFFICIENCY AS AIM

A conception which made nature supply the end of a true education and society the end of an evil one, could hardly fail to call out a protest. The opposing emphasis took the form of a doctrine that the business of education is to supply precisely what nature fails to secure; namely, habituation of an individual to social control; subordination of natural powers to social rules. It is not surprising to find that the value in the idea of social efficiency resides largely in its protest against the points at which the doctrine of natural development went astray; while its misuse comes when it is employed to slur over the truth in that conception. It is a fact that we must look to the activities and achievements of associated life to find what the development of power—that is to say, efficiency—means. The error is in implying that we must adopt measures of subordination rather than of utilization to secure efficiency. The doctrine is rendered adequate when we recognize that social efficiency is attained not by negative constraint but by positive use of native individual capacities in occupations having a social meaning.

(1) Translated into specific aims, social efficiency indicates the importance of industrial competency. Persons cannot live without means of subsistence; the ways in which these means are employed and consumed have a profound influence upon all the relationships of persons to one another. If an individual is not able to earn his own living and that of the children dependent upon him, he is a drag or parasite upon the activities of others. He misses for himself one of the most educative experiences of life. If he is not trained in the right use of the products of industry, there is grave danger that he may deprave himself and injure others in his possession of wealth. No scheme of education can afford to neglect such basic considerations. Yet in the name of higher and more spiritual ideals, the arrangements for higher education have often not only neglected them, but looked at them with scorn as beneath the level of educative concern. With the change from an oligarchical to a democratic society, it is natural that the significance of an education which should have as a result ability to make one's way economically in the world, and to manage economic resources usefully instead of for mere display and luxury, should receive emphasis.

There is, however, grave danger that in insisting upon this end, existing economic conditions and standards will be accepted as final. A democratic criterion requires us to develop capacity to the point of competency to choose and make its own career. This principle is violated when the attempt is made to fit individuals in advance for definite industrial callings, selected not on the basis of trained original capacities, but on that of the wealth or social status of parents. As a matter of fact, industry at the present time undergoes rapid and abrupt changes through the evolution of new inventions. New industries spring up, and old ones are revolutionized. Consequently an attempt to train for too specific a mode of efficiency defeats its own purpose. When the occupation changes its methods, such individuals are left behind with even less ability to readjust themselves than if they had a less definite training. But, most of all, the present industrial constitution of society is, like every society which has ever existed, full of inequities. It is the aim of progressive education to take part in correcting unfair privilege and unfair deprivation, not to perpetuate them. Wherever social control means subordination of individual activities to class authority, there is danger that industrial education will be dominated by acceptance of the *status quo*. Differences of economic opportunity then dictate what the future callings of individuals are to be. We have an unconscious revival of the defects of the Platonic scheme without its enlightened method of selection.

(2) Civic efficiency, or good citizenship. It is, of course, arbitrary to separate industrial competency from capacity in good citizenship. But the latter term may be used to indicate a number of qualifications which are vaguer than vocational ability. These traits run from whatever make an individual a more agreeable companion to citizenship in the political sense: it denotes ability to judge men and measures wisely and to take a determining part in making as well as obeying laws. The aim of civic efficiency has at least the merit of protecting us from the notion of a training of mental power at large. It calls attention to the fact that power must be relative to doing something, and to the fact that the things which most need to be done are things which involve one's relationships with others.

Here again we have to be on guard against understanding the aim too narrowly. An overdefinite interpretation would at certain periods have excluded scientific discoveries, in spite of the fact that in the last analysis security of social progress depends upon them. For scientific men would have been thought to be mere theoretical dreamers, totally lacking in social efficiency. It must be borne in mind that ultimately social efficiency means neither more nor less than capacity to share in a give and take of experience. It covers all that makes one's own experience more worth while to others, and all that enables one to participate more richly in the worth-while experiences of others. Ability to produce and to enjoy art, capacity for recreation, the significant utilization of leisure, are more important elements in it than elements conventionally associated oftentimes with citizenship.

In the broadest sense, social efficiency is nothing less than that socialization of *mind* which is actively concerned in making experiences more communicable; in breaking down the barriers of social stratification which make individuals impervious to the interests of others. When social efficiency is confined to the service rendered by overt acts, its chief constituent (because its only guarantee) is omitted,—intelligent sympathy or good will. For sympathy as a desirable quality is something more than mere feeling; it is a cultivated imagination for what men have in common and a rebellion at whatever unnecessarily divides them. What is sometimes called a benevolent interest in others may be but an unwitting mask for an attempt to dictate to them what their good shall be, instead of an endeavor to free them so that they may seek and find the good of their own choice. Social efficiency, even social service, are hard and metallic things when severed from an active acknowledgment of the diversity of goods which life may afford to different persons, and from faith in the social utility of encouraging every individual to make his own choice intelligent.

III. CULTURE AS AIM

Whether or not social efficiency is an aim which is consistent with culture turns upon these considerations. Culture means at least something cultivated, something ripened; it is opposed to the raw and crude. When the "natural" is identified with this rawness, culture is opposed to what is called natural development. Culture is also something personal; it is cultivation with respect to appreciation of ideas and art and broad human interests. When efficiency is identified with a narrow range of *acts*, instead of with the spirit and meaning of *activity*, culture is opposed to efficiency. Whether called culture or complete development of personality, the outcome is identical with the true meaning of social efficiency whenever attention is given to what is unique in an individual—and he would not be an individual if there were not something incommensurable about him. Its opposite is the mediocre, the average. Whenever distinctive quality is developed, distinction of personality results, and with it greater promise for a social service which goes beyond the supply in quantity of material commodities. For how can there be a society really worth serving unless it is constituted of individuals of significant personal qualities?

The fact is that the opposition of high worth of personality to social efficiency is a product of a feudally organized society with its rigid division of inferior and superior. The latter are supposed to have time and opportunity to develop themselves as human beings; the former are confined to providing external products. When social efficiency as measured by product or output is urged as an ideal in a would-be democratic society, it means that the depreciatory estimate of the masses characteristic of an aristocratic community is accepted and carried over. But if democracy has a moral and ideal meaning, it is that a social return be demanded from all and that opportunity for development of distinctive capacities be afforded all. The separation of the two aims in education is fatal to democracy; the adoption of the narrower meaning of efficiency deprives it of its essential justification.

The aim of efficiency (like any educational aim) must be included within the process of experience. When it is measured by tangible external products, and not by the achieving of a distinctively valuable experience, it becomes materialistic. Results in the way of commodities which may be the outgrowth of an efficient personality are, in the strictest sense, by-products of education: by-products which are inevitable and important, but nevertheless by-products. To set up an external aim strengthens by reaction the false conception of culture which identifies it with something purely "inner." And the idea of perfecting an "inner" personality is a sure sign of social divisions. What is called inner is simply that which does not connect with others—which is not capable of free and full communication. What is termed spiritual culture has usually been futile, with something rotten about it, just because it has been conceived as a thing which a man might have internally—and therefore exclusively. What one is as a person is what one is as associated with others, in a free give and take of intercourse. This transcends both the efficiency which consists in supplying products to others and the culture which is an exclusive refinement and polish.

Any individual has missed his calling, farmer, physician, teacher, student, who does not find that the accomplishments of results of value to others is an accompaniment of a process of experience inherently worth while. Why then should it be thought that one must take his choice between sacrificing himself to doing useful things for others, or sacrificing them to pursuit of his own exclusive ends, whether the saving of his own soul or the building of an inner spiritual life and personality? What happens is that since neither of these things is persistently possible, we get a compromise and an alternation. One tries each course by turns. There is no greater tragedy than that so much of the professedly spiritual and religious thought of the world has emphasized the two ideals of self-sacrifice and spiritual self-perfecting instead of throwing its weight against this dualism of life. The dualism is too deeply established to be easily overthrown; for that reason, it is the particular task of education at the present time to struggle in behalf of an aim in which social efficiency and personal culture are synonyms instead of antagonists.

SUMMARY

General or comprehensive aims are points of view for surveying the specific problems of education. Consequently it is a test of the value of the manner in which any large end is stated to see if it will translate readily and consistently into the procedures which are suggested by another. We have applied this test to three general aims: Development according to nature, social efficiency, and culture or personal mental enrichment. In each case we have seen that the aims when partially stated come into conflict with each other. The partial statement of natural development takes the primitive powers in an alleged spontaneous development as the end-all. From this point of view training which renders them useful to others is an abnormal constraint; one which profoundly modifies them through deliberate nurture is corrupting. But when we recognize that natural activities mean native activities which develop only through the uses in which they are nurtured, the conflict disappears. Similarly a social efficiency which is defined in terms of rendering external service to others is of necessity opposed to the aim of enriching the meaning of experience, while a culture which is taken to consist in an internal refinement of a mind is opposed to a socialized disposition. But social efficiency as an educational purpose should mean cultivation of power to join freely and fully in shared or common activities. This is impossible without culture, while it brings a reward in culture, because one cannot share in intercourse with others without learning—without getting a broader point of view and perceiving things of which one would otherwise be ignorant. And there is perhaps no better definition of culture than that it is the capacity for constantly expanding the range and accuracy of one's perception of meanings.

NOTES

[MW 9:118–30.]
1. Donaldson, *The Growth of the Brain*, p. 357.
2. We must not forget that Rousseau had the idea of a radically different sort of society, a fraternal society whose end should be identical with the good of all its members, which he thought to be as much better than existing states as these are worse than the state of nature.

The words nation and national have two quite different meanings. We cannot profitably discuss the nationalizing of education unless we are clear as to the difference between the two. For one meaning indicates something desirable, something to be cultivated by education, while the other stands for something to be avoided as an evil plague. The idea which has given the movement toward nationality which has been such a feature of the last century its social vitality is the consciousness of a community of history and purpose larger than that of the family, the parish, the sect and the province. The upbuilding of national states has substituted a unity of feeling and aim, a freedom of intercourse, over wide areas for earlier local isolations, suspicions, jealousies and hatreds. It has forced men out of narrow sectionalisms into membership in a larger social unit, and created loyalty to a state which subordinates petty and selfish interests.

One cannot say this, however, without being at once reminded that nationalism has had another side. With the possible exception of our own country the national states of the modern world have been built up through conflict. The development of a sense of unity within a charmed area has been accompanied by dislike, by hostility, to all without. Skilful politicians and other self-seekers have always known how to play cleverly upon patriotism, and upon ignorance of other peoples, to identify nationalism with latent hatred of other nations. Without exaggeration, the present world war may be said to be the outcome of this aspect of nationalism, and to present it in its naked unloveliness.

In the past, our geographical isolation has largely protected us from the harsh, selfish and exclusive aspect of nationalism. The absence of pressure from without, the absence of active and urgent rivalry and hostility of powerful neighbors, has perhaps played a part in the failure to develop an adequate unity of sentiment and idea for the country as a whole. Individualism of a go-as-you-please type has had too full swing. We have an inherited jealousy of any strong national governing agencies, and we have been inclined to let things drift rather than to think out a central, controlling policy. But the effect of the war has been to

Nationalizing Education

(1916)

make us aware that the days of geographical isolation are at an end, and also to make us conscious that we are lacking in an integrated social sense and policy for our country as a whole, irrespective of classes and sections.

We are now faced by the difficulty of developing the good aspect of nationalism without its evil side; of developing a nationalism which is the friend and not the foe of internationalism. Since this is a matter of ideas, of emotions, of intellectual and moral disposition and outlook, it depends for its accomplishment upon educational agencies, not upon outward machinery. Among these educational agencies, the public school takes first rank. When sometime in the remote future the tale is summed up and the public as distinct from the private and merely personal achievement of the common school is recorded, the question which will have to be answered is, What has the American public school done toward subordinating a local, provincial, sectarian and partisan spirit of mind to aims and interests which are common to all the men and women of the country—to what extent has it taught men to think and feel in ideas broad enough to be inclusive of the purposes and happiness of all sections and classes? For unless the agencies which form the mind and morals of the community can prevent the operation of those forces which are always making for a division of interests, class and sectional ideas and feelings will become dominant, and our democracy will fall to pieces.

Unfortunately at the present time one result of the excitement which the war has produced is that many influential and well-meaning persons attempt to foster the growth of an inclusive nationalism by appeal to our fears, our suspicions, our jealousies and our latent hatreds. They would make the measure of our national preparedness our readiness to meet other nations in destructive war rather than our fitness to cooperate with them in the constructive tasks of peace. They are so disturbed by what has been revealed of internal division, of lack of complete national integration, that they have lost faith in the slow policies of education. They would kindle a sense of our dependence upon one another by making us afraid of peoples outside of our border; they would bring about unity within by laying stress upon our separateness from others. The situation makes it all the more necessary that those concerned with education should withstand popular clamor for a nationalism based upon hysterical excitedness or mechanical drill, or a combination of the two. We must ask what a real nationalism, a real Americanism, is like. For unless we know our own character and purpose we are not likely to be intelligent in our selection of the means to further them.

I want to mention only two elements in the nationalism which our education should cultivate. The first is that the American nation is itself complex and compound. Strictly speaking it is interracial and international in its make-up. It is composed of a multitude of peoples speaking different tongues, inheriting diverse traditions, cherishing varying ideals of life. This fact is basic to *our* nationalism as distinct from that of other peoples. Our national motto, "One from Many," cuts deep and extends far. It denotes a fact which doubtless adds to the difficulty of getting a genuine unity. But it also immensely enriches the possibilities of the result to be attained. No matter how loudly any one proclaims his Americanism, if he assumes that any one racial strain, any one component culture, no matter how early settled it was in our territory, or how effective it has proved in its own land, is to furnish a pattern to which all other strains and cultures are to conform, he is a traitor to an American nationalism. Our unity cannot be a homogeneous thing like that of the separate states of Europe from which our population is drawn; it must be a unity created by drawing out and composing into a harmonious whole the best, the most characteristic which each contributing race and people has to offer.

I find that many who talk the loudest about the need of a supreme and unified Americanism of spirit really mean some special code or tradition to which they happen to be attached. They have some pet tradition which they would impose upon all. In thus measuring the scope of Americanism by some single element which enters into it they are themselves false to the spirit of America. Neither Englandism nor New-Englandism, neither Puritan nor Cavalier any more than Teuton or Slav, can do anything but furnish one note in a vast symphony.

The way to deal with hyphenism, in other words, is to welcome it, but to welcome it in the sense of extracting from each people its special good, so that it shall surrender into a common fund of wisdom and experience what it especially has to contribute. All of these surrenders and contributions taken together create the national spirit of America. The dangerous thing is for each factor to isolate itself, to try to live off its past, and then to attempt to impose itself upon other elements, or, at least, to keep itself intact and thus refuse to accept what other cultures have to offer, so as thereby to be transmuted into authentic Americanism.

In what is rightly objected to as hyphenism the hyphen has become something which separates one people from other peoples—and thereby prevents American nationalism. Such terms as Irish-American or Hebrew-American or German-American are false terms because they seem to assume something which is already in existence called America to which the other factor may be externally hitched on. The fact is the genuine American, the typical American, is himself a hyphenated character. This does not mean that he is part American, and that some foreign ingredient is then added. It means that, as I have said, he is international and interracial in his make-up. He is not American plus Pole or German. But the American is himself Pole-German-English-French-Spanish-Italian-Greek-Irish-Scandinavian-Bohemian-Jew-and so on. The point is to see to it that the hyphen connects instead of separates. And this means at least that our public schools shall teach each factor to respect every other, and shall take pains to enlighten all as to the great past contributions of every strain in our composite make-up. I wish our teaching of American history in the schools would take more account of the great waves of migration by which our land for over three centuries has been continuously built up, and make every pupil conscious of the rich breadth of our national make-up. When every pupil recognizes all the factors which have gone into our being, he will continue to prize and reverence that coming from his own past, but he will think of it as honored in being simply one factor in forming a whole, nobler and finer than itself.

In short, unless our education is nationalized in a way which recognizes that the peculiarity of *our* nationalism is its internationalism, we shall breed enmity and division in our frantic efforts to secure unity. The teachers of the country know this fact much better than do many of its politicians. While too often politicians have been fostering a vicious hyphenatedism and sectionalism as a bid for votes, teachers have been engaged in transmuting beliefs and feelings once divided and opposed into a new thing under the sun—a national spirit inclusive not exclusive, friendly not jealous. This they have done by the influence of personal contact, cooperative intercourse and sharing in common tasks and hopes. The teacher who has been an active agent in furthering the common struggle of native born, African, Jew, Italian and perhaps a score of other peoples to attain emancipation and enlightenment will never become a party to a conception of America as a nation which conceives of its history and its hopes as less broad than those of humanity—let politicians clamor for their own ends as they will.

The other point in the constitution of a genuine American nationalism to which I invite attention is that we have been occupied during the greater part of our history in subduing nature, not one another or other peoples. I once heard two foreign visitors coming from different countries discuss what had been impressed upon them as the chief trait of the American people. One said vigor, youthful and buoyant energy. The other said it was kindness, the disposition to live and let live, the absence of envy at the success of others. I like to think that while both of these ascribed traits have the same cause back of them, the latter statement goes deeper. Not that we have more virtue, native or acquired, than others, but that we have had more room, more opportunity. Consequently the same conditions which have put a premium upon active and hopeful energy have permitted the kindlier instincts of man to express themselves. The spaciousness of a continent not previously monopolized by man has stimulated vigor and has also diverted activity from the struggle against fellow-man into the struggle against nature. When men make their gains by fighting in common a wilderness, they have not the motive for mutual distrust which comes when they get ahead only by fighting one another. I recently heard a story which seems to me to have something typical about it. Some manufacturers were discussing the problem of labor; they were loud in their complaints. They were bitter against the exactions of unions, and full of tales of an inefficiency which seemed to them calculated. Then one of them said: "Oh, well, poor devils! They haven't much of a chance and have to do what they can to hold their own. If we were in their place, we should be just the same." And the others nodded assent and the conversation lapsed. I call this characteristic, for if there was not an ardent sympathy, there was at least a spirit of toleration and passive recognition.

But with respect to this point as well as with respect to our composite make-up, the situation is changing. We no longer have a large unoccupied continent. Pioneer days are past, and natural resources are possessed. There is danger that the same causes which have set the hand of man against his neighbor in other countries will have the same effect here. Instead of sharing in a common fight against nature, we are already starting to fight against one another, class against class, haves against have-nots. The change puts a definite responsibility upon the schools to sustain our true national spirit. The virtues of mutual esteem, of human forbearance and well-wishing which in our earlier days were the unconscious products of circumstances must now be the conscious fruit of an education which forms the deepest springs of character.

Teachers above all others have occasion to be distressed when the earlier idealism of welcome to the oppressed is treated as a weak sentimentalism, when sympathy for the unfortunate and those who have not had a fair chance is regarded as a weak indulgence fatal to efficiency. Our traditional disposition in these respects must now become a central motive in public education, not as a matter of condescension or patronizing, but as essential to the maintenance of a truly American spirit. All this puts a responsibility upon the schools which can be met only by widening the scope of educational facilities. The schools have now to make up to the disinherited masses by conscious instruction, by the development of personal power, skill, ability and initiative, for the loss of external opportunities consequent upon the passing of our pioneer days. Otherwise power is likely to pass more and more into the hands of the wealthy, and we shall end with this same alliance between intellectual and artistic culture and economic power due to riches which has been the curse of every civilization in the past, and which our fathers in their democratic idealism thought this nation was to put an end to.

Since the idea of the nation is equal opportunity for all, to nationalize education means to use the schools as a means for making this idea effective. There was a time when this could be done more or less well simply by providing schoolhouses, desks, blackboards and perhaps books. But that day has passed. Opportunities can be equalized only as the schools make it their active serious business to enable all alike to become masters of their own industrial fate. That growing movement which is called industrial or vocational education now hangs in the scales. If it is so constructed in practice as to produce merely more competent hands for subordinate clerical and shop positions, if its purpose is shaped to drill boys and girls into certain forms of automatic skill which will make them useful in carrying out the plans of others, it means that instead of nationalizing education in the spirit of our nation, we have given up the battle, and decided to refeudalize education.

I have said nothing about the point which my title most naturally suggests—changes in administrative methods which will put the resources of the whole nation at the disposition of the more backward and less fortunate portions, meaning by resources not only money but expert advice and guidance of every sort. I have no doubt that we shall move in the future away from a merely regional control of the public schools in the direction of a more central regulation. I say nothing about this phase of the matter at this time not only because it brings up technical questions, but because this side of the matter is but the body, the mechanism of a nationalized education. To nationalize American education is to use education to promote our national idea,—which is the idea of democracy. This is the soul, the spirit, of a nationalized education, and unless the administrative changes are executed so as to embody this soul, they will mean simply the development of red tape, a mechanical uniformity and a deadening supervision from above.

Just because the circumstances of the war have brought the idea of the nation and the national to the foreground of everyone's thoughts, the most important thing is to bear in mind that there are nations and nations, this kind of nationalism and that. Unless I am mistaken there are some now using the cry of an American nationalism, of an intensified national patriotism, to further ideas which characterize the European nations, especially those most active in the war, but which are treasonable to the ideal of *our* nation. Therefore, I have taken this part of your time to remind you of the fact that our nation and democracy are equivalent terms; that our democracy means amity and good will to all humanity (including those beyond our border) and equal opportunity for all within. Since as a nation we are composed of representatives of all nations who have come here to live in peace with one another and to escape the enmities and jealousies which characterize old-world nations, to nationalize our education means to make it an instrument in the active and constant suppression of the war spirit, and in the positive cultivation of sentiments of respect and friendship for all men and women wherever they live. Since our democracy means the substitution of equal opportunity for all for the old-world ideal of unequal opportunity for different classes and the limitation of the individual by the class to which he belongs, to nationalize our education is to make the public school an energetic and willing instrument in developing initiative, courage, power and personal ability in each individual. If we can get our education nationalized in spirit in these directions, the nationalizing of the administrative machinery will in the end take care of itself. So I appeal to teachers in the face of every hysterical wave of emotion, and of every subtle appeal of sinister class interest, to remember that they above all others are the consecrated servants of the democratic ideas in which alone this country is truly a distinctive nation—ideas of friendly and helpful intercourse between all and the equipment of every individual to serve the community by his own best powers in his own best way.

NOTES

[First published in *Journal of Education* 84 (1916): 425–28. Republished in *Addresses and Proceedings* of the National Education Association, 1916, pp. 183–89; and in *Education Today*, ed. Joseph Ratner (New York: G. P. Putnam's Sons, 1940), pp. 112–21. MW 10:202–10.]

Education
as Engineering

(1922)

Mrs. Mary Austin in her illuminating article on "The Need for a New Social Concept" gives an apt expression of the contrast in contemporary behavior between our power in physical engineering and in basic human concerns. We can, as she points out, easily construct a new type of bridge; we cannot create a new type of education. It would be a comparatively simple matter if schools were destroyed to restore them out of a denuded social consciousness; it would be very difficult under like circumstances to recover ability to make a modern bridge. "The reason is that we have been thinking about education long enough to form a pattern in our minds but not long enough of the multitudinous processes involved in the building of steel bridges."

The meaning is clear, and there is nothing to be gained by a meticulous critique of words. But for radical renovation of the school system, a revision, almost a reversal, of wording would seem to be required. Instead of saying that we have thought so long about education—if thinking means anything intellectual—it would be closer to the realities of the situation to say we have only just begun to think about it. The school system represents not thinking but the domination of thought by the inertia of immemorial customs. Modern bridge building, on the other hand, is quite inconceivable apart from the use of materials determined by purely intellectual methods. Our steel cantilever bridges represent precisely the kind of thing that custom unmodified by thought could never achieve no matter how far it was carried. Because bridge building is dependent upon thinking it is easy for thinking to change the mode; because education depends upon habits which arose before there was scientific method, thinking with great difficulty makes even a little dent.

Consequently if our school system were destroyed, we should not have to recover our "minds"—our intellectual equipment—to restore our schools. It would be enough if we retained our habits. To restore modern bridges we could dispense with formed habits provided we retained our intellectual technique. There is an ambiguity in referring to a "mental pattern" in connection with schools. The pattern is not mental, if we mean a pattern formed *by* mind. There is doubtless a pattern *in* our minds, but that signifies only a sense of a comfortable scheme of action which has been deposited by wont and use. The pattern is so deep-seated and clearly outlined that the ease of its recognition gives rise to a deceptive sense that there is something intellectual in the pattern itself. In engineering the pattern is mental in quite a different way. It summarizes a distinctively intellectual type of behavior.

A sense of this contrast seems essential to adequate reflection on the question of how educational procedure is to become a form of constructive engineering. William James said that anyone grasps the significance of a generalization only in the degree in which he is familiar with the detail covered by it. Now detail means things in concrete existence. We are familiar only with things which specifically enter into our lives and with which we steadily reckon and deal. All concepts, theories, general ideas are thin, meagre and ineffectual in the degree in which they are not reflective expressions of acts and events already embodied, achieved, in experience. New conceptions in education will not of themselves carry us far in modifying schools, for until the schools are modified the new conceptions will be themselves pale, remote, vague, formal. They will become thick, substantial, only in the degree in which they are not indispensably required. For they will offer precise and definite modes of thinking only when new meanings and values have become embodied in concrete life-experiences and are thus sustained by them. Till that time arrives the importance of new concepts is mainly negative and critical. They enable us to criticize existing modes of practice; they point out to us the fact that concrete detail of the right sort does *not* exist. Their positive function is to inspire experimental action rather than to give information as to how to execute it.

There was, I take it, no definite art or science of modern bridge building until after bridges of the new sort had been constructed. It was impossible that the new art should precede the new achievement. The formulae for construction, the rules of specific procedure, the specific classification of types of problems and solutions had to wait upon presentation of appropriate concrete material, that is upon successful experimentation. Nevertheless the pioneers had something to go upon and go ahead with, even if they had no specified art of bridge building to rely upon. They had a certain amount of dependable knowledge in mathematics and physics. The difficulty they suffered from was that no one before them had employed this knowledge in building the kind of bridge that new social conditions called for. When they tried to imagine a new type, the minds of all but a few were surely held in bondage by habituation to what was already familiar.

The essential need was thus human rather than scientific. Some one had to have the imagination to get away from the "thought" of the existing easily recognized pattern. This took daring, the courage to think out of line with convention and custom; it took inventiveness in using existing scientific material in a new way, for new consequences. It took intellectual initiative to conduct experiment against almost universal indifference or reprobation; it took intellectual honesty to learn from failure as well as from success in experimentation. The pioneer succeeded in making his bridge—and ultimately making a new art or scientific technique—because he had the courage of a creative mind. Consider the history of any significant invention or discovery, and you will find a period when there was enough knowledge to make a new mode of action or observation possible but no definite information or instruction as to how to make it actual. Every time it was a courageous imagination, a quality which is personal, human, moral, rather than scientific or technical, which built the bridge—in every sense of the word bridge.

There is at present no art of educational engineering. There will not be any such art until considerable progress has been made in creating new modes of education in the home and school. But there does already exist a considerable body of observations and ideas in biology, psychology and the like which serves to criticize and condemn much of our existing practice, and to suggest to a mind not weighed down by fear the possibility of new leads and openings. Given imagination, courage and the desire to experiment and to learn from its results, there is a push toward, a momentum for creative work. Its concrete consequences if subjected to honest or discriminating reflection will afford material for the elaboration of an art, a fairly definite body of suggestions and instructions for the later intelligent conduct of an educative art. But this technique will be largely ex post facto. It is equally fatal to postpone effort till we have the art and to try to deduce the art in advance from the scientific knowledge in biology, psychology and sociology we actually possess. If earlier mathematicians and physicists had attempted to anticipate the result of inventive experimentation in bridge building by deducing from their sciences the rules of the new art, it is certain that they would have arrived only at improved rules for making the old and familiar type of bridge; they would have retarded the day of the new type; they would have concealed from view the necessity of the indispensable human factor—emancipation from routine and timidity. The case is the same with the creation of new types of schools and the ulterior development of an art of education.

There is no question that would-be pioneers in the educational field need an extensive and severe intellectual equipment. Experimentation is something other than blindly trying one's luck or mussing around in the hope that something nice will be the result. Teachers who are to develop a new type of education need a more exacting and comprehensive training in science, philosophy and history than teachers who follow conventionally safe lines. But they do not at present need a translation of this knowledge into a science and art of education. They do not need it because it cannot be had and the pretence of supplying it makes conditions worse rather than better. When, for example, psychology is employed simply to improve the existing teaching of arithmetic or spelling for pre-existing ends, or to measure the technical results of such teaching, let that fact be clearly acknowledged. Let it not be supposed that there is really any advance in the science of education merely because there is a technical improvement in the tools of managing an educational scheme conspicuous for its formation prior to the rise of science. Such "science" only rationalizes old, customary education while improving it in minor details. Given the required intellectual equipment, the further immediate demand is for human qualities of honesty, courage and invention which will enable one to go ahead without the props of custom or the specious pretensions of custom masquerading in the terminology of science.

At present we are still largely in the "rationalizing" stage. Consequently, as was pointed out in an earlier article on "Education as a Religion," educational concepts nominally as diverse as culture, discipline, social service-ableness work out in practice to mean only a little more of this or that study. The scope of our rationalizing is seen in the fact that educational theory as taught in our teachers' training schools has been revolutionized in the last generation, largely in a decade. But where is the evidence of any corresponding change in practice? The most optimistic soul, if candid, will admit that we are mostly doing the old things with new names attached. The change makes little difference—except for advertising purposes. We used to lay out a course prescribed by authority for the improvement of the minds of the young. Now we initiate them into their cultural heritage. The staples used to be taught in certain ways on the ground that the crude and lawless minds of the young needed to be chastened by discipline in things above and beyond them. Now we appeal to "inner motivation." But we teach much the same topics, only in a more gracious, less repellent way. Strange, though, that the opposed needs of external discipline and of inner purpose should be met by so nearly the same subjects and topics!

I am not insinuating that there is personal insincerity in this state of affairs. In part it is due to the fact that docility has been emphasized in education, plus the fact that in the main the most docile among the young are the ones who become teachers when they are adults. Consequently they still listen docilely to the voice of authority. More fundamentally the outcome is due to the fact that a premature attempt is being made to lay down a procedure, definite proper courses of subjects and methods, by which teachers may guide themselves, the procedure being nominally derived from our new knowledge in biology, psychology, etc. But as we have seen, this cannot be done; no results so definite as this can be reached until after the change in educational practice is well under way. When the attempt is made in advance to answer specific questions which will arise in the course of employing the new knowledge, to supply in advance definite suggestions as to courses of procedure, it is inevitable that the minds both of "authorities" and of students intending to teach should fall back upon just the old practices which they are nominally striving to get away from. For here alone is there material concrete enough to permit the formulation of definite problems, answers and steps to be undertaken.

In short, at present, both students and teachers of education are excessively concerned with trying to evolve a body of definite, usable, educational directions out of the new body of science. The attempt is only too natural. But it is pathetic. The endeavor to forestall experiment and its failures and achievements, the attempt to tell in advance how successfully to do a new kind of thing ends, at most, in a rectification of old ways and results, plus a complacent assurance that the best methods of modern science are employed and sanction what is done. This sense of being scientifically up-to-date does endless harm. It retards the creation of a new type of education, because it obscures the one thing deeply needful: a new personal attitude in which a teacher shall be an inventive pioneer in use of what is known, and shall learn in the process of experience to formulate and deal with those problems which

a premature "science" of education now tries to state and solve in advance of experience.

I do not underestimate the value of the guidance which some time in the future individuals may derive from the results of prior collective experience. I only say that the benefit of such an art cannot be had until a sufficient number of individuals have experimented without its beneficial aid in order to provide its materials. And what they need above all else is the creatively courageous disposition. Fear, routine, sloth, identification of success with ease, and approbation of others are the enemies that now stand in the way of educational advance. Too much of what is called educational science and art only perpetuate a régime of wont and use by pretending to give scientific guidance and guarantees in advance. There is in existence knowledge which gives a compass to those who enter on the uncharted seas, but only a stupid insincerity will claim that a compass is a chart. The call is to the creative adventurous mind. Religious faith in education working through this medium of individual courage with the aid of non-educational science will end in achieving education as a science and an art. But as usual we confuse faith with worship, and term science what is only justification of habit.

NOTES

[First published in *New Republic* 32 (1922): 89–91. Republished in *Education Today*, ed. Joseph Ratner (New York: G. P. Putnam's Sons, 1940), pp. 150–56. MW 13:323–328.]

Education in Relation to Form

From *How We Think* (1933)

LEARNING IS LEARNING TO THINK

From what has been said, however, it is evident that education, *upon its intellectual side*, is vitally concerned with cultivating the attitude of reflective thinking, preserving it where it already exists, and changing looser methods of thought into stricter ones whenever possible. Of course, education is not exhausted in its intellectual aspect; there are practical attitudes of efficiency to be formed, moral dispositions to be strengthened and developed, esthetic appreciations to be cultivated. But in all these things there is at least an element of conscious meaning and hence of thought. Otherwise, practical activity is mechanical and routine, morals are blind and arbitrary, and esthetic appreciation is sentimental gush. In what follows we shall confine ourselves, however, to the intellectual side. We state emphatically that, *upon its intellectual side education consists in the formation of wideawake, careful, thorough habits of thinking.*

Of course intellectual learning includes the amassing and retention of information. But information is an undigested burden unless it is understood. It is *knowledge* only as its material is *comprehended*. And understanding, comprehension, means that the various parts of the information acquired are grasped in their relations to one another—a result that is attained only when acquisition is accompanied by constant reflection upon the meaning of what is studied. There is an important distinction between verbal, mechanical memory and what older writers called "judicious memory." The latter seizes the *bearings* of what is retained and recalled; it can, therefore, use the material in new situations where verbal memory would be completely at a loss.

What we have called "psychological thinking" is just the actual process that takes place. This, in particular cases, may be random and disorderly or else a mere play of fantasy. But if it were *always* nothing but that, not only would thinking be of no use, but life could hardly be even maintained. If thought had nothing to do with real conditions and if it did not move logically from these conditions to the thought of ends to be reached, we should never invent, or plan, or know how to get out of any trouble or predicament. As we have already noted, there are both intrinsic elements and pressure of circumstances that introduce into thinking genuinely logical or reflective qualities.

THE CONNECTION BETWEEN PROCESS AND PRODUCT OF THINKING OVERLOOKED BY TWO EDUCATIONAL SCHOOLS

Curiously enough, the internal and necessary connection between the actual process of thinking and its intellectual product is overlooked by two opposite educational schools.

One of these schools thinks that the mind is naturally so illogical in its processes that logical form must be impressed upon it from without. It assumes that logical quality belongs only to organized knowledge and that the operations of the mind become logical only through absorption of logically formulated, ready-made material. In this case, the logical formulations are not the outcome of any process of thinking that is personally undertaken and carried out; the formulation has been made by another mind and is presented in a finished form, apart from the processes by which it was arrived at. Then it is assumed that by some magic its logical character will be transferred into the minds of pupils.

An illustration or two will make clear what is meant by the foregoing statements. Suppose the subject is geography. The first thing is to give its definition, marking it off from every other subject. Then the various abstract terms upon which depends the scientific development of the science are stated and defined one by one—pole, equator, ecliptic, zone—from the simpler units to the more complex that are formed out of them; then the more concrete elements are taken in similar series—continent, island, coast, promontory, cape, isthmus, peninsula, ocean, lake, coast, gulf, bay, and so on. In acquiring this material the pupil's mind is supposed not only to gain important information, but, by accommodating itself to ready-made logical definitions, generalizations, and classifications, gradually also to acquire logical habits.

This type of method has been applied to every subject taught in the schools—reading, writing, music, physics, grammar, arithmetic. Drawing, for example, has been taught on the theory that, since all pictorial representation is a matter of combining straight and curved lines, the simplest procedure is to have the pupil acquire the ability first to draw straight lines in various positions (horizontal, perpendicular, diagonals at various angles), then typical curves; and finally, to combine straight and curved lines in various permutations to construct actual pictures. This seemed to give the ideal "logical" method, beginning with analysis into elements, and then proceeding in regular order to more and more complex syntheses, each element being defined when used, and thereby clearly understood.

Even when this method in its extreme form is not followed, few schools (especially of the middle or upper elementary grades) are free from an exaggerated attention to forms supposedly necessary for the pupil to use if he is to get his result logically. It is held that there are certain steps, arranged in a certain order, that express preeminently an understanding of the subject, and the pupil is made to "analyze" his procedure into these steps; *i.e.*, to learn a certain routine formula of statement. While this method is usually at its height in grammar and arithmetic, it invades also history and even literature, which are then reduced, under plea of intellectual training, to outlines, diagrams, and other schemes of division and subdivision. In memorizing this simulated cut-and-dried copy of the logic of an adult, the child is generally made to stultify his own vital logical movement. The adoption by teachers of this misconception of logical method has probably done more than anything else to bring pedagogy into disrepute, for to many persons "pedagogy" means precisely a set of mechanical, self-conscious devices for replacing by some cast-iron external scheme the personal mental movement of the individual.

It is evident from these examples that in such a scheme of instruction, the logical is identified exclusively with certain formal properties of subject matter; with subject matter defined, refined, subdivided, classified, organized according to certain principles of connection that have been worked out by persons who are expert in that particular field. It conceives the method of instruction to be the devices by which similar traits are imported into the mind by careful reproduction of the given material in arithmetic, geography, grammar, physics, biology, or whatnot. The natural operations of the mind are supposed to be indifferent or even averse to all logical achievement. Hence the mottoes of this school are "discipline," "restraint," "conscious effort," "the necessity of tasks," and so on. From this point of view studies, rather than attitudes and habits, embody the logical factor in education. The mind becomes logical only by learning to conform to an external subject matter. To produce this conformity, the study should first be analyzed (by textbook or teacher) into its logical elements; then each of these elements should be defined; finally, all the elements should be arranged in series or classes according to logical formulae or general principles. Then the pupil learns the definitions one by one and, progressively adding one to another, builds up the logical system, and thereby is himself gradually imbued, from without, with logical quality.

A reaction inevitably occurs from the poor results that accrue from these professedly "logical" methods. Lack of interest in study, habits of inattention and procrastination, positive aversion to intellectual application, dependence upon sheer memorizing and mechanical routine with only a modicum of understanding by the pupil of what he is about, show that the theory of logical definition, division, gradation, and system does not work out practically as it is theoretically supposed to do. The consequent disposition—as in every reaction—is to go to the opposite extreme. The "logical" is thought to be wholly artificial and extraneous; teacher and pupil alike are to turn their backs upon it, and to give free rein to the expression of existing aptitudes and tastes. Emphasis upon natural tendencies and powers as the only possible starting point of development is indeed wholesome. But the reaction is false, and hence misleading, in what it ignores and denies: the presence of genuinely intellectual factors in existing powers and interests.

The other type of school really accepts the underlying premise of the opposite educational theory. It also assumes that the mind is naturally averse to logical form; it grounds this conviction upon the fact that many minds *are* rebellious to the particular logical forms in which a certain type of textbook presents its material. From this fact it is inferred that logical order is so foreign to the natural operations of the mind that it is of slight importance in education, at least in that of the young, and that the main thing is just to give free play to impulses and desires without regard to any definitely *intellectual* growth. Hence the mottoes of this school are "freedom," "self-expression," "individuality," "spontaneity," "play," "interest," "natural unfolding," and so on. In its emphasis upon individual attitude and activity, it sets slight store upon organized subject matter. It conceives *method* to consist of various devices for stimulating and evoking, in their natural order of growth, the native potentialities of individuals.

THE BASIC ERROR OF THE TWO SCHOOLS IS THE SAME

Thus the basic error of the two schools is the same. Both ignore and virtually deny the fact that tendencies toward a reflective and truly logical activity are native to the mind, and that they show themselves at an early period, since they are demanded by outer conditions and stimulated by native curiosity. There is an innate disposition to draw inferences, and an inherent desire to experiment and test. The mind at every stage of growth has its own logic. It entertains suggestions, tests them by observation of objects and events, reaches conclusions, tries them in action, finds them confirmed or in need of correction or rejection. A baby, even at a comparatively early period, makes inferences in the way of expectations from what is observed, interpreting what it sees as a sign or evidence of something it does not observe with the senses. The school of so-called "free self-expression" thus fails to note that one thing that is urgent for expression in the spontaneous activity of the young is *intellectual* in character. Since this factor is predominantly the *educative* one, as far as instruction is concerned, other aspects of activity should be made means to its effective operation.

Any teacher who is alive to the modes of thought operative in the natural experience of the normal child will have no difficulty in avoiding the identification of the logical with a ready-made organization of subject matter, as well as the notion that the way to escape this error is to pay no attention to logical considerations. Such a teacher will have no difficulty in seeing that the real problem of intellectual education is the *transformation* of natural powers into expert, tested powers: the transformation of more or less casual curiosity and sporadic suggestion into attitudes of alert, cautious, and thorough inquiry. He will see that the *psychological* and the *logical*, instead of being opposed to each other (or even independent of each other), are connected as the earlier and the terminal, or concluding, stages of the same process. He will recognize, moreover, that the kind of logical arrangement that marks subject matter at the stage of maturity is not the only kind possible; that the kind found in scientifically organized material is actually undesirable until the mind has reached a point of maturity where it is capable of understanding just *why* this form, rather than some other, is adopted.

That which is strictly logical from the standpoint of subject matter really represents the conclusions of an expert, trained mind. The definitions, divisions, and classifications of the conventional text represent these conclusions boiled down. The only way in which a person can reach ability to make accurate definitions, penetrating classifications, and comprehensive generalizations is by thinking alertly and carefully on his own *present* level. Some kind of intellectual organization must be required, or else habits of vagueness, disorder, and incoherent "thinking" will be formed. But

the organization need not be that which would satisfy the mature expert. For the immature mind is still in process of gaining the intellectual skill that the latter has already achieved. It is absurd to suppose that the beginner can commence where the adept stops. But the beginner should be trained to demand from himself careful examination, consecutiveness, and some sort of summary and formulation of *his* conclusions, together with a statement of the reasons for them.

IN SUMMARY

We may summarize by saying that "logical" has at least three different meanings. In its widest sense, any thinking that is intended to reach a conclusion that is to be accepted and believed in is logical, even though the actual operations are *il*-logical. In the narrowest sense, "logical" signifies that which is demonstrated, according to certain approved forms, to follow from premises the terms of which have clear and definite meanings; it signifies *proof of a stringent character*. Between the two lies the meaning, which is educationally vital: systematic care to safeguard the processes of thinking so that it is truly reflective. In this connection, "logical" signifies the *regulation* of natural and spontaneous processes of observation, suggestion, and testing; that is, thinking as an *art*.

NOTES

[LW 8:176–82.]

P A R T   6

*The Individual,
the Community, and
Democracy*

If one wishes to realize the distance which may lie between "facts" and the meaning of facts, let one go to the field of social discussion. Many persons seem to suppose that facts carry their meaning along with themselves on their face. Accumulate enough of them, and their interpretation stares out at you. The development of physical science is thought to confirm the idea. But the power of physical facts to coerce belief does not reside in the bare phenomena. It proceeds from method, from the technique of research and calculation. No one is ever forced by just the collection of facts to accept a particular theory of their meaning, so long as one retains intact some other doctrine by which he can marshal them. Only when the facts are allowed free play for the suggestion of new points of view is any significant conversion of conviction as to meaning possible. Take away from physical science its laboratory apparatus and its mathematical technique, and the human imagination might run wild in its theories of interpretation even if we suppose the brute facts to remain the same.

In any event, social philosophy exhibits an immense gap between facts and doctrines. Compare, for example, the facts of politics with the theories which are extant regarding the nature of the state. If inquirers confine themselves to observed phenomena, the behavior of kings, presidents, legislators, judges, sheriffs, assessors and all other public officials, surely a reasonable consensus is not difficult to attain. Contrast with this agreement the differences which exist as to the basis, nature, functions and justification of the state, and note the seemingly hopeless disagreement. If one asks not for an enumeration of facts, but for a definition of the state, one is plunged into controversy, into a medley of contradictory clamors. According to one tradition, which claims to derive from Aristotle, the state is associated and harmonized life lifted to its highest potency; the state is at once the keystone of the social arch and is the arch in its wholeness. According to another view, it is just one of many social institutions, having a narrow but important function, that of arbiter in the conflict of other social units. Every group springs out of and realizes a positive human interest; the church, religious values; guilds,

Search for the Public

From *The Public and Its Problems* (1927)

unions and corporations, material economic interests, and so on. The state, however, has no concern of its own; its purpose is formal, like that of the leader of the orchestra who plays no instrument and makes no music, but who serves to keep other players who do produce music in unison with one another. Still a third view has it that the state is organized oppression, at once a social excrescence, a parasite and a tyrant. A fourth is that it is an instrument more or less clumsy for keeping individuals from quarreling too much with one another.

Confusion grows when we enter subdivisions of these different views and the grounds offered for them. In one philosophy, the state is the apex and completion of human association, and manifests the highest realization of all distinctively human capacities. The view had a certain pertinency when it was first formulated. It developed in an antique city-state, where to be fully a free man and to be a citizen participating in the drama, the sports, the religion and the government of the community were equivalent affairs. But the view persists and is applied to the state of to-day. Another view coordinates the state with the church (or as a variant view slightly subordinates it to the latter) as the secular arm of Deity maintaining outward order and decorum among men. A modern theory idealizes the state and its activities by borrowing the conceptions of reason and will, magnifying them till the state appears as the objectified manifestation of a will and reason which far transcend the desires and purposes which can be found among individuals or assemblages of individuals.

We are not concerned, however, with writing either a cyclopedia or history of political doctrines. So we pause with these arbitrary illustrations of the proposition that little common ground has been discovered between the factual phenomena of political behavior and the interpretation of the meaning of these phenomena. One way out of the impasse is to consign the whole matter of meaning and interpretation to political philosophy as distinguished from political science. Then it can be pointed out that futile speculation is a companion of all philosophy. The moral is to drop all doctrines of this kind overboard, and stick to facts verifiably ascertained.

The remedy urged is simple and attractive. But it is not possible to employ it. Political facts are not outside human desire and judgment. Change men's estimate of the *value* of existing political agencies and forms, and the latter change more or less. The different theories which mark political philosophy do not grow up externally to the facts which they aim to interpret; they are amplifications of selected factors among those facts. Modifiable and altering human habits sustain and generate political phenomena. These habits are not wholly informed by reasoned purpose and deliberate choice—far from it—but they are more or less amenable to them. Bodies of men are constantly engaged in attacking and trying to change some political habits, while other bodies of men are actively supporting and justifying them. It is mere pretense, then, to suppose that we can stick by the *de facto*, and not raise at some points the question of *de jure*: the question of by what right, the question of legitimacy. And such a question has a way of growing until it has become a question as to the nature of the state itself. The alternatives before us are not factually limited science on one hand and uncontrolled speculation on the other. The choice is between blind, unreasoned attack and defense on the one hand, and discriminating criticism employing intelligent method and a conscious criterion on the other.

The prestige of the mathematical and physical sciences is great, and properly so. But the difference between facts which are what they are independent of human desire and endeavor and facts which are to some extent what they are because of human interest and purpose, and which alter with alteration in the latter, cannot be got rid of by any methodology. The more sincerely we appeal to facts, the greater is the importance of the distinction between facts which condition human activity and facts which are conditioned by human activity. In the degree which we ignore this difference, social science becomes pseudo-science. Jeffersonian and Hamiltonian political ideas are not merely theories dwelling in the human mind remote from facts of American political behavior. They are expressions of chosen phases and factors among those facts, but they are also something more: namely, forces which have shaped those facts and which are still contending to shape them in the future this way and that. There is more than a speculative difference between a theory of the state which regards it as an instrument in protecting individuals in the rights they already have, and one which conceives its function to be the effecting of a more equitable distribution of rights among individuals. For the theories are held and applied by legislators in congress and by judges on the bench and make a difference in the subsequent facts themselves.

I make no doubt that the practical influence of the political philosophies of Aristotle, the Stoics, St. Thomas, Locke, Rousseau, Kant and Hegel has often been exaggerated in comparison with the influence of circumstances. But a due measure of efficacy cannot be denied them on the ground which is sometimes proffered; it cannot be denied on the ground that ideas are without potency. For ideas belong to human beings who have bodies, and there is no separation between the structures and processes of the part of the body that entertains the ideas and the part that performs acts. Brain and muscles work together, and the brains of men are much more important data for social science than are their muscular system and their sense organs.

It is not our intention to engage in a discussion of political philosophies. The concept of the state, like most concepts which are introduced by "The," is both too rigid and too tied up with controversies to be of ready use. It is a concept which can be approached by a flank movement more easily than by a frontal attack. The moment we utter the words "The State" a score of intellectual ghosts rise to obscure our vision. Without our intention and without our notice, the notion of "The State" draws us imperceptibly into a consideration of the logical relationship of various ideas to one another, and away from facts of human activity. It is better, if possible, to start from the latter and see if we are not led thereby into an idea of something which will turn out to implicate the marks and signs which characterize political behavior.

There is nothing novel in this method of approach. But very much depends upon what we select from which to start and very much depends upon whether we select our point of departure in order to tell at the terminus what the state *ought* to be or what it *is*. If we are too concerned with the former, there is a likelihood that we shall unwittingly have doctored the facts selected in order to come out at a predetermined point. The phase of human action we should *not* start with is that to which direct causative power is attributed. We should not look for state-forming forces. If we do, we are likely to get involved in mythology. To explain the origin of the state by saying that man is a political animal is to travel in a verbal circle. It is like attributing religion to a religious instinct, the family to marital and parental affection, and language to a natural endowment which impels men to speech. Such theories merely reduplicate in a so-called causal force the effects to be accounted for. They are of a piece with the notorious potency of opium to put men to sleep because of its dormitive power.

The warning is not directed against a man of straw. The attempt to derive the state, or any other social institution, from strictly "psychological" data is in point. Appeal to a gregarious instinct to account for social arrangements is the outstanding example of the lazy fallacy. Men do not run together and join in a larger mass as do drops of quicksilver, and if they did the result would not be a state nor any mode of human association. The instincts, whether named gregariousness, or sympathy, or the sense of mutual dependence, or domination on one side and abasement and subjection on the other, at best account for everything in general and nothing in particular. And at worst, the alleged instinct and natural endowment appealed to as a causal force themselves represent physiological tendencies which have previously been shaped into habits of action and expectation by means of the very social conditions they are supposed to explain. Men who have lived in herds develop attachment to the horde to which they have become used; children who have perforce lived in dependence grow into habits of dependence and subjection. The inferiority complex is socially acquired, and the "instinct" of display and mastery is but its other face. There are structural organs which physiologically manifest themselves in vocalizations as the organs of a bird induce song. But the barking of dogs and the song of birds are enough to prove that these native tendencies do not generate language. In order to be converted into language, native vocalization requires transformation by extrinsic conditions, both organic and extra-organic or environmental: formation, be it noted, not just stimulation. The cry of a baby can doubtless be described in purely organic terms, but the wail becomes a noun or verb only by its consequences in the responsive behavior of others. This responsive behavior takes the form of nurture and care, themselves dependent upon tradition, custom and social patterns. Why not postulate an "instinct" of infanticide as well as one of guidance and instruction? Or an "instinct" of exposing girls and taking care of boys?

We may, however, take the argument in a less mythological form than is found in the current appeal to social instincts of one sort or another. The activities of animals, like those of minerals and plants, are correlated with their structure. Quadrupeds run, worms crawl, fish swim, birds fly. They are made that way; it is "the nature of the beast." We do not gain anything by inserting instincts to run, creep, swim and fly between the structure and the act. But the strictly organic conditions which lead men to join, assemble, foregather, combine, are just those which lead other animals to unite in swarms and packs and herds. In describing what is common in human and other animal junctions and consolidations we fail to touch what is distinctively human in human associations. These structural conditions and acts may be *sine qua nons* of human societies; but so are the attractions and repulsions which are exhibited in inanimate things. Physics and chemistry as well as zoology may inform us of some of the conditions without which human beings would not associate. But they do not furnish us with the *sufficient* conditions of community life and of the forms which it takes.

We must in any case start from acts which are performed, not from hypothetical causes for those acts, and consider their consequences. We must also introduce intelligence, or the observation of consequences *as* consequences, that is, in connection with the acts from which they proceed. Since we must introduce it, it is better to do so knowingly than it is to smuggle it in in a way which deceives not only the customs officer—the reader—but ourselves as well. We take then our point of departure from the objective fact that human acts have consequences upon others, that some of these consequences are perceived, and that their perception leads to subsequent effort to control action so as to secure some consequences and avoid others. Following this clew, we are led to remark that the consequences are of two kinds, those which affect the persons directly engaged in a transaction, and those which affect others beyond those immediately concerned. In this distinction we find the germ of the distinction between the private and the public. When indirect consequences are recognized and there is effort to regulate them, something having the traits of a state comes into existence. When the consequences of an action are confined, or are thought to be confined, mainly to the persons directly engaged in it, the transaction is a private one. When A and B carry on a conversation together the action is a trans-action: both are concerned in it; its results pass, as it were, across from one to the other. One or other or both may be helped or harmed thereby. But, presumably, the consequences of advantage and injury do not extend beyond A and B; the activity lies between them; it is private. Yet if it is found that the consequences of conversation extend beyond the two directly concerned, that they affect the welfare of many others, the act acquires a public capacity, whether the conversation be carried on by a king and his prime minister or by Catiline and a fellow conspirator or by merchants planning to monopolize a market.

The distinction between private and public is thus in no sense equivalent to the distinction between individual and social, even if we suppose that the latter distinction has a definite meaning. Many private acts are social; their consequences contribute to the welfare of the community or affect its status and prospects. In the broad sense any transaction deliberately carried on between two or more persons is social in quality. It is a form of associated behavior and its consequences may influence further associations. A man may serve others, even in the community at large, in carrying on a private business. To some extent it is true, as Adam Smith asserted, that our breakfast table is better supplied by the convergent outcome of activities of farmers, grocers and butchers carrying on private affairs with a view to private profit than it would be if we were served on a basis of philanthropy or public spirit. Communities have been supplied with works of art, with scientific discoveries, because of the personal delight found by private persons in engaging in these activities. There are private philanthropists who act so that needy persons or the community as a whole profit by the endowment of libraries, hospitals and educational institutions. In short, private acts may be socially valuable both by indirect consequences and by direct intention.

There is therefore no necessary connection between the private character of an act and its non-social or anti-social character. The public, moreover, cannot be identified with the socially useful. One of the most regular activities of the politically organized community has been waging war. Even the most bellicose of militarists will hardly contend that all wars have been socially helpful, or deny that some have been so destructive of social values that it would have been infinitely better if they had not been waged. The argument for the non-equivalence of the public and the social, in any praiseworthy sense of social, does not rest upon the case of war alone. There is no one, I suppose, so enamored of political action as to hold that it has never been short-sighted, foolish and harmful. There are even those who hold that the presumption is always that social loss will result from agents of the public doing anything which could be done by persons in their private capacity. There are many more who protest that some special public activity, whether prohibition, a protective tariff or the expanded meaning given the Monroe Doctrine, is baleful to society. Indeed every serious political dispute turns upon the question whether a given political act is socially beneficial or harmful.

Just as behavior is not anti-social or non-social because privately undertaken, it is not necessarily socially valuable because carried on in the name of the public by public agents.

The argument has not carried us far, but at least it has warned us against identifying the community and its interests with the state or the politically organized community. And the differentiation may dispose us to look with more favor upon the proposition already advanced: namely, that the line between private and public is to be drawn on the basis of the extent and scope of the consequences of acts which are so important as to need control, whether by inhibition or by promotion. We distinguish private and public buildings, private and public schools, private paths and public highways, private assets and public funds, private persons and public officials. It is our thesis that in this distinction we find the key to the nature and office of the state. It is not without significance that etymologically "private" is defined in opposition to "official," a private person being one deprived of public position. The public consists of all those who are affected by the indirect consequences of transactions to such an extent that it is deemed necessary to have those consequences systematically cared for. Officials are those who look out for and take care of the interests thus affected. Since those who are indirectly affected are not direct participants in the transactions in question, it is necessary that certain persons be set apart to represent them, and see to it that their interests are conserved and protected. The buildings, property, funds, and other physical resources involved in the performance of this office are *res publica*, the common-wealth. The public as far as organized by means of officials and material agencies to care for the extensive and enduring indirect consequences of transactions between persons is the *Populus*.

It is a commonplace that legal agencies for protecting the persons and properties of members of a community, and for redressing wrongs which they suffer, did not always exist. Legal institutions derive from an earlier period when the right of self-help obtained. If a person was harmed, it was strictly up to him what he should do to get even. Injuring another and exacting a penalty for an injury received were private transactions. They were the affairs of those directly concerned and nobody else's direct business. But the injured party obtained readily the help of friends and relatives, and the aggressor did likewise. Hence consequences of the quarrel did not remain confined to those immediately concerned. Feuds ensued, and the blood-quarrel might implicate large numbers and endure for generations. The recognition of this extensive and lasting embroilment and the harm wrought by it to whole families brought a public into existence. The transaction ceased to concern only the immediate parties to it. Those indirectly affected formed a public which took steps to conserve its interests by instituting composition and other means of pacification to localize the trouble.

The facts are simple and familiar. But they seem to present in embryonic form the traits that define a state, its agencies and officers. The instance illustrates what was meant when it said that it is fallacy to try to determine the nature of the state in terms of direct causal factors. Its essential point has to do with the enduring and extensive consequences of behavior, which like all behavior proceeds in ultimate analysis through individual human beings. Recognition of evil consequences brought about a common interest which required for its maintenance certain measures and rules, together with the selection of certain persons as their guardians, interpreters, and, if need be, their executors.

If the account given is at all in the right direction, it explains the gap already mentioned between the facts of political action and theories of the state. Men have looked in the wrong place. They have sought for the key to the nature of the state in the field of agencies, in that of doers of deeds, or in some will or purpose back of the deeds. They have sought to explain the state in terms of authorship. Ultimately all deliberate choices proceed from somebody in particular; acts are performed by somebody, and all arrangements and plans are made by somebody in the most concrete sense of "somebody." Some John Doe and Richard Roe figure in every transaction. We shall not, then, find the public if we look for it on the side of originators of voluntary actions. Some John Smith and his congeners decide whether or not to grow wheat and how much, where and how to invest money, what roads to build and travel, whether to wage war and if so how,

what laws to pass and which to obey and disobey. The actual alternative to deliberate acts of individuals is not action by the public; it is routine, impulsive and other unreflected acts also performed by individuals.

Individual human beings may lose their identity in a mob or in a political convention or in a joint-stock corporation or at the polls. But this does not mean that some mysterious collective agency is making decisions, but that some few persons who know what they are about are taking advantage of massed force to conduct the mob their way, boss a political machine, and manage the affairs of corporate business. When the public or state is involved in making social arrangements like passing laws, enforcing a contract, conferring a franchise, it still acts through concrete persons. The persons are now officers, representatives of a public and shared interest. The difference is an important one. But it is not a difference between single human beings and a collective impersonal will. It is between persons in their private and in their official or representative character. The quality presented is not authorship but authority, the authority of recognized consequences to control the behavior which generates and averts extensive and enduring results of weal and woe. Officials are indeed public agents, but agents in the sense of factors doing the business of others in securing and obviating consequences that concern them.

When we look in the wrong place we naturally do not find what we are looking for. The worst of it is, however, that looking in the wrong place, to causal forces instead of consequences, the outcome of the looking becomes arbitrary. There is no check on it. "Interpretation" runs wild. Hence the variety of conflicting theories and the lack of consensus of opinion. One might argue *a priori* that the continual conflict of theories about the state is itself proof that the problem has been wrongly posed. For, as we have previously remarked, the main facts of political action, while the phenomena vary immensely with diversity of time and place, are not hidden even when they are complex. They are facts of human behavior accessible to human observation. Existence of a multitude of contradictory theories of the state, which is so baffling from the standpoint of the theories themselves, is readily explicable the moment we see that all the theories, in spite of their divergence from one another, spring from a root of shared error: the taking of causal agency instead of consequences as the heart of the problem.

Given this attitude and postulate, some men at some time will find the causal agency in a metaphysical nisus attributed to nature; and the state will then be explained in terms of an "essence" of man realizing itself in an end of perfected Society. Others, influenced by other preconceptions and other desires, will find the required author in the will of God reproducing through the medium of fallen humanity such an image of divine order and justice as the corrupt material allows. Others seek for it in the meeting of the wills of individuals who come together and by contract or mutual pledging of loyalties bring a state into existence. Still others find it in an autonomous and transcendent will embodied in all men as a universal within their particular beings, a will which by its own inner nature commands the establishment of external conditions in which it is possible for will to express outwardly its freedom. Others find it in the fact that mind or reason is either an attribute of reality or is reality itself, while they condole that difference and plurality of minds, individuality, is an illusion attributable to sense, or is merely an appearance in contrast with the monistic reality of reason. When various opinions all spring from a common and shared error, one is as good as another, and the accidents of education, temperament, class interest and the dominant circumstances of the age decide which is adopted. Reason comes into play only to find justification for the opinion which has been adopted, instead of to analyze human behavior with respect to its consequences and to frame polities accordingly. It is an old story that natural philosophy steadily progressed only after an intellectual revolution. This consisted in abandoning the search for causes and forces and turning to the analysis of what is going on and how it goes on. Political philosophy has still in large measure to take to heart this lesson.

The failure to note that the problem is that of perceiving in a discriminating and thorough way the consequences of human action (including negligence and inaction) and of instituting measures and means of caring for these consequences is not confined to production of conflicting and irreconcilable theories of the state. The failure has also had the effect of perverting the views of those who, up to a certain point, perceived the truth. We have asserted that all deliberate choices and plans are finally the work of single human beings. Thoroughly false conclusions have been drawn from this observation. By thinking still in terms of causal forces, the conclusion has been drawn from this fact that the state, the public, is a fiction, a mask for private desires for power and position. Not only the state but society itself has been pulverized into an aggregate of unrelated wants and wills. As a logical consequence, the state is conceived either as sheer oppression born of arbitrary power and sustained in fraud, or as a pooling of the forces of single men into a massive force which single persons are unable to resist, the pooling being a measure of desperation since its sole alternative is the conflict of all with all which generates a life that is helpless and brutish. Thus the state appears either a monster to be destroyed or as a Leviathan to be cherished. In short, under the influence of the prime fallacy that the problem of the state concerns causal forces, individualism, as an ism, as a philosophy, has been generated.

While the doctrine is false, it sets out from a fact. Wants, choices and purposes have their locus in single beings; behavior which manifests desire, intent and resolution proceeds from them in their singularity. But only intellectual laziness leads us to conclude that since the form of thought and decision is individual, their content, their subject-matter, is also something purely personal. Even if "consciousness" were the wholly private matter that the individualistic tradition in philosophy and psychology supposes it to be, it would still be true that consciousness is *of* objects, not of itself. Association in the sense of connection and combination is a "law" of everything known to exist. Singular things act, but they act together. Nothing has been discovered which acts in entire isolation. The action of everything is along with the action of other things. The "along with" is of such a kind that the behavior of each is modified by its connection with others. There are trees which can grow only in a forest. Seeds of many plants can successfully germinate and develop only under conditions furnished by the presence of other plants. Reproduction of kind is dependent upon the activities of insects which bring about fertilization. The life-history of an animal cell is conditioned upon connection with what other cells are doing. Electrons, atoms and molecules exemplify the omnipresence of conjoint behavior.

There is no mystery about the fact of association, of an interconnected action which affects the activity of singular elements. There is no sense in asking how individuals come to be associated. They exist and operate in association. If there is any mystery about the matter, it is the mystery that the universe is the kind of universe it is. Such a mystery could not be explained without going outside the universe. And if one should go to an outside source to account for it, some logician, without an excessive draft upon his ingenuity, would rise to remark that the outsider would have to be connected with the universe in order to account for anything in it. We should still be just where we started, with the fact of connection as a fact to be accepted.

There is, however, an intelligible question about human association:—Not the question how individuals or singular beings come to be connected, but how they come to be connected in just those ways which give human communities traits so different from those which mark assemblies of electrons, unions of trees in forests, swarms of insects, herds of sheep, and constellations of stars. When we consider the difference we at once come upon the fact that the consequences of conjoint action take on a new value when they are observed. For notice of the effects of connected action forces men to reflect upon the connection itself; it makes it an object of attention and interest. Each acts, in so far as the connection is known, in view of the connection. Individuals still do the thinking, desiring and purposing, but *what* they think of is the consequences of their behavior upon that of others and that of others upon themselves.

Each human being is born an infant. He is immature, helpless, dependent upon the activities of others. That many of these dependent beings survive is proof that others in some measure look out for them, take care of them. Mature and better equipped beings are aware of the consequences of their acts upon those of the young. They not only act conjointly with them, but they act in that especial kind of association which manifests interest in the consequences of their conduct upon the life and growth of the young.

Continued physiological existence of the young is only one phase of interest in the consequences of association. Adults are equally concerned to act so that the immature learn to think, feel, desire and habitually conduct themselves in certain ways. Not the least of the consequences which are striven for is that the young shall themselves learn to judge, purpose and choose from the standpoint of associated behavior and its consequences. In fact, only too often this interest takes the form of endeavoring to make the young believe and plan just as adults do. This instance alone is enough to show that while singular beings in their singularity think, want and decide, *what* they think and strive for, the content of their beliefs and intentions is a subject-matter provided by association. Thus man is not merely *de facto* associated, but he *becomes* a social animal in the make-up of his ideas, sentiments and deliberate behavior. *What* he believes, hopes for and aims at is the outcome of association and intercourse. The only thing which imports obscurity and mystery into the influence of association upon what individual persons want and act for is the effort to discover alleged, special, original, society-making causal forces, whether instincts, fiats of will, personal, or an immanent, universal, practical reason, or an indwelling, metaphysical, social essence and nature. These things do not explain, for they are more mysterious than are the facts they are evoked to account for. The planets in a constellation would form a community if they were aware of the connections of the activities of each with those of the others and could use this knowledge to direct behavior.

We have made a digression from consideration of the state to the wider topic of society. However, the excursion enables us to distinguish the state from other forms of social life. There is an old tradition which regards the state and completely organized society as the same thing. The state is said to be the complete and inclusive realization of all social institutions. Whatever values result from any and every social arrangement are gathered together and asserted to be the work of the state. The counterpart of this method is that philosophical anarchism which assembles all the evils that result from all forms of human grouping and attributes them *en masse* to the state, whose elimination would then bring in a millennium of voluntary fraternal organization. That the state should be to some a deity and to others a devil is another evidence of the defects of the premises from which discussion sets out. One theory is as indiscriminate as the other.

There is, however, a definite criterion by which to demarcate the organized public from other modes of community life. Friendships, for example, are non-political forms of association. They are characterized by an intimate and subtle sense of the fruits of intercourse. They contribute to experience some of its most precious values. Only the exigencies of a preconceived theory would confuse with the state that texture of friendships and attachments which is the chief bond in any community, or would insist that the former depends upon the latter for existence. Men group themselves also for scientific inquiry, for religious worship, for artistic production and enjoyment, for sport, for giving and receiving instruction, for industrial and commercial undertakings. In each case some combined or conjoint action, which has grown up out of "natural," that is, biological, conditions and from local contiguity, results in producing distinctive consequences— that is, consequences which differ in kind from those of isolated behavior.

When these consequences are intellectually and emotionally appreciated, a shared interest is generated and the nature of the interconnected behavior is thereby transformed. Each form of association has its own peculiar quality and value, and no person in his senses confuses one with another. The characteristic

of the public as a state springs from the fact that all modes of associated behavior may have extensive and enduring consequences which involve others beyond those directly engaged in them. When these consequences are in turn realized in thought and sentiment, recognition of them reacts to remake the conditions out of which they arose. Consequences have to be taken care of, looked out for. This supervision and regulation cannot be effected by the primary groupings themselves. For the essence of the consequences which call a public into being is the fact that they expand beyond those directly engaged in producing them. Consequently special agencies and measures must be formed if they are to be attended to; or else some existing group must take on new functions. The obvious external mark of the organization of a public or of a state is thus the existence of officials. Government is not the state, for that includes the public as well as the rulers charged with special duties and powers. The public, however, is organized in and through those officers who act in behalf of its interests.

Thus the state represents an important although distinctive and restricted social interest. From this point of view there is nothing extraordinary in the preeminence of the claims of the organized public over other interests when once they are called into play, nor in its total indifference and irrelevancy to friendships, associations for science, art and religion under most circumstances. If the consequences of a friendship threaten the public, then it is treated as a conspiracy; usually it is not the state's business or concern. Men join each other in partnership as a matter of course to do a piece of work more profitably or for mutual defense. Let its operations exceed a certain limit, and others not participating in it find their security or prosperity menaced by it, and suddenly the gears of the state are in mesh. Thus it happens that the state, instead of being all absorbing and inclusive, is under some circumstances the most idle and empty of social arrangements. Nevertheless, the temptation to generalize from these instances and conclude that the state generically is of no significance is at once challenged by the fact that when a family connection, a church, a trade union, a business corporation, or an educational institution conducts itself so as to affect large numbers outside of itself, those who are affected form a public which endeavors to act through suitable structures, and thus to organize itself for oversight and regulation.

I know of no better way in which to apprehend the absurdity of the claims which are sometimes made in behalf of society politically organized than to call to mind the influence upon community life of Socrates, Buddha, Jesus, Aristotle, Confucius, Homer, Vergil, Dante, St. Thomas, Shakespeare, Copernicus, Galileo, Newton, Boyle, Locke, Rousseau and countless others, and then to ask ourselves if we conceive these men to be officers of the state. Any method which so broadens the scope of the state as to lead to such conclusion merely makes the state a name for the totality of all kinds of associations. The moment we have taken the word as loosely as that, it is at once necessary to distinguish, within it, the state in its usual political and legal sense. On the other hand, if one is tempted to eliminate or disregard the state, one may think of Pericles, Alexander, Julius and Augustus Caesar, Elizabeth, Cromwell, Richelieu, Napoleon, Bismarck and hundreds of names of that kind. One dimly feels that they must have had a private life, but how insignificant it bulks in comparison with their action as representatives of a state!

This conception of statehood does not imply any belief as to the propriety or reasonableness of any particular political act, measure or system. Observations of consequences are at least as subject to error and illusion as is perception of natural objects. Judgments about what to undertake so as to regulate them, and how to do it, are as fallible as other plans. Mistakes pile up and consolidate themselves into laws and methods of administration which are more harmful than the consequences which they were originally intended to control. And as all political history shows, the power and prestige which attend command of official position render rule something to be grasped and exploited for its own sake. Power to govern is distributed by the accident of birth or by the possession of qualities which enable a person to obtain office, but which are quite irrelevant

to the performance of its representative functions. But the need which calls forth the organization of the public by means of rulers and agencies of government persists and to some extent is incarnated in political fact. Such progress as political history records depends upon some luminous emergence of the idea from the mass of irrelevancies which obscure and clutter it. Then some reconstruction occurs which provides the function with organs more apt for its fulfillment. Progress is not steady and continuous. Retrogression is as periodic as advance. Industry and inventions in technology, for example, create means which alter the modes of associated behavior and which radically change the quantity, character and place of impact of their indirect consequences.

These changes are extrinsic to political forms which, once established, persist of their own momentum. The new public which is generated remains long inchoate, unorganized, because it cannot use inherited political agencies. The latter, if elaborate and well institutionalized, obstruct the organization of the new public. They prevent that development of new forms of the state which might grow up rapidly were social life more fluid, less precipitated into set political and legal molds. To form itself, the public has to break existing political forms. This is hard to do because these forms are themselves the regular means of instituting change. The public which generated political forms is passing away, but the power and lust of possession remains in the hands of the officers and agencies which the dying public instituted. This is why the change of the form of states is so often effected only by revolution. The creation of adequately flexible and responsive political and legal machinery has so far been beyond the wit of man. An epoch in which the needs of a newly forming public are counteracted by established forms of the state is one in which there is increasing disparagement and disregard of the state. General apathy, neglect and contempt find expression in resort to various short-cuts of direct action. And direct action is taken by many other interests than those which employ "direct action" as a slogan, often most energetically by intrenched class-interests which profess the greatest reverence for the established "law and order" of the existing state. By its very nature, a state is ever something to be scrutinized, investigated, searched for. Almost as soon as its form is stabilized, it needs to be re-made.

Thus the problem of discovering the state is not a problem for theoretical inquirers engaged solely in surveying institutions which already exist. It is a practical problem of human beings living in association with one another, of mankind generically. It is a complex problem. It demands power to perceive and recognize the consequences of the behavior of individuals joined in groups and to trace them to their source and origin. It involves selection of persons to serve as representatives of the interests created by these perceived consequences and to define the functions which they shall possess and employ. It requires institution of a government such that those having the renown and power which goes with the exercise of these functions shall employ them for the public and not turn them to their own private benefit. It is no cause for wonder, then, that states have been many, not only in number but in type and kind. For there have been countless forms of joint activity with correspondingly diverse consequences. Power to detect consequences has varied especially with the instrumentalities of knowledge at hand. Rulers have been selected on all kinds of different grounds. Their functions have varied and so have their will and zeal to represent common interests. Only the exigencies of a rigid philosophy can lead us to suppose that there is some one form or idea of The State which these protean historic states have realized in various degrees of perfection. The only statement which can be made is a purely formal one: the state is the organization of the public effected through officials for the protection of the interests shared by its members. But what the public may be, what the officials are, how adequately they perform their function, are things we have to go to history to discover.

Nevertheless, our conception gives a criterion for determining how good a particular state is: namely, the degree of organization of the public which is attained, and the degree in which its officers are so constituted as to perform their function of caring for public inter-

ests. But there is no *a priori* rule which can be laid down and by which when it is followed a good state will be brought into existence. In no two ages or places is there the same public. Conditions make the consequences of associated action and the knowledge of them different. In addition the means by which a public can determine the government to serve its interests vary. Only formally can we say what the best state would be. In concrete fact, in actual and concrete organization and structure, there is no form of state which can be said to be the best: not at least till history is ended, and one can survey all its varied forms. The formation of states must be an experimental process. The trial process may go on with diverse degrees of blindness and accident, and at the cost of unregulated procedures of cut and try, of fumbling and groping, without insight into what men are after or clear knowledge of a good state even when it is achieved. Or it may proceed more intelligently, because guided by knowledge of the conditions which must be fulfilled. But it is still experimental. And since conditions of action and of inquiry and knowledge are always changing, the experiment must always be retried; the State must always be rediscovered. Except, once more, in formal statement of conditions to be met, we have no idea what history may still bring forth. It is not the business of political philosophy and science to determine what the state in general should or must be. What they may do is to aid in creation of methods such that experimentation may go on less blindly, less at the mercy of accident, more intelligently, so that men may learn from their errors and profit by their successes. The belief in political fixity, of the sanctity of some form of state consecrated by the efforts of our fathers and hallowed by tradition, is one of the stumbling-blocks in the way of orderly and directed change; it is an invitation to revolt and revolution.

As the argument has moved to and fro, it will conduce to clearness to summarize its steps. Conjoint, combined, associated action is a universal trait of the behavior of things. Such action has results. Some of the results of human collective action are perceived, that is, they are noted in such ways that they are taken account of. Then there arise purposes, plans, measures and means, to secure consequences which are liked and eliminate those which are found obnoxious. Thus perception generates a common interest; that is, those affected by the consequences are perforce concerned in conduct of all those who along with themselves share in bringing about the results. Sometimes the consequences are confined to those who directly share in the transaction which produces them. In other cases they extend far beyond those immediately engaged in producing them. Thus two kinds of interests and of measures of regulation of acts in view of consequences are generated. In the first, interest and control are limited to those directly engaged; in the second, they extend to those who do not directly share in the performance of acts. If, then, the interest constituted by their being affected by the actions in question is to have any practical influence, control over the actions which produce them must occur by some indirect means.

So far the statements, it is submitted, set forth matters of actual and ascertainable fact. Now follows the hypothesis. Those indirectly and seriously affected for good or for evil form a group distinctive enough to require recognition and a name. The name selected is The Public. This public is organized and made effective by means of representatives who as guardians of custom, as legislators, as executives, judges, etc., care for its especial interests by methods intended to regulate the conjoint actions of individuals and groups. Then and in so far, association adds to itself political organization, and something which may be government comes into being: the public is a political state.

The direct confirmation of the hypothesis is found in the statement of the series of observable and verifiable matters of fact. These constitute conditions which are sufficient to account, so it is held, for the characteristic phenomena of political life, or state activity. If they do, it is superfluous to seek for other explanation. In conclusion, two qualifications should be added. The account just given is meant to be generic; it is consequently schematic, and omits many differential conditions, some of which receive attention in subsequent chapters. The other point is that in the negative part of the argument, the attack upon theories which would explain the state by means of special causal forces and agencies, there is no denial of causal relations or connections among phenomena themselves. That is obviously assumed at every point. There can be no consequences and measures to regulate the mode and quality of their occurrence without the causal nexus. What is denied is an appeal to *special* forces outside the series of observable connected phenomena. Such causal powers are no different in kind to the occult forces from which physical science had to emancipate itself. At best, they are but phases of the related phenomena themselves which are then employed to account for the facts. What is needed to direct and make fruitful social inquiry is a method which proceeds on the basis of the interrelations of observable acts and their results. Such is the gist of the method we propose to follow.

NOTES

[LW 2:238–58.]

We have had occasion to refer in passing to the distinction between democracy as a social idea and political democracy as a system of government. The two are, of course, connected. The idea remains barren and empty save as it is incarnated in human relationships. Yet in discussion they must be distinguished. The idea of democracy is a wider and fuller idea than can be exemplified in the state even at its best. To be realized it must affect all modes of human association, the family, the school, industry, religion. And even as far as political arrangements are concerned, governmental institutions are but a mechanism for securing to an idea channels of effective operation. It will hardly do to say that criticisms of the political machinery leave the believer in the idea untouched. For, as far as they are justified—and no candid believer can deny that many of them are only too well grounded—they arouse him to bestir himself in order that the idea may find a more adequate machinery through which to work. What the faithful insist upon, however, is that the idea and its external organs and structures are not to be identified. We object to the common supposition of the foes of existing democratic government that the accusations against it touch the social and moral aspirations and ideas which underlie the political forms. The old saying that the cure for the ills of democracy is more democracy is not apt if it means that the evils may be remedied by introducing more machinery of the same kind as that which already exists, or by refining and perfecting that machinery. But the phrase may also indicate the need of returning to the idea itself, of clarifying and deepening our apprehension of it, and of employing our sense of its meaning to criticize and re-make its political manifestations.

Confining ourselves, for the moment, to political democracy, we must, in any case, renew our protest against the assumption that the idea has itself produced the governmental practices which obtain in democratic states: General suffrage, elected representatives, majority rule, and so on. The idea has influenced the concrete political movement, but it has not caused it. The transition from family and dynastic government supported by the loyalties of tradition to popular government was the

Search for the Great Community

From *The Public and Its Problems* (1927)

outcome primarily of technological discoveries and inventions working a change in the customs by which men had been bound together. It was not due to the doctrines of doctrinaires. The forms to which we are accustomed in democratic governments represent the cumulative effect of a multitude of events, unpremeditated as far as political effects were concerned and having unpredictable consequences. There is no sanctity in universal suffrage, frequent elections, majority rule, congressional and cabinet government. These things are devices evolved in the direction in which the current was moving, each wave of which involved at the time of its impulsion a minimum of departure from antecedent custom and law. The devices served a purpose; but the purpose was rather that of meeting existing needs which had become too intense to be ignored, than that of forwarding the democratic idea. In spite of all defects, they served their own purpose well.

Looking back, with the aid which *ex post facto* experience can give, it would be hard for the wisest to devise schemes which, under the circumstances, would have met the needs better. In this retrospective glance, it is possible, however, to see how the doctrinal formulations which accompanied them were inadequate, one-sided and positively erroneous. In fact they were hardly more than political warcries adopted to help in carrying on some immediate agitation or in justifying some particular practical polity struggling for recognition, even though they were asserted to be absolute truths of human nature or of morals. The doctrines served a particular local pragmatic need. But often their very adaptation to immediate circumstances unfitted them, pragmatically, to meet more enduring and more extensive needs. They lived to cumber the political ground, obstructing progress, all the more so because they were uttered and held not as hypotheses with which to direct social experimentation but as final truths, dogmas. No wonder they call urgently for revision and displacement.

Nevertheless the current has set steadily in one direction: toward democratic forms. That government exists to serve its community, and that this purpose cannot be achieved unless the community itself shares in selecting its governors and determining their policies, are a deposit of fact left, as far as we can see, permanently in the wake of doctrines and forms, however transitory the latter. They are not the whole of the democratic idea, but they express it in its political phase. Belief in this political aspect is not a mystic faith as if in some overruling providence that cares for children, drunkards and others unable to help themselves. It marks a well-attested conclusion from historic facts. We have every reason to think that whatever changes may take place in existing democratic machinery, they will be of a sort to make the interest of the public a more supreme guide and criterion of governmental activity, and to enable the public to form and manifest its purposes still more authoritatively. In this sense the cure for the ailments of democracy is more democracy. The prime difficulty, as we have seen, is that of discovering the means by which a scattered, mobile and manifold public may so recognize itself as to define and express its interests. This discovery is necessarily precedent to any fundamental change in the machinery. We are not concerned therefore to set forth counsels as to advisable improvements in the political forms of democracy. Many have been suggested. It is no derogation of their relative worth to say that consideration of these changes is not at present an affair of primary importance. The problem lies deeper; it is in the first instance an intellectual problem: the search for conditions under which the Great Society may become the Great Community. When these conditions are brought into being they will make their own forms. Until they have come about, it is somewhat futile to consider what political machinery will suit them.

In a search for the conditions under which the inchoate public now extant may function democratically, we may proceed from a statement of the nature of the democratic idea in its generic social sense.[1] From the standpoint of the individual, it consists in having a responsible share according to capacity in forming and directing the activities of the groups to which one belongs and in participating according to need in the values which the groups sustain. From the standpoint of the groups, it demands liberation of the potentialities of members of a group in harmony with the interests and goods which are common. Since every individual is a member of many groups, this specification cannot be fulfilled except when different groups interact flexibly and fully in connection with other groups. A member of a robber band may express his powers in a way consonant with belonging to that group and be directed by the interest common to its members. But he does so only at the cost of repression of those of his potentialities which can be realized only through membership in other groups. The robber band cannot interact flexibly with other groups; it can act only through isolating itself. It must prevent the operation of all interests save those which circumscribe it in its separateness. But a good citizen finds his conduct as a member of a political group enriching and enriched by his participation in family life, industry, scientific and artistic associations. There is a free give-and-take: fullness of integrated personality is therefore possible of achievement, since the pulls and responses of different groups reenforce one another and their values accord.

Regarded as an idea, democracy is not an alternative to other principles of associated life. It is the idea of community life itself. It is an ideal in the only intelligible sense of an ideal: namely, the tendency and movement of some thing which exists carried to its final limit, viewed as completed, perfected. Since things do not attain such fulfillment but are in actuality distracted and interfered with, democracy in this sense is not a fact and never will be. But neither in this sense is there or has there ever been anything which is a community in its full measure, a community unalloyed by alien elements. The idea or ideal of a community presents, however, actual phases of associated life as they are freed from restrictive and disturbing elements, and are contemplated as having attained their limit of development. Wherever there is conjoint activity whose consequences are appreciated as good by all singular persons who take part in it, and where the realization of the good is such as to effect an energetic desire and effort to sustain it in being just because it is a good shared by all, there is in so far a community. The clear consciousness of a communal life, in all its implications, constitutes the idea of democracy.

Only when we start from a community as a fact, grasp the fact in thought so as to clarify and enhance its constituent elements, can we reach an idea of democracy which is not utopian. The conceptions and shibboleths which are traditionally associated with the idea of democracy take on a veridical and directive meaning only when they are construed as marks and traits of an association which realizes the defining characteristics of a community. Fraternity, liberty and equality isolated from communal life are hopeless abstractions. Their separate assertion leads to mushy sentimentalism or else to extravagant and fanatical violence which in the end defeats its own aims. Equality then becomes a creed of mechanical identity which is false to facts and impossible of realization. Effort to attain it is divisive of the vital bonds which hold men together; as far as it puts forth issue, the outcome is a mediocrity in which good is common only in the sense of being average and vulgar. Liberty is then thought of as independence of social ties, and ends in dissolution and anarchy. It is more difficult to sever the idea of brotherhood from that of a community, and hence it is either practically ignored in the movements which identify democracy with Individualism, or else it is a sentimentally appended tag. In its just connection with communal experience, fraternity is another name for the consciously appreciated goods which accrue from an association in which all share, and which give direction to the conduct of each. Liberty is that secure release and fulfillment of personal potentialities which take place only in rich and manifold association with others: the power to be an individualized self making a distinctive contribution and enjoying in its own way the fruits of association. Equality denotes the unhampered share which each individual member of the community has in the consequences of associated action. It is equitable because it is measured only by need and capacity to utilize, not by extraneous factors which deprive one in order that another may take and have. A baby in the family is equal with others, not because of some antecedent and structural quality which is the same as that of others, but in so far as his needs for care and development are attended to without being sacrificed to the superior strength, possessions and matured abilities of others. Equality does not signify that kind of mathematical or physical equivalence in virtue of which any one element may be substituted for another. It denotes effective regard for whatever is distinctive and unique in each, irrespective of physical and psychological inequalities. It is not a natural possession but is a fruit of the community when its action is directed by its character as a community.

Associated or joint activity is a condition of the creation of a community. But association itself is physical and organic, while communal life is moral, that is emotionally, intellectually, consciously sustained. Human beings combine in behavior as directly and unconsciously as do atoms, stellar masses and cells; as directly and unknowingly as they divide and repel. They do so in virtue of their own structure, as man and woman unite, as the baby seeks the breast and the breast is there to supply its need. They do so from external circumstances, pressure from without, as atoms combine or separate in presence of an electric charge, or as sheep huddle together from the cold. Associated activity needs no explanation; things are made that way. But no amount of aggregated collective action of itself constitutes a community. For beings who observe and think, and whose ideas are absorbed by impulses and become sentiments and interests, "we" is as inevitable as "I." But "we" and "our" exist only when the consequences of combined action are perceived and become an object of desire and effort, just as "I" and "mine" appear on the scene only when a distinctive share in mutual action is consciously asserted or claimed. Human associations may be ever so organic in origin and firm in operation, but they develop into societies in a human sense only as their consequences, being known, are esteemed and sought for. Even if "society" were as much an organism as some writers have held, it would not on that account be society. Interactions, transactions, occur *de facto* and the results of interdependence follow. But participation in activities and sharing in results are additive concerns. They demand *communication* as a prerequisite.

Combined activity happens among human beings; but when nothing else happens it passes as inevitably into some other mode of interconnected activity as does the interplay of iron and the oxygen of water. What takes place is wholly describable in terms of energy, or, as we say in the case of human interactions, of force. Only when there exist *signs* or *symbols* of activities and of their outcome can the flux be viewed as from without, be arrested for consideration and esteem, and be regulated. Lightning strikes and rives a tree or rock, and the resulting fragments take up and continue the process of interaction, and so on and on. But when phases of the process are represented by signs, a new medium is interposed. As symbols are related to one another, the important relations of a course of events are recorded and are preserved as meanings. Recollection and foresight are possible; the new medium facilitates calculation, planning, and a new kind of action which intervenes in what happens to direct its course in the interest of what is foreseen and desired.

Symbols in turn depend upon and promote communication. The results of conjoint experience are considered and transmitted. Events cannot be passed from one to another, but meanings may be shared by means of signs. Wants and impulses are then attached to common meanings. They are thereby transformed into desires and purposes, which, since they implicate a common or mutually understood meaning, present new ties, converting a conjoint activity into a community of interest and endeavor. Thus there is generated what, metaphorically, may be termed a general will and social consciousness: desire and choice on the part of individuals in behalf of activities that, by means of symbols, are communicable and shared by all concerned. A community thus presents an order of energies transmuted into one of meanings which are appreciated and mutually referred by each to every other on the part of those engaged in combined action. "Force" is not eliminated but is transformed in use and direction by ideas and sentiments made possible by means of symbols.

The work of conversion of the physical and organic phase of associated behavior into a community of action saturated and regulated by mutual interest in shared meanings, consequences which are translated into ideas and desired objects by means of symbols, does not occur all at once nor completely. At any given time, it sets a problem rather than marks a settled achievement. We are born organic beings associated with others, but we are not born members of a community. The young have to be brought within the traditions, outlook and interests which characterize a community by means of education: by unremitting instruction and by learning in connection with the phenomena of overt association. Everything which is distinctively human is learned, not native, even though it could not be learned without native structures which mark man off from other animals. To learn in a human way and to human effect is not just to acquire added skill through refinement of original capacities.

To learn to be human is to develop through the give-and-take of communication an effective sense of being an individually distinctive member of a community; one who understands and appreciates its beliefs, desires and methods, and who contributes to a further conversion of organic powers into human resources and values. But this translation is never finished. The old Adam, the unregenerate element in human nature, persists. It shows itself wherever the method obtains of attaining results by use of force instead of by the method of communication and enlightenment. It manifests itself more subtly, pervasively and effectually when knowledge and the instrumentalities of skill which are the product of communal life are employed in the service of wants and impulses which have not themselves been modified by reference to a shared interest. To the doctrine of "natural" economy which held that commercial exchange would bring about such an interdependence that harmony would automatically result, Rousseau gave an adequate answer in advance. He pointed out that interdependence provides just the situation which makes it possible and worth while for the stronger and abler to exploit others for their own ends, to keep others in a state of subjection where they can be utilized as animated tools. The remedy he suggested, a return to a condition of independence based on isolation, was hardly seriously meant. But its

desperateness is evidence of the urgency of the problem. Its negative character was equivalent to surrender of any hope of solution. By contrast it indicates the nature of the only possible solution: the perfecting of the means and ways of communication of meanings so that genuinely shared interest in the consequences of interdependent activities may inform desire and effort and thereby direct action.

This is the meaning of the statement that the problem is a moral one dependent upon intelligence and education. We have in our prior account sufficiently emphasized the role of technological and industrial factors in creating the Great Society. What was said may even have seemed to imply acceptance of the deterministic version of an economic interpretation of history and institutions. It is silly and futile to ignore and deny economic facts. They do not cease to operate because we refuse to note them, or because we smear them over with sentimental idealizations. As we have also noted, they generate as their result overt and external conditions of action and these are known with various degrees of adequacy. What actually happens in consequence of industrial forces is dependent upon the presence or absence of perception and communication of consequences, upon foresight and its effect upon desire and endeavor. Economic agencies produce one result when they are left to work themselves out on the merely physical level, or on that level modified only as the knowledge, skill and technique which the community has accumulated are transmitted to its members unequally and by chance. They have a different outcome in the degree in which knowledge of consequences is equitably distributed, and action is animated by an informed and lively sense of a shared interest. The doctrine of economic interpretation as usually stated ignores the transformation which meanings may effect; it passes over the new medium which communication may interpose between industry and its eventual consequences. It is obsessed by the illusion which vitiated the "natural economy": an illusion due to failure to note the difference made in action by perception and publication of its consequences, actual and possible. It thinks in terms of antecedents, not of the eventual; of origins, not fruits.

We have returned, through this apparent excursion, to the question in which our earlier discussion culminated: What are the conditions under which it is possible for the Great Society to approach more closely and vitally the status of a Great Community, and thus take form in genuinely democratic societies and state? What are the conditions under which we may reasonably picture the Public emerging from its eclipse?

The study will be an intellectual or hypothetical one. There will be no attempt to state how the required conditions might come into existence, nor to prophesy that they will occur. The object of the analysis will be to show that *unless* ascertained specifications are realized, the Community cannot be organized as a democratically effective Public. It is not claimed that the conditions which will be noted will suffice, but only that at least they are indispensable. In other words, we shall endeavor to frame a hypothesis regarding the democratic state to stand in contrast with the earlier doctrine which has been nullified by the course of events.

Two essential constituents in that older theory, as will be recalled, were the notions that each individual is of himself equipped with the intelligence needed, under the operation of self-interest, to engage in political affairs; and that general suffrage, frequent elections of officials and majority rule are sufficient to ensure the responsibility of elected rulers to the desires and interests of the public. As we shall see, the second conception is logically bound up with the first and stands or falls with it. At the basis of the scheme lies what Lippmann has well called the idea of the "omnicompetent" individual: competent to frame policies, to judge their results; competent to know in all situations demanding political action what is for his own good, and competent to enforce his idea of good and the will to effect it against contrary forces. Subsequent history has proved that the assumption involved illusion. Had it not been for the misleading influence of a false psychology, the illusion might have been detected in advance. But current philosophy held that ideas and knowledge were functions of a mind or consciousness which originated in individuals by means of isolated contact with objects. But in fact, knowledge is a function of association and communication; it depends upon tradition, upon tools and methods socially transmitted, developed and sanctioned. Faculties of effectual observation, reflection and desire are habits acquired under the influence of the culture and institutions of society, not ready-made inherent powers. The fact that man acts from crudely intelligized emotion and from habit rather than from rational consideration, is now so familiar that it is not easy to appreciate that the other idea was taken seriously as the basis of economic and political philosophy. The measure of truth which it contains was derived from observation of a relatively small group of shrewd business men who regulated their enterprises by calculation and accounting, and of citizens of small and stable local communities who were so intimately acquainted with the persons and affairs of their locality that they could pass competent judgment upon the bearing of proposed measures upon their own concerns.

Habit is the mainspring of human action, and habits are formed for the most part under the influence of the customs of a group. The organic structure of man entails the formation of habit, for, whether we wish it or not, whether we are aware of it or not, every act effects a modification of attitude and set which directs future behavior. The dependence of habit-forming upon those habits of a group which constitute customs and institutions is a natural consequence of the helplessness of infancy. The social consequences of habit have been stated once for all by James: "Habit is the enormous fly-wheel of society, its most precious conservative influence. It alone is what keeps us within the bounds of ordinance, and saves the children of fortune from the uprisings of the poor. It alone prevents the hardest and most repulsive walks of life from being deserted by those brought up to tread therein. It keeps the fisherman and the deck-hand at sea through the winter; it holds the miner in his darkness, and nails the countryman to his log-cabin and his lonely farm through all the months of snow; it protects us from invasion by the natives of the desert and the frozen zone. It dooms us all to fight out the battle of life upon the lines of our nurture or our early choice, and to make the best of a pursuit that disagrees, because there is no other for which we are fitted and it is too late to begin again. It keeps different social strata from mixing."

The influence of habit is decisive because all distinctively human action has to be learned, and the very heart, blood and sinews of learning is creation of habitudes. Habits bind us to orderly and established ways of action because they generate ease, skill and interest in things to which we have grown used and because they instigate fear to walk in different ways, and because they leave us incapacitated for the trial of them. Habit does not preclude the use of thought, but it determines the channels within which it operates. Thinking is secreted in the interstices of habits. The sailor, miner, fisherman and farmer think, but their thoughts fall within the framework of accustomed occupations and relationships. We dream beyond the limits of use and wont, but only rarely does revery become a source of acts which break bounds; so rarely that we name those in whom it happens demonic geniuses and marvel at the spectacle. Thinking itself becomes habitual along certain lines; a specialized occupation. Scientific men, philosophers, literary persons, are not men and women who have so broken the bonds of habits that pure reason and emotion undefiled by use and wont speak through them. They are persons of a specialized infrequent habit. Hence the idea that men are moved by an intelligent and calculated regard for their own good is pure mythology. Even if the principle of self-love actuated behavior, it would still be true that the *objects* in which men find their love manifested, the objects which they take as constituting their peculiar interests, are set by habits reflecting social customs.

These facts explain why the social doctrinaires of the new industrial movement had so little prescience of what was to follow in consequence of it. These facts explain why the more things changed, the more they were the same; they account, that is, for the fact that instead of the sweeping revolution which was expected to result from democratic political machinery, there was in the main but a transfer of vested power from one class to another. A few men, whether or not they were good judges of their own true interest and good, were competent judges of the conduct of business for pecuniary profit, and of how the new governmental machinery could be made to serve their ends. It would have taken a new race of human beings to escape, in the use made of political forms, from the influence of deeply engrained habits, of old institutions and customary social status, with their inwrought limitations of expectation, desire and demand. And such a race, unless of disembodied angelic constitution, would simply have taken up the task where human beings assumed it upon emergence from the condition of anthropoid apes. In spite of sudden and catastrophic revolutions, the essential continuity of history is doubly guaranteed. Not only are personal desire and belief functions of habit and custom, but the objective conditions which provide the resources and tools of action, together with its limitations, obstructions and traps, are precipitates of the past, perpetuating, willy-nilly, its hold and power. The creation of a *tabula rasa* in order to permit the creation of a new order is so impossible as to set at naught both the hope of buoyant revolutionaries and the timidity of scared conservatives.

Nevertheless, changes take place and are cumulative in character. Observation of them in the light of their recognized consequences arouses reflection, discovery, invention, experimentation. When a certain state of accumulated knowledge, of techniques and instrumentalities is attained, the process of change is so accelerated, that, as to-day, it appears externally to be the dominant trait. But there is a marked lag in any corresponding change of ideas and desires. Habits of opinion are the toughest of all habits; when they have become second nature, and are supposedly thrown out of the door, they creep in again as stealthily and surely as does first nature. And as they are modified, the alteration first shows itself negatively, in the disintegration of old beliefs, to be replaced by floating, volatile and accidentally snatched up opinions. Of course there has been an enormous increase in the amount of knowledge possessed by mankind, but it does not equal, probably, the increase in the amount of errors and half-truths which have got into circulation. In social and human matters, especially, the development of a critical sense and methods of discriminating judgment has not kept pace with the growth of careless reports and of motives for positive misrepresentation.

What is more important, however, is that so much of knowledge is not knowledge in the ordinary sense of the word, but is "science." The quotation marks are not used disrespectfully, but to suggest the technical character of scientific material. The layman takes certain conclusions which get into circulation to be science. But the scientific inquirer knows that they constitute science only in connection with the methods by which they are reached. Even when true, they are not science in virtue of their correctness, but by reason of the apparatus which is employed in reaching them. This apparatus is so highly specialized that it requires more labor to acquire ability to use and understand it than to get skill in any other instrumentalities possessed by man. Science, in other words, is a highly specialized language, more difficult to learn than any natural language. It is an artificial language, not in the sense of being factitious, but in that of being a work of intricate art, devoted to a particular purpose and not capable of being acquired nor understood in the way in which the mother tongue is learned. It is, indeed, conceivable that sometime methods of instruction will be devised which will enable laymen to read and hear scientific material with comprehension, even when they do not themselves use the apparatus which is science. The latter may then become for large numbers what students of language call a passive, if not an active, vocabulary. But that time is in the future.

For most men, save the scientific workers, science is a mystery in the hands of initiates, who have become adepts in virtue of following ritualistic ceremonies from which the profane herd is excluded. They are fortunate who get as far as a sympathetic appreciation of the methods which give pattern to the complicated apparatus: methods of analytic, experimental observation, mathematical formulation and deduction, constant and elaborate check and test. For most persons, the reality of the apparatus is found only in its embodiments in practical affairs, in mechanical devices and in techniques which touch life as it is lived. For them, electricity is *known* by means of the telephones, bells and lights they use, by the generators and magnetos in the automobiles they drive, by the trolley cars in which they ride. The physiology and biology they are acquainted with is that they have learned in taking precautions against germs and from the physicians they depend upon for health. The science of what might be supposed to be closest to them, of human nature, was for them an esoteric mystery until it was applied in advertising, salesmanship and personnel selection and management, and until, through psychiatry, it spilled over into life and popular consciousness, through its bearings upon "nerves," the morbidities and common forms of crankiness which make it difficult for persons to get along with one another and with themselves. Even now, popular psychology is a mass of cant, of slush and of superstition worthy of the most flourishing days of the medicine man.

Meanwhile the technological application of the complex apparatus which is science has revolutionized the conditions under which associated life goes on. This may be known as a fact which is stated in a proposition and assented to. But it is not known in the sense that men understand it. They do not know it as they know some machine which they operate, or as they know electric light and steam locomotives. They do not understand *how* the change has gone on nor *how* it affects their conduct. Not understanding its "how," they cannot use and control its manifestations. They undergo the consequences, they are affected by them. They cannot manage them, though some are fortunate enough—what is commonly called good fortune—to be able to exploit some phase of the process for their own personal profit. But even the most shrewd and successful man does not in any analytic and systematic way—in a way worthy to compare with the knowledge which he has won in lesser affairs by means of the stress of experience—know the system within which he operates. Skill and ability work within a framework which we have not created and do not comprehend. Some occupy strategic positions which give them advance information of forces that affect the market; and by training and an innate turn that way they have acquired a special technique which enables them to use the vast impersonal tide to turn their own wheels. They can dam the current here and release it there. The current itself is as much beyond them as was ever the river by the side of which some ingenious mechanic, employing a knowledge which was transmitted to him, erected his sawmill to make boards of trees which he had not grown. That within limits those successful in affairs have knowledge and skill is not to be doubted. But such knowledge goes relatively but little further than that of the competent skilled operator who manages a machine. It suffices to employ the conditions which are before him. Skill enables him to turn the flux of events this way or that in his own neighborhood. It gives him no control of the flux.

Why should the public and its officers, even if the latter are termed statesmen, be wiser and more effective? The prime condition of a democratically organized public is a kind of knowledge and insight which does not yet exist. In its absence, it would be the height of absurdity to try to tell what it would be like if it existed. But some of the conditions which must be fulfilled if it is to exist can be indicated. We can borrow that much from the spirit and method of science even if we are ignorant of it as a specialized apparatus. An obvious requirement is freedom of social inquiry and of distribution of its conclusions. The notion that men may be free in their thought even when they are not in its expression and dissemination has been sedulously propagated. It had its origin in the idea of a mind complete in itself, apart from action and from objects. Such a consciousness presents in fact the spectacle of mind deprived of its normal functioning, because it is baffled by the actualities in connection with which alone it is truly mind, and is driven back into secluded and impotent revery.

There can be no public without full publicity in respect to all consequences which concern it. Whatever obstructs and restricts publicity, limits and distorts public opinion and checks and distorts thinking on social affairs. Without freedom of expression, not even methods of social inquiry can be developed. For tools can be evolved and perfected only in operation; in application to observing, reporting and organizing actual subject-matter; and this application cannot occur save through free and systematic communication. The early history of physical knowledge, of Greek conceptions of natural phenomena, proves how inept become the conceptions of the best endowed minds when those ideas are elaborated apart from the closest contact with the events which they purport to state and explain. The ruling ideas and methods of the human sciences are in much the same condition to-day. They are also evolved on the basis of past gross observations, remote from constant use in regulation of the material of new observations.

The belief that thought and its communication are now free simply because legal restrictions which once obtained have been done away with is absurd. Its currency perpetuates the infantile state of social knowledge. For it blurs recognition of our central need to possess conceptions which are used as tools of directed inquiry and which are tested, rectified and caused to grow in actual use. No man and no mind was ever emancipated merely by being left alone. Removal of formal limitations is but a negative condition; positive freedom is not a state but an act which involves methods and instrumentalities for control of conditions. Experience shows that sometimes the sense of external oppression, as by censorship, acts as a challenge and arouses intellectual energy and excites courage. But a belief in intellectual freedom where it does not exist contributes only to complacency in virtual enslavement, to sloppiness, superficiality and recourse to sensations as a substitute for ideas: marked traits of our present estate with respect to social knowledge. On one hand, thinking deprived of its normal course takes refuge in academic specialism, comparable in its way to what is called scholasticism. On the other hand, the physical agencies of publicity which exist in such abundance are utilized in ways which constitute a large part of the present meaning of publicity: advertising, propaganda, invasion of private life, the "featuring" of passing incidents in a way which violates all the moving logic of continuity, and which leaves us with those isolated intrusions and shocks which are the essence of "sensations."

It would be a mistake to identify the conditions which limit free communication and circulation of facts and ideas, and which thereby arrest and pervert social thought or inquiry, merely with overt forces which are obstructive. It is true that those who have ability to manipulate social relations for their own advantage have to be reckoned with. They have an uncanny instinct for detecting whatever intellectual tendencies even remotely threaten to encroach upon their control. They have developed an extraordinary facility in enlisting upon their side the inertia, prejudices and emotional partisanship of the masses by use of a technique which impedes free inquiry and expression. We seem to be approaching a state of government by hired promoters of opinion called publicity agents. But the more serious enemy is deeply concealed in hidden entrenchments.

Emotional habituations and intellectual habitudes on the part of the mass of men create the conditions of which the exploiters of sentiment and opinion only take advantage. Men have got used to an experimental method in physical and technical matters. They are still afraid of it in human concerns. The fear is the more efficacious because like all deep-lying fears it is covered up and disguised by all kinds of rationalizations. One of its commonest forms is a truly religious idealization of, and reverence for, established institutions; for example in our own politics, the Constitution, the Supreme Court, private property, free contract and so on. The words "sacred" and "sanctity" come readily to our lips when such things come under discussion. They testify to the religious aureole which protects the institutions. If "holy" means that which is not to be approached nor touched, save with ceremonial precautions and by specially anointed officials, then such things are holy in contemporary political life. As supernatural matters have progressively been left high and dry upon a secluded beach, the actuality of religious taboos has more and more gathered about secular institutions, especially those connected with the nationalistic state.[2] Psychiatrists have discovered that one of the commonest causes of mental disturbance is an underlying fear of which the subject is not aware, but which leads to withdrawal from reality and to unwillingness to think things through. There is a social pathology which works powerfully against effective inquiry into social institutions and conditions. It manifests itself in a thousand ways; in querulousness, in impotent drifting, in uneasy snatching at distractions, in idealization of the long established, in a facile optimism assumed as a cloak, in riotous glorification of things "as they are," in intimidation of all dissenters—ways which depress and dissipate thought all the more effectually because they operate with subtle and unconscious pervasiveness.

The backwardness of social knowledge is marked in its division into independent and insulated branches of learning. Anthropology, history, sociology, morals, economics, political science, go their own ways without constant and systematized fruitful interaction. Only in appearance is there a similar division in physical knowledge. There is continuous cross-fertilization between astronomy, physics, chemistry and the biological sciences. Discoveries and improved methods are so recorded and organized that constant exchange and intercommunication take place. The isolation of the humane subjects from one another is connected with their aloofness from physical knowledge. The mind still draws a sharp separation between the world in which man lives and the life of man in and by that world, a cleft reflected in the separation of man himself into a body and a mind, which, it is currently supposed, can be known and dealt with apart. That for the past three centuries energy should have gone chiefly into physical inquiry, beginning with the things most remote from man such as heavenly bodies, was to have been expected. The history of the physical sciences reveals a certain order in which they developed. Mathematical tools had to be employed before a new astronomy could be constructed. Physics advanced when ideas worked out in connection with the solar system were used to describe happenings on the earth. Chemistry waited on the advance of physics; the sciences of living things required the material and methods of physics and chemistry in order to make headway. Human psychology ceased to be chiefly speculative opinion only when biological and physiological conclusions were available. All this is natural and seemingly inevitable. Things which had the most outlying and indirect connection with human interests had to be mastered in some degree before inquiries could competently converge upon man himself.

Nevertheless the course of development has left us of this age in a plight. When we say that a subject of science is technically specialized, or that it is highly "abstract," what we practically mean is that it is not conceived in terms of its bearing upon human life. All *merely* physical knowledge is technical, couched in a technical vocabulary communicable only to the few. Even physical knowledge which does affect human conduct, which does modify what we do and undergo, is also technical and remote in the degree in which its bearings are not understood and used. The sunlight, rain, air and soil have always entered in visible ways into human experience; atoms and molecules and cells and most other things with which the sciences are occupied affect us, but not visibly. Because they enter life and modify experience in imperceptible ways, and their consequences are not realized, speech about them is technical; communication is by means of peculiar symbols. One would think, then, that a fundamental and ever-operating aim would be to translate knowledge of the subject-matter of physical conditions into terms which are generally understood, into signs denoting human consequences of services and disservices rendered. For ultimately all consequences which enter human life depend upon physical conditions; they can be understood and mastered only as the latter are taken into account. One would think, then, that any state of affairs which tends to render the things of the environment unknown and incommunicable by human beings in terms of their own activities and sufferings would be deplored as a disaster, that it would be felt to be intolerable, and to be put up with only as far as it is, at any given time, inevitable.

But the facts are to the contrary. Matter and the material are words which in the minds of many convey a note of disparagement. They are taken to be foes of whatever is of ideal value in life, instead of as conditions of its manifestation and sustained being. In consequence of this division, they do become in fact enemies, for whatever is consistently kept apart from human values depresses thought and renders values sparse and precarious in fact. There are even some who regard the materialism and dominance of commercialism of modern life as fruits of undue devotion to physical science, not seeing that the split between man and nature, artificially made by a tradition which originated before there was understanding of the physical conditions that are the medium of human activities, is the benumbing factor. The most influential form of the divorce is separation between pure and applied science. Since "application" signifies recognized bearing upon human experience and well-being, honor of what is "pure" and contempt for what is "applied" has for its outcome a science which is remote and technical, communicable only to specialists, and a conduct of human affairs which is haphazard, biased, unfair in distribution of values. What is applied and employed as the alternative to knowledge in regulation of society is ignorance, prejudice, class-interest and accident. Science is converted into knowledge in its honorable and emphatic sense *only* in application. Otherwise it is truncated, blind, distorted. When it is then applied, it is in ways which explain the unfavorable sense so often attached to "application" and the "utilitarian": namely, use for pecuniary ends to the profit of a few.

At present, the application of physical science is rather *to* human concerns than *in* them. That is, it is external, made in the interests of its consequences for a possessing and acquisitive class. Application *in* life would signify that science was absorbed and distributed; that it was the instrumentality of that common understanding and thorough communication which is the precondition of the existence of a genuine and effective public. The use of science to regulate industry and trade has gone on steadily. The scientific revolution of the seventeenth century was the precursor of the industrial revolution of the eighteenth and nineteenth. In consequence, man has suffered the impact of an enormously enlarged control of physical energies without any corresponding ability to control himself and his own affairs. Knowledge divided against itself, a science to whose incompleteness is added an artificial split, has played its part in generating enslavement of men, women and children in factories in which they are animated machines to tend inanimate machines. It has maintained sordid slums, flurried and discontented careers, grinding poverty and luxurious wealth, brutal exploitation of nature and man in times of peace and high explosives and noxious gases in times of war. Man, a child in understanding of himself, has placed in his hands physical tools of incalculable power. He plays with them like a child, and whether they work harm or good is largely a matter of accident. The instrumentality becomes a master and works fatally as if possessed of a will of its own—not because it has a will but because man has not.

The glorification of "pure" science under such conditions is a rationalization of an escape; it marks a construction of an asylum of refuge, a shirking of responsibility. The true purity of knowledge exists not when it is uncontaminated by contact with use and service. It is wholly a moral matter, an affair of honesty, impartiality and generous breadth of intent in search and communication. The adulteration of knowledge is due not to its use, but to vested bias and prejudice, to one-sidedness of outlook, to vanity, to conceit of possession and authority, to contempt or disregard of human concern in its use. Humanity is not, as was once thought, the end for which all things were formed; it is but a slight and feeble thing, perhaps an episodic one, in the vast stretch of the universe. But for man, man is the centre of interest and the measure of importance. The magnifying of the physical realm at the cost of man is but an abdication and a flight. To make physical science a rival of human interests is bad enough, for it forms a diversion of energy which can ill be afforded. But the evil does not stop there. The ultimate harm is that the understanding by man of his own affairs and his ability to direct them are sapped at their root when knowledge of nature is disconnected from its human function.

It has been implied throughout that knowledge is communication as well as understanding. I well remember the saying of a man, uneducated from the standpoint of the schools, in speaking of certain matters: "Sometime they will be found out and not only found out, but they will be known." The schools may suppose that a thing is known when it is found out. My old friend was aware that a thing is fully known only when it is published, shared, socially accessible. Record and communication are indispensable to knowledge. Knowledge cooped up in a private consciousness is a myth, and knowledge of social phenomena is peculiarly dependent upon dissemination, for only by distribution can such knowledge be either obtained or tested. A fact of community life which is not spread abroad so as to be a common possession is a contradiction in terms. Dissemination is something other than scattering at large. Seeds are sown, not by virtue of being thrown out at random, but by being so distributed as to take root and have a chance of growth. Communication of the results of social inquiry is the same thing as the formation of public opinion. This marks one of the first ideas framed in the growth of political democracy as it will be one of the last to be fulfilled. For public opinion is judgment which is formed and entertained by those who constitute the public and is about public affairs. Each of the two phases imposes for its realization conditions hard to meet.

Opinions and beliefs concerning the public presuppose effective and organized inquiry. Unless there are methods for detecting the energies which are at work and tracing them through an intricate network of interactions to their consequences, what passes as public opinion will be "opinion" in its derogatory sense rather than truly public, no matter how widespread the opinion is. The number who share error as to fact and who partake of a false belief measures power for harm. Opinion casually formed and formed under the direction of those who have something at stake in having a lie believed can be *public* opinion only in name. Calling it by this name, acceptance of the name as a kind of warrant, magnifies its capacity to lead action estray. The more who share it, the more injurious its influence. Public opinion, even if it happens to be correct, is intermittent when it is not the product of methods of investigation and reporting constantly at work. It appears only in crises. Hence its "rightness" concerns only an immediate emergency. Its lack of continuity makes it wrong from the standpoint of the course of events. It is as if a physician were able to deal for the moment with an emergency in disease but could not adapt his treatment of it to the underlying conditions which brought it about. He may then "cure" the disease—that is, cause its present alarming symptoms to subside—but he does not modify its causes; his treatment may even affect them for the worse. Only continuous inquiry, continuous in the sense of being connected as well as persistent, can provide the material of enduring opinion about public matters.

There is a sense in which "opinion" rather than knowledge, even under the most favorable circumstances, is the proper term to use—namely, in the sense of judgment, estimate. For in its strict sense, knowledge can refer only to what *has* happened and been done. What is still *to be* done involves a forecast of a future still contingent, and cannot escape the liability to error in judgment involved in all anticipation of probabilities. There may well be honest divergence as to policies to be pursued, even when plans spring from knowledge of the same facts. But genuinely public policy cannot be generated unless it be informed by knowledge, and this knowledge does not exist except when there is systematic, thorough, and well-equipped search and record.

Moreover, inquiry must be as nearly contemporaneous as possible; otherwise it is only of antiquarian interest. Knowledge of history is evidently necessary for connectedness of knowledge. But history which is not brought down close to the actual scene of events leaves a gap and exercises influence upon the formation of judgments about the public interest only by guess-work about intervening events. Here, only too conspicuously, is a limitation of the existing social sciences. Their material comes too late, too far after the event, to enter effectively into the formation of public opinion about the immediate public concern and what is to be done about it.

A glance at the situation shows that the physical and external means of collecting information in regard to what is happening in the world have far outrun the intellectual phase of inquiry and organization of its results. Telegraph, telephone, and now the radio, cheap and quick mails, the printing press, capable of swift reduplication of material at low cost, have attained a remarkable development. But when we ask what sort of material is recorded and how it is organized, when we ask about the intellectual form in which the material is presented, the tale to be told is very different. "News" signifies something which has just happened, and which is new just because it deviates from the old and regular. But its *meaning* depends upon relation to what it imports, to what its social consequences are. This import cannot be determined unless the new is placed in relation to the old, to what has happened and been integrated into the course of events. Without coordination and consecutiveness, events are not events, but mere occurrences, intrusions; an event implies that out of which a happening proceeds. Hence even if we discount the influence of private interests in procuring suppression, secrecy and misrepresentation, we have here an explanation of the triviality and "sensational" quality of so much of what passes as news. The catastrophic, namely, crime, accident, family rows, personal clashes and conflicts, are the most obvious forms of breaches of continuity; they supply the element of shock which is the strictest meaning of sensation; they are the *new* par excellence, even though only the date of the newspaper could inform us whether they happened last year or this, so completely are they isolated from their connections.

So accustomed are we to this method of collecting, recording and presenting social changes, that it may well sound ridiculous to say that a genuine social science would manifest its reality in the daily press, while learned books and articles supply and polish tools of inquiry. But the inquiry which alone can furnish knowledge as a precondition of public judgments must be contemporary and quotidian. Even if social sciences as a specialized apparatus of inquiry were more advanced than they are, they would be comparatively impotent in the office of directing opinion on matters of concern to the public as long as they are remote from application in the daily and unremitting assembly and interpretation of "news."

On the other hand, the tools of social inquiry will be clumsy as long as they are forged in places and under conditions remote from contemporary events.

What has been said about the formation of ideas and judgments concerning the public apply as well to the distribution of the knowledge which makes it an effective possession of the members of the public. Any separation between the two sides of the problem is artificial. The discussion of propaganda and propagandism would alone, however, demand a volume, and could be written only by one much more experienced than the present writer. Propaganda can accordingly only be mentioned, with the remark that the present situation is one unprecedented in history. The political forms of democracy and quasi-democratic habits of thought on social matters have compelled a certain amount of public discussion and at least the simulation of general consultation in arriving at political decisions. Representative government must at least seem to be founded on public interests as they are revealed to public belief. The days are past when government can be carried on without any pretense of ascertaining the wishes of the governed. In theory, their assent must be secured. Under the older forms, there was no need to muddy the sources of opinion on political matters. No current of energy flowed from them. To-day the judgments popularly formed on political matters are so important, in spite of all factors to the contrary, that there is an enormous premium upon all methods which affect their formation.

The smoothest road to control of political conduct is by control of opinion. As long as interests of pecuniary profit are powerful, and a public has not located and identified itself, those who have this interest will have an unresisted motive for tampering with the springs of political action in all that affects them. Just as in the conduct of industry and exchange generally the technological factor is obscured, deflected and defeated by "business," so specifically in the management of publicity. The gathering and sale of subject-matter having a public import is part of the existing pecuniary system. Just as industry conducted by engineers on a factual techno-logical basis would be a very different thing from what it actually is, so the assembling and reporting of news would be a very different thing if the genuine interests of reporters were permitted to work freely.

One aspect of the matter concerns particularly the side of dissemination. It is often said, and with a great appearance of truth, that the freeing and perfecting of inquiry would not have any especial effect. For, it is argued, the mass of the reading public is not interested in learning and assimilating the results of accurate investigation. Unless these are read, they cannot seriously affect the thought and action of members of the public; they remain in secluded library alcoves, and are studied and understood only by a few intellectuals. The objection is well taken save as the potency of art is taken into account. A technical high-brow presentation would appeal only to those technically high-brow; it would not be news to the masses. Presentation is fundamentally important, and presentation is a question of art. A newspaper which was only a daily edition of a quarterly journal of sociology or political science would undoubtedly possess a limited circulation and a narrow influence. Even at that, however, the mere existence and accessibility of such material would have some regulative effect. But we can look much further than that. The material would have such an enormous and widespread human bearing that its bare existence would be an irresistible invitation to a presentation of it which would have a direct popular appeal. The freeing of the artist in literary presentation, in other words, is as much a precondition of the desirable creation of adequate opinion on public matters as is the freeing of social inquiry. Men's conscious life of opinion and judgment often proceeds on a superficial and trivial plane. But their lives reach a deeper level. The function of art has always been to break through the crust of conventionalized and routine consciousness. Common things, a flower, a gleam of moonlight, the song of a bird, not things rare and remote, are means with which the deeper levels of life are touched so that they spring up as desire and thought. This process is art. Poetry, the drama, the novel, are proofs that the problem of presentation is not insoluble. Artists have always been the real purveyors of news, for it is not the outward happening in itself which is new, but the kindling by it of emotion, perception and appreciation.

We have but touched lightly and in passing upon the conditions which must be fulfilled if the Great Society is to become a Great Community; a society in which the ever-expanding and intricately ramifying consequences of associated activities shall be known in the full sense of that word, so that an organized, articulate Public comes into being. The highest and most difficult kind of inquiry and a subtle, delicate, vivid and responsive art of communication must take possession of the physical machinery of transmission and circulation and breathe life into it. When the machine age has thus perfected its machinery it will be a means of life and not its despotic master. Democracy will come into its own, for democracy is a name for a life of free and enriching communion. It had its seer in Walt Whitman. It will have its consummation when free social inquiry is indissolubly wedded to the art of full and moving communication.

NOTES

[LW 2:325–50.]

1. The most adequate discussion of this ideal with which I am acquainted is T. V. Smith's *The Democratic Way of Life*.

2. The religious character of nationalism has been forcibly brought out by Carlton Hayes, in his *Essays on Nationalism*, especially Chap. 4.

The Inclusive Philosophic Idea

(1928)

There are at the present time a considerable number of persons who habitually employ the social as a principle of philosophic reflection and who assign it a force equal and even superior to that ascribed to the physical, vital and mental. There are others, probably a greater number, who decline to take "social" seriously as a category of description and interpretation for purposes of philosophy, and who conceive any attempt so to take it as involving a confusion of anthropology and sociology with metaphysics. The most they would concede is that cultural material may throw light on the genesis and history of human beliefs about ultimate subject-matter. Then it is asserted that it is but a case of the familiar genetic fallacy, the confusion of the history of belief with the nature of that believed, to assign to such an account a place anywhere except within the history of human culture. Such a situation solicits attention; and I desire to state as far as space permits what is the intent of those who attribute genuine philosophic import to the idea of the social.

A start may be conveniently made by noting that associated or conjoint behavior is a universal characteristic of all existences. Knowledge is in terms of related objects and unless it is supposed that relations are a subjective intrusion, or that, *a la* Hume, only *ideas* are associated, relation as the nerve of science correlates with association among things. This fact being noted, we observe that the qualities of things associated are displayed only in association, since in interactions alone are potentialities released and actualized. Furthermore, the manifestation of potentialities varies with the manner and range of association. This statement is only a formal way of calling attention to the fact that we characterize an element, say hydrogen, not only, as the name implies, in terms of its water-forming potentiality but ultimately in terms of consequences effected in a whole range of modes of conjoint behavior.[1]

These considerations being premised, attention fastens upon the fact that the more numerous and varied the forms of association into which anything enters, the better basis we have for describing and understanding it, for the more complex is an association the more fully are potentialities released for observation. Since things present themselves to us in such fashion that narrower and wider ranges, simpler and more complex ones, are readily distinguished, it would appear that metaphysical description and understanding is demarcated as that which has to do with the widest and fullest range of associated activity. And I remark that if the phrase "degrees of reality" can be given an empirically intelligible meaning, that meaning would seem to depend upon following out the line of thought thus suggested.[2] In short, there appears to be a fairly straight road to the conclusion that a just gauge of the adequacy of any philosophic account of things is found in the extent to which that account is based upon taking things in the widest and most complex scale of associations open to observation.

In making this statement I am not unaware that the opposite method has been pursued and is still recommended by philosophers in good repute: namely, a method based on predilection for ultimate and unattached simples, called by various writers essences, data, etc. The question of whether we should begin with the simple or the complex appears to me the most important problem in philosophic method at the present time, cutting under, for example, the traditional distinctions of real and ideal. Or, if it be said that while perforce we are compelled psychologically and practically to begin with the complex, *philosophy* begins only when we have come upon simples, the problem of method still remains. Are these simples isolated and self-sufficient, or are they the results of intellectual analysis, themselves intellectual rather than existential in quality, and therefore of value only in the degree in which they afford us means of arriving at a better understanding of the complex wholes with which we began? Time forbids consideration of this fundamental question. I content myself with observing that the hypothesis that ultimate and detached simples are the only reals for philosophy seems to be the sole logical alternative to the position that the wider and more complex the range of associated interaction with which we deal the more fully is the nature of the object of philosophic thought revealed to us. Hence, the issue as to

method reduces itself to the question whether isolated simples can be asserted without self-contradiction to be ultimate and self-sufficient on their own account. Those who do not accept them as the real, appear committed to the position herein stated.

While the fact of association and of range of associations as determining "degrees of reality" gives us our starting point, it gives *only* a starting point for discussing the value of "social" as a philosophic category. For by the social as a distinctive mode of association is denoted specifically human forms of grouping, and these according to the findings of science appear only late in time. Hence, the objection which readily occurs to mind. The view that "social" in its characteristically human sense is an important category is met with the retort that, on the contrary, it is but a highly special case of association and as such is restricted in significance, humanly interesting of course, but a matter of detail rather than of an important principle. My introductory remarks were intended as an anticipatory reply to such an objection. Association barely by itself is a wholly formal category. It acquires content only by considering the different forms of association which constitute the material of experience. Thus, while it is admitted that society, in the human sense, is a form of association that is restricted in its space-time manifestation, it cannot be placed in contrast with association in general. Its import can be determined not by comparing it with association in its generic formal sense, but only by comparing and contrasting it with other special types of association.

This fact gives what has been said regarding the importance of range and complexity of association as a philosophic measure its special import. If reference to association is to be anything more than a ceremonial and barren act of deference, if it is to be used in an enterprise of philosophic description and understanding, it indicates the necessity of study and analysis of the different modes of association that present themselves in experience. And the implication of our argument is that in such a comparison of definite types of association, the social, in its human sense, is the richest, fullest and most delicately subtle of any mode actually experienced. There is no need to go through the form of discovering, as if for the first time, the different typical modes which are to be compared and contrasted. They have been made familiar enough in the course of thought. Aside from social, whose thoroughgoing admission still awaits adequate acknowledgment, they are the physical, the vital or organic, and the mental. The gist of our problem consists in deciding which of these forms presents the broader and fuller range of associations. Association in general is but a matrix; its filling is the facts of association actually displayed in nature. Indeed, the category of association is but a highly abstract notation of what is formally common to the special modes.

Before coming, however, to this affair of comparison, which constitutes the main topic of this paper, it will be well to clear the ground of certain notions which led to misconstruction and depreciation of the meaning of "social" as a category. A moment ago I referred to the facts of association as they are actually displayed in human life. The reference implied that social facts are themselves natural facts. This implication goes against preconceptions engendered by the common opposition of the physical and the social sciences; by the tacit identification, in other words, of the natural sciences with the purely physical. As far as this idea lingers in the back of the head, social and natural are oppositional conceptions; the attempt to find a key by which to read the cipher of nature in the social is then immediately felt to be absurd; this feeling then operates to effect the contemptuous dismissal of the "social." Denial of opposition between the social and natural is, however, an important element of the *meaning* of "social" as a category; and if anyone is interested in finding out the intent of those who would employ "social" as a philosophic category, that one should begin by asking himself what are the implications of the current separation of natural and social sciences, and whether upon reflection he is willing to stand by them. A denial of the separation is not only possible to a sane mind, but is demanded by any methodological adoption of the principle of continuity, and also, as will be indicated later, by social phenomena themselves. Upon the hypothesis of continuity—if

that is to be termed a hypothesis which cannot be denied without self-contradiction—the social, in spite of whatever may be said regarding the temporal and spatial limitation of its manifestations, furnishes philosophically the inclusive category.

A two-fold harm is wrought by the current separation of social and natural science and by accepting the meaning which attaches to social after it has been thus divorced. The chief point at which philosophy may be of aid in the pursuits of the social sciences lies precisely here. In the degree in which what passes for social science is built upon the notion of a gap between natural and social phenomena, that science is truncated, arbitrary and insecure. An analytic survey of the present status of the social sciences would be needed to justify this remark. But there are only a few sociologists who have ventured as yet to assert that there is something distinctive or unique in social phenomena; so we are met with a paradoxical situation in which social phenomena are isolated from physical and organic considerations and yet are explained in physical, organic or psychological terms instead of in characteristically social terms. In psychology the persisting tradition of a purely individualistic and private subject-matter is to be attributed directly to neglect of the social conditions of mental phenomena, while indirectly this neglect goes back to a separation of social from natural: since only acknowledgment of the continuity of the social and the natural provides the intermediary terms which link psychological phenomena with others. Some forms of behaviorism, in reaction against the unnatural isolation of the physical and mental, merely throw the latter overboard entirely, and reduce them to the terms of the material dealt with in purely physical science. In political science may be noted an oscillation between the adoption of non-natural categories, such as a transcendent "will," and the resolution of political phenomena into physical terms of conflict and adjustment of forces. A recent economic writer has asserted that economic science has so neglected the place of technology in industry that a generation has gone forth which, although "educated" in economic science, is almost wholly ignorant of economic affairs.[3] Technology is evidently a matter that connects directly with the development of physical science; the point, instead of being an incidental one, can be shown to be intimately connected with all the sound objections brought against the abstraction of the "economic man." The economic man cannot be set in his place in social phenomena, in his actual relations to legal, political, technological and other cultural institutions, until these are connected with natural phenomena.

These are but too casual and abbreviated hints of the meaning of the assertion that the performance of the service which philosophy might theoretically render to the social sciences waits upon the frank acknowledgment of the social as a category continuous with and inclusive of the categories of the physical, vital and mental.

This reference to the sciences is not to be regarded, however, as implying an adoption of that conception of philosophy which identifies it exclusively with either an analysis or a synthesis of the premises or results of the special sciences. On the contrary, the sciences themselves are outgrowths of some phase of social culture, from which they derive their instruments, physical and intellectual, and by which their problems and aims are set. The only philosophy that can "criticize" the premises of the special sciences without running the danger of being itself a pseudo-science is that which takes into account the anthropological (in its broadest sense) basis of the sciences, just as the only one that can synthesize their conclusions, without running a like danger, is the one which steps outside these conclusions to place them in the broader context of social life.

In now turning to the main point, the social as a ranking philosophic category, on the ground that it is indicative of the widest and richest range of association empirically accessible (and no apology is offered for basing philosophy upon the empirically manifest rather than upon the occult), it is necessary to point out a certain ambiguity of language which because of brevity of exposition, necessarily attaches to our statement. Social *phenomena* are not of themselves, of course, equivalent to social as a *category*. The latter is derived from the former by means of an intel-

lectual analysis which determines what is their distinctive character. Now I am not here dealing with the important and eventually imperative problem of the category *of* the social, or the determination of the characteristics which constitute the distinguishing nature of the social, but rather with social phenomena *en gross* as comprehending, for philosophic analysis, physical, organic and mental phenomena in a mode of association in which the latter take on new properties and exercise new functions. In other words, I am here implying that social phenomena do as a matter of fact manifest *something* distinctive, and that that something affords the key to a naturalistic account of phenomena baffling philosophic interpretation when it is left out of account. To those who accept this view, the burden of proof as to the value of "social" as a metaphysical category lies upon those who habitually treat its worth as trivial. For what do *they* mean by social phenomena? If social phenomena are not an exemplification upon the widest and most intricate scale of the generic trait of associated behavior or interaction, what do they signify? I see but one kind of answer open to them, covering two alternatives: Either social phenomena are anomalous, an excrescence or intrusion, supervening in an accidental and meaningless way upon other phenomena, or else they have no distinctive import, being in reality *nothing but* physical, vital or psychological phenomena. Does not each of these views contradict the observable traits of social phenomena?

Upon a *prima facie* view, social phenomena take up and incorporate within themselves things associated in the narrower way which we term the physical. It gives a ludicrous result to think of social phenomena merely as lying on top of physical phenomena; such a notion is negated by the most casual observation of the facts. What would social phenomena be without the physical factor of land, including all the natural resources (and obstacles) and forms of energy for which the word "land" stands? What would social phenomena be without the tools and machines by which physical energies are utilized? Or what would they be without physical appliances and apparatus, from clothes and houses to railways, temples and printing-presses? No, it is not the social which is a superficial category. The view is superficial of those who fail to see that in the social the physical is taken up into a wider and more complex and delicate system of interactions so that it takes on new properties by release of potentialities previously confined because of absence of full interaction.

The same consideration applies to the inclusion within the social of the vital or organic. The members of society are living human beings with the characteristics of living creatures; but as they enter into distinctively human associations strictly organic properties are modified and even transformed. Certain physiological factors of sex, of procreation, immaturity and need of care, are assuredly implicated in the functions expressed in family life. But however great the role of animal lust, there is something more in any family association than bare physiological factors. The fact of transformation of the purely organic by inclusion within the scope of human association is so obvious—note the significant case of change of cries into speech—that it has indeed led to belief in the intrusive intervention of unnatural and supernatural factors in order to account for the differences between the animal and the human. The disjunction between the assertion that the human is the merely animal and the assertion that an extraneous force is obtruded is not, however, exhaustive. There remains an alternative which is most fully confirmed by empirical fact, namely that the difference is made when new potentialities are actualized, when the range of interactions that delimits the organic is taken up into the wider and more subtly complex association which forms human society.

Since traits derived from the physical mode have been admitted into philosophy (materialism in other words is at least grudgingly admitted into philosophic companionship); and since organic philosophies, framed on the pattern of vital phenomena, upon conceptions of species, development and purpose, are freely admitted, it seems arbitrary, to say the least, to exclude the social from the role of a legitimate category.

That the mental has a recognized claim to serve as a category of description and interpretation of natural existence is evident in the very existence of idealistic philosophies. There are those who deny the ability of these theories to execute their claim, just as there are those who deny the capacity of the physical and vital to make good. But thought, as well as matter and life, is at least admitted to rank as a respectable figure in the gallery of categories. Now of the mental as of the physical and organic it may be said that it operates as an included factor within social phenomena, since the mental is empirically discernible only where association is manifested in the form of participation and communication. It would therefore appear legitimate to adopt as a hypothesis worthy of being tried out the idea that the ulterior meaning of the mental as well as of the physical and vital is revealed in this form of associational interaction. The implication is not that they have no describable *existence* outside the social, but that in so far as they appear and operate outside of that large interaction which forms the social they do not reveal that full force and import with which it is the traditional business of philosophy to occupy itself.

After this statement of the intent of the enterprise of employing the social as a category, it remains to sketch in a summary fashion a few specimens of its implications which are relevant to the clarification of some outstanding philosophic issues. We may conveniently begin with the matter just referred to, the place of the mental in the existential scheme of things, using for purposes of our discussion as the equivalent of "mental" the fact of *meaning*, whether direct as in cognition of objects, or indirect as in esthetic, affectional and moral relations. The state of philosophic discussion exhibits a dilemma, or rather a trilemma. The mental is viewed (i) as a mysterious intrusion occurring in some unaccountable way in the order of nature; (ii) as illusory, or, in current language, as an epiphenomenon; and (iii) as ontological, whether as a section of being on the same level with the physical section, or as the Being of which so-called physical things are but disguised forms or "appearances." It may be argued that the persistence of the problem and of these widely opposed modes of solution is itself strongly indicative that some factor of the situation, the one which is the key to understanding, has been omitted. In any case, the persistence of these unreconcilable conceptions is a challenge to search for something which will eliminate the scandal of such sharp antagonisms in interpretation. Now when we turn to the social, we find *communication* to be an existential occurrence involved in all distinctively communal life, and we find that communication requires meaning and understanding as conditions of unity or agreement in conjoint behavior. We find, that is, meaning to be not an anomaly nor an accidentally supervening quality but a constitutive ingredient of existential events. We find meaning as a describable, verifiable empirical phenomenon whose genesis, modes and consequences can be concretely examined and traced. It presents itself not as an intrusion, nor as an accidental and impotent iridescence, nor as the reduplication of a structure already inhering in antecedent existence, but as an additive quality realized in the process of wider and more complex interaction of physical and vital phenomena; and as having a distinctive and concretely verifiable office in sustaining and developing a distinctive kind of observable facts, those namely which are termed social. We do not then have to resort to purely metaphysical and dialectical considerations, adopted *ad hoc*, in order to "save" the reality and importance of the mental. The realm of meanings, of mind, is at home, securely located and anchored in an empirically observable order of existence. And this order stands in genetic continuity with physical and vital phenomena, being, indeed, these phenomena taken up into and incorporated within a wider scope of associated interactions. We do not have to read the mental back into the antecedent physical, much less resort to the desperate measure of making it so all-inclusive that the physical is treated as a disguised and illusory "appearance" of the mental. The social affords us an observable instance of a "realm of mind" objective to an individual, by entering into which as a participating member organic activities are transformed into acts having a mental quality.

These considerations are not supposed to demonstrate the truth of the position taken; but they are seriously proposed to indicate a hypothesis which is worthy of trial; as a hypothesis which starts from a *vera causa*, that is, from an empirically verifiable fact, instead of from concepts which have no such observed locus of their own but which are invented simply to account for facts otherwise inexplicable. In the second place, the actual structure of knowledge viewed in relation to the operations by which it is concretely established to be knowledge in the honorific sense, that is as tested and justified, as grounded, instead of as mere opinion and fantastic belief, can be understood only in social terms. By knowledge as grounded I mean belief in relation to evidence that substantiates it. Now the simplest distinction that can be drawn between objects of knowledge in this sense and mere matters of opinion and credulity, or even of thought however internally self-consistent and formally valid, is the distinction between the socially confirmed and the privately entertained. Opinion and theory as long as they are uncommunicated, or as long as, even if communicated and shared, they are unconfirmed in conjoint behavior are at best but candidates for membership within the system of knowledge. To labor this point is to weaken it. It is a truism that science is science because observations, experiments and calculations are so conducted as to be capable of report to others and repetition by others. Now this report and repetition are wholly misconceived when thought of simply as external additions to a thought complete in itself. They signify that thought itself is conceived and developed in such terms as to be capable of communication to others, of understanding by them, and of adoption and utilization in cooperative action. Report, communication, is not a bare emission of thoughts framed and completed in private soliloquy or solipsistic observation. The entire operation of individual experimentation and soliloquizing has been influenced at every point by reference to the social medium in which their results are to be set forth and responded to. Indeed what has been said is an understatement. It is not simply that the characteristic findings of thought cannot pass into knowledge save when framed with reference to social submission and adoption, but that language and thought in their relation to signs and symbols are inconceivable save as ways of achieving concerted action.

In passing, it may also be remarked that the reference to private thought as a *candidate* for knowledge through incorporation into conjoint associated action (which also involves, be it recalled, physical conditions and hence is subject to test by physical consequences), throws light upon and may give the key to another mystery of philosophic speculation—namely the nature of mind as subjective. For the latter when it is interpreted from the standpoint of the social as a category, does not appear as an anomaly, much less as a bogey, an intrusive and wholly undesirable source of error. Thinking and its results present themselves as indeed hypothetical, demanding trial in terms of social action, and hence as subject to error and defeat. But they also offer themselves as having a positive and constructive office. For they are not merely candidates for reception into the social *status quo*, the received and established order of associated behavior; they are rather claimants for a changed social order to be effected in the very action which they promote and by which they are to be tested. Sometimes the claim is narrow, affecting only the behavior of a selected group who are experts in the particular field; sometimes, as in the proposal of new policies, it is wide in the appeal which it virtually makes. But the former type, addressed primarily say to a group of scientific specialists, has a way of expanding; it cannot be kept cooped up; and in any case there is no difference in principle.

In giving illustrations, one is embarrassed by the range of philosophic problems which suggest themselves as receiving illumination and clarification when the social is employed as a category of description and interpretation. We may, however, draw, almost at random, upon the moral field. Consider the recurrent discussion concerning the objectivity of moral distinctions and judgments, with its ceaseless vibration between reduction of them to private preferences, none the less private when they happen to be collectively entertained, and recourse to purely transcendent considerations in order to "secure" their objectivity. It would be dogmatic to assert in this casual allusion that the problem is solved when the social is

used as a category, and the social is seen to incorporate the physical, organic and psychological; but no one can reasonably deny that the whole problem takes on a very different aspect when its elements are placed in this context.[4]

An allied topic concerns the "naturalness" of the moral life of man. Those who assert that it is natural are met by the counter-assertion that such a view reduces the moral life to a strictly animal plane. This sharp disjunction falls to the ground, however, when the distinctive forms of association characteristic of the life of man in social relations are recognized, for this recognition not only admits but asserts that these relations realize new and unique qualities not manifested in the lesser areas of natural association. A generalization of what is involved in this issue is found in a theory familiar to students of the history of thought. A succession of thinkers, from Herder and Kant to Hegel, have asserted that the significance of the history of humanity is found in the struggle of man to emerge from a state in which he was wholly immersed in "nature" to a state in which "spirit" is wholly triumphant, and where triumph involves a sublimated cancellation of the physical and animal. It is submitted that whatever is empirically verifiable in such a doctrine is better stated in terms of the constant remaking of the physical environment and the living organism which occurs when the latter come within the scope of the culture carried in human society. It is a fact rather than a speculation that physical and animal nature are transformed in the process of education and of incorporation in the means and consequences of associated political, legal, religious, industrial, and scientific and artistic institutions. "Spirit" in the doctrine referred to is a transcendent and blind name for something which exhibits itself empirically as that phase of social phenomena called civilization.

The philosophic issues mentioned are cited only as illustrative specimens. They afford at most but a skeleton-like table of contents and a highly incomplete one at that. They are given as indications of a scheme of philosophic description and interpretation that has to be rounded out and filled in in order to realize and to test what is signified by "social" as a philosophic category. It is the historic claim of philosophy that it occupies itself with the ideal of wholes and the whole. It is submitted that either the whole is manifested in concretely empirical ways, and in ways consonant with infinite variety, or else wholeness is but a dialectical speculation. I do not say that the social as we know it *is* the whole, but I do emphatically suggest that it is the widest and richest manifestation of the whole accessible to our observation. As such it is at least the proper point of departure for any more imaginative construings of the whole one may wish to undertake. And in any case it furnishes the terms in which any consistent *empirical* philosophy must speak. Only by whole-hearted adoption of it as a ranking fact and idea can empirical philosophy come into its own, and escape the impotency and one-sidedness which has dogged the traditional sensationalistic empiricism. The commitment of Lockean empiricism to a doctrine that ignored the associative property of all things experienced is the source of that particularistic nominalism whose goal is solipsistic scepticism. In consequence empiricism ceased to be empirical and became a dialectic construction of the implications of absolute particularism. By rebound, it induced recourse to principles of connection extraneously supplied, whether by "synthetic action of thought" or by eternal essences. In the end,

these systems rise or fall with the truth of the empirical particularism against which they have reacted. Thus the social as a category is as important in the critical evaluation of recent systems of thought as it is in direct application to problems of matter, life and mind.

NOTES

[First published in *Monist* 38 (1928): 161–77, from an address to the Eastern Division of the American Philosophical Association at the University of Chicago, December 1927. LW 3:41–54.]

1. In case there is objection to the use of the conceptions of potentiality and actualization, it may be pointed out that the same facts may be stated, though as it seems to me more awkwardly, by saying that things in different modes of association occasion different effects and that our knowledge of them is adequate in the degree in which it includes a broad range of effects due to a variety of associated operations.

2. It is perhaps worth while in passing to note also that such concepts as "levels" and "emergence" seem to be most readily definable upon the basis of this consideration.

3. Tugwell, *Industry's Coming of Age*, p. vii.

4. Compare the treatment of the objectivity of esthetic judgments in the article "On the Genesis of the Aesthetic Categories" by J. H. Tufts, *Decennial Publications of the University of Chicago*, Volume III.

A Critique of American Civilization

(1928)

When Robinson Crusoe sat down to make a debit-credit list of his blessings and his troubles, he did it in order to cheer himself up. One has a feeling that when one is engaged in undertaking a somewhat similar appraisal of our civilization, one is doing something of the same sort, indulging in social apologetics. Nor is this the only embarrassment. A person can put down in black and white his financial resources and liabilities, but the result will not shed light upon his state of health and his intellectual and moral well-being. So it is possible to itemize with more or less accuracy certain gains and losses in American life, and yet not know what they import for the prosperity of our social body. There is for example a great gain, a gain of two hundred and fifty per cent in ten years in the number of students in our secondary schools and colleges. But what does it signify? There is a great increase in crime and disregard of law. But what does it mean? Neither the causes nor the consequences of such gains and losses are apparent, and without an insight into reasons and effects, we can hardly even guess what these things portend for good and ill in our civilization. One foreign visitor says a number of nice things about our country, and another one may pass a number of harsh criticisms. We may agree as to the substantial truth of both statements, and experience a glow of pride at one and a sense of irritation at the other. But what do these things mean? Has either of them got below the surface? I should not feel greater assurance if I tried to strike a balance sheet of gains and losses in American civilization.

Fortunately for me this is not my task. It has been accomplished in various fields by those competent to speak, each in his and her own special territory. Yet when I am called upon to try and sum up and to tell what it all comes to in the direction and quality of American life, I experience a profound misgiving. Where are we going? Toward what are we moving? The value of any changing thing lies in its consequences, and the consequences of the present conditions and forces are not here. To make an evaluation is to prophesy, and where is there the astronomer who can predict the future of our social system?

I should not, however, indulge in the expression of these doubts if they were merely personal misgivings. They seem rather to be indicative, evidential, in a peculiar way of the state and prospects of American civilization. By this I mean something more than the platitude that we are in a state of social transition and flux. I mean in the first place, that when we list items of gain and loss in opposite columns, we find paradoxes, contradictions of extraordinary range and depth; and in the second place, that these contradictions are evidence of what seems to be the most marked trait of our present state—namely, its inner tension and conflict. If ever there was a house of civilization divided within itself and against itself, it is our own today. If one were to take only some symptoms and ignore others, one might make either a gloomy or a glowing report, and each with equal justice—as far as each went.

If one looks at the overt and outer phenomena, at what I may call the public and official, the externally organized, side of our life, my own feeling about it would be one of discouragement. We seem to find everywhere a hardness, a tightness, a clamping down of the lid, a regimentation and standardization, a devotion to efficiency and prosperity of a mechanical and quantitative sort. If one looks exclusively at the activities of a great number of individuals in different spheres (and by individuals I mean voluntary groups as well), there is a scene of immense vitality that is stimulating to the point of inspiration. This contradiction between the inner and the outer, the private and the public, phases of our civilization, seems to be its most significant feature; the sense of its existence and scope furnishes the gist of all I have to say.

One finds, I think, the fact of this opposition reflected, at least implicitly, in all the articles that report upon special phases of our life. Let me note, almost at random, some of its obviously visible signs. In domestic politics, there is an extraordinary apathy, indicated not only by abstention from the polls, but in the seemingly calm indifference with which the public takes the revelation of corruption in high places. On the other hand, there was never previously so much publicity, so much investigation and exposure having a genuinely scientific quality. And unless one thinks that the cynical indifference of the public is an evidence of thorough-going corruption not merely of some officials and business men, but of the heart of the American people, there is ground for thinking that the prevailing attitude toward political life is itself an indication of a growing sense that our reliance and hope is being increasingly put on agencies that lie deeper than the political; that there is a feeling, as yet inarticulate and groping, that the real needs of the American people must be met by means more fundamental than our traditional political institutions put at our disposal. If, and as far as, our political apathy is due to widespread distrust of the reality, under present conditions, of existing political forms, there is ground for belief that social forces that are much more truly characteristic of our social life than is our inherited political machinery are destined to change the latter, when there will be a revival of political interest, and only then.

The domestic political scene presents a still more obvious contradiction in connection with the matter of intolerance. Never have the forces of bigotry and intolerance been so well organized and so active. It is enough to refer to the Ku Klux Klan, not yet negligible. On the other hand, for the first time in history there is a possibility of the election of a Roman Catholic for the office of the presidency. This contradiction may not seem very significant, but to me at least it seems deeply symptomatic of our entire condition, that which I have called inner division and tension. The very factors that have produced the tightening up and solidifying of the forces of reaction are also producing a more conscious and determined liberal attitude. Organization and outer power still lie with the former; but the latter is in process of fermentation and inner growth, and the future may be on its side. So viewed, I would assign to the fact just cited a significance that taken in isolation it does not possess.

A more important if vaguer illustration of the point is found in the whole situation as regards freedom of thought and speech. It goes without saying that never before in our history have there been such flagrant violations of what one would have supposed to be fundamental in the American system. It is customary to refer this particular reenforcement of reaction to the war. Undoubtedly the reference is correct, and yet the war was an opportunity rather than the decisive cause. The sources lie further back in the development of our regime of control of economic forces. On the other hand, never was the spirit of self-criticism so alert and penetrating. If our complacency has grown more strident and self-conscious, so has our spirit of self-examination and discrimination. This fact has been noted sufficiently in special articles so that there is no need to dwell upon it or cite evidence. If we are our own "best pals" we are now also our own "severest critics." Public and organized censorship and repression has its counterpart in spontaneous and private exploration and exhibition of shortcomings and evils. To all appearance, the age of muckraking has disappeared. But by contrast, that outburst was comparatively external and superficial. It dealt with specific and outward ailments. If the fervor of exposure and condemnation that marked the nineties has vanished, it is also true that the critical spirit has turned inward and is now concerned with underlying intellectual and moral causes.

As I recently read Arthur Garfield Hays' *Let Freedom Ring*, I was of two minds. One was of profound shame and depression that we had so far departed from the principles that were supposed to be the foundation of our political and social structure. But then there is the book itself and still more there is the gallant fight for freedom it records. And I wondered whether, if any previous time exhibited such a record of suppression, it also manifested any more courageous and unremitting battle for the maintenance of civil liberties. And it occurred to me that the consolidation of the energy of the forces of reaction was perhaps a sign of their well-grounded fear that after all, contrary social forces were working against them. After all, blacklists and "key-sheets" have some occasion, and the ridiculous fear of the Bolshevizing of our country may be a symptom that those in power are not entirely at ease in their Zion.

In international matters, there is, it seems to me, a like contradiction. That imperialistic policy is now, in an economic form, our domi-nating note seems to me too evident to need proof. But, in spite of the pious words of the Hughes-Coolidge regime, it is becoming recognized for what it is. Only occasionally perhaps does the protest due to its recognition find effective expression in action, as it did in the case of Mexico noted in the article by Norman Thomas. But nevertheless we are not so somnolent as we once were. Our economic policy in Nicaragua goes marching on with the support of marines; but there was a time when similar interventions (with apologies to our authorities for not calling them "interpositions") went almost without notice, beyond the pious hope that we were instilling some decent fear of God in a lot of semi-savages. Perception of great social changes usually lags far behind the changes themselves, so far behind that it is incapable of modifying their operation. But perception of the growth of economic imperialism is not perhaps so far behind the fact, and consequently so important, as has been the case in other matters. There are some grounds for hoping that it is nearly enough up to date so as to exercise a contemporary influence.

That an immediate effect of the war and of the "peace" in which it issued was to intensify and make more conscious our international isolation, there can hardly be a doubt. Silly as it is, the mere word "international" is suspect in many quarters; it smells of Russia and the Third International. While "Americanization" processes are not so drastic as they were a few years ago, the older immigrants to this country, who arrogate to themselves the title of "Americans," still display fear of late comers. Persons are blacklisted for no greater crime than favoring the outlawry of war or adherence of the United States to the World Court. But on the other side individuals have a much wider and more sympathetic interest in foreign affairs than ever before, and numerous voluntary associations stimulate and feed the interest. If overtly and outwardly we are more nationalistic than at any previous time, we are also, as far as intellectual and moral currents are concerned, more internationally inclined. The entire peace movement is less negative, less merely anti-war and more bent on establishing positive international cooperation. As the chapter on "Advances in the Quest for Peace" notes, it is also much more realistic. While, during the war, a man might find himself in jail for a too emphatic declaration that the causes of the war were economic rivalries, that is now a commonplace of discussion from admirals to the man in the street. It is a great gain that intelligent people now know where to look, what to give attention to, in all cases of international friction. While there is not adequate evidence that this enlightenment is sufficient to withstand organized propaganda in the case of a crisis, it is still true, I think, that glittering generalities about freedom, justice, and an end to all war as the objectives of a war have lost much of their force.

It has long been a moot question how civilization is to be measured. What is the gauge of its status and degree of advance? Shall it be judged by its *élite*, by its artistic and scientific products, by the depth and fervor of its religious devotion? Or by the level of the masses, by the amount of ease and security attained by the common man? Was pre-revolutionary Russia at the acme of European civilization because of its achievements in literature, music and the drama? Or will the new Russia if it succeeds, even at the expense of retrogression in these matters, in elevating the life of the masses, stand at a higher level? As between the two sides to the controversy, there is no common premise, and hence no possibility of a solution. One side can claim to stand for ideal attainments as the ultimate measure and accuse the other side of having a low and merely materialistic criterion. This other side can retort with a charge of aristocratic harsh indifference to the well-being and security of the great number to whom the struggle for life is all important, and inquire what is the value of an art and a science from which most are excluded, or of a religion that for the many is merely a dream of a remote bliss compensatory to the suffering of present evils.

The question is evidently crucial for an appraisal of gains in American civilization. From what base line shall we set out to measure? Those who engage in glorification of American life uniformly point to the fact that the lot of the common man (however poor it may still be from an absolute standard) is at least better than that of his fellow in other countries or at other epochs.

If we ask for the intellectual and ideal content of this common life, the tale is not so reassuring. Even when we have discounted the exaggerations of the now familiar denunciations of the yokelry and the booboisie, enough truth remains to be depressing. It would probably be easy to fill my allotted space with evidences of the triviality and superficiality of life as it is lived by the masses. It is perhaps enough to refer for a good-humored depiction of the scene to Charles Merz's *The Great American Band Wagon*. And if we take achievements in higher culture as our standard of valuation, not even the most optimistic can give our civilization a very high rating. To take one illustration, our physical plant for scientific study is far superior to that of any European country; measured by capital invested, it might even be equal to that of all Europe. The results hardly correspond. The pressure toward immediate commercial application is great, and the popular hero is the inventor, not the investigator and discoverer. Burbank and Edison are names to conjure with, while those of Willard Gibbs and Michelson are faint rumors on a thin air.

The dispute concerns ultimate standards, and hence, as has been said, cannot be settled—except by taking sides. But one can say that in the end the value of elevation of the common man in security, ease and comfort of living is to be viewed as an opportunity for a possible participation in more ideal values; and that there is something defective, to say the least, in a civilization wherein achievements in the former do not terminate in a general participation in spiritual values. To bring about opportunities is to have done much; but if the opportunities are not utilized, the actual outcome is a reproach and condemnation. Here then is the issue: Admitting that our civilization displays a relative superiority in its material basis, what are we likely to build upon it in religion, science and art, and in the amenities and graces of life?

The question is framed with respect to the future. There is some truth in the old saying that we have been too occupied with the material conquest of a continent to occupy ourselves with higher things. But since the former task is fairly accomplished, we may well ask ourselves how it stands with the other part of the saying: that when we get around to it, we shall make "culture hum"? The distinctive pioneer virtues have departed with the pioneer age. Where is the enormous and vital energy that marked this age now directing itself? Survey of the immediate scene would seem to indicate that much of it is going into a frenzied money-making, an equally frenzied material enjoyment of the money that is made, and an imitative "having a good time" on the part of those who haven't made much money. There are those who think that in conquering a continent, our own souls have been subdued by the material fruits of the victory. Prosperity is our God.

The case has been so put as to suggest the worst possibility. There is much to be said on the other side; there are many hopeful signs that might be pointed to. In a series devoted to gains in American civilization, I seem to be emphasizing losses. Yet what has been said may be relevant in at least bringing to the fore the ultimate problem, that of the measure of gain and loss. It is also tributary, I think, to my main point—that we are in the throes of an inner conflict and division. For the situation taken at its worst is that of the overt and public phase of our life, while the things that may be set forth on the other side of the account have to do with forces that are as yet unorganized and inchoate. One may point to our newspaper press and to the type of periodical that one finds on the news-stands as representing the organized aspect of our intellectual life in its public impact. A tabloid, with all that that implies, having a circulation of over a million—almost three times that of the other style of papers—and the multitudes of "confession" magazines, would then seem to tell a large part of the story. But on the other hand there is the unprecedented appearance and astonishing popular welcome of books that popularize and humanize serious subjects. I find this fact to be illustrative of something real and vital which is stirring, and which in the outcome may have a potency greater than that of the factors externally dominant. As an isolated fact, it proves nothing. As a symptom, it is perhaps highly significant. The spontaneous local developments of interest in painting, music, drama, and the vogue of poetry go deeper. "Best sellers" are certainly of much higher average type than a generation ago.

Reference to the educational situation is pertinent at this point. It is unnecessary to review what has already been said by Mr. Sharp in his article. Yet the rapid and intense extension of interest and activity in adult, parental and pre-school education, in education at both ends of the scale, is an indication that cannot be ignored, any more than can the remarkable development of progressive schools. The most extraordinary matter, however, is the expansion of secondary and higher education. No one can tell its cause or import, but in velocity and extent it marks nothing less than a revolutionary change. It used to be said that only one in twenty of the elementary pupils found their way into high school, and only one in a hundred into college. Now the number in the lower schools is only five times that in the secondary schools, and there is one student in a college to twenty in the elementary. And the astonishing thing is that the expansion has occurred at an accelerating rate since 1910. There are for example at least six times as many students in colleges and professional schools as there were thirty years ago, and tenfold more in secondary schools. Let the worst possible be said about the quality of the education received, and it remains true that we are in the presence of one of the most remarkable social phenomena of history. It is impossible to gauge the release of potentialities contained in this change; it is incredible that it should not eventuate in the future in a corresponding intellectual harvest. While, as I have said, it is impossible to determine its causes, it at least shows that we are finally beginning to make good our ideal of equal educational opportunity for all. I believe that a considerable part of the development is due to the rise in status of immigrants of the second and third generation; and in spite of all that is said in depreciation of those from southern and southeastern Europe, I believe that when our artistic renascence comes, it will proceed largely from this source.

The reverse side of the pattern is, of course, the intensification of efforts of special interests to control public and private education for their own ends, mainly under the guise of a nationalistic patriotism. The recent revelations of the efforts of the Electric Light and Power Companies to utilize the schools are much in point. I know of nothing more significant than the fact that the instructions sent out to publicity agents for manufacturing public opinion and sentiment uniformly combine "press and schools" as the agencies to be influenced. In some respects these revelations seem to me more sinister than those of the oil scandals, in that they represent an attempt at corruption of the source of public action. In any case, we have a striking instance of what I have called our inner conflict and tension. Our democracy is at least far enough advanced so that there is a premium put on the control of popular opinion and beliefs. There was a time in history when the few did not have to go through the form of consulting the opinion of the many. Government by press agents, by "counsellors of public relations," by propaganda in press and school, is at least evidence that that time has passed. We have enough government by public opinion so that it is necessary for the economic powers that govern to strive to regulate the agencies by which that opinion is created.

If we ask which forces are to win, those that are organized, that know what they are after and that take systematic means to accomplish their end, or those that are spontaneous, private and scattered—like those that have resulted in the expansion of our higher school population—we have, I think, the problem of our civilization before us. To answer the problem is to engage in prophecy that may well be gratuitous. It goes back to faith rather than to proof by sight and touch. Yet there *are* reasons for hoping for a favorable issue. One of them is the fact that our civilization, whatever else it may be, is one of diffusion, of ready circulation. It is a fancy of mine to picture the essence of our life in terms of the Ford car. On the one side, there is the acme of mechanization, of standardization, of external efficiency. On the other, there is, as the effect, a vast mobility, a restless movement of individuals. The resulting mobility is aimless and blind; it can be easily represented as exhibiting a mere love of

movement for its own sake, an abandonment to speed of change for its own sake. But nevertheless the movement, the instability, is there. The industrial forces that would control it for their own purposes automatically, and as by some principle of fate, multiply and intensify it. Thus the division, the tension, increases. A standardized, regimented technology of industry continually releases unexpected and unforeseen forces of individuality. In its effort to control their operation, it redoubles its repressive and mechanizing efforts. Is it a mere compensatory fantasy to suppose that in the process it is inevitably and unwittingly working its own doom? The answer given will depend upon one's conceptions of the ultimate structure of individual human nature, of what its potentialities will do when they are liberated.

It is a trite saying that our social experiment, that of raising the level of the mass, is an unprecedented one. It is impossible, however, to separate the scope of the endeavor from that side of our civilization that is most open to criticism—its devotion to quantity at the expense of quality. It is as true of civilizations as of persons that their defects and their qualities of value go together. Moreover the ideal of mass elevation is intimately connected with the fact of diffusion. Our democratic fathers apparently thought that the desired elevation of the mass would automatically occur if certain political agencies were instituted. By one of the ironies of history, these political agencies are just the thing that lent themselves, indirectly rather than directly, to appropriation and manipulation by the few in possession of ultimate economic power. But meantime the very forces of industry have created mechanisms that operate to bring about diffusion on an unprecedented scale. European critics of our culture often ignore the fact that many of the things they criticize are due to the fact that we have been compelled perforce to undertake the task which Europe shirked. In their animadversions upon our lack in higher culture, they pass over the fact that millions of European immigrants have, and have realized, opportunities here that they never had at home. The mass and quantitative aspect of our civilization has thus a uniquely positive significance. All the facts indicate that if we should attain the higher values by which civilization is to be ultimately measured, it will be by a mass achievement, and not be the work of a chosen few, of an *élite*. It will be by social osmosis, by diffusion.

If, then, I have not touched specifically upon the industrial and technological phase of our life, it is because I regard it as central and dominant. It is the prepared mechanism of diffusion and distribution. And the ultimate question about it is not the distribution of pecuniary incomes that it finally effects. That question is, indeed, of an importance not to be ignored. But its last importance is its bearing upon the distribution of imponderables, the diffusion of education and of a share in the values of intellectual and artistic life. While it is true that devotion to the economic phase of life is materialism, and that so judged our civilization is materialistic, it is also true that we have broken down the age-long old world separation of the material and the ideal, and that the destruction of this dualism is a necessary precondition of any elevated culture that is the property of a people as a whole. The constructive function, that of using the economic and material basis as a means for widely shared ideal ends, is only begun. But it is far enough along to provide what never existed before: operative agencies of diffusion. Even though it be of the nature of prophecy rather than of record, I do not believe that in the long run anything can defeat or seriously deflect the normal diffusion effect of our economic forces.

The tightening-up, the repression, the mechanical standardization, to which allusion has been made, presents the attempt at obstruction and diversion of this normal tendency. The liberation of individual potentialities, the evocation of personal and voluntary associated energies, manifest the actual effect still expressed in a form as inchoate as the effort in the opposite direction is organic. Our faith is ultimately in individuals and their potentialities. In saying this, I do not mean what is sometimes called individualism as opposed to association. I mean rather an individuality that operates in and through voluntary associations. If our outward scene is one of externally imposed organization, behind and beneath there is working the force of liberated individualities, experimenting in their own ways to find and realize their own ends. The testimony of history is that in the end such a force, however scattered and inchoate, ultimately prevails over all set institutionalized forms, however firmly established the latter may seem to be.

In concluding, let me confess that I am aware that as I have been writing I have been influenced, and unduly so I think, by the mood of self-conscious criticism that has overtaken us. In reality, I believe that we have already accomplished very much in the way of diffusion of culture—whatever that elusive word may signify. It is a part of any humane culture to be concerned to see that others share in it. Our newly acquired self-consciousness makes one hesitant to speak of social service and practical idealism; the overworked words have taken on a somewhat ridiculous color. But it is true that no other people at any other age has been so permeated with the spirit of sharing as our own. If defects go with qualities, so do qualities with defects. The excessive sociability that breeds conformity also makes us uneasy till advantages are shared with the less fortunate. Every significant civilization gives a new meaning to "culture." If this new spirit, so unlike that of old-world charity and benevolence, does not already mark an attainment of a distinctive culture on the part of American civilization, and give the promise and potency of a new civilization, Columbus merely extended and diluted the Old World. But I still believe that he discovered a New World.

NOTES

[First published in *World Tomorrow* 11 (1928): 391–95. Republished, with additions, in *Recent Gains in American Civilization*, ed. Kirby Page (New York: Harcourt, Brace and Co., 1928), pp. 253–76. LW 3:133–44.]

Nothing is blinder than the supposition that we live in a society and world so static that either nothing new will happen or else it will happen because of the use of violence. Social change is here as a fact, a fact having multifarious forms and marked in intensity. Changes that are revolutionary in effect are in process in every phase of life. Transformations in the family, the church, the school, in science and art, in economic and political relations, are occurring so swiftly that imagination is baffled in attempt to lay hold of them. Flux does not have to be created. But it does have to be directed. It has to be so controlled that it will move to some end in accordance with the principles of life, since life itself is development. Liberalism is committed to an end that is at once enduring and flexible: the liberation of individuals so that realization of their capacities may be the law of their life. It is committed to the use of freed intelligence as the method of directing change. In any case, civilization is faced with the problem of uniting the changes that are going on into a coherent pattern of social organization. The liberal spirit is marked by its own picture of the pattern that is required: a social organization that will make possible effective liberty and opportunity for personal growth in mind and spirit in all individuals. Its present need is recognition that established material security is a prerequisite of the ends which it cherishes, so that, the basis of life being secure, individuals may actively share in the wealth of cultural resources that now exist and may contribute, each in his own way, to their further enrichment.

The fact of change has been so continual and so intense that it overwhelms our minds. We are bewildered by the spectacle of its rapidity, scope and intensity. It is not surprising that men have protected themselves from the impact of such vast change by resorting to what psycho-analysis has taught us to call rationalizations, in other words, protective fantasies. The Victorian idea that change is a part of an evolution that necessarily leads through successive stages to some preordained divine far-off event is one rationalization. The conception of a sudden, complete, almost catastrophic, transformation, to be brought about

Renascent Liberalism

From *Liberalism and Social Action* (1935)

by the victory of the proletariat over the class now dominant, is a similar rationalization. But men have met the impact of change in the realm of actuality, mostly by drift and by temporary, usually incoherent, improvisations. Liberalism, like every other theory of life, has suffered from the state of confused uncertainty that is the lot of a world suffering from rapid and varied change for which there is no intellectual and moral preparation.

Because of this lack of mental and moral preparation the impact of swiftly moving changes produced, as I have just said, confusion, uncertainty and drift. Change in patterns of belief, desire and purpose has lagged behind the modification of the external conditions under which men associate. Industrial habits have changed most rapidly; there has followed at considerable distance, change in political relations; alterations in legal relations and methods have lagged even more, while changes in the institutions that deal most directly with patterns of thought and belief have taken place to the least extent. This fact defines the primary, though not by any means the ultimate, responsibility of a liberalism that intends to be a vital force. Its work is first of all education, in the broadest sense of that term. Schooling is a part of the work of education, but education in its full meaning includes all the influences that go to form the attitudes and dispositions (of desire as well as of belief), which constitute dominant habits of mind and character.

Let me mention three changes that have taken place in one of the institutions in which immense shifts have occurred, but that are still relatively external—external in the sense that the pattern of intelligent purpose and emotion has not been correspondingly modified. Civilization existed for most of human history in a state of scarcity in the material basis for a humane life. Our ways of thinking, planning and working have been attuned to this fact. Thanks to science and technology we now live in an age of potential plenty. The immediate effect of the emergence of the new possibility was simply to stimulate, to a point of incredible exaggeration, the striving for the material resources, called wealth, opened to men in the new vista. It is a characteristic of all development, physiological and mental, that when a new force and factor appears, it is first pushed to an extreme. Only when its possibilities have been exhausted (at least relatively) does it take its place in the life perspective. The economic-material phase of life, which belongs in the basal ganglia of society, has usurped for more than a century the cortex of the social body. The habits of desire and effort that were bred in the age of scarcity do not readily subordinate themselves and take the place of the matter-of-course routine that becomes appropriate to them when machines and impersonal power have the capacity to liberate man from bondage to the strivings that were once needed to make secure his physical basis. Even now when there is a vision of an age of abundance and when the vision is supported by hard fact, it is material security as an end that appeals to most rather than the way of living which this security makes possible. Men's minds are still pathetically held in the clutch of old habits and haunted by old memories.

For, in the second place, insecurity is the natural child and the foster child, too, of scarcity. Early liberalism emphasized the importance of insecurity as a fundamentally necessary economic motive, holding that without this goad men would not work, abstain or accumulate. Formulation of this conception was new. But the fact that was formulated was nothing new. It was deeply rooted in the habits that were formed in the long struggle against material scarcity. The system that goes by the name of capitalism is a systematic manifestation of desires and purposes built up in an age of ever threatening want and now carried over into a time of ever increasing potential plenty. The conditions that generate insecurity for the many no longer spring from nature. They are found in institutions and arrangements that are within deliberate human control. Surely this change marks one of the greatest revolutions that has taken place in all human history. Because of it, insecurity is not now the motive to work and sacrifice but to despair. It is not an instigation to put forth energy but to an impotency that can be converted from death into endurance only by charity. But the habits of mind and action that modify institutions to make potential abundance an actuality are still so inchoate that most of us discuss labels like individualism, socialism and communism instead of even perceiving the possibility, much less the necessity for realizing what can and should be.

In the third place, the patterns of belief and purpose that still dominate economic institutions were formed when individuals produced with their hands, alone or in small groups. The notion that society in general is served by the unplanned coincidence of the consequences of a vast multitude of efforts put forth by isolated individuals without reference to any social end, was also something new as a formulation. But it also formulated the working principle of an epoch which the advent of new forces of production was to bring to an end. It demands no great power of intelligence to see that under present conditions the isolated individual is well-nigh helpless. Concentration and corporate organization are the rule. But the concentration and corporate organization are still controlled in their operation by ideas that were institutionalized in eons of separate individual effort. The attempts at cooperation for mutual benefit that are put forth are precious as experimental moves. But that society itself should see to it that a cooperative industrial order be instituted, one that is consonant with the realities of production enforced by an era of machinery and power, is so novel an idea to the general mind that its mere suggestion is hailed with abusive epithets— sometimes with imprisonment.

When, then, I say that the first object of a renascent liberalism is education, I mean that its task is to aid in producing the habits of mind and character, the intellectual and moral patterns, that are somewhere near even with the actual movements of events. It is, I repeat, the split between the latter as they have externally occurred and the ways of desiring, thinking, and of putting emotion and purpose into execution that is the basic cause of present confusion in mind and paralysis in action. The educational task cannot be accomplished merely by working upon men's minds, without action that effects actual change in institutions. The idea that dispositions and attitudes can be altered by merely "moral" means conceived of as something that goes on wholly inside of persons is itself one of the old patterns that has to

be changed. Thought, desire and purpose exist in a constant give and take of interaction with environing conditions. But resolute thought is the first step in that change of action that will itself carry further the needed change in patterns of mind and character.

In short, liberalism must now become radical, meaning by "radical" perception of the necessity of thoroughgoing changes in the setup of institutions and corresponding activity to bring the changes to pass. For the gulf between what the actual situation makes possible and the actual state itself is so great that it cannot be bridged by piecemeal policies undertaken *ad hoc*. The process of producing the changes will be, in any case, a gradual one. But "reforms" that deal now with this abuse and now with that without having a social goal based upon an inclusive plan, differ entirely from effort at reforming, in its literal sense, the institutional scheme of things. The liberals of more than a century ago were denounced in their time as subversive radicals, and only when the new economic order was established did they become apologists for the *status quo* or else content with social patchwork. If radicalism be defined as perception of need for radical change, then today any liberalism which is not also radicalism is irrelevant and doomed.

But radicalism also means, in the minds of many, both supporters and opponents, dependence upon use of violence as the main method of effecting drastic changes. Here the liberal parts company. For he is committed to the organization of intelligent action as the chief method. Any frank discussion of the issue must recognize the extent to which those who decry the use of any violence are themselves willing to resort to violence and are ready to put their will into operation. Their fundamental objection is to change in the economic institution that now exists, and for its maintenance they resort to the use of the force that is placed in their hands by this very institution. They do not need to advocate the use of force; their only need is to employ it. Force, rather than intelligence, is built into the procedures of the existing social system, regularly as coercion, in times of crisis as overt violence. The legal system, conspicuously in its penal aspect, more subtly in civil practice, rests upon coercion.

Wars are the methods recurrently used in settlement of disputes between nations. One school of radicals dwells upon the fact that in the past the transfer of power in one society has either been accomplished by or attended with violence. But what we need to realize is that physical force is used, at least in the form of coercion, in the very set-up of our society. That the competitive system, which was thought of by early liberals as the means by which the latent abilities of individuals were to be evoked and directed into socially useful channels, is now in fact a state of scarcely disguised battle hardly needs to be dwelt upon. That the control of the means of production by the few in legal possession operates as a standing agency of coercion of the many, may need emphasis in statement, but is surely evident to one who is willing to observe and honestly report the existing scene. It is foolish to regard the political state as the only agency now endowed with coercive power. Its exercise of this power is pale in contrast with that exercised by concentrated and organized property interests.

It is not surprising in view of our standing dependence upon the use of coercive force that at every time of crisis coercion breaks out into open violence. In this country, with its tradition of violence fostered by frontier conditions and by the conditions under which immigration went on during the greater part of our history, resort to violence is especially recurrent on the part of those who are in power. In times of imminent change, our verbal and sentimental worship of the Constitution, with its guarantees of civil liberties of expression, publication and assemblage, readily goes overboard. Often the officials of the law are the worst offenders, acting as agents of some power that rules the economic life of a community. What is said about the value of free speech as a safety valve is then forgotten with the utmost of ease: a comment, perhaps, upon the weakness of the defense of freedom of expression that values it simply as a means of blowing-off steam.

It is not pleasant to face the extent to which, as matter of fact, coercive and violent force is relied upon in the present social system as a means of social control. It is much more agreeable to evade the fact. But unless the fact is acknowledged as a fact in its full depth and breadth, the meaning of dependence upon intelligence as the alternative method of social direction will not be grasped. Failure in acknowledgment signifies, among other things, failure to realize that those who propagate the dogma of dependence upon force have the sanction of much that is already entrenched in the existing system. They would but turn the use of it to opposite ends. The assumption that the method of intelligence already rules and that those who urge the use of violence are introducing a new element into the social picture may not be hypocritical but it is unintelligently unaware of what is actually involved in intelligence as an alternative method of social action.

I begin with an example of what is really involved in the issue. Why is it, apart from our tradition of violence, that liberty of expression is tolerated and even lauded when social affairs seem to be going in a quiet fashion, and yet is so readily destroyed whenever matters grow critical? The general answer, of course, is that at bottom social institutions have habituated us to the use of force in some veiled form. But a part of the answer is found in our ingrained habit of regarding intelligence as an individual possession and its exercise as an individual right. It is false that freedom of inquiry and of expression are not modes of action. They are exceedingly potent modes of action. The reactionary grasps this fact, in practice if not in express idea, more quickly than the liberal, who is too much given to holding that this freedom is innocent of consequences, as well as being a merely individual right. The result is that this liberty is tolerated as long as it does not seem to menace in any way the *status quo* of society. When it does, every effort is put forth to identify the established order with the public good. When this identification is established, it follows that any merely individual right must yield to the general welfare. As long as freedom of thought and speech is claimed as a merely individual right, it will give way, as do other merely personal claims, when it is, or is successfully represented to be, in opposition to the general welfare.

I would not in the least disparage the noble fight waged by early liberals in behalf of individual freedom of thought and expression. We owe more to them than it is possible to record in words. No more eloquent words have ever come from any one than those of Justice Brandeis in the case of a legislative act that in fact restrained freedom of political expression. He said: "Those who won our independence believed that the final end of the State was to make men free to develop their faculties, and that in its government the deliberative forces should prevail over the arbitrary. They valued liberty both as an end and as a means. They believed liberty to be the secret of happiness and courage to be the secret of liberty. They believed that freedom to think as you will and to speak as you think are means indispensable to the discovery and spread of political truth; that without free speech and assembly discussion would be futile; that with them, discussion affords ordinarily adequate protection against the dissemination of noxious doctrines; that the greatest menace to freedom is an inert people; that public discussion is a political duty; and that this should be a fundamental principle of the American Government." This is the creed of a fighting liberalism. But the issue I am raising is connected with the fact that these words are found in a dissenting, a minority opinion of the Supreme Court of the United States. The public function of free individual thought and speech is clearly recognized in the words quoted. But the reception of the truth of the words is met by an obstacle: the old habit of defending liberty of thought and expression as something inhering in individuals apart from and even in opposition to social claims.

Liberalism has to assume the responsibility for making it clear that intelligence is a social asset and is clothed with a function as public as is its origin, in the concrete, in social cooperation. It was Comte who, in reaction against the purely individualistic ideas that seemed to him to underlie the French Revolution, said that in mathematics, physics and astronomy there is no right of private conscience. If we remove the statement from the context of actual scientific procedure, it is dangerous because it is false. The individual inquirer has not only the right but the duty to criticize the ideas, theories and "laws" that are current in science. But if we take the statement in the context of scientific method, it indicates that he carries on this criticism in virtue of a socially generated body of knowledge and by means of methods that are not of private origin and possession. He uses a method that retains public validity even when innovations are introduced in its use and application.

Henry George, speaking of ships that ply the ocean with a velocity of five or six hundred miles a day, remarked, "There is nothing whatever to show that the men who to-day build and navigate and use such ships are one whit superior in any physical or mental quality to their ancestors, whose best vessel was a coracle of wicker and hide. The enormous improvement which these ships show is not an improvement of human nature; it is an improvement of society—it is due to a wider and fuller union of individual efforts in accomplishment of common ends." This single instance, duly pondered, gives a better idea of the nature of intelligence and its social office than would a volume of abstract dissertation. Consider merely two of the factors that enter in and their social consequences. Consider what is involved in the production of steel, from the first use of fire and then the crude smelting of ore, to the processes that now effect the mass production of steel. Consider also the development of the power of guiding ships across trackless wastes from the day when they hugged the shore, steering by visible sun and stars, to the appliances that now enable a sure course to be taken. It would require a heavy tome to describe the advances in science, in mathematics, astronomy, physics, chemistry, that have made these two things possible. The record would be an account of a vast multitude of cooperative efforts, in which one individual uses the results provided for him by a countless number of other individuals, and uses them so as to add to the common and public store. A survey of such facts brings home the actual social character of intelligence as it actually develops and makes its way. Survey of the consequences upon the ways of living of individuals and upon the terms on which men associate together, due to the new method of transportation would take us to the wheat farmer of the prairies, the cattle raiser of the plains, the cotton grower of the

South; into a multitude of mills and factories, and to the counting-room of banks, and what would be seen in this country would be repeated in every country of the globe.

It is to such things as these, rather than to abstract and formal psychology that we must go if we would learn the nature of intelligence: in itself, in its origin and development, and its uses and consequences. At this point, I should like to recur to an idea put forward in the preceding chapter. I then referred to the contempt often expressed for reliance upon intelligence as a social method, and I said this scorn is due to the identification of intelligence with native endowments of individuals. In contrast to this notion, I spoke of the power of individuals to appropriate and respond to the intelligence, the knowledge, ideas and purposes that have been integrated in the medium in which individuals live. Each of us knows, for example, some mechanic of ordinary native capacity who is intelligent within the matters of his calling. He has lived in an environment in which the cumulative intelligence of a multitude of cooperating individuals is embodied, and by the use of his native capacities he makes some phase of this intelligence his own. Given a social medium in whose institutions the available knowledge, ideas and art of humanity were incarnate, and the average individual would rise to undreamed heights of social and political intelligence.

The rub, the problem is found in the proviso. Can the intelligence actually existent and potentially available be embodied in that institutional medium in which an individual thinks, desires and acts? Before dealing directly with this question, I wish to say something about the operation of intelligence in our present political institutions, as exemplified by current practices of democratic government. I would not minimize the advance scored in substitution of methods of discussion and conference for the method of arbitrary rule. But the better is too often the enemy of the still better. Discussion, as the manifestation of intelligence in political life, stimulates publicity; by its means sore spots are brought to light that would otherwise remain hidden. It affords opportunity for promulgation of new ideas. Compared with despotic rule, it is an invitation to individuals to concern themselves with public affairs. But discussion and dialectic, however indispensable they are to the elaboration of ideas and policies after ideas are once put forth, are weak reeds to depend upon for systematic origination of comprehensive plans, the plans that are required if the problem of social organization is to be met. There was a time when discussion, the comparison of ideas already current so as to purify and clarify them, was thought to be sufficient in discovery of the structure and laws of physical nature. In the latter field, the method was displaced by that of experimental observation guided by comprehensive working hypotheses, and using all the resources made available by mathematics.

But we still depend upon the method of discussion, with only incidental scientific control, in politics. Our system of popular suffrage, immensely valuable as it is in comparison with what preceded it, exhibits the idea that intelligence is an individualistic possession, at best enlarged by public discussion. Existing political practice, with its complete ignoring of occupational groups and the organized knowledge and purposes that are involved in the existence of such groups, manifests a dependence upon a summation of individuals quantitatively, similar to Bentham's purely quantitative formula of the greatest sum of pleasures of the greatest possible number. The formation of parties or, as the eighteenth-century writers called them, factions, and the system of party government is the practically necessary counterweight to a numerical and atomistic individualism. The idea that the conflict of parties will, by means of public discussion, bring out necessary public truths is a kind of political watered-down version of the Hegelian dialectic, with its synthesis arrived at by a union of antithetical conceptions. The method has nothing in common with the procedure of organized cooperative inquiry which has won the triumphs of science in the field of physical nature.

Intelligence in politics when it is identified with discussion means reliance upon symbols. The invention of language is probably the greatest single invention achieved by humanity. The development of political forms that promote the use of symbols in place of arbitrary power was another great invention. The nineteenth-century establishment of parliamentary institutions, written constitutions and the suffrage as means of political rule, is a tribute to the power of symbols. But symbols are significant only in connection with realities behind them. No intelligent observer can deny, I think, that they are often used in party politics as a substitute for realities instead of as means of contact with them. Popular literacy, in connection with the telegraph, cheap postage and the printing press, has enormously multiplied the number of those influenced. That which we term education has done a good deal to generate habits that put symbols in the place of realities. The forms of popular government make necessary the elaborate use of words to influence political action. "Propaganda" is the inevitable consequence of the combination of these influences and it extends to every area of life. Words not only take the place of realities but are themselves debauched. Decline in the prestige of suffrage and of parliamentary government are intimately associated with the belief, manifest in practice even if not expressed in words, that intelligence is an individual possession to be reached by means of verbal persuasion.

This fact suggests, by way of contrast, the genuine meaning of intelligence in connection with public opinion, sentiment and action. The crisis in democracy demands the substitution of the intelligence that is exemplified in scientific procedure for the kind of intelligence that is now accepted. The need for this change is not exhausted in the demand for greater honesty and impartiality, even though these qualities be now corrupted by discussion carried on mainly for purposes of party supremacy and for imposition of some special but concealed interest. These qualities need to be restored. But the need goes further. The social use of intelligence would remain deficient even if these moral traits were exalted, and yet intelligence continued to be identified simply with discussion and persuasion, necessary as are these things. Approximation to use of scientific method in investigation and of the engineering mind in the invention and projection of far-reaching social plans is demanded. The habit of considering social realities in terms of

cause and effect and social policies in terms of means and consequences is still inchoate. The contrast between the state of intelligence in politics and in the physical control of nature is to be taken literally. What has happened in this latter is the outstanding demonstration of the meaning of organized intelligence. The combined effect of science and technology has released more productive energies in a bare hundred years than stands to the credit of prior human history in its entirety. Productively it has multiplied nine million times in the last generation alone. The prophetic vision of Francis Bacon of subjugation of the energies of nature through change in methods of inquiry has well-nigh been realized. The stationary engine, the locomotive, the dynamo, the motor car, turbine, telegraph, telephone, radio and moving picture are not the products of either isolated individual minds nor of the particular economic régime called capitalism. They are the fruit of methods that first penetrated to the working causalities of nature and then utilized the resulting knowledge in bold imaginative ventures of invention and construction.

We hear a great deal in these days about class conflict. The past history of man is held up to us as almost exclusively a record of struggles between classes, ending in the victory of a class that had been oppressed and the transfer of power to it. It is difficult to avoid reading the past in terms of the contemporary scene. Indeed, fundamentally it is impossible to avoid this course. With a certain proviso, it is highly important that we are compelled to follow this path. For the past as past is gone, save for esthetic enjoyment and refreshment, while the present is with us. Knowledge of the past is significant only as it deepens and extends our understanding of the present. Yet there is a proviso. We must grasp the things that are most important in the present when we turn to the past and not allow ourselves to be misled by secondary phenomena no matter how intense and immediately urgent they are. Viewed from this standpoint, the rise of scientific method and of technology based upon it is the genuinely active force in producing the vast complex of changes the world is now undergoing, not the class struggle whose spirit and method are opposed to science. If we lay hold upon the causal force exercised by this embodiment of intelligence we shall know where to turn for the means of directing further change.

When I say that scientific method and technology have been the active force in producing the revolutionary transformations society is undergoing, I do not imply no other forces have been at work to arrest, deflect and corrupt their operation. Rather this fact is positively implied. At this point, indeed, is located the conflict that underlies the confusions and uncertainties of the present scene. The conflict is between institutions and habits originating in the pre-scientific and pre-technological age and the new forces generated by science and technology. The application of science, to a considerable degree, even its own growth, has been conditioned by the system to which the name of capitalism is given, a rough designation of a complex of political and legal arrangements centering about a particular mode of economic relations. Because of the conditioning of science and technology by this setting, the second and humanly most important part of Bacon's prediction has so far largely missed realization. The conquest of natural energies has not accrued to the betterment of the common human estate in anything like the degree he anticipated.

Because of conditions that were set by the legal institutions and the moral ideas existing when the scientific and industrial revolutions came into being, the chief usufruct of the latter has been appropriated by a relatively small class. Industrial entrepreneurs have reaped out of all proportion to what they sowed. By obtaining private ownership of the means of production and exchange they deflected a considerable share of the results of increased productivity to their private pockets. This appropriation was not the fruit of criminal conspiracy or of sinister intent. It was sanctioned not only by legal institutions of age-long standing but by the entire prevailing moral code. The institution of private property long antedated feudal times. It is the institution with which men have lived, with few exceptions, since the dawn of civilization. Its existence has deeply impressed itself upon mankind's moral conceptions. Moreover, the new industrial forces tended to break down many of the rigid class barriers that had been in force, and to give to millions a new outlook and inspire a new hope;—especially in this country with no feudal background and no fixed class system.

Since the legal institutions and the patterns of mind characteristic of ages of civilization still endure, there exists the conflict that brings confusion into every phase of present life. The problem of bringing into being a new social orientation and organization is, when reduced to its ultimates, the problem of using the new resources of production, made possible by the advance of physical science, for social ends, for what Bentham called the greatest good of the greatest number. Institutional relationships fixed in the pre-scientific age stand in the way of accomplishing this great transformation. Lag in mental and moral patterns provides the bulwark of the older institutions; in expressing the past they still express present beliefs, outlooks and purposes. Here is the place where the problem of liberalism centres today.

The argument drawn from past history that radical change must be effected by means of class struggle, culminating in open war, fails to discriminate between the two forces, one active, the other resistant and deflecting, that have produced the social scene in which we live. The active force is, as I have said, scientific method and technological application. The opposite force is that of older institutions and the habits that have grown up around them. Instead of discrimination between forces and distribution of their consequences, we find the two things lumped together. The compound is labeled the capitalistic or the bourgeois class, and to this class as a class is imputed all the important features of present industrialized society—much as the defenders of the régime of economic liberty exercised for private property are accustomed to attribute every improvement made in the last century and a half to the same capitalistic régime. Thus in orthodox communist literature, from the *Communist Manifesto* of 1848 to the present day, we are told that the bourgeoisie, the name for a distinctive class, has done this and that. It has, so it is said, given a cosmopolitan character to production and consumption; has destroyed the national basis of industry; has agglomerated population in urban centres; has transferred power from the country to the city, in the process of creating colossal productive force, its chief achievement. In addition, it has created crises of ever renewed intensity; has created imperialism of a new type in frantic effort to control raw materials and markets. Finally, it has created a new class, the proletariat, and has created it as a class having a common interest opposed to that of the bourgeoisie, and is giving an irresistible stimulus to its organization, first as a class and then as a political power. According to the economic version of the Hegelian dialectic, the bourgeois class is thus creating its own complete and polar opposite, and this in time will end the old power and rule. The class struggle of veiled civil war will finally burst into open revolution and the result will be either the common ruin of the contending parties or a revolutionary reconstitution of society at large through a transfer of power from one class to another.

The position thus sketched unites vast sweep with great simplicity. I am concerned with it here only as far as it emphasizes the idea of a struggle between classes, culminating in open and violent warfare as being the method for production of radical social change. For, be it noted, the issue is not whether some amount of violence will accompany the effectuation of radical change of institutions. The question is whether force or intelligence is to be the method upon which we consistently rely and to whose promotion we devote our energies. Insistence that the use of violent force is *inevitable* limits the use of available intelligence, for wherever the inevitable reigns intelligence cannot be used. Commitment to inevitability is always the fruit of dogma; intelligence does not pretend to *know* save as a result of experimentation, the opposite of preconceived dogma. Moreover, acceptance in advance of the inevitability of violence tends to produce the use of violence in cases where peaceful methods might otherwise avail. The curious fact is that while it is generally admitted that this and that particular social problem, say of the family, or railroads or banking, must be solved, if at all, by the method of intelligence, yet there is supposed to be some one all-inclusive social problem which can be solved only by the use of violence. This fact would be inexplicable were it not a conclusion from dogma as its premise.

It is frequently asserted that the method of experimental intelligence can be applied to physical facts because physical nature does not present conflicts of class interests, while it is inapplicable to society because the latter is so deeply marked by incompatible interests. It is then assumed that the "experimentalist" is one who has chosen to ignore the uncomfortable fact of conflicting interests. Of course, there *are* conflicting interests; otherwise there would be no social problems. The problem under discussion is precisely *how* conflicting claims are to be settled in the interest of the widest possible contribution to the interests of all—or at least of the great majority. The method of democracy—inasfar as it is that of organized intelligence—is to bring these conflicts out into the open where their special claims can be seen and appraised, where they can be discussed and judged in the light of more inclusive interests than are represented by either of them separately. There is, for example, a clash of interests between munition manufacturers and most of the rest of the population. The more the respective claims of the two are publicly and scientifically weighed, the more likely it is that the public interest will be disclosed and be made effective. There is an undoubted objective clash of interests between finance-capitalism that controls the means of production and whose profit is served by maintaining relative scarcity, and idle workers and hungry consumers. But what generates violent strife is failure to bring the conflict into the light of intelligence where the conflicting interests can be adjudicated in behalf of the interest of the great majority. Those most committed to the dogma of inevitable force recognize the need for intelligently discovering and expressing the dominant social interest up to a certain point and then draw back. The "experimentalist" is one who would see to it that the method depended upon by all in some degree in every democratic community be followed through to completion.

In spite of the existence of class conflicts,

amounting at times to veiled civil war, any one habituated to the use of the method of science will view with considerable suspicion the erection of actual human beings into fixed entities called classes, having no overlapping interests and so internally unified and externally separated that they are made the protagonists of history—itself hypothetical. Such an idea of classes is a survival of a rigid logic that once prevailed in the sciences of nature, but that no longer has any place there. This conversion of abstractions into entities smells more of a dialectic of concepts than of a realistic examination of facts, even though it makes more of an emotional appeal to many than do the results of the latter. To say that all past historic social progress has been the result of cooperation and not of conflict would be also an exaggeration. But exaggeration against exaggeration, it is the more reasonable of the two. And it is no exaggeration to say that the measure of civilization is the degree in which the method of cooperative intelligence replaces the method of brute conflict.

But the point I am especially concerned with just here is the indiscriminate lumping together as a single force of two different things—the results of scientific technology and of a legal system of property relations. It is science and technology that have had the revolutionary social effect while the legal system has been the relatively static element. According to the Marxians themselves, the economic foundations of society consist of two things, the forces of production on one side and, on the other side, the social relations of production, that is, the legal property system under which the former operates. The latter lags behind, and "revolutions" are produced by the power of the forces of production to change the system of institutional relations. But what are the modern forces of production save those of scientific technology? And what is scientific technology save a large-scale demonstration of organized intelligence in action?

It is quite true that what is happening socially is the result of the combination of the two factors, one dynamic, the other relatively static. If we choose to call the combination by the name of capitalism, then it is true, or a truism, that capitalism is the "cause" of all the important social changes that have occurred—an argument that the representatives of capitalism are eager to put forward whenever the increase of productivity is in question. But if we want to *understand*, and not just to paste labels, unfavorable or favorable as the case may be, we shall certainly begin and end with discrimination. Colossal increase in productivity, the bringing of men together in cities and large factories, the elimination of distance, the accumulation of capital, fixed and liquid—these things would have come about, at a certain stage, no matter what the established institutional system. They are the consequence of the new means of technological production. Certain other things have happened because of inherited institutions and the habits of belief and character that accompany and support them. If we begin at this point, we shall see that the release of productivity is the product of cooperatively organized intelligence, and shall also see that the institutional framework is precisely that which is not subjected as yet, in any considerable measure, to the impact of inventive and constructive intelligence. That coercion and oppression on a large scale exist, no honest person can deny. But these things are not the product of science and technology but of the perpetuation of old institutions and patterns untouched by scientific method. The inference to be drawn is clear.

The argument, drawn from history, that great social changes have been effected only by violent means, needs considerable qualification, in view of the vast scope of changes that are taking place without the use of violence. But even if it be admitted to hold of the past, the conclusion that violence is the method now to be depended upon does not follow—unless one is committed to a dogmatic philosophy of history. The radical who insists that the future method of change must be like that of the past has much in common with the hide-bound reactionary who holds to the past as an ultimate fact. Both overlook the *fact that history in being a process of change generates change not only in details but also in the method of directing social change*. I recur to what I said at the beginning of this chapter. It is true that the social order is largely conditioned by the use of coercive force, bursting at times into open violence. But what is also true is that mankind now has in its possession a new method, that of cooperative and experimental science which expresses the method of intelligence. I should be meeting dogmatism with dogmatism if I asserted that the existence of this historically new factor completely invalidates all arguments drawn from the effect of force in the past. But it is within the bounds of reason to assert that the presence of this social factor demands that the present situation be analyzed on its own terms, and not be rigidly subsumed under fixed conceptions drawn from the past.

Any analysis made in terms of the present situation will not fail to note one fact that militates powerfully against arguments drawn from past use of violence. Modern warfare is destructive beyond anything known in older times. This increased destructiveness is due primarily, of course, to the fact that science has raised to a new pitch of destructive power all the agencies of armed hostility. But it is also due to the much greater interdependence of all the elements of society. The bonds that hold modern communities and states together are as delicate as they are numerous. The self-sufficiency and independence of a local community, characteristic of more primitive societies, have disappeared in every highly industrialized country. The gulf that once separated the civilian population from the military has virtually gone. War involves paralysis of all normal social activities, and not merely the meeting of armed forces in the field. The *Communist Manifesto* presented two alternatives: *either* the revolutionary change and transfer of power to the proletariat, *or* the common ruin of the contending parties. Today, the civil war that would be adequate to effect transfer of power and a reconstitution of society at large, as understood by official Communists, would seem to present but one possible consequence: the ruin of all parties and the destruction of civilized life. This fact alone is enough to lead us to consider the potentialities of the method of intelligence.

The argument for putting chief dependence upon violence as the method of effecting radical change is, moreover, usually put in a way that proves altogether too much for its own case. It is said that the dominant eco-nomic class has all the agencies of power in its hands, directly the army, militia and police; indirectly, the courts, schools, press and radio. I shall not stop to analyze this statement. But if one admits it to be valid, the conclusion to be drawn is surely the folly of resorting to a use of force against force that is so well intrenched. The positive conclusion that emerges is that conditions that would promise success in the case of use of force are such as to make possible great change without any great recourse to such a method.[1]

Those who uphold the necessity of dependence upon violence usually much oversimplify the case by setting up a disjunction they regard as self-evident. They say that the sole alternative is putting our trust in parliamentary procedures as they now exist. This isolation of law-making from other social forces and agencies that are constantly operative is wholly unrealistic. Legislatures and congresses do not exist in a vacuum—not even the judges on the bench live in completely secluded sound-proof chambers. The assumption that it is possible for the constitution and activities of law-making bodies to persist unchanged while society itself is undergoing great change is an exercise in verbal formal logic.

It is true that in this country, because of the interpretations made by courts of a written constitution, our political institutions are unusually inflexible. It is also true, as well as even more important (because it is a factor in causing this rigidity) that our institutions, democratic in form, tend to favor in substance a privileged plutocracy. Nevertheless, it is sheer defeatism to assume in advance of actual trial that democratic political institutions are incapable either of further development or of constructive social application. Even as they now exist, the forms of representative government are potentially capable of expressing the public will when that assumes anything like unification. And there is nothing inherent in them that forbids their supplementation by political agencies that represent definitely economic social interests, like those of producers and consumers.

The final argument in behalf of the use of intelligence is that as are the means used so are the actual ends achieved—that is, the consequences. I know of no greater fallacy than the claim of those who hold to the dogma of the necessity of brute force that this use will be the method of calling genuine democracy into existence—of which they profess themselves the simon-pure adherents. It requires an unusually credulous faith in the Hegelian dialectic of opposites to think that all of a sudden the use of force by a class will be transmuted into a democratic classless society. Force breeds counterforce; the Newtonian law of action and reaction still holds in physics, and violence is physical. To profess democracy as an ultimate ideal and the suppression of democracy as a means to the ideal may be possible in a country that has never known even rudimentary democracy, but when professed in a country that has anything of a genuine democratic spirit in its traditions, it signifies desire for possession and retention of power by a class, whether that class be called Fascist or Proletarian. In the light of what happens in non-democratic countries, it is pertinent to ask whether the rule of a class signifies the dictatorship of the majority, or dictatorship over the chosen class by a minority party; whether dissenters are allowed even within the class the party claims to represent; and whether the development of literature and the other arts proceeds according to a formula prescribed by a party in conformity with a doctrinaire dogma of history and of infallible leadership, or whether artists are free from regimentation? Until these questions are satisfactorily answered, it is permissible to look with considerable suspicion upon those who assert that suppression of democracy is the road to the adequate establishment of genuine democracy. The one exception—and that apparent rather than real—to dependence upon organized intelligence as the method for directing social change is found when society through an authorized majority has entered upon the path of social experimentation leading to great social change, and a minority refuses by force to permit the method of intelligent action to go into effect. Then force may be intelligently employed to subdue and disarm the recalcitrant minority.

There may be some who think I am unduly dignifying a position held by a comparatively small group by taking their arguments as seriously as I have done. But their position serves to bring into strong relief the alternatives before us. It makes clear the meaning of renascent liberalism. The alternatives are continuation of drift with attendant improvisations to meet special emergencies; dependence upon violence; dependence upon socially organized intelligence. The first two alternatives, however, are not mutually exclusive, for if things are allowed to drift the result may be some sort of social change effected by the use of force, whether so planned or not. Upon the whole, the recent policy of liberalism has been to further "social legislation"; that is, measures which add performance of social services to the older functions of government. The value of this addition is not to be despised. It marks a decided move away from *laissez faire* liberalism, and has considerable importance in educating the public mind to a realization of the possibilities of organized social control. It has helped to develop some of the techniques that in any case will be needed in a socialized economy. But the cause of liberalism will be lost for a considerable period if it is not prepared to go further and socialize the forces of production, now at hand, so that the liberty of individuals will be supported by the very structure of economic organization.

The ultimate place of economic organization in human life is to assure the secure basis for an ordered expression of individual capacity and for the satisfaction of the needs of man in non-economic directions. The effort of mankind in connection with material production belongs, as I said earlier, among interests and activities that are, relatively speaking, routine in character, "routine" being defined as that which, without absorbing attention and energy, provides a constant basis for liberation of the values of intellectual, esthetic and companionship life. Every significant religious and moral teacher and prophet has asserted that the material is instrumental to the good life. Nominally at least, this idea is accepted by every civilized community. The transfer of the burden of material production from human muscles and brain to steam, electricity and chemical processes now makes possible the effective actualization of this ideal. Needs, wants and desires are always the moving force in generating creative action. When these wants are compelled by force of conditions to be directed for the most part, among the mass of mankind, into obtaining the means of subsistence, what should be a means becomes perforce an end in itself. Up to the present the new mechanical forces of production, which are the means of emancipation from this state of affairs, have been employed to intensify and exaggerate the reversal of the true relation between means and ends. Humanly speaking, I do not see how it would have been possible to avoid an epoch having this character. But its perpetuation is the cause of the continually growing social chaos and strife. Its termination cannot be effected by preaching to individuals that they should place spiritual ends above material means. It can be brought about by organized social reconstruction that puts the results of the mechanism of abundance at the free disposal of individuals. The actual corrosive "materialism" of our times does not proceed from science. It springs from the notion, sedulously cultivated by the class in power, that the creative capacities of individuals can be evoked and developed only in a struggle for material possessions and material gain. We either should surrender our professed belief in the supremacy of ideal and spiritual values and accommodate our beliefs to the predominant material orientation, or we should through organized endeavor institute the socialized economy of material security and plenty that will release human energy for pursuit of higher values.

Since liberation of the capacities of individuals for free, self-initiated expression is an essential part of the creed of liberalism, liberalism that is sincere must will the means that condition the achieving of its ends. Regimentation of material and mechanical forces is the only way by which the mass of individuals can be released from regimentation and consequent suppression of their cultural possibilities. The eclipse of liberalism is due to the fact that it has not faced the alternatives and adopted the means upon which realization of its professed aims depends. Liberalism can be true to its ideals only as it takes the course that leads to their attainment. The notion that organized social control of economic forces lies

outside the historic path of liberalism shows that liberalism is still impeded by remnants of its earlier *laissez faire* phase, with its opposition of society and the individual. The thing which now dampens liberal ardor and paralyzes its efforts is the conception that liberty and development of individuality as ends exclude the use of organized social effort as means. Earlier liberalism regarded the separate and competing economic action of individuals as the means to social well-being as the end. We must reverse the perspective and see that socialized economy is the means of free individual development as the end.

That liberals are divided in outlook and endeavor while reactionaries are held together by community of interests and the ties of custom is well-nigh a commonplace. Organization of standpoint and belief among liberals can be achieved only in and by unity of endeavor. Organized unity of action attended by consensus of beliefs will come about in the degree in which social control of economic forces is made the goal of liberal action. The greatest educational power, the greatest force in shaping the dispositions and attitudes of individuals, is the social medium in which they live. The medium that now lies closest to us is that of unified action for the inclusive end of a socialized economy. The attainment of a state of society in which a basis of material security will release the powers of individuals for cultural expression is not the work of a day. But by concentrating upon the task of securing a socialized economy as the ground and medium for release of the impulses and capacities men agree to call ideal, the now scattered and often conflicting activities of liberals can be brought to effective unity.

It is no part of my task to outline in detail a program for renascent liberalism. But the question of "what is to be done" cannot be ignored. Ideas must be organized, and this organization implies an organization of individuals who hold these ideas and whose faith is ready to translate itself into action. Translation into action signifies that the general creed of liberalism be formulated as a concrete program of action. It is in organization for action that liberals are weak, and without this organization there is danger that democratic ideals may go by default. Democracy has been a fighting faith. When its ideals are reenforced by those of scientific method and experimental intelligence, it cannot be that it is incapable of evoking discipline, ardor and organization. To narrow the issue for the future to a struggle between Fascism and Communism is to invite a catastrophe that may carry civilization down in the struggle. Vital and courageous democratic liberalism is the one force that can surely avoid such a disastrous narrowing of the issue. I for one do not believe that Americans living in the tradition of Jefferson and Lincoln will weaken and give up without a whole-hearted effort to make democracy a living reality. This, I repeat, involves organization.

The question cannot be answered by argument. Experimental method means experiment, and the question can be answered only by trying, by organized effort. The reasons for making the trial are not abstract or recondite. They are found in the confusion, uncertainty and conflict that mark the modern world. The reasons for thinking that the effort if made will be successful are also not abstract and remote. They lie in what the method of experimental and cooperative intelligence has already accomplished in subduing to potential human use the energies of physical nature. In material production, the method of intelligence is now the established rule; to abandon it would be to revert to savagery. The task is to go on, and not backward, until the method of intelligence and experimental control is the rule in social relations and social direction. Either we take this road or we admit that the problem of social organization in behalf of human liberty and the flowering of human capacities is insoluble.

It would be fantastic folly to ignore or to belittle the obstacles that stand in the way. But what has taken place, also against great odds, in the scientific and industrial revolutions, is an accomplished fact; the way is marked out. It may be that the way will remain untrodden. If so, the future holds the menace of confusion moving into chaos, a chaos that will be externally masked for a time by an organization of force, coercive and violent, in which the liberties of men will all but disappear. Even so, the cause of the liberty of the human spirit, the cause of opportunity of human beings for full development of their powers, the cause for which liberalism enduringly stands, is too precious and too ingrained in the human constitution to be forever obscured. Intelligence after millions of years of errancy has found itself as a method, and it will not be lost forever in the blackness of night. The business of liberalism is to bend every energy and exhibit every courage so that these precious goods may not even be temporarily lost but be intensified and expanded here and now.

NOTES

[LW 11:41–65.]

1. It should be noted that Marx himself was not completely committed to the dogma of the inevitability of force as the means of effecting revolutionary changes in the system of "social relations." For at one time he contemplated that the change might occur in Great Britain and the United States, and possibly in Holland, by peaceful means.

There is comparatively little difference among the groups at the left as to the social ends to be reached. There is a great deal of difference as to the means by which these ends should be reached and by which they can be reached. This difference as to means is the tragedy of democracy in the world today. The rulers of Soviet Russia announce that with the adoption of the new constitution they have for the first time in history created a democracy. At almost the same time, Goebbels announces that German Nazi-socialism is the only possible form of democracy for the future. Possibly there is some faint cheer for those who believe in democracy in these expressions. It is something that after a period in which democracy was scorned and laughed at, it is now acclaimed.

No one outside of Germany will take seriously the claim that Germany is a democracy, to say nothing of its being the perfected form of democracy. But there is something to be said for the assertion that the so-called democratic states of the world have achieved only "bourgeois" democracy. By "bourgeois" democracy is meant one in which power rests finally in the hands of finance capitalism, no matter what claims are made for government of, by and for all the people. In the perspective of history it is clear that the rise of democratic governments has been an accompaniment of the transfer of power from agrarian interests to industrial and commercial interests.

This transfer did not take place without a struggle. In this struggle, the representatives of the new forces of production asserted that their cause was that of liberty and of the free choice and initiative of individuals. Upon the continent and to a less degree in Great Britain, the political manifestation of free economic enterprise took the name of liberalism. So-called liberal parties were those which strove for a maximum of individualistic economic action with a minimum of social control, and did so in the interest of those engaged in manufacturing and commerce. If this manifestation expresses the full meaning of liberalism, then liberalism has served its time and it is social folly to try to resurrect it.

For the movement has definitely failed to realize the ends of liberty and individuality

Democracy Is Radical

(1937)

which were the goals it set up and in the name of which it proclaimed its rightful political supremacy. The movement for which it stood gave power to a few over the lives and thoughts of the many. Ability to command the conditions under which the mass of people have access to the means of production and to the products that result from their activity has been the fundamental feature of repression of freedom and the bar to development of individuality through all the ages. It is silly to deny that there has been gain to the masses accompanying the change of masters. But to glorify these gains and to give no attention to the brutalities and inequities, the regimentation and suppression, the war, open and covert, that attend the present system is intellectual and moral hypocrisy. Distortion and stultification of human personality by the existing pecuniary and competitive regime give the lie to the claim that the present social system is one of freedom and individualism in any sense in which liberty and individuality exist for all.

The United States is the outstanding exception to the statement that democracy arose historically in the interest of an industrial and commercial class, although it is true that in the formation of the federal constitution this class reaped much more than its fair share of the fruits of the revolution. And it is also true that as this group rose to economic power it appropriated also more and more political power. But it is simply false that this country, even politically, is merely a capitalistic democracy. The present struggle in this country is something more than a protest of a new class, whether called the proletariat or given any other name, against an established industrial autocracy. It is a manifestation of the native and enduring spirit of the nation against the destructive encroachments of forces that are alien to democracy.

This country has never had a political party of the European "liberal" type, although in recent campaigns the Republican party has taken over most of the slogans of the latter. But the attacks of leaders of the party upon liberalism as one form of the red menace show that liberalism has a different origin, setting and aim in the United States. It is fundamentally an attempt to realize democratic modes of life in their full meaning and far-reaching scope. There is no particular sense in trying to save the *word* "liberal." There is every reason for not permitting the methods and aims of *democracy* to be obscured by denunciations of liberalism. The danger of this eclipse is not a theoretical matter; it is intensely practical.

For democracy means not only the ends which even dictatorships now assert are their ends, security for individuals and opportunity for their development as personalities. It signifies also primary emphasis upon the *means* by which these ends are to be fulfilled. The means to which it is devoted are the voluntary activities of individuals in opposition to coercion; they are assent and consent in opposition to violence; they are the force of intelligent organization versus that of organization imposed from outside and above. *The fundamental principle of democracy is that the ends of freedom and individuality for all can be attained only by means that accord with those ends*. The value of upholding the banner of liberalism in this country, no matter what it has come to mean in Europe, is its insistence upon freedom of belief, of inquiry, of discussion, of assembly, of education: upon the method of public intelligence in opposition to even a coercion that claims to be exercised in behalf of the ultimate freedom of all individuals. There is intellectual hypocrisy and moral contradiction in the creed of those who uphold the need for at least a temporary dictatorship of a class as well as in the position of those who assert that the present economic system is one of freedom of initiative and of opportunity for all.

There is no opposition in standing for liberal democratic means combined with ends that are socially radical. There is not only no contradiction, but neither history nor human nature gives any reason for supposing that socially radical ends can be attained by any other than liberal democratic means. The idea that those who possess power never surrender it save when forced to do so by superior physical power, applies to dictatorships that claim to operate in behalf of the oppressed masses while actually operating to wield power against the masses. *The end of democracy is a radical end. For it is an end that has not been adequately realized in any country at any time.* It is radical because it requires great change in existing social institutions, economic, legal and cultural. A democratic liberalism that does not recognize these things in thought and action is not awake to its own meaning and to what that meaning demands.

There is, moreover, nothing more radical than insistence upon democratic methods as the means by which radical social changes be effected. It is not a merely verbal statement to say that reliance upon superior physical force is the reactionary position. For it is the method that the world has depended upon in the past and that the world is now arming in order to perpetuate. It is easy to understand why those who are in close contact with the inequities and tragedies of life that mark the present system, and who are aware that we now have the resources for initiating a social system of security and opportunity for all, should be impatient and long for the overthrow of the existing system by any means whatever. But democratic means and the attainment of democratic ends are one and inseparable. The revival of democratic faith as a buoyant, crusading and militant faith is a consummation to be devoutly wished for. But the crusade can win at the best but partial victory unless it springs from a living faith in our common human nature and in the power of voluntary action based upon public collective intelligence.

NOTES

[First published in *Common Sense* 6 (January 1937): 10–11. LW 11:296–99.]

Creative Democracy— The Task Before Us

(1939)

Under present circumstances I cannot hope to conceal the fact that I have managed to exist eighty years. Mention of the fact may suggest to you a more important fact—namely, that events of the utmost significance for the destiny of this country have taken place during the past four-fifths of a century, a period that covers more than half of its national life in its present form. For obvious reasons I shall not attempt a summary of even the more important of these events. I refer here to them because of their bearing upon the issue to which this country committed itself when the nation took shape—the creation of democracy, an issue which is now as urgent as it was a hundred and fifty years ago when the most experienced and wisest men of the country gathered to take stock of conditions and to create the political structure of a self-governing society.

For the net import of the changes that have taken place in these later years is that ways of life and institutions which were once the natural, almost the inevitable, product of fortunate conditions have now to be won by conscious and resolute effort. Not all the country was in a pioneer state eighty years ago. But it was still, save perhaps in a few large cities, so close to the pioneer stage of American life that the traditions of the pioneer, indeed of the frontier, were active agencies in forming the thoughts and shaping the beliefs of those who were born into its life. In imagination at least the country was still having an open frontier, one of unused and unappropriated resources. It was a country of physical opportunity and invitation. Even so, there was more than a marvelous conjunction of physical circumstances involved in bringing to birth this new nation. There was in existence a group of men who were capable of readapting older institutions and ideas to meet the situations provided by new physical conditions—a group of men extraordinarily gifted in political inventiveness.

At the present time, the frontier is moral, not physical. The period of free lands that seemed boundless in extent has vanished. Unused resources are now human rather than material. They are found in the waste of grown men and women who are without the chance to work, and in the young men and young women who find doors closed where there was once opportunity. The crisis that one hundred and fifty years ago called out social and political inventiveness is with us in a form which puts a heavier demand on human creativeness.

At all events this is what I mean when I say that we now have to re-create by deliberate and determined endeavor the kind of democracy which in its origin one hundred and fifty years ago was largely the product of a fortunate combination of men and circumstances. We have lived for a long time upon the heritage that came to us from the happy conjunction of men and events in an earlier day. The present state of the world is more than a reminder that we have now to put forth every energy of our own to prove worthy of our heritage. It is a challenge to do for the critical and complex conditions of today what the men of an earlier day did for simpler conditions.

If I emphasize that the task can be accomplished only by inventive effort and creative activity, it is in part because the depth of the present crisis is due in considerable part to the fact that for a long period we acted as if our democracy were something that perpetuated itself automatically; as if our ancestors had succeeded in setting up a machine that solved the problem of perpetual motion in politics. We acted as if democracy were something that took place mainly at Washington and Albany— or some other state capital—under the impetus of what happened when men and women went to the polls once a year or so—which is a somewhat extreme way of saying that we have had the habit of thinking of democracy as a kind of political mechanism that will work as long as citizens were reasonably faithful in performing political duties.

Of late years we have heard more and more frequently that this is not enough; that democracy is a way of life. This saying gets down to hard pan. But I am not sure that something of the externality of the old idea does not cling to the new and better statement. In any case we can escape from this external way of thinking only as we realize in thought and act that democracy is a *personal* way of individual life; that it signifies the possession and continual use of certain attitudes, forming personal character and determining desire and purpose in all the relations of life. Instead of thinking of our own dispositions and habits as accommodated to certain institutions we have to learn to think of the latter as expressions, projections and extensions of habitually dominant personal attitudes.

Democracy as a personal, an individual, way of life involves nothing fundamentally new. But when applied it puts a new practical meaning in old ideas. Put into effect it signifies that powerful present enemies of democracy can be successfully met only by the creation of personal attitudes in individual human beings; that we must get over our tendency to think that its defense can be found in any external means whatever, whether military or civil, if they are separated from individual attitudes so deep-seated as to constitute personal character.

Democracy is a way of life controlled by a working faith in the possibilities of human nature. Belief in the Common Man is a familiar article in the democratic creed. That belief is without basis and significance save as it means faith in the potentialities of human nature as that nature is exhibited in every human being irrespective of race, color, sex, birth and family, of material or cultural wealth. This faith may be enacted in statutes, but it is only on paper unless it is put in force in the attitudes which human beings display to one another in all the incidents and relations of daily life. To denounce Naziism for intolerance, cruelty and stimulation of hatred amounts to fostering insincerity if, in our personal relations to other persons, if, in our daily walk and conversation, we are moved by racial, color or other class prejudice; indeed, by anything save a generous belief in their possibilities as human beings, a belief which brings with it the need for providing conditions which will enable these capacities to reach fulfilment. The democratic faith in human equality is belief that every human being, independent of the quantity or range of his personal endowment, has the right to equal opportunity with every other person for development of whatever gifts he has. The democratic belief in the principle of leadership is a generous one. It is universal. It is belief in the capacity of every person to lead his own life free from coercion and imposition by others provided right conditions are supplied.

Democracy is a way of personal life controlled not merely by faith in human nature in general but by faith in the capacity of human beings for intelligent judgment and action if proper conditions are furnished. I have been accused more than once and from opposed quarters of an undue, a utopian, faith in the possibilities of intelligence and in education as a correlate of intelligence. At all events, I did not invent this faith. I acquired it from my surroundings as far as those surroundings were animated by the democratic spirit. For what is the faith of democracy in the role of consultation, of conference, of persuasion, of discussion, in formation of public opinion, which in the long run is self-corrective, except faith in the capacity of the intelligence of the common man to respond with commonsense to the free play of facts and ideas which are secured by effective guarantees of free inquiry, free assembly and free communication? I am willing to leave to upholders of totalitarian states of the right and the left the view that faith in the capacities of intelligence is utopian. For the faith is so deeply embedded in the methods which are intrinsic to democracy that when a professed democrat denies the faith he convicts himself of treachery to his profession.

When I think of the conditions under which men and women are living in many foreign countries today, fear of espionage, with danger hanging over the meeting of friends for friendly conversation in private gatherings, I am inclined to believe that the heart and final guarantee of democracy is in free gatherings of neighbors on the street corner to discuss back and forth what is read in uncensored news of the day, and in gatherings of friends in the living rooms of houses and apartments to converse freely with one another. Intolerance, abuse, calling of names because of differences of opinion about religion or politics or business, as well as because of differences of race, color, wealth or degree of culture are treason to the democratic way of life. For everything which bars freedom and fullness of communication sets up barriers that divide human beings into sets and cliques, into antagonistic sects and factions, and thereby undermines the democratic way of life. Merely legal guarantees of the civil liberties of free belief, free expression, free assembly are of little avail if in daily life freedom of communication, the give and take of ideas, facts, experiences, is choked by mutual suspicion, by abuse, by fear and hatred. These things destroy the essential condition of the democratic way of living even more effectually than open coercion which—as the example of totalitarian states proves—is effective only when it succeeds in breeding hate, suspicion, intolerance in the minds of individual human beings.

Finally, given the two conditions just mentioned, democracy as a way of life is controlled by personal faith in personal day-by-day working together with others. Democracy is the belief that even when needs and ends or consequences are different for each individual, the habit of amicable cooperation—which may include, as in sport, rivalry and competition—is itself a priceless addition to life. To take as far as possible every conflict which arises—and they are bound to arise—out of the atmosphere and medium of force, of violence as a means of settlement into that of discussion and of intelligence is to treat those who disagree—even profoundly—with us as those from whom we may learn, and in so far, as friends. A genuinely democratic faith in peace is faith in the possibility of conducting disputes, controversies and conflicts as cooperative undertakings in which both parties learn by giving the other a chance to express itself, instead of having one party conquer by forceful suppression of the other—a suppression which is none the less one of violence when it takes place by psychological means of ridicule, abuse, intimidation, instead of by overt imprisonment or in concentration camps. To cooperate by giving differences a chance to show themselves because of the belief that the expression of difference is not only a right of the other persons but is a means of enriching one's own life-experience, is inherent in the democratic personal way of life.

If what has been said is charged with being a set of moral commonplaces, my only reply is that that is just the point in saying them. For to get rid of the habit of thinking of democracy as something institutional and external and to acquire the habit of treating it as a way of personal life is to realize that democracy is a moral ideal and so far as it becomes a fact is a moral fact. It is to realize that democracy is a reality only as it is indeed a commonplace of living.

Since my adult years have been given to the pursuit of philosophy, I shall ask your indulgence if in concluding I state briefly the democratic faith in the formal terms of a philosophic position. So stated, democracy is belief in the ability of human experience to generate the aims and methods by which further experience will grow in ordered richness. Every other form of moral and social faith rests upon the idea that experience must be subjected at some point or other to some form of external control; to some "authority" alleged to exist outside the processes of experience. Democracy is the faith that the process of experience is more important than any special result attained, so that special results achieved are of ultimate value only as they are used to enrich and order the ongoing process. Since the process of experience is capable of being educative, faith in democracy is all one with faith in experience and education. All ends and values that are cut off from the ongoing process become arrests, fixations. They strive to fixate what has been gained instead of using it to open the road and point the way to new and better experiences.

If one asks what is meant by experience in this connection my reply is that it is that free interaction of individual human beings with surrounding conditions, especially the human surroundings, which develops and satisfies need and desire by increasing knowledge of things as they are. Knowledge of conditions as they are is the only solid ground for communication and sharing; all other communication means the subjection of some persons to the personal opinion of other persons. Need and desire—out of which grow purpose and direction of energy—go beyond what exists, and hence beyond knowledge, beyond science. They continually open the way into the unexplored and unattained future.

Democracy as compared with other ways of life is the sole way of living which believes wholeheartedly in the process of experience as end and as means; as that which is capable of generating the science which is the sole dependable authority for the direction of further experience and which releases emotions, needs and desires so as to call into being the things that have not existed in the past. For every way of life that fails in its democracy limits the contacts, the exchanges, the communications, the interactions by which experience is steadied while it is also enlarged and enriched. The task of this release and enrichment is one that has to be carried on day by day. Since it is one that can have no end till experience itself comes to an end, the task of democracy is forever that of creation of a freer and more humane experience in which all share and to which all contribute.

NOTES

[First published in *John Dewey and the Promise of America*, Progressive Education Booklet No. 14 (Columbus, Ohio: American Education Press, 1939), pp. 12–17, from an address read by Horace M. Kallen at the dinner in honor of Dewey in New York City on 20 October 1939. LW 14:224–30.]

PART 7

Pragmatism and Culture: Science and Technology, Art, and Religion

It is an old story that the right name is half the battle in moral and social disputes. With the fundamentalists, their key-word, whether or no it turn out to be half the battle, is nine-tenths of their case, perhaps ninety-nine one-hundredths. The craving of human beings for something solid and unshakable upon which to rest is ultimate and unappeasable. Many philosophers have made the search for a principle of certitude their chief quest. They sought certainty, however, not because they were philosophers but because they were human. Certainty merely happened to be the name given to the object of their particular human desire for a harbor that cannot be troubled, a support that cannot be weakened. Fundamentals are the answer to man's cry for security, living as he does a life of uncertainty in a world that is always on the move.

Just what is taken to be so fixed and final that man may repose upon it, differs with race, clime, epoch and temperament. Looking at the variety of philosophic and religious ideas of the basic and ultimate which history displays, it seems hopeless to try to define fundamentals except in a circular manner. They are whatever afford a considerable group of men living amid troubles and vicissitudes a sense of stability, safety, peace. There have even been those who carried doubt to such a point that it ceased to be a torturing perplexity, a harassing of the soul. To them scepticism became an ultimate exercise, something so certain that nothing could affect it. The mere act of doubting became a sacred rite; the performance of it afforded the requisite sense of the solid and unshakable.

Two things are equally inept. One is to forget that human nature must have something upon which to rest; the other is to fancy that one's own preferred foundation-stones are the only things that will bring stability and security to others.

As far as names go, the fundamentalists have shrewdly stolen a march on their foes in the title they have given themselves. In putting their opponents in the light of having incidentals instead of fundamentals, they have shifted the issue. Instead of raising the question, what truths and beliefs are likely at the present day to provide needed foundations, they have cre-

Fundamentals

(1924)

ated a presumption that theirs is the only brand of fundamentals. One can hear them reiterating on every hand: Take ours, or go entirely without.

Between fundamentalism and modernism as tendencies within ecclesiastical denominations, this seizure of strategic ground by one party is of no great interest to outsiders; the war is civil, domestic. But it is always of public interest that issues should not be confused; there should be at least intellectual clarity as to what is at stake. And the very names under which contending parties are now ranked is proof that the issue has not been clarified; there is no real joining of issues. In consequence, a controversy which has tremendously caught the popular imagination and aroused public interest—conceive religion on the first page!—is likely to produce too much heat and smoke where light is needed.

Obviously there is no inherent conflict between fundamentalism and modernism. Modernism joins issue with traditionalism. The respective claims over human life of traditions and of novel discoveries is a matter which is unsettled and which is of immense import for the conduct of life. There is much to be said on both sides. Yet it has hardly begun to be faced as an intellectual question. Such consideration of it as has been undertaken is entangled in questions of the merits of some particular tradition and some particular discovery—such as the Mosaic tradition of the world's creation against the discovery of the principle of evolution. If the issue had taken the form of literalism versus symbolism, controversy would have been enlightening as well as important. There are doubtless some matters which have to be taken with a certain literalness or not taken at all; brute matters of fact, for instance. There are other matters which lend themselves naturally to poetry, and where a vesture of emotion and imagination is favorable to the apprehension of the meanings involved. Honesty demands that things of the first kind be taken literally. Only crude, illiterate Philistinism will insist upon translating poetic symbolism into the prose of the first reader. But just where is the division line to be drawn in religious beliefs at present?

Just what in religion today, in the Christian religion in particular, is matter of fact to be accepted as such? Just what is symbolism, of value as far as it fulfills the functions of ready conveyance of moral truths and of inspiriting men to their observation in life? If existing controversy were definitely devoted to clearing up such questions as these it would get somewhere over and above a victory of one faction over another. Yet while those who follow the discussion find this issue touched upon here and there, they do not find it, it seems to me, clearly faced. The presentation of the issue as between fundamentalism and modernism tends to create only obscuration.

Again, one finds involved in the discussion the issue of the claims of institutional authority versus personal liberty of judgment. This issue is probably one in which the average person is most interested; the one in which he understands the controversy now raging in the churches. For this is an issue with which most men are already familiar; they have met it in politics. They have become used to thinking of a struggle between institutional authoritarianism and personal libertarianism as the fundamental thing in political history. But it may be doubted whether the issue is being clearly joined in the existing controversy. If one wants to find an uncompromising expression of the claims of the institution over the individual, one has to go beyond the High Church party in the Episcopal Church, to the Roman Catholic Church. And if one wants to find an unqualified assertion of liberty of personal belief, one has for the most part to travel outside the bounds of even liberal Protestant churches. Hence compromise, ambiguity of statement, vague qualifying clauses, hang like a fog over the discussion within the Protestant churches.

The traditionalist and literalist—I cannot strain my conscience to the point of calling him a fundamentalist—asserts an inerrant written authoritative truth—the scriptures. But no written document interprets itself, least of all such a collection of documents spread over a long period of history as the Bible. Where is the inerrant interpreter in Protestantism to correspond with the inerrant document? If it is the redeemed soul, enlightened in the very fact of its redemption, how is it that the testimony of the saints varies so much? And if it is the authority of church conferences, synods, presbyteries and conventicles in the past, why should continued power of interpretation have departed? Why do not their successors yearly, yes weekly, employ newly gained knowledge to issue pronunciamentoes as to the right interpretation of the inerrant scriptures? And, since such a course implies training and information, why are not inquiry and discussion encouraged to the uttermost?—not in the name of liberalism, but in the name of the supreme importance of a correct understanding of the one ultimate inerrant authority bequeathed to man.

These questions are intended to suggest the impenetrable confusion which surrounds the thinking of the traditionalist party when one takes their own standpoint. Denying infallibility in man and to any body of men, in effect they proclaim the infallibility of men who lived many centuries ago in periods of widespread ignorance, of unscientific methods of inquiry, of intolerance and persecuting animosity, when demonstrably the object in many cases was not so much to find truth as to down an opponent.

On the other hand, it is almost impossible to find from the side of the liberal a clear statement of just what method and criterion he holds to and is willing to see carried through to the end. He is identified with some church. Therefore he obviously believes in the value for religion of corporate tradition and organization. It is surprising to find so many persons carried away by the argument that if a clergyman does not accept the faith of his ecclesiastic institution in the sense in which it is understood by the majority, or by those in chief authority, he should "get out." Just because such a one is devoted to his corporate organization and finds himself at one with it in spirit, he clings to the fact that it is *his* church, that he belongs there, and feels assured that it will move toward fuller light. Such persons may perhaps be reproached with too great hopefulness or emotionality, but hardly with disloyalty; perhaps they suffer from too great loyalty. In any case, the question that the liberal element needs to answer in order to clarify the situation, is how they conceive the church. To what extent is it a doctrinal institution? To what extent a social-moral institution? Or if the answer is that it exists for spiritual pur-

poses, surely there is demanded some idea of what "spiritual" means, less vague than that current in liberal circles, and a more definite conception of the relation of organized institutions to spirituality.

If the nature and office of organized association for religious ends is one "fundamental" in the existing situation, another, equally important, is the method of ascertaining and testing truth. Those traditionalists and literalists who have arrogated to themselves the title of fundamentalists recognize of course no mean between their dogmas and blank, dark, hopeless uncertainty and unsettlement. Until they have been reborn into the life of intelligence, they will not be aware that there are a steadily increasing number of persons who find security in *methods* of inquiry, of observation, experiment, of forming and following working hypotheses. Such persons are not unsettled by the upsetting of any special belief, because they retain security of procedure. They can say, borrowing language from another context, though this method slay my most cherished belief, yet will I trust it. The growth of this sense, even if only half-consciously, is the cause of the increased indifference of large numbers of persons to organized religion. It is not that they are especially excited about this or that doctrine, but that the guardianship of truth seems to them to have passed over to the *method* of attaining and testing beliefs. In this latter fundamental they rest in intellectual and emotional peace.

Just where does the modernist group in the church stand as to this particular fundamental? What do they conceive to be the ultimate source and authority, the criterion, for belief? With the best will in the world to side with them as against literal traditionalists, one may find it hard to secure from them anything but a cloudy answer to this question. Looking at the present controversy from the outside, one may believe that it is thoroughly wholesome, humane and emancipating in effect, that it will make for tolerance and open-mindedness, greater sincerity and directness of experience and statement. And yet one may believe that it will not accomplish anything fundamental, until the liberal protesting elements have cleared up their minds on at least just these two points: What is the relation of a specially organized community and institution like the church, whatever be the church, to religious experience? What is the place of belief in religion and by what methods is true belief achieved and tested?

NOTES

[First published in *New Republic* 37 (1924): 275–76. Republished in *Characters and Events*, ed. Joseph Ratner (New York: Henry Holt and Co., 1929), 2:453–58. MW 15:3–7.]

The old issue between science and religion, or as many preferred to call it between science and theology, has slowly but surely changed its aspect. The operation of four rather than two forces is clearly evident in the current fundamentalist controversy. Instead of an alignment of two opposing tendencies, there is now a quadrilateral situation. The "people" have been called in, so that public opinion and sentiment are a power to be reckoned with; because of this fact the state of general education is a new and decisive factor in shaping the course and outcome of the old struggle.

When a glance is cast upon the earlier conflict between the new science of nature and traditional dogmas, the mass of the people is seen to be indifferent and unconcerned; they are hardly even spectators of the combat. On one side there are a few scientific inquirers, men like Galileo, who in the course of their scientific investigations reach results, especially about astronomical matters and the place of the earth in the scheme of things, directly contrary to those contained in the official doctrines of the church. On the other hand, there are the official representatives of the church, aggrieved and insulted by the challenge of a few scientific heretics. Outside of these limited circles, few knew or cared about what was going on. But the printing press, cheap newspapers, mails and telegraph and the extension of schooling have changed all that.

Even in the few years since Darwin published his *Origin of Species* affairs have moved rapidly. The rise of Protestantism and the increased active participation of laymen in matters of religious beliefs had indeed aroused a much wider public concern about the new views regarding the development of life and a naturalistic interpretation of the Descent of Man, than had the older scientific heresies. The issue was no longer wholly between scientific men on one side and established official authorities of the church on the other. Hot debate took place in widely circulated books and magazines, and large numbers were stirred to passionate adherence and more passionate denunciations. But I should guess that the number of daily newspapers was small that concerned themselves with the issue beyond reviews in their literary columns; it would be, I

Science, Belief and the Public

(1924)

fancy, a safe wager that the controversy did not make the first page of newspapers, with glaring headlines, nor cause anything approaching the stir excited today by a single sermon by a well-known clergyman. Certain it is that bills were not introduced in legislatures and parliaments. For geology and biology not being at that time regular parts of even higher schooling, except perhaps for a few, there was nothing for statutes to regulate, unless the state was to emulate the Inquisition in regulating the diffusion of all scientific notions about the world.

These considerations help explain, it seems to me, a fact which has puzzled so many. For a long time it looked as if the conception of continuity of organic development had, in some version or other, become about as firmly entrenched in science and as accepted from science by the public mind as Copernican astronomy. Many of us imagined that a serious attack upon evolutionary views with a revival of pre-Darwinian biology was as improbable as an attack upon the astronomy of Galileo, or a wide-spread and influential campaign in behalf of the Ptolemaic system. Certainly, from the specialized scientific point of view, the anti-evolutionary campaign comes about three centuries too late. If it were to affect seriously the course of scientific inquiries, a number of persons should have been strangled in their cradles some three hundred years ago. Nevertheless, the issue is for the public actual and vital today, in spite of the elapse of a generation in which we prided ourselves—just as we prided ourselves that a great war was henceforth impossible—upon the advance of the scientific spirit, and the accommodation of the public mind to the conclusions of scientific inquiries.

The moral is inevitable. The public, the popular mass that the enlightened could once refer to as canaille, has taken an active part; but the conditions which have enabled the public actively to intervene have failed in providing an education which would enable the public to discriminate, with respect to the matters upon which it is most given to vehement expression, between opinions untouched by scientific method and attitude and the weight of evidence.

This to my mind is the salient aspect of the present situation. In the large, the controversy between science and dogma in the old sense is over and done with. There are many individuals, believers and others, to whom the question of adjusting their religious conceptions to the conclusions of science is still a vital one. But as a technical and professional cause, science has won its freedom. Scientists in the field and the laboratory may be discommoded at times, individual inquirers and teachers may lose their jobs. But the scientific revolution is nevertheless accomplished; and it is one of the revolutions that do not turn backwards. Inquirers will go on inquiring, and the results of their inquiries will be disseminated at least among their fellow-workers, and will make their way—even if they are as revolutionary as are the discoveries of the last thirty years regarding the constitution of matter and energy, ideas more upsetting of older conceptions in many ways than were those of the intellectual pioneers of the seventeenth century. The real issue is not here. It concerns the growing influence of the general public in matters of thought and belief, and the comparative failure of schooling up to the present time to instil even the rudiments of the scientific attitude in vast numbers of persons, so as to enable them to distinguish between matters of mere opinion and argument and those of fact and ascertainment of fact.

Americans who have been abroad tell of the amused incredulity of educated Europeans over reports of the state of scientific and theological controversy in this country; the reports seem incredible except upon the basis of an almost barbaric state of culture. Yet it may be doubted whether if numbers alone were taken into account, there would not be a larger proportion of persons in this country who could give an intelligent statement of the scientific conceptions involved than in most European countries. The difference is that in those countries those who could not give an intelligent exposition hardly count at all. Here, owing to the spread of democracy in social relations and in education, they count for a great deal. They feel themselves concerned and have channels through which they can make their influence felt.

Naturally such a situation is sport for those hostile to democracy and to universal schooling. They are entitled to chuckle and to make the most of it in their indictments. But, after all, it is a condition and not a theory that confronts us. Defences of democracy are about as much out of place in any scheme of action as are attacks. No social creed produced the present situation. The consequences of the industrialization of affairs in such things as change of population from rural to urban, quick and easy transportation of persons and goods, cheap communications and the rise of cheap printing-matter, have created that state of society which we call democratic, and the democratic creed. Unless the movement of forces is radically altered, attacks upon democracy are about as effective as shooting paper-wads at a battle-ship—an occupation that may also conceivably relieve the feelings under certain conditions.

The realities of the situation centre about what can be done to ally the forces which create the democratizing of society with the mental and moral attitudes of science. The worst of the predicament is a tendency toward a vicious circle. The forces that compel some degree of general schooling also make for a loose, scrappy and talkative education, and this education in turn reenforces the bad features of the underlying forces. But it is some gain to know where the issue actually lies; to be compelled to face the fact that while schooling has been extended and scientific subjects have found their way into the regular course of studies, little has been accomplished as yet in converting prejudiced and emotional habits of mind into scientific interest and capacity.

This generic diagnosis of the disease may be specified in two particulars. There is a considerable class of influential persons, enlightened and liberal in technical, scientific and religious matters, who are only too ready to make use of appeal to authority, prejudice, emotion and ignorance to serve their purposes in political and economic affairs. Having done whatever they can do to debauch the habit of the public mind in these respects, they then sit back in amazed sorrow when this same habit of mind displays itself violently with regard, say, to the use of established methods of his-toric and literary interpretations of the scriptures or with regard to the animal origin of man. "Fundamentalism" might have been revived even if the Great War had not occurred. But it is reasonable to suppose that it would have not assumed such an intolerant and vituperative form, if so many educated men, in positions of leadership, had not deliberately cultivated resort to bitter intolerance and to coercive suppression of disliked opinions during the war.

Again, a man may be thoroughly convinced that the spread of certain economic ideas is dangerous to society; but if he encourages, even by passivity, recourse to coercion and intimidation in order to resist the holding and teaching of these ideas, he should not be surprised if others fail to draw the line of persecution and intolerance just where he personally would draw it. The statement that as we sow, so shall we reap, is trite. But there is no field of life in which it applies so aptly and fully as in that of belief and the methods employed to affect belief. Until highly respectable and cultivated classes of men cease to suppose that in economic and political matters the importance of the end of social stability and security justifies the use of means other than those of reason, the intellectual habit of the public will continue to be corrupted at the root, and by those from whom enlightenment should be expected.

The other point concerns the kind of education given in the schools, as that is affected by the temper of actual and professed pillars of society. There are at the best plenty of obstacles in the way of thinking in general, and in particular of using school instruction so as to further discriminating and circumspect thought. The weight of authority, custom, imitation, pressure of time, large numbers, the need of "covering the ground," of securing mechanical skill, of uniformity in administrative matters, of sparing tax-payers, all conspire to depress thinking. These extraneous obstacles are consolidated and held together by the fear entertained by many "best minds" lest the schools promote habits of independent thinking. Fundamentally, fear of the consequences of thought underlies most professions of reverence for culture, respect for quantity of information and emphasis upon discipline. The fundamental defect in the present state of democracy is the assumption that political and economic freedom can be achieved without first freeing the mind. Freedom of mind is not something that spontaneously happens. It is not achieved by the mere absence of obvious restraints. It is a product of constant, unremitting nurture of right habits of observation and reflection. Until the taboos that hedge social topics from contact with thought are removed, scientific method and results in subjects far removed from social themes will make little impression upon the public mind. Prejudice, fervor of emotion, bunkum, opinion and irrelevant argument will weigh as heavily as fact and knowledge. Intellectual confusion will continue to encourage the men who are intolerant and who fake their beliefs in the interests of their feelings and fancies.

NOTES

[First published in *New Republic* 38 (1924): 143–45. Republished in *Characters and Events*, ed. Joseph Ratner (New York: Henry Holt and Co., 1929), 2:459–64. MW 15:47–52.]

Human conduct, broadly viewed, falls into two sorts: Particular cases overlap, but the difference is discernible in any large scale consideration of conduct. Sometimes human beings act with a minimum of foresight, without examination of what they are doing and its probable consequences. They act not upon deliberation, but from routine, instinct, the direct pressure of appetite, or a blind "hunch." It would be a mistake to suppose that such behavior is always inefficient or unsuccessful. When we do not like it, we condemn it as capricious, arbitrary, careless, negligent. But in other cases we praise the marvellous rectitude of instinct or intuition; we are inclined to accept the offhand appraisal of an expert in preference to elaborately calculated conclusions of a man who is ill-informed. There is the old story of the layman who was appointed to a position in India where he would have to pass in his official capacity on various matters in controversy between natives. Upon consulting a legal friend, he was told to use his common-sense and announce his decisions firmly; in the majority of cases his natural decision as to what was fair and reasonable would suffice. But, his friend added: "Never try to give reasons, for they will usually be wrong."

In the other sort of case, action follows upon a decision, and the decision is the outcome of inquiry, comparison of alternatives, weighing of facts; deliberation or thinking has intervened. Considerations which have weight in reaching the conclusion as to what is to be done, or which are employed to justify it when it is questioned, are called "reasons." If they are stated in sufficiently general terms, they are "principles." When the operation is formulated in a compact way, the decision is called a conclusion, and the considerations which led up to it are called the premises. Decisions of the first type may be reasonable: that is, they may be adapted to good results; those of the second type are reasoned or rational, increasingly so, in the degree of care and thoroughness with which inquiry has been conducted and the order in which connections have been established between the considerations dealt with.

Now I define logical theory as an account of the procedures followed in reaching deci-

Logical Method and Law

(1924)

sions of the second type, in those cases in which subsequent experience shows that they were the best which could have been used under the conditions. This definition would be questioned by many authorities, and it is only fair to say that it does not represent the orthodox or the prevailing view. But it is stated at the outset so that the reader may be aware of the conception of logic which underlies the following discussion. If we take an objection which will be brought against this conception by adherents of the traditional notion, it will serve to clarify its meaning. It will be said that the definition restricts thinking to the processes antecedent to making a decision or a deliberate choice; and, thereby, in confining logical procedure to practical matters, fails to take even a glance at those cases in which true logical method is best exemplified: namely, scientific, especially mathematical, subjects.

A partial answer to this objection is that the especial topic of our present discussion is logical method in legal reasoning and judicial decision; and that such cases at least are similar in general type to decisions made by engineers, merchants, physicians, bankers, etc., in the pursuit of their callings. In law we are certainly concerned with the necessity of settling upon a course of action to be pursued, giving judgment of one sort or another in favor of adoption of one mode of conduct and against another. But the scope of the position taken will appear more clearly if we do not content ourselves with this *ad hoc* reply.

If we consider the procedure of the mathematician or of any man of science, as it concretely occurs, instead of considering simply the relations of consistent implication which subsist between the propositions in which his finally approved conclusions are set forth, we find that he, as well as an intelligent farmer or business-man or physician, is constantly engaged in making decisions; and that in order to make them wisely he summons before his mental gaze various considerations and accepts and rejects them with a view to making his decision as rational as possible. The concrete subject with which he deals, the material he investigates, accepts, rejects, employs in reaching and justifying his decision, is different from that of farmer, lawyer or merchant, but the

course of the operation, the form of the procedure, is similar. The scientific man has the advantage of working under much more narrowly and exactly controlled conditions, with the aid of symbols artfully devised to protect his procedure. For that reason it is natural and proper that we should, in our formal treatises, take operations of this type as standards and models, and should treat ordinary "practical" reasonings leading up to decisions as to what is to be done as only approximations. But every thinker, as an investigator, mathematician or physicist, as well as "practical man," thinks in order to determine *his* decisions and conduct—his conduct as a specialized agent working in a carefully delimited field.

It may be replied, of course, that this is an arbitrary notion of logic, and that in reality logic is an affair of the relations and orders of relations which subsist between propositions which constitute the accepted subject-matter of a science; that relations are independent of operations of inquiry and of reaching conclusions or decisions. I shall not stop to try to controvert this position, but shall use it to point the essential difference between it and the position taken in this article. According to the latter, logical systematization with a view to the utmost generality and consistency of propositions is indispensable but is not ultimate. It is an instrumentality, not an end. It is a means of improving, facilitating, clarifying the inquiry that leads up to concrete decisions; primarily that particular inquiry which has just been engaged in, but secondarily, and of greater ultimate importance, other inquiries directed at making other decisions in similar fields. And here at least I may fall back for confirmation upon the special theme of law. It is most important that rules of law should form as coherent and generalized logical systems as possible. But these logical systematizations of law in any field, whether of crime, contracts or torts, with their reduction of a multitude of decisions to a few general principles that are logically consistent with one another, while they may be an end in itself for a particular student, are clearly in last resort subservient to the economical and effective reaching of decisions in particular cases.

It follows that logic is ultimately an empirical and concrete discipline. Men first employ certain ways of investigating, and of collecting, recording and using data in reaching conclusions, in making decisions; they draw inferences and make their checks and tests in various ways. These different ways constitute the empirical raw material of logical theory. The latter thus comes into existence without any conscious thought of logic, just as forms of speech take place without conscious reference to rules of syntax or of rhetorical propriety. But it is gradually learned that some methods which are used work better than others. Some yield conclusions that do not stand the test of further situations; they produce conflicts and confusion; decisions dependent upon them have to be retracted or revised. Other methods are found to yield conclusions which are available in subsequent inquiries as well as confirmed by them. There first occurs a kind of natural selection of the methods which afford the better type of conclusion, better for subsequent usage, just as happens in the development of rules for conducting any art. Afterwards the methods are themselves studied critically. Successful ones are not only selected and collated, but the causes of their effective operation are discovered. Thus logical theory becomes scientific.

The bearing of the conception of logic which is here advanced upon legal thinking and decisions may be brought out by examining the apparent disparity which exists between actual legal development and the strict requirements of logical theory. Justice Holmes has generalized the situation by saying that "the whole outline of the law is the resultant of a conflict at every point between logic and good sense—the one striving to work fiction out to consistent results, the other restraining and at last overcoming that effort when the results become too manifestly unjust."[1] This statement he substantiates by a thorough examination of the development of certain legal notions. Upon its surface, such a statement implies a different view of the nature of logic than that stated. It implies that logic is not the method *of* good sense, that it has as it were a substance and life of its own which conflicts with the requirements of good decisions with respect to concrete subject-matters. The differ-

ence, however, is largely verbal. What Justice Holmes terms logic is formal consistency, consistency of concepts with one another irrespective of the consequences of their application to concrete matters-of-fact. We might state the fact by saying that concepts once developed have a kind of intrinsic inertia on their own account; once developed the law of habit applies to them. It is practically economical to use a concept ready at hand rather than to take time and trouble and effort to change it or to devise a new one. The use of prior ready-made and familiar concepts also gives rise to a sense of stability, of guarantee against sudden and arbitrary changes of the rules which determine the consequences which legally attend acts. It is the nature of any concept, as it is of any habit, to change more slowly than do the concrete circumstances with reference to which it is employed. Experience shows that the relative fixity of concepts affords men with a specious sense of protection, of assurance against the troublesome flux of events. Thus Justice Holmes says, "The language of judicial decision is mainly the language of logic. And the logical method and form flatter that longing for certainty and for repose which is in every human mind. But certainty generally is an illusion."[2] From the view of logical method here set forth, however, the undoubted facts which Justice Holmes has in mind do not concern logic, but rather certain tendencies of the human creatures who use logic, tendencies which a sound logic will guard against. For they spring from the momentum of habit once formed, and express the effect of habit upon our feelings of ease and stability—feelings which have little to do with the actual facts of the case.

However this is only part of the story. The rest of the story is brought to light in some other passages of Justice Holmes. "The actual life of the law has not been logic: it has been experience. The felt necessities of the times, the prevalent moral and political theories, intuitions of public policy, avowed or unconscious, even the prejudices which judges share with their fellow-men, have had a good deal more to do than the syllogism in determining the rules by which men should be governed."[3] In other words, Justice Holmes is thinking of logic as equivalent with the syllogism, as he is quite entitled to do in accord with the ortho-dox tradition. From the standpoint of the syl-logism as the logical model which was made current by scholasticism there *is* an antithesis between experience and logic, between logic and good sense. For the philosophy embodied in the formal theory of the syllogism asserted that thought or reason has fixed forms of its own, anterior to and independent of concrete subject-matters, and to which the latter have to be adapted whether or no. This defines the negative aspect of this discussion; and it shows by contrast the need of another kind of logic which shall reduce the influence of habit, and shall facilitate the use of good sense regarding matters of social consequence.

In other words, there are different logics in use. One of these, the one which has had greatest historic currency and exercised great-est influence on legal decisions, is that of the syllogism. To this logic the strictures of Justice Holmes apply in full force. For it purports to be a logic of rigid demonstration, not of search and discovery. It claims to be a logic of fixed forms, rather than of methods of reaching in-telligent decisions in concrete situations, or of methods employed in adjusting disputed is-sues in behalf of the public and enduring inter-est. Those ignorant of formal logic, the logic of the abstract relations of ready-made concep-tions to one another, have at least heard of the standard syllogism: "All men are mortal; Soc-rates is a man; therefore he is mortal." This is offered as the model of all proof or demonstra-tion. It implies that what we need and must procure is first a fixed general *principle*, the so-called major premiss, such as: "all men are mortal"; then, in the second place, a *fact* which belongs intrinsically and obviously to a class of things to which the general principle ap-plies: "Socrates is a man." Then the conclusion automatically follows: "Socrates is mortal." According to this model every demonstrative or strictly logical conclusion "subsumes" a par-ticular under an appropriate universal. It im-plies the prior and given existence of particu-lars and universals.

It thus implies that for every possible case which may arise, there is a fixed antecedent rule already at hand; that the case in question is either simple and unambiguous or is resolv-able by direct inspection into a collection of simple and indubitable facts, such as, "Socrates is a man." It thus tends, when it is accepted, to produce and confirm what Professor Pound has called mechanical jurisprudence; it flatters that longing for certainty of which Justice Holmes speaks; it reinforces those inert factors in human nature which make men hug as long as possible any idea which has once gained lodgment in the mind.

In a certain sense it is foolish to criticize the model supplied by the syllogism. The state-ments made about men and Socrates are obvi-ously true and the connection between them is undoubted. The trouble is that while the syllo-gism sets forth the *results* of thinking, it has nothing to do with the *operation* of thinking. Take the case of Socrates being tried before the Athenian citizens, and the thinking which had to be done to reach a decision. Certainly the issue was not whether Socrates was mortal; the point was whether this mortality would or should occur at a specified date and in a specified way. Now that is just what does not and cannot follow from a general principle or a major premiss. Again, to quote Justice Holmes, "General propositions do not decide concrete cases." No concrete proposition, that is to say one with its material dated in time and placed in space, follows from any general statements or from any connection between them.

If we trust to an experimental logic, we find that general principles emerge as state-ments of generic ways in which it has been found helpful to treat concrete cases. The real force of the proposition that all men are mortal is found in the expectancy tables of insurance companies, which, with their accompanying rates, show how it is prudent and socially useful to deal with human mortality. The "uni-versal" stated in the major premiss is not out-side of and antecedent to particular cases; nei-ther is it a selection of something found in a variety of cases. It is an indication of a unified way of treating cases for certain purposes or consequences in spite of their diversity. Hence its meaning and worth are subject to inquiry and revision in view of what happens, what the consequences are, when it is used as a method of treatment.

As a matter of fact, men do not begin

thinking with premisses. They begin with some complicated and confused case, apparently admitting of alternative modes of treatment and solution. Premisses only gradually emerge from analysis of the total situation. The problem is not to draw a conclusion from given premisses; that can best be done by a piece of inanimate machinery, by fingering a key-board. The problem is to *find* statements, of general principle and of particular fact, which are worthy to serve as premisses. As matter of actual fact, we generally begin with some vague anticipation of a conclusion (or at least of alternative conclusions), and then we look around for principles and data which will substantiate it or which will enable us to choose intelligently between rival conclusions. No lawyer ever thought out the case of a client in terms of the syllogism. He begins with a conclusion which he intends to reach, favorable to his client of course, and then analyzes the facts of the situation to find material out of which to construct a favorable statement of facts, to *form* a minor premiss. At the same time he goes over recorded cases to find rules of law employed in cases which can be presented as similar, rules which will substantiate a certain way of looking at and interpreting the facts. And as his acquaintance with rules of law judged applicable widens, he probably alters perspective and emphasis in selection of the facts which are to form his evidential data. And as he learns more of the facts of the case, he may modify his selection of rules of law upon which he bases his case.

I do not for a moment set up this procedure as a model of scientific method; it is too precommitted to the establishment of a particular and partisan conclusion to serve as such a model. But it does illustrate, in spite of this deficiency, the particular point which is being made here: namely, that thinking actually sets out from a more or less confused situation, which is vague and ambiguous with respect to the conclusion it indicates, and that the formation of both major premiss and minor proceeds tentatively and correlatively in the course of analysis of this situation and of prior rules. As soon as acceptable premisses are given—and of course the judge and jury have eventually to do with their becoming accepted—the conclusion is also given. In strict logic, the conclusion does not follow from premisses; conclusions and premisses are two ways of stating the same thing. Thinking may be defined either as a development of premisses or development of a conclusion; as far as it is one operation it is the other.

Courts not only reach decisions; they expound them, and the exposition must state justifying reasons. The mental operations therein involved are somewhat different from those involved in arriving at a conclusion. The logic of exposition is different from that of search and inquiry. In the latter, the situation as it exists is more or less doubtful, indeterminate and problematic with respect to what it signifies. It unfolds itself gradually and is susceptible of dramatic surprise; at all events it has, for the time being, two sides. Exposition implies that a definitive solution is reached, that the situation is now determinate with respect to its legal implications. Its purpose is to set forth grounds for the decision reached so that it will not appear as an arbitrary dictum, and so that it will indicate a rule for dealing with similar cases in the future. It is highly probable that the need of justifying to others conclusions reached and decisions made has been the chief cause of the origin and development of logical operations in the precise sense; of abstraction, generalization, regard for consistency of implications. It is quite conceivable that if no one had ever had to account to others for his decisions, logical operations would never have developed, but men would use exclusively methods of inarticulate intuition and impression, feeling; so that only after considerable experience in accounting for their decisions to others who demanded a reason, or exculpation, and were not satisfied till they got it, did men begin to give an account to themselves of the process of reaching a conclusion in a justified way. However this may be, it is certain that in judicial decisions the only alternative to arbitrary dicta, accepted by the parties to a controversy only because of the authority or prestige of the judge, is a rational statement which formulates grounds and exposes connecting or logical links.

It is at this point that the chief stimulus and temptation to mechanical logic and abstract use of formal concepts come in. Just because the personal element cannot be entirely excluded, while at the same time the decision must assume as nearly as possible an impersonal, objective, rational form, the temptation is to surrender the vital logic which has actually yielded the conclusion, and to substitute for it forms of speech which are rigorous in appearance and which give an illusion of certitude. Another moving force is the undoubted need for the maximum possible of stability and regularity of expectation in determining courses of conduct. Men need to know the legal consequences which society through the courts will attach to their specific transactions, the liabilities they are assuming, the fruits they may count upon in entering upon a given course of action.

This is a legitimate requirement from the standpoint of the interests of the community and of particular individuals. Enormous confusion has resulted, however, from confusion of *theoretical* certainty with *practical* certainty. There is a wide gap separating the reasonable proposition that judicial decisions should possess the maximum possible regularity in order to enable persons in planning their conduct to foresee the legal import of their acts, and the absurd because impossible proposition that every decision should flow with formal logical necessity from antecedently known premises. To attain the former result there are required general principles of interpreting cases—rules of law—and procedures of pleading and trying cases which do not alter arbitrarily. But principles of interpretation do not signify rules so rigid that they can be stated once for all and then be literally and mechanically adhered to. For the situations to which they are to be applied do not literally repeat one another in all details; and questions of degree of this factor or that have the chief weight in determining which general rule will be employed to judge the situation in question. A large part of what has been asserted concerning the necessity of absolutely uniform and immutable antecedent rules of law is in effect an attempt to evade the really important issue of finding and employing rules of law, substantive and procedural, which will actually secure to the members of the community a reasonable measure of practi-

cal certainty of expectation in framing their courses of conduct. The mechanical ease of the court in disposing of cases and not the actual security of agents is the real cause, for example, of making rules of pleading hard and fast. The result introduces an unnecessary element of gamble into the behavior of those seeking settlement of disputes, while it affords to the judges only that factitious ease and simplicity which is supplied by any routine habit of action. It substitutes a mechanical procedure for the need of analytic thought.

There is of course every reason why rules of law should be as regular and as definite as possible. But the amount and kind of antecedent assurance which is actually attainable is a matter of fact, not of form. It is large wherever social conditions are pretty uniform, and when industry, commerce, transportation, etc., move in the channels of old customs. It is much less wherever invention is active, and when new devices in business and communication bring about new forms of human relationship. Thus the use of power machinery radically modifies the old terms of association of master and servant and fellow servants; rapid transportation brings into general use commercial bills of lading; mass production engenders organization of laborers and collective bargaining; industrial conditions favor concentration of capital. In part legislation endeavors to reshape old rules of law to make them applicable to new conditions. But statutes have never kept up with the variety and subtlety of social change. They cannot at the very best avoid some ambiguity, which is due not only to carelessness but also to the intrinsic impossibility of foreseeing all possible circumstances, since without such foresight definitions must be vague and classifications indeterminate. Hence to claim that old forms are ready at hand that cover every case and that may be applied by formal syllogizing, is to pretend to a certainty and regularity which cannot exist in fact. The effect of the pretension is to increase practical uncertainty and social instability. Just because circumstances are really novel and not covered by old rules, it is a gamble which old rule will be declared regulative of a particular case, so that shrewd and enterprising men are encouraged to sail close to the wind and trust to ingenious lawyers to find some rule under which they can get off scot free.

The facts involved in this discussion are commonplace and they are not offered as presenting anything original or novel. What we are concerned with is their bearing upon the logic of judicial decisions. For the implications are more revolutionary than they might at first seem to be. They indicate either that logic must be abandoned or that it must be a logic *relative to consequences rather than to antecedents*, a logic of prediction of probabilities rather than one of deduction of certainties. For the purposes of a logic of inquiry into probable consequences, general principles can only be tools justified by the work they do. They are means of intellectual survey, analysis and insight into the factors of the situation to be dealt with. Like other tools they must be modified when they are applied to new conditions and new results have to be achieved. Here is where the great practical evil of the doctrine of immutable and necessary antecedent rules comes in. It sanctifies the old; adherence to it in practice constantly widens the gap between current social conditions and the principles used by the courts. The effect is to breed irritation, disrespect for law, together with virtual alliance between the judiciary and entrenched interests that correspond most nearly to the conditions under which the rules of law were previously laid down.

Failure to recognize that general legal rules and principles are working hypotheses, needing to be constantly tested by the way in which they work out in application to concrete situations, explains the otherwise paradoxical fact that the slogans of the liberalism of one period often become the bulwarks of reaction in a subsequent era. There was a time in the eighteenth century when the great social need was emancipation of industry and trade from a multitude of restrictions which held over from the feudal estate of Europe. Adapted well enough to the localized and fixed conditions of that earlier age, they became hindrances and annoyances as the effects of new methods, use of coal and steam, emerged. The movement of emancipation expressed itself in principles of liberty in use of property, and freedom of contract, which were embodied in a mass of legal decisions. But the absolutistic logic of rigid syllogistic forms infected these ideas. It was soon forgotten that they were relative to analysis of existing situations in order to secure orderly methods in behalf of economic social welfare. Thus these principles became in turn so rigid as to be almost as socially obstructive as "immutable" feudal laws had been in their day.

That the remarks which have been made, commonplace as they are in themselves, have a profound practical import may also be seen in the present reaction against the individualistic formulae of an older liberalism. The last thirty years have seen an intermittent tendency in the direction of legislation, and to a less extent of judicial decision, towards what is vaguely known as "social justice," toward formulae of a collectivistic character. Now it is quite possible that the newer rules may be needed and useful at a certain juncture, and yet that they may also become harmful and socially obstructive if they are hardened into absolute and fixed antecedent premises. But if they are conceived as tools to be adapted to the conditions in which they are employed rather than as absolute and intrinsic "principles," attention will go to the facts of social life, and the rules will not be allowed to engross attention and become absolute truths to be maintained intact at all costs. Otherwise we shall in the end merely have substituted one set of formally absolute and immutable syllogistic premises for another set.

If we recur then to our introductory conception that logic is really a theory about empirical phenomena, subject to growth and improvement like any other empirical discipline, we recur to it with an added conviction: namely, that the issue is not a purely speculative one but implies consequences vastly significant for practice. I should indeed not hesitate to assert that the sanctification of ready-made antecedent universal principles as methods of thinking is the chief obstacle to the kind of thinking which is the indispensable prerequisite of steady, secure and intelligent social reforms in general, and social advance by means of law in particular. If this be so, infiltration into law of a more experimental and flexible logic is a social as well as an intellectual need.

NOTES

[First published in *Philosophical Review* 33 (1924): 560–72. Republished in *Cornell Law Quarterly* 10 (1924): 17–27, and in *Philosophy and Civilization* (New York: Minton, Balch and Co., 1931), pp. 126–40. MW 15:65–77.]

1. *Collected Legal Papers*, p. 50.
2. *Ibid.*, p. 181.
3. *The Common Law*, p. 1.

The significant outward forms of the civilization of the western world are the product of the machine and its technology. Indirectly, they are the product of the scientific revolution which took place in the seventeenth century. In its effect upon men's external habits, dominant interests, the conditions under which they work and associate, whether in the family, the factory, the state, or internationally, science is by far the most potent social factor in the modern world. It operates, however, through its undesigned effects rather than as a transforming influence of men's thoughts and purposes. This contrast between outer and inner operation is the great contradiction in our lives. Habits of thought and desire remain in substance what they were before the rise of science, while the conditions under which they take effect have been radically altered by science.

When we look at the external social consequences of science, we find it impossible to apprehend the extent or gauge the rapidity of their occurrence. Alfred North Whitehead has recently called attention to the progressive shortening of the time-span of social change. That due to basic conditions seems to be of the order of half a million years; that due to lesser physical conditions, like alterations in climate, to be of the order of five thousand years. Until almost our own day the time-span of sporadic technological changes was of the order of five hundred years; according to him, no great technological changes took place between, say, 100 A.D. and 1400 A.D. With the introduction of steam-power, the fifty years from 1780 to 1830 were marked by more changes than are found in any previous thousand years. The advance of chemical techniques and in use of electricity and radio-energy in the last forty years makes even this last change seem slow and awkward.

Domestic life, political institutions, international relations and personal contacts are shifting with kaleidoscopic rapidity before our eyes. We cannot appreciate and weigh the changes; they occur too swiftly. We do not have time to take them in. No sooner do we begin to understand the meaning of one such change than another comes and displaces the former. Our minds are dulled by the sudden and repeated impacts. Externally, science through its

Science and Society

From *Philosophy and Civilization* (1931)

applications is manufacturing the conditions of our institutions at such a speed that we are too bewildered to know what sort of civilization is in process of making.

Because of this confusion, we cannot even draw up a ledger account of social gains and losses due to the operation of science. But at least we know that the earlier optimism which thought that the advance of natural science was to dispel superstition, ignorance, and oppression, by placing reason on the throne, was unjustified. Some superstitions have given way, but the mechanical devices due to science have made it possible to spread new kinds of error and delusion among a larger multitude. The fact is that it is foolish to try to draw up a debit and credit account for science. To do so is to mythologize; it is to personify science and impute to it a will and an energy on its own account. In truth science is strictly impersonal; a method and a body of knowledge. It owes its operation and its consequences to the human beings who use it. It adapts itself passively to the purposes and desires which animate these human beings. It lends itself with equal impartiality to the kindly offices of medicine and hygiene and the destructive deeds of war. It elevates some through opening new horizons; it depresses others by making them slaves of machines operated for the pecuniary gain of owners.

The neutrality of science to the uses made of it renders it silly to talk about its bankruptcy, or to worship it as the usherer in of a new age. In the degree in which we realize this fact, we shall devote our attention to the human purposes and motives which control its application. Science is an instrument, a method, a body of technique. While it is an end for those inquirers who are engaged in its pursuit, in the large human sense it is a means, a tool. For what ends shall it be used? Shall it be used deliberately, systematically, for the promotion of social well-being, or shall it be employed primarily for private aggrandizement, leaving its larger social results to chance? Shall the scientific attitude be used to create new mental and moral attitudes, or shall it continue to be subordinated to service of desires, purposes and institutions which were formed before science came into existence? Can the attitudes which control the use of science be themselves so influenced by scientific technique that they will harmonize with its spirit?

The beginning of wisdom is, I repeat, the realization that science itself is an instrument which is indifferent to the external uses to which it is put. Steam and electricity remain natural forces when they operate through mechanisms; the only problem is the purposes for which men set the mechanisms to work. The essential technique of gunpowder is the same whether it be used to blast rocks from the quarry to build better human habitations, or to hurl death upon men at war with one another. The airplane binds men at a distance in closer bonds of intercourse and understanding, or it rains missiles of death upon hapless populations. We are forced to consider the relation of human ideas and ideals to the social consequences which are produced by science as an instrument.

The problem involved is the greatest which civilization has ever had to face. It is, without exaggeration, the most serious issue of contemporary life. Here is the instrumentality, the most powerful, for good and evil, the world has ever known. What are we going to do with it? Shall we leave our underlying aims unaffected by it, treating it merely as a means by which uncooperative individuals may advance their own fortunes? Shall we try to improve the hearts of men without regard to the new methods which science puts at our disposal? There are those, men in high position in church and state, who urge this course. They trust to a transforming influence of a morals and religion which have not been affected by science to change human desire and purpose, so that they will employ science and machine technology for beneficent social ends. The recent Encyclical of the Pope is a classic document in expression of a point of view which would rely wholly upon inner regeneration to protect society from the injurious uses to which science may be put. Quite apart from any ecclesiastical connection, there are many "intellectuals" who appeal to inner "spiritual" concepts, totally divorced from scientific intelligence, to effect the needed work. But there is another alternative: to take the method of science home into our own controlling attitudes and dispositions, to employ the new techniques as means of directing our thoughts and efforts to a planned control of social forces.

Science and machine technology are young from the standpoint of human history. Though vast in stature, they are infants in age. Three hundred years are but a moment in comparison with thousands of centuries man has lived on the earth. In view of the inertia of institutions and of the mental habits they breed, it is not surprising that the new technique of apparatus and calculation, which is the essence of science, has made so little impression on underlying human attitudes. The momentum of traditions and purposes that preceded its rise took possession of the new instrument and turned it to their ends. Moreover, science had to struggle for existence. It had powerful enemies in church and state. It needed friends and it welcomed alliance with the rising capitalism which it so effectively promoted. If it tended to foster secularism and to create predominantly material interests, it could still be argued that it was in essential harmony with traditional morals and religion. But there were lacking the conditions which are indispensable to the serious application of scientific method in reconstruction of fundamental beliefs and attitudes. In addition, the development of the new science was attended with so many internal difficulties that energy had to go to perfecting the instrument just as an instrument. Because of all these circumstances the fact that science was used in behalf of old interests is nothing to be wondered at.

The conditions have now changed, radically so. The claims of natural science in the physical field are undisputed. Indeed, its prestige is so great that an almost superstitious aura gathers about its name and work. Its progress is no longer dependent upon the adventurous inquiry of a few untrammeled souls. Not only are universities organized to promote scientific research and learning, but one may almost imagine the university laboratories abolished and still feel confident of the continued advance of science. The development of industry has compelled the inclusion of scientific inquiry within the processes of production and distribution. We find in the public prints as many demonstrations of the benefits of science from a business point of view as there are proofs of its harmony with religion.

It is not possible that, under such conditions, the subordination of scientific techniques to purposes and institutions that flourished before its rise can indefinitely continue. In all affairs there comes a time when a cycle of growth reaches maturity. When this stage is reached, the period of protective nursing comes to an end. The problem of securing proper use succeeds to that of securing conditions of growth. Now that science has established itself and has created a new social environment, it has (if I may for the moment personify it) to face the issue of its social responsibilities. Speaking without personification, we who have a powerful and perfected instrument in our hands, one which is determining the quality of social changes, must ask what changes we want to see achieved and what we want to see averted. We must, in short, plan its social effects with the same care with which in the past we have planned its physical operation and consequences. Till now we have employed science absent-mindedly as far as its effects upon human beings are concerned. The present situation with its extraordinary control of natural energies and its totally unplanned and haphazard social economy is a dire demonstration of the folly of continuing this course.

The social effects of the application of science have been accidental, even though they are intrinsic to the private and unorganized motives which we have permitted to control that application. It would be hard to find a better proof that such is the fact than the vogue of the theory that such unregulated use of science is in accord with "natural law," and that all effort at planned control of its social effects is an interference with nature. The use which has been made of a peculiar idea of personal liberty to justify the dominion of accident in social affairs is another convincing proof. The doctrine that the most potent instrument of widespread, enduring, and objective social changes must be left at the mercy of purely private desires for purely personal gain is a doctrine of anarchy. Our present insecurity of life is the fruit of the adoption in practice of this anarchic doctrine.

The technologies of industry have flowed

from the intrinsic nature of science. For that is itself essentially a technology of apparatus, materials and numbers. But the pecuniary aims which have decided the social results of the use of these technologies have not flowed from the inherent nature of science. They have been derived from institutions and attendant mental and moral habits which were entrenched before there was any such thing as science and the machine. In consequence, science has operated as a means for extending the influence of the institution of private property and connected legal relations far beyond their former limits. It has operated as a device to carry an enormous load of stocks and bonds and to make the reward of investment in the way of profit and power one out of all proportion to that accruing from actual work and service.

Here lies the heart of our present social problem. Science has hardly been used to modify men's fundamental acts and attitudes in social matters. It has been used to extend enormously the scope and power of interests and values which anteceded its rise. Here is the contradiction in our civilization. The potentiality of science as the most powerful instrument of control which has ever existed puts to mankind its one outstanding present challenge.

There is one field in which science has been somewhat systematically employed as an agent of social control. Condorcet, writing during the French Revolution in the prison from which he went to the guillotine, hailed the invention of the calculus of probabilities as the opening of a new era. He saw in this new mathematical technique the promise of methods of insurance which should distribute evenly and widely the impact of the disasters to which humanity is subject. Insurance against death, fire, hurricanes and so on have in a measure confirmed his prediction. Nevertheless, in large and important social areas, we have only made the merest beginning of the method of insurance against the hazards of life and death. Insurance against the risks of maternity, of sickness, old age, unemployment, is still rudimentary; its idea is fought by all reactionary forces. Witness the obstacles against which social insurance with respect to accidents incurred in industrial employment had to contend. The anarchy called natural law and personal liberty still operates with success against a planned social use of the resources of scientific knowledge.

Yet insurance against perils and hazards is the place where the application of science has gone the furthest, not the least, distance in present society. The fact that motor cars kill and maim more persons yearly than all factories, shops, and farms is a fair symbol of how backward we are in that province where we have done most. Here, however, is one field in which at least the idea of planned use of scientific knowledge for social welfare has received recognition. We no longer regard plagues, famine and disease as visitations of necessary "natural law" or of a power beyond nature. By preventive means of medicine and public hygiene as well as by various remedial measures we have in idea, if not in fact, placed technique in the stead of magic and chance and uncontrollable necessity in this one area of life. And yet, as I have said, here is where the socially planned use of science has made the most, not least, progress. Were it not for the youth of science and the historically demonstrated slowness of all basic mental and moral change, we could hardly find language to express astonishment at the situation in which we have an extensive and precise control of physical energies and conditions, and in which we leave the social consequences of their operation to chance, *laissez-faire*, privileged pecuniary status, and the inertia of tradition and old institutions.

Condorcet thought and worked in the Baconian strain. But the Baconian ideal of the systematic organization of all knowledge, the planned control of discovery and invention, for the relief and advancement of the human estate, remains almost as purely an ideal as when Francis Bacon put it forward centuries ago. And this is true in spite of the fact that the physical and mathematical technique upon which a planned control of social results depends has made in the meantime incalculable progress. The conclusion is inevitable. The outer arena of life has been transformed by science. The effectively working mind and character of man have hardly been touched.

Consider that phase of social action where science might theoretically be supposed to have taken effect most rapidly, namely, education. In dealing with the young, it would seem as if scientific methods might at once take effect in transformation of mental attitudes, without meeting the obstacles which have to be overcome in dealing with adults. In higher education, in universities and technical schools, a great amount of research is done and much scientific knowledge is imparted. But it is a principle of modern psychology that the basic attitudes of mind are formed in the earlier years. And I venture the assertion that for the most part the formation of intellectual habits in elementary education, in the home and school, is hardly affected by scientific method. Even in our so-called progressive schools, science is usually treated as a side line, an ornamental extra, not as the chief means of developing the right mental attitudes. It is treated generally as one more body of ready-made information to be acquired by traditional methods, or else as an occasional diversion. That it is the method of all effective mental approach and attack in all subjects has not gained even a foothold. Yet if scientific method is not something esoteric but is a realization of the most effective operation of intelligence, it should be axiomatic that the development of scientific attitudes of thought, observation, and inquiry is the chief business of study and learning.

Two phases of the contradiction inhering in our civilization may be especially mentioned. We have long been committed in theory and words to the principle of democracy. But criticism of democracy, assertions that it is failing to work and even to exist are everywhere rife. In the last few months we have become accustomed to similar assertions regarding our economic and industrial system. Mr. Ivy Lee, for example, in a recent commencement address, entitled "This Hour of Bewilderment," quoted from a representative clergyman, a railway president, and a publicist, to the effect that our capitalistic system is on trial. And yet the statements had to do with only one feature of that system: the prevalence of unemployment and attendant insecurity. It is not necessary for me to invade the territory of economics and politics. The essential fact is that if both democracy and capitalism are on trial, it is in reality our collective intelligence which is on trial. We have displayed enough intelligence in the physical field to create the new and powerful instrument of science and technology. We have not as yet had enough intelligence to use this instrument deliberately and systematically to control its social operations and consequences.

The first lesson which the use of scientific method teaches is that control is coordinate with knowledge and understanding. Where there is technique there is the possibility of administering forces and conditions in the region where the technique applies. Our lack of control in the sphere of human relations, national, domestic, international, requires no emphasis of notice. It is proof that we have not begun to operate scientifically in such matters. The public press is full of discussion of the five-year plan and the ten-year plan in Russia. But the fact that the plan is being tried by a country which has a dictatorship foreign to all our beliefs tends to divert attention from the fundamental consideration. The point for us is not this political setting nor its communistic context. It is that by the use of all available resources of knowledge and experts an attempt is being made at organized social planning and control. Were we to forget for the moment the special Russian political setting, we should see here an effort to use coordinated knowledge and technical skill to direct economic resources toward social order and stability.

To hold that such organized planning is possible only in a communistic society is to surrender the case to communism. Upon any other basis, the effort of Russia is a challenge and a warning to those who live under another political and economic regime. It is a call to use our more advanced knowledge and technology in scientific thinking about our own needs, problems, evils, and possibilities so as to achieve some degree of control of the social consequences which the application of science is, willy-nilly, bringing about. What stands in the way is a lot of outworn traditions, motheaten slogans and catchwords, that do substitute duty for thought, as well as our entrenched predatory self-interest. We shall only make a real beginning in intelligent thought when we cease mouthing platitudes; stop confining our idea to antitheses of individualism and socialism, capitalism and communism, and realize that the issue is between chaos and order, chance and control: the haphazard use and the planned use of scientific techniques.

Thus the statement with which we began, namely, that we are living in a world of change extraordinary in range and speed, is only half true. It holds of the outward applications of science. It does not hold of our intellectual and moral attitudes. About physical conditions and energies we think scientifically; at least, some men do, and the results of their thinking enter into the experiences of all of us. But the entrenched and stubborn institutions of the past stand in the way of our thinking scientifically about human relations and social issues. Our mental habits in these respects are dominated by institutions of family, state, church, and business that were formed long before men had an effective technique of inquiry and validation. It is this contradiction from which we suffer to-day.

Disaster follows in its wake. It is impossible to overstate the mental confusion and the practical disorder which are bound to result when external and physical effects are planned and regulated, while the attitudes of mind upon which the direction of external results depends are left to the medley of chance, tradition, and dogma. It is a common saying that our physical science has far outrun our social knowledge; that our physical skill has become exact and comprehensive while our humane arts are vague, opinionated, and narrow. The fundamental trouble, however, is not lack of sufficient information about social facts, but unwillingness to adopt the scientific attitude in what we do know. Men floundered in a morass of opinion about physical matters for thousands of years. It was when they began to use their ideas experimentally and to create a technique or direction of experimentation that physical science advanced with system and surety. No amount of mere fact-finding develops science nor the scientific attitude in either physics or social affairs. Facts merely amassed and piled up are dead; a burden which only adds to confusion. When ideas, hypotheses, begin to play upon facts, when they are methods for experimental use in action, then light dawns; then it becomes possible to discriminate significant from trivial facts, and relations take the place of isolated scraps. Just as soon as we begin to use the knowledge and skills we have to control social consequences in the interest of shared abundant and secured life, we shall cease to complain of the backwardness of our social knowledge. We shall take the road which leads to the assured building up of social science just as men built up physical science when they actively used the techniques of tools and numbers in physical experimentation.

In spite, then, of all the record of the past, the great scientific revolution is still to come. It will ensue when men collectively and cooperatively organize their knowledge for application to achieve and make secure social values; when they systematically use scientific procedures for the control of human relationships and the direction of the social effects of our vast technological machinery. Great as have been the social changes of the last century, they are not to be compared with those which will emerge when our faith in scientific method is made manifest in social works. We are living in a period of depression. The intellectual function of trouble is to lead men to think. The depression is a small price to pay if it induces us to think about the cause of the disorder, confusion, and insecurity which are the outstanding traits of our social life. If we do not go back to their cause, namely our half-way and accidental use of science, mankind will pass through depressions, for they are the graphic record of our unplanned social life. The story of the achievement of science in physical control is evidence of the possibility of control in social affairs. It is our human intelligence and human courage which are on trial; it is incredible that men who have brought the technique of physical discovery, invention, and use to such a pitch of perfection will abdicate in the face of the infinitely more important human problem.

NOTES

[First published in *Philosophy and Civilization* (New York: Minton, Balch and Co., 1931), pp. 318–30. LW 6:53–63.]

It would require a technical survey, which would be out of place here, to prove that the existing limitations of "social science" are due mainly to unreasoning devotion to physical science as a model, and to a misconception of physical science at that. Without making any such survey, attention may be directly called to one outstanding difference between physical and social facts. The ideal of the knowledge dealing with the former is the elimination of all factors dependent upon distinctively human response. "Fact," physically speaking, is the ultimate residue after human purposes, desires, emotions, ideas and ideals have been systematically excluded. A social "fact," on the other hand, is a concretion in external form of precisely these human factors.

An occurrence is a physical fact only when its constituents and their relations remain the same, irrespective of the human attitude toward them. A species of mosquitoes is the carrier of the germs of malaria, whether we like or dislike malaria. Drainage and oil-spraying to destroy mosquitoes are a social fact because their use depends upon human purpose and desire. A steam locomotive or a dynamo is a physical fact in its structure; it is a social fact when its existence depends upon the desire for rapid and cheap transportation and communication. The machine itself may be understood physically without reference to human aim and motive. But the railway or public-utility system cannot be understood without reference to human purposes and human consequences.

I may illustrate the present practice of slavishly following the technique of physical science and the uselessness of its results by the present zeal for "fact finding." Of course, one cannot think, understand and plan without a basis of fact, and since facts do not lie around in plain view, they have to be discovered. But for the most part, the data which now are so carefully sought and so elaborately scheduled are not social facts at all. For their connection with any system of human purposes and consequences, their bearing as means and as results upon human action, are left out of the picture. At best they are mere physical and external facts. They are unlike the facts of physical science, because the latter are found

Social Science and Social Control

(1931)

by methods which make their interrelations and their laws apparent, while the facts of social "fact finding" remain a miscellaneous pile of meaningless items. Since their connections with human wants and their effect on human values are neglected, there is nothing which binds them together into an intelligible whole.

It may be retorted that to connect facts with human desires and their effect upon human values is subjective and moral, and to an extent that makes it impossible to establish any conclusions upon an objective basis: that to attempt inference on this point would land us in a morass of speculative opinion. Suppose, for example, all the facts about the working of the prohibition law and its enforcement were much more completely known than they are; even so, to establish a connection between these facts and the human attitudes lying back of them would be a matter of guess work. As things stand, there is much force in the objection. But if made universal, it would overlook the possibility of another kind of situation.

Wherever purposes are employed deliberately and systematically for the sake of certain desired social results, there it is possible, within limits, to determine the connection between the human factor and the actual occurrence, and thus to get a complete social fact, namely, the actual external occurrence in its human relationships. Prohibition, whether noble or not, is not an experiment in any intelligent scientific sense of the term. For it was undertaken without the effort to obtain the conditions of control which are essential to any experimental determination of fact. The Five Year Plan of Russia, on the other hand, whether noble or the reverse, has many of the traits of a social experiment, for it is an attempt to obtain certain specified social results by the use of specified definite measures, exercised under conditions of considerable, if not complete, control.

The point I am making may be summed up by saying that it is a complete error to suppose that efforts at social control depend upon the prior existence of a social science. The reverse is the case. The building up of social science, that is, of a body of knowledge in which facts are ascertained in their significant relations, is dependent upon putting social planning into effect. It is at this point that the misconception about physical science, when it is taken as a model for social knowledge, is important. Physical science did not develop because inquirers piled up a mass of facts about observed phenomena. It came into being when men intentionally experimented, on the basis of ideas and hypotheses, with observed phenomena to modify them and disclose new observations. This process is self-corrective and self-developing. Imperfect and even wrong hypotheses, when *acted upon*, brought to light significant phenomena which made improved ideas and improved experimentations possible. The change from a passive and accumulative attitude into an active and productive one is the secret revealed by the progress of physical inquiry. Men obtained knowledge of natural energies by trying deliberately to control the conditions of their operation. The result was knowledge, and then control on a larger scale by the application of what was learned.

It is a commonplace of logical theory that laws are of the "if-then" type. *If* something occurs, *then* something else happens; if certain conditions exist, they are accompanied by certain other conditions. Such knowledge alone is knowledge of a fact in any intelligible sense of the word. Although we have to act in order to discover the conditions underlying the "if" in physical matters, yet the material constituting the "if" is there apart from our action; like the movements of sun and earth in an eclipse. But in social phenomena the relation is: "If we *do* something, something else will happen." The objective material constituting the "if" belongs to us, not to something wholly independent of us. We are concerned, not with a bare relation of cause and effect, but with one of means and consequences, that is, of causes deliberately used for the sake of producing certain effects. As far as we intentionally do and make, we shall know; as far as we "know" without making, our so-called knowledge is a miscellany, or at most antiquarian, and hence without relevance to future planning. Only the knowledge which is itself the fruit of a technology can breed further technology.

I want to make the same point with reference to social prediction. Here, too, the assumption is generally made that we must be able to predict before we can plan and control. Here again the reverse is the case. We can predict the occurrence of an eclipse precisely because we cannot control it. If we could control it, we could not predict, except contingently; just as we can predict a collision when we see two trains approaching on the same track—provided that a human being does not foresee the possibility and take measures to avert its happening. The other day I ran across a remark of Alexander Hamilton's to the effect that instead of awaiting an event to know what measures to take, we should take measures to bring the event to pass. And I would add that only then can we genuinely forecast the future in the world of social matters.

Empirical rule-of-thumb practices were the mothers of the arts. But the practices of the arts were in turn the source of science, when once the empirical methods were freed in imagination and used with some degree of freedom of experimentation. There cannot be a science of an art until the art has itself made some advance, and the significant development occurs when men intentionally try to use such art as they have already achieved in order to obtain results which they conceive to be desirable. If we have no social technique at all, it is impossible to bring planning and control into being. If we do have at hand a reasonable amount of technique, then it is by deliberately using what we have that we shall in the end develop a dependable body of social knowledge. If we want foresight, we shall not obtain it by any amount of fact finding so long as we disregard the human aims and desires producing the facts which we find. But if we decide upon what we want socially, what sort of social consequences we wish to occur, and then use whatever means we possess to effect these intended consequences, we shall find the road that leads to foresight. Forethought and planning must come before foresight.

I am not arguing here for the desirability of social planning and control. That is another question. Those who are satisfied with present conditions and who are hopeful of turning them to account for personal profit and power will answer it in the negative. What I am saying is that if we want something to which the name "social science" may be given, there is only one way to go about it, namely, by entering upon the path of social planning and control. Observing, collecting, recording and filing tomes of social phenomena without deliberately trying to do something to bring a desired state of society into existence only encourages a conflict of opinion and dogma in their interpretation. If the social situation out of which these facts emerge is itself confused and chaotic because it expresses socially unregulated purpose and haphazard private intent, the facts themselves will be confused, and we shall add only intellectual confusion to practical disorder. When we deliberately employ whatever skill we possess in order to serve the ends which we desire, we shall begin to attain a measure of at least intellectual order and understanding. And if past history teaches anything, it is that with intellectual order we have the surest possible promise of advancement to practical order.

NOTES

[First published in *New Republic* 67 (29 July 1931): 276–77. LW 6:64–68.]

By Nature and by Art

(1944)

Current philosophical theories of knowledge are strangely neglectful of the implications and consequences of the revolution that has taken place in the actual subject-matter and methods of scientific knowledge. In substance, this revolution may be said to be one from knowledge that is such "by nature" to scientific subject-matter which is what it is because it is "by art." The classic scheme, following Aristotle, held that the subject-matter of science, as the highest grade of knowledge, is what it is because of certain inherent forms, essences, or natures. These indwelling and constitutive natures are eternal, immutable, and necessary. It followed that in the Greek-medieval system all *sciences*, from astronomy to biology, were concerned with species or kinds, which are immutably the same and eternally separated from one another by the fixed natures forming their inherent essences or Being.

Other forms of knowledge, such as were called sense-perception and opinion, were also what they were by the nature of their inherent Beings; or, more strictly, by the unchangeable and incorrigible partiality or defect of Being which marked them. For over against fixed and eternal species constituted by inherent essential forms were the things that change; things that are generated and perish. Alteration, modifiability, mutability, are *ipso facto* proof of instability and inconstancy. These in turn are proof of lack of Being in its full sense. It is because of lack, or privation, of self-contained and self-sufficient Being that some things are variable and transient, now one thing and now another. The lack of inherent natures or essences is equivalent to dependence upon circumstances that are external, this dependence upon what is outside being manifested in their variability. In classic terminology, science is concerned with "formal causes," that is, with inherent natures which "cause" things to be *what* they are. Sense-knowledge and opinion are inferior forms of knowledge concerned with things which by their natures are so mutable that knowledge of them is itself unstable and shifting—as in the case of things touched, heard, seen.

It should not be necessary to dwell upon

the fact that according to what is now science what the ancient scheme relegated to an inferior position, namely, efficient and material "causes," constitutes the only legitimate subject-matter of natural science, acceptance of the view that essential forms or natures are its subject-matter accounting for the sterility of science during the period before the scientific revolution occurred. According to the ancient doctrine, the subject-matter of sense-knowledge and opinion on one side, and of science on the other, are forever separated by a gulf that is impassable for the reason that it is cosmological and ontological—that is, due to the very "being" of the subjects involved. In what now constitutes science, the difference is methodological. For it is due to *methods of inquiry*, not to inherent natures. Potentially the subject-matters of sense and opinion are science in the making; they are its raw material. Increased maturity of the procedures and techniques of inquiry will transform their material into scientific knowledge. On the other side, there is no subject-matter of the scientific kind which is eternally the same and not subject to improvement with further development of efficacy in inquiry-procedures.

The scientific revolution, which put science upon the road of steady advance and ever increasing fertility, is connected with substitution of knowledge "by art" for that said to be "by nature." The connection is not remote nor recondite. The arts are concerned with production, with generation, with doing and making. They fall, therefore, within the domain of things which in the classic scheme are mutable, and of which, according to that scheme, scientific knowledge is impossible. According to the present conduct of science and according to its conclusions, science consists of knowledge of *orders of change*. While this fact marks a complete departure from the classic view, it does not suffice of itself to justify calling scientific knowledge an art, though it provides a condition without which that designation is not warranted; for it completely breaks down the grounds upon which a fixed and impassable line was originally drawn between the subject-matters of science and of art. For it connects science with change. The consideration that completes the ground for assimilat-

ing science to art is the fact that assignment of scientific status in any given case rests upon facts which are experimentally produced. Science is now the product of operations deliberately undertaken in conformity with a plan or project that has the properties of a working hypothesis. The value or validity of the latter is tested, as in the case of any art, by what happens in consequence of the operations it instigates and directs. Moreover, science is assimilated to the conditions defining an art by the fact that, as in the case of any industrial art, production of relevant and effective consequences depends upon use of artificially designed appliances and apparatus as means of execution of the plan that directs the operations which are undertaken.

II

It is an old and familiar story that "nature" is a word of many senses. One of its senses has been mentioned. According to it, the nature of that which is undergoing investigation, say combustion, electricity, or whatever, is the subject-matter of scientific generalizations. We still use the expression "the nature" of something or other in this sense, though, I imagine, with decreasing frequency. But when we do use it in this sense, its meaning is radically different from that possessed by the same expression in the classic scheme. For it no longer designates a fixed and inherent essence, or Being, that makes facts to *be* what they are. Instead, it signifies an order of connected changes, an order which is found to be fruitfully effective in understanding and dealing with particular changes. The difference is radical.[1]

Another meaning of "nature" is *cosmological*. The word is used to stand for the world, for the universe, for the sum total of facts which actually and potentially are the subject of inquiry and knowledge. With respect to this sense of "nature," ancient philosophy has an important advantage over the general tenor of modern philosophy. For while modern philosophy is conformable to actual scientific practice in eliminating an ontological difference, or a difference in kinds of Being, between the eternal and the changing, it has, unfortunately, tended to substitute for this difference one equally fixed between supposed subjective and objective orders of Being.[2] "Unfortunately" is in fact too mild and neutral a word. For the net effect has been to set up a seat and agency of knowing over against Nature as that known. Hence the "knower" becomes in effect extra-natural. Historically, the facts of the case are easily explainable. For while in the Greek version mind in both its sensible and its rational operations was a culminating manifestation or terminal "end," of natural facts, in the medieval version (out of which modern theory grew without outgrowing some of its major tenets) soul and mind took on definitely supernatural traits. These traits, in a more or less attenuated form, reappear in the extra-natural knowing "subject" of modern philosophy as that is set over against the natural world as "object."

To complete the statement of the terms of the question under discussion, it is necessary to note explicitly the sense of "nature" and "natural" in which they contrast with "art" and "artificial." For in the cosmological sense of nature, the saying of Shakespeare holds to the effect that nature is made better by no mean but nature makes that mean; in the third sense of natural (that just mentioned), science is definitely and conclusively a matter of art, not of nature.

We most readily lay hold of the meaning of this statement by presenting to ourselves a picture of an astronomical observatory or a physical laboratory. And we have to include as part of the picture the role of collections of books and periodicals, which operate in the most intimate and vital working connection with the other means by which science is carried on. For the body of printed matter is what enables the otherwise highly restricted material of immediate perception to be linked with subject-matters having an indefinitely wide spatial and temporal range. For only in fusion with book-material does what is immediately present take on scientific status, and only in fusion with the latter does the former cease to be "theoretical" in the hypothetical sense of that word. For only as culturally transmitted material with its deep and wide scope is anchored, refreshed, and tested continually through *here-and-now* materials provided by

direct experimental observations does it become a warranted part of authentic science.

A further qualification has to be added to complete the statement that science with respect to both method and conclusions is an art. For there is a sense in which every form of knowledge is an affair of art. For all knowledge, even the most rudimentary such as is attributable to low-grade organisms, is an expression of skill in selection and arrangement of materials so as to contribute to maintenance of the processes and operations constituting life. It is not a metaphorical expression to say that at the very least all animals know *how*, in virtue of organic structure and physiological processes in connection with trans-cuticular conditions, to do things of this sort. When, then, it is said that science, as distinct from other modes of knowledge, is an art, the word "art" is used with a differential property. The operations of *search* that constitute the art or skill marking other modes of knowledge develop into re-search.

A more concrete qualification of the art which constitutes scientific knowledge is its dependence upon *extra-organic* appliances and instrumentalities, themselves artificially devised. The scientific revolution may be said to have been initiated when investigators borrowed apparatus and processes from the industrial arts and used them as means of obtaining dependable scientific data. The use of the lens was of itself almost enough to revolutionize the science of astronomy. As we look back, we note that the bulk of early knowledge was in fact built up through the pursuit of industrial and mechanical arts. The low social status of artisans (in which class were included sculptors, architects, painters of pictures, musicians, in fact all producers save those working with words) was "rationalized" in the doctrine of the inherently inferior state of all knowledge of this kind. At best, it was "empirical" in the disparaging sense of that word. Fundamentally, the scientific revolution consisted of transformation of "empirical" into *experimental*. The transformation was effected, historically, by adoption, as means of obtaining scientific knowledge, of devices and processes previously employed in industry to obtain "material" ends—in that sense of "material" which identifies "matter" with the menial and servile. After a period in which natural knowledge progressed by *borrowing* from the industrial crafts, science entered upon a period of steady and ever-accelerated growth by means of deliberate invention of such appliances on its own account. In order to mark this differential feature of the art which is science, I shall now use the word "technology."[3]

Because of technologies, a circular relationship between the arts of production and science has been established. I have already spoken of the dependence of science as now conducted upon the use of appliances and processes such as were once confined to the "utilitarian" and "practical" ends to which a subordinate and "base" status was attributed socially and morally. On the other hand, before the application in a return movement of science in the industrial arts, production was a routine affair. It was marked by imitation and by following established models and precedents. Innovation and invention were accidental rather than systematic. Application of scientific conclusions and methods liberated production from this state—a state justifying use of the adjective "empirical" in its disparaging sense. Through incorporation into the arts of production of the methods and conclusions of science, they are capable of becoming "rational" in the honorific sense of that word. The phrase "rationalization of production" states a fact. Indeed, it may be said that the distinction between science and other technologies is not intrinsic. It is dependent upon cultural conditions that are extrinsic to both science and industry. Were it not for the influence exerted by these conditions, the difference between them would be conventional to the point of being verbal. But as long as some technologies are carried on for personal profit at the expense of promotion of the common welfare, the stigma of "materialism" will continue to be attached to industrial technologies, and the honorific adjective "idealistic" will be monopolized by the technology which yields knowledge—especially if that knowledge is "pure"— that is, in the classic view, uncontaminated by being put to "practical" use.

III

Valuable instruction concerning a number of mooted problems in the theory of knowledge may be derived from the underlying principles of the prior discussion. One of them, perhaps the most obvious on the surface, is the fact that many classifications and distinctions which have been supposed to be inherent or intrinsic to knowing and knowledge are in fact due to socio-cultural conditions of a historical, and therefore temporal and local, sort. There is the fact (upon which I have dwelt at length in previous writings) of the arbitrary and irrelevant nature of the sharp line drawn in the classic philosophical tradition between "theoretical" and "practical" knowledge. The gulf that was supposed to separate them is in fact merely a logical corollary of the view that the proper subject of scientific knowledge is eternal and immutable. The connection of science with change and the connection of the methods of science with experimental production of change have completely vitiated this doctrine. The infertility of natural knowledge before adoption of the experimental method is attributable, in large measure, to the fact that ancient and medieval science took the material of ordinary observation "as is"; that is, in lumps and chunks as given "naturally" in a ready-made state. In consequence, the only treatment to which it could be subjected was dialectical.

What is not so obvious upon the surface is that a theory of knowledge based upon the conduct and conclusions of science does away, once and for all, with the fixed difference supposed to exist between sense-knowledge and rational-knowledge. The sensory aspect of knowledge is strictly an *aspect*. It is distinguishable in intellectual analyses that are undertaken for special purposes. But it is not, as it was long taken to be, a special kind of knowledge nor yet a separate component in knowledge. It is that aspect of the system of knowledge in and by which knowledge extending across an indefinitely extensive spatial and temporal range of facts is anchored and focalized in that which is *here-and-now*. Without demonstrated anchorage of this sort, any system, no matter how well organized with respect to internal consistency, is "theoretical" in the sense of being hypothetical. On the other hand, the "rational" aspect of knowledge is constituted by the corpus of extant knowledge which has been constituted by prior inquiries and which is so organized as to be communicable—and hence applicable to results of further inquiry by which the old system is corrected and extended.

The principle underlying these special matters is that the legitimate subject-matter of a *theory* of knowledge consists of *facts* that are known at a given time, with, of course, the proviso that the procedures by which this body of knowledge has been built up are an integral part of it. This view of the grounds of a competent theory of knowledge stands in open opposition to that which underlies the *epistemological* theory: the postulate, namely, that no subject-matter is entitled to be called knowledge until it has been shown to satisfy conditions that are laid down prior to any case of actual knowledge and independently of any conclusion reached in the course of the inquiries by which knowledge in the concrete is arrived at. The completeness of the opposition between the two postulates may be judged from the following consideration. Upon the ground of the first postulate subject-matter is entitled to the name of knowledge when it is determined by the methods of inquiry, test, verification, and systematic arrangement, or organization, which are factually employed in the sciences. Upon the other basis, the antecedent conditions apply to any and every case, good, bad, and indifferent. Hence they are of an entirely different order from the facts of actual investigation, test, and verification, which warrant use of the name "knowledge" in its honorific sense in actual instances.

It was then inevitable, from the standpoint of logic, that the epistemological approach culminated in the Kantian question: How is knowledge possible anyway (*ueberhaupt*)? If the question were put with reference to the "possibility" of any other subject under investigation, the *existence* of the subject-matter under inquiry would be the starting point. It suffices, for example, to show that cancer exists for the question as to its possibility to be

simply the question of the specific conditions of an *actuality*. Only in the case of knowledge is it supposed that the question of its "possibility" is one which puts actuality into total doubt until certain universal antecedent conditions have been laid down and shown to be satisfied.

In the case of cancer, for example, the question of possibility means that our knowledge is still in a doubtful and indeterminate state, so that research is going on to discover the characteristic properties, conditions, and consequences of facts whose actual existence sets the problem. Yet strangely enough (strangely, provided, that is, historical-cultural facts are left out of account) the dogmatic and contradictory assumption that there exists knowledge of the conditions of knowledge prior to and conditioning every specific instance of knowledge arrogated to itself the name of a *critical* theory of knowledge!

IV

I do not propose to discuss further this contradiction, beyond saying that the contradiction will be obvious to anyone who views the matter in terms of the facts of knowledge, instead of in terms supplied by the history of philosophical systems viewed in isolation from other cultural events. I propose rather to set forth some of the historical-cultural conditions which generated in general the epistemological assumption of prior conditions to be satisfied; and which, in particular, led to the "subject-object" formula about these conditions. One of the influential factors consists of the conditions existing when the scientific revolution took place. It is hardly possible to over-emphasize the fact that these conditions were those of revolt not merely against long accepted intellectual doctrines but also against customs and institutions which were the carriers of these doctrines, and which gave them a support extraneous to their own constituents. Because of causes which are psychologically adequate, if not factually so, the word "social" has come to be regarded as applicable to that which is institutionally established and which exerts authority because of this fact. The adjective "individual" is identified on this basis with that which marks a departure from the traditionally and institutionally established, especially if the departure is of a quality involving revolt and a challenge to the rightful authority of tradition and custom.

These conditions were fully and strikingly present at the time of the rise of modern science. Every book on the history of philosophy mentions the fact that the philosophical literature of the fifteenth and subsequent centuries is marked by treatises, essays, tractates, that deal with the methods to be adopted and pursued if scientific knowledge is to be actually obtained. The negative aspect of these new ventures is assault, overt or implicit, upon all that had long been accepted as science. There was in effect, if not openly, an assertion that currently accepted subject-matter was hardly more than a systematized collection of errors and falsities. The necessity of radically new procedures of assault upon existing "science" was uniformly treated as an affair of *method*. It was because of the *methods* habitually used and sanctioned that existing "science" was stagnant, and so far removed from its proper mark—understanding of nature. Other documents upon right methods may not have used the words of Francis Bacon's *Novum Organum*, much less endorsed its precepts. But they were at one with him in proclaiming the necessity of a complete break with traditional methods and in stark opposition to the tenets of the *Organon* of Aristotle.

If the movement of protest, revolt, and innovation that was expressed in these documents and put in practice in the new astronomy and "natural philosophy" had been confined to "science" in its technical and isolated aspect, there would not have been the crisis that actually occurred. The facts constituting what is called "the conflict of science with religion"—or theology—clearly and convincingly prove that the movement of innovation, protest, and revolt was not so confined. The new science was treated as morally heretical and as a dangerous menace to the very foundations of a stable and just social order. Upon the Continent, especially, it was treated as rebellion against divinely established authority. In a more fundamental way than in the ecclesiastic movement named Protestantism, it was a protest against established foundations in morals and religion. Its opponents made this point clear when its proponents failed to do so.

Stated in slightly different terms, the subject-object formulation of the conditions to be satisfied before any subject-matter has a right to the honorable title of "knowledge" has to be viewed in vitally intimate connection with those movements in political and economic institutions which popularly bear the name "individualism." For, as has been already remarked, any departure from traditions and customs that are incorporated in and backed by institutions having firmly established authority is regarded as "individual" in a non-social and *anti*-social sense by the guardians of old forms in church and state. Only at a later time, when it is possible to place events in a long historic perspective instead of in the short-time crowded and broken perspective of what is immediately contemporary, can so-called "individualism" be seen to be as "social" in origin, content, and consequences as are the customs and institutions which are in process of modification.

In this cultural situation, the fact that philosophers as unlike as Descartes and Berkeley both refer to the seat and agent of knowledge as "I" or an "ego," a personal self, has more than casual significance. This reference is especially significant as evidence of the new climate of opinion just because no attempt at justification accompanied it. It was taken to be such an evident matter that no argument in its behalf was called for. References and allusions of this kind are the forerunners of the allegedly "critical" attempt of Kant to frame an account of the conditions of knowledge in terms of a "transcendental ego," after Hume had demonstrated the shaky character of the "empirical" self as the source and agent of authentic knowledge.

If we adopt the customary course of isolating philosophies in their historical appearance which is their actuality from other socio-cultural facts, if we treat the history of philosophy as something capable of being understood in the exclusive terms of documents labeled philosophical, we shall look at the outstanding feature of modern philosophy as one of a conflict between doctrines appealing to "sense-experience" as ultimate authority and theories appealing to intuition and reason, a conflict reaching a supposed solution in the Kantian reconciliation of the *a priori* and the *a posteriori*. When these philosophies are placed in their cultural context, they are seen to be partners in a common movement, both schools being in revolt against traditional science in its methods, premises, and conclusions, while both schools are engaged in search for a new and different seat of intellectual and moral authority. There are indeed significant differences between the two schools. But when these are historically viewed, they appear as differences of emphasis, one school inclining to the "conservative" phase of cultural institutions, and the other school to the "progressive" or radical phase.

While those aspects of the new science which express initiative, invention, enterprise, and independence of custom (on the ground that customs are more likely to be distorting and misleading than helpful in attaining scientific knowledge) are necessary conditions for generation of the subject-object formulation, they are far from being its sufficient condition. Unquestioned persistence of fundamental tradition controlled protest against other customs. Medieval institutions centered in belief in an immaterial soul or spirit. This belief was no separate item. It permeated every aspect of life. The drama of the fall, the redemption, and the eternal destiny for weal or woe, of the soul was all-controlling in the accepted view of the creation and history of the universe and of man. Belief in the soul was so far from being just an intellectual tenet that poignant emotion and the deepest and most vivid images of which man is capable centered about it. The church that administered the concerns of the soul was in effect the dominant educational and political institution of the period.

Secularizing movements gradually undermined the monopoly of authority possessed by the church. Although interests of a natural type did not supersede supernatural interests, they tended to push them out of a central into a peripheral position. But supernatural concerns retained such force in moral and religious matters that the theory of knowledge was routed through the channels they had worn after the

facts of science were wearing a natural channel. This roundabout channel seemed, because of the force of habit, more "natural" than any indicated by the facts of science. The enormous gap between knowledge-facts and epistemological theory which marks modern philosophy was instituted.

In spite of revolt and innovation, the hold of the belief in the soul as knowing subject upon the attitudes which controlled the formation of the theory of knowledge was so firm that it could not be broken until the institutions, upon which the belief in its concrete validity depended had undergone definite degeneration.

Revolt and innovation were sufficient, however, to bring to explicit and emphatic statement one aspect of the Christian doctrine of the soul, an aspect which was kept covert and hidden in the dominant institutionalism of the Middle Ages. This aspect was the *individual* or singular nature of the subject of sin, redemption, punishment, and reward. Protestantism insisted upon making this aspect of the Christian position overt and central in religious matters. The writers who were concerned with the new science performed a similar task in the theories of knowledge they promulgated. The hold of the old doctrine, even upon those most indifferent to its theological phases, is shown in the persistence of belief in an immaterial mind, consciousness, or whatever, as being the seat and agent of knowledge. The influence of the belief upon the new science, even with its fundamental revolt and innovation, is exhibited in identification of the subject and agent of sound knowledge with "individuals" who had freed themselves from the perverting and deadening effect of custom and tradition. Even today those who deny in words that mind and consciousness are organs of knowledge, replacing them with an organic body or with the nervous system of the organism, attribute to the latter an isolation from the rest of nature (including transmitted and communicated culture) which is much more than reminiscent of the lonely isolation of the medieval soul.

It took more than the undeniable but negative fact of the gradual attenuation and decay of the importance once attached to the soul as seat of knowledge to effect an adequate elimination. The new movement of science had to achieve, on the ground of its own methods and conclusions, a positive conquest of those aspects of natural fact that deal with life and human history before complete elimination could occur. Only during the last hundred years (less than that in fact) have the sciences of biology, cultural anthropology, and history, especially of "origins," reached a stage of development which places man and his works squarely within nature. In so doing they have supplied the concrete and verified positive facts that make possible and imperatively demand formation of a systematic theory of knowledge in which the facts of knowledge are specified or described and organized exactly as are the facts of the sciences which are the relevant subject-matter of a theory of knowledge. Only in this way will the facts of our knowledge-systems and those of the theory of knowledge be brought into harmony with one another, and the present glaring discrepancy between them be done away with.

NOTES

[First published in *Journal of Philosophy* 41 (25 May 1944): 281–92. LW 15:84–96.]

1. It may be remarked in passing that the *old* sense of the "nature" of a thing still prevails in discussion of moral and social subjects; and this fact may explain the continued stagnation and infertility of inquiry in these fields.

2. Virtual synonyms are "mental" and "physical" orders, and "personal" and "impersonal," taken as separate and opposed with reference to their inherent stuffs or subject-matters.

3. While a number of writers have brought forward the facts which are involved in this view, Dr. Clarence Ayres, as far as I am aware, was the first one explicitly to call science a mode of technology. It is probable that I might have avoided a considerable amount of misunderstanding if I had systematically used "technology" instead of "instrumentalism" in connection with the view I put forth regarding the distinctive quality of science as knowledge.

Common Sense and Scientific Inquiry

From *Logic: The Theory of Inquiry* (1938)

Upon the biological level, organisms have to respond to conditions about them in ways that modify those conditions and the relations of organisms to them so as to restore the reciprocal adaptation that is required for the maintenance of life-functions. Human organisms are involved in the same sort of predicament. Because of the effect of cultural conditions, the problems involved not only have different contents but are capable of statement *as* problems so that inquiry can enter as a factor in their resolution. For in a cultural environment, physical conditions are modified by the complex of customs, traditions, occupations, interests and purposes which envelops them. Modes of response are correspondingly transformed. They avail themselves of the significance which things have acquired, and of the *meanings* provided by language. Obviously, rocks as minerals signify something more in a group that has learned to work iron than is signified either to sheep and tigers or to a pastoral or agricultural group. The meanings of related symbols, which form the language of a group, also, as was shown in the last chapter, introduce a new type of attitudes and hence of modes of response. I shall designate the environment in which human beings are *directly* involved the common sense environment or "world," and inquiries that take place in making the required adjustments in behavior common sense inquiries.

As is brought out later, the problems that arise in such situations of interaction may be reduced to problems of the use and enjoyment of the objects, activities and products, material and ideological, (or "ideal") of the world in which individuals live. Such inquiries are, accordingly, different from those which have knowledge as their goal. The attainment of knowledge of some things is necessarily involved in common sense inquiries, but it occurs for the sake of settlement of some issue of use and enjoyment, and not, as in scientific inquiry, for its own sake. In the latter, there is no *direct* involvement of human beings in the *immediate* environment—a fact which carries with it the ground of distinguishing the theoretical from the practical.

The use of the term *common sense* is somewhat arbitrary from a linguistic point of view.

But the existence of the kinds of situations referred to and of the kind of inquiries that deal with the difficulties and predicaments they present cannot be doubted. They are those which continuously arise in the conduct of life and the ordering of day-by-day behavior. They are such as constantly arise in the development of the young as they learn to make their way in the physical and social environments in which they live; they occur and recur in the life-activity of every adult, whether farmer, artisan, professional man, law-maker or administrator; citizen of a state, husband, wife, or parent. On their very face they need to be discriminated from inquiries that are distinctively scientific, or that aim at attaining confirmed facts, "laws" and theories.

They need, accordingly, to be designated by some distinctive word, and *common sense* is used for that purpose. Moreover, the term is not wholly arbitrary even from the standpoint of linguistic usage. In the *Oxford Dictionary*, for example, is found the following definition of common sense: "Good sound practical sense; combined tact and readiness in dealing with the ordinary affairs of life." Common sense in this signification applies to behavior in its connection with the *significance* of things.

There is, clearly, a distinctively intellectual content involved; *good sense* is, in ordinary language, good *judgment*. Sagacity is power to discriminate the factors that are relevant and important in significance in given situations; it is power of discernment; in a proverbial phrase, ability to tell a hawk from a hernshaw, chalk from cheese, and to bring the discriminations made to bear upon what is to be done and what is to be abstained from, in the "ordinary affairs of life." That which, in the opening paragraphs, was called the mode of inquiry dealing with situations of use and enjoyment, is, after all, but a formal way of saying what the dictionary states in its definition of common sense.

There is, however, another dictionary definition: "The general sense, feeling, judgement of mankind or a community." It is in this sense that we speak of the *deliverances* of common sense as if they were a body of settled truths. It applies not to things in their significance but to *meanings* accepted. When the Scottish school of Reid and Stewart erected "common sense" into an ultimate authority and arbiter of philosophic questions, they were carrying this signification to its limit. The reference to practical sagacity in dealing with problems of response and adaptation in use and enjoyment has now gone into the background. "Common" now means "*general*." It designates the conceptions and beliefs that are currently accepted without question by a given group or by mankind in general. They are *common* in the sense of being widely, if not universally, accepted. They are *sense*, in the way in which we speak of the "sense of a meeting" and in which we say things do or do not "make sense." They have something of the same ultimacy and immediacy for a group that "sensation" and "feeling" have for an individual in his contact with surrounding objects. It is a commonplace that every cultural group possesses a set of meanings which are so deeply embedded in its customs, occupations, traditions and ways of interpreting its physical environment and group-life, that they form the basic categories of the language-system by which details are interpreted. Hence they are regulative and "normative" of specific beliefs and judgments.

There is a genuine difference between the two meanings of common sense. But from the standpoint of a given group there is a definite deposit of agreement. They are both of them connected with the conduct of life in relation to an existing environment: one of them in judging the significance of things and events with reference to what should be done; the other, in the ideas that are used to direct and justify activities and judgments. Tabus are, first, customary ways of activities. To us they are mistaken rather than sagacious ways of action. But the system of meanings embodied in the language that carries tradition gives them authority in such highly practical matters as the eating of food and the behavior that is proper in the presence of chieftains and members of the family configuration, so that they control the relations of males and females and persons of various kinship degrees. To us, such conceptions and beliefs are highly impractical; to those who held them they were matters of higher practical importance than were special modes of behavior in dealing with particular objects. For they set the standards for judging the latter and acting in reference to them. It is possible today, along with our knowledge of the enormous differences that characterize various cultures, to find some unified deposit of activities and of meanings in the "common sense and feeling of *mankind*," especially in matters of basic social cohesion.

In any case, the difference between the two meanings may be reduced, without doing violence to the facts, to the difference between phases and aspects of special practical situations that are looked into, questioned and examined with reference to what may or should be done at a particular time and place and the rules and precepts that are taken for granted in reaching all conclusions and in all socially correct behavior. Both are concerned, one directly and the other indirectly, with "the ordinary affairs of life," in the broad sense of life.

I do not suppose that a generalization of the inquiries and conclusions of this type under the caption of "use and enjoyment" needs much exposition for its support. Use and enjoyment are the ways in which human beings are directly connected with the world about them. Questions of food, shelter, protection, defense, etc., are questions of the use to be made of materials of the environment and of the attitudes to be taken practically towards members of the same group and to other groups taken as wholes. Use, in turn, is for the sake of some consummation or enjoyment. Some things that are far beyond the scope of direct use, like stars and dead ancestors, are objects of magical use, and of enjoyment in rites and legends. If we include the correlative negative ideas of disuse, of abstinence from use, and toleration and suffering, problems of use and enjoyment may be safely said to exhaust the domain of common sense inquiry.

There is direct connection between this fact and the concern of common sense with the *qualitative*. It is by discernment of qualities that the fitness and capacity of things and events for use is decided; that proper foodstuffs, for example, are told or discriminated from those that are unfit, poisonous or tabued. That enjoyment-suffering is qualitative through and through and is concerned with situations in their pervasive qualitative character, is almost too obvious for mention. Furthermore, the

operations and responses that are engaged in use and enjoyment of situations are qualitatively marked off. Tanning skins is a process qualitatively different from that of weaving baskets or shaping clay into jars; the rites that are responsive to death are qualitatively different from those appropriate to birth and weddings. Inferiors, superiors and equals are treated in modes of greeting and approach that are qualitatively unlike.

The reason for calling attention to these commonplace facts is that they bring out the basic difference between the subject-matters characteristic of common sense and of scientific inquiries; and they also indicate the differences between the problems and procedures of inquiry that are characteristic of common sense in different stages of culture. I shall first consider the latter point. Common sense in respect to both its content of ideas and beliefs, and its methods of procedure, is anything but a constant. Both its content and its methods alter from time to time not merely in detail but in general pattern. Every invention of a new tool and utensil, every improvement in technique, makes some difference in what is used and enjoyed and in the inquiries that arise with reference to use and enjoyment, with respect to both significance and meaning. Changes in the regulative scheme of relations within a group, family, clan or nation, react even more intensively into some older system of uses and enjoyments.

One has only to note the enormous differences in the contents and methods of common sense in modes of life that are respectively dominantly nomadic, agricultural and industrial. Much that was once taken without question as a matter of common sense is forgotten or actively condemned. Other old conceptions and convictions continue to receive theoretical assent and strong emotional attachment because of their prestige. But they have little hold and application in the ordinary affairs of life. For example, ideas and practices which, in primitive tribes, were interwoven with practically every concern of ordinary affairs, are later relegated to a separate domain, religious or esthetic.

The business of one age becomes the sport and amusement of another age. Even scientific theories and interpretations continue to be affected by conceptions that have ceased to be determinative in the actual practice of inquiry. The special bearing of the fact that "common sense" is anything but a constant upon logical formulations, will concern us in the sequel. Here it is enough to call attention to a point which will later receive detailed examination: namely, the very fitness of the Aristotelian logical organon in respect to the culture and common sense of a certain group in the period in which it was formulated unfits it to be a logical formulation of not only the science but even of the common sense of the present cultural epoch.

I recur now to the bearing of the fact that common sense inquiries are concerned with qualitative matter and operations upon their distinction from scientific inquiries. Fundamentally, the distinction is that brought out in the previous chapter: Namely, that between significances and meanings that are determined in reference to pretty direct existential application and those that are determined on the ground of their systematic relations of coherence and consistency with one another. All that the present mode of statement adds is that, in the first case, "existential application" means application in *qualitative* use and enjoyment of the environment. On the other hand, both the history of science and the present state of science prove that the goal of the systematic relationship of facts and conceptions to one another is dependent upon *elimination* of the qualitative as such and upon reduction to non-qualitative formulation.

The problem of the relation of the domain of common sense to that of science has notoriously taken the form of opposition of the qualitative to the non-qualitative; largely, but not exclusively, the quantitative. The difference has often been formulated as the difference between perceptual material and a system of conceptual constructions. In this form it has constituted, in recent centuries, the chief theme of epistemology and metaphysics. From the standpoint that controls the present discussion, the problem is not epistemological (save as that word means the *logical*) nor is it metaphysical or ontological. In saying that it is logical, it is affirmed that the question at issue is that of the relation to each other of different kinds of *problems*, since difference in the type of problem demands different emphases in inquiry. It is because of this fact that different logical forms accrue to common sense and scientific objects. From this point of view, the question, summarily stated, is that of the relation to each other of the subject-matters of practical uses and concrete enjoyments and of scientific conclusions; not the subject matters of two different domains whether epistemological or ontological.

The conclusion to be later reached is here anticipated to serve as a guide in following the further discussion. (1) Scientific subject-matter and procedures grow out of the direct problems and methods of common sense, of practical uses and enjoyments, and (2) react into the latter in a way that enormously refines, expands and liberates the contents and the agencies at the disposal of common sense. The separation and opposition of scientific subject-matter to that of common sense, when it is taken to be final, generates those controversial problems of epistemology and metaphysics that still dog the course of philosophy. When scientific subject-matter is seen to bear genetic and functional relation to the subject-matter of common sense, these problems disappear. Scientific subject-matter is intermediate, not final and complete in itself.

I begin the discussion by introducing and explaining the denotative force of the word *situation*. Its import may perhaps be most readily indicated by means of a preliminary negative statement. What is designated by the word "situation" is *not* a single object or event or set of objects and events. For we never experience nor form judgments about objects and events in isolation, but only in connection with a contextual whole. This latter is what is called a "situation." I have mentioned the extent in which modern philosophy had been concerned with the problem of existence as perceptually and conceptually determined. The confusions and fallacies that attend the discussion of this problem have a direct and close connection with the difference between an object and a situation. Psychology has paid much attention to the question of the *process* of perception, and has for its purpose described the perceived object in terms of the results of analysis of the process.

I pass over the fact that, no matter how legitimate the virtual identification of process and product may be for the special purpose of *psychological* theory, the identification is thoroughly dubious as a generalized ground of philosophical discussion and theory. I do so in order to call attention to the fact that by the very nature of the case the psychological treatment takes a *singular* object or event for the subject-matter of its analysis. In actual experience, there is never any such isolated singular object or event; *an* object or event is always a special part, phase, or aspect, of an environing experienced world—a situation. The singular object stands out conspicuously because of its especially focal and crucial position at a given time in determination of some problem of use or enjoyment which the *total* complex environment presents. There is always a *field* in which observation of *this* or *that* object or event occurs. Observation of the latter is made for the sake of finding out what that *field* is with reference to some active adaptive response to be made in carrying forward a *course* of behavior. One has only to recur to animal perception, occurring by means of sense organs, to note that isolation of what is perceived from the course of life-behavior would be not only futile, but obstructive, in many cases fatally so.

A further conclusion follows. When the act and object of perception are isolated from their place and function in promoting and directing a successful course of activities in behalf of use-enjoyment, they are taken to be exclusively *cognitive*. The perceived object, orange, rock, piece of gold, or whatever, is taken to be an object of *knowledge per se*. In the sense of being discriminatingly noticed, it *is* an object of knowledge, but not of knowledge as ultimate and self-sufficient. It is noted or "known" only so far as guidance is thereby given to direction of behavior; so that the situation in which it is found can be appropriately enjoyed or some of its conditions be so used that enjoyment will result or suffering be obviated. It is only when an object of focal observation is regarded as an object of knowledge in isolation that there arises the notion that there are two kinds of knowledge, and two kinds of

objects of knowledge, so opposed to each other that philosophy must either choose which is "real" or find some way of reconciling their respective "realities." When it is seen that in common sense inquiry there is no attempt made to know the object or event *as such* but only to determine what it signifies with respect to the way in which the entire situation should be dealt with, the opposition and conflict do not arise. The object or event in question is perceived as part of the environing world, not in and by itself; it is rightly (validly) perceived if and when it acts as clew and guide in use-enjoyment. We live and act in connection with the existing environment, not in connection with isolated objects, even though a singular thing may be crucially significant in deciding how to respond to total environment.

Recurring to the main topic, it is to be remarked that a situation is a whole in virtue of its immediately pervasive quality. When we describe it from the psychological side, we have to say that the situation as a qualitative whole is sensed or *felt*. Such an expression is, however, valuable only as it is taken negatively to indicate that it is *not*, as such, an object in *discourse*. Stating that it is *felt* is wholly misleading if it gives the impression that the situation *is* a feeling or an emotion or anything mentalistic. On the contrary, feeling, sensation and emotion have themselves to be identified and described in terms of the immediate presence of a total qualitative situation.

The pervasively qualitative is not only that which binds all constituents into a whole but it is also unique; it constitutes in each situation an *individual* situation, indivisible and unduplicable. Distinctions and relations are instituted *within* a situation; *they* are recurrent and repeatable in different situations. Discourse that is not controlled by reference to a situation is not discourse, but a meaningless jumble, just as a mass of pied type is not a font much less a sentence. A universe of experience is the precondition of a universe of discourse. Without its controlling presence, there is no way to determine the relevancy, weight or coherence of any designated distinction or relation. The universe of experience surrounds and regulates the universe of discourse but never appears as such within the latter. It may be objected that what was previously said contradicts this statement. For we have been discoursing about universes of experience and situations, so that the latter have been brought within the domain of symbols. The objection, when examined, serves to elicit an important consideration. It is a commonplace that a universe of discourse cannot be a term or element within itself. One universe of discourse may, however, be a term of discourse within *another* universe. The same principle applies in the case of universes of experience.

The reader, whether he agrees or not with what has been said, whether he understands it or not, *has*, as he reads the above passages, a uniquely qualified experienced situation, and his reflective understanding of what is said is controlled by the nature of that immediate situation. One cannot decline to *have* a situation for that is equivalent to having no experience, not even one of disagreement. The most that can be refused or declined is the having of that *specific* situation in which there is reflective recognition (discourse) of the presence of former situations of the kind stated. This very declination is, nevertheless, identical with initiation of another encompassing qualitative experience as a unique whole.

In other words, it *would* be a contradiction if I attempted to demonstrate by means of discourse, the existence of universes of experience. It is not a contradiction by means of discourse to *invite* the reader to have for himself that kind of an immediately experienced situation in which the presence of a situation as a universe of experience is seen to be the encompassing and regulating condition of all discourse.

There is another difficulty in grasping the meaning of what has been said. It concerns the use of the word "quality." The word is usually associated with something specific, like *red, hard, sweet*; that is, with distinctions made within a total experience. The intended contrasting meaning may be suggested, although not adequately exemplified, by considering such qualities as are designated by the terms distressing, perplexing, cheerful, disconsolate. For these words do not designate specific qualities in the way in which *hard*, say, designates a particular quality of a rock. For such qualities

permeate and color *all* the objects and events that are involved in an experience. The phrase "tertiary qualities," happily introduced by Santayana, does not refer to a third quality like in kind to the "primary" and "secondary" qualities of Locke and merely happening to differ in content. For a tertiary quality qualifies *all* the constituents to which it applies in thoroughgoing fashion.

Probably the meaning of *quality*, in the sense in which quality is said to pervade all elements and relations that are or can be instituted in discourse and thereby to constitute them an individual whole, can be most readily apprehended by referring to the esthetic use of the word. A painting is said to have quality, or a particular painting to have a Titian or Rembrandt quality. The word thus used most certainly does not refer to any particular line, color or part of the painting. It is something that affects and modifies all the constituents of the picture and all of their relations. It is not anything that can be expressed in words for it is something that must be *had*. Discourse may, however, point out the qualities, lines and relations by means of which pervasive and unifying quality is achieved. But so far as this discourse is separated from *having* the immediate total experience, a reflective object takes the place of an esthetic one. Esthetic experience, in its emphatic sense, is mentioned as a way of calling attention to situations and universes of experience. The intended force of the illustration would be lost if esthetic experience as such were supposed to exhaust the scope and significance of a "situation." As has been said, a qualitative and qualifying situation is present as the background and the control of *every* experience. It was for a similar reason that it was earlier stated that reference to tertiary qualities was not adequately exemplary. For such qualities as are designated by "distressing," "cheerful," etc., are *general*, while the quality of distress and cheer that marks an existent situation is not general but is unique and inexpressible in words.

I give one further illustration from a different angle of approach. It is more or less a commonplace that it is possible to carry on observations that amass facts tirelessly and yet the observed "facts" lead nowhere. On the other hand, it is possible to have the work of observation so controlled by a conceptual framework fixed in advance that the very things which are genuinely decisive in the problem in hand and its solution, are completely overlooked. Everything is forced into the predetermined conceptual and theoretical scheme. The way, and the only way, to escape these two evils, is sensitivity to the quality of a situation as a whole. In ordinary language, a problem must be felt before it can be stated. If the unique quality of the situation is *had* immediately, then there is something that regulates the selection and the weighing of observed facts and their conceptual ordering.

The discussion has reached the point where the basic problem of the relation of common sense material and methods to that of scientific subject-material and method, can be explicitly discussed. In the first place, science takes its departure of necessity from the qualitative objects, processes, and instruments of the common sense world of use and concrete enjoyments and sufferings. The scientific theory of colors and light is extremely abstract and technical. But it is *about* the colors and light involved in everyday affairs. Upon the common sense level, light and colors are not experienced or inquired into as things in isolation nor yet as qualities of objects viewed in isolation. They are experienced, weighed and judged in reference to their place in the occupations and arts (including social ceremonial arts as well as fine arts) the group carries on. Light is a dominant factor in the daily routine of rising from sleep and going about one's business. Differences in the duration of the light of sun and moon interpenetrate almost every tribal custom. Colors are signs of what can be done and of how it should be done in some inclusive situation—such as, judging the prospects of the morrow's weather; selection of appropriate clothing for various occasions; dyeing, making rugs, baskets and jars; and so on in diverse ways too obvious and tedious to enumerate. They play their part either in practical decisions and activities or in enjoyed celebrations, dances, wakes, feasts, etc. What holds of light and color applies to all objects, events and qualities that enter into everyday common sense affairs.

Gradually and by processes that are more or less tortuous and originally unplanned, definite technical processes and instrumentalities are formed and transmitted. Information about things, their properties and behaviors, is amassed, independently of any particular immediate application. It becomes increasingly remote from the situations of use and enjoyment in which it originated. There is then a background of materials and operations available for the development of what we term science, although there is still no sharp dividing line between common sense and science. For purposes of illustration, it may be supposed that primitive astronomy and primitive methods of keeping track of time (closely connected with astronomical observations) grew out of the practical necessities of groups with herds in care of animals with respect to mating and reproduction, and of agricultural groups with reference to sowing, tilling and reaping. Observation of the change of position of constellations and stars, of the relation of the length of daylight to the sun's place in relation to the constellations along the line of the equinox provided the required information. Instrumental devices were developed in order that the observations might be made; definite techniques for using the instruments followed.

Measurement of angles of inclination and declination was a practical part of meeting a practical need. The illustration is, from a historical point of view, more or less speculative. But something of this general kind certainly effected the transition from what we call common sense to what we call science. If we were to take the practical needs of medicine in healing the sick and dealing with wounds, in their relation to the growth of physiological and anatomical knowledge, the case would be even clearer. In the early history of Greek reflective thought, art, or *techne*, and science, were synonymous.

But this is not the whole of the story. Oriental cultures, especially the Assyrian, Babylonian and Egyptian, developed a division between "lower" and "higher" techniques and kinds of knowledge. The lower, roughly speaking, was in possession of those who did the daily practical work; carpentering, dyeing, weaving, making pottery, trading, etc. The higher came to be the possession of a special class, priests and the successors of primitive medicine men. Their knowledge and techniques were "higher" because they were concerned with what were supposed to be matters of ultimate concern; the welfare of the people and especially its rulers—and this welfare involved transactions with the powers that ruled the universe. *Their* kind of practical activity was so different from that of artisans and traders, the objects involved were so different, the social status of the persons engaged in carrying on the activities in question was so enormously different, that the activity of the guardians and administrators of the higher knowledge and techniques was not "practical" in the sense of practical that applied to the ordinary useful worker. These facts contained dualism in embryo, indeed in more or less mature form. This, when it was reflectively formulated, became the dualism of the empirical and rational, of theory and practice, and, in our own day, of common sense and science.[1]

The Greeks were much less subject to ecclesiastic and autocratic political control than were the peoples mentioned. The Greeks are pointed to with considerable justice as those who freed thought and knowledge from external control. But in one fundamentally important way they fixed, for subsequent intellectual history, the division just mentioned—although changing its direction and interpretation. Science and philosophy (which were still one) constituted the higher form of knowledge and activity. It alone was "rational" and alone deserved the names of knowledge and of activity that was "pure" because liberated from the constraints of practice. Experiential knowledge was confined to the artisan and trader, and their activity was "practical" because it was concerned with satisfaction of needs and desires—most of the latter, as in the case of the trader, being base and unworthy anyway.

The free citizen was not supposed to engage in any of these pursuits but to devote himself to politics and the defense of the city-state. Although the scientist-philosopher was compelled by constraint of the body to give some time and thought to satisfaction of wants, *as* a scientist-philosopher he was engaged in exercising his reason upon rational objects,

thereby attaining the only possible complete freedom and perfect enjoyment. The definitely socio-practical division between workers and non-citizens who were servile, and the members of the leisure class who were free citizens, was converted by philosophic formulation into a division between practice and theory, experience and reason. Strictly scientific-philosophic knowledge and activity were finally conceived to be supra-social as well as supra-empirical. They connected those who pursued them with the divine and cut them off from their fellows.

I have engaged in what seems to be a historical excursus not for the sake of giving historical information but in order to indicate the origin of the distinction between empirical knowledge and practice on one hand and rational knowledge and pure activity on the other; between knowledge and practice that are admittedly of social origin and intent and the insight and activity that were supposed to have no social and practical bearings. This origin is itself social-cultural. Such is the irony of the situation. Relatively free as were the minds of Greek thinkers, momentous as were their accomplishments in certain directions, after Greek culture ceased to be a living thing and its products were carried over into different cultures, the inheritance from the Greeks became an incubus upon the progress of experience and of science, save in mathematics. Even in the latter field it kept mathematics for a long time subservient to strictly geometrical formulation.

The later revival of genuine science undoubtedly drew stimulus and inspiration from the products of Greek thought. But these products were reanimated by contact and interaction with just the things of ordinary experience and the instruments of use in practical arts which in classic Greek thought were supposed to contaminate the purity of science. There was a return to the conditions and factors mentioned earlier: qualitative materials, processes and instruments. Phenomena of heat, light and electricity became matters to be experienced under controlled conditions instead of matters to receive rational formulation through pure intellect. The lens and compass and a multitude of the tools and processes of the practical arts were borrowed and adapted to the needs of scientific inquiry. The ordinary processes that had long been at home in the arts, weakening and intensifying, combining and separating, dissolving and evaporating, precipitating and infusing, heating and cooling, etc. etc., were no longer scorned. They were adopted as means of finding out something about nature, instead of being employed only for the sake of accomplishing objects of use and enjoyment.

Symbolic instrumentalities, especially, underwent tremendous reconstruction; they were refined as well as expanded. On one hand they were constructed and related together on the basis of their applicability, through operations, to existence, and they were freed, on the other hand, from reference to direct application in use and enjoyment. The physical problems that emerged in pursuit of experiential knowledge of nature thus required and evoked new symbolic means of registration and manipulation. Analytic geometry and calculus became primary modes of conceptual response as quantity, change and motion were found to be not irrational accidents but the keys with which to solve the mysteries of natural existence. Language was, nonetheless, an old and familiar qualitative achievement. The most exact comprehensive mathematical language hardly compares as an achievement with the creation of intelligible speech by primitive peoples. Finally, the test of the validity of conceptions formulated and developed in rational discourse was found to reside in their applicability to existential qualitative material. They were no longer taken to be "true" as constituents of rational discourse in isolation but valid in the degree in which they were capable of organizing the qualitative materials of common sense and of instituting control over them. Those semantic-conceptual constructions that indicate with the greatest degree of definiteness the way in which they are to be applied are, even as conceptions, the most truly rational ones. At every point in the practice of scientific inquiry, the old separation between experience and reason, between theory and doing, was destroyed.

In consequence, the contents and techniques of common sense underwent a revolutionary change. It was noted earlier that common sense is not a constant. But the most revolutionary change it has ever undergone is that effected by the infiltration and incorporation of scientific conclusions and methods into itself. Even the procedures and materials that are connected with elementary environmental conditions of life, such things as food, clothing, shelter and locomotion, have undergone tremendous transformation, while unprecedented needs and unprecedented powers of satisfying them have also emerged. The effect of the embodiment of science in the common sense world and the activities that deal with it in the domain of human relationships is as great as that which has taken place in relation to physical nature. It is only necessary to mention the social changes and problems that have arisen from the new technologies of production and distribution of goods and services. For these technologies are the direct product of the new science. To relate in detail the ways in which science has affected the area of common sense in respect to the relationships of person to person, group to group, people to people, would be to relate the story of social change in the last few centuries. Applications of science in revolutionizing the forces and conditions of production, distribution and communication have of necessity tremendously modified the conditions under which human beings live and act in connection with one another, whether the conditions be those of interchange and friendly association or of opposition and war.

It is not intimated that the incorporation of scientific conclusions and operations into the common sense attitudes, beliefs and intellectual methods of what is now taken for granted as matters of common sense is as yet complete or coherent. The opposite is the case. In the most important matters the effect of science upon the content and procedures of common sense has been disintegrative. This disintegrative influence is a social, not a logical, fact. But it is the chief reason why it seems so easy, so "natural," to make a sharp division between common sense inquiry and its logic and scientific inquiry and its logic.

Two aspects of the disintegration which creates the semblance of complete opposition and conflict will be noted. One of them is the fact, already noted, that common sense is concerned with a field that is dominantly qualitative, while science is compelled by its own problems and goals to state its subject-matter in terms of magnitude and other mathematical relations which are non-qualitative. The other fact is that since common sense is concerned, directly and indirectly, with problems of use and enjoyment, it is inherently teleological. Science, on the other hand, has progressed by elimination of "final causes" from every domain with which it is concerned, substituting measured correspondences of change. It operates, to use the old terminology, in terms of "efficient causation," irrespective of ends and values. Upon the basis of the position here taken, these differences are due to the fact that different types of problems demand different modes of inquiry for their solution, not to any ultimate division in existential subject-matter.

The subject-matter of science is stated in symbol-constellations that are radically unlike those familiar to common sense; in what, in effect, is a different language. Moreover, there is much highly technical material that has not been incorporated into common sense even by way of technological application in "material" affairs. In the region of highest importance to common sense, namely, that of moral, political, economic ideas and beliefs, and the methods of forming and confirming them, science has had even less effect. Conceptions and methods in the field of human relationships are in much the same state as were the beliefs and methods of common sense in relation to physical nature before the rise of experimental science. These considerations fix the meaning of the statement that the difference that now exists between common sense and science is a social, rather than a logical, matter. If the word "language" is used not just formally, but to include its content of substantial meanings, the difference is a difference of languages.

The problems of science demand a set of data and a system of meanings and symbols so differentiated that science cannot rightly be called "organized common sense." But it is a potential organ for *organizing* common sense in its dealing with its own subject-matter and problems and this potentiality is far from actualization. In the techniques which affect human use of the materials of physical nature in production, science has become a powerful agency of organization. As far as issues of enjoyment, of consumption, are concerned, it has taken little effect. Morals and the problems of social control are hardly touched. Beliefs, conceptions, customs and institutions, whose rise antedated the modern period, still have possession of the field. The union of this fact with the highly technical and remote language of science creates and maintains the feeling and idea of a complete gap. The paths of communication between common sense and science are as yet largely one-way lanes. Science takes its departure from common sense, but the return road into common sense is devious and blocked by existing social conditions.

In the things of greatest import there is little intercommunication. Pre-scientific ideas and beliefs in morals and politics are, moreover, so deeply ingrained in tradition and habit and institutions, that the impact of scientific method is feared as something profoundly hostile to mankind's dearest and deepest interests and values. On the side of philosophical formulation, highly influential schools of thought are devoted to maintaining the domain of values, ideas and ideals as something wholly apart from any possibility of application of scientific methods. Earlier philosophic conceptions of the necessary separation between reason and experience, theory and practice, higher and lower activities, are used to justify the necessity of the division.

With respect to the second point, that of a seeming fundamental difference due to the fact that common sense is profoundly teleological in its controlling ideas and methods while science is deliberately indifferent to teleology, it must be noted that in spite of the theoretical difference, physical science has, in practical fact, liberated and vastly extended the range of ends open to common sense and has enormously increased the range and power of the means available for attaining them. In ancient thought, ends were fixed by nature; departure from those ends that were antecedently set and fixed by the very nature of things, was impossible; the attempt to institute ends of human devising was taken to be the sure road to confusion and chaos. In the moral field, this conception still exists and is even probably dominant. But in respect to "material" affairs, it has been completely abandoned. Inventions of new agencies and instruments create new ends; they create new consequences which stir men to form new purposes.

The original philosophical meaning of "ends" as fixed completions is almost forgotten. Instead of science eliminating ends and inquiries controlled by teleological considerations, it has, on the contrary, enormously freed and expanded activity and thought in telic matters. This effect is not a matter of opinion but of facts too obvious to be denied. The same sort of thing holds of the qualities with which common sense is inextricably concerned. Multitudes of new qualities have been brought into existence by the applications of physical science, and, what is even more important, our power to bring qualities within actual experience when we so desire, has been intensified almost beyond the possibility of estimate. Consider, as one instance alone, our powers with respect to qualities generated by light and electricity.

The foregoing survey is made for a double purpose. On the one hand the outstanding problem of our civilization is set by the fact that common sense in its content, its "world" and methods, is a house divided against itself. It consists in part, and that part the most vital, of regulative meanings and procedures that antedate the rise of experimental science in its conclusions and methods. In another part, it is what it is because of application of science. This cleavage marks every phase and aspect of modern life: religious, economic, political, legal, and even artistic.

The existence of this split is put in evidence by those who condemn the "modern" and who hold that the only solution of the chaos in civilization is to revert to the intellectual beliefs and methods that were authoritative in past ages, as well as by radicals and "revolutionaries." Between the two stand the multitude that is confused and insecure. It is for this reason that it is here affirmed that the basic problem of present culture and associated living is that of effecting integration where division now exists. The problem cannot be solved apart from a unified logical method of attack and procedure. The attainment of uni-

fied method means that the fundamental unity of the structure of inquiry in common sense and science be recognized, their difference being one in the problems with which they are directly concerned, not in their respective logics. It is not urged that attainment of a unified logic, a theory of inquiry, will resolve the split in our beliefs and procedures. But it is affirmed that it will not be resolved without it.

On the other hand, the problem of unification is one in and for logical theory itself. At the present time logics in vogue do not claim for the most part to be logics of inquiry. In the main, we are asked to take our choice between the traditional logic, which was formulated not only long before the rise of science but when also the content and methods of science were in radical opposition to those of present science, and the new purely "symbolistic logic" that recognizes only mathematics, and even at that is not so much concerned with methods of mathematics as with linguistic formulation of its results. The logic of science is not only separated from common sense, but the best that can be done is to speak of logic *and* scientific method as two different and independent matters. Logic in being "purified" from all experiential taint has become so formalistic that it applies only to itself.

The next chapter deals explicitly with the traditional logic as derived from Aristotle, with a view to showing (1) that of necessity the scientific conditions under which it was formulated are so different from those of existing knowledge that it has been transformed from what it originally was, a logic of *knowledge*, into a purely formal affair, and (2) that there is a necessity for a logical theory based upon scientific conclusions and methods. These are so unlike those of classic science that the need is not revision and extension of the old logic here and there, but a radically different standpoint and a different treatment to be carried through all logical subject matter.

NOTES

[LW 12:66–85.]
1. See L. Hogben, *Mathematics for the Million*, Ch. 1.

By one of the ironic perversities that often attend the course of affairs, the existence of the works of art upon which formation of an esthetic theory depends has become an obstruction to theory about them. For one reason, these works are products that exist externally and physically. In common conception, the work of art is often identified with the building, book, painting, or statue in its existence apart from human experience. Since the actual work of art is what the product does with and in experience, the result is not favorable to understanding. In addition, the very perfection of some of these products, the prestige they possess because of a long history of unquestioned admiration, creates conventions that get in the way of fresh insight. When an art product once attains classic status, it somehow becomes isolated from the human conditions under which it was brought into being and from the human consequences it engenders in actual life-experience.

When artistic objects are separated from both conditions of origin and operation in experience, a wall is built around them that renders almost opaque their general significance, with which esthetic theory deals. Art is remitted to a separate realm, where it is cut off from that association with the materials and aims of every other form of human effort, undergoing, and achievement. A primary task is thus imposed upon one who undertakes to write upon the philosophy of the fine arts. This task is to restore continuity between the refined and intensified forms of experience that are works of art and the everyday events, doings, and sufferings that are universally recognized to constitute experience. Mountain peaks do not float unsupported; they do not even just rest upon the earth. They *are* the earth in one of its manifest operations. It is the business of those who are concerned with the theory of the earth, geographers and geologists, to make this fact evident in its various implications. The theorist who would deal philosophically with fine art has a like task to accomplish.

If one is willing to grant this position, even if only by way of temporary experiment, he will see that there follows a conclusion at first sight surprising. In order to understand the meaning of artistic products, we have to forget them for

The Live Creature

From *Art as Experience* (1934)

a time, to turn aside from them and have recourse to the ordinary forces and conditions of experience that we do not usually regard as esthetic. We must arrive at the theory of art by means of a detour. For theory is concerned with understanding, insight, not without exclamations of admiration, and stimulation of that emotional outburst often called appreciation. It is quite possible to enjoy flowers in their colored form and delicate fragrance without knowing anything about plants theoretically. But if one sets out to *understand* the flowering of plants, he is committed to finding out something about the interactions of soil, air, water and sunlight that condition the growth of plants.

By common consent, the Parthenon is a great work of art. Yet it has esthetic standing only as the work becomes an experience for a human being. And, if one is to go beyond personal enjoyment into the formation of a theory about that large republic of art of which the building is one member, one has to be willing at some point in his reflections to turn from it to the bustling, arguing, acutely sensitive Athenian citizens, with civic sense identified with a civic religion, of whose experience the temple was an expression, and who built it not as a work of art but as a civic commemoration. The turning to them is as human beings who had needs that were a demand for the building and that were carried to fulfillment in it; it is not an examination such as might be carried on by a sociologist in search for material relevant to his purpose. The one who sets out to theorize about the esthetic experience embodied in the Parthenon must realize in thought what the people into whose lives it entered had in common, as creators and as those who were satisfied with it, with people in our own homes and on our own streets.

In order to *understand* the esthetic in its ultimate and approved forms, one must begin with it in the raw; in the events and scenes that hold the attentive eye and ear of man, arousing his interest and affording him enjoyment as he looks and listens: the sights that hold the crowd—the fire-engine rushing by; the machines excavating enormous holes in the earth; the human-fly climbing the steeple-side; the men perched high in air on girders, throwing

and catching red-hot bolts. The sources of art in human experience will be learned by him who sees how the tense grace of the ball-player infects the onlooking crowd; who notes the delight of the housewife in tending her plants, and the intent interest of her goodman in tending the patch of green in front of the house; the zest of the spectator in poking the wood burning on the hearth and in watching the darting flames and crumbling coals. These people, if questioned as to the reason for their actions, would doubtless return reasonable answers. The man who poked the sticks of burning wood would say he did it to make the fire burn better; but he is none the less fascinated by the colorful drama of change enacted before his eyes and imaginatively partakes in it. He does not remain a cold spectator. What Coleridge said of the reader of poetry is true in its way of all who are happily absorbed in their activities of mind and body: "The reader should be carried forward, not merely or chiefly by the mechanical impulse of curiosity, not by a restless desire to arrive at the final solution, but by the pleasurable activity of the journey itself."

The intelligent mechanic engaged in his job, interested in doing well and finding satisfaction in his handiwork, caring for his materials and tools with genuine affection, is artistically engaged. The difference between such a worker and the inept and careless bungler is as great in the shop as it is in the studio. Oftentimes the product may not appeal to the esthetic sense of those who use the product. The fault, however, is oftentimes not so much with the worker as with the conditions of the market for which his product is designed. Were conditions and opportunities different, things as significant to the eye as those produced by earlier craftsmen would be made.

So extensive and subtly pervasive are the ideas that set Art upon a remote pedestal, that many a person would be repelled rather than pleased if told that he enjoyed his casual recreations, in part at least, because of their esthetic quality. The arts which today have most vitality for the average person are things he does not take to be arts: for instance, the movie, jazzed music, the comic strip, and, too frequently, newspaper accounts of love-nests, murders, and exploits of bandits. For, when what he knows as art is relegated to the museum and gallery, the unconquerable impulse towards experiences enjoyable in themselves finds such outlet as the daily environment provides. Many a person who protests against the museum conception of art, still shares the fallacy from which that conception springs. For the popular notion comes from a separation of art from the objects and scenes of ordinary experience that many theorists and critics pride themselves upon holding and even elaborating. The times when select and distinguished objects are closely connected with the products of usual vocations are the times when appreciation of the former is most rife and most keen. When, because of their remoteness, the objects acknowledged by the cultivated to be works of fine art seem anemic to the mass of people, esthetic hunger is likely to seek the cheap and the vulgar.

The factors that have glorified fine art by setting it upon a far-off pedestal did not arise within the realm of art nor is their influence confined to the arts. For many persons an aura of mingled awe and unreality encompasses the "spiritual" and the "ideal" while "matter" has become by contrast a term of depreciation, something to be explained away or apologized for. The forces at work are those that have removed religion as well as fine art from the scope of the common or community life. These forces have historically produced so many of the dislocations and divisions of modern life and thought that art could not escape their influence. We do not have to travel to the ends of the earth nor return many millennia in time to find peoples for whom everything that intensifies the sense of immediate living is an object of intense admiration. Bodily scarification, waving feathers, gaudy robes, shining ornaments of gold and silver, of emerald and jade, formed the contents of esthetic arts, and, presumably, without the vulgarity of class exhibitionism that attends their analogues today. Domestic utensils, furnishings of tent and house, rugs, mats, jars, pots, bows, spears, were wrought with such delighted care that today we hunt them out and give them places of honor in our art museums. Yet in their own time and place, such things were enhancements of the processes of everyday life. Instead

of being elevated to a niche apart, they belonged to display of prowess, the manifestation of group and clan membership, worship of gods, feasting and fasting, fighting, hunting, and all the rhythmic crises that punctuate the stream of living.

Dancing and pantomime, the sources of the art of the theater, flourished as part of religious rites and celebrations. Musical art abounded in the fingering of the stretched string, the beating of the taut skin, the blowing with reeds. Even in the caves, human habitations were adorned with colored pictures that kept alive to the senses experiences with the animals that were so closely bound with the lives of humans. Structures that housed their gods and the instrumentalities that facilitated commerce with the higher powers were wrought with especial fineness. But the arts of the drama, music, painting, and architecture thus exemplified had no peculiar connection with theaters, galleries, museums. They were part of the significant life of an organized community.

The collective life that was manifested in war, worship, the forum, knew no division between what was characteristic of these places and operations, and the arts that brought color, grace, and dignity, into them. Painting and sculpture were organically one with architecture, as that was one with the social purpose that buildings served. Music and song were intimate parts of the rites and ceremonies in which the meaning of group life was consummated. Drama was a vital reenactment of the legends and history of group life. Not even in Athens can such arts be torn loose from this setting in direct experience and yet retain their significant character. Athletic sports, as well as drama, celebrated and enforced traditions of race and group, instructing the people, commemorating glories, and strengthening their civic pride.

Under such conditions, it is not surprising that the Athenian Greeks, when they came to reflect upon art, formed the idea that it is an act of reproduction, or imitation. There are many objections to this conception. But the vogue of the theory is testimony to the close connection of the fine arts with daily life; the idea would not have occurred to any one had art been remote from the interests of life. For the doctrine did not signify that art was a literal copying of objects, but that it reflected the emotions and ideas that are associated with the chief institutions of social life. Plato felt this connection so strongly that it led him to his idea of the necessity of censorship of poets, dramatists, and musicians. Perhaps he exaggerated when he said that a change from the Doric to the Lydian mode in music would be the sure precursor of civic degeneration. But no contemporary would have doubted that music was an integral part of the ethos and the institutions of the community. The idea of "art for art's sake" would not have been even understood.

There must then be historic reasons for the rise of the compartmental conception of fine art. Our present museums and galleries to which works of fine art are removed and stored illustrate some of the causes that have operated to segregate art instead of finding it an attendant of temple, forum, and other forms of associated life. An instructive history of modern art could be written in terms of the formation of the distinctively modern institutions of museum and exhibition gallery. I may point to a few outstanding facts. Most European museums are, among other things, memorials of the rise of nationalism and imperialism. Every capital must have its own museum of painting, sculpture, etc., devoted in part to exhibiting the greatness of its artistic past, and, in other part, to exhibiting the loot gathered by its monarchs in conquest of other nations; for instance, the accumulations of the spoils of Napoleon that are in the Louvre. They testify to the connection between the modern segregation of art and nationalism and militarism. Doubtless this connection has served at times a useful purpose, as in the case of Japan, who, when she was in the process of westernization, saved much of her art treasures by nationalizing the temples that contained them.

The growth of capitalism has been a powerful influence in the development of the museum as the proper home for works of art, and in the promotion of the idea that they are apart from the common life. The *nouveaux riches*, who are an important by-product of the capitalist system, have felt especially bound to surround themselves with works of fine art which, being rare, are also costly. Generally speaking, the typical collector is the typical capitalist. For evidence of good standing in the realm of higher culture, he amasses paintings, statuary, and artistic *bijoux*, as his stocks and bonds certify to his standing in the economic world.

Not merely individuals, but communities and nations, put their cultural good taste in evidence by building opera houses, galleries, and museums. These show that a community is not wholly absorbed in material wealth, because it is willing to spend its gains in patronage of art. It erects these buildings and collects their contents as it now builds a cathedral. These things reflect and establish superior cultural status, while their segregation from the common life reflects the fact that they are not part of a native and spontaneous culture. They are a kind of counterpart of a holier-than-thou attitude, exhibited not toward persons as such but toward the interests and occupations that absorb most of the community's time and energy.

Modern industry and commerce have an international scope. The contents of galleries and museums testify to the growth of economic cosmopolitanism. The mobility of trade and of populations, due to the economic system, has weakened or destroyed the connection between works of art and the *genius loci* of which they were once the natural expression. As works of art have lost their indigenous status, they have acquired a new one—that of being specimens of fine art and nothing else. Moreover, works of art are now produced, like other articles, for sale in the market. Economic patronage by wealthy and powerful individuals has at many times played a part in the encouragement of artistic production. Probably many a savage tribe had its Maecenas. But now even that much of intimate social connection is lost in the impersonality of a world market. Objects that were in the past valid and significant because of their place in the life of a community now function in isolation from the conditions of their origin. By that fact they are also set apart from common experience, and serve as insignia of taste and certificates of special culture.

Because of changes in industrial conditions the artist has been pushed to one side from the main streams of active interest. Industry has been mechanized and an artist cannot work mechanically for mass production. He is less integrated than formerly in the normal flow of social services. A peculiar esthetic "individualism" results. Artists find it incumbent upon them to betake themselves to their work as an isolated means of "self-expression." In order not to cater to the trend of economic forces, they often feel obliged to exaggerate their separateness to the point of eccentricity. Consequently artistic products take on to a still greater degree the air of something independent and esoteric.

Put the action of all such forces together, and the conditions that create the gulf which exists generally between producer and consumer in modern society operate to create also a chasm between ordinary and esthetic experience. Finally we have, as the record of this chasm, accepted as if it were normal, the philosophies of art that locate it in a region inhabited by no other creature, and that emphasize beyond all reason the merely contemplative character of the esthetic. Confusion of values enters in to accentuate the separation. Adventitious matters, like the pleasure of collecting, of exhibiting, of ownership and display, simulate esthetic values. Criticism is affected. There is much applause for the wonders of appreciation and the glories of the transcendent beauty of art indulged in without much regard to capacity for esthetic perception in the concrete.

My purpose, however, is not to engage in an economic interpretation of the history of the arts, much less to argue that economic conditions are either invariably or directly relevant to perception and enjoyment, or even to interpretation of individual works of art. It is to indicate that *theories* which isolate art and its appreciation by placing them in a realm of their own, disconnected from other modes of experiencing, are not inherent in the subject-matter but arise because of specifiable extraneous conditions. Embedded as they are in institutions and in habits of life, these conditions operate effectively because they work so unconsciously. Then the theorist assumes they are embedded in the nature of things. Nevertheless, the influence of these conditions is not confined to theory. As I have already indicated, it deeply affects the practice of living, driving away esthetic perceptions that are necessary ingredients of happiness, or reducing them to the level of compensating transient pleasurable excitations.

Even to readers who are adversely inclined to what has been said, the implications of the statements that have been made may be useful in defining the nature of the problem: that of recovering the continuity of esthetic experience with normal processes of living. The understanding of art and of its role in civilization is not furthered by setting out with eulogies of it nor by occupying ourselves exclusively at the outset with great works of art recognized as such. The comprehension which theory essays will be arrived at by a detour; by going back to experience of the common or mill run of things to discover the esthetic quality such experience possesses. Theory can start with and from acknowledged works of art only when the esthetic is already compartmentalized, or only when works of art are set in a niche apart instead of being celebrations, recognized as such, of the things of ordinary experience. Even a crude experience, if authentically an experience, is more fit to give a clue to the intrinsic nature of esthetic experience than is an object already set apart from any other mode of experience. Following this clue we can discover how the work of art develops and accentuates what is characteristically valuable in things of everyday enjoyment. The art product will then be seen to issue from the latter, when the full meaning of ordinary experience is expressed, as dyes come out of coal tar products when they receive special treatment.

Many theories about art already exist. If there is justification for proposing yet another philosophy of the esthetic, it must be found in a new mode of approach. Combinations and permutations among existing theories can easily be brought forth by those so inclined. But, to my mind, the trouble with existing theories is that they start from a ready-made compartmentalization, or from a conception of art that "spiritualizes" it out of connection with the objects of concrete experience. The alternative, however, to such spiritualization is not a degrading and Philistinish materialization of works of fine art, but a conception that discloses the way in which these works idealize qualities found in common experience. Were works of art placed in a directly human context in popular esteem, they would have a much wider appeal than they can have when pigeonhole theories of art win general acceptance.

A conception of fine art that sets out from its connection with discovered qualities of ordinary experience will be able to indicate the factors and forces that favor the normal development of common human activities into matters of artistic value. It will also be able to point out those conditions that arrest its normal growth. Writers on esthetic theory often raise the question of whether esthetic philosophy can aid in cultivation of esthetic appreciation. The question is a branch of the general theory of criticism, which, it seems to me, fails to accomplish its full office if it does not indicate what to look for and what to find in concrete esthetic objects. But, in any case, it is safe to say that a philosophy of art is sterilized unless it makes us aware of the function of art in relation to other modes of experience, and unless it indicates why this function is so inadequately realized, and unless it suggests the conditions under which the office would be successfully performed.

The comparison of the emergence of works of art out of ordinary experiences to the refining of raw materials into valuable products may seem to some unworthy, if not an actual attempt to reduce works of art to the status of articles manufactured for commercial purposes. The point, however, is that no amount of ecstatic eulogy of finished works can of itself assist the understanding or the generation of such works. Flowers can be enjoyed without knowing about the interactions of soil, air, moisture, and seeds of which they are the result. But they cannot be *understood* without taking just these interactions into account—and theory is a matter of understanding. Theory is concerned with discovering the nature of the production of works of art and of their enjoyment in perception. How is it that the everyday making of things grows into that form of making which is genuinely artistic?

How is it that our everyday enjoyment of scenes and situations develops into the peculiar satisfaction that attends the experience which is emphatically esthetic? These are the questions theory must answer. The answers cannot be found, unless we are willing to find the germs and roots in matters of experience that we do not currently regard as esthetic. Having discovered these active seeds, we may follow the course of their growth into the highest forms of finished and refined art.

It is a commonplace that we cannot direct, save accidentally, the growth and flowering of plants, however lovely and enjoyed, without understanding their causal conditions. It should be just a commonplace that esthetic understanding—as distinct from sheer personal enjoyment—must start with the soil, air, and light out of which things esthetically admirable arise. And these conditions are the conditions and factors that make an ordinary experience complete. The more we recognize this fact, the more we shall find ourselves faced with a problem rather than with a final solution. *If* artistic and esthetic quality is implicit in every normal experience, how shall we explain how and why it so generally fails to become explicit? Why is it that to multitudes art seems to be an importation into experience from a foreign country and the esthetic to be a synonym for something artificial?

We cannot answer these questions any more than we can trace the development of art out of everyday experience, unless we have a clear and coherent idea of what is meant when we say "normal experience." Fortunately, the road to arriving at such an idea is open and well marked. The nature of experience is determined by the essential conditions of life. While man is other than bird and beast, he shares basic vital functions with them and has to make the same basal adjustments if he is to continue the process of living. Having the same vital needs, man derives the means by which he breathes, moves, looks and listens, the very brain with which he coordinates his senses and his movements, from his animal forbears. The organs with which he maintains himself in being are not of himself alone, but by the grace of struggles and achievements of a long line of animal ancestry.

Fortunately a theory of the place of the esthetic in experience does not have to lose itself in minute details when it starts with experience in its elemental form. Broad outlines suffice. The first great consideration is that life goes on in an environment; not merely *in* it but because of it, through interaction with it. No creature lives merely under its skin; its subcutaneous organs are means of connection with what lies beyond its bodily frame, and to which, in order to live, it must adjust itself, by accommodation and defense but also by conquest. At every moment, the living creature is exposed to dangers from its surroundings, and at every moment, it must draw upon something in its surroundings to satisfy its needs. The career and destiny of a living being are bound up with its interchanges with its environment, not externally but in the most intimate way.

The growl of a dog crouching over his food, his howl in time of loss and loneliness, the wagging of his tail at the return of his human friend are expressions of the implication of a living in a natural medium which includes man along with the animal he has domesticated. Every need, say hunger for fresh air or food, is a lack that denotes at least a temporary absence of adequate adjustment with surroundings. But it is also a demand, a reaching out into the environment to make good the lack and to restore adjustment by building at least a temporary equilibrium. Life itself consists of phases in which the organism falls out of step with the march of surrounding things and then recovers unison with it—either through effort or by some happy chance. And, in a growing life, the recovery is never mere return to a prior state, for it is enriched by the state of disparity and resistance through which it has successfully passed. If the gap between organism and environment is too wide, the creature dies. If its activity is not enhanced by the temporary alienation, it merely subsists. Life grows when a temporary falling out is a transition to a more extensive balance of the energies of the organism with those of the conditions under which it lives.

These biological commonplaces are something more than that; they reach to the roots of the esthetic in experience. The world is full of things that are indifferent and even hostile to life; the very processes by which life is maintained tend to throw it out of gear with its surroundings. Nevertheless, if life continues and if in continuing it expands, there is an overcoming of factors of opposition and conflict; there is a transformation of them into differentiated aspects of a higher powered and more significant life. The marvel of organic, of vital, adaptation through expansion (instead of by contraction and passive accommodation) actually takes place. Here in germ are balance and harmony attained through rhythm. Equilibrium comes about not mechanically and inertly but out of, and because of, tension.

There is in nature, even below the level of life, something more than mere flux and change. Form is arrived at whenever a stable, even though moving, equilibrium is reached. Changes interlock and sustain one another. Wherever there is this coherence there is endurance. Order is not imposed from without but is made out of the relations of harmonious interactions that energies bear to one another. Because it is active (not anything static because foreign to what goes on) order itself develops. It comes to include within its balanced movement a greater variety of changes.

Order cannot but be admirable in a world constantly threatened with disorder—in a world where living creatures can go on living only by taking advantage of whatever order exists about them, incorporating it into themselves. In a world like ours, every living creature that attains sensibility welcomes order with a response of harmonious feeling whenever it finds a congruous order about it.

For only when an organism shares in the ordered relations of its environment does it secure the stability essential to living. And when the participation comes after a phase of disruption and conflict, it bears within itself the germs of a consummation akin to the esthetic.

The rhythm of loss of integration with environment and recovery of union not only persists in man but becomes conscious with him; its conditions are material out of which he forms purposes. Emotion is the conscious sign of a break, actual or impending. The discord is the occasion that induces reflection.

Desire for restoration of the union converts mere emotion into interest in objects as conditions of realization of harmony. With the realization, material of reflection is incorporated into objects as their meaning. Since the artist cares in a peculiar way for the phase of experience in which union is achieved, he does not shun moments of resistance and tension. He rather cultivates them, not for their own sake but because of their potentialities, bringing to living consciousness an experience that is unified and total. In contrast with the person whose purpose is esthetic, the scientific man is interested in problems, in situations wherein tension between the matter of observation and of thought is marked. Of course he cares for their resolution. But he does not rest in it; he passes on to another problem using an attained solution only as a stepping stone from which to set on foot further inquiries.

The difference between the esthetic and the intellectual is thus one of the place where emphasis falls in the constant rhythm that marks the interaction of the live creature with his surroundings. The ultimate matter of both emphases in experience is the same, as is also their general form. The odd notion that an artist does not think and a scientific inquirer does nothing else is the result of converting a difference of tempo and emphasis into a difference in kind. The thinker has his esthetic moment when his ideas cease to be mere ideas and become the corporate meanings of objects. The artist has his problems and thinks as he works. But his thought is more immediately embodied in the object. Because of the comparative remoteness of his end, the scientific worker operates with symbols, words and mathematical signs. The artist does his thinking in the very qualitative media he works in, and the terms lie so close to the object that he is producing that they merge directly into it.

The live animal does not have to project emotions into the objects experienced. Nature is kind and hateful, bland and morose, irritating and comforting, long before she is mathematically qualified or even a congeries of "secondary" qualities like colors and their shapes. Even such words as long and short, solid and hollow, still carry to all but those who are intellectually specialized, a moral and emotional connotation. The dictionary will inform any one who consults it that the early use of words like sweet and bitter was not to denote qualities of sense as such but to discriminate things as favorable and hostile. How could it be otherwise? Direct experience comes from nature and man interacting with each other. In this interaction, human energy gathers, is released, dammed up, frustrated and victorious. There are rhythmic beats of want and fulfillment, pulses of doing and being withheld from doing.

All interactions that effect stability and order in the whirling flux of change are rhythms. There is ebb and flow, systole and diastole: ordered change. The latter moves within bounds. To overpass the limits that are set is destruction and death, out of which, however, new rhythms are built up. The proportionate interception of changes establishes an order that is spatially, not merely temporally patterned: like the waves of the sea, the ripples of sand where waves have flowed back and forth, the fleecy and the black-bottomed cloud. Contrast of lack and fullness, of struggle and achievement, of adjustment after consummated irregularity, form the drama in which action, feeling, and meaning are one. The outcome is balance and counterbalance. These are not static nor mechanical. They express power that is intense because measured through overcoming resistance. Environing objects avail and counteravail.

There are two sorts of possible worlds in which esthetic experience would not occur. In a world of mere flux, change would not be cumulative; it would not move toward a close. Stability and rest would have no being. Equally is it true, however, that a world that is finished, ended, would have no traits of suspense and crisis, and would offer no opportunity for resolution. Where everything is already complete, there is no fulfillment. We envisage with pleasure Nirvana and a uniform heavenly bliss only because they are projected upon the background of our present world of stress and conflict. Because the actual world, that in which we live, is a combination of movement and culmination, of breaks and re-unions, the experience of a living creature is capable of esthetic quality. The live being recurrently loses and reestablishes equilibrium with his surroundings. The moment of passage from disturbance into harmony is that of intensest life. In a finished world, sleep and waking could not be distinguished. In one wholly perturbed, conditions could not even be struggled with. In a world made after the pattern of ours, moments of fulfillment punctuate experience with rhythmically enjoyed intervals.

Inner harmony is attained only when, by some means, terms are made with the environment. When it occurs on any other than an "objective" basis, it is illusory—in extreme cases to the point of insanity. Fortunately for variety in experience, terms are made in many ways—ways ultimately decided by selective interest. Pleasures may come about through chance contact and stimulation; such pleasures are not to be despised in a world full of pain. But happiness and delight are a different sort of thing. They come to be through a fulfillment that reaches to the depths of our being—one that is an adjustment of our whole being with the conditions of existence. In the process of living, attainment of a period of equilibrium is at the same time the initiation of a new relation to the environment, one that brings with it potency of new adjustments to be made through struggle. The time of consummation is also one of beginning anew. Any attempt to perpetuate beyond its term the enjoyment attending the time of fulfillment and harmony constitutes withdrawal from the world. Hence it marks the lowering and loss of vitality. But, through the phases of perturbation and conflict, there abides the deep-seated memory of an underlying harmony, the sense of which haunts life like the sense of being founded on a rock.

Most mortals are conscious that a split often occurs between their present living and their past and future. Then the past hangs upon them as a burden; it invades the present with a sense of regret, of opportunities not used, and of consequences we wish undone. It rests upon the present as an oppression, instead of being a storehouse of resources by which to move confidently forward. But the live creature adopts its past; it can make friends with even its stupidities, using them as warnings that increase present wariness. Instead of

trying to live upon whatever may have been achieved in the past, it uses past successes to inform the present. Every living experience owes its richness to what Santayana well calls "hushed reverberations."[1]

To the being fully alive, the future is not ominous but a promise; it surrounds the present as a halo. It consists of possibilities that are felt as a possession of what is now and here. In life that is truly life, everything overlaps and merges. But all too often we exist in apprehensions of what the future may bring, and are divided within ourselves. Even when not overanxious, we do not enjoy the present because we subordinate it to that which is absent. Because of the frequency of this abandonment of the present to the past and future, the happy periods of an experience that is now complete because it absorbs into itself memories of the past and anticipations of the future, come to constitute an esthetic ideal. Only when the past ceases to trouble and anticipations of the future are not perturbing is a being wholly united with his environment and therefore fully alive. Art celebrates with peculiar intensity the moments in which the past reenforces the present and in which the future is a quickening of what now is.

To grasp the sources of esthetic experience it is, therefore, necessary to have recourse to animal life below the human scale. The activities of the fox, the dog, and the thrush may at least stand as reminders and symbols of that unity of experience which we so fractionize when work is labor, and thought withdraws us from the world. The live animal is fully present, all there, in all of its actions: in its wary glances, its sharp sniffings, its abrupt cocking of ears. All senses are equally on the *qui vive*. As you watch, you see motion merging into sense and sense into motion—constituting that animal grace so hard for man to rival. What the live creature retains from the past and what it expects from the future operate as directions in the present. The dog is never pedantic nor academic; for these things arise only when the past is severed in consciousness from the present and is set up as a model to copy or a storehouse upon which to draw. The past absorbed into the present carries on; it presses forward.

There is much in the life of the savage that is sodden. But, when the savage is most alive, he is most observant of the world about him and most taut with energy. As he watches what stirs about him, he, too, is stirred. His observation is both action in preparation and foresight of the future. He is as active through his whole being when he looks and listens as when he stalks his quarry or stealthily retreats from a foe. His senses are sentinels of immediate thought and outposts of action, and not, as they so often are with us, mere pathways along which material is gathered to be stored away for a delayed and remote possibility.

It is mere ignorance that leads then to the supposition that connection of art and esthetic perception with experience signifies a lowering of their significance and dignity. Experience in the degree in which it *is* experience is heightened vitality. Instead of signifying being shut up within one's own private feelings and sensations, it signifies active and alert commerce with the world; at its height it signifies complete interpenetration of self and the world of objects and events. Instead of signifying surrender to caprice and disorder, it affords our sole demonstration of a stability that is not stagnation but is rhythmic and developing. Because experience is the fulfillment of an organism in its struggles and achievements in a world of things, it is art in germ. Even in its rudimentary forms, it contains the promise of that delightful perception which is esthetic experience.

NOTES

[LW 10:9–25.]

1. "These familiar flowers, these well-remembered bird-notes, this sky with its fitful brightness, these furrowed and grassy fields, each with a sort of personality given to it by the capricious hedge, such things as these are the mother-tongue of our imagination, the language that is laden with all the subtle inextricable associations the fleeting hours of our childhood left behind them. Our delight in the sunshine on the deep-bladed grass to-day might be no more than the faint perception of wearied souls, if it were not for the sunshine and grass of far-off years, which still live in us and transform our perception into love." George Eliot in *The Mill on the Floss*.

Never before in history has mankind been so much of two minds, so divided into two camps, as it is today. Religions have traditionally been allied with ideas of the supernatural, and often have been based upon explicit beliefs about it. Today there are many who hold that nothing worthy of being called religious is possible apart from the supernatural. Those who hold this belief differ in many respects. They range from those who accept the dogmas and sacraments of the Greek and Roman Catholic church as the only sure means of access to the supernatural to the theist or mild deist. Between them are the many Protestant denominations who think the Scriptures, aided by a pure conscience, are adequate avenues to supernatural truth and power. But they agree in one point: the necessity for a Supernatural Being and for an immortality that is beyond the power of nature.

The opposed group consists of those who think the advance of culture and science has completely discredited the supernatural and with it all religions that were allied with belief in it. But they go beyond this point. The extremists in this group believe that with elimination of the supernatural not only must historic religions be dismissed but with them everything of a religious nature. When historical knowledge has discredited the claims made for the supernatural character of the persons said to have founded historic religions; when the supernatural inspiration attributed to literatures held sacred has been riddled, and when anthropological and psychological knowledge has disclosed the all-too-human source from which religious beliefs and practices have sprung, everything religious must, they say, also go.

There is one idea held in common by these two opposite groups: identification of the religious with the supernatural. The question I shall raise in these chapters concerns the ground for and the consequences of this identification: its reasons and its value. In the discussion I shall develop another conception of the nature of the religious phase of experience, one that separates it from the supernatural and the things that have grown up about it. I shall try to show that these derivations are encumbrances and that what is genuinely religious

Religion versus the Religious

From *A Common Faith* (1934)

will undergo an emancipation when it is re-lieved from them; that then, for the first time, the religious aspect of experience will be free to develop freely on its own account.

This view is exposed to attack from both the other camps. It goes contrary to traditional religions, including those that have the greatest hold upon the religiously minded today. The view announced will seem to them to cut the vital nerve of the religious element itself in taking away the basis upon which traditional religions and institutions have been founded. From the other side, the position I am taking seems like a timid halfway position, a concession and compromise unworthy of thought that is thoroughgoing. It is regarded as a view entertained from mere tendermindedness, as an emotional hangover from childhood indoctrination, or even as a manifestation of a desire to avoid disapproval and curry favor.

The heart of my point, as far as I shall develop it in this first section, is that there is a difference between religion, a religion, and the religious; between anything that may be denoted by a noun substantive and the quality of experience that is designated by an adjective. It is not easy to find a definition of religion in the substantive sense that wins general acceptance. However, in the *Oxford Dictionary* I find the following: "Recognition on the part of man of some unseen higher power as having control of his destiny and as being entitled to obedience, reverence and worship."

This particular definition is less explicit in assertion of the supernatural character of the higher unseen power than are others that might be cited. It is, however, surcharged with implications having their source in ideas connected with the belief in the supernatural, characteristic of historic religions. Let us suppose that one familiar with the history of religions, including those called primitive, compares the definition with the variety of known facts and by means of the comparison sets out to determine just what the definition means. I think he will be struck by three facts that reduce the terms of the definition to such a low common denominator that little meaning is left.

He will note that the "unseen powers" referred to have been conceived in a multitude of incompatible ways. Eliminating the differ-ences, nothing is left beyond the bare reference to something unseen and powerful. This has been conceived as the vague and undefined Mana of the Melanesians; the Kami of primitive Shintoism; the fetish of the Africans; spirits, having some human properties, that pervade natural places and animate natural forces; the ultimate and impersonal principle of Buddhism; the unmoved mover of Greek thought; the gods and semi-divine heroes of the Greek and Roman Pantheons; the personal and loving Providence of Christianity, omnipotent, and limited by a corresponding evil power; the arbitrary Will of Moslemism; the supreme legislator and judge of deism. And these are but a few of the outstanding varieties of ways in which the invisible power has been conceived.

There is no greater similarity in the ways in which obedience and reverence have been expressed. There has been worship of animals, of ghosts, of ancestors, phallic worship, as well as of a Being of dread power and of love and wisdom. Reverence has been expressed in the human sacrifices of the Peruvians and Aztecs; the sexual orgies of some Oriental religions; exorcisms and ablutions; the offering of the humble and contrite mind of the Hebrew prophet, the elaborate rituals of the Greek and Roman Churches. Not even sacrifice has been uniform; it is highly sublimated in Protestant denominations and in Moslemism. Where it has existed it has taken all kinds of forms and been directed to a great variety of powers and spirits. It has been used for expiation, for propitiation and for buying special favors. There is no conceivable purpose for which rites have not been employed.

Finally, there is no discernible unity in the moral motivations appealed to and utilized. They have been as far apart as fear of lasting torture, hope of enduring bliss in which sexual enjoyment has sometimes been a conspicuous element; mortification of the flesh and extreme asceticism; prostitution and chastity; wars to extirpate the unbeliever; persecution to convert or punish the unbeliever, and philanthropic zeal; servile acceptance of imposed dogma, along with brotherly love and aspiration for a reign of justice among men.

I have, of course, mentioned only a sparse number of the facts which fill volumes in any well-stocked library. It may be asked by those who do not like to look upon the darker side of the history of religions why the darker facts should be brought up. We all know that civilized man has a background of bestiality and superstition and that these elements are still with us. Indeed, have not some religions, including the most influential forms of Christianity, taught that the heart of man is totally corrupt? How could the course of religion in its entire sweep not be marked by practices that are shameful in their cruelty and lustfulness, and by beliefs that are degraded and intellectually incredible? What else than what we find could be expected, in the case of people having little knowledge and no secure method of knowing; with primitive institutions, and with so little control of natural forces that they lived in a constant state of fear?

I gladly admit that historic religions have been relative to the conditions of social culture in which peoples lived. Indeed, what I am concerned with is to press home the logic of this method of disposal of outgrown traits of past religions. Beliefs and practices in a religion that now prevails are by this logic relative to the present state of culture. If so much flexibility has obtained in the past regarding an unseen power, the way it affects human destiny, and the attitudes we are to take toward it, why should it be assumed that change in conception and action has now come to an end? The logic involved in getting rid of inconvenient aspects of past religions compels us to inquire how much in religions now accepted are survivals from outgrown cultures. It compels us to ask what conception of unseen powers and our relations to them would be consonant with the best achievements and aspirations of the present. It demands that in imagination we wipe the slate clean and start afresh by asking what would be the idea of the unseen, of the manner of its control over us and the ways in which reverence and obedience would be manifested, if whatever is basically religious in experience had the opportunity to express itself free from all historic encumbrances.

So we return to the elements of the definition that has been given. What boots it to accept, in defense of the universality of religion, a definition that applies equally to the most savage and degraded beliefs and practices that have related to unseen powers and to noble ideals of a religion having the greatest share of moral content? There are two points involved. One of them is that there is nothing left worth preserving in the notions of unseen powers, controlling human destiny to which obedience, reverence and worship are due, if we glide silently over the nature that has been attributed to the powers, the radically diverse ways in which they have been supposed to control human destiny, and in which submission and awe have been manifested. The other point is that when we begin to select, to choose, and say that some present ways of thinking about the unseen powers are better than others; that the reverence shown by a free and self-respecting human being is better than the servile obedience rendered to an arbitrary power by frightened men; that we should believe that control of human destiny is exercised by a wise and loving spirit rather than by madcap ghosts or sheer force—when I say, we begin to choose, we have entered upon a road that has not yet come to an end. We have reached a point that invites us to proceed farther.

For we are forced to acknowledge that concretely there is no such thing as religion in the singular. There is only a multitude of religions. "Religion" is a strictly collective term and the collection it stands for is not even of the kind illustrated in textbooks of logic. It has not the unity of a regiment or assembly but that of any miscellaneous aggregate. Attempts to prove the universality prove too much or too little. It is probable that religions have been universal in the sense that all the peoples we know anything about have had a religion. But the differences among them are so great and so shocking that any common element that can be extracted is meaningless. The idea that religion is universal proves too little in that the older apologists for Christianity seem to have been better advised than some modern ones in condemning every religion but one as an impostor, as at bottom some kind of demon worship or at any rate a superstitious figment. Choice among religions is imperative, and the necessity for choice leaves nothing of any force in the argument from universality. Moreover, when once we enter upon the road of choice, there is at once presented a possibility not yet generally realized.

For the historic increase of the ethical and ideal content of religions suggests that the process of purification may be carried further. It indicates that further choice is imminent in which certain values and functions in experience may be selected. This possibility is what I had in mind in speaking of the difference between the religious and a religion. I am not proposing a religion, but rather the emancipation of elements and outlooks that may be called religious. For the moment we have a religion, whether that of the Sioux Indian or of Judaism or of Christianity, that moment the ideal factors in experience that may be called religious take on a load that is not inherent in them, a load of current beliefs and of institutional practices that are irrelevant to them.

I can illustrate what I mean by a common phenomenon in contemporary life. It is widely supposed that a person who does not accept any religion is thereby shown to be a non-religious person. Yet it is conceivable that the present depression in religion is closely connected with the fact that religions now prevent, because of their weight of historic encumbrances, the religious quality of experience from coming to consciousness and finding the expression that is appropriate to present conditions, intellectual and moral. I believe that such is the case. I believe that many persons are so repelled from what exists as a religion by its intellectual and moral implications, that they are not even aware of attitudes in themselves that if they came to fruition would be genuinely religious. I hope that this remark may help make clear what I mean by the distinction between "religion" as a noun substantive and "religious" as adjectival.

To be somewhat more explicit, a religion (and as I have just said there is no such thing as religion in general) always signifies a special body of beliefs and practices having some kind of institutional organization, loose or tight. In contrast, the adjective "religious" denotes nothing in the way of a specifiable entity, either institutional or as a system of beliefs. It does not denote anything to which one can specifically point as one can point to this and that historic religion or existing church. For it does not denote anything that can exist by itself or that can be organized into a particular and distinctive form of existence. It denotes attitudes that may be taken toward every object and every proposed end or ideal.

Before, however, I develop my suggestion that realization of the distinction just made would operate to emancipate the religious quality from encumbrances that now smother or limit it, I must refer to a position that in some respects is similar in words to the position I have taken, but that in fact is a whole world removed from it. I have several times used the phrase "religious elements of experience." Now at present there is much talk, especially in liberal circles, of religious experience as vouching for the authenticity of certain beliefs and the desirability of certain practices, such as particular forms of prayer and worship. It is even asserted that religious experience is the ultimate basis of religion itself. The gulf between this position and that which I have taken is what I am now concerned to point out.

Those who hold to the notion that there is a definite kind of experience which is itself religious, by that very fact make out of it something specific, as a kind of experience that is marked off from experience as aesthetic, scientific, moral, political; from experience as companionship and friendship. But "religious" as a quality of experience signifies something that may belong to all these experiences. It is the polar opposite of some type of experience that can exist by itself. The distinction comes out clearly when it is noted that the concept of this distinct kind of experience is used to validate a belief in some special kind of object and also to justify some special kind of practice.

For there are many religionists who are now dissatisfied with the older "proofs" of the existence of God, those that go by the name of ontological, cosmological and teleological. The cause of the dissatisfaction is perhaps not so much the arguments that Kant used to show the insufficiency of these alleged proofs, as it is the growing feeling that they are too formal to offer any support to religion in action. Anyway, the dissatisfaction exists. Moreover, these religionists are moved by the rise of the experimental method in other fields. What is more natural and proper, accordingly, than that they should affirm they are just as good empiricists as anybody else—indeed, as good as the scientists themselves? As the latter rely upon certain kinds of experience to prove the existence of certain kinds of objects, so the religionists rely upon a certain kind of experience to prove the existence of the object of religion, especially the supreme object, God.

The discussion may be made more definite by introducing, at this point, a particular illustration of this type of reasoning. A writer says: "I broke down from overwork and soon came to the verge of nervous prostration. One morning after a long and sleepless night . . . I resolved to stop drawing upon myself so continuously and begin drawing upon God. I determined to set apart a quiet time every day in which I could relate my life to its Ultimate Source, regain the consciousness that in God I live, move and have my being. That was thirty years ago. Since then I have had literally not one hour of darkness or despair."

This is an impressive record. I do not doubt its authenticity nor that of the experience related. It illustrates a religious aspect of experience. But it illustrates also the use of that quality to carry a superimposed load of a particular religion. For having been brought up in the Christian religion, its subject interprets it in the terms of the personal God characteristic of that religion. Taoists, Buddhists, Moslems, persons of no religion including those who reject all supernatural influence and power, have had experiences similar in their effect. Yet another author commenting upon the passage says: "The religious expert can be more sure that this God exists than he can of either the cosmological God of speculative surmise or the Christlike God involved in the validity of moral optimism," and goes on to add that such experiences "mean that God the Savior, the Power that gives victory over sin on certain conditions that man can fulfill, is an existent, accessible and scientifically knowable reality." It should be clear that this inference is sound only if the conditions, of whatever sort, that produce the effect are called "God." But most readers will take the inference to mean that the existence of a particular

Being, of the type called "God" in the Christian religion, is proved by a method akin to that of experimental science.

In reality, the only thing that can be said to be "proved" is the existence of some complex of conditions that have operated to effect an adjustment in life, an orientation, that brings with it a sense of security and peace. The particular interpretation given to this complex of conditions is not inherent in the experience itself. It is derived from the culture with which a particular person has been imbued. A fatalist will give one name to it; a Christian Scientist another, and the one who rejects all supernatural being still another. The determining factor in the interpretation of the experience is the particular doctrinal apparatus into which a person has been inducted. The emotional deposit connected with prior teaching floods the whole situation. It may readily confer upon the experience such a peculiarly sacred preciousness that all inquiry into its causation is barred. The stable outcome is so invaluable that the cause to which it is referred is usually nothing but a reduplication of the thing that has occurred, plus some name that has acquired a deeply emotional quality.

The intent of this discussion is not to deny the genuineness of the result nor its importance in life. It is not, save incidentally, to point out the possibility of a purely naturalistic explanation of the event. My purpose is to indicate what happens when religious experience is already set aside as something *sui generis*. The actual religious quality in the experience described is the *effect* produced, the better adjustment in life and its conditions, not the manner and cause of its production. The way in which the experience operated, its function, determines its religious value. If the reorientation actually occurs, it, and the sense of security and stability accompanying it, are forces on their own account. It takes place in different persons in a multitude of ways. It is sometimes brought about by devotion to a cause; sometimes by a passage of poetry that opens a new perspective; sometimes as was the case with Spinoza—deemed an atheist in his day—through philosophical reflection.

The difference between an experience having a religious force because of what it does in and to the processes of living and religious experience as a separate kind of thing gives me occasion to refer to a previous remark. If this function were rescued through emancipation from dependence upon specific types of beliefs and practices, from those elements that constitute a religion, many individuals would find that experiences having the force of bringing about a better, deeper and enduring adjustment in life are not so rare and infrequent as they are commonly supposed to be. They occur frequently in connection with many significant moments of living. The idea of invisible powers would take on the meaning of all the conditions of nature and human association that support and deepen the sense of values which carry one through periods of darkness and despair to such an extent that they lose their usual depressive character.

I do not suppose for many minds the dislocation of the religious from a religion is easy to effect. Tradition and custom, especially when emotionally charged, are a part of the habits that have become one with our very being. But the possibility of the transfer is demonstrated by its actuality. Let us then for the moment drop the term "religious," and ask what are the attitudes that lend deep and enduring support to the processes of living. I have, for example, used the words "adjustment" and "orientation." What do they signify?

While the words "accommodation," "adaptation," and "adjustment" are frequently employed as synonyms, attitudes exist that are so different that for the sake of clear thought they should be discriminated. There are conditions we meet that cannot be changed. If they are particular and limited, we modify our own particular attitudes in accordance with them. Thus we accommodate ourselves to changes in weather, to alterations in income when we have no other recourse. When the external conditions are lasting we become inured, habituated, or, as the process is now often called, conditioned. The two main traits of this attitude, which I should like to call accommodation, are that it affects *particular* modes of conduct, not the entire self, and that the process is mainly *passive*. It may, however, become general and then it becomes fatalistic resignation or submission. There are other attitudes toward the environment that are also particular but that are more active. We re-act against conditions and endeavor to change them to meet our wants and demands. Plays in a foreign language are "adapted" to meet the needs of an American audience. A house is rebuilt to suit changed conditions of the household; the telephone is invented to serve the demand for speedy communication at a distance; dry soils are irrigated so that they may bear abundant crops. Instead of accommodating ourselves to conditions, we modify conditions so that they will be accommodated to our wants and purposes. This process may be called adaptation.

Now both of these processes are often called by the more general name of adjustment. But there are also changes in ourselves in relation to the world in which we live that are much more inclusive and deep seated. They relate not to this and that want in relation to this and that condition of our surroundings, but pertain to our being in its entirety. Because of their scope, this modification of ourselves is enduring. It lasts through any amount of vicissitude of circumstances, internal and external. There is a composing and harmonizing of the various elements of our being such that, in spite of changes in the special conditions that surround us, these conditions are also arranged, settled, in relation to us. This attitude includes a note of submission. But it is voluntary, not externally imposed; and as voluntary it is something more than a mere Stoical resolution to endure unperturbed throughout the buffetings of fortune. It is more outgoing, more ready and glad, than the latter attitude, and it is more active than the former. And in calling it voluntary, it is not meant that it depends upon a particular resolve or volition. It is a change *of* will conceived as the organic plenitude of our being, rather than any special change *in* will.

It is the claim of religions that they effect this generic and enduring change in attitude. I should like to turn the statement around and say that whenever this change takes place there is a definitely religious attitude. It is not *a* religion that brings it about, but when it occurs, from whatever cause and by whatever means, there is a religious outlook and function. As I have said before, the doctrinal or intellectual apparatus and the institutional accretions that grow up are, in a strict sense, adventitious to the intrinsic quality of such experiences. For they are affairs of the traditions of the culture with which individuals are inoculated. Mr. Santayana has connected the religious quality of experience with the imaginative, as that is expressed in poetry. "Religion and poetry," he says, "are identical in essence, and differ merely in the way in which they are attached to practical affairs. Poetry is called religion when it intervenes in life, and religion, when it merely supervenes upon life, is seen to be nothing but poetry." The difference between intervening *in* and supervening *upon* is as important as is the identity set forth. Imagination may play upon life or it may enter profoundly into it. As Mr. Santayana puts it, "poetry has a universal and a moral function," for "its highest power lies in its relevance to the ideals and purposes of life." Except as it intervenes, "all observation is observation of brute fact, all discipline is mere repression, until these facts digested and this discipline embodied in humane impulses become the starting-point for a creative movement of the imagination, the firm basis for ideal constructions in society, religion, and art."

If I may make a comment upon this penetrating insight of Mr. Santayana, I would say that the difference between imagination that only supervenes and imagination that intervenes is the difference between one that completely interpenetrates all the elements of our being and one that is interwoven with only special and partial factors. There actually occurs extremely little observation of brute facts merely for the sake of the facts, just as there is little discipline that is repression and nothing but repression. Facts are usually observed with reference to some practical end and purpose, and that end is presented only imaginatively. The most repressive discipline has some end in view to which there is at least imputed an ideal quality; otherwise it is purely sadistic. But in such cases of observation and discipline imagination is limited and partial. It does not extend far; it does not permeate deeply and widely.

The connection between imagination and the harmonizing of the self is closer than is usually thought. The idea of a whole, whether of the whole personal being or of the world, is an imaginative, not a literal, idea. The limited world of our observation and reflection becomes the Universe only through imaginative extension. It cannot be apprehended in knowledge nor realized in reflection. Neither observation, thought, nor practical activity can attain that complete unification of the self which is called a whole. The *whole* self is an ideal, an imaginative projection. Hence the idea of a thoroughgoing and deep-seated harmonizing of the self with the Universe (as a name for the totality of conditions with which the self is connected) operates only through imagination—which is one reason why this composing of the self is not voluntary in the sense of an act of special volition or resolution. An "adjustment" possesses the will rather than is its express product. Religionists have been right in thinking of it as an influx from sources beyond conscious deliberation and purpose—a fact that helps explain, psychologically, why it has so generally been attributed to a supernatural source and that, perhaps, throws some light upon the reference of it by William James to unconscious factors. And it is pertinent to note that the unification of the self throughout the ceaseless flux of what it does, suffers, and achieves, cannot be attained in terms of itself. The self is always directed toward something beyond itself and so its own unification depends upon the idea of the integration of the shifting scenes of the world into that imaginative totality we call the Universe.

The intimate connection of imagination with ideal elements in experience is generally recognized. Such is not the case with respect to its connection with faith. The latter has been regarded as a substitute for knowledge, for sight. It is defined, in the Christian religion, as *evidence* of things not seen. The implication is that faith is a kind of anticipatory vision of things that are now invisible because of the limitations of our finite and erring nature. Because it is a substitute for knowledge, its material and object are intellectual in quality. As John Locke summed up the matter, faith is "assent to a proposition . . . on the credit of its proposer." Religious faith is then given to a body of propositions as true on the credit of their supernatural author, reason coming in to demonstrate the reasonableness of giving such credit. Of necessity there results the development of theologies, or bodies of systematic propositions, to make explicit in organized form the content of the propositions to which belief is attached and assent given. Given the point of view, those who hold that religion necessarily implies a theology are correct.

But belief or faith has also a moral and practical import. Even devils, according to the older theologians, believe—and tremble. A distinction was made, therefore, between "speculative" or intellectual belief and an act called "justifying" faith. Apart from any theological context, there is a difference between belief that is a conviction that some end should be supreme over conduct, and belief that some object or being exists as a truth for the intellect. Conviction in the moral sense signifies being conquered, vanquished, in our active nature by an ideal end; it signifies acknowledgment of its rightful claim over our desires and purposes. Such acknowledgment is practical, not primarily intellectual. It goes beyond evidence that can be presented to *any* possible observer. Reflection, often long and arduous, may be involved in arriving at the conviction, but the import of thought is not exhausted in discovery of evidence that can justify intellectual assent. The authority of an ideal over choice and conduct is the authority of an ideal, not of a fact, of a truth guaranteed to intellect, not of the status of the one who propounds the truth.

Such moral faith is not easy. It was questioned of old whether the Son of Man should find faith on the earth in his coming. Moral faith has been bolstered by all sorts of arguments intended to prove that its object is not ideal and that its claim upon us is not primarily moral or practical, since the ideal in question is already embedded in the existent frame of things. It is argued that the ideal is already the final reality at the heart of things that exist, and that only our senses or the corruption of our natures prevent us from apprehending its prior existential being. Starting, say, from such an idea as that justice is more than a moral ideal because it is embedded in the very make-up of the actually existent world, men have gone on to build up vast intellectual schemes, philosophies, and theologies, to prove that ideals are real not as ideals but as antecedently existing actualities. They have failed to see that in converting moral realities into matters of intellectual assent they have evinced lack of *moral* faith. Faith that something should be in existence as far as lies in our power is changed into the intellectual belief that it is already in existence. When physical existence does not bear out the assertion, the physical is subtly changed into the metaphysical. In this way, moral faith has been inextricably tied up with intellectual beliefs about the supernatural.

The tendency to convert ends of moral faith and action into articles of an intellectual creed has been furthered by a tendency of which psychologists are well aware. What we ardently desire to have thus and so, we tend to believe is already so. Desire has a powerful influence upon intellectual beliefs. Moreover, when conditions are adverse to realization of the objects of our desire—and in the case of significant ideals they are extremely adverse— it is an easy way out to assume that after all they are already embodied in the ultimate structure of what is, and that appearances to the contrary are *merely* appearances. Imagination then merely supervenes and is freed from the responsibility for intervening. Weak natures take to reverie as a refuge as strong ones do to fanaticism. Those who dissent are mourned over by the first class and converted through the use of force by the second.

What has been said does not imply that all moral faith in ideal ends is by virtue of that fact religious in quality. The religious is "morality touched by emotion" only when the ends of moral conviction arouse emotions that are not only intense but are actuated and supported by ends so inclusive that they unify the self. The inclusiveness of the end in relation to both self and the "universe" to which an inclusive self is related is indispensable. According to the best authorities, "religion" comes from a root that means being bound or tied. Originally, it meant being bound by vows to a particular way of life—as *les religieux* were monks and nuns who had assumed certain vows. The religious attitude signifies something that is bound through imagination to a *general* attitude. This comprehensive attitude, moreover, is much broader than anything indicated by "moral" in its usual sense. The quality of attitude is displayed in art, science and good citizenship.

If we apply the conception set forth to the terms of the definition earlier quoted, these terms take on a new significance. An unseen power controlling our destiny becomes the power of an ideal. All possibilities, as possibilities, are ideal in character. The artist, scientist, citizen, parent, as far as they are actuated by the spirit of their callings, are controlled by the unseen. For all endeavor for the better is moved by faith in what is possible, not by adherence to the actual. Nor does this faith depend for its moving power upon intellectual assurance or belief that the things worked for must surely prevail and come into embodied existence. For the authority of the object to determine our attitude and conduct, the right that is given it to claim our allegiance and devotion is based on the intrinsic nature of the ideal. The outcome, given our best endeavor, is not with us. The inherent vice of all intellectual schemes of idealism is that they convert the idealism of action into a system of beliefs about antecedent reality. The character assigned this reality is so different from that which observation and reflection lead to and support that these schemes inevitably glide into alliance with the supernatural.

All religions, marked by elevated ideal quality, have dwelt upon the power of religion to introduce perspective into the piecemeal and shifting episodes of existence. Here too we need to reverse the ordinary statement and say that whatever introduces genuine perspective is religious, not that religion is something that introduces it. There can be no doubt (referring to the second element of the definition) of our dependence upon forces beyond our control. Primitive man was so impotent in the face of these forces that, especially in an unfavorable natural environment, fear became a dominant attitude, and, as the old saying goes, fear created the gods.

With increase of mechanisms of control, the element of fear has, relatively speaking, subsided. Some optimistic souls have even concluded that the forces about us are on the whole essentially benign. But every crisis, whether of the individual or of the community, reminds man of the precarious and partial nature of the control he exercises. When man, individually and collectively, has done his uttermost, conditions that at different times and places have given rise to the ideas of Fate and Fortune, of Chance and Providence, remain. It is the part of manliness to insist upon the capacity of mankind to strive to direct natural and social forces to humane ends. But unqualified absolutistic statements about the omnipotence of such endeavors reflect egoism rather than intelligent courage.

The fact that human destiny is so interwoven with forces beyond human control renders it unnecessary to suppose that dependence and the humility that accompanies it have to find the particular channel that is prescribed by traditional doctrines. What is especially significant is rather the form which the sense of dependence takes. Fear never gave stable perspective in the life of anyone. It is dispersive and withdrawing. Most religions have in fact added rites of communion to those of expiation and propitiation. For our dependence is manifested in those relations to the environment that support our undertakings and aspirations as much as it is in the defeats inflicted upon us. The essentially unreligious attitude is that which attributes human achievement and purpose to man in isolation from the world of physical nature and his fellows. Our successes are dependent upon the cooperation of nature. The sense of the dignity of human nature is as religious as is the sense of awe and reverence when it rests upon a sense of human nature as a cooperating part of a larger whole. Natural piety is not of necessity either a fatalistic acquiescence in natural happenings or a romantic idealization of the world. It may rest upon a just sense of nature as the whole of which we are parts, while it also recognizes that we are parts that are marked by intelligence and purpose, having the capacity to strive by their aid to bring conditions into greater consonance with what is humanly desirable. Such piety is an inherent constituent of a just perspective in life.

Understanding and knowledge also enter into a perspective that is religious in quality. Faith in the continued disclosing of truth through directed cooperative human endeavor is more religious in quality than is any faith in a completed revelation. It is of course now usual to hold that revelation is not completed in the sense of being ended. But religions hold that the essential framework is settled in its significant moral features at least, and that new elements that are offered must be judged by conformity to this framework. Some fixed doctrinal apparatus is necessary for *a* religion. But faith in the possibilities of continued and rigorous inquiry does not limit access to truth to any channel or scheme of things. It does not first say that truth is universal and then add there is but one road to it. It does not depend for assurance upon subjection to any dogma or item of doctrine. It trusts that the natural interactions between man and his environment will breed more intelligence and generate more knowledge provided the scientific methods that define intelligence in operation are pushed further into the mysteries of the world, being themselves promoted and improved in the operation. There is such a thing as faith in intelligence becoming religious in quality—a fact that perhaps explains the efforts of some religionists to disparage the possibilities of intelligence as a force. They properly feel such faith to be a dangerous rival.

Lives that are consciously inspired by loyalty to such ideals as have been mentioned are still comparatively infrequent to the extent of that comprehensiveness and intensity which arouse an ardor religious in function. But before we infer the incompetency of such ideals and of the actions they inspire, we should at least ask ourselves how much of the existing situation is due to the fact that the religious factors of experience have been drafted into supernatural channels and thereby loaded with irrelevant encumbrances. A body of beliefs and practices that are apart from the common and natural relations of mankind must, in the de-gree in which it is influential, weaken and sap the force of the possibilities inherent in such relations. Here lies one aspect of the emancipation of the religious from religion.

Any activity pursued in behalf of an ideal end against obstacles and in spite of threats of personal loss because of conviction of its general and enduring value is religious in quality. Many a person, inquirer, artist, philanthropist, citizen, men and women in the humblest walks of life, have achieved, without presumption and without display, such unification of themselves and of their relations to the conditions of existence. It remains to extend their spirit and inspiration to ever wider numbers. If I have said anything about religions and religion that seems harsh, I have said those things because of a firm belief that the claim on the part of religions to possess a monopoly of ideals and of the supernatural means by which alone, it is alleged, they can be furthered, stands in the way of the realization of distinctively religious values inherent in natural experience. For that reason, if for no other, I should be sorry if any were misled by the frequency with which I have employed the adjective "religious" to conceive of what I have said as a disguised apology for what have passed as religions. The opposition between religious values as I conceive them and religions is not to be bridged. Just because the release of these values is so important, their identification with the creeds and cults of religions must be dissolved.

NOTES

[LW 9:3–20.]

INDEX

Epistemology, xi, 78; industry, 56; modern, 125
Equality, 295; democratic, 77–78
Error, 150
Essence, xii, 373; teleological, 10
Essences, eternal, 315
Esthetic, the, 392; related to the intellectual, 398; sources of, 399
Ethics, Aristotelian, 99
Event, 181–82; distinguished from becoming, 183; as eventful, 210; as eventuation, 210
Events, 184; natural, 149
Evil, 92
Evolution, 4, 176, 177, 179, 223, 323; as biological continuity, 57; doctrine of, 180; of mind, 145
Examinations, 231
Existence, 4, 51, 131; as history, 157; metaphysical, 92; as process, 157; relation to value, 92–93
Experience, 121, 154, 155, 215, 241, 397; as able to create technologies, 23; of the child, 237, 238; as cognitive, 116; conditions of, 49; crude, 395; definition of, 58; determinate, 117; development of, 242; as end and means, 343; esthetic, 400; experimental, 48; to *have* an, 385; meaning of, 115; non-cognitive, 160; one-sided, 27; orthodox description of, 47; pregnant with connections, 48; primarily a process of undergoing, 49; relation to connections, 51; relation to scientific methods, 23; religious, 404
Experimentalism, 3, 12
Experimental method, 336
External world: problem of, 146

Facts: and truths, 239; logical, 201; physical, 369
Facts-of-the-case, 209
Faith, 7, 409–10; as acceptance of intellectual propositions, 22; ends of, 408; that experience is ultimate authority, 22; experimental, 31; moral, 408; in possibilities of human experience, 26; pragmatic, 31; as tendency toward action, 22; utopian, 342
Fallacy: analytic, 208; genetic, 308; of unlimited universalization, 209, 213
Fate, 217
Feelings, 138–39, 198, 229
Finance capitalism, 331
Fine art. *See* Art, fine
Fixity, types of, 39
Form: degrees of, 309; logical, 275, 276
Formulations, logical, 197
Foundations, xii; in morals, 377; in religion, 377
Freedom, 76
Frontier, moral, 340
Functionalism, 115
Functions, 186
Fundamentalism, religious, 348, 349, 351, 353
Fundamentalists, 347
Fundamentals, 347
Future, the, 181

Galileo, 41, 290, 351, 352
Generalizations, empirical, 51; vs. matters of fact, 51
George, Henry, 327
Gibbs, Willard, 319
Gifford Lectures, x
Gilded Age, 33
God, 109, 170, 220; concept of, 6; knowledge of, 56; proofs of existence of, 404; as Ultimate Source, 405; will of, 67, 185, 287
Goebbels, Paul J., 337
Goethe, Johann Wolfgang von, 127

Goods, immediate, 86
Government, representative, 306
Gravitation, law of, 220
Gray, Asa, 42
Great Community, the, xii, 293, 294, 298, 307
Great Society, the, 294, 298, 307
Green, Thomas Hill, 5, 10, 17
Growth-process, 144

Habit, 147; and custom, 299; as flywheel of society, 298; as mainspring of human action, 298
Habit-formation, 146
Habits, 4, 6, 52, 229, 254; of action, 5; of speech, 207; mental, 211; moral, 248
Hall, G. Stanley, xi
Hallucination, 58, 64
Hamilton, Alexander, 371
Hamiltonian political ideas, 282
Harmony, 398, 399
Harris, William Torrey, xi, 16
Hays, Arthur Garfield, 318
Heaven, 105
Hegel, G. W. F., 15, 16, 72, 283; influence on Dewey, 18
Hellenistic thought, 135
History: as method of directing change, 332; as process of change, 332
History of thought: competing views of, 80
Hobbes, Thomas, 136
Hocking, Ernest, 158, 160, 161
Hodgson, Shadworth, 13n7
Holmes, Oliver Wendell, 93, 357, 358
Homer, 290
Human conduct, 303, 355
Humanism, 115, 165
Human nature, 347
Hume, David, 10, 13, 51, 215, 308, 377
Huxley, Thomas Henry, 14
Hypothesis, 7, 159, 361

Ideal: authority of, over choice, 408
Ideal, the: and the real, 92; as sacred, 93
Idealism, 57, 106, 123, 165, 219; German, 17; Kantian, 9; neo-Hegelian, 11; neo-Kantian, 5; objective, 62; panpsychic, 136; vice of, 409
Idealists, 125
Ideals, 36, 410
Ideas, 202; as discrete, 10; pre-scientific, 389
Identity, 203
Imagination, 407; objects of, 95
Immediate Empiricism: as method of philosophical analysis, 118; postulate of, 115, 118; significance of, as principle, 118
Immediate Experience, 119
Immigrants, xii; European, 321
Imperialism, 394
Individual, 219, 376; social, 230
Individual, the, 367; and the social, 284
Individual differences: among children, 259
Individualism, 322, 367, 377; active, 12; atomic, xii, 77; egoistic, 12; esthetic, 395; fixed, 12; laissez-faire, 170; of the past, 27; "ragged," xii
Individuality, 217, 224, 297; qualitative, 91
Individuals, 288; native endowments of, 328
Industrial: autocracy, 338; conditions, 395
Industrial Revolution, 24, 303
Industry, 310, 365, 387; forces of, 26
Inference, 191, 276; no conscious experience without, 48
Inhibitions, organic, 128

Inquiry, 176, 305, 381; Greek methods of, 191; metaphysical, 175; methods of, 373; scientific, 107, 380; tools of, xii

Instincts, organic, 52

Institutionalism: of Middle Ages, 378

Instrument: teleological, 10, 11

Instrumentalism, ix, x, 3; attempts to universalize, 36; biological influences on, 9; historical antecedents of, 9; psychological influences on, 9; as reflective of American scene, 35

Instrumentalities, 299, 301, 364, 386; symbolic, 388

Instruments, x, 91

Intellectual, the: related to the esthetic, 398

Intelligence: argument in behalf of the use of, 333; constructive, 52; creative, 367; defined, 52, 101; and education, 297; as experimental, 331; faith in, 13; method of, 101; nature of, 328; in politics, 328; pragmatic theory of, 67; and reason, 12; reflective, 55; as social asset, 327; as social method, 328–29; socially organized, 334

Intelligence, method of, 326

Interactionism, 136

Interest, selective, 212

Intuition, 64, 198

Intuitionalism, 16

Inventor, the: as hero, 319

James, William, ix, 3, 5–7, 9, 10, 13n7, 19, 20, 30, 34, 36, 78, 86, 120n5, 201, 218, 219, 271, 298, 407; as intellectual nonconformist, 33

Jazz, 392

Jeffersonian political ideas, 282

Jesus, 165, 290

Johns Hopkins University, 16, 17

Judgment, 102, 204; copula of, 10; object of, 11; perceptual, 11; subject of, 10; theory of, 10

Judgments: as valuations, x

Judicial decision: language of, 357

Kant, Immanuel, 4, 13n7, 15, 51, 79, 81, 109, 163, 164, 200, 283, 376, 377

Kepler, Johannes, 41

Knowing: defined according to pragmatism, 66; as one mode of experiencing, 116; philosophic, 65

Knowledge, 54, 63; adulteration of, 304; as art, 374; and belief, 95, 96, 102; critical theory of, 376; definition of, 61; defined, 57; as disclosure of reality, 110; genuine, 40; kinds of, 386; as mode of interaction, 100; objectives of, 61; per se, 384; possibility of, 376; and practice, 387; problem of, 56; rational, 375; as science, 92; sense, 375; spectator theory of, 65; subject-matter for, 61; teleological phase of, 12; theory of, 375

Ku Klux Klan, 317

Labor, 399

Language: no thought without, 207

Laplace, Pierre Simon, 222

Law, 355; natural, 366

Law, rules of: as antecedent assurance, 360; as uniform, 360

Laws: as formulation of frequency distributions, 222; fundamental, 182

Learning, 297

Legal rules, general, 361

Lens, the, 387

Liberalism, xii, 323, 338; early, 324; first object of, 325;

laissez-faire, 334; must become radical, 325; renascent, 325, 335

Liberals, early, 326

Liberty: definition of, 76

Life, 134; conditions of, 388; growth of, 397; meaning of, 25; phases of, 397

Life-process, the, 240

Lippmann, Walter, 298

Locke, John, 10, 12, 13n7, 72, 200, 208, 283, 290, 407

Logic: Aristotelian, 196; classic, 43; confusion of, with physiological psychology, 63; Darwinian, 43; as deduction of certainties, 361; experimental, 358; mechanical, 359; new, 44; as prediction of probabilities, 361; and realistic metaphysics, 11; relative to consequences, 361; as theory about empirical phenomena, 361; ultimately concrete, 357; ultimately empirical, 356; as use of meanings in dialectical manner, 149

Logical method, 355, 356

Logical theory, 370; defined, 355

Logicians, idealistic, 201

Lotze, Rudolf Hermann, 9

Louvre, the, 394

Machine, the, 369

Majority rule, 293

Malinowski, Bronislaw, 206

Marsh, James, 14

Marx, Karl, 170

Marxians, 332

Material, the: as instrumental to the good life, 334

Materialism, 6, 76, 335; mechanistic, 145; metaphysical, 140

Matter, 393; concept of, 6; not an event or existence, 139

Matters of fact: vs. empirical generalizations, 51

Mazzini, Giuseppe, 127

McDougall, William, 164

McGilvary, Evander Bradley, 121–23

Meaning, 142; having a, 153n1; relation to truth, 82

Meanings, 4, 380, 381; having, 150; ownership of, 149; always meanings of, 149; related to true and false, 91; as reveries, 150; system of, 381; using, 150

Means: and consequences, 85

Means: and ends, 107, 333

Mechanism, 219

Meliorism, 9

Mental, the, 139; as description, 312; as mysterious intrusion into nature, 312; as ontological, 312

Merz, Charles, 319

Metaphysical puzzles, 133n2

Metaphysics, 176, 195; mechanistic, 144; spiritualistic, 144

Method, pragmatic, 3, 5

Michelson, Albert, 319

Mill, James, 208

Mill, John Stuart, 13n7, 100, 208

Millennium: Christian idea of, 218

Mind, 135, 138, 145; emergent theory of, 143; function of, 67; vs. matter, 42; property of field of interacting events, 139; relation to body, 63

Mind-body problem: solution of, 140

Modernism, religious, 348–49

Monism, 6–7

Monroe Doctrine, 285

Montague, William Pepperell, 133n3

Moral goodness: experience of, 96

Moral life, 314

Morals: conscience in, 87; marking the converging forces of life, 27; naturalistic, 169; not a theme by itself, 27
Morris, George Sylvester, 17
Movies, 392
Mumford, Lewis, 33–36
Museums, 394
Myths: of historic interpretation, 33; of literary criticism, 33

Napoleon, 394
Nationalism, 265, 394
Naturalism, xi, 166, 167, 169; anthropocentric, 161; and materialism, 163; most urgent task of, 164; philosophical, 162, 164
Naturalists, 168
Natural law, 367
Natural selection, 42
Nature, 42, 134, 152, 154, 175, 314, 372; continuity of, 144; many senses of, 373; objective, 145; traits of, 92, 95
Nazism, 164, 341
Nazi-socialism, 337
Needs: intrinsic, 254
Nervous system, 9, 152
New England culture, 17
Newman, Cardinal, 162, 169
New Realists, 64
News: meaning of, 305
Newton, Isaac, 12, 213, 290
New York Times, ix
Nominalism, ix
Non-Being, 117
Noumena, 191

Object, 129; intelligible, 191; perceptible, 191; properties and relations of, 88; of thought, 122, 201
Objectification, 138
Objectivity, 95
Objects, 139, 394; artistic, 391; of belief, 89; eternal, 101; fixed and immutable, 104; fixed properties of, 196; of knowledge, 160; of physical science, 195; qualitative, 195; tendency to seek non-communicating compartments, 90
Occasionalism, 136
Ogden, C. K., 206
One, the: and the Many, 6
Ontological argument, 404
Opinion, 321; control of, 306; opposed to knowledge, 305
Organism, 152, 175, 219; and environment, xii, 49, 139, 397; power of, 52; relation to world, 50
Organization, 152
Origin, 177; ultimate, 176
Origin of Species: theological response to, 39

Pantheism, 15
Parallelism, 136; psycho-physical, 148
Parthenon, 392
Paul, Saint, 162
Peirce, Charles Sanders, ix, 3, 6, 9, 13n7, 30
Perception: modes of, 87; relativity in, 59
Phenomena, 190; antecedent, 8
Phenomenalism, 57, 125
Philosophic discourse: scientific and literary, 89
Philosophies: classical, 106; of compensation, 23; of escape, 23; materialistic, 24; spiritual, 24
Philosophy, 66, 71, 215; as allied with theology, 46; anti-naturalistic, 162, 167; artificiality of, 47; association with academic teaching, 46; characteristic defect of, 208; compared with science, 72; constructive, 27; as critical method, 101; as criticism, 215; as criticism of criticisms, 86; defined, 86; and democracy, 72, 75; Dewey's prescription for, 57; as distinct from science, 158; does not furnish motives, 94; emancipation of, 47; of experience, 24; and fixed degrees of truth, 77; function of, 6, 158; future of, in America, 68; Greek, 77, 80, 84, 102, 103; has moral function, 158; has practical function, 158; historical existence, 80; historically largely transcendental, 22; historic role of, 79, 80, 82; as liaison officer, 90; as linked to feudalism, 72; as linked to particular social order, 72; Medieval, 77; as messenger, 90; and metaphysics of feudalism, 77; modern, 95, 374; not analysis of past, 63; not form or science of knowledge, 74; as one mode of knowing, 63; not contemplative survey of existence, 63; as outlook on future possibilities, 63; pragmatic, 34, 66; problem of, 107; professionalization of, 47; and ranks of reality, 77; reconstruction of, 158; related to its social medium, 34; relation to absolute origins, 43; relation to specific values, 43; Scholastic, 46; schools of, 47; source in entire human predicament, 94; as subject-matter, 158; subject-matter for, 214; proper task of, 91; technical, 65; usually conservative, 46; wholesale type of, 44
Philosophy, modern: subjectivity in, 95
Philosophy, speculative: technical blunder of, 55
Philosophy of nature, 39
Physical, 139, 157
Physical mobility: in children, 259
Physical science, 370
Plan and control, 371
Plato, xi, 81, 135, 214; influence on Dewey, 18; as metaphysician, 18; as misrepresented, 18
Pluralism, 6; ontological, 50
Poetry: moral function of, 407; as universal, 407
Political institutions, democratic, 333
Political philosophy: as distinguished from political science, 282
Pope, the, 364
Potentialities, 223; as phases of civilization, 317
Potentiality, 179
Practical, the, 5
Practicalism, 3
Practice: and knowledge, 387
Pragmatism, x, 3–7, 12, 29, 115, 120n8, 132n1; as Anglo-Saxon reaction to Latin mind, 13; arguments against, 126; as connected with intelligence, 55; definition of, 126; metaphysical implication of, 8; narrow, 55; as reflective of American scene, 35; as revision of English empiricism, 9
Pre-established harmony, 136
Predicate: correlative with subject, 200
Predication, 201; defined, 200
Prejudice, 26
Principles, ethical, 246
Private, the: and the public, 284, 317
Problems: artificial, 47; philosophic, 7
Process Philosophy, xi
Production, 5; rationalization of, 375
Progress, 27, 218
Progressive Era, ix
Prohibition, 370
Properties, 196–97

Social prediction, 371
Social reform: defined, 91
Social science, 369–71; and natural science, 310
Social sciences, 83
Society, 287, 289; and science, 363; self governing, 340
Sociology, 330; confusion with metaphysics, 308
Socrates, 203, 290, 358
Solipsism, 213
Soul, 135; Dewey's reconstruction of term, 151; as inhabiting the body, 152
Species: classic notion of, 42; as final cause, 40; as fixed, 40; as understood by the Greeks, 40
Speech, free, 317, 326
Spencer, Herbert, 10, 147, 148, 164; on God as "unknowable energy," 43
Spencerians, 52
Spinoza, Benedict, 59, 92, 162
Spirit, 135, 314
Spiritual, the, 349, 364, 393
Spiritualism, 163; metaphysical, 167
State, the, 281, 283, 287, 289; determining goodness of, 291; purpose of, 282
Stimulations, organic, 128
Stoics, the, 283
Subject: correlative with predicate, 200; as given, 196
Subject-matter: of common sense, 383; double aspect of, 243; metaphysical, 176; of science, 383
Subjectivism, 12, 124
Subjectivity, 60
Succession: opposed to series, 142
Suffrage, 293
Summum Bonum, 4, 99
Supernatural, the, 402
Supernatural Being, 401
Supernaturalism, 23, 163, 167; in Greece, 81; medieval Christian, 81
Supernaturalists, 168
Syllogism, 359; has nothing to do with operation of thinking, 358; as setting forth the results of thinking, 358
Symbols, 296; meaning of not inherited, 207

Taste, cultivated, 86
Technique, mathematical, 281
Technologies, 375, 388
Technology, x, xii, 23, 24, 224, 300, 310, 329, 330, 363, 365; and economic forces, 26; idealization of, 36
Teleological argument, 404
Teleology, spiritualistic, 145
Temporal development, 224
Tendencies: observation of, by teachers, 260
Texts, 238
Theism, 6, 165
Theological philosophy: of the Roman Catholic Church, 165
Theology: Christian, 103; and science, 351
Theories, 100
Theory: epistemological, 376; and practice, 106
Thing: as cognitive, 117; as cognized, 117; as known object, 117
Things: logical status of, 196; qualitative, 196
Things-in-themselves, 119n4
Thinking: as controlled association, 204; as existential process, 204; mechanics of, 202; objective in, 212; psychological, 274; temporal background of, 211
Thinking, constructive: value of, 53
Thomas, Norman, 318

Thoreau, Henry David, 36
Thought, 206; freedom of, 317; as intrinsic feature of experience, 53; object of, 191, 201; as partial experimentation, 97; qualitative, 195, 200; teleological phase of, 12; Victorian, 27
Time, 217, 224; absolute, 221; as connected with individuality, 219, 223; as measure of motion in space, 220; mystery of, 225; in physical science, 220; as a problem, 219
Tolstoy, Leo, 76
Tools, mathematical, 302
Tools and machines, 311
Torrey, H. A. P., 15
Traditionalism, religious, 348, 349
Traditions, 12
Training: separation of intellectual and moral, 248
Traits, 312; of existences, 177; found in things experienced, 156; irreducible, 176, 179; logical, 62; of natural existence, 139; of things, 138
Transcendentalism, 119, 165; German, 13
True, the: traditional discussion of, 89
Truth, 120n5; coherence theory of, 8; correspondence theory of, 8, 148; and error, 59; eternal, 79; immutable, 168; love of, 29, 32; meaning of, 7; philosophy a recipient and not a donor of, 90; relation to meaning, 82; transcendent standard of, 97; as verification, 7
Truth of things: synonymous with realness of things, 130
Truths: and facts, 239; necessary, 10

Uncertainty principle, 222
United States Constitution, 302, 326
United States Supreme Court, 302, 327
Universals: meanings of, 100
Universe, the: as block, 96; as closed, 35; constitution of, 44; as indeterminate, 35; as open, 35; purpose of, 25; as rigid, 6; as static, 125
Utensils, domestic, 393
Utilitarianism, 104

Valuation, 98
Value, 84–85; as such, 86; relation to existence, 92
Value-objects, 88
Values, 6, 156; enduring, 88; ideal, 44; theory of, 86; transcendent, 14; ultimate, 104; unstable, 86
Values, immediate: defined, 88
Vergil, 290
Verification, experimental, 8
Vermont, University of, 14
Victorian Age, 27
Violence, 333

Wallace, William, 17
War, 26, 333, 393
Wars: waged in the name of supernaturalism, 165
Watson, John B., 9
Welt-Anschauung, 35
Whitehead, Alfred North, 181, 219, 363
Whitman, Walt, 36, 307
Wisdom: as moral term, 73; defined, 73
Women: contributions to philosophy, 73
Woodbridge, F. J. E., 119
Work, 399
World formulas, 6
Worship, 393

Larry A. Hickman is Director of the Center for Dewey Studies and Professor of Philosophy at Southern Illinois University at Carbondale. He is author of *John Dewey's Pragmatic Technology* and editor of *Technology as a Human Affair* and *Reading Dewey.* He is also general editor of *The Collected Works of John Dewey, 1882–1953: The Electronic Edition.*

Thomas M. Alexander is Professor of Philosophy at Southern Illinois University at Carbondale. He is author of *John Dewey's Theory of Art, Experience and Nature: The Horizons of Feeling.*